The Radical Vision

ESSAYS FOR THE SEVENTIES

The Radical Vision

ESSAYS FOR THE SEVENTIES

EDITED BY

Leo Hamaliam and Frederick R. Karl
CITY COLLEGE OF THE CITY UNIVERSITY OF NEW YORK

THOMAS Y. CROWELL COMPANY
NEW YORK • ESTABLISHED 1834.

Acknowledgment is gratefully made
to New Directions Publishing Corporation for permission to use a passage
from Henry Miller, *The Air-Conditioned Nightmare,* as an epigraph to
this volume. Copyright 1945 by New
Directions Publishing Corporation.
Reprinted by permission.

We are not kept alive by legislators and militarists, that's fairly obvious. We are kept alive by men of faith, men of vision. They are like vital germs in the endless process of becoming. Make room, then, for the life-giving ones!

HENRY MILLER, *The Air-Conditioned Nightmare*

Contents

III / Campus Agonistes: The Students Rebel

IV / Escape from History? The Present Imperative

VIII / Counterpoints

Introduction

Every age has its radicalism, and every age considers itself more radical than the one before. Yet, surely, ours is the most radical in recent times, and America is the most radical of all nations, while, paradoxically, it may also be among the most conservative. Affluence, like poverty, may act as both stimulant and anesthetic, but clearly it is always the few, not the many, who make revolutions under any conditions. And revolutions need not be only political: in our version of the radical vision, politics plays a relatively small part. Nor must "radical" mean "fanatic," as it often does in many minds. The "radical" positions presented on these pages share nothing with the narrow and parochial views of the eccentric extremist.

Furthermore, every age gets the radicals it deserves. And every age defines its radicals differently, whether they be Voltaire in the eighteenth century, Thoreau in the nineteenth, or Sartre and Ginsberg in the twentieth. By contemporary "radicals" we mean those who want to go to the root of things, who wish to expose the core of the matter. In the past, too many radicals were satisfied with modest reforms. They did not go to the roots; they settled for modification, for small, minor alterations. At present, the radical seeks substantive reform. When he says he wants change—whether in the college, in the cities, or in our very consciousness—he means just that: CHANGE. "Radical," then, at the present indicates the toppling of the past insofar as that past constricts the possibilities of the future. If we had to characterize "radical" in one word, we would say that it is anti-authoritarian. In every area where radicalism of thought or feeling has penetrated, we have seen the toppling of authority figures or institutions, whether they be Lyndon Johnson, Grayson Kirk of Columbia, or old conceptions of art, literature, music, race, and psychology. Authoritarianism embraces the status quo or at best gradualism; radicalism accepts constant flux as a condition of living today.

This sense of radical change, this desire to topple unserviceable monuments of the past, is not always accompanied by applicable alternatives. We deceive ourselves if we demand consistent philosophies in the radical vision. The vision itself is too new, too inchoate, and too much in movement. But the shape is discernible: history is out, the present is in; strict intellectualism is out, consciousness is in; old complacencies are out, new awareness of one's self and of others is in. Often the very sense of a radical vision is contempt, arrogance, and condescension. There is little sympathy for safe, trodden ways, and no easy forgiveness of the older generation's mistakes. The radical vision is tough, sometimes harsh, even when the visionary is a former flower child. The radical vision writes off large chunks of the past as unworkable, insists on a clean slate, and works best with improvisation.

The radical visionary is willing to experiment, to risk failure, rather than to play it tidy with acceptable forms and conventions. In keeping with the principle that unifies this book, we have chosen forms of writing that do not ordinarily appear in collections of expository prose—the interview, the dialogue, the open essay, which is like a memoir or a diary. If the message is radical—that is, searching for the roots—then the form cannot always be the familiar and tried. Ginsberg, Burroughs, and Cleaver, for example, are perhaps best apprehended and appreciated when they are encouraged to talk freely. Spontaneous, creative people cannot be shackled. To hear them speaking in their own unique voices is to hear them at the grass-roots, so to speak, of their being. Genuineness is a key quality of the radical vision. Thus, for the radical it is important to allow the matter to acquire its own form if it will, not to superimpose authority on what may be a freely associative interior monologue.

Collectively, these selections stand as a comprehensive critique of the very assumptions many of us will carry well into the coming decade. Each writer or speaker challenges some cherished conviction by which we live. The targets of attack include moral rigidity, evasions of inner consciousness, attempts to restrict the body and the senses, the slow unchecked stain of urban decay, the official lie which poses as national policy, the strait-jacket of Establishment status quo, the daily equivocations that have become part of the American fabric, the masks of privilege and power, the terrible silence of the decent in the face of injustice or misrule, and public reluctance to accept fresh thought and feeling in the arts. In brief, this book is indirectly an indictment of the visible failure of the great society. In the radical vision, the only greatness in personal life comes from living with awareness, individuality, and without fear.

These writers do not limit themselves to the safety of a specialty, nor do they always speak as sages who advocate balance and rationality. Their inspiration is intuition, and in spirit they are often more like Hotspur than Socrates. They have in common the courage, the insight, and the breadth of perception that permits them to range widely over the subject at hand, exposing spurious values, false standards, and the decline of imagination that have brought us, in their eyes, to the brink of disaster both in our personal lives and in our public affairs. They are daring because they know ideas have consequences, and they are willing to confront the consequences.

Some of these writers may seem to be far apart in either their ideological or intellectual positions, but they are united by the act of vision: each writer creates out of the ashes of his criticism a unique phoenix, his own particular proposal for transforming some aspect of society, for disclosing the latent, unfulfilled possibilities of man. These writers are committed to elevating, broadening, or refining the resources we have only partially discovered in ourselves. And even when the writer is advocating a cause or defining a position that the majority may now regard as hostile to our present interests, his vision contains a new, exciting possibility for the future.

For the opposing point of view—not necessarily reactionary, by any means—we have included a section called "Counterpoints." These essays and essayists offer critiques of contemporary radical thought, whether it is wholesale repudiation of the generation as in George Kennan, or distaste at what would appear to be a decline in intellectual standards as in Theodore Roszak.

In the past, men have aspired to utopias, have proposed countless panaceas for our ills. Often their visions were either impractical or unrealizable because men lacked the means to implement them. In the affluence of today, these limitations have been abolished. Given the will and the vision, man can make his reach and grasp cohere. Because these writers combine a keen sense of reality with their proposals, their visions have the virtue of being viable as well as visionary. The gunpowder of the seventies is implicit in their dreams. For students willing to align their lives with fresh ideas rather than with received tradition, these essays and interviews will be at the least like Keats' travels "in the realms of gold" and at the most like Shelley's driven leaves that "quicken a new birth." Either way, as the student reads, the radical vision is changing the world under his very eyes.

I / The "Now" Generation: Values in Transition

Most people pretend to themselves that they are deeply interested in innovation, but what they really want are moderate changes that can be handled in the same old ways by the same old people with the same old attitudes. The "Now" generation defines itself as "new" people with "new" attitudes seeking "new" ways to think and to act. Whether or not the "Now" generation has made this breakthrough, it is difficult to think of any area of American life that has remained untouched by its values. From the election of public officials to the resignation of college administrators, American adults have either rejected "Now" values or have tried to move to this "different drummer." We cannot underestimate the significance of the movement, fragmented and disparate as it appears. If anything, its importance seems to be increasing as we enter the decade of the seventies.

The mass media have not done a responsible job reporting what the "Now" generation stands for. About the only thing the media have conveyed accurately is that a small minority indeed is involved *actively*. Less concerned with sense than with the sensational, they have failed to stress that these values have spread to huge numbers of the young and the middle-aged who are not part of "the action," but who, nevertheless, quietly support the radicals. The movies we see, the books we read, the religious beliefs we hold, the political ideas and ideals we espouse, the art we look at in the museums, the music we hear, the clothes we wear, the sense of sex and body we envision, the way we view the past and the present, and the way we plan for the future, the

3

very moral values we applaud and embrace—all of these have been influenced in one dimension or another by the new values.

We should always keep in mind that vast changes such as our current cultural revolution has brought will not stand still, and we cannot accurately predict the sense of a future decade based on the values of the previous one. But we can assume that the technological "spirit" is intensifying, and will continue to intensify; and that the reaction to it—in sexual morality, in art, in feeling, in political philosophy—will concurrently intensify at the other pole. The material may destroy materialism. Thus, even if and when the Vietnam War ends, protest will not die down. Once a technique has been perfected, it becomes an established method, with a life of its own. Similarly, the hair and clothing styles that were only a short time ago exclusively the hippie's symbol of identity have now been adopted by a majority of the young. Drugs, too, have followed this pattern, becoming more and more socially acceptable. Thus, at no one point in time can we say what forms the life styles of the "Now" generation will take; but we can safely assume that a movement generated by such far-reaching social and psychological forces will itself form and re-form when it appears to be finished, like the mythological Proteus himself taking new shapes from the circumstances of his environment.

The essays selected for this section include two by active members of the "Now" generation, Ronald McGuire, a former student at The City College of New York, and Jerry Rubin, one of the founders of the Yippies (Youth International Party). Perhaps better than the philosophers and psychologists who follow with their analyses, they can give the sense and substance of the movement as it appears to those on the firing line of dissent, rebellion, and rejection. An obvious key to their position is their hatred of authority, their realization that they must go their own way, do "their own thing." Many of their critics have perhaps forgotten how completely this is an American way of seeing and doing. But more than that, McGuire and Rubin are describing a revolt—though masked in many ways—not against capitalism or white supremacy or even the repressive attitudes of college administrators—but against the age itself, against people who have made a mess of the world, setting themselves as the arbiters of good and evil in everything.

It is not even a revolt against authority as such, for these students are willing to submit to the authority of their peers. McGuire and Rubin, in language that will infuriate their elders, are reacting against the stupidity, hypocrisy, apathy, and lack of vision that are sending the twentieth century to hell in a technological handbasket. Yet implicit in their statements is the hope that America may still be an open society, open, that is, to alternate styles of thinking and living. Rooted in desperation and joy, their rebellion is a tactic for keeping that society open.

For Gary Snyder, in his "Passage to More Than India," from *Earth House Hold*, this new style has arrived and is being practiced by thousands of young people all over the United States. Basing their style on Indian tribal culture, these young people have, like the Indians, tried to exorcise the demons that would destroy their lives; only in their case, the demons are the familiar modern ones of technology, monogamy, and pragmatism. They have refused to become detribalized, that is, corrupted by values that uncritically pass as "civilized."

The essay by Robert Jay Lifton is a sympathetic study of the "Now" movement from the standpoint of both philosophy and psychiatry. Professor Lifton describes the young person of today as the "protean man" who is seeking some general pattern of self-process in his own aspirations and beliefs, even when those aspirations are absurd and the beliefs worth nothing more than mockery. The ego, as Hesse explored it in *Steppenwolf,* is a manifold entity whose nature is lost in the optical illusion of a single undeniable body. The pageant of life is unsubstantial, and out of such insubstantiality "protean man" lives his dream of life, faces the flux of existence. If this seems at times like mystical nonsense, who can deny that in the process of becoming "protean" (since World War II, according to Lifton) the young have redeemed the idea of spontaneity, of improvisation in daily life? Thus, the "protean man" enacts the existential moment that Sartre has made central in our consciousness. (See the section called "Apostles of the Age" and Sartre's own essay in Part IV.)

A significant aspect of the movement is its attempt to open up the self that lies behind consciousness and rationality. Often this aspect conflicts with the political strategy of the committed "Now" generation, simply because individual expression or private experience does not count as heavily as cooperation when concerted effort is called for. But for many of the young, even this gap may be closed so long as the drug experience does not pre-empt other activities. For some, the use of drugs derives from a larger impulse, the desire to follow one's self into the farthest reaches of the unknown, much as an explorer seeks out new territory. For others, drugs provide an *escape* from the self, from pressures of school and work, from the demands of parents, teachers, and peers. This group of drug users, of course, would need help with or without drugs. Alan Watts is concerned with the first group, those who use drugs to expand their consciousness, rather than to escape overwhelming problems. Whether drugs can expand *anyone's* awareness has been challenged recently by the medical profession, but Watts argues historically and philosophically for his position, without the taint of special pleading.

Despite the secular humanism of the younger generation in revolt, there has been a keen respect for the basic Christian values as represented by the figure of Jesus Christ. Hidden by the disguises of formal religion, the vision of Christ remains essentially radical. Communal living among the young has become commonplace, and the values that lead to this life are those of the early Christians: a return to simplicity, far from social pressures and governmental big brotherhood. It is not surprising that many spokesmen for the church, like Malcolm Boyd, himself an Episcopal clergyman, have felt the ground swell of resentment against organized, affluent religion and have responded. Their radicalism springs from their determination to make the Christian vision of social justice viable now. Like most of our authors, they reject the Christian promise of heaven thereafter and believe that whatever heaven there is and whatever it offers must be enjoyed here and now. They believe fervently that the so-called underground church is the essence of Christianity, and that the established churches no longer carry God's word. The transcendental experience must be found outside the church (compare this view with Watts'). Like the acid rock enthusiasts, like the hippies and the Yippies, like the other radical critics of our civilization, they hold that man must look within for his disciplines—not to the church, or to the school, or to the government.

1 / Cry of the Wild

RONALD MCGUIRE

What have / *they done to the Earth?*
What have they done to our fair sister?
Ravaged and plundered and ripped her and bit her
Stuck her with knives in the side of the dawn,
Tied her with fences and dragged her down.
I hear a very gentle sound.
With your ear down to the ground
We want the world and we want it ...
now.
now?
NOW ! ! !

JIM MORRISON

I am a monster. I am writing this but soon I will have forgotten how to write. Even now the words come hard and I know that some of what I say will be twisted around by liberals without balls to salve the embers/infernos of their consciences.

I am a monster, but it wasn't always so. I used to be able to write well and my teachers were proud of me. They taught me about Nuremberg before I even learned how to read. And they taught me about the Constitution and the thing that said "all men are created equal" and about the rights we all had under the law and about the awful thing that happened in Germany which could never happen here because we had the Constitution, the laws, the Declaration of Independence, and most of all, the tradition of a free people willing to fight any oppressor to guard their cherished liberty. I was a good pupil. I learned and I remembered. But things have changed since then.

SOURCE: *Observation Post* (The City College of New York), January 30, 1969.
Ronald McGuire is a former student at The City College of New York, uptown campus, where he was active in many demonstrations before his expulsion in 1969.

I think it was in the basement of Park Gym during the hut thing when three of New York's Finest kicked the shit out of me. John Stark, President Buell G. Gallagher's administrative assistant came along and told me that the blood streaming down my face and the cracked teeth were probably the result of some accident. Anyway, I didn't recall their badge numbers. I think the punches must have done something to my brain because I thought that Stark was wearing a pig uniform.

It was in Chicago after the pig car drove through the crowd and ran over the little black girl's legs that something else happened to me. I clenched my fist and found a spray can of Day-Glo, an iridescent paint best seen in black light, in my hand.

There was a dump truck with four pigs in back spraying tear gas. I waited for the truck to pass, hiding behind a tree.

The can hit the pig in the mouth. He went down and stopped spraying tear gas.

I now feel sorry for letting the heat of the moment get the best of me. Day-Glo is highly inflammable. Light a match to a can and you have an effective torch or, at short range, a flame thrower. Empty cannisters can be refilled with other, more potent chemicals. I should have thought before I acted.

I will remember next time.

Martin Luther King, my old guru, is dead. Now I am free to listen to the stirrings within my soul. I will never again go smiling at the cameras as I get arrested to awaken the conscience of middle class America.

I am white and have middle class roots and, if I cut my hair, finish school and recant, I could be a junior executive in some department store. Or I could be a professor in some college. And then I wouldn't have to recant, just keep quiet long enough to get tenure.

But I want no part of the Great Society. That society doesn't see me. They see hippies. The media class us flower children. The designers sell Nehru shirts at forty dollars each, mod haircuts are "in," and rock music saturates the airwaves.

We are not flower children. We love, but we have also learned to hate. Two years ago chicks were giving flowers to cops. No one gave flowers to the pigs in Chicago.

The society made a fatal mistake with us. They saw the form of our rebellion, but either they didn't perceive or were afraid to face its substance. We didn't drop out to wear our hair long. Our revolution isn't aimed at having a Harlow's replace the local Bijou. We want to legalize LSD, not marijuana.

We want to affirm life, not package it and sell it.

This society treats us like children. But it is to our advantage to be treated as children. It gives us a freedom of movement that we wouldn't have otherwise. But the time will come when the love will turn to fear and we will have to fight for our right to exist. We will then be monsters no longer, but men.

For the time being, we must study and prepare. And we are doing that.

We must educate people. But our revolution, because it is a revolution of life styles, must be a revolution of the young. The middle-aged middle-class liberals will be useful, but they will be midwives to a difficult birth. A man who has already found a secure place in this society will not fight to change it. While they can give aid and comfort to those who are, we recognize that politics must be rooted in experience.

Radicals must reach the young. And we are. A look at the turmoil on the campuses and now the elementary and secondary schools throughout the nation is indicative of the direction that the youth of America is moving in. The movement is to the left, and time is on our side.

Enough of our culture has been assimilated to have an affect on the society. The media unwittingly disseminating our propaganda in the form of rock music and mod styles.

Rather than being assimilated into the society we are awakening a soul that has been in suspended animation. Our dances and our music lead to a thirst for life that cannot be quenched by the putrid offerings of Madison Avenue. There will have to be changes made, we will have to make room to dance without stepping on each other's toes.

We reject Marxism and classical socialist thinking because it was predicated on an economy of scarcity, not abundance. We are the alienated children of the middle class, not the proletariat.

We are not rebelling because we need bread, food or a place to sleep. We want freedom and an alternative to the anonymity of the mass society.

We see the potential in this society to abolish economic deprivation. We see, through technology, the potential to abolish most of the labor that man has been cursed with since the dawn of time. Total unemployment, rather than an evil would be the goal of an enlightened economy, thus liberating people from the onus of being compelled to work. Technology should be used, as much as possible, to limit the amount of human labor necessary for running the economy to the absolute minimum.

Our politics is a politics of joy. Our life style is our politics. Our activity is aimed at liberating the human soul. As ROTC has a death drill we have the dance of life.

We are learning that a closeness can exist between us that we do not see in the IBM push button world of depersonalized persons and personalized machines. We have learned to share; to give and take are the same. Gracious giving is as important as gracious taking. We are against charity because we truly believe that there is no sacrifice involved in giving, but rather a positive joy.

When one of us asks for "spare change," it is not a beggar asking for charity. We're saying, "Dig it, I am a person, just like you but you have an abundance of the means of obtaining the goods of life.

Wouldn't you like to share it?"

Our politics is the politics of youth. We are cultural revolutionaries. LSD is our textbook, Day-Glo our weapon and orgasm our victory. Older people find it hard to imitate our dance, impossible to understand our music and afraid to experience our drugs. I don't care to speculate about the quality of sex in suburbia, but I will just observe the number of middle-aged housewives who try to seduce dirty, unwashed hippies and the number of pigs who try to make it with the chicks they bust.

Attempts at reaching the middle-aged middle-class community are fruitless. We should rather direct our efforts toward our potential brothers, the young, the blacks, the bikers, hippies and junkies.

We must recognize that students in high school are already ahead of us, rejecting even the rhetoric of the dying society. They, not the middle class, are the ones we should address ourselves to.

Our politics is the politics of education. Radical education is aimed at finding contradictions in the society and confronting

10

them. All perception is rooted in prior experience. The ivory tower is a vantage point we cannot accept.

Intellectual analysis is never more valid than emotional commitment. Just as consciousness begins at birth with an inarticulate, guttural expression of need, radicalism begins with an unspoken feeling inside one's guts of alienation. An emotional statement lies at the basis of all thought.

We must strive to end the divorce between thought and emotion imposed upon us by a sterile society. Our minds must be tools to act upon our emotions until thought and action become one.

We cannot be dispassionate intellectuals. We are passionate men.

Our politics is the politics of experience, and we reject all politics not rooted in experience. We reject liberalism because the politics of liberals is based on sympathy. No slave has ever won his freedom through the generosity of his master. We will struggle to get our freedom or it will not be worth having.

Our experience is the experience of outlaws. We cannot drop out. Many have tried. Drug busts, draft cards, landlords who won't rent to hippies, employers who won't hire us because of our appearance have all forced us to come back to the society.

We are coming back, but we will not play the game. We will define ourselves.

We are persecuted. Many of our brothers are in jail for drugs or the draft.

Our gurus, Huey Newton, Eldridge Cleaver and Timothy Leary are outlaws. We too are outlaws, but we are less visible than our leaders.

We are seen but not yet recognized.

Older, calmer heads cannot understand our desperation, cannot understand that in the eyes of society we are or will be outlaws, condemned to imprisonment because of our life style. On the one hand we are chastised for imposing our morality on others, while on the other hand we are forced day by day to struggle with that deadening, hypocritical morality that is force fed to us.

Drug laws and draft laws are used as an instrument of the establishment to smash our subculture. The draft keeps us visible and most of us are subject to arrest at any time under the drug laws. These and other similar conventions by the society made "dropping out" impossible.

Our politics is the politics of struggle. We did not create that struggle, we recognized its existence. We are persecuted and we have to fight back.

We also recognize the loss of control of modern man over his institutions. There is no position of meaningful influence in the society because of the built-in conservative nature of the institutions of that society. These institutions of society can only be changed through struggle.

Our politics must be the politics of community. We need to build radical communities in order to provide alternate life styles to the automaton-suburbia syndrome. We need radical communities to provide staging grounds for our struggle and bases of operation for that struggle. We need radical communities to further enjoy those experiences denied to us by the society.

There are certain things that we must guard against in our communities.

We must guard against our communities becoming havens for drop-outs. Communities must be movement centers in the real sense of the word. If a community attempts to remove itself from confrontations with the contradictions in the society then it becomes irrelevant as a force for change. We as an underground culture can never gloss over the fact that we are in conflict with the society.

Now, while we are still in a nascent stage, while we are not yet recognized for what we are by the major part of society, we could easily follow the path of least resistance. We could allow the media to define us in a way which will make us irrelevant as a force for social change (flower children-hippies).

Our communes must give us a sense of cultural identity that is our own, and not Madison Avenue's. Toward this end we must realize that our education must be internal as well as external.

Most important of all, our communities must provide an alternative life style by replacing complete namelessness with communities based on interpersonal relations.

Our communes will not be ivory towers. We cannot draw away from confrontation with society. We must come to realize that our every aspiration, our every move, our every thought brings us into conflict with the society.

We are not an underground, but we must prepare to be an underground.

2 / A Yippie Manifesto

JERRY RUBIN

This is a Viet Cong flag on my back. During the recent hearings of the House UnAmerican Activities Committee in Washington, a friend and I are walking down the street en route to Congress— he's wearing an American flag and I'm wearing this VC flag.

The cops mass, and boom! all of a sudden they come toward us. I think: Oh, man, curtains. I am going to be arrested for treason, for supporting the enemy.

And who do the cops grab and throw in the paddy wagon?

My friend with the American flag!

And I'm left all alone in the VC flag.

"What kind of a country is this?" I shout at the cops. "YOU COMMUNISTS!"

Everything is cool en route to Canada until the border. An official motions me into a small room and pulls out a five-page questionnaire.

"Do you use drugs?" he asks quite seriously.

"Yeah," I say.

"Which?"

"Coca Cola."

"I mean DRUGS!" he shouts.

SOURCE: *Evergreen Review* 13 (May 1969), 41–43, 83–92. Copyright © 1969 by Jerry Rubin. Reprinted by permission of Brandt & Brandt.

Jerry Rubin is a founder of the Yippies (Youth International Party); since 1964, he has participated in and led numerous demonstrations, including the one in Chicago during the Democratic National Convention of 1968. He has recently published his manifesto, *Do It!*

"Coca Cola is more dangerous for you than marijuana," I say. "Fucks up your body, and it's addictive."

"Have you ever advocated the overthrow of the Canadian government?" he asks.

"Not until I get into Canada."

"Have you ever been arrested for inciting to riot?"

I reply no, and it is true. In August I was arrested in Chicago for something similar, "solicitation to mob action," a violation of a sex statute.

Finally I ask the border official to drop out. "Man, your job is irrelevant," I say. "The Canadian-American border does not exist. There are no such things as borders. The border exists only in your head.

"No state has the right to ask me these questions. The answers are mine. Next thing I know you guys will be tapping my brain!"

I try to get the cat to take off his uniform right there. But he refuses, saying, "I've got a job to do and a family to support."

So goes the cancer of the Western world: everyone just doing his "job." Nobody learned the lesson of Eichmann. Everyone still points the finger elsewhere.

America and the West suffer from a great spiritual crisis. And so the yippies are a revolutionary religious movement.

We do not advocate political solutions that you can vote for. You are never going to be able to *vote* for the revolution. Get that hope out of your mind.

And you are not going to be able to buy the revolution in a supermarket, in the tradition of our consumer society. The revolution is not a can of goods.

Revolution only comes through personal transformation: finding God and changing your life. Then millions of converts will create a massive social upheaval.

The religion of the yippies is: "RISE UP AND ABANDON THE CREEPING MEATBALL!!"

That means anything you want it to mean. Which is why it is so powerful a revolutionary slogan. The best picket sign I ever saw was blank. Next best was: "We Protest ———!"

Slogans like "Get out of Vietnam" are informative, but they do not create myths. They don't ask you to do anything but carry them.

14

Political demonstrations should make people dream and fantasize. A religious-political movement is concerned with people's souls, with the creation of a magic world which we make real.

When the national media first heard our slogan, they reported that the "creeping meatball" was Lyndon Johnson. Which was weird and unfair, because we liked Lyndon Johnson.

We cried when LBJ dropped out. "LBJ, you took us too literally! We didn't mean YOU should drop out! Where would WE be if it weren't for you, LBJ?"

Is there any kid in America, or anywhere in the world, who wants to be like LBJ when he grows up?

As a society falls apart, its children reject their parents. The elders offer us Johnsons, Agnews, and Nixons, dead symbols of a dying past.

The war between THEM and US will be decided by the seven-year-olds.

We offer: sex, drugs, rebellion, heroism, brotherhood.

They offer: responsibility, fear, puritanism, repression.

Dig the movie *Wild in the Streets*! A teenage rock-and-roll singer campaigns for a Bobby Kennedy-type politician.

Suddenly he realizes: "We're all young! Let's run the country ourselves!"

"Lower the voting age to 14!"

"14 or FIGHT!"

They put LSD in the water fountains of Congress and the Congressmen have a beautiful trip. Congress votes to lower the voting age to 14.

The rock-and-roll singer is elected President, but the CIA and military refuse to recognize the vote. Thousands of longhairs storm the White House, and six die in the siege. Finally the kids take power, and they put all people over 30 into camps and give them LSD every day. (Some movies are even stranger than OUR fantasies.)

"Don't trust anyone over 30!" say the yippies—a much-quoted warning.

I am four years old.

We are born twice. My first birth was in 1938, but I was reborn in Berkeley in 1964 in the Free Speech Movement.

When we say "Don't trust anyone over 30," we're talking about the second birth. I got 26 more years.

When people 40 years old come up to me and say, "Well, I guess I can't be part of your movement," I say, "What do you mean? You could have been born yesterday. Age exists in your head."

Bertrand Russell is our leader. He's 90 years old.

Another yippie saying is: "THE GROUND YOU STAND ON IS LIBERATED TERRITORY!"

Everybody in this society is a policeman. We all police ourselves. When we free ourselves, the real cops take over.

I don't smoke pot in public often, although I love to. I don't want to be arrested: that's the only reason.

I police myself.

We do not own our own bodies.

We fight to regain our bodies—to make love in the parks, say "fuck" on television, do what we want to do whenever we want to do it.

Prohibitions should be prohibited.

Rules are made to be broken.

Never say "no."

The yippies say: "PROPERTY IS THEFT."

What America got, she stole.

How was this country built? By the forced labor of slaves. America owes black people billions in compensation.

"Capitalism" is just a polite schoolbook way of saying: "Stealing."

Who deserves what they get in America? Do the Rockefellers deserve their wealth? HELL NO!

Do the poor deserve their poverty? HELL NO!!

America says that people work only for money. But check it out: those who don't have money work the hardest, and those who have money take very long lunch hours.

When I was born I had food on my table and a roof over my head. Most babies born in the world face hunger and cold. What is the difference between them and me?

Every well-off white American better ask himself that question or he will never understand why people hate America.

The enemy is this dollar bill right here in my hand.

Now if I get a match, I'll show you what I think of it.

This burning gets some political radicals very uptight. I don't know exactly why. They burn a lot of money putting out leaflets nobody reads.

I think it is more important today to burn a dollar bill than it is to burn a draft card.

(Hmmm, pretty resilient. Hard to burn. Anybody got a lighter?)

We go to the New York Stock Exchange, about 20 of us, our pockets stuffed with dollar bills. We want to throw real dollars down at all those people on the floor playing monopoly games with numbers.

An official stops us at the door and says, "You can't come in. You are hippies and you are coming to demonstrate."

With TV cameras flying away, we reply: "Hippies? Demonstrate? We're Jews. And we're coming to see the stock market."

Well, that gets the guy uptight, and he lets us in. We get to the top, and the dollars start raining down on the floor below.

These guys deal in millions of dollars as a game, never connecting it to people starving. Have they ever seen a real dollar bill?

"This is what it is all about, you sonavabitches!!"

Look at them: wild animals chasing and fighting each other for the dollar bills thrown by the hippies!

And then the cops come. The cops are a necessary part of any demonstration theater. When you are planning a demonstration, always include a role for the cops. Cops legitimize demonstrations.

The cops throw us out.

It is noon. Wall Street. Businessmen with briefcases and suits and ties. Money freaks going to lunch. Important business deals. Time. Appointments.

And there we are in the middle of it, burning five-dollar bills. Burning their world. Burning their Christ.

"Don't! Don't!" some scream, grasping for the sacred paper. Several near fist-fights break out.

We escape with our lives.

Weeks later *The New York Times* publishes a short item revealing that the New York Stock Exchange is installing a bulletproof glass window between the visitors' platform and the floor, so that "nobody can shoot a stockbroker."

(In Chicago 5,000 yippies come, armed only with our skin. The cops bring tanks, dogs, guns, gas, long-range rifles, missiles. Is it South Vietnam or Chicago? America always overreacts.)

The American economy is doomed to collapse because it has no soul. Its stability is war and preparation for war. Consumer products are built to break, and advertising brainwashes us to consume new ones.

The rich feel guilty. The poor are taught to hate themselves. The guilty and the wretched are on a collision course.

If the men who control the technology used it for human needs and not profit and murder, every human being on the planet could be free from starvation. Machines could do most of the work: people would be free to do what they want.

We should be very realistic and demand the impossible. Food, housing, clothing, medicine, and color TV free for all!!

People would work because of love, creativity, and brotherhood. A new economic structure would produce a new man.

That new structure will be created by new men.

American society, because of its Western-Christian-Capitalist bag, is organized on the fundamental premise that man is bad, society evil, and that: People must be motivated and forced by external reward and punishment.

We are a new generation, species, race. We are bred on affluence, turned on by drugs, at home in our bodies, and excited by the future and its possibilities.

Everything for us is an experience, done for love or not done at all.

We live off the fat of society. Our fathers worked all-year-round for a two-week vacation. Our entire life is a vacation!

Every moment, every day we decide what we are going to do.

We do not groove with Christianity, the idea that people go to heaven after they are dead. We want HEAVEN NOW!

We do not believe in studying to obtain degrees in school. Degrees and grades are like money and credit, good only for burning.

There is a war going on in the Western world: a war of genocide by the old against the young.

The economy is closed. It does not need us. Everything is built.

So the purpose of universities is: to get us off the streets. Schools are baby-sitting agencies.

The purpose of the Vietnam war is: to get rid of blacks. They are a nuisance. America got the work she needed out of blacks, but now she has no use for them.

It is a psychological war. The old say, "We want you to die for us." The old send the young to die for the old.

Our response? Draft-card burning and draft dodging! We won't die for you.

Young whites are dropping out of white society. We are getting our heads straight, creating new identities. We're dropping out of middle-class institutions, leaving their schools, running away from their homes, and forming our own communities.

We are becoming the new niggers.

I'm getting on a plane en route to Washington. An airline official comes up to me and says, "You can't go on this airplane."

"Why not?" I ask.

"Because you smell."

That's what they used to say about black people, remember?

They don't say that about black people anymore. They'd get punched in their fucking mouths.

Our long hair communicates disrespect to America. A racist, short-hair society gets freaked by long hair. It blinds people. In Vietnam, America bombs the Vietnamese, but cannot see them because they are brown.

Long hair is vital to us because it enables us to recognize each other. We have white skin like our oppressors. Long hair ties us together into a visible counter-community.

A car drives down the street, parents in front, and 15-year-old longhair kid in back. The kid gives me the "V" sign! That's the kind of communication taking place.

Within our community we have the seeds of a new society. We have our own communications network, the underground press. We have the beginnings of a new family structure in communes. We have our own stimulants.

When the cops broke into my home on the Lower East Side to arrest me for possession of pot, it was like American soldiers invading a Vietnamese village. They experienced cultural shock.

Fidel Castro was on the wall. They couldn't believe it! Beads! They played with my beads for 20 minutes.

When the cops kidnapped me in Chicago, they interviewed me as if I had just landed from Mars.

"Do you fuck each other?"

"What is it like on LSD?"

"Do you talk directly with the Viet Cong?"

The two generations cannot communicate with one another because of our different historical experiences.

Our parents suffered through the Depression and World War II. We experience the consumer economy and the U.S.A. as a military bully in Vietnam.

From 1964 to 1968 the movement has been involved in the destruction of the old symbols of America. Through our actions we have redefined those symbols for the youth.

Kids growing up today expect school to be a place to demonstrate, sit-in, fight authority, and maybe get arrested.

Demonstrations become the initiation rites, rituals, and social celebrations of a new generation.

Remember the Pentagon, center of the military ego? We urinated on it. Thousands of stoned freaks stormed the place, carrying Che's picture and stuffing flowers in the rifles of the 82nd Airborne.

Remember the Democratic Convention? Who, after Chicago, can read schoolbook descriptions of national political conventions with a straight face anymore? The farce within the convention became clear because of the war between the yippies and the cops in the streets.

We are calling the bluff on the myths of America. Once the myth is exposed, the structure behind it crumbles like sand. Chaos results. People must create new realities.

In the process we create new myths, and these new myths forecast the future.

In America in 1969 old myths can be destroyed overnight, and new ones created overnight because of the power of television. By making communications instantaneous, television telescopes the revolution by centuries. What might have taken 100 years will now take 20. What used to happen in 10 years now happens in two. In a dying society, television becomes a revolutionary instrument.

For her own protection, the government is soon going to have to suppress freedom of the press and take direct control over what goes on television, especially the news.

TV has dramatized the longhair drop-out movement so well that virtually every young kid in the country wants to grow up and be a demonstrator.

What do you want to be when you grow up? A fireman? A cop? A professor?

"I want to grow up and make history."

Young kids watch TV's thrill-packed coverage of demonstrations—including the violence and excitement—and dream about being in them. They look like fun.

Mayor Daley put out this television film about Chicago. It had cops beating up young longhairs. In one scene, the cops threw a tear-gas canister into the crowd, and one demonstrator picked it up and heaved it right back.

Who do you think every kid in the country identified with?

Then the announcer said the chiller: "These demonstrations are Communist led! . . ."

Communism? Who the hell knows from Communism? We never lived through Stalin. We read about it, but it doesn't affect us emotionally. Our emotional reaction to Communism is Fidel marching into Havana in 1959.

There is NO WORD that the Man has to turn off your youth, no scare word.

"They're for ANARCHY!"

Damn right, we're for anarchy! This country is fucking over-organized anyway.

"DON'T DO THIS, DON'T DO THAT, DON'T!"

Growing up in America is learning what NOT to do.

We say: "DO IT, DO IT. DO WHATEVER YOU WANT TO DO."

Our battlegrounds are the campuses of America. White middle-class youth are strategically located in the high schools and colleges of this country. They are our power bases.

If one day 100 campuses were closed in a nationally coordinated rebellion, we could force the President of the United States to sue for peace at the conference table.

As long as we are in school we are prisoners. Schools are voluntary jails. We must liberate ourselves.

Dig the geography of a university. You can always tell what the rulers have up their sleeves when you check out the physical environment they create. The buildings tell you how to behave. Then there is less need for burdensome rules and cops. They designed classrooms so that students sit in rows, one after the other, hierarchically, facing the professor who stands up front talking to all of them.

Classrooms say:

"Listen to the Professor.

"He teaches you.

"Keep your place.

"Don't stretch out.

"Don't lie on the floor.

"Don't relax.

"Don't speak out of turn.

"Don't take off your clothes.

"Don't get emotional.

"Let the mind rule the body.

"Let the needs of the classroom rule the mind."

Classrooms are totalitarian environments. The main purpose of school and education in America is to force you to accept and love authority, and to distrust your own spontaneity and emotions.

How can you grow in such an over-structured environment? You can't. Schools aren't for learning.

Classrooms should be organized in circles, with the professor one part of the circle. A circle is a democratic environment.

Try breaking up the environment. Scream "Fuck" in the middle of your prof's lecture.

So, we organize a University of the Flesh. Four of us go into a classroom. We sit in the middle of the class. The lecture is on "Thinking."

Thinking!

We take off our shirts, smoke joints, and start French kissing. A lot of students get nervous. This goes on for 10–15 minutes, and the professor goes on with his lecture like nothing is happening.

Finally a girl says, "The people there are causing a distraction, and could they either put their shirts back on or could they please leave."

And the prof says, "Well, I agree with that. I think that if you're not here to hear what I'm saying . . ."

We shout: "You can't separate thinking from loving! We are hard in thought!!"

And the prof says, "Well, in my classroom I give the lessons."

Scratch a professor deep and you find a cop!

Fucking milquetoast! Didn't have the guts to throw us out, but in his classroom, HE GIVES the lesson. So he sends his teaching assistant to get the cops, and we split.

We must bring psychological guerrilla war to the university.

The mind is programmed. Get in there and break that bloody program!

Can you imagine what a feeling a professor has standing in front of a class and looking at a room full of bright faces taking down every word he says, raising their hands and asking him questions? It really makes someone think he is God. And to top it off, he has the power to reward and punish you, to decide whether or not you are fit to advance in the academic rat race.

Is this environment the right one for teacher and student?

Socrates is turning in his grave.

I was telling a professor of philosophy at Berkeley that many of his students were wiser men than he, even though he may have read more books and memorized more theories.

He replied, "Well, I must take the lead in the transfer of knowledge."

Transfer of knowledge! What is knowledge?

How to Live.

How to Legalize Marijuana.

How to Make a Revolution.

How to Free People from Jail.

How to Organize Against the CIA.

When a professor takes off his suit and tie, and joins us in the streets, then I say, "Hey man, what's your first name? You're my brother. Let's go. We're together."

I don't dig the "professor" bullshit. I am more interested in a 15-year-old stoned dope freak living on street corners than I am in a Ph.D.

There is anti-intellectualism in America because professors have created an artificial environment. That is why the average working guy does not respect professors.

The university is a protective and plastic scene, shielding people from the reality of life, the reality of suffering, of ecstasy, of struggle. The university converts the agony of life into the security of words and books.

You can't learn anything in school. Spend one hour in a jail or a courtroom and you will learn more than in five years spent in a university.

All I learned in school was how to beat the system, how to fake answers. But there are no answers. There are only more questions. Life is a long journey of questions, answered through the challenge of living. You would never know that, living in a university ruled by the "right" answers to the wrong questions.

Graffiti in school bathrooms tells you more about what's on people's minds than all the books in the library.

We must liberate ourselves. I dropped out. The shit got up to my neck and I stopped eating. I said: NO. NO. NO!! I'm dropping out.

People at Columbia found out what it felt like to learn when they seized buildings and lived in communes for days.

We have to redesign the environment and remake human relationships. But if you try it, you will be kicked out.

You know what professors and deans will say? "If you don't like it here, why don't you go back to Russia!"

A lot is demanded of white, middle-class youth in 1969. The whole thing about technological and bureaucratic society is that it is not made for heroes. We must become heroes.

The young kids living in the streets as new niggers are the pioneers of tomorrow, living dangerously and existentially.

The yippies went to Chicago to have our own counter-festival, a "Festival of Life" in the parks of Chicago, as a human contrast to the "Convention of Death" of the Democrats.

I get a phone call on Christmas Day, 1967 from Marvin Garson, the editor of the *San Francisco Express-Times,* and he says, "Hey, it looks like the Peace and Freedom Party is not going to get on the ballot."

I say, "I don't care. I'm not interested in electoral politics anyway."

And he says, "Let's run a pig for President."

An arrow shoots through my brain. Yeah! A pig, with buttons, posters, bumper stickers.

"America, why take half a hog, when you can have the whole hog?"

At the Democratic convention, the pigs nominate the President and he eats the people.

At the yippie convention, we nominate our pig and after he makes his nominating speech, we eat him. The contrast is clear: Should the President eat the people or the people eat the President?

Well, we didn't kill our pig. If there is one issue that could split the yippies, it is the issue of vegetarianism. A lot of yippies don't believe in killing and eating animals, so I had to be less militant on that point.

We bring Pigasus to Chicago, and he is arrested in Civic Center. The cops grab him. They grab seven of us, and they throw us in the paddy wagon with Pigasus.

The thing about running a pig for President is that it cuts through the shit. People's minds are full of things like, "You may elect a greater evil." We must break through their logic. Once we get caught in their logic, we're trapped in it.

Just freak it all out and proclaim: "This country is run on the principles of garbage. The Democratic and Republican parties have nominated a pig. So have we. We're honest about it."

In Chicago, Pigasus was a hell of a lot more effective than all those lackeys running around getting votes for the politicians. It turned out that the pig was more relevant to the current American political scene than Senator Eugene McCarthy. I never thought McCarthy could reform the Democratic party. Hell, McCarthy barely got into the convention himself. He had to have a ticket. That's how controlled the damn thing was. Finally, we forced McCarthy out into the streets with the people.

The election was not fair because every time we brought the pig out to give a campaign speech, they arrested him. It happened in Chicago, in New York, in San Francisco, even in London.

The yippies asked that the presidential elections be canceled until the rules of the game were changed. We said that everyone in the world should vote in the American election because America controls the world.

Free elections are elections in which the people who vote are the people affected by the results. The Vietnamese have more right to vote in the American elections than some 80-year-old grandmother in Omaha. They're being bombed by America! They should have at least some choice about if, how, and by whom they are going to be bombed.

I have nothing in particular against 80-year-old grandmothers, but I am in favor of lowering the voting age to 12 or 14 years. And I am not sure whether people over 50 should vote.

It is the young kids who are going to live in this world in the next 50 years. They should choose what they want for themselves.

Most people over 50 don't think about the potentialities of the future: they are preoccupied with justifying their past.

The only people who can choose change without suffering blows to their egos are the young, and change is the rhythm of the universe.

Many older people are constantly warning: "The right wing will get you." "George Wallace will get your momma."

I am so scared of George Wallace that I wore his fucking campaign button. I went to his campaign rally—all old ladies.

There are six Nazis who come with black gloves and mouthpieces, looking for a fight. And two fights break out. Two guys with long hair beat the shit out of them.

I am not afraid of the right wing because the right wing does not have the youth behind it.

"Straight" people get very freaked by Wallace. "Freaks" know the best way to fuck Wallace up. We support him.

At Wallace's rally in the Cow Palace in San Francisco, we come with signs saying "CUT THEIR HAIR!" "SEND THEM BACK TO AFRICA!" "BOMB THE VIETNAMESE BACK TO THE STONE AGE!"

When we arrive there is a picket line going on in front of the rally. I recognize it is the Communist Party picketing.

What? Picketing Wallace?

I walk up to my friend Bettina Aptheker and say, "Bettina, you're legitimizing him. You're legitimizing him by picketing. Instead, support him, kiss him. When he says the next hippie in front of his car will be the last hippie, cheer! Loudly!"

26

We have about two hundred people there, and we are the loudest people at the rally. Every five seconds we are jumping up and swearing, "Heil! Hitler! Heil! Hitler!"

Wallace is a sick man. America is the loony bin. The only way to cure her is through theatrical shock. Wallace is necessary because he brings to the surface the racism and hate that is deep within the country.

The yippie Fugs spearheaded the anti-war movement of the past five years by touring theaters and dance halls shouting into a microphone: "KILL, KILL, KILL FOR PEACE! KILL, KILL, KILL FOR PEACE!"

Wallace says aloud what most people say privately. He exposes the beast within liberal America. He embarrasses the liberal who says in one breath, "Oh, I like Negroes," and then in another breath, "We must eliminate crime in the streets."

Remember what Huey Long said: "When fascism comes to America, it will come as Americanism."

Wallace may be the best thing for those of us who are fighting him. You can only fight a disease after you recognize and diagnose it. America does not suffer from a cold: she has cancer.

The liberals who run this country agree with Wallace more than they disagree with him. George tells tales out of school. The liberals are going to have to shut that honest motherfucker up.

Do you dig that most cops support Wallace? Cops—the people who make and enforce the law in the streets! Wallace speaks FOR them.

Isn't that scary? Can't you see why blacks are getting guns and organizing into small self-defense units? Wouldn't you, if you were in *their* situation? Shouldn't *you* be?

Make America see her vampire face in the mirror. Destroy that gap between public talk and private behavior. Only when people see what's happening can they hear our screams, and feel our passion.

The Vietnam war is an education for America. It is an expensive teaching experience, but the American people are the most brainwashed people in the world.

At least the youth are learning that this country is no paradise

—America kills infants and children in Vietnam without blinking. Only professional killers can be so cool.

If you become hip to America in Vietnam, you can understand the reaction against the red-white-and-blue in Latin America, and you can feel why China hates us.

They are not irrational—America is.

Wallace is a left-wing agitator. Dig him. He speaks to the same anxiety and powerlessness that the New Left and yippies talk about.

Do you feel overwhelmed by bigness, including Big Government?

Do you lack control over your own life?

Are you distrustful of the politicians and bureaucrats in Washington?

Are you part of the "little people"?

Wallace stirs the masses. Revolutions should do that too.

When is the left going to produce an inflammatory and authentic voice of the people? A guy who reaches people's emotions? Who talks about revolution the way some of those nuts rap about Christ?

Wallace says: "We're against niggers, intellectuals, liberals, hippies."

Everybody! He puts us all together. He organizes us for us.

We must analyze how America keeps people down. Not by physical force, but by fear. From the second kids are hatched, we are taught fear. If we can overcome fear, we will discover that we are Davids fighting Goliath.

In late September a friend calls and says, "Hey, I just got a subpoena from HUAC."

I say, "Yeah? I didn't. What's going on here? I'm angry. I want a subpoena too."

It's called subpoenas envy.

So I telephone a confidante to the Red Squad, a fascist creep who works for the *San Francisco Examiner*, and I say, "Hey, Ed, baby, what about HUAC? Are they having hearings?"

He answers, "Well, I don't know. Are they?"

"Well, my friend just got a subpoena," I say. "I'd like one, too. If you can manage it."

He says, "Call me back in a few hours."

I call him back that afternoon and he says, "Well, I just talked to HUAC in Washington, and you are right. They are having hearings, and they are looking for you in New York."

"In NEW YORK? I've been in Berkeley a week! You guys are sure doing a shitty job trying to save this country!"

We exaggerate the surveillance powers of cops. We shouldn't. They are lazy. Their laziness may be the one reason why America doesn't yet have a totally efficient police state.

The cops were not lazy in Chicago. They followed "the leaders" continuously, 24 hours a day. If you are trailed by four cops just six steps behind you, you can't do very much.

But the people really doing things—why, the cops didn't even know who they were!

Pigs cannot relate to anarchy. They do not understand a movement based on personal freedom. When they look at our movement, they look for a hierarchy: leaders, lieutenants, followers.

The pigs think that we are organized like their pig department. We are not, and that's why we are going to win. A hierarchical, top-down organization is no match for the free and loose energy of the people.

As the pigs check with their higher-ups to find out what to do next, we have already switched the tactics and scene of the battle. They are watching one guy over there, and it is happening over here!

I come to the HUAC hearings wearing a bandolero of real bullets and carrying a toy M-16 rifle on my shoulder. The rifle was a model of the rifles the Viet Cong steal and then use to kill American soldiers in Vietnam.

The pigs stop me at the door of the hearings. They grab the bullets and the gun. It is a dramatic moment. Press and yippies pack us in tightly. The pigs drag me down three flights of stairs and remove the bullets, leaving the gun, Viet Cong pajamas, Eldridge Cleaver buttons, Black Panther beret, war paint, earrings, bandolero, and the bells which ring every time I move my body. My costume carried a nonverbal message: "We must all become stoned guerrillas."

The secret to the costume was the painted tits. Guerrilla war in America is going to come in psychedelic colors. We are hippie-guerrillas.

In HUAC's chambers Abbie Hoffman jumps up and yells out, "May I go to the bathroom?" Young kids reading that in their hometown papers giggle because they have to ask permission every time they want to go to the bathroom in school.

The message of my costume flipped across the country in one day: an example of our use of the enemy's institutions—her mass media—to turn on and communicate with one another.

I wore a Santa Claus costume to HUAC two months later in a direct attempt to reach the head of every child in the country.

Our victories are catching up with us: America isn't ready to napalm us yet, but the future doesn't look easy.

From June to November 1968, when I was helping to organize the demonstrations against the Democratic convention in Chicago, I experienced the following example of Americana:

New York pigs use a phony search warrant to bust into my apartment, question me, beat me, search the apartment, and arrest me for alleged felonious possession of marijuana; a pig in Chicago disguises himself as a biker to "infiltrate" the yippies as an agent provocateur and spy; he busts me on a frame-up, "solicitation to mob action," a felony punishable by five years in the pen; the judge imposes $25,000 bail and restricts my travel to Illinois; then the Justice Department in a document to a Virginia court admits that it maintains "electronic surveillance . . . of Jerry Rubin . . . in the interests of national security."

To try to suppress youth, Nixon will have to destroy the Constitution.

We will be presumed guilty until proven innocent.

Our privacy will vanish. Big Brother will spy on all of us and dominate our lives.

Every cop will become a law unto himself.

The courts will become automatic transmission belts sending us to detention camps and prisons.

People will be arrested for what they write and say.

Congress will impose censorship on the mass media, unless the media first censors itself, which is more likely.

To be young will be a crime.

In response, we must never become cynical, or lose our capacity for anger. We must stay on the offensive and be aggressive: AMERICA: IF YOU INJURE ONE, YOU MUST FIGHT ALL.

If our opposition is united, the repression may backfire and fail. The government may find the costs too heavy.

Don't think, "They can never get ME."

They can.

You are either on the side of the cops or on the side of human beings.

YIPPIE!

3 / Passage to More Than India

GARY SNYDER

It will be a revival, in higher form, of the liberty, equality, and fraternity of the ancient gentes.

LEWIS HENRY MORGAN

The Tribe

The celebrated human Be-In in San Francisco, January of 1967, was called "A Gathering of the Tribes." The two posters: one based on a photograph of a Shaivite sadhu with his long matted hair, ashes and beard; the other based on an old etching of a Plains Indian approaching a powwow on his horse—the carbine that had been cradled in his left arm replaced by a guitar. The Indians, and the Indian. The tribes were Berkeley, North Beach, Big Sur, Marin County, Los Angeles, and the host, Haight-Ashbury. Outriders were present from New York, London and Amsterdam. Out on the polo field that day the splendidly clad

SOURCE: Gary Snyder, *Earth House Hold* (New York: New Directions, 1968), pp. 103–16. Copyright © 1968, 1969 by Gary Snyder. "Passage to More Than India" was first published in *Evergreen Review*. Reprinted by permission of New Directions Publishing Corp.

Gary Snyder was born in San Francisco and studied Oriental languages at Berkeley. With Allen Ginsberg, Jack Kerouac, Philip Whalen, and Michael McClure, he helped to initiate and to introduce to the public what developed into the "beat movement" in literature. His main interests are Neolithic primitive and American Indian shamanism, nature, sexual intercourse, ritual and order, Buddhist thought, Chinese poetry, and Western science.

ab/originals often fell into clusters, with children, a few even under banners. These were the clans.

Large old houses are rented communally by a group, occupied by couples and singles (or whatever combinations) and their children. In some cases, especially in the rock-and-roll business and with light-show groups, they are all working together on the same creative job. They might even be a legal corporation. Some are subsistence farmers out in the country, some are contractors and carpenters in small coast towns. One girl can stay home and look after all the children while the other girls hold jobs. They will all be cooking and eating together and they may well be brown-rice vegetarians. There might not be much alcohol or tobacco around the house, but there will certainly be a stash of marijuana and probably some LSD. If the group has been together for some time it may be known by some informal name, magical and natural. These house-holds provide centers in the city and also out in the country for loners and rangers; gathering places for the scattered smaller hip families and havens for the questing adolescent children of the neighborhood. The clan sachems will sometimes gather to talk about larger issues—police or sheriff department harassments, busts, anti-Vietnam projects, dances and gatherings.

All this is known fact. The number of committed total tribesmen is not so great, but there is a large population of crypto-members who move through many walks of life undetected and only put on their beads and feathers for special occasions. Some are in the academies, others in the legal or psychiatric professions—very useful friends indeed. The number of people who use marijuana regularly and have experienced LSD is (considering it's all illegal) staggering. The impact of all this on the cultural and imaginative life of the nation—even the politics—is enormous.

And yet, there's nothing very new about it, in spite of young hippies just in from the suburbs for whom the "beat generation" is a kalpa away. For several centuries now Western Man has been ponderously preparing himself for a new look at the inner world and the spiritual realms. Even in the centers of nineteenth-century materialism there were dedicated seekers—some within Christianity, some in the arts, some within the occult circles. Witness William Butler Yeats. My own opinion is that we are now experiencing a surfacing (in a specifically "American" incarnation) of the Great Subculture which goes back as far perhaps as the late Paleolithic.

This subculture of illuminati has been a powerful undercurrent in all higher civilizations. In China it manifested as Taoism, not only Lao-tzu but the later Yellow Turban revolt and medieval Taoist secret societies; and the Zen Buddhists up till early Sung. Within Islam the Sufis; in India the various threads converged to produce Tantrism. In the West it has been represented largely by a string of heresies starting with the Gnostics, and on the folk level by "witchcraft."

Buddhist Tantrism, or Vajrayana as it's also known, is probably the finest and most modern statement of this ancient shamanistic-yogic-gnostic-socioeconomic view: that mankind's mother is Nature and Nature should be tenderly respected; that man's life and destiny is growth and enlightenment in self-disciplined freedom; that the divine has been made flesh and that flesh is divine; that we not only should but *do* love one another. This view has been harshly suppressed in the past as threatening to both Church and State. Today, on the contrary, these values seem almost biologically essential to the survival of humanity.

The Family

Lewis Henry Morgan (d. 1881) was a New York lawyer. He was asked by his club to reorganize it "after the pattern of the Iroquois confederacy." His research converted him into a defender of tribal rights and started him on his career as an amateur anthropologist. His major contribution was a broad theory of social evolution which is still useful. Morgan's *Ancient Society* inspired Engels to write *Origins of the Family, Private Property and the State* (1884, and still in print in both Russia and China), in which the relations between the rights of women, sexuality and the family, and attitudes toward property and power are tentatively explored. The pivot is the revolutionary implications of the custom of matrilineal descent, which Engels learned from Morgan; the Iroquois are matrilineal.

A schematic history of the family:

Hunters and gatherers—a loose monogamy within communal clans usually reckoning descent in the female line, i.e., matrilineal.

Early agriculturalists—a tendency toward group and polyandrous marriage, continued matrilineal descent and smaller-sized clans.

Pastoral nomads—a tendency toward stricter monogamy and patrilineal descent; but much premarital sexual freedom.

Iron-Age agriculturalists—property begins to accumulate and the family system changes to monogamy or polygyny with patrilineal descent. Concern with the legitimacy of heirs.

Civilization so far has implied a patriarchal, patrilineal family. Any other system allows too much creative sexual energy to be released into channels which are "unproductive." In the West, the clan, or gens, disappeared gradually, and social organization was ultimately replaced by political organization, within which separate male-oriented families compete: the modern state.

Engels' Marxian classic implies that the revolution cannot be completely achieved in merely political terms. Monogamy and patrilineal descent may well be great obstructions to the inner changes required for a people to truly live by "communism." Marxists after Engels let these questions lie. Russia and China today are among the world's staunchest supporters of monogamous, sexually turned-off families. Yet Engels' insights were not entirely ignored. The Anarcho-Syndicalists showed a sense for experimental social reorganization. American anarchists and the I.W.W. lived a kind of communalism, with some lovely stories handed down of free love—their slogan was more than just words: "Forming the new society within the shell of the old." San Francisco poets and gurus were attending meetings of the "Anarchist Circle"—old Italians and Finns—in the 1940's.

The Redskins

In many American Indian cultures it is obligatory for every member to get out of the society, out of the human nexus, and "out of his head," at least once in his life. He returns from his solitary vision quest with a secret name, a protective animal spirit, a secret song. It is his "power." The culture honors the man who has visited other realms.

Peyote, the mushroom, morning-glory seeds and Jimson-weed are some of the best-known herbal aids used by Indian cultures to assist in the quest. Most tribes apparently achieved these results simply through yogic-type disciplines: including sweat-baths, hours of dancing, fasting and total isolation. After the decline of the apocalyptic fervor of Wovoka's Ghost Dance religion (a pan-Indian movement of the 1880's and 1890's which believed that if all the Indians would dance the Ghost Dance with their Ghost shirts on, the Buffalo would rise from the ground, trample the white men to death in their dreams, and all the dead game would return; America would be restored to the Indians), the peyote cult spread and established itself in most of the western American tribes. Although the peyote religion conflicts with pre-existing tribal religions in a few cases (notably with the Pueblo), there is no doubt that the cult has been a positive force, helping the Indians maintain a reverence for their traditions and land through their period of greatest weakness— which is now over. European scholars were investigating peyote in the twenties. It is even rumored that Dr. Carl Jung was experimenting with peyote then. A small band of white peyote users emerged, and peyote was easily available in San Francisco by the late 1940's. In Europe some researchers on these alkaloid compounds were beginning to synthesize them. There is a karmic connection between the peyote cult of the Indians and the discovery of lysergic acid in Switzerland.

Peyote and acid have a curious way of tuning some people in to the local soil. The strains and stresses deep beneath one in the rock, the flow and fabric of wildlife around, the human history of Indians on this continent. Older powers become evident: west of the Rockies, the ancient creator-trickster, Coyote. Jaime de Angulo, a now-legendary departed Spanish shaman and anthropologist, was an authentic Coyote-medium. One of the most relevant poetry magazines is called *Coyote's Journal*. For many, the invisible presence of the Indian, and the heartbreaking beauty of America work without fasting or herbs. We make these contacts simply by walking the Sierra or Mohave, learning the old edibles, singing and watching.

The Jewel in the Lotus

At the Congress of World Religions in Chicago in the 1890's, two of the most striking figures were Swami Vivekananda (Shri Ramakrishna's disciple) and Shaku Soyen, the Zen Master and Abbot of Engaku-ji, representing Japanese Rinzai Zen. Shaku Soyen's interpreter was a college student named Teitaro Suzuki. The Ramakrishna-Vivekananda line produced scores of books and established Vedanta centers all through the Western world. A small band of Zen monks under Shaku Sokatsu (disciple of Shaku Soyen) was raising strawberries in Hayward, California, in 1907. Shigetsu Sasaki, later to be known as the Zen Master Sokei-an, was roaming the timberlands of the Pacific Northwest just before World War I, and living on a Puget Sound Island with Indians for neighbors. D. T. Suzuki's books are to be found today in the libraries of biochemists and on stone ledges under laurel trees in the open-air camps of Big Sur gypsies.

A Californian named Walter Y. Evans-Wentz, who sensed that the mountains on his family's vast grazing lands really did have spirits in them, went to Oxford to study the Celtic belief in fairies and then to Sikkim to study Vajrayana under a lama. His best-known book is *The Tibetan Book of the Dead.*

Those who do not have the money or time to go to India or Japan, but who think a great deal about the wisdom traditions, have remarkable results when they take LSD. The *Bhagavad-Gita,* the Hindu mythologies, *The Serpent Power,* the *Lanka-vatara-sūtra,* the *Upanishads,* the *Hevajra-tantra,* the *Maha-nirvana-tantra*—to name a few texts—become, they say, finally clear to them. They often feel they must radically reorganize their lives to harmonize with such insights.

In several American cities traditional meditation halls of both Rinzai and Soto Zen are flourishing. Many of the newcomers turned to traditional meditation after initial acid experience. The two types of experience seem to inform each other.

The Heretics

When Adam delved and Eve span,
Who was then a gentleman?

The memories of a Golden Age—the Garden of Eden—the Age of the Yellow Ancestor—were genuine expressions of civilization and its discontents. Harking back to societies where women and men were more free with each other; where there was more singing and dancing; where there were no serfs and priests and kings.

Projected into future time in Christian culture, this dream of the Millennium became the soil of many heresies. It is a dream handed down right to our own time—of ecological balance, classless society, social and economic freedom. It is actually one of the possible futures open to us. To those who stubbornly argue "it's against human nature," we can only patiently reply that you must know your own nature before you can say this. Those who have gone into their own natures deeply have, for several thousand years now, been reporting that we have nothing to fear if we are willing to train ourselves, to open up, explore and grow.

One of the most significant medieval heresies was the Brotherhood of the Free Spirit, of which Hieronymus Bosch was probably a member. The Brotherhood believed that God was immanent in everything, and that once one had experienced this God-presence in himself he became a Free Spirit; he was again living in the Garden of Eden. The brothers and sisters held their meetings naked, and practiced much sharing. They "confounded clerics with the subtlety of their arguments." It was complained that "they have no uniform . . . sometimes they dress in a costly and dissolute fashion, sometimes most miserably, all according to time and place." The Free Spirits had communal houses in secret all through Germany and the Lowlands, and wandered freely among them. Their main supporters were the well-organized and affluent weavers.

When brought before the Inquisition they were not charged with witchcraft, but with believing that man was divine, and with making love too freely, with orgies. Thousands were burned. There are some who have as much hostility to the adepts of the subculture today. This may be caused not so much by the outlandish clothes and dope, as by the nutty insistence on "love." The West and Christian culture on one level deeply wants love to win—and having decided (after several sad tries) that love can't, people who still say it will are like ghosts from an old dream.

Love begins with the family and its network of erotic and responsible relationships. A slight alteration of family structure will project a different love-and-property outlook through a whole culture . . . thus the communism and free love of the Christian heresies. This is a real razor's edge. Shall the lion lie down with the lamb? And make love even? The Garden of Eden.

White Indians

The modern American family is the smallest and most barren family that has ever existed. Each newly-married couple moves to a new house or apartment—no uncles or grandmothers come to live with them. There are seldom more than two or three children. The children live with their peers and leave home early. Many have never had the least sense of family.

I remember sitting down to Christmas dinner eighteen years ago in a communal house in Portland, Oregon, with about twelve others my own age, all of whom had no place they wished to go home to. That house was my first discovery of harmony and community with fellow beings. This has been the experience of hundreds of thousands of men and women all over America since the end of World War II. Hence the talk about the growth of a "new society." But more; these gatherings have been people spending time with each other—talking, delving, making love. Because of the sheer amount of time "wasted" together (without TV) they know each other better than most Americans know their own family. Add to this the mind-opening and personality-revealing effects of grass and acid, and it becomes possible to predict the emergence of groups who live by mutual illumination—have seen themselves as of one mind and one flesh—the "single eye" of the heretical English Ranters; the meaning of sahajiya, "born together"—the name of the latest flower of the Tantric community tradition in Bengal.

Industrial society indeed appears to be finished. Many of us are, again, hunters and gatherers. Poets, musicians, nomadic engineers and scholars; fact-diggers, searchers and re-searchers scoring in rich foundation territory. Horse-traders in lore and magic. The super hunting-bands of mercenaries like Rand or CIA may in some ways belong to the future, if they can be transformed by the ecological conscience, or acid, to which they are very vulnerable. A few of us are literally hunters and gatherers, playfully studying the old techniques of acorn flour, seaweed-gathering, yucca-fiber, rabbit snaring and bow hunting. The densest Indian population in pre-Columbian America north of Mexico was in Marin, Sonoma and Napa Counties, California.

And finally, to go back to Morgan and Engels, sexual mores and the family are changing in the same direction. Rather than the "breakdown of the family" we should see this as the transition to a new form of family. In the near future, I think it likely that the freedom of women and the tribal spirit will make it possible for us to formalize our marriage relationships in any way we please—as groups, or polygynously or polyandrously, as well as monogamously. I use the word "formalize" only in the sense of make public and open the relationships, and to sacramentalize them; to see family as part of the divine ecology. Because it is simpler, more natural, and breaks up tendencies toward property accumulation by individual families, matrilineal descent seems ultimately indicated. Such families already exist. Their children are different in personality structure and outlook from anybody in the history of Western culture since the destruction of Knossos.

The American Indian is the vengeful ghost lurking in the back of the troubled American mind. Which is why we lash out with such ferocity and passion, so muddied a heart, at the black-haired young peasants and soldiers who are the "Viet Cong." That ghost will claim the next generation as its own. When this has happened, citizens of the USA will at last begin to be Americans, truly at home on the continent, in love with their land. The chorus of a Cheyenne Indian Ghost dance song—"hi-niswa' vita'ki'ni"—"We shall live again."

> Passage to more than India!
> Are thy wings plumed indeed for such far flights?
> O soul, voyagest thou indeed on voyages like those?

Why Tribe

We use the term Tribe because it suggests the type of new society now emerging within the industrial nations. In America of course the word has associations with the American Indians, which we like. This new subculture is in fact more similar to that ancient and successful tribe, the European Gypies—a group without nation or territory which maintains its own values, its language and religion, no matter what country it may be in.

The Tribe proposes a totally different style: based on community houses, villages and ashrams; tribe-run farms or workshops or companies; large open families; pilgrimages and wanderings from center to center. A synthesis of Gandhian "village anarchism" and I.W.W. syndicalism. Interesting visionary pamphlets along these lines were written several years ago by Gandhians Richard Gregg and Appa Patwardhan. The Tribe proposes personal responsibilities rather than abstract centralized government, taxes and advertising-agency-plus-Mafia type international brainwashing corporations.

In the United States and Europe the Tribe has evolved gradually over the last fifty years—since the end of World War I—in response to the increasing insanity of the modern nations. As the number of alienated intellectuals, creative types and general social misfits grew, they came to recognize each other by various minute signals. Much of this energy was channeled into Communism in the thirties and early forties. All the anarchists and left-deviationists—and many Trotskyites—were tribesmen at heart. After World War II, another generation looked at Communist rhetoric with a fresh eye and saw that within the Communist governments (and states of mind) there are too many of the same things as are wrong with "capitalism"—too much anger and murder. The suspicion grew that perhaps the whole Western Tradition, of which Marxism is but a (Millennial Protestant) part, is off the track. This led many people to study other major civilizations—India and China—to see what they could learn.

It's an easy step from the dialectic of Marx and Hegel to an interest in the dialectic of early Taoism, the *I Ching,* and the yin-yang theories. From Taoism it is another easy step to the philosophies and mythologies of India—vast, touching the deepest areas of the mind, and with a view of the ultimate nature of the universe which is almost identical with the most sophisticated thought in modern physics—that truth, whatever it is, which is called "The Dharma."

Next comes a concern with deepening one's understanding in an experiential way: abstract philosophical understanding is simply not enough. At this point many, myself included, found in the Buddha-Dharma a practical method for clearing one's mind of the trivia, prejudices and false values that our conditioning had laid on us—and more important, an approach to the basic problem of how to penetrate to the deepest non-self Self. Today we have many who are exploring the Ways of Zen, Vajrayāna, Yoga, Shamanism, Psychedelics. The Buddha-Dharma is a long, gentle, human dialog—2,500 years of quiet conversation—on the nature of human nature and the eternal Dharma—and practical methods of realization.

In the course of these studies it became evident that the "truth" in Buddhism and Hinduism is not dependent in any sense on Indian or Chinese culture; and that "India" and "China"—as societies—are as burdensome to human beings as any others; perhaps more so. It became clear that "Hinduism" and "Buddhism" as social institutions had long been accomplices of the State in burdening and binding people, rather than serving to liberate them. Just like the other Great Religions.

At this point, looking once more quite closely at history both East and West, some of us noticed the similarities in certain small but influential heretical and esoteric movements. These schools of thought and practice were usually suppressed, or diluted and made harmless, in whatever society they appeared. Peasant witchcraft in Europe, Tantrism in Bengal, Quakers in England, Tachikawa-ryū in Japan, Ch'an in China. These are all outcroppings of the Great Subculture which runs underground all through history. This is the tradition that runs without break from Paleo-Siberian Shamanism and Magdalenian cave-painting; through megaliths and Mysteries, astronomers, ritualists, alchemists and Albigensians; gnostics and vagantes, right down to Golden Gate Park.

The Great Subculture has been attached in part to the official religions but is different in that it transmits a community style of life, with an ecstatically positive vision of spiritual and physical love; and is opposed for very fundamental reasons to the Civilization Establishment.

It has taught that man's natural being is to be trusted and followed; that we need not look to a model or rule imposed from outside in searching for the center; and that in following the grain, one is being truly "moral." It has recognized that for one to "follow the grain" it is necessary to look exhaustively into the negative and demonic potentials of the Unconscious, and by recognizing these powers—symbolically acting them out—one releases himself from these forces. By this profound exorcism and ritual drama, the Great Subculture destroys the one credible claim of Church and State to a necessary function.

All this is subversive to civilization: for civilization is built on hierarchy and specialization. A ruling class, to survive, must propose a Law: a law to work must have a hook into the social psyche—and the most effective way to achieve this is to make people doubt their natural worth and instincts, especially sexual. To make "human nature" suspect is also to make Nature—the wilderness—the adversary. Hence the ecological crisis of today.

We came, therefore, (and with many Western thinkers before us) to suspect that civilization may be overvalued. Before anyone says "This is ridiculous, we all know civilization is a necessary thing," let him read some cultural anthropology. Take a look at the lives of South African Bushmen, Micronesian navigators, the Indians of California; the researches of Claude Lévi-Strauss. Everything we have thought about man's welfare needs to be rethought. The Tribe, it seems, is the newest development in the Great Subculture. We have almost unintentionally linked ourselves to a transmission of gnosis, a potential social order, and techniques of enlightenment, surviving from prehistoric times.

The most advanced developments of modern science and technology have come to support some of these views. Consequently the modern Tribesman, rather than being old-fashioned in his criticism of civilization, is the most relevant type in contemporary society. Nationalism, warfare, heavy industry and consumership, are already outdated and useless. The next great step of mankind is to step into the nature of his own mind—the real question is "just what is consciousness?"—and we must make the most intelligent and creative use of science in exploring these questions. The man of wide international experience, much learning and leisure—luxurious product of our long and sophisticated history—may with good reason wish to live simply, with few tools and minimal clothes, close to nature.

The Revolution has ceased to be an ideological concern. Instead, people are trying it out right now—communism in small communities, new family organization. A million people in America and another million in England and Europe. A vast underground in Russia, which will come out in the open four or five years hence, is now biding. How do they recognize each other? Not always by beards, long hair, bare feet or beads. The signal is a bright and tender look; calmness and gentleness, freshness and ease of manner. Men, women and children—all of whom together hope to follow the timeless path of love and wisdom, in affectionate company with the sky, winds, clouds, trees, waters, animals and grasses—this is the tribe.

4 / Protean Man

ROBERT JAY LIFTON

I should like to examine a set of psychological patterns characteristic of contemporary life, which are creating a new kind of man—a "protean man." As my stress is upon change and flux, I shall not speak much of "character" and "personality," both of which suggest fixity and permanence. Erikson's concept of identity has been, among other things, an effort to get away from this principle of fixity; and I have been using the term self-process to convey still more specifically the idea of flow. For it is quite possible that even the image of personal identity, in so far as it suggests inner stability and sameness, is derived from a vision of a traditional culture in which man's relationship to his institutions and symbols are still relatively intact—which is hardly the case today. If we understand the self to be the person's symbol of his own organism, then self-process refers to the continuous psychic recreation of that symbol.

I came to this emphasis through work in cultures far removed from my own, studies of young (and not so young) Chinese and Japanese. Observations I was able to make in America also led

SOURCE: *Partisan Review* 35 (Winter 1968), 13–27. Copyright © 1968 by Robert Jay Lifton. Reprinted by permission of the author.

Robert Jay Lifton is research professor of psychiatry at Yale University and author of *Death in Life: Survivors of Hiroshima*.

me to the conviction that a very general process was taking place. I do not mean to suggest that everybody is becoming the same, or that a totally new "world-self" is taking shape. But I am convinced that a new style of self-process is emerging everywhere. It derives from the interplay of three factors responsible for human behavior: the psychobiological potential common to all mankind at any moment in time; those traits given special emphasis in a particular cultural tradition; and those related to modern (and particularly contemporary) historical forces. My thesis is that this third factor plays an increasingly important part in shaping self-process.

My work with Chinese was done in Hong Kong, in connection with a study of the process of "thought reform" (or "brainwashing") as conducted on the mainland. I found that Chinese intellectuals of varying ages, whatever their experience with thought reform itself, had gone through an extraordinary set of what I at that time called identity fragments—of combinations of belief and emotional involvement—each of which they could readily abandon in favor of another. I remember particularly the profound impression made upon me by the extraordinary history of one young man in particular: beginning as a "filial son" or "young master," that elite status of an only son in an upper-class Chinese family; then feeling himself an abandoned and betrayed victim, as traditional forms collapsed during civil war and general chaos, and his father, for whom he was to long all his life, was separated from him by political and military duties; then a "student activist" in rebellion against the traditional culture in which he had been so recently immersed (as well as against a Nationalist Regime whose abuses he had personally experienced); leading him to Marxism and to strong emotional involvement in the Communist movement; then, because of remaining "imperfections," becoming a participant in a thought reform program for a more complete ideological conversion; but which, in his case, had the opposite effect, alienating him, so he came into conflict with the reformers and fled the country; then, in Hong Kong, struggling to establish himself as an "anti-Communist writer"; after a variety of difficulties, finding solace and meaning in becoming a Protestant convert; and following that, still just thirty, apparently poised for some new internal (and perhaps external) move.

44

Even more dramatic were the shifts in self-process of a young Japanese whom I interviewed in Tokyo and Kyoto from 1960 to 1962. I shall mention one in particular as an extreme example of this protean pattern, though there were many others who in various ways resembled him. Before the age of twenty-five he had been all of the following: a proper middle-class Japanese boy, brought up in a professional family within a well-established framework of dependency and obligation; then, due to extensive contact with farmers' and fishermen's sons brought about by wartime evacuation, a "country boy" who was to retain what he described as a life-long attraction to the tastes of the common man; then, a fiery young patriot who "hated the Americans" and whose older brother, a kamikaze pilot, was saved from death only by the war's end; then a youngster confused in his beliefs after Japan's surrender, but curious about rather than hostile toward American soldiers; soon an eager young exponent of democracy, caught up in the "democracy boom" which swept Japan; at the same time a youthful devotee of traditional Japanese arts—old novels, Chinese poems, kabuki and flower arrangement; during junior high and high school, an all-round leader, outstanding in studies, student self-government and general social and athletic activities; almost simultaneously, an outspoken critic of society at large and of fellow students in particular for their narrow careerism, on the basis of Marxist ideas current in Japanese intellectual circles; yet also an English-speaking student, which meant, in effect, being in still another vanguard and having strong interest in things American; then, midway through high school, experiencing what he called a "kind of neurosis" in which he lost interest in everything he was doing and, in quest of a "change in mood," took advantage of an opportunity to become an exchange student for one year at an American high school; became a convert to many aspects of American life, including actually being baptized as a Christian under the influence of a minister he admired who was also his American "father," and returned to Japan only reluctantly; as a "returnee," found himself in many ways at odds with his friends and was accused by one of "smelling like butter" (a traditional Japanese phrase for Westerners); therefore reimmersed himself in "Japanese" experience—sitting on *tatami*, indulging in quiet, melancholy moods, drinking tea and so on; then became a *ronin*—in feudal days, a samurai without a master, now a student without a university—because of failing his examinations for Tokyo University (a sort of Harvard, Yale, Columbia and Berkeley rolled into one), and as is the custom, spending the following year preparing for the next round rather than attend a lesser institution; once admitted, found little to interest him until becoming an enthusiastic *Zengakuren* activist, with full embrace of its ideal of "pure Communism" and a profound sense of fulfillment in taking part in the planning and carrying out of student demonstrations; but when offered a high position in the organization during his junior year, abruptly became an *ex-Zengakuren* activist by resigning, because he felt he was not suited for "the life of a revolutionary"; then an aimless dissipator, as he drifted into a pattern of heavy drinking, marathon mah-jongg games and affairs with bargirls; but when the time came, had no difficulty gaining employment with one of Japan's mammoth industrial organizations (and one of the *bêtes noires* of his Marxist days) and embarking upon the life of a young executive or *sarariman* (salaried man)—in fact doing so with eagerness, careful preparation and relief, but at the same time having fantasies and dreams of kicking over the traces, sometimes violently, and embarking upon a world tour (largely Hollywood-inspired) of exotic and sophisticated pleasure-seeking.

There are, of course, important differences between the protean life styles of the two young men, and between them and their American counterparts—differences which have to do with cultural emphases and which contribute to what is generally called national character. But such is the intensity of the shared aspects of historical experience that contemporary Chinese, Japanese and American self-process turn out to have striking points of convergence.

I would stress two historical developments as having special importance for creating protean man. The first is the worldwide sense of what I have called *historical* (or *psychohistorical) dislocation,* the break in the sense of connection which men have long felt with the vital and nourishing symbols of their cultural tradition—symbols revolving around family, idea systems, religions, and the life cycle in general. In our contemporary world one perceives these traditional symbols (as I have suggested elsewhere, using the Japanese as a paradigm) as irrelevant, burdensome or inactivating, and yet one cannot avoid carrying them within or having one's self-process profoundly affected by them. The second large historical tendency is the *flooding of imagery* produced by the extraordinary flow of postmodern cultural influences over mass communication networks. These cross readily over local and national boundaries, and permit each individual to be touched by everything, but at the same time cause him to be overwhelmed by superficial messages and undigested cultural elements, by headlines and by endless partial alternatives in every sphere of life. These alternatives, moreover, are universally and simultaneously shared —if not as courses of action, at least in the form of significant inner imagery.

We know from Greek mythology that Proteus was able to change his shape with relative ease—from wild boar to lion to dragon to fire to flood. But what he did find difficult, and would not do unless seized and chained, was to commit himself to a single form, the form most his own, and carry out his function of prophecy. We can say the same of protean man, but we must keep in mind his possibilities as well as his difficulties.

The protean style of self-process, then, is characterized by an interminable series of experiments and explorations—some shallow, some profound—each of which may be readily abandoned in favor of still new psychological quests. The pattern in many ways resembles what Erik Erikson has called "identity diffusion" or "identity confusion," and the impaired psychological functioning which those terms suggest can be very much present. But I would stress that the protean style is by no means pathological as such, and, in fact, may well be one of the functional patterns of our day. It extends to all areas of human experience—to political as well as sexual behavior, to the holding and promulgating of ideas and to the general organization of lives.

I would like to suggest a few illustrations of the protean style, as expressed in America and Europe, drawn both from psychotherapeutic work with patients and from observations on various forms of literature and art.

One patient of mine, a gifted young teacher, spoke of himself in this way:

> I have an extraordinary number of masks I can put on or take off. The question is: is there, or should there be, one face which should be authentic? I'm not sure that there is one for me. I can think of other parallels to this, especially in literature. There are representations of every kind of crime, every kind of sin. For me, there is not a single act I cannot imagine myself committing.

He went on to compare himself to an actor on the stage who "performs with a certain kind of polymorphous versatility"— and here he was referring, slightly mockingly, to Freud's term, "polymorphous perversity," for diffusely inclusive (also protean) infantile sexuality. And he asked:

> Which is the real person, so far as an actor is concerned? Is he more real when performing on the stage—or when he is at home? I tend to think that for people who have these many, many masks, there is no home. Is it a futile gesture for the actor to try to find his real face?

My patient was by no means a happy man, but neither was he incapacitated. And although we can see the strain with which he carries his "polymorphous versatility," it could also be said that, as a teacher and a thinker, and in some ways as a man, it served him well.

In contemporary American literature, Saul Bellow is notable for the protean men he has created. In *The Adventures of Augie March,* one of his earlier novels, we meet a picaresque hero with a notable talent for adapting himself to divergent social worlds. Augie himself says: "I touched all sides, and nobody knew where I belonged. I had no good idea of that myself." And a perceptive young English critic, Tony Tanner, tells us: "Augie indeed celebrates the self, but he can find nothing to do with it." Tanner goes on to describe Bellow's more recent protean hero, Herzog, as "a representative modern intelligence, swamped with ideas, metaphysics, and values, and surrounded by messy facts. It labours to cope with them all."

A distinguished French literary spokesman for the protean style—in his life and in his work—is, of course, Jean-Paul Sartre. Indeed, I believe that it is precisely because of these protean traits that Sartre strikes us as such an embodiment of twentieth-century man. An American critic, Theodore Solotaroff, speaks of Sartre's fundamental assumption that "there is no such thing as even a relatively fixed sense of self, ego, or identity—rather there is only the subjective mind in motion in relationship to that which it confronts." And Sartre himself refers to human consciousness as "a sheer activity transcending toward objects," and "a great emptiness, a wind blowing toward objects." These might be overstatements, but I doubt that they could have been written thirty years ago. Solotaroff further characterizes Sartre as

> constantly on the go, hurrying from point to point, subject to subject; fiercely intentional, his thought occupies, fills, and distends its material as he endeavors to lose and find himself in his encounters with other lives, disciplines, books, and situations.

This image of repeated, autonomously willed death and rebirth of the self, so central to the protean style, becomes associated with the themes of fatherlessness—as Sartre goes on to tell us in his autobiography with his characteristic tone of serious self-mockery:

> There is no good father, that's the rule. Don't lay the blame on men but on the bond of paternity, which is rotten. To beget children, nothing better; *to have* them, what iniquity! Had my father lived, he would have lain on me at full length and would have crushed me. . . . Amidst Aeneas and his fellows who carry their Anchises on their backs, I move from shore to shore, alone and hating those invisible begetters who bestraddle their sons all their life long. I left behind me a young man who did not have time to be my father and who could now be my son. Was it a good thing or bad? I don't know. But I readily subscribed to the verdict of an eminent psychoanalyst: I have no Superego.

ROBERT JAY LIFTON 49

We note Sartre's image of interchangeability of father and son, of "a young man who did not have time to be my father and who could now be my son"—which, in a literal sense refers to the age at which his father died, but symbolically suggests an extension of the protean style to intimate family relationships. And such reversals indeed become necessary in a rapidly changing world in which the sons must constantly "carry their fathers on their backs," teach them new things which they, as older people, cannot possibly know. The judgment of the absent superego, however, may be misleading, especially if we equate superego with susceptibility to guilt. What has actually disappeared—in Sartre and in protean man in general—is the *classic* superego, the internalization of clearly defined criteria of right and wrong transmitted within a particular culture by parents to their children. Protean man requires freedom from precisely that kind of superego—he requires a symbolic fatherlessness—in order to carry out his explorations. But rather than being free of guilt, we shall see that his guilt takes on a different form from that of his predecessors.

There are many other representations of protean man among contemporary novelists: in the constant internal and external motion of "beat generation" writings, such as Jack Kerouac's *On the Road;* in the novels of a gifted successor to that generation, J. P. Donleavy, particularly *The Ginger Man;* and of course in the work of European novelists such as Günter Grass, whose *The Tin Drum* is a breathtaking evocation of prewar Polish-German, wartime German and postwar German environments, in which the protagonist combines protean adaptability with a kind of perpetual physical-mental "strike" against any change at all.

In the visual arts, one of the most important postwar movements has been aptly named "action painting" to convey its stress upon process rather than fixed completion. And a more recent and related movement in sculpture, called Kinetic Art, goes further. According to Jean Tinguely, one of its leading practitioners, "artists are putting themselves in rhythm with their time, in contact with their epic, especially with permanent and perpetual movement." As revolutionary as any style or approach is the stress upon innovation per se which now dominates painting. I have frequently heard artists, themselves considered radical innovators, complain bitterly of the current standards dictating that "innovation is all," and of a turnover in art movements so rapid as to discourage the idea of holding still long enough to develop a particular style.

We also learn much from film stars. Marcello Mastroianni, when asked whether he agreed with *Time* magazine's characterization of him as "the neo-capitalist hero," gave the following answer:

> In many ways, yes. But I don't think I'm any kind of hero, neo-capitalist or otherwise. If anything I am an *anti*-hero or at most a *non*-hero. *Time* said I had the frightened, characteristically 20th-century look, with a spine made of plastic napkin rings. I accepted this—because modern man is that way; and being a product of my time and an artist, I can represent him. If humanity were all one piece, I would be considered a weakling.

Mastroianni accepts his destiny as protean man; he seems to realize that there are certain advantages to having a spine made of plastic napkins rings, or at least that it is an appropriate kind of spine to have these days.

John Cage, the composer, is an extreme exponent of the protean style, both in his music and in his sense of all of us as listeners. He concluded a recent letter to the *Village Voice* with the sentence: "Nowadays, everything happens at once and our souls are conveniently electronic, omniattentive." The comment is McLuhan-like, but what I wish to stress particularly is the idea of omniattention—the sense of contemporary man as having the possibility of "receiving" and "taking in" everything. In attending, as in being, nothing is "off limits."

To be sure, one can observe in contemporary man a tendency which seems to be precisely the opposite of the protean style. I refer to the closing off of identity or constriction of self-process, to a straight-and-narrow specialization in psychological as well as in intellectual life, and to reluctance to let in any "extraneous" influences. But I would emphasize that where this kind of constricted or "one-dimensional" self-process exists, it has an essentially reactive and compensatory quality. In this it differs from earlier characterological styles it may seem to resemble (such as the "inner-directed" man described by Riesman, and still earlier patterns in traditional society). For these were direct outgrowths of societies which then existed, and in harmony with those societies, while at the present time a constricted self-process requires continuous "psychological work" to fend off protean influences which are always abroad.

Protean man has a particular relationship to the holding of ideas which has, I believe, great significance for the politics, religion, and general intellectual life of the future. For just as elements of the self can be experimented with and readily altered, so can idea systems and ideologies be embraced, modified, let go of and reembraced, all with a new ease that stands in sharp contrast to the inner struggle we have in the past associated with these shifts. Until relatively recently, no more than one major ideological shift was likely to occur in a lifetime, and that one would be long remembered as a significant individual turning-point accompanied by profound soul-searching and conflict. But today it is not unusual to encounter several such shifts, accomplished relatively painlessly, within a year or even a month; and among many groups, the rarity is a man who has gone through life holding firmly to a single ideological vision.

In one sense, this tendency is related to "the end of ideology" spoken of by Daniel Bell, since protean man is incapable of enduring an unquestioning allegiance to the large ideologies and utopian thought of the nineteenth and early twentieth centuries. One must be cautious about speaking of the end of anything, however, especially ideology, and one also encounters in protean man what I would call strong ideological hunger. He is starved for ideas and feelings that can give coherence to his world, but here too his taste is toward new combinations. While he is by no means without yearning for the absolute, what he finds most acceptable are images of a more fragmentary nature than those of the ideologies of the past; and these images, although limited and often fleeting, can have great influence upon his psychological life. Thus political and religious movements, as they confront protean man, are likely to experience less difficulty convincing him to alter previous convictions than they do providing him a set of beliefs which can command his allegiance for more than a brief experimental interlude.

Intimately bound up with his flux in emotions and beliefs is a profound inner sense of absurdity, which finds expression in a tone of mockery. The sense and the tone are related to a perception of surrounding activities and belief as profoundly strange and inappropriate. They stem from a breakdown in the relationship between inner and outer worlds—that is, in the sense of symbolic integrity—and are part of the pattern of psychohistorical dislocation I mentioned earlier. For if we view man as primarily a symbol-forming organism, we must recognize that he has constant need of a meaningful inner formulation of self and world in which his own actions, and even his impulses, have some kind of "fit" with the "outside" as he perceives it.

The sense of absurdity, of course, has a considerable modern tradition, and has been discussed by such writers as Camus as a function of man's spiritual homelessness and inability to find any meaning in traditional belief systems. But absurdity and mockery have taken much more extreme form in the post-World War II world, and have in fact become a prominent part of a universal life style.

In American life, absurdity and mockery are everywhere. Perhaps their most vivid expression can be found in such areas as Pop Art and the more general burgeoning of "pop culture." Important here is the complex stance of the pop artist toward the objects he depicts. On the one hand he embraces the materials of the everyday world, celebrates and even exalts them—boldly asserting his creative return to representational art (in active rebellion against the previously reigning nonobjective school), and his psychological return to the "real world" of *things*. On the other hand, everything he touches he mocks. "Thingness" is pressed to the point of caricature. He is indeed artistically reborn as he moves freely among the physical and symbolic materials of his environment, but mockery is his birth certificate and his passport. This kind of duality of approach is formalized in the stated "duplicity" of Camp, a poorly-defined aesthetic in which (among other things) all varieties of mockery converge under the guiding influence of the homosexual's subversion of a heterosexual world.

Also relevant are a group of expressions in current slang, some of them derived originally from jazz. The "dry mock" has replaced the dry wit; one refers to a segment of life experience as a "bit," "bag," "caper," "game" (or "con game"), "scene," "show" or "scenario"; and one seeks to "make the scene" (or "make it"), "beat the system" or "pull it off"—or else one "cools it" ("plays it cool") or "cops out." The thing to be experienced, in other words, is too absurd to be taken at its face value; one must either keep most of the self aloof from it, or if not one must lubricate the encounter with mockery.

A similar spirit seems to pervade literature and social action alike. What is best termed a "literature of mockery" has come to dominate fiction and other forms of writing on an international scale. Again Günter Grass's *The Tin Drum* comes to mind, and is probably the greatest single example of this literature—a work, I believe, which will eventually be appreciated as much as a general evocation of contemporary man as of the particular German experience with Nazism. In this country the divergent group of novelists known as "black humorists" also fit into the general category—related as they are to a trend in the American literary consciousness which R. W. B. Lewis has called a "savagely comical apocalypse" or a "new kind of ironic literary form and disturbing vision, the joining of the dark thread of apocalypse with the nervous detonations of satiric laughter." For it is precisely death itself, and particularly threats of the contemporary apocalypse, that protean man ultimately mocks.

The relationship of mockery to political and social action has been less apparent, but is, I would claim, equally significant. There is more than coincidence in the fact that the largest American student uprising of recent decades, the Berkeley Free Speech Movement of 1965, was followed immediately by a "Dirty Speech Movement." While the object of the Dirty Speech Movement—achieving free expression of forbidden language, particularly of four-letter words—can be viewed as a serious one, the predominant effect, even in the matter of names, was that of a mocking caricature of the movement which preceded it. But if mockery can undermine protest, it can also enliven it. There have been signs of craving for it in major American expressions of protest such as the Negro movement and the opposition to the war in Vietnam. In the former a certain chord can be struck by the comedian Dick Gregory, and in the latter by the use of satirical skits and parodies, that revives the flagging attention of protestors becoming gradually bored with the repetition of their "straight" slogans and goals. And on an international scale, I would say that, during the past decade, Russian intellectual life has been enriched by a leavening spirit of mockery—against which the Chinese leaders are now, in the extremes of their "Cultural Revolution," fighting a vigorous but ultimately losing battle.

Closely related to the sense of absurdity and the spirit of mockery is another characteristic of protean man which can be called "suspicion of counterfeit nurturance." Involved here is a severe conflict of dependency, a core problem of protean man. I first began to think of the concept several years ago while working with survivors of the atomic bomb in Hiroshima. I found that these survivors both felt themselves in need of special help, and resented whatever help was offered them because they equated it with weakness and inferiority. In considering the matter more generally, I found this equation of nurturance with a threat to autonomy a major theme of contemporary life. The increased dependency needs resulting from the breakdown of traditional institutions lead protean man to seek out replacements wherever he can find them. The large organizations (government, business, academic, etc.) to which he turns, and which contemporary society more and more holds out as a substitute for traditional institutions, present an ambivalent threat to his autonomy in one way; and the intense individual relationships in which he seeks to anchor himself in another. Both are therefore likely to be perceived as counterfeit. But the obverse side of this tendency is an expanding sensitivity to the unauthentic, which may be just beginning to exert its general creative force on man's behalf.

Technology (and technique in general), together with science, have special significance for protean man. Technical achievement of any kind can be strongly embraced to combat inner tendencies toward diffusion, and to transcend feelings of absurdity and conflicts over counterfeit nurturance. The image of science itself, however, as the ultimate power behind technology and, to a considerable extent, behind contemporary thought in general, becomes much more difficult to cope with. Only in certain underdeveloped countries can one find, in relatively pure form, those expectations of scientific-utopian deliverance from all human want and conflict which were characteristic of eighteenth- and nineteenth-century Western thought. Protean man retains much of this utopian imagery, but he finds it increasingly undermined by massive disillusionment. More and more he calls forth the other side of the God-devil polarity generally applied to science, and sees it as a purveyor of total destructiveness. This kind of profound ambivalence creates for him the most extreme psychic paradox: the very force he still feels to be his liberator from the heavy burdens of past irrationality also threatens him with absolute annihilation, even extinction. But this paradox may well be—in fact, I believe, already has been—the source of imaginative efforts to achieve new relationships between science and man, and indeed, new visions of science itself.

I suggested before that protean man was not free of guilt. He indeed suffers from it considerably, but often without awareness of what is causing his suffering. For his is a form of hidden guilt: a vague but persistent kind of self-condemnation related to the symbolic disharmonies I have described, a sense of having no outlet for his loyalties and no symbolic structure for his achievements. This is the guilt of social breakdown, and it includes various forms of historical and racial guilt experienced by whole nations and peoples, both by the privileged and the abused. Rather than a clear feeling of evil or sinfulness, it takes the form of a nagging sense of unworthiness all the more troublesome for its lack of clear origin.

Protean man experiences similarly vague constellations of anxiety and resentment. These too have origin in symbolic impairments and are particularly tied-in with suspicion of counterfeit nurturance. Often feeling himself uncared for, even abandoned, protean man responds with diffuse fear and anger. But he can neither find a good cause for the former, nor a consistent target for the latter. He nonetheless cultivates his anger because he finds it more serviceable than anxiety, because there are plenty of targets of one kind or another beckoning, and because even moving targets are better than none. His difficulty is that focused indignation is as hard for him to sustain as is any single identification or conviction.

Involved in all of these patterns is a profound psychic struggle with the idea of change itself. For here too protean man finds himself ambivalent in the extreme. He is profoundly attracted to the idea of making all things, including himself, totally new—to the "mode of transformation." But he is equally drawn to an image of a mythical past of perfect harmony and prescientific wholeness, to the "mode of restoration." Moreover, beneath his transformationism is nostalgia, and beneath his restorationism is his fascinated attraction to contemporary forms and symbols. Constantly balancing these elements midst the extraordinarily rapid change surrounding his own life, the nostalgia is pervasive, and can be one of his most explosive and dangerous emotions. This longing for a "Golden Age" of absolute oneness, prior to individual and cultural separation or delineation, not only sets the tone for the restorationism of the politically Rightist antagonists of history: the still-extant Emperor-worshipping assassins in Japan, the Colons in France and the John Birchites and Ku Klux Klanners in this country. It also, in more disguised form, energizes that transformationist totalism of the Left which courts violence, and is even willing to risk nuclear violence, in a similarly elusive quest.

Following upon all that I have said are radical impairments to the symbolism of transition within the life cycle—the *rites de passage* surrounding birth, entry into adulthood, marriage and death. Whatever rites remain seem shallow, inappropriate, fragmentary. Protean man cannot take them seriously, and often seeks to improvise new ones with whatever contemporary materials he has available, including cars and drugs. Perhaps the central impairment here is that of symbolic immortality—of the universal need for imagery of connection predating and extending beyond the individual life span, whether the idiom of this immortality is biological (living on through children and grandchildren), theological (through a life after death), natural (*in* nature itself which outlasts all) or creative (through what man makes and does). I have suggested elsewhere that this sense of immortality is a fundamental component of ordinary psychic life, and that it is now being profoundly threatened: by simple historical velocity, which subverts the idioms (notably the theological) in which it has traditionally been maintained; and, of particular importance to protean man, by the existence of nuclear weapons, which, even without being used, call into question all modes of immortality. (Who can be certain of living on through children and grandchildren, through teachings or kindnesses?)

Protean man is left with two paths to symbolic immortality which he tries to cultivate, sometimes pleasurably and sometimes desperately. One is the natural mode we have mentioned. His attraction to nature and concern at its desecration has to do with an unconscious sense that, in whatever holocaust, at least nature will endure—though such are the dimensions of our present weapons that he cannot be absolutely certain even of this. His second path may be termed that of "experiential transcendence"—of seeking a sense of immortality in the way that mystics always have, through psychic experience of such great intensity that time and death are, in effect, eliminated. This, I believe, is the larger meaning of the "drug revolution," of protean man's hunger for chemical aids to "expanded consciousness." And indeed all revolutions may be thought of, at bottom, as innovations in the struggle for immortality, as new combinations of old modes.

We have seen that young adults individually, and youth movements collectively, express most vividly the psychological themes of protean man. And although it is true that these themes make contact with what we sometimes call the "psychology of adolescence," we err badly if we overlook their expression in all age groups and dismiss them as "mere adolescent phenomena." Rather, protean man's affinity for the young—his being metaphorically and psychologically so young in spirit—has to do with his never-ceasing quest for imagery of rebirth. He seeks such imagery from all sources: from ideas, techniques, religious and political systems, mass movements and drugs; or from special individuals of his own kind whom he sees as possessing that problematic gift of his namesake, the gift of prophecy. The dangers inherent in the quest seem hardly to require emphasis. What perhaps needs most to be kept in mind is the general principle that renewal on a large scale is impossible to achieve without forays into danger, destruction and negativity. The principle of "death and rebirth" is as valid psychohistorically as it is mythologically. However misguided many of his forays may be, protean man also carries with him an extraordinary range of possibility for man's betterment, or more important, for his survival.

5 / A Psychedelic Experience: Fact or Fantasy?

ALAN WATTS

Since at least 1500 B.c. men have, from time to time, held the view that our normal vision of the world is a hallucination—a dream, a figment of the mind, or, to use the Hindu word which means both art and illusion, a *maya*. The implication is that, if this is so, life need never be taken seriously. It is a fantasy, a play, a drama to be enjoyed. It does not really *matter*, for one day (perhaps in the moment of death) the illusion will dissolve, and each one of us will awaken to discover that he himself is *what* there is and *all* that there is—the very root and ground of the universe, or the ultimate and eternal space in which things and events come and go.

This is not simply an idea which someone "thought up," like science fiction or a philosophical theory. It is the attempt to express an experience in which consciousness itself, the basic sensation of being "I," undergoes a remarkable change. We do not know much about these experiences. They are relatively common, and arise in every part of the world. They occur to both children and adults. They may last for a few seconds and come once in a lifetime, or they may happen repeatedly and constitute a permanent change of consciousness. With baffling impartiality they may descend upon those who never heard of them, as upon those who have spent years trying to cultivate them by some type of discipline. They have been regarded, equally, as a disease of consciousness with symptoms everywhere the same, like measles, and as a vision of higher reality such as comes in moments of scientific or psychological insight. They may turn people into monsters and megalomaniacs, or transform them into saints and

SOURCE: David Solomon, ed., *LSD: The Consciousness-Expanding Drug* (New York: G. P. Putnam's Sons, 1964), pp. 114–27. Copyright © 1964 by David Solomon. Reprinted by permission of G. P. Putnam's Sons.

Alan Watts, a minister and philosopher, has been a kind of guru for the drug and Zen scene; he is the author of *The Way of Zen* and several other books.

sages. While there is no sure way of inducing these experiences, a favorable atmosphere may be created by intense concentration, by fasting, by sensory deprivation, by hyper-oxygenation, by prolonged emotional stress, by profound relaxation, or by the use of certain drugs.

Experiences of this kind underlie some of the great world religions—Hinduism, Buddhism and Taoism in particular, and, to a much lesser extent, Judaism, Christianity, and Islam. As expressed in the doctrines of these religions, they purport to be an account of "the way things are" and therefore invite comparison with descriptions of the universe and of man given by physicists and biologists. They contradict common sense so violently and are accompanied with such a powerful sense of authenticity and reality (*more* real than reality is a common description) that men have always wondered whether they are divine revelations or insidious delusions.

This problem becomes all the more urgent now that the general public has become aware that experiences of this type are available, with relative ease, through the use of such chemicals as the so-called psychedelic drugs—LSD-25, mescaline, psilocybin, hashish, and marijuana, to name only the better known. The reality status of the modes of consciousness induced by these chemicals becomes, then, a matter of most serious concern for the guardians of our mental health, for psychiatrists and psychologists, philosophers and ministers, for every scientific investigator of the nature of consciousness, and, above all, for a large section of the general public curious and eager to get "the experience" for reasons of all kinds.

A proper study of the question runs, at the very beginning, into two obstacles. The first is that we know very little indeed about the structure and chemistry of the brain. We do not know enough of the ways in which it gleans information about the outside world and about itself to know whether these chemicals help it (as lenses help the eyes) or confuse it. The second is that the nature and use of these chemicals is surrounded with an immense semantic fog, whose density is increased by people who ought to know better. I mean psychiatrists.

What we know, positively and scientifically, about psychedelic chemicals is that they bring about certain alterations of sense perception, of emotional level and tone, of identity feeling, of the interpretation of sense data, and of the sensations of time and space. The nature of these alterations depends on three variables: the chemical itself (type and dosage), the psycho-physiological state of the subject, and the social and aesthetic context of the experiment. Their physiological side effects are minimal, though there are conditions (e.g., disease of the liver) in which some of them may be harmful. They are not physiologically habit-forming in the same way as alcohol and tobacco, though some individuals may come to depend upon them for other (i.e., "neurotic") reasons. Their results are not easily predictable since they depend so largely upon such imponderables as the setting, and the attitudes and expectations of both the supervisor and the subject. The (enormous) scientific literature on the subject indicates that a majority of people have pleasant reactions, a largish minority have unpleasant but instructive and helpful reactions, while a very small minority have psychotic reactions lasting from hours to months. It has never been definitely established that they have led directly to a suicide. (I am referring specifically here to LSD-25, mescaline, the mushroom-derivative psilocybin, and the various forms of *cannabis,* such as hashish and marijuana.)

Thus what we know for certain implies that these chemicals cannot be used without caution. But this applies equally to antibiotics, whiskey, household ammonia, the automobile, the kitchen knife, electricity, and matches. No worthwhile life can be lived without risks, despite current American superstitions to the contrary—as that passing laws can prevent people from being immoral and that technological power can be made foolproof. The question is therefore whether the risks involved in using these chemicals are worthwhile, and it seems to me that what is worthwhile should be judged not only in terms of useful knowledge or therapeutic effect, but also in terms of simple pleasure. (I have heard addiction to music described in just the same vocabulary as addiction to drugs.) If it turns out that psychedelics offer valid ways of exploring man's "inner world," the hidden ways of the mind and brain, we should surely admit that new knowledge of this inmost frontier may be worth quite serious risks. Psychoses and compulsive delusions are, after all, no more dangerous than the Indians and the mountain ranges that stood in the way of the first settlers of the American West.

ALAN WATTS 61

Psychiatrists often wonder why colleagues in other branches of medicine and specialists in other fields of science do not take them quite seriously. A typical reason may be found in their haste to define the nature and effects of these chemicals in terms which are simply prejudicial, and which boil down to nothing more than gobbledygook with an authoritative rumble. For example, the chemicals in question are commonly classified as "hallucinogenics" or "psychotomimetics." The first word means that they generate hallucinations, and the second that their effects resemble, or mimic, certain forms of psychosis or insanity. Only rarely do they give the impression of events in the external world which are not actually happening (i.e., hallucinations) and the ten-year-old notion that they induce "model psychoses" such as temporary schizophrenia has long been abandoned by those who are still in active research. But even if these findings were to be contested, the words "hallucination" and "psychosis" are loaded: they designate *bad* states of mind, whereas a clean scientific language should say only that these chemicals induce different and unusual states of mind.

It is almost a standard joke that psychiatry has pejorative or "put-down" words for every human emotion, as "euphoric" for happy, "fixated" for interested, and "compulsive" for determined. The discussion of psychedelic chemicals, both in the scientific literature and the public press, is thoroughly swamped with question-begging language of this kind in articles that purport to be impartial and authoritative. Right from the start the very word "drug," when used in this connection, evokes the socially reprehensible image of people who are "drugged" or "doped"—glassy-eyed, staggering, or recumbent wrecks of humanity, withdrawn from reality into a diabolical paradise of bizarre or lascivious dreams. The image of the Fu Manchu opium den, with screaming meemies at the end of the line.

Thus it is most common to find the action of psychedelics called "toxic" (i.e., poisonous), and the sensory and emotional changes induced referred to as "distortions," "delusive mechanisms," "dissociations," and "regressions," or as "loss of ego structure" and "abnormal perception of body image." This is the language of pathology. Used without explicit qualification, it implies that a consciousness so changed is sick. Likewise, when —in the context of a scientific article—the writer reports, "Subjects experienced religious exaltation, and some described sensations of being one with God," and leaves it at that, the implication is plainly that they went crazy. For in our own culture, to feel that you are God is insanity almost by definition. But, in Hindu culture, when someone says, "I have just found out that I am God," they say, "Congratulations! You at last got the point." Obviously, the word "God" does not mean the same thing in both cultures. Yet psychiatrists toss off such utterly damning remarks without scruple, and feel free to use their diagnostic jargon of mental pathology for states of consciousness which many of them have never even bothered to experience. For they expect to get accurate information about these states from subjects untrained in scientific description, fearing that if they themselves entered into any new mode of consciousness it would impair their scientific objectivity. This is pure scholasticism, as when the theologians said to Galileo, "We will not look through your telescope because we already know how the universe is ordered. If your telescope were to show us anything different, it would be an instrument of the devil."

Similarly, so many practitioners of the inexact sciences (e.g., psychology, anthropology, sociology) let it be known most clearly that they already know what reality is, and therefore what sanity is. For these poor drudges reality is the world of nonpoetry: it is the reduction of the physical universe to the most banal and dessicated terms conceivable, in accordance with the great Western myth that all nature outside the human skin is a stupid and unfeeling mechanism. There is a sort of "official psychiatry" of the army, state mental hospital, and of what, in California, they call "correctional facility" (i.e., prison), which defends this impoverished reality with a strange passion.

To come, then, to any effective evaluation of these chemicals and the changed states of consciousness and perception which they induce, we must begin with a highly detailed and accurate description of what they do, both from the standpoint of the subject and of the neutral observer, despite the fact that in experiments of this kind it becomes startlingly obvious that the observer cannot be neutral, and that the posture of "objectivity" is itself one of the determinants of the outcome. As the physicist well knows, to observe a process is to change it. But the importance of careful description is that it may help us to understand the kind or level of reality upon which these changes in consciousness are taking place.

For undoubtedly they are happening. The dancing, kaleidoscopic arabesques which appear before closed eyes are surely an observation of *some* reality, though not, perhaps, in the physical world outside the skin. But are they rearranged memories? Structures in the nervous system? Archetypes of the collective unconscious? Electronic patterns such as often dance on the TV screen? What, too, are the fernlike structures which are so often seen—the infinitude of branches upon branches upon branches, or analogous shapes? Are these a glimpse of some kind of analytical process in the brain, similar to the wiring patterns in a computer? We really have no idea, but the more carefully observers can record verbal descriptions and visual pictures of these phenomena, the more likely that neurologists or physicists or even mathematicians will turn up the physical processes to which they correspond. The point is that these visions are not *mere* imagination, as if there had ever been anything mere about imagination! The human mind does not just perversely invent utterly useless images out of nowhere at all. Every image tells us something about the mind or the brain or the organism in which it is found.

The effects of the psychedelics vary so much from person to person and from situation to situation that it is well nigh impossible to say with any exactitude that they create certain particular and invariable changes of consciousness. I would not go so far as to say that the chemical effects are simply featureless, providing no more than a vivid mirror to reflect the fantasies and unconscious dispositions of the individuals involved. For there are certain types of change which are usual enough to be considered characteristic of psychedelics: the sense of slowed or arrested time, and the alteration of "ego boundary"—that is, of the sensation of one's own identity.

The feeling that time has relaxed its pace may, to some extent, be the result of having set aside the better part of a day just to observe one's own consciousness, and to watch for interesting changes in one's perception of such ordinary things as reflected sunlight on the floor, the grain in wood, the texture of linen, or the sound of voices across the street. My own experience has never been of a distortion of these perceptions, as in looking at oneself in a concave mirror. It is rather that every perception becomes—to use a metaphor—more resonant. The chemical seems to provide consciousness with a sounding box, or its equivalent, for all the senses, so that sight, touch, taste, smell, and imagination are intensified like the voice of someone singing in the bathtub.

The change of ego boundary sometimes begins from this very resonance of the senses. The intensification and "deepening" of color, sound and texture lends them a peculiar transparency. One seems to be aware of them more than ever as vibration, electronic and luminous. As this feeling develops it appears that these vibrations are continuous with one's own consciousness and that the external world is in some odd way inside the mind-brain. It appears, too, with overwhelming obviousness, that the inside and the outside do not exclude one another and are not actually separate. They go together; they imply one another, like front and back, in such a way that they become polarized. As, therefore, the poles of a magnet are the extremities of a single body, it appears that the inside and the outside, the subject and the object, the self and the world, the voluntary and the involuntary, are the poles of a single process which is my real and hitherto unknown self. This new self has no location. It is not something like a traditional soul, using the body as a temporary house. To ask *where* it is, is like asking where the universe is. Things in space have a where, but the thing that space is in doesn't need to be anywhere. It is simply what there is, just plain basic isness!

How easily, then, an unsophisticated person might exclaim, "I have just discovered that I am God!" Yet if, during such an experience, one retains any critical faculties at all, it will be clear that anyone else in the same state of consciousness will also be God. It will be clear, too, that the "God" in question is not the God of popular theology, the Master Technician who controls, creates, and understands everything in the universe. Were it so, a person in this state should be able to give correct answers to all questions of fact. He would know the exact height of Mount Whitney in millimeters. On the other hand, this awareness of a deeper and universal self would correspond exactly with that other type of God which mystics have called the "divine ground" of the universe, a sort of intelligent and super-conscious space containing the whole cosmos as a mirror contains images . . . though the analogy fails in so far as it suggests something immense: we cannot picture sizelessness.

Anyone moving into completely unfamiliar territory may at first misunderstand and misinterpret what he sees, as is so evident from the first impressions of visitors to foreign lands where patterns of culture differ radically from their own. When Europeans depicted their first impressions of China, they made the roofs of houses exaggeratedly curly and people's eyes slanted at least 45 degrees from the horizontal. Contrariwise, the Japanese saw all Europeans as red-haired, sunken-eyed goblins with immensely long noses. But the unfamiliarities of foreign cultures are nothing to those of one's own inner workings. What is there in the experience of clear blue sky to suggest the structure of the optical nerves? Comparably, what is there in the sound of a human voice on the radio to suggest the formations of tubes and transistors? I raise this question because it is obvious that any chemically induced alteration of the nervous system must draw the attention of that system to itself. I am not normally aware that the sensation of blue sky is a state of the eyes and brain, but if I see wandering spots that are neither birds nor flying saucers, I know that these are an abnormality within the optical system itself. In other words, I am enabled, by virtue of this abnormality, to become conscious of one of the instruments of consciousness. But this is most unfamiliar territory.

Ordinarily, we remain quite unaware of the fact that the whole field of vision with its vast multiplicity of colors and shapes is a state of affairs inside our heads. Only eyes within a nervous system within a whole biological organism can translate the particles and /or waves of the physical world into light, color, and form, just as only the skin of a drum can make a moving hand go "Boom!" Psychedelics induce subtle alterations of perception which make the nervous system aware of itself, and the individual suddenly and unaccustomedly becomes conscious of the external world as a state of his own body. He may even go so far as to feel a confusion between what other people and things are doing, on the one hand, and his own volition, on the other. The particular feeling, or "cue," attached to thoughts and actions normally understood to be voluntary may then be attached to what is ordinarily classified as involuntary. (Similarly,

66

in *déjà vu* or "hasn't-this-happened-before?" experiences, perceptions of the immediate here and now come through with the cue or signal usually attached to memories.)

Under such circumstances the naive observer might well take these impressions so literally as to feel that the universe and his own body are *in fact* one and the same, that he is willing everything that happens, and that he is indeed the God of popular theology. If that were all, the psychedelics might certainly be dismissed as hallucinogens. We might conclude that they merely confuse the "wiring" of the nervous system in such a way that volition or "I-am-doing-this" signals get mixed up with messages about the external world.

Yet the problem cannot be set aside so simply. Let us suppose that a biologist wants to make a very detailed and accurate description of the behavior of some particular organism, perhaps of a sea bird feeding on the beach. He will be unable to describe the behavior of the bird without also describing the behavior of the water, of the sandworms or shellfish which the bird is eating, of seasonal changes of tide, temperature, and weather, all of which go together with the behavior of the bird. He cannot describe the behavior of the organism without also describing the behavior of its environment. We used to attribute this to the fact that organisms are always reacting to things that happen in their environments, and are even determined by their environments in all that they do. But this is to speak as if things were a collection of perfectly separate billiard balls banging against one another. Today, however, the scientist tends more and more to speak of the behavior of the organism and the behavior of the environment as the behavior of a single "field," somewhat awkwardly named the "organism/environment." Instead of talking about actions and reactions between different things and events, he prefers to speak of transactions. In the transaction of buying and selling, there is no selling unless there is simultaneously buying, and *vice versa*. The relation of organism to environment is also considered a transaction, because it has been found that living creatures exist only in a balanced relationship to one another. The present natural state of this planet "goes with" the existence of human beings, just as buying goes with selling. In any radically different environment, man could survive only by becoming a different type of being.

The implications of this organism/environment relationship are somewhat startling, for what is really being said is this: The entity we are describing is not an organism *in* an environment; it is a unified field or process, because it is more simple and more convenient to think of what the organism does and what the environment does as a single "behavior." Now substitute for "entity we are describing" the idea of the self. I myself am not just what is bounded by my skin. I myself (the organism) am what my whole environmental field (the universe) is doing. It is, then, simply a convention, a fashion, an arbitrary social institution, to confine the self to some center of decision and energy located within this bag of skin. This is no more than the rule of a particular social game of cops and robbers, that is, of who shall we praise and reward, and who shall we blame and punish? To play this game, we pretend that the origin of actions is something inside each human skin. But only force of long ingrained habit makes it hard to realize that we could define and actually *feel* ourselves to be the total pattern of the cosmos as focused or expressed *here*. This would be a sense of our identity consistent with the scientific description of man and other organisms. It would involve, too, the sensation that the external world is continuous with and one with our own bodies—a sensation very seriously needed in a civilization where men are destroying their environment by misapplied technology. This is the technology of man's *conquest* of nature, as if the external world were his enemy and not the very matrix in which he is brought forth and sustained. This is the technology of the dust bowls, of polluted air, poisoned streams, chemical chickens, pseudo-vegetables, foam-rubber bread, and the total Los Angelization of man.

Yet how is this long-ingrained sense of insular identity to be overcome? How is twentieth-century man to gain a feeling of his existence consistent with twentieth-century knowledge? We need very urgently to know that we are not strangers and aliens in the physical universe. We were not dropped here by divine whim or mechanical fluke out of some other universe altogether. We did not arrive, like birds on barren branches; we grew out of this world, like leaves and fruit. Our universe "humans" just as a rosebush "flowers." We are living in a world where men all over the planet are linked by an immense network of communications, and where science has made us theoretically aware of our interdependence with the entire domain of organic and inorganic nature. But our ego-feeling, our style of personal identity, is more appropriate to men living in fortified castles.

There seems to me a strong possibility that the psychedelics (as a medicine rather than a diet) may help us to "trigger" a new sense of identity, providing the initial boost to get us out of the habit of restricting "I" to a vague center within the skin. That they make us aware that our whole knowledge of the external world is a state of our own bodies is not a merely technical and trivial discovery. It is the obverse of the fact that our own bodies are functions, or behaviors, of the whole external world. This—at first—weird and mystical sensation of "unity with the cosmos" has been objectively verified. The mystic's subjective experience of his identity with "the All" is the scientist's objective description of ecological relationship, of the organism/environment as a unified field.

Our general failure (over the past three thousand years of human history) to notice the inseparability of things, and to be aware of our own basic unity with the external world, is the result of specializing in a particular kind of consciousness. For we have very largely based culture and civilization on concentrated attention, on using the mind as a spotlight rather than a floodlight, and by this means analyzing the world into separate bits. Concentrated attention is drummed into us in schools; it is essential to the three R's; it is the foundation of all careful thought and detailed description, all high artistic technique and intellectual discipline. But the price we pay for this vision of the world in vivid detail, bit by bit, is that we lose sight of the relationships and unities between the bits. Furthermore, a form of attention which looks at the world bit by bit doesn't have time to examine all possible bits; it has to be programmed (or prejudiced) to look only at *significant* bits, at things and events which are relevant to certain preselected ends—survival, social or financial advancement, and other fixed goals which exclude the possibility of being open to surprises, and to those delights which are extra special because they come without being sought.

In my own experience, which is shared by very many others, the psychedelics expand attention. They make the spotlight of consciousness a floodlight which not only exposes ignored relationships and unities but also brings to light unsuspected details —details normally ignored because of their lack of significance, or their irrelevance to some prejudice of what ought to be. (For example, the tiniest hairs on people's faces and blotchy variations of skin color, not really supposed to be there, become marvelously visible.) There is thus good reason to believe that the psychedelics are the opposite of hallucinogens insofar as they decrease the selectivity of the senses and expose consciousness to events beyond those that are supposed to deserve notice.

Time after time, this unprogrammed mode of attention, looking *at* things without looking *for* things, reveals the unbelievable beauty of the everyday world. Under the influence of programmed attention, our vision of the world tends to be somewhat dusty and drab. This is for the same reason that *staring* at things makes them blurred, and that trying to get the utmost out of a particular pleasure makes it something of a disappointment. Intense beauty and intense pleasure are always gratuitous, and are revealed only to senses that are not seeking and straining. For our nerves are not muscles; to push them is to reduce their efficiency.

What, finally, of the strong impression delivered both by the psychedelics and by many forms of mystical experience that the world is in some way an illusion? A difficulty here is that the word "illusion" is currently used pejoratively, as the negative of everything real, serious, important, valuable, and worthwhile. Is this because moralists and metaphysicians are apt to be personality types lacking the light touch? Illusion is related etymologically to the Latin *ludere,* to play, and thus is distinguished from reality as the drama is distinguished from "real life." In Hindu philosophy, the world is seen as a drama in which all the parts—each person, animal, flower, stone, and star—are roles or masks of the one supreme Self, which plays the *lila* or game of hide and seek with itself for ever and ever, dismembering itself as the Many and remembering itself as the One through endless cycles of time, in the spirit of a child tossing stones into a pond through a long afternoon in summer. The sudden awakening of the mystical experience is therefore the one Self remembering itself as the real foundation of the seemingly individual and separate organism.

Thus the Hindu *maya,* or world illusion, is not necessarily something bad. *Maya* is a complex word signifying the art, skill, dexterity, and cunning of the supreme Self in the exercise of its playful, magical, and creative power. The power of an actor so superb that he is taken in by his own performance. The Godhead amazing itself, getting lost in a maze.

Classical illustrations of *maya* include the apparently continuous circle of fire made by a whirling torch, and of the continuity of time and moving events by the whirring succession of *ksana,* or atomic instants. Physicists use similar metaphors in trying to explain how vibrating wavicles produce the illusion of solid material. The impenetrability of granite, they say, is something like the apparently solid disk made by the blades of an electric fan: it is an intensely rapid motion of the same minute orbits of light that constitute our fingers. Physics and optics have also much to say about the fact that all reality, all existence is a matter of relationship and transaction. Consider the formula

$$\frac{a \qquad b}{c} = \text{Rainbow},$$

where *a* is the sun, *b* is moisture in the atmosphere, and *c* is an observer, all three being at the same time in a certain angular relationship. Deduct any one term, *a, b* or *c,* or arrange them in positions outside the correct angular relationship, and the phenomenon "rainbow" will not exist. In other words, the actual existence of rainbows depends as much upon creatures with eyes as it depends upon the sun and moisture in the atmosphere. Common sense accepts this in respect to diaphanous things like rainbows which back off into the distance when we try to reach them. But it has great difficulty in accepting the fact that chunky things like apartment buildings and basic things like time and space exist in just the same way—*only* in relation to certain structures known as organisms with nervous systems.

Our difficulty in accepting for ourselves so important a part in the actual creation or manifestation of the world comes, of course, from this thorough habituation to the feeling that we are strangers in the universe—that human consciousness is a fluke of nature, that the world is an external object which we confront, that its immense size reduces us to pitiful unimportance, or that geological and astronomical structures are somehow more real (hard and solid?) than organisms. But these are actually mythological images of the nineteenth and early twentieth centuries—ideas which, for a while, seemed extremely plausible, mostly for the reason that they appeared to be hardboiled, down to earth and toughminded, a currently fashionable posture for the scientist. Despite the lag between advanced scientific ideas and the common sense of even the educated public, the mythology of man as a hapless fluke trapped in a mindless mechanism is breaking down. The end of this century may find us, at last, thoroughly at home in our own world, swimming in the ocean of relativity as joyously as dolphins in the water.

II / Apostles of the Age:
Their Creeds and Causes

The term "apostles" commonly refers to the earliest missionaries of Christendom, but here we are using it to identify modern advocates of any influential moral, philosophical, or political reforms. Nothing demonstrates the diversity of the radical vision better than the diversity of its apostles.

Herbert Marcuse is a German-born professor with deep debts to Hegel, Marx, and Freud; Malcolm X was a former criminal who made Islam into a rallying cause for blacks; Allen Ginsberg is a "beat" poet from New Jersey whose message and manner have turned him into a spokesman for nearly every cause that the young espouse; H. D. Laing is a British psychoanalyst; Norman O. Brown is a professor of classics.

What they have in common is both a desire to see a new society develop from the trappings of the old and the gift of speaking with "the trumpet of prophecy." Strikingly, despite all the talk of "generation gap"—which is a handy phrase for journalists —these apostles are not under thirty; in fact, many have reached their fifties and sixties. It is the style of the man, the posture he assumes, the force with which he develops his ideas, and the integrity with which he holds them that determine whether he will have meaning to the younger generation.

Differences among the age's apostles are indeed huge. Politically, Che Guevara has been the most striking, although his popularity may prove transitory as another even more daring and dashing figure undertakes dangerous missions in the name of the people. The chief appeal of Che rests on his talent for turning ideas into direct action. That he refused to accept revolution when it became static, that he left Cuba once its revolution seemed solidified, marks him as a radical figure of the present. For he pursued his ideas in the backwashes of the jungle among the dispossessed, and the jungles of South America, for many disaffected Americans, are analogous to the ghettoes of our large cities. Che, for many Latin Americans as well, was a martyr, the opposite of the Johnson-Rusk-McNamara image that the United States projected in the late sixties.

For the blacks, Malcolm X filled the role that Che did for many white radical students. After rejecting his earlier life as a criminal, Malcolm X transformed himself through diligent reading and through a growing self-awareness into the man most capable of expressing black aspirations for the future. He was probably the one figure who could have prevented the black quest for political power and recognition from fragmenting itself into divisory factions. By the time of his assassination, in 1965, he had become a dynamic, charismatic figure, flexible enough in his vision to revise his earlier views while arousing the blacks to growing self-consciousness and pride.

Both Herbert Marcuse and Norman O. Brown are professorial types who refuse to be traditional academicians. Both are concerned with the loss of Eros in a one-dimensional society; both believe that technology destroys while it claims to be saving; and both feel that disaffection, alienation, the growth of self, and the rejection of bourgeois values are more significant than acquiescence to an affluent society that equates happiness with consumption. In his two major books, *Life Against Death* and *Love's Body,* Brown is groping for ways which will permit the body to live. In page after page, he speaks of renting the veil, breaking the seal, making the unconscious conscious—of finding the "key to the cipher: the sudden sight of the real Israel, the true bread, the real lamb." These are paths to the discovery of what and who we are, and, in their quasi-religious and apocalyptic formulations, they remind us of that remarkable pioneer for the united kingdom of the flesh-and-spirit, D. H. Lawrence.

More political than Brown, Marcuse attempts to strike a balance between man's instinctive needs and the social pressures which stifle them. In this respect, the British psychoanalyst, R. D. Laing, is somewhat similar, for Laing refuses to accept a so-called rational society as truly rational, and, as a psychologist, he refuses to call the disaffected "mad" or "insane." Instead, like Marcuse, he regards disaffection as the normal response to a technological society run along mechanical principles by madmen who seem sane. While Laing lacks Marcuse's historical and theoretical base for his arguments, he brings to bear many years of experience in treating the mentally maladjusted. His refusal to regard so-called mad behavior according to society's dictates immediately makes him attractive to a generation which sees true madness in our support of distant wars, armament races, and nuclear deterrents while entire generations of poor and underprivileged are sacrificed to these priorities.

Although Marshall McLuhan does not have the personal charisma of a Che Guevara or an R. D. Laing, his pronouncements on the mass media have become common coinage, so common that the editors have only provided, not McLuhan himself but, in Part VIII, a sharp criticism of his work. This is not the place to debate whether McLuhan is serious or not, whether he is a passing fad, or whether he really wants to do away with the printed page—the student will have to reach those conclusions himself. McLuhan's importance, apart from other considerations, is that he has dramatically called our attention to certain significant implications derived from the study of the mass media. He maintains that we can no longer hold the same assumptions about the printed word, about the past, and about our ways of gaining knowledge; that we must take into account the media themselves and how they modify the "message." McLuhan has won recognition as the high priest of the revolution in communications media, but it is unlikely that the full impact of his ideas has yet been absorbed or appreciated, especially his contention that the human nervous system is being changed by the electronic media.

We close this section appropriately with Allen Ginsberg. His interview embodies, albeit gently and calmly, all of the views we have discussed above. Ginsberg's concern has been to make of his life a poem. Against great opposition, he has followed his own sense of himself, at a time when it was not easy to proclaim oneself a homosexual, a beatnik, and a smoker of pot. The climate of the 1950s, when Ginsberg was developing his muse, was dominated by Congressional investigating committees who did not take kindly to deviation or dissent, no matter how real or genuine. Somewhat like Shelley or Blake, earlier dissenters under different conditions with different tastes, he has pursued an inner voice of his own, a voice that was to speak for millions of young people in the generation after his own. As we move into the seventies, we feel that he will continue to be present wherever he has a chance to express his faith in individual expression and spirit.

6 / The Black Revolution[1]

MALCOLM X

Friends and enemies: Tonight I hope that we can have a little fireside chat with as few sparks as possible being tossed around. Especially because of the very explosive condition that the world is in today. Sometimes, when a person's house is on fire and someone comes in yelling fire, instead of the person who is awakened by the yell being thankful, he makes the mistake of charging the one who awakened him with having set the fire. I hope that this little conversation tonight about the black revolution won't cause many of you to accuse us of igniting it when you find it at your doorstep. . . .

---

[1] On April 8, 1964, Malcolm X gave a speech on "The Black Revolution" at a meeting sponsored by the Militant Labor Forum at Palm Gardens in New York. This forum is connected with *The Militant*, a socialist weekly, which Malcolm considered "one of the best newspapers anywhere."

The talk gave Malcolm an opportunity for a fuller presentation of his arguments for internationalizing the black struggle by indicting the United States government before the United Nations for racism. It is notable also for his statement that a "bloodless revolution" was still possible in the United States under certain circumstances.

SOURCE: George Breitman, ed., *Malcolm X Speaks* (New York: Grove Press, 1966), pp. 45–57. Copyright © 1965 by Merit Publishers and Betty Shabazz. "The Black Revolution" was originally a speech given April 8, 1964.

Malcolm X (born Malcolm Little), after serving a prison sentence for burglary, turned to Islam, helped build the Black Muslim movement, left that organization, and was in the process of structuring his own black power movement when he was assassinated on February 21, 1965, in New York. His life story is recounted in *The Autobiography of Malcolm X*.

During recent years there has been much talk about a population explosion. Whenever they are speaking of the population explosion, in my opinion they are referring primarily to the people in Asia or in Africa—the black, brown, red, and yellow people. It is seen by people of the West that, as soon as the standard of living is raised in Africa and Asia, automatically the people begin to reproduce abundantly. And there has been a great deal of fear engendered by this in the minds of the people of the West, who happen to be, on this earth, a very small minority.

In fact, in most of the thinking and planning of whites in the West today, it's easy to see the fear in their minds, conscious minds and subconscious minds, that the masses of dark people in the East, who already outnumber them, will continue to increase and multiply and grow until they eventually overrun the people of the West like a human sea, a human tide, a human flood. And the fear of this can be seen in the minds, in the actions, of most of the people here in the West in practically everything that they do. It governs their political views and it governs their economic views and it governs most of their attitudes toward the present society.

I was listening to Dirksen, the senator from Illinois, in Washington, D.C., filibustering the civil-rights bill; and one thing that he kept stressing over and over and over was that if this bill is passed, it will change the social structure of America. Well, I know what he's getting at, and I think that most other people today, and especially our people, know what is meant when these whites, who filibuster these bills, express fears of changes in the social structure. Our people are beginning to realize what they mean.

Just as we can see that all over the world one of the main problems facing the West is race, likewise here in America today, most of your Negro leaders as well as the whites agree that 1964 itself appears to be one of the most explosive years yet in the history of America on the racial front, on the racial scene. Not only is this racial explosion probably to take place in America, but all of the ingredients for this racial explosion in America to blossom into a world-wide racial explosion present themselves right here in front of us. America's racial powder keg, in short, can actually fuse or ignite a world-wide powder keg.

There are whites in this country who are still complacent when they see the possibilities of racial strife getting out of hand. You are complacent simply because you think you outnumber the racial minority in this country; what you have to bear in mind is whereas you might outnumber us in this country, you don't outnumber us all over the earth.

Any kind of racial explosion that takes place in this country today, in 1964, is not a racial explosion that can be confined to the shores of America. It is a racial explosion that can ignite the racial powder keg that exists all over the planet that we call earth. I think that nobody would disagree that the dark masses of Africa and Asia and Latin America are already seething with bitterness, animosity, hostility, unrest, and impatience with the racial intolerance that they themselves have experienced at the hands of the white West.

And just as they have the ingredients of hostility toward the West in general, here we also have 22 million African-Americans, black, brown, red, and yellow people, in this country who are also seething with bitterness and impatience and hostility and animosity at the racial intolerance not only of the white West but of white America in particular.

And by the hundreds of thousands today we find our own people have become impatient, turning away from your white nationalism, which you call democracy, toward the militant, uncompromising policy of black nationalism. I point out right here that as soon as we announced we were going to start a black nationalist party in this country, we received mail from coast to coast, especially from young people at the college level, the university level, who expressed complete sympathy and support and a desire to take an active part in any kind of political action based on black nationalism, designed to correct or eliminate immediately evils that our people have suffered here for 400 years.

The black nationalists to many of you may represent only a minority in the community. And therefore you might have a tendency to classify them as something insignificant. But just as the fuse is the smallest part or the smallest piece in the powder keg, it is yet that little fuse that ignites the entire powder keg. The black nationalists to you may represent a small minority in the so-called Negro community. But they just happen to be composed of the type of ingredient necessary to fuse or ignite the entire black community.

And this is one thing that whites—whether you call yourselves liberals or conservatives or racists or whatever else you might choose to be—one thing that you have to realize is, where the black community is concerned, although the large majority you come in contact with may impress you as being moderate and patient and loving and long-suffering and all that kind of stuff, the minority who you consider to be Muslims or nationalists happen to be made of the type of ingredient that can easily spark the black community. This should be understood. Because to me a powder keg is nothing without a fuse.

1964 will be America's hottest year; her hottest year yet; a year of much racial violence and much racial bloodshed. But it won't be blood that's going to flow only on one side. The new generation of black people that have grown up in this country during recent years are already forming the opinion, and it's a just opinion, that if there is to be bleeding, it should be reciprocal—bleeding on both sides.

It should also be understood that the racial sparks that are ignited here in America today could easily turn into a flaming fire abroad, which means it could engulf all the people of this earth into a giant race war. You cannot confine it to one little neighborhood, or one little community, or one little country. What happens to a black man in America today happens to the black man in Africa. What happens to a black man in America and Africa happens to the black man in Asia and to the man down in Latin America. What happens to one of us today happens to all of us. And when this is realized, I think that the whites—who are intelligent even if they aren't moral or aren't just or aren't impressed by legalities—those who are intelligent will realize that when they touch this one, they are touching all of them, and this in itself will have a tendency to be a checking factor.

The seriousness of this situation must be faced up to. I was in Cleveland last night, Cleveland, Ohio. In fact I was there Friday, Saturday and yesterday. Last Friday the warning was given that this is a year of bloodshed, that the black man has ceased to turn the other cheek, that he has ceased to be nonviolent, that he has ceased to feel that he must be confined by all these restraints that are put upon him by white society in struggling for what white society says he was supposed to have had a hundred years ago.

So today, when the black man starts reaching out for what America says are his rights, the black man feels that he is within his rights—when he becomes the victim of brutality by those who are depriving him of his rights—to do whatever is necessary to protect himself. An example of this was taking place last night at this same time in Cleveland, where the police were putting water hoses on our people there and also throwing tear gas at them—and they met a hail of stones, a hail of rocks, a hail of bricks. A couple of weeks ago in Jacksonville, Florida, a young teen-age Negro was throwing Molotov cocktails.

Well, Negroes didn't do this ten years ago. But what you should learn from this is that they are waking up. It was stones yesterday, Molotov cocktails today; it will be hand grenades tomorrow and whatever else is available the next day. The seriousness of this situation must be faced up to. You should not feel that I am inciting someone to violence. I'm only warning of a powder-keg situation. You can take it or leave it. If you take the warning, perhaps you can still save yourself. But if you ignore it or ridicule it, well, death is already at your doorstep. There are 22 million African-Americans who are ready to fight for independence right here. When I say fight for independence right here, I don't mean any nonviolent fight, or turn-the-other-cheek fight. Those days are gone. Those days are over.

If George Washington didn't get independence for this country nonviolently, and if Patrick Henry didn't come up with a nonviolent statement, and you taught me to look upon them as patriots and heroes, then it's time for you to realize that I have studied your books well. . . .

1964 will see the Negro revolt evolve and merge into the worldwide black revolution that has been taking place on this earth since 1945. The so-called revolt will become a real black revolution. Now the black revolution has been taking place in Africa and Asia and Latin America; when I say black, I mean nonwhite—black, brown, red or yellow. Our brothers and sisters in Asia, who were colonized by the Europeans, our brothers and sisters in Africa, who were colonized by the Europeans, and in Latin America, the peasants, who were colonized by the Europeans, have been involved in a struggle since 1945 to get the colonialists, or the colonizing powers, the Europeans, off their land, out of their country.

This is a real revolution. Revolution is always based on land. Revolution is never based on begging somebody for an integrated cup of coffee. Revolutions are never fought by turning the other cheek. Revolutions are never based upon love-your-enemy and pray-for-those-who-spitefully-use-you. And revolutions are never waged singing "We Shall Overcome." Revolutions are based upon bloodshed. Revolutions are never compromising. Revolutions are never based upon negotiations. Revolutions are never based upon any kind of tokenism whatsoever. Revolutions are never even based upon that which is begging a corrupt society or a corrupt system to accept us into it. Revolutions overturn systems. And there is no system on this earth which has proven itself more corrupt, more criminal, than this system that in 1964 still colonizes 22 million African-Americans, still enslaves 22 million Afro-Americans.

There is no system more corrupt than a system that represents itself as the example of freedom, the example of democracy, and can go all over this earth telling other people how to straighten out their house, when you have citizens of this country who have to use bullets if they want to cast a ballot.

The greatest weapon the colonial powers have used in the past against our people has always been divide-and-conquer. America is a colonial power. She has colonized 22 million Afro-Americans by depriving us of first-class citizenship, by depriving us of civil rights, actually by depriving us of human rights. She has not only deprived us of the right to be a citizen, she has deprived us of the right to be human beings, the right to be recognized and respected as men and women. In this country the black can be fifty years old and he is still a "boy."

I grew up with white people. I was integrated before they even invented the word and I have never met white people yet—if you are around them long enough—who won't refer to you as a "boy" or a "gal," no matter how old you are or what school you came out of, no matter what your intellectual or professional level is. In this society we remain "boys."

So America's strategy is the same strategy as that which was used in the past by the colonial powers: divide and conquer. She plays one Negro leader against the other. She plays one Negro organization against the other. She makes us think we have different objectives, different goals. As soon as one Negro says something, she runs to this Negro and asks him, "What do you think about what he said?" Why, anybody can see through that today—except some of the Negro leaders.

All of our people have the same goals, the same objective. That objective is freedom, justice, equality. All of us want recognition and respect as human beings. We don't want to be integrationists. Nor do we want to be separationists. We want to be human beings. Integration is only a method that is used by some groups to obtain freedom, justice, equality and respect as human beings. Separation is only a method that is used by other groups to obtain freedom, justice, equality or human dignity.

Our people have made the mistake of confusing the methods with the objectives. As long as we agree on objectives, we should never fall out with each other just because we believe in different methods or tactics or strategy to reach a common objective.

We have to keep in mind at all times that we are not fighting for integration, nor are we fighting for separation. We are fighting for recognition as human beings. We are fighting for the right to live as free humans in this society. In fact, we are actually fighting for rights that are even greater than civil rights and that is human rights. . . .

Among the so-called Negroes in this country, as a rule the civil-rights groups, those who believe in civil rights, spend most of their time trying to prove they are Americans. Their thinking is usually domestic, confined to the boundaries of America, and they always look upon themselves as a minority. When they look upon themselves upon the American stage, the American stage is a white stage. So a black man standing on that stage in America automatically is in the minority. He is the underdog, and in his struggle he always uses an approach that is a begging, hat-in-hand, compromising approach.

Whereas the other segment or section in America, known as the black nationalists, are more interested in human rights than they are in civil rights. And they place more stress on human rights than they do on civil rights. The difference between the thinking and the scope of the Negroes who are involved in the human-rights struggle and those who are involved in the civil-rights struggle is that those so-called Negroes involved in the human-rights struggle don't look upon themselves as Americans.

They look upon themselves as a part of dark mankind. They see the whole struggle not within the confines of the American stage, but they look upon the struggle on the world stage. And, in the world context, they see that the dark man outnumbers the white man. On the world stage the white man is just a microscopic minority.

So in this country you find two different types of Afro-Americans—the type who looks upon himself as a minority and you as the majority, because his scope is limited to the American scene; and then you have the type who looks upon himself as part of the majority and you as part of a microscopic minority. And this one uses a different approach in trying to struggle for his rights. He doesn't beg. He doesn't thank you for what you give him, because you are only giving him what he should have had a hundred years ago. He doesn't think you are doing him any favors.

He doesn't see any progress that he has made since the Civil War. He sees not one iota of progress because, number one, if the Civil War had freed him, he wouldn't need civil-rights legislation today. If the Emancipation Proclamation, issued by that great shining liberal called Lincoln, had freed him, he wouldn't be singing "We Shall Overcome" today. If the amendments to the Constitution had solved his problem, his problem wouldn't still be here today. And if the Supreme Court desegregation decision of 1954 was genuinely and sincerely designed to solve his problem, his problem wouldn't be with us today.

So this kind of black man is thinking. He can see where every maneuver that America has made, supposedly to solve this problem, has been nothing but political trickery and treachery of the worst order. Today he doesn't have any confidence in these so-called liberals. (I know that all that have come in here tonight don't call yourselves liberals. Because that's a nasty name today. It represents hypocrisy.) So these two different types of black people exist in the so-called Negro community and they are beginning to wake up and their awakening is producing a very dangerous situation.

You have whites in the community who express sincerity when they say they want to help. Well, how can they help? How can a white person help the black man solve his problem? Number one, you can't solve it for him. You can help him solve it, but you can't solve it for him today. One of the best ways that you can help him solve it is to let the so-called Negro, who has been involved in the civil-rights struggle, see that the civil-rights struggle must be expanded beyond the level of civil rights to human rights. Once it is expanded beyond the level of civil rights to the level of human rights, it opens the door for all of our brothers and sisters in Africa and Asia, who have their independence, to come to our rescue.

When you go to Washington, D.C., expecting those crooks down there—and that's what they are—to pass some kind of civil-rights legislation to correct a very criminal situation, what you are doing is encouraging the black man, who is the victim, to take his case into the court that's controlled by the criminal that made him the victim. It will never be solved in that way. . . .

The civil-rights struggle involves the black man taking his case to the white man's court. But when he fights it at the human-rights level, it is a different situation. It opens the door to take Uncle Sam to the world court. The black man doesn't have to go to court to be free. Uncle Sam should be taken to court and made to tell why the black man is not free in a so-called free society. Uncle Sam should be taken into the United Nations and charged with violating the UN charter of human rights.

You can forget civil rights. How are you going to get civil rights with men like Eastland and men like Dirksen and men like Johnson? It has to be taken out of their hands and taken into the hands of those whose power and authority exceed theirs. Washington has become too corrupt. Uncle Sam has become bankrupt when it comes to a conscience—it is impossible for Uncle Sam to solve the problem of 22 million black people in this country. It is absolutely impossible to do it in Uncle Sam's courts— whether it is the Supreme Court or any other kind of court that comes under Uncle Sam's jurisdiction.

The only alternative that the black man has in America today is to take it out of Senator Dirksen's and Senator Eastland's and President Johnson's jurisdiction and take it downtown on the East River and place it before that body of men who represent international law, and let them know that the human rights of black people are being violated in a country that professes to be the moral leader of the free world.

86

Any time you have a filibuster in America, in the Senate, in 1964 over the rights of 22 million black people, over the citizenship of 22 million black people, or that will affect the freedom and justice and equality of 22 million black people, it's time for that government itself to be taken before a world court. How can you condemn South Africa? There are only 11 million of our people in South Africa, there are 22 million of them here. And we are receiving an injustice which is just as criminal as that which is being done to the black people of South Africa.

So today those whites who profess to be liberals—and as far as I am concerned it's just lip-profession—you understand why our people don't have civil rights. You're white. You can go and hang out with another white liberal and see how hypocritical they are. A lot of you sitting right here know that you've seen whites up in a Negro's face with flowery words, and as soon as that Negro walks away you listen to how your white friend talks. We have black people who can pass as white. We know how you talk.

We can see that it is nothing but a governmental conspiracy to continue to deprive the black people in this country of their rights. And the only way we will get these rights restored is by taking it out of Uncle Sam's hands. Take him to court and charge him with genocide, the mass murder of millions of black people in this country—political murder, economic murder, social murder, mental murder. This is the crime that this government has committed, and if you yourself don't do something about it in time, you are going to open the doors for something to be done about it from outside forces.

I read in the paper yesterday where one of the Supreme Court justices, Goldberg, was crying about the violation of human rights of three million Jews in the Soviet Union. Imagine this. I haven't got anything against Jews, but that's their problem. How in the world are you going to cry about problems on the other side of the world when you haven't got the problems straightened out here? How can the plight of three million Jews in Russia be qualified to be taken to the United Nations by a man who is a justice in this Supreme Court, and is supposed to be a liberal, supposed to be a friend of black people, and hasn't opened up his mouth one time about taking the plight of black people down here to the United Nations? . . .

MALCOLM X 87

If Negroes could vote south of the—yes, if Negroes could vote south of the Canadian border—south South, if Negroes could vote in the Southern part of the South, Ellender wouldn't be the head of the Agricultural and Forestry Committee, Richard Russell wouldn't be head of the Armed Services Committee, Robertson of Virginia wouldn't be head of the Banking and Currency Committee. Imagine that, all of the banking and currency of the government is in the hands of a cracker.

In fact, when you see how many of these committee men are from the South, you can see that we have nothing but a cracker government in Washington, D.C. And their head is a cracker president. I said a cracker president. Texas is just as much a cracker state as Mississippi. . . .

The first thing this man did when he came in office was invite all the big Negroes down for coffee. James Farmer was one of the first ones, the head of CORE. I have nothing against him. He's all right—Farmer, that is. But could that same president have invited James Farmer to Texas for coffee? And if James Farmer went to Texas, could he have taken his white wife with him to have coffee with the president? Any time you have a man who can't straighten out Texas, how can he straighten out the country? No, you're barking up the wrong tree.

If Negroes in the South could vote, the Dixiecrats would lose power. When the Dixiecrats lost power, the Democrats would lose power. A Dixiecrat lost is a Democrat lost. Therefore the two of them have to conspire with each other to stay in power. The Northern Dixiecrat puts all the blame on the Southern Dixiecrat. It's a con grame, a giant political con game. The job of the Northern Democrat is to make the Negro think that he is our friend. He is always smiling and wagging his tail and telling us how much he can do for us if we vote for him. But at the same time that he's out in front telling us what he's going to do, behind the door he's in cahoots with the Southern Democrat setting up the machinery to make sure he'll never have to keep his promise.

This is the conspiracy that our people have faced in this country for the past hundred years. And today you have a new generation of black people who have come on the scene, who have become disenchanted with the entire system, who have become disillusioned over the system, and who are ready now and willing to do something about it.

So, in my conclusion, in speaking about the black revolution, America today is at a time or in a day or at an hour where she is the first country on this earth that can actually have a bloodless revolution. In the past, revolutions have been bloody. Historically you just don't have a peaceful revolution. Revolutions are bloody, revolutions are violent, revolutions cause bloodshed and death follows in their paths. America is the only country in history in a position to bring about a revolution without violence and bloodshed. But America is not morally equipped to do so.

Why is America in a position to bring about a bloodless revolution? Because the Negro in this country holds the balance of power, and if the Negro in this country were given what the Constitution says he is supposed to have, the added power of the Negro in this country would sweep all of the racists and the segregationists out of office. It would change the entire political structure of the country. It would wipe out the Southern segregationism that now controls America's foreign policy, as well as America's domestic policy.

And the only way without bloodshed that this can be brought about is that the black man has to be given full use of the ballot in every one of the fifty states. But if the black man doesn't get the ballot, then you are going to be faced with another man who forgets the ballot and starts using the bullet.

Revolutions are fought to get control of land, to remove the absentee landlord and gain control of the land and the institutions that flow from that land. The black man has been in a very low condition because he has had no control whatsoever over any land. He has been a beggar economically, a beggar politically, a beggar socially, a begger even when it comes to trying to get some education. The past type of mentality, that was developed in this colonial system among our people, today is being overcome. And as the young ones come up, they know what they want. And as they listen to your beautiful preaching about democracy and all those other flowery words, they know what they're supposed to have.

So you have a people today who not only know what they want, but also know what they are supposed to have. And they themselves are creating another generation that is coming up that not only will know what it wants and know what it should have, but also will be ready and willing to do whatever is necessary to

see that what they should have materializes immediately.
Thank you.

7 / Liberation from the Affluent Society

HERBERT MARCUSE

I am very happy to see so many flowers here and that is why I
want to remind you that flowers, by themselves, have no power
whatsoever, other than the power of men and women who protect them and take care of them against aggression and destruction.

As a hopeless philosopher for whom philosophy has become inseparable from politics, I am afraid I have to give here today a
rather philosophical speech, and I must ask your indulgence. We
are dealing with the dialectics of liberation (actually a redundant phrase, because I believe that all dialectic is liberation) and
not only liberation in an intellectual sense, but liberation involving the mind and the body, liberation involving entire human
existence. Think of Plato: the liberation from the existence in
the cave. Think of Hegel: liberation in the sense of progress and
freedom on the historical scale. Think of Marx. Now in what
sense is all dialectic liberation? It is liberation from the repressive, from a bad, a false system—be it an organic system, be it a
social system, be it a mental or intellectual system: liberation
by forces developing within such a system. That is a decisive
point. And liberation by virtue of the contradiction generated by
the system, precisely because it is a bad, a false system.

SOURCE: David Cooper, ed., *To Free a Generation* (New York: Collier Books, 1968),
pp. 175–92. Copyright © 1967 by The Institute of Phenomenological Studies. All
rights reserved. Reprinted by permission.
  Herbert Marcuse, the German-born philosopher, is the author of several influential books, including *Eros and Civilization, Repressive Tolerance, An Essay on
Liberation, One-Dimensional Man, Reason and Revolution: Hegel and the Rise
of Social Theory,* and *Negations: Essays in Critical Theory.*

I am intentionally using here moral, philosophical terms, values: 'bad', 'false'. For without an objectively justifiable goal of a better, a free human existence, all liberation must remain meaningless—at best, progress in servitude. I believe that in Marx too socialism *ought* to be. This 'ought' belongs to the very essence of scientific socialism. It *ought* to be; it is, we may almost say, a biological, sociological and political necessity. It is a biological necessity in as much as a socialist society, according to Marx, would conform with the very *logos* of life, with the essential possibilities of a human existence, not only mentally, not only intellectually, but also organically.

Now as to today and our own situation. I think we are faced with a novel situation in history, because today we have to be liberated from a relatively well-functioning, rich, powerful society. I am speaking here about liberation from the affluent society, that is to say, the advanced industrial societies. The problem we are facing is the need for liberation not from a poor society, not from a disintegrating society, not even in most cases from a terroristic society, but from a society which develops to a great extent the material and even cultural needs of man—a society which, to use a slogan, delivers the goods to an ever larger part of the population. And that implies, we are facing liberation from a society where liberation is apparently without a mass basis. We know very well the social mechanisms of manipulation, indoctrination, repression which are responsible for this lack of a mass basis, for the integration of the majority of the oppositional forces into the established social system. But I must emphasize again that this is not merely an ideological integration; that it is not merely a social integration; that it takes place precisely on the strong and rich basis which enables the society to develop and satisfy material and cultural needs better than before.

But knowledge of the mechanisms of manipulation or repression, which go down into the very unconscious of man, is not the whole story. I believe that we (and I will use 'we' throughout my talk) have been too hesitant, that we have been too ashamed, understandably ashamed, to insist on the integral, radical features of a socialist society, its qualitative difference from all the established societies: the qualitative difference by virtue of which socialism is indeed the negation of the established systems, no matter how productive, no matter how powerful they are or they may appear. In other words—and this is one of the many points where I disagree with Paul Goodman—our fault was not that we have been too immodest, but that we have been too modest. We have, as it were, repressed a great deal of what we should have said and what we should have emphasized.

If today these integral features, these truly radical features which make a socialist society a definite negation of the existing societies, if this qualitative difference today appears as Utopian, as idealistic, as metaphysical, this is precisely the form in which these radical features must appear if they are really to be a definite negation of the established society: if socialism is indeed the rupture of history, the radical break, the leap into the realm of freedom—a total rupture.

Let us give one illustration of how this awareness, or half-awareness, of the need for such a total rupture was present in some of the great social struggles of our period. Walter Benjamin quotes reports that during the Paris Commune, in all corners of the city of Paris there were people shooting at the clocks on the towers of the churches, palaces and so on, thereby consciously or half-consciously expressing the need that somehow time has to be arrested; that at least the prevailing, the established time continuum has to be arrested, and that a new time has to begin—a very strong emphasis on the qualitative difference and on the totality of the rupture between the new society and the old.

In this sense, I should like to discuss here with you the repressed prerequisites of qualitative change. I say intentionally 'of qualitative change', not 'of revolution', because we know of too many revolutions through which the continuum of repression has been sustained, revolutions which have replaced one system of domination by another. We must become aware of the essentially new features which distinguish a free society as a definite negation of the established societies, and we must begin formulating these features, no matter how metaphysical, no matter how Utopian, I would even say no matter how ridiculous we may appear to the normal people in all camps, on the right as well as on the left.

What is the dialectic of liberation with which we here are concerned? It is the construction of a free society, a construction which depends in the first place on the prevalence of the vital need for abolishing the established systems of servitude; and secondly, and this is decisive, it depends on the vital commitment, the striving, conscious as well as sub- and un-conscious, for the qualitatively different values of a free human existence. Without the emergence of such new needs and satisfactions, the needs and satisfactions of free men, all change in the social institutions, no matter how great, would only replace one system of servitude by another system of servitude. Nor can the emergence—and I should like to emphasize this—nor can the emergence of such new needs and satisfactions be envisaged as a mere by-product, the mere result, of changed social institutions. We have seen this; it is a fact of experience. The development of the new institutions must already be carried out and carried through by men with the new needs. That, by the way, is the basic idea underlying Marx's own concept of the proletariat as the historical agent of revolution. He saw the industrial proletariat as the historical agent of revolution, not only because it was the basic class in the material process of production, not only because it was at that time the majority of the population, but also because this class was 'free' from the repressive and aggressive competitive needs of capitalist society and therefore, at least potentially, the carrier of essentially new needs, goals and satisfactions.

We can formulate this dialectic of liberation also in a more brutal way, as a vicious circle. The transition from voluntary servitude (as it exists to a great extent in the affluent society) to freedom presupposes the abolition of the institutions and mechanisms of repression. And the abolition of the institutions and mechanisms of repression already presupposes liberation from servitude, prevalence of the need for liberation. As to needs, I think we have to distinguish between the need for changing intolerable conditions of existence, and the need for changing the society as a whole. The two are by no means identical, they are by no means in harmony. *If* the need is for changing intolerable conditions of existence, with at least a reasonable chance that this can be achieved within the established society, with the growth and progress of the established society, then this is merely quantitative change. Qualitative change is a change of the very system as a whole.

I would like to point out that the distinction between quantitative and qualitative change is not identical with the distinction between reform and revolution. Quantitative change can mean and can lead to revolution. Only the conjunction, I suggest, of these two is revolution in the essential sense of the leap from pre-history into the history of man. In other words, the problem with which we are faced is the point where quantity can turn into quality, where the quantitative change in the conditions and institutions can become a qualitative change affecting all human existence.

Today the two potential factors of revolution which I have just mentioned are disjointed. The first is most prevalent in the underdeveloped countries, where quantitative change—that is to say, the creation of human living conditions—is in itself qualitative change, but is not yet freedom. The second potential factor of revolution, the prerequisites of liberation, are potentially there in the advanced industrial countries, but are contained and perverted by the capitalist organization of society.

I think we are faced with a situation in which this advanced capitalist society has reached a point where quantitative change can technically be turned into qualitative change, into authentic liberation. And it is precisely against this truly fatal possibility that the affluent society, advanced capitalism, is mobilized and organized on all fronts, at home as well as abroad.

Before I go on, let me give a brief definition of what I mean by an affluent society. A model, of course, is American society today, although even in the U.S. it is more a tendency, not yet entirely translated into reality. In the first place, it is a capitalist society. It seems to be necessary to remind ourselves of this because there are some people, even on the left, who believe that American society is no longer a class society. I can assure you that it is a class society. It is a capitalist society with a high concentration of economic and political power; with an enlarged and enlarging sector of automation and coordination of production, distribution and communication; with private ownership in the means of production, which however depends increasingly on ever more active and wide intervention by the government. It is a society in which, as I mentioned, the material as well as cultural needs of the underlying population are satisfied on a scale larger than ever before—but they are satisfied in line with the requirements and interests of the apparatus and of the powers which control the apparatus. And it is a society growing on the condition of accelerating waste, planned obsolescence and destruction, while the substratum of the population continues to live in poverty and misery.

I believe that these factors are internally interrelated, that they constitute the syndrome of late capitalism: namely, the apparently inseparable unity—inseparable for the system—of productivity and destruction, of satisfaction of needs and repression, of liberty within a system of servitude—that is to say, the subjugation of man to the apparatus, and the inseparable unity of rational and irrational. We can say that the rationality of the society lies in its very insanity, and that the insanity of the society is rational to the degree to which it is efficient, to the degree to which it delivers the goods.

Now the question we must raise is: why do we need liberation from such a society if it is capable—perhaps in the distant future, but apparently capable—of conquering poverty to a greater degree than ever before, of reducing the toil of labour and the time of labour, and of raising the standard of living? If the price for all goods delivered, the price for this comfortable servitude, for all these achievements, is exacted from people far away from the metropolis and far away from its affluence? If the affluent society itself hardly notices what it is doing, how it is spreading terror and enslavement, how it is fighting liberation in all corners of the globe?

We know the traditional weakness of emotional, moral and humanitarian arguments in the face of such technological achievement, in the face of the irrational rationality of such a power. These arguments do not seem to carry any weight against the brute facts—we might say brutal facts—of the society and its productivity. And yet, it is only the insistence on the real possibilities of a free society, which is blocked by the affluent society—it is only this insistence in practice as well as in theory, in demonstration as well as in discussion, which still stands in the way of the complete degradation of man to an object, or rather subject/object, of total administration. It is only this insistence which still stands in the way of the progressive brutalization and moronization of man. For—and I should like to emphasize this—the capitalist Welfare State is a Warfare State.

HERBERT MARCUSE 95

It must have an Enemy, with a capital E, a total Enemy; because the perpetuation of servitude, the perpetuation of the miserable struggle for existence in the very face of the new possibilities of freedom, activates and intensifies in this society a primary aggressiveness to a degree, I think, hitherto unknown in history. And this primary aggressiveness must be mobilized in socially useful ways, lest it explode the system itself. Therefore the need for an Enemy, who must be there, and who must be created if he does not exist. Fortunately, I dare say, the Enemy does exist. But his image and his power must, in this society, be inflated beyond all proportions in order to be able to mobilize this aggressiveness of the affluent society in socially useful ways.

The result is a mutilated, crippled and frustrated human existence: a human existence that is violently defending its own servitude.

We can sum up the fatal situation with which we are confronted. Radical social change is objectively necessary, in the dual sense that it is the only chance to save the possibilities of human freedom and, furthermore, in the sense that the technical and material resources for the realization of freedom are available. But while this objective need is demonstrably there, the subjective need for such a change does not prevail. It does not prevail precisely among those parts of the population that are traditionally considered the agents of historical change. The subjective need is repressed, again on a dual ground: firstly, by virtue of the actual satisfaction of needs, and secondly, by a massive scientific manipulation and administration of needs —that is, by a systematic social control not only of the consciousness, but also of the unconscious of man. This control has been made possible by the very achievements of the greatest liberating sciences of our time, in psychology, mainly psychoanalysis and psychiatry. That they could become and have become at the same time powerful instruments of suppression, one of the most effective engines of suppression, is again one of the terrible aspects of the dialectic of liberation.

This divergence between the objective and the subjective need changes completely, I suggest, the basis, the prospects and the strategy of liberation. This situation presupposes the emergence of new needs, qualitatively different and even opposed to

96

the prevailing aggressive and repressive needs: the emergence of a new type of man, with a vital, biological drive for liberation, and with a consciousness capable of breaking through the material as well as ideological veil of the affluent society. In other words, liberation seems to be predicated upon the opening and the activation of a depth dimension of human existence, this side of and underneath the traditional material base: not an idealistic dimension, over and above the material base, but a dimension even more material than the material base, a dimension underneath the material base. I will illustrate presently what I mean.

The emphasis on this new dimension does not mean replacing politics by psychology, but rather the other way around. It means finally taking account of the fact that society has invaded even the deepest roots of individual existence, even the unconscious of man. *We* must get at the roots of society in the individuals themselves, the individuals who, because of social engineering, constantly reproduce the continuum of repression even through the great revolution.

This change is, I suggest, not an ideological change. It is dictated by the actual development of an industrial society, which has introduced factors which our theory could formerly correctly neglect. It is dictated by the actual development of industrial society, by the tremendous growth of its material and technical productivity, which has surpassed and rendered obsolete the traditional goals and preconditions of liberation.

Here we are faced with the question: is liberation from the affluent society identical with the transition from capitalism to socialism? The answer I suggest is: It is not identical, if socialism is defined merely as the planned development of the productive forces, and the rationalization of resources (although this remains a precondition for all liberation). It is identical with the transition from capitalism to socialism, if socialism is defined in its most Utopian terms: namely, among others, the abolition of labour, the termination of the struggle for existence —that is to say, life as an end in itself and no longer as a means to an end—and the liberation of human sensibility and sensitivity, not as a private factor, but as a force for transformation of human existence and of its environment. To give sensitivity and sensibility their own right is, I think, one of the basic goals of integral socialism. These are the qualitatively different features of a free society. They presuppose, as you may already have seen, a total trans-valuation of values, a new anthropology. They presuppose a type of man who rejects the performance principles governing the established societies; a type of man who has rid himself of the aggressiveness and brutality that are inherent in the organization of established society, and in their hypocritical, puritan morality; a type of man who is biologically incapable of fighting wars and creating suffering; a type of man who has a good conscience of joy and pleasure, and who works, collectively and individually, for a social and natural environment in which such an existence becomes possible.

The dialectic of liberation, as turned from quantity into quality, thus involves, I repeat, a break in the continuum of repression which reaches into the depth dimension of the organism itself. Or, we may say that today qualitative change, liberation, involves organic, instinctual, biological changes at the same time as political and social changes.

The new needs and satisfactions have a very material basis, as I have indicated. They are not thought out but are the logical derivation from the technical, material and intellectual possibilities of advanced, industrial society. They are inherent in, and the expression of, the productivity of advanced industrial society, which has long since made obsolete all kinds of inner-worldly asceticism, the entire work discipline on which Judaeo-Christian morality has been based.

Why is this society surpassing and negating this type of man, the traditional type of man, and the forms of his existence, as well as the morality to which it owes much of its origins and foundations? This new, unheard-of and not anticipated productivity allows the concept of a technology of liberation. Here I can only briefly indicate what I have in mind: such amazing and indeed apparently Utopian tendencies as the convergence of technique and art, the convergence of work and play, the convergence of the realm of necessity and the realm of freedom. How? No longer subjected to the dictates of capitalist profitability and of efficiency, no longer to the dictates of scarcity, which today are perpetuated by the capitalist organization of society; socially necessary labour, material production, would and could become (we see the tendency already) increasingly scientific. Technical experimentation, science and technology would and could become a play with the hitherto hidden—methodically hidden and blocked—potentialities of men and things, of society and nature.

This means one of the oldest dreams of all radical theory and practice. It means that the creative imagination, and not only the rationality of the performance principle, would become a productive force applied to the transformation of the social and natural universe. It would mean the emergence of a form of reality which is the work and the medium of the developing sensibility and sensitivity of man.

And now I throw in the terrible concept: it would mean an 'aesthetic' reality—society as a work of art. This is the most Utopian, the most radical possibility of liberation today.

What does this mean, in concrete terms? I said, we are not concerned here with private sensitivity and sensibility, but with sensitivity and sensibility, creative imagination and play, becoming forces of transformation. As such they would guide, for example, the total reconstruction of our cities and of the countryside; the restoration of nature after the elimination of the violence and destruction of capitalist industrialization; the creation of internal and external space for privacy, individual autonomy, tranquillity; the elimination of noise, of captive audiences, of enforced togetherness, of pollution, of ugliness. These are not—and I cannot emphasize this strongly enough—snobbish and romantic demands. Biologists today have emphasized that these are organic needs for the human organism, and that their arrest, their perversion and destruction by capitalist society, actually mutilates the human organism, not only in a figurative way but in a very real and literal sense.

I believe that it is only in such a universe that man can be truly free, and truly human relationships between free beings can be established. I believe that the idea of such a universe guided also Marx's concept of socialism, and that these aesthetic needs and goals must from the beginning be present in the reconstruction of society, and not only at the end or in the far future. Otherwise, the needs and satisfactions which reproduce a repressive society would be carried over into the new society. Repressive men would carry over their repression into the new society.

HERBERT MARCUSE 99

Now, at this farthest point, the question is: how can we possibly envisage the emergence of such qualitatively different needs and goals as organic, biological needs and goals and not as superimposed values? How can we envisage the emergence of these needs and satisfactions within and against the established society—that is to say, prior to liberation? That was the dialectic with which I started, that in a very definite sense we have to be free from in order to create a free society.

Needless to say, the dissolution of the existing system is the precondition for such qualitative change. And the more efficiently the repressive apparatus of the affluent societies operates, the less likely is a gradual transition from servitude to freedom. The fact that today we cannot identify any specific class or any specific group as a revolutionary force, this fact is no excuse for not using any and every possibility and method to arrest the engines of repression in the individual. The diffusion of potential opposition among the entire underlying population corresponds precisely to the total character of our advanced capitalist society. The internal contradictions of the system are as grave as ever before and likely to be aggravated by the violent expansion of capitalist imperialism. Not only the most general contradictions between the tremendous social wealth on the one hand, and the destructive, aggressive and wasteful use of this wealth on the other; but far more concrete contradictions such as the necessity for the system to automate, the continued reduction of the human base in physical labour-power in the material reproduction of society and thereby the tendency towards the draining of the sources of surplus profit. Finally, there is the threat of technological unemployment which even the most affluent society may no longer be capable of compensating by the creation of ever more parasitic and unproductive labour: all these contradictions exist. In reaction to them suppression, manipulation and integration are likely to increase.

But fulfilment is there, the ground can and must be prepared. The mutilated consciousness and the mutilated instincts must be broken. The sensitivity and the awareness of the new transcending, antagonistic values—they are there. And they are there, they are here, precisely among the still non-integrated social groups and among those who, by virtue of their privileged position, can pierce the ideological and material veil of mass communication and indoctrination—namely, the intelligentsia.

We all know the fatal prejudice, practically from the beginning, in the Labour Movement against the intelligentsia as catalyst of historical change. It is time to ask whether this prejudice against the intellectuals, and the inferiority complex of the⁄intellectuals resulting from it, was not an essential factor in the development of the capitalist as well as the socialist societies: in the development and weakening of the opposition. The intellectuals usually went out to organize the others, to organize in the communities. They certainly did not use the potentiality they had to organize themselves, to organize among themselves not only on a regional, not only on a national, but on an international level. That is, in my view, today one of the most urgent tasks. Can we say that the intelligentsia is the agent of historical change? Can we say that the intelligentsia today is a revolutionary class? The answer I would give is: No, we cannot say that. But we can say, and I think we must say, that the intelligentsia has a decisive preparatory function, not more; and I suggest that this is plenty. By itself it is not and cannot be a revolutionary class, but it can become the catalyst, and it has a preparatory function—certainly not for the first time, that is in fact the way all revolution starts—but more, perhaps, today than ever before. Because—and for this too we have a very material and very concrete basis—it is from this group that the holders of decisive positions in the productive process will be recruited, in the future even more than hitherto. I refer to what we may call the increasingly scientific character of the material process of production, by virtue of which the role of the intelligentsia changes. It is the group from which the decisive holders of decisive positions will be recruited: scientists, researchers, technicians, engineers, even psychologists—because psychology will continue to be a socially necessary instrument, either of servitude or of liberation.

This class, this intelligentsia has been called the new working class. I believe this term is at best premature. They are—and this we should not forget—today the pet beneficiaries of the established system. But they are also at the very source of the glaring contradictions between the liberating capacity of science and its repressive and enslaving use. To activate the repressed and manipulated contradiction, to make it operate as a catalyst of change, that is one of the main tasks of the opposition today. It remains and must remain a political task.

Education is our job, but education in a new sense. Being theory as well as practice, political practice, education today is more than discussion, more than teaching and learning and writing. Unless and until it goes beyond the classroom, until and unless it goes beyond the college, the school, the university, it will remain powerless. Education today must involve the mind *and* the body, reason *and* imagination, the intellectual *and* the instinctual needs, because our entire existence has become the subject/object of politics, of social engineering. I emphasize, it is not a question of making the schools and universities, of making the educational system political. The educational system is political already. I need only remind you of the incredible degree to which (I am speaking of the U.S.) universities are involved in huge research grants (the nature of which you know in many cases) by the government and the various quasi-governmental agencies.

The educational system *is* political, so it is not we who want to politicize the educational system. What we want is a counter-policy against the established policy. And in this sense we must meet this society on its own ground of total mobilization. We must confront indoctrination in servitude with indoctrination in freedom. We must each of us generate in ourselves, and try to generate in others, the instinctual need for a life without fear, without brutality, and without stupidity. And we must see that we can generate the instinctual and intellectual revulsion against the values of an affluence which spreads aggressiveness and suppression throughout the world.

Before I conclude I would like to say my bit about the Hippies. It seems to me a serious phenomenon. If we are talking of the emergence of an instinctual revulsion against the values of the affluent society, I think here is a place where we should look for it. It seems to me that the Hippies, like any non-conformist movement on the left, are split. That there are two parts, or parties, or tendencies. Much of it is mere masquerade and clownery on the private level, and therefore indeed, as Gerassi suggested, completely harmless, very nice and charming in many cases, but that is all there is to it. But that is not the whole story. There is in the Hippies, and especially in such tendencies in the Hippies as the Diggers and the Provos, an inherent political element—perhaps even more so in the U.S. than here. It is the appearance indeed of new instinctual needs and values. This experience is there. There is a new sensibility against efficient and insane reasonableness. There is the refusal to play the rules of a rigid game, a game which one knows is rigid from the beginning, and the revolt against the compulsive cleanliness of puritan morality and the aggression bred by this puritan morality as we see it today in Vietnam among other things.

At least this part of the Hippies, in which sexual, moral and political rebellion are somehow united, is indeed a non-aggressive form of life: a demonstration of an aggressive non-aggressiveness which achieves, at least potentially, the demonstration of qualitatively different values, a trans-valuation of values.

All education today is therapy: therapy in the sense of liberating man by all available means from a society in which, sooner or later, he is going to be transformed into a brute, even if he doesn't notice it any more. Education in this sense is therapy, and all therapy today is political theory and practice. What kind of political practice? That depends entirely on the situation. It is hardly imaginable that we should discuss this here in detail. I will only remind you of the various possibilities of demonstrations, of finding out flexible modes of demonstration which can cope with the use of institutionalized violence, of boycott, many other things—anything goes which is such that it indeed has a reasonable chance of strengthening the forces of the opposition.

We can prepare for it as educators, as students. Again I say, our role is limited. We are no mass movement. I do not believe that in the near future we will see such a mass movement.

I want to add one word about the so-called Third World. I have not spoken of the Third World because my topic was strictly liberation from the affluent society. I agree entirely with Paul Sweezy, that without putting the affluent society in the framework of the Third World it is not understandable. I also believe that here and now our emphasis must be on the advanced industrial societies—not forgetting to do whatever we can and in whatever way we can to support, theoretically and practically, the struggle for liberation in the neo-colonial countries which, if again they are not the final force of liberation, at least contribute their share—and it is a considerable share—to the potential weakening and disintegration of the imperialist world system.

Our role as intellectuals is a limited role. On no account should we succumb to any illusions. But even worse than this is to succumb to the wide-spread defeatism which we witness. The preparatory role today is an indispensable role. I believe I am not being too optimistic—I have not in general the reputation of being too optimistic—when I say that we can already see the signs, not only that *They* are getting frightened and worried but that there are far more concrete, far more tangible manifestations of the essential weakness of the system. Therefore, let us continue with whatever we can—no illusions, but even more, no defeatism.

8 / Apocalypse: The Place of Mystery in the Life of the Mind

NORMAN O. BROWN

Introductory Comment by Benjamin Nelson

It is hardly likely that a more controversial Phi Beta Kappa Oration has ever been delivered on an American campus than the following statement made by Professor Norman O. Brown to the Columbia University Chapter toward the close of the last academic year. The only comparable declaration in the 184 years since the founding of the honorary fraternity is the historic address by Ralph Waldo Emerson, "The American Scholar," spoken at Harvard College in 1837. As tempting as

SOURCE: *Harper's,* May 1961, pp. 47–49. Copyright © 1961, by Harper's Magazine, Inc. Reprinted by permission of the author.

Norman O. Brown, professor of classics and comparative literature at the University of Rochester, is the author of *Life Against Death,* one of the most significant non-fiction books of the last decade, and *Love's Body.*

it would be to compare and contrast these two statements in these pages, I must forgo the pleasure and concentrate upon Professor Brown's Summons to a New Beginning.

To read Professor Brown's pages as literal prose would be to neglect their expressive purpose. A brilliant young classicist of Wesleyan University, Professor Brown has for some years now been engaged in dredging below the surfaces of the mind and culture of contemporary man. In the manner of Freud— with whose writings he has wrestled in his much-discussed book entitled Life Against Death—*Professor Brown wishes to "awaken man from his slumbers." Unlike Freud, however, who placed his faith in the "small voice of reason," Norman Brown assumes the stance of the mystic and the prophet; he laments our present plight, he reveals our brighter future, and adjures us to follow him in taking the first steps out of the darkness of our own devising into the path of grace.*

If we falter as we read his glowing words, the blame is not altogether his. We are, indeed, unmindful of our possibilities and ignorant of our first natures. Professor Brown finds decisive proof of this in the fact that we have become deaf to the music of the luminous visionaries and tortured ecstatics from Dionysius to D. H. Lawrence, who suffered both in the flesh and the spirit so that their fellow men might be restored to the Eternal Life they had heedlessly abdicated.

We will not understand Professor Brown if we fail to recognize in him a latter-day poet who aspires to be a legislator of mankind. Plato, the mystics of both East and West, the Theosophist cabalists of the Florentine Academy, George Fox, William Blake, the New England Transcendentalists, and above all Nietzsche are his spiritual ancestors. Emulating, indeed going beyond Emerson, he calls upon all of us to discard the reasonings and to shed the rationalizations which have brought us to our present impasse.

Convinced of the importance of Norman Brown's oration, I still cannot agree with his view that the ills of contemporary man and society are due to the malicious and foolish workings of man's reason. H. G. Wells was surely not at the peak of his power when he wrote that mind was at the end of its tether. Nor would I agree that the way out of the present juncture is through Dionysian frenzy, Orphic mystery, or the "no-mind"

NORMAN O. BROWN 105

of Zen Buddhism, as Professor Brown suggests. The Greeks, from whom Professor Brown has learned so much, were perhaps more correct than he supposes, when they emphasized man's need both for Love (Eros) and Reason (Logos).

There is no denying that the American scholar and the American college need today—as they will need tomorrow— to dedicate themselves anew to the unending quest of spiritual creativity. In the midst of our massive organizations of teaching and research we are prone to forget that the "letter killeth and the spirit giveth life." Professor Brown is evidently horrified by the "routinization of the imaginative" which occurs in the contemporary academy and in the world at large and this is one of the most valuable themes of his message. But does he present truly the relation between vision and technique? In his world, time ceases to run, space vanishes, history ends, as men turn in final commitment to the quest of salvation. Paradox and dilemma and tragic ambiguity do not seem to becloud his horizons. Once the soul made newly active becomes aflame with love, he supposes, there is inextinguishable illumination, and the complex tangles of history and the actual conflicts of interest dissolve forevermore.

I see little basis for these assumptions. So long as men inhabit their earthly abodes, I think they will need knowledge, skill, patience, and even cunning to moderate the antagonisms and untangle the knots which their human condition and all-too-human differences spawn. As much as I applaud Professor Brown's integrity of purpose, I frankly feel that the uncritical adoption of his teachings would involve risk to many of our most precious if unspectacular achievements. For many of us who shared—and still share—the agonies of the present century, the very foundations of society and culture are too precarious to allow for the abandonment of logic, learning, experience, method, ingenuity, art, wisdom, and even wit. The melioration of social and political problems requires realism and prudence at least as much as mystical withdrawal. Love must have a mind as well as heart if it is to avail man here below. "Commissar" and "Yogi," "Square" and "Beat" do not exhaust the alternatives.

This, at least, is one dissenting, if sympathetic, reaction to the oration that follows. But readers must encounter its chal-

lenge—*its poetry as well as its prose—for themselves. We dare not let voices such as Professor Brown's go unheard.*

Columbia University
May 31, 1960

I didn't know whether I should appear before you—there is a time to show and a time to hide; there is a time to speak, and also a time to be silent. What time is it? It is fifteen years since H. G. Wells said Mind was at the End of its Tether—with a frightful queerness come into life: there is no way out or around or through, he said; it is the end. It is because I think mind is at the end of its tether that I would be silent. It is because I think there is a way out—a way down and out—the title of Mr. John Senior's new book on the occult tradition in literature—that I will speak.

Mind at the end of its tether: I can guess what some of you are thinking—*his* mind is at the end of its tether—and this could be; it scares me but it deters me not. The alternative to mind is certainly madness. Our greatest blessings, says Socrates in the *Phaedrus,* come to us by way of madness—provided, he adds, that the madness comes from the god. Our real choice is between holy and unholy madness: open your eyes and look around you—madness is in the saddle anyhow. Freud is the measure of our unholy madness, as Nietzsche is the prophet of the holy madness, of Dionysus, the mad truth. Dionysus has returned to his native Thebes; mind—at the end of its tether—is another Pentheus, up a tree. Resisting madness can be the maddest way of being mad.

And there is a way out—the blessed madness of the maenad and the bacchant: "Blessed is he who has the good fortune to know the mysteries of the gods, who sanctifies his life and initiates his soul, a bacchant on the mountains, in holy purifications." It is possible to be mad and to be unblest; but it is not possible to get the blessing without the madness; it is not possible to get the illuminations without the derangement. Derangement is disorder: the Dionysian faith is that order as we have known it is crippling, and for cripples; that what is past is prologue; that we can throw away our crutches and discover the supernatural power of walking; that human history goes from man to superman.

NORMAN O. BROWN 107

No superman I; I come to you not as one who has supernatural powers, but as one who seeks for them, and who has some notions which way to go to find them.

Sometimes—most times—I think that the way down and out leads out of the university, out of the academy. But perhaps it is rather that we should recover the academy of earlier days—the Academy of Plato in Athens, the Academy of Ficino in Florence, Ficino who says, "The spirit of the god Dionysus was believed by the ancient theologians and Platonists to be the ecstasy and abandon of disencumbered minds, when partly by innate love, partly at the instigation of the god, they transgress the natural limits of intelligence and are miraculously transformed into the beloved god himself: where, inebriated by a certain new draft of nectar and by an immeasurable joy, they rage, as it were, in a bacchic frenzy. In the drunkenness of this Dionysian wine, our Dionysius (the Areopagite) expresses his exultation. He pours forth enigmas, he sings in dithyrambs. To penetrate the profundity of his meanings, to imitate his quasi-Orphic manner of speech, we too require the divine fury."

At any rate the point is first of all to find again the mysteries. By which I do not mean simply the sense of wonder—that sense of wonder which is indeed the source of all true philosophy—by mystery I mean secret and occult; therefore unpublishable; therefore outside the university as we know it; but not outside Plato's Academy, or Ficino's.

Why are mysteries unpublishable? First because they cannot be put into words, at least not the kind of words which earned you your Phi Beta Kappa keys. Mysteries display themselves in words only if they can remain concealed; this is poetry, isn't it? We must return to the old doctrine of the Platonists and Neo-Platonists, that poetry is veiled truth; as Dionysus is the god who is both manifest and hidden; and as John Donne declared, with the Pillar of Fire goes the Pillar of Cloud. This is also the new doctrine of Ezra Pound, who says: "Prose is not education but the outer courts of the same. Beyond its doors are the mysteries. Eleusis. Things not to be spoken of save in secret. The mysteries self-defended, the mysteries that cannot be revealed. Fools can only profane them. The dull can neither penetrate the secretum nor divulge it to others." The mystic academies, whether Plato's or Ficino's, knew the limitations of words and drove us on beyond them, to go over, to go under, to the learned ignorance, in which God is better honored and loved by silence than by words, and better seen by closing the eyes to images than by opening them.

And second, mysteries are unpublishable because only some can see them, not all. Mysteries are intrinsically esoteric, and as such an offense to democracy: is not publicity a democratic principle? Publication makes it republican—a thing of the people. The pristine academies were esoteric and aristocratic, self-consciously separate from the profane vulgar. Democratic resentment denies that there can be anything that can't be seen by everybody; in the democratic academy truth is subject to public verification; truth is what any fool can see. This is what is meant by the so-called scientific method: so-called science is the attempt to democratize knowledge—the attempt to substitute method for insight, mediocrity for genius, by getting a standard operating procedure. The great equalizers dispensed by the scientific method are the tools, those analytical tools. The miracle of genius is replaced by the standardized mechanism. But fools with tools are still fools, and don't let your Phi Beta Kappa key fool you. Tibetan prayer wheels are another way of arriving at the same result: the degeneration of mysticism into mechanism—so that any fool can do it. Perhaps the advantage is with Tibet: for there the mechanism is external while the mind is left vacant; and vacancy is not the worst condition of the mind. And the resultant prayers make no futile claim to originality or immortality; being nonexistent, they do not have to be catalogued or stored.

The sociologist Simmel sees showing and hiding, secrecy and publicity, as two poles, like Yin and Yang, between which societies oscillate in their historical development. I sometimes think I see that civilizations originate in the disclosure of some mystery, some secret; and expand with the progressive publication of their secret; and end in exhaustion when there is no longer any secret, when the mystery has been divulged, that is to say profaned. The whole story is illustrated in the difference between ideogram and alphabet. The alphabet is indeed a democratic triumph; and the enigmatic ideogram, as Ezra Pound has taught us, is a piece of mystery, a piece of poetry, not yet profaned. And so there comes a time—I believe we are in such a time—when civilization has to be renewed by the discovery of new mysteries, by the undemocratic but sovereign power of the imagination, by the undemocratic power which makes poets the unacknowledged legislators of mankind, the power which makes all things new.

The power which makes all things new is magic. What our time needs is mystery: what our time needs is magic. Who would not say that only a miracle can save us? In Tibet the degree-granting institution is, or used to be, the College of Magic Ritual. It offers courses in such fields as clairvoyance and telepathy; also (attention physics majors) internal heat: internal heat is a yoga bestowing supernatural control over body temperature. Let me succumb for a moment to the fascination of the mysterious East and tell you of the examination procedure for the course in internal heat. Candidates assemble naked, in midwinter, at night, on a frozen Himalayan lake. Beside each one is placed a pile of wet frozen undershirts; the assignment is to wear, until they are dry, as many as possible of these undershirts before dawn. Where the power is real, the test is real, and the grading system dumfoundingly objective. I say no more. I say no more; Eastern Yoga does indeed demonstrate the existence of supernatural powers, but it does not have the particular power our Western society needs; or rather I think that each society has access only to its own proper powers; or rather each society will only get the kind of power it knows how to ask for.

The Western consciousness has always asked for freedom: the human mind was born free, or at any rate born to be free, but everywhere it is in chains; and now at the end of its tether. It will take a miracle to free the human mind: because the chains are magical in the first place. We are in bondage to authority outside ourselves: most obviously—here in a great university it must be said—in bondage to the authority of books. There is a Transcendentalist anticipation of what I want to say in Emerson's Phi Beta Kappa address on the American Scholar:

"The books of an older period will not fit this. Yet hence arises a grave mischief. The sacredness which attaches to the act of creation, the act of thought, is transferred to the record. Instantly the book becomes noxious: the guide is a tyrant. The sluggish and perverted mind of the multitude having once received this book, stands upon it, and makes an outcry if it is destroyed. Colleges are built on it. Meek young men grow up in libraries. Hence, instead of Man Thinking, we have the book-worm. I had better never see a book than to be warped by its attraction clean out of my own orbit, and make a satellite instead of a system. The one thing in the world, of value, is the active soul."

How far this university is from that ideal is the measure of the defeat of our American dream.

This bondage to books compels us not to see with our own eyes; compels us to see with the eyes of the dead, with dead eyes. Whitman, likewise in a Transcendentalist sermon, says, "You shall no longer take things at second or third hand, nor look through the eyes of the dead, nor feed on the specters in books." There is a hex on us, the specters in books, the authority of the past; and to exorcise these ghosts is the great work of magical self-liberation. Then the eyes of the spirit would become one with the eyes of the body, and god would be in us, not outside. God in us: *entheos:* enthusiasm; this is the essence of the holy madness. In the fire of the holy madness even books lose their gravity, and let themselves go up into the flame: "Properly," says Ezra Pound, "we should read for power. Man reading should be man intensely alive. The book should be a ball of light in one's hand."

I began with the name of Dionysus; let me be permitted to end with the name of Christ: for the power I seek is also Christian. Nietzsche indeed said the whole question was Dionysus versus Christ; but only the fool will take these as mutually exclusive opposites. There is a Dionysian Christianity, an apocalyptic Christianity, a Christianity of miracles and revelations. And there always have been some Christians for whom the age of miracle and revelation is not over; Christians who claim the spirit; enthusiasts. The power I look for is the power of enthusiasm; as condemned by John Locke; as possessed by George Fox, the Quaker; through whom the houses were shaken; who saw the channel of blood running down the streets of the city of Litchfield; to whom, as a matter of fact, was even given the magic internal heat—"The fire of the Lord was so in my feet, and all around me, that I did not matter to put on my shoes any more."

Read again the controversies of the seventeenth century and discover our choice: we are either in an age of miracles, says Hobbes, miracles which authenticate fresh revelations; or else we are in an age of reasoning from already received Scripture. Either miracle or Scripture. George Fox, who came up in spirit through the flaming sword into the paradise of God, so that all things were new, he being renewed to the state of Adam which he was in before he fell, sees that none can read Moses aright without Moses' spirit; none can read John's words aright, and with a true understanding of them, but in and with the same divine spirit by which John spake them, and by his burning shining light which is sent from God. Thus the authority of the past is swallowed up in new creation; the word is made flesh. We see with our own eyes and to see with our own eyes is second sight. To see with our own eyes is second sight.

> Twofold Always. May God us keep
> From single vision and Newton's sleep.

9 / The Obvious

R. D. LAING

. . . A recent study of the American public's view of U.S. policy towards China (prepared for the Council on Foreign Relations by the Survey Research Center at the University of Michigan) reports that one out of every four Americans still does not know that the Chinese people have a communist government.

I would not be surprised if over half of those of us who know that the people of China have a communist government, do *not* know that one quarter of the population do *not*, if this report is to be believed.

I want to draw attention to a few of those features of North American and European society that seem to be most dangerous,

SOURCE: David Cooper, ed., *To Free a Generation* (New York: Collier Books, 1968), pp. 13–33. Reprinted by permission of Deborah Rogers Ltd., London.

R. D. Laing, a young British psychiatrist, has written two books which have strongly influenced the younger generation of the late sixties, *The Divided Self* and *The Politics of Experience*.

because they seem to help, or perhaps even to be necessary, to maintain and to perpetuate our component of a social world system that as a whole presents more and more the appearance of total irrationality.

To a considerable extent what follows is an essay in stating what I take to be obvious. It is obvious that the social world situation is endangering the future of all life on this planet. To state the obvious is to share with you what (in your view) my misconceptions might be. The obvious can be dangerous. The deluded man frequently finds his delusions so obvious that he can hardly credit the good faith of those who do not share them. Hitler regarded it as perfectly obvious that the Jews were a poison to the Aryan race and hence required to be exterminated. What is obvious to Lyndon Johnson is not at all obvious to Ho Chi Minh. What is obvious to me might not be obvious to anyone else. The obvious is literally that which stands in one's way, in front of or over against oneself. One has to begin by recognizing that it exists for oneself.

This talk is also an attempt to exhibit for your inspection some facets of my present effort to diagnose, to see into and through social reality. I at most am presuming to try to articulate what seems to me to be the case, in some very limited aspects, in respect of what is going on in the human sector of the planet. I shall have to deal for the most part in generalities. I am not sure whether these are clichés to many of you. One man's revolution is another's platitude.

The Invisibility of Social Events

The study of social events presents an almost insurmountable difficulty, in that their visibility, as one might say, is very low. In social *space* one's direct immediate capacity to see what is happening does not extend any further than one's own senses extend. Beyond that one has to make inferences based on hearsay evidence, reports of one kind or another of what other human beings are able to see within *their* equally limited field of observation. As in space, so in *time*. Our capacity to probe back into history is extraordinarily limited. Even in the most detailed investigations of small fragments of micro-history, in studies of families, one finds it difficult to get past two or three generations. Beyond that, how things have come to be as they are disappears into mist.

They often go out of view in space and time at a boundary between here and now, and there and then—a boundary which unfortunately consigns here and now to unintelligibility without information from there and then, which is, however, beyond our reach.

Context of Social Events

A fundamental lesson that almost all social scientists have learned is that the intelligibility of social events requires that they be always seen in a context that extends both spatially and in time. The dilemma is that this is often as impossible as it is necessary. The fabric of sociality is an interlaced set of contexts, of sub-systems interlaced with other sub-systems, of contexts interlaced with metacontexts and metametacontexts and so on until it reaches a theoretical limit, the context of all possible social contexts, comprising together with all the contexts that are subsumed within it, what one might call the *total social world system*. Beyond this total social world system—as there is no larger social context that we can define—there is no further *social* context to which one can refer the intelligibility of the total social world system.

As we begin from micro-situations and work up to macro-situations we find that the apparent irrationality of behaviour on a small scale takes on a certain form of intelligibility when one sees it in context. One moves, for example, from the apparent irrationality of the single 'psychotic' individual to the intelligibility of that irrationality within the context of the family. The irrationality of the family in its turn must be placed within the context of its encompassing networks. These further networks must be seen within the context of yet larger organizations and institutions. These larger contexts do not exist out there on some periphery of social space: they pervade the interstices of all that is comprised by them.

The Paradox of the Irrationality of the Whole

It is terrifying that having moved up through the irrationality/rationality of sets of sub-systems until we reach the total social context, we there seem to glimpse a total system that appears to be dangerously out of the control of the sub-systems or sub-contexts that comprise it. Here we face a theoretical, logical and practical dilemma. Namely, we seem to arrive at an empirical limit which itself appears to be without obvious intelligibility, and beyond this limiting context we do not know what further context there may be that may help us to set the total social world system in a larger pattern or design in which it finds its rationality. Some people think that it may be possible to do this within a cosmic pattern. On the other hand, more than one person has said—and usually been regarded as mad for having said it—that perhaps God is not dead: perhaps God is Himself mad.

Mediations

We have a theoretical and practical problem of finding the mediations between the different levels of contexts: between the different systems and metasystems, extending all the way from the smallest micro- to the largest macro-social systems. The intermediate systems that lie on this range have to be studied not only in themselves, but as conditioning and conditioned media between the individual parts and the whole.

In our society, at certain times, this interlaced set of systems may lend itself to revolutionary change, not at the extreme micro or macro ends; that is, not through the individual pirouette of solitary repentance on the one hand, or by a seizure of the machinery of the state on the other; but by sudden, structural, radical qualitative changes in the intermediate system levels: changes in a factory, a hospital, a school, a university, a set of schools, or a whole area of industry, medicine, education, etc.

The Example of Psychiatry

I started to try to see through the dense opacity of social events from the study of certain people who were labelled psychotic or neurotic, as seen in mental hospitals, psychiatric units and out-patient clinics. I began to see that I was involved in the study of *situations* and not simply of individuals. It seemed (and this still seems to be the case) that the study of such situations was arrested in three principal ways. In the first place the behaviour of such people was regarded as signs of a pathological process that was going on *in* them, and only secondarily of anything else. The whole subject was enclosed in a medical metaphor. In the second place this medical metaphor conditioned the conduct of all those who were enclosed by it, doctors and patients. Thirdly, through this metaphor the person who was the patient in the system, being isolated from the system, could no longer be seen as a person: as a corollary, it was also difficult for the doctor to behave as a person. A person does not exist without a social context. You cannot take a person out of his social context and still see him as a person, or *act* towards him as a person. It one does not *act* towards the other as a person, one depersonalizes *oneself*.

Someone is gibbering away on his knees, talking to someone who is not there. Yes, he is praying. If one does not accord him the social intelligibility of this behaviour, he can only be seen as mad. Out of social context, his behaviour can only be the outcome of an unintelligible 'psychological' and/or 'physical' process, for which he requires treatment. This metaphor sanctions a massive ignorance of the social context within which the person was interacting. It also renders any genuine reciprocity between the process of labelling (the practice of psychiatry) and of being labelled (the role of patient) as impossible to conceive as it is to observe. Someone whose mind is imprisoned in the metaphor cannot see it as a metaphor. It is just *obvious*. How, he will say, can diagnosing someone as ill who is obviously ill, make him ill? Or make him better, for that matter? Some of us began to realize that this aspect of the theory and practice of psychiatry was an essay in non-dialectical thinking and practice. However, once one had got oneself out of the straitjacket of this metaphor, it was possible to see the function of this anti-dialectical exercise. The unintelligibility of the experience and behaviour of the diagnosed person is created by the person diagnosing him, as well as by the person diagnosed. This stratagem seems to serve specific functions within the structure of the system in which it occurs.

To work smoothly, it is necessary that those who use this stratagem do not themselves know that it is a stratagem. They should not be cynical or ruthless: they should be sincere and concerned. Indeed, the more 'treatment' is escalated—through negotiation (psychotherapy), pacification (tranquillization), physical struggle (cold-packs and straitjackets), through at one and the same time more and more *humane* and *effective* forms of destruction (electroshocks and insulin comas), to the final solution of cutting a person's brain in two or more slices by psycho-surgery—the more the human beings who do these things to other people tend to feel sincere concern, dedication, pity; and they can hardly help but feel more and more indignant, sorrowful, horrified and scandalized at those of their colleagues who are horrified and scandalized by their actions. As for the patients, the more they protest, the less insight they display; the more they fight back, clearly the more they need to be pacified; the more persecuted they feel at being destroyed, the more necessary to destroy them. And at the end of it all, they may indeed be 'cured', they may even express gratitude for no longer having the brains left to protest against persecution. But many do not. This only goes to show, as one leading psychiatrist said to me: 'It's the white man's burden, Ronald. We can't expect any thanks, but we must go on.'

Hundreds of thousands of people are involved in this amazing political operation. Many patients in their innocence continue to flock for help to psychiatrists who honestly feel they are giving people what they ask for: relief from suffering. This is but one example of the diametric irrationality of much of our social scene. The *exact* opposite is achieved to what is intended. Doctors in all ages have made fortunes by killing their patients by means of their cures. The difference in psychiatry is that it is the death of the soul.

Those who think they have seen through this to some extent see it as a system of violence and counter-violence. People called brain surgeons have stuck knives into the brains of hundreds and thousands of people in the last twenty years: people who may never have used a knife against anyone themselves; they may have broken a few windows, sometimes screamed, but they have killed fewer people than the rest of the population, many many fewer if we count the mass-exterminations of wars, declared and undeclared, waged by the legalized 'sane' members of our society.

Such institutionalized, organized violence seems to begin to be called into play at certain moments in a micro-political power struggle, often but not necessarily involving a family, always involving a network of people, more or less extended. The apparent irrationality and sometimes apparently senseless violence of one person in this group—not necessarily the 'patient'—finds its intelligibility in the social context. This apparently senseless violence is a moment in an ongoing set of reciprocals of violence and counter-violence. However, the worst violence of all is the reciprocal denial of reciprocity, the creation of a frozen, non-dialectical *impasse,* both by the patient who refuses to communicate, and by the psychiatrist, who double-stamps this *refusal* as *inability.*

To cut a long story very short: the context of the individual at first appears as his immediate network, and the contexts of that network come into view as larger social frameworks that have not by any means been adequately identified. However, we can theoretically reach farther than our empirical research can go, in the hope that our theoretical reach can help us to extend our practical grasp. So we may postulate that there is no end to context upon context until one reaches a total social world system which comprises a hierarchy of contexts, metacontexts, meta-metacontexts: interlaced patterns of control, frequently violent control, no part of which is understandable if extrapolated from the whole of which it is a part. Nevertheless, some components of this do seem to be more irremediably irrational[1] than others.

I sometimes think that the danger of the interlaced sets of psychiatric systems in our society (to their homeostasis, equilibrium, steady state) is not where most people in the system suppose it to be. In the mental-health field there is some anxiety lest we may not have enough mental hospitals, research workers, nurses, etc. to cope with the continued increase in the incidence of mental illness, so-called. It may be that the problem is not that there will be too *few* psychiatrists for too many patients, but that there will be *too few patients* coming along in the next ten or twenty years.

It may be that what our system needs is a sufficient number of people to be elected patients and treated accordingly. To each network of perhaps 20 or 30 people some sort of human lightning

---

[1] An action can be regarded as irrational if it is ostensibly a means towards an end, such that this means leads to an end it purports to avoid. One attempts to avoid an outcome by certain means. Such means are irrational when they bring about the end they are intended to avoid—a common finding in the psychoanalysis of 'neurotic' defense against anxiety. The defenses generate the anxieties they are defenses against. I am putting in parenthesis the question of the rationality of the

conductor may be required into which 'bad vibrations' from un-lived living may be channelled—a sort of human earthing device. In the intermediate zone we appear to deal with our violence by such elective focusing (scapegoating being but one obvious example). This is not only in terms of psychiatry. Think how networks selectively funnel people into the criminal chan-nel. On the intermediate levels between macro and micro we see all the time how one out of so many people is nominated as he or she who is felt to epitomize a violence that justifies violence from US. It is plausible to me that this represents a desperate stratagem to keep the system ongoing. If this sounds a bit mad to you, you will be not entirely wrong. This is the type of theory that psychiatric patients often bring forward. They are labelled psychotic partly *because* they bring forward this type of theory.

I have so far sketched some ways violence may be *focused* on single persons. Let us now look at the other end of the scale, the macro end of the intermediate zone. Here violence is pro-jected in an antithetical way, not on any individual *within* the system, but on some vague mass being *outside* the subsystem—THEM. Here we are concerned with the massive actions of the largest groups of people in the world. I want to consider for a moment some facets of the macro-situation. Again, I am going to state only what seems to me obvious, for the same reasons I gave before: that it might not be obvious to others and it will give you the opportunity to make up your minds as to how misguided or naïve I am.

Looking at the whole world scene, it seems that transecting existing human divisions and struggles in terms of race, nation-ality or geopolitical blocs a new transworld polarization is rapidly occurring between Haves and Have-nots. Most of the Have-nots are peasants. Their age-long misery seems to be more in the process of being deepened by the minority of the Haves than otherwise. It seems that an increasing number of the Have-nots are beginning to become restive and to be no longer resigned to this state of affairs. Armed struggles are current in Asia, Latin America and Africa. As far as I know the Have-nots do not tend to look to the U.S.A. or Western Europe for help, although their governments (who belong to the Haves) may do so. The Have-nots are not sophisticated in Western economics. Rightly or wrongly, I have formed the impression that many of them have begun to feel that the U.S.A. and Western Europe have been exploiting them for too long. They look, rightly or wrongly, to Russia, to an increasing extent to China, and to a growing extent to themselves for their help. Looking at this situation, on a worldwide scale, it seems to me as though a World War (World Wars I and II being the prodromata of the real global involvement) is well under way. The world revolution, Arnold Toynbee has suggested, has begun. But who will eventually be fighting whom is still not clear. Ten years from now the U.S.A. and China may be in alliance against Africa. Provisionally, for the time being, it seems that *our* slice of the world cake (since practically all of us here are from Western Europe or the U.S.A.) has a certain homogeneity despite the heterogeneity of very intricate interlacing of its multiple subsystems, and despite its plurality of contradictions. But many of these contradictions are more apparent than real. They arise from our belief in our own lies and mystifications. Many people are tortured by contradictions that exist only between facts and propaganda, not in the facts themselves. For instance, we have *not* abolished poverty within our own territory; the U.S.A. is *not* a democracy. Once you do not think that the U.S.A. is a democracy, then there are a great many problems that do not have to be solved because they do not exist. Many people in the U.K. still believe that the U.K. is one of the most peace-loving countries in the world. It has fought more wars, I believe, in the last 300 years than any other nation on earth.

I am not going to enumerate the mystifications to which I think we are subject. I shall take most of that for granted. I find no problem in the fact that a growing number of the people in Africa, Asia, Latin America—the local inhabitants (called, by *us,* terrorists)—are fighting against the white invaders of their countries. This violence is not problematical. Where is the problem? What does puzzle me somewhat, however, is that the spokesmen of the U.S.A. and of this country sometimes seem to think that the violence of the inhabitants of Latin America, Asia and Africa can only be explained as the outcome of a communist plot to overthrow the U.S.A. and Europe.

Suppose the Chinese had 600,000 troops in Southern Mexico engaged in slaughtering the local inhabitants, devastating the ecology and dropping more bombs on Northern Mexico each month than were dropped on the whole of Germany during the whole of World War II. Suppose the Chinese had encircled the U.S.A. with missile bases in Canada, Cuba, the Pacific Islands; that China's fleets patrolled the seas and its atomic submarines appeared to be ubiquitous; and that all this was deployed, according to the Chinese, for no other purpose than directly to put down a threat to the Chinese people by the people of the U.S.A. And suppose that China had made it quite clear into the bargain that it regarded the U.S.A. as the greatest threat to world peace, and that if the U.S.A. sent any troops into Northern Mexico, they would give them all they'd got and smash them back into the Stone Age. Then I would have no difficulty in understanding the anxieties of the people of the U.S.A. and its leaders about such a policy of 'containment,' whether or not they were aware that the people of China had a communist government.

But that is not what we have got to understand. We can more profitably exercise ourselves by trying to understand how the statements of the leaders of the U.S.A. often seem to attribute to the Chinese precisely the policy they themselves seem to be pursuing towards the Chinese.

In Vietnam several million men, women and children, mainly peasants, are exposed to indiscriminate death and mutilation. When they fight, they are fighting on their own land for their own land. On the other side, thousands of miles away from their homes, are mercenaries, well-paid, well-fed, steel-trained specialists in the technology of killing. There are people fighting to destroy all forms of life over a sector of the earth's surface, because somewhere in that space there may be some human beings who have inside them the 'wrong' ideology.

We do not have to ask why an increasing number of the world's inhabitants hate us Europeans and the U.S.A. We do not have to go into extraordinary psychological explanations of why I would hate someone who had napalmed my children. It is no more complicated than black and white.

Consider Vietnam again. It is not at all obvious why it is going on. No purely economic explanation seems adequate. It may be imperialism gone mad. U Thant has proposed that it is a sort of Holy War. The theoreticians in the Pentagon say that it is a global operation in order to contain the advance of communist

R. D. LAING 121

imperialism. It may be much more primitive. President Johnson says to combat commanders in the Officers' Mess at Qumran Bay: 'Come home with that coonskin on the wall.' One hears extraordinary statements from U.S. politicians, such as 'Bringing Red China to her knees'. What we have here is the most primitive analogical 'thinking', behind which lies a hinterland of fantasy one hardly dares contemplate.

Many people feel ashamed and disgusted by Vietnam. Nevertheless, some of us have to grasp the full implications of the fact that a great number of people have got to the state where they feel guilty if they are turned down by the draft; that a great number of people feel ashamed and guilty if they *don't* manufacture, deliver or drop napalm, etc.

This whole system and the eager and active human perpetuation of it is almost beyond comprehension, because it defies imagination if one is not in it, and its horror is so stark that it is almost unbearable if one is in it.

Multiple Ignorance

Moreover, the system itself generates ignorance of itself, and ignorance of this ignorance. I would guess that *at least* three out of four of the three quarters of Americans whom we are assured are aware that the Chinese people have a communist government would not believe this figure. Let us suppose that one in four do not know—and do not know they do not know. Let us suppose that three out of four of the remainder do not know that one out of four does not know he does not know. So how many sane men can we address?

But this is just the beginning. Three out of four *do* know that the people of China have a communist government—and By God we better do something about it before it is too late: we must contain it, if not destroy it, before It destroys Us. I would guess that *at least* three quarters of the three quarters who 'know' that the people of China have a communist government have a reflex of horror and terror at the thought. But perhaps the worst of all reflexes is *pity*: 'How can we sit idly by and let this happen to our brothers and sisters the Chinese. Look what they did to our missionaries—you can't blame them *all* for that of course. Dear Chiang, he did his best.'

The dear little old lady investor in tennis shoes has her nephew the General. He thinks she is too soft. She has always thought more of others than herself. 'I believe that a people gets the government it deserves. Look at our country for example. If the Chinese have a communist government it must be their fault to some extent—you can't just let them get away with that. If they don't want to get what's coming to them, they know what to do about it.'

There are those who know they don't know, those who don't know they don't know, and legions of those who find denser and denser realms of darkness in which to veil their own ignorance from themselves. And there are those who, no matter what they think they know or don't know to any metalevel, will *just do what they are told* when it comes to the bit. Those that are left, who know they don't know and who will not necessarily do what they are told—it is to them that this speech is addressed, which I hope may be of some service, if only as a joke, to the last surviving *human beings* on the planet. The privilege of being one of this number I hardly dare claim.

Once you are hooked you don't know you are hooked. One comes to be ashamed of one's original nature, terrified of it, and ready to destroy evidence of it in oneself and anyone else. This has been achieved—one can see it being achieved—not only by families but by all the institutions that are brought to bear on children. First, in babies, through the kinesics of handling and the suppression of their immediate instinctive intelligence of smell and touch and taste; thereafter through kinesics and *para*-linguistics—words are of tertiary significance. The product of this is a young man of eighteen who is ripe to volunteer to be (or at the very least to acquiesce in being) a hired killer. Who is *proud* to be processed to be a hired killer, deeply guilty and ashamed of himself if he is frightened, *even* in his guts, and guilty and ashamed if he feels guilty and ashamed of killing simply because he is told to do so.

For far too long psychologists have given a disproportionate amount of time and effort to the psychopathology of the abnormal. We need to catch up on the *normal* psychological correlates of the *normal* state of affairs, of which Vietnam is only one of the most obvious *normal* manifestations. I shall give you an example, a story of a type which has been told me so often that I regard it as only slightly excessively normal. A boy of three is held by his mother out of a sixth-storey window by his neck. His mother says: 'See how much I love you.' The demonstration being that if she did not love him she would drop him.

One could go through many speculations as to why a woman could be so warped as to terrorize her own son in such a way. When one has been through all that, one comes back, I think, to the obvious: the reason why she was doing this to him was exactly the reason she gave him. It was to show him that she loved him. Why else should she do it? That is what she said she was doing it for, and evidently to her no clearer proof of love could be vouchsafed. In that case, one has got to move into the psychology of that woman, and that is the psychology of normality. This is an example of *extreme normality*. The *normal* way parents get their children to love them is to terrorize them, to say to them in effect: 'Because I am not dropping you, because I am not killing you, this shows that I love you, and therefore you should come for the assuagement of your terror to the person who is generating the terror that you are seeking to have assuaged.' The above mother is rather hyper-normal.

To understand her one has to go back to her parents. Let us suppose she really meant what she said. She was doing this to the child in order to show him that she loved him. She has remained constantly puzzled and hurt that he did not exhibit the gratitude she would expect for taking this trouble. Other children are grateful when their parents do a lot *less* for them than *we* have done for you. What did her mother do to her? In what way did her mother not love her? Possibly her mother never held her out of a high window and showed her how much she loved her, as she should have done. And why not? You have to ask what her great-grandmother did or did not do for her grandmother, and so on.

The whole system, in any of its aspects, is so well into such multi-generational spiral effects that it is very difficult to see how the spiral can be turned round. The psychoanalyst Winnicott recently posed the question: One looks into the mirror to see oneself—what antecedes the mirror? He suggests that what comes before the mirror is one's mother's face. So that if one's mother's face is a mirror, when one looks in one's mother's face one sees oneself. What else can one see? That is fine so long as

one's mother, in looking at oneself, sees oneself. But if in looking
at oneself she sees herself—sees oneself as an extension of herself, but in so doing is unaware of so doing, so that she *thinks*
she sees oneself—out of that deep spiral of misapprehension
however is one to find oneself again? Nor is it *herself* that she
sees in the baby. She is seeing what her mother saw, and her
mother saw, and so on. The spiral of alienation goes whirling
back, way out of sight. And by the time one has lost oneself in
the nth turn of this spiral of alienation and grown up to see,
without knowing that one sees, one's mirror image in the face of
one's enemy; to become the Other to an Other who is himself
Other than himself; then we are just beginning to get to the precondition of the possibility of the amazing collective paranoid
projective systems that operate on large scales. We attribute to
Them exactly what We are doing to Them. Because We are seeing ourselves in Them, but we do not know that we are. We think
that They are Them, but They are actually Us.

For instance, one of the ironies of history: 'All men are created
equal. They are endowed by their creator with certain inalien-
able rights: among these are life, liberty and the pursuit of happiness.' It is the opening sentence of the Declaration of Independence of the Democratic Republic of Vietnam.

Can we find some way of disarticulating the circuit somewhere from within? We might be able to consider what are the
weakest, what the strongest threads that maintain the tapestry
in its tightly woven state.

I was struck by a remark that Sir Julian Huxley made to me a
few years ago. He said he thought the most dangerous link in the
chain was *obedience*. That we have been trained, and we train
our children, so that we and they are prepared to do practically
anything if told to do it by a sufficient authority. It is always
said, 'it couldn't happen here', but it is always happening here.[2]
It is particularly important to study the nature of obedience. Our
system operates through a network of common-obedience rec-
iprocities. What is the organization structure of this net? Clearly
we have not all equal discretion in the exercise of power. In an
ultimate sense we may wish to take on equal responsibility, but
there is a vast differential in power in all sectors of the total

[2] *No doubt,* it is happening *there* as well.

world system. The people who exercise power can do so only if people carry out their orders. We have the spectacle at this very moment in the earth's history of white troops in the middle of jungle darkness blazing away at the darkness, for reasons they do not know—except that if they were forced to, I would think they would probably come down to saying, 'Well, ours is not to reason why. We are carrying out orders.' Some of them want to be heroes. I do not think many of them do.

The following is a simple morality tale from Yale University, an experiment conducted by Dr. Stanley Milgram.

Dr. Milgram recruited 40 male volunteers who believed they were to take part in an experimental study of memory and learning at Yale University. The 40 men were between the ages of 20 and 50 and represented a wide range of occupations. Typical subjects were postal clerks, high school teachers, salesmen, engineers and laborers. One subject had not finished elementary school, but some others had doctorate and other professional degrees.

The role of experimenter was played by a 31-year-old high school teacher of biology. His manner was impassive but he maintained a somewhat stern appearance during the experiment. The experimenter was aided by a mild-mannered and likable man, who acted as a 'victim'. The experimenter interviewed each volunteer and, with him, the 'victim' masquerading as another volunteer. He told the two of them that the intention was to investigate the effects of punishment on learning, and in particular the differential effects of varying degrees of punishment and various types of teacher. The drawing of lots was rigged so that the volunteer was always the teacher and the 'victim' was always the learner. The victim was strapped into an 'electric chair' apparatus and electrode paste and an electrode were applied. The teacher-volunteer was then taken into an adjacent room and placed before a complex instrument labeled 'Shock Generator'. The teacher-volunteer was given a 45-volt shock to demonstrate the apparent authenticity of the machine.

Pulling the Switch

A row of 30 switches on the 'shock generator' were labeled from 15 to 450 volts by 15-volt steps. In addition, groups of switches were labeled from 'slight shock' to 'danger: severe shock'. Following instructions and in the context of a mock learning experiment, the teacher-volunteer was led to believe that he was administering increasingly more severe punishment to the learner-victim, who made prearranged responses. The learner-victim gave incorrect answers to three out of every four questions and received shocks as punishment for his errors. When the punitive shock reached the 300-volt level, the learner-victim—as had been prearranged—kicked on the wall of the room in which he was bound to the electric chair. At this point teacher-volunteers turned to the experimenter for guidance. The teacher-volunteer was advised to continue after a 5–10 second pause. After the 315-volt shock, the pounding was heard again. Silence followed. At this point in the experiment the teacher-volunteers began to react in various ways. But they were verbally encouraged, and even ordered in a firm manner, to proceed right up to the maximum level of voltage.

Test Results

. . . Dr. Milgram states that contrary to all expectations 26 of the 40 subjects completed the series, finally administering 450 volts to the now silent 'victim'. Only 5 refused to carry on after the victim's first protest when 300-volts were apparently administered. Many continued, even though they experienced considerable emotional disturbance, as clearly shown by their spoken comments, profuse sweating, tremor, stuttering and bizarre nervous laughter and smiling. Three subjects had uncontrollable seizures. The teacher-volunteers who continued the shock frequently voiced their concern for the learner-victim, but the majority overcame their humane reactions and continued as ordered right up to the maximum punishment.

One observer related: 'I observed a mature and initially poised businessman enter the laboratory smiling and confident. Within 20 minutes he was reduced to a twitching, stuttering wreck, who was rapidly approaching a point of nervous collapse. He constantly pulled on his earlobe and twisted his hands. At one point he pushed his fist into his forehead and muttered: "Oh God, let's stop it." And yet he continued to respond to every word of the experimenter, and obeyed to the end.'

The conflict that the subjects faced in this experiment was between obeying an authority they trusted and respected, and doing something they felt to be wrong. The real-life situation is more horrible. There is, for many, perhaps no conflict at all. My guess is that *most* people feel guilty at *not* doing what they are told, even though they think it is wrong, and even though they mistrust those who give the orders. They feel guilty at trusting their own mistrust.

It would be nice to live in a world where we could feel that if one of the authorities of society—whether Mao, the Pope, or Lyndon Johnson, and their acolytes—told us something, the fact that they said so would make it more likely to be true than false. It would be nice, even, if one could believe that something that appears in any of our journals of scholarship, or medical or social-science research, was more likely to be true than false by the fact of its publication. Unfortunately we are forced by the cynical lies, multifarious deceptions and sincerely held delusions to which we are now subjected through all media—even the organs of scholarship and science—to a position of almost total social scepticism. There is almost nothing we *can* know about the total social world system, or any of the systems for several levels down from there. But it is possible to know that we cannot so know—this being a historical contingency of the present world situation, but given that situation, a necessity of that situation. Yet we are so 'programmed' to believe that what we are told is more likely to be true than false because we are told it, that almost all of us are liable to be caught out occasionally. We have all a 'reflex' towards believing and doing what we are told.

We can put no trust in princes, popes, politicians, scholars or scientists, our worst enemy or our best friend. With the greatest precautions, we may put trust in a source that is much deeper than our egos—if we can trust ourselves to have found it, or rather, to have been found by it. It is obvious that it is hidden, but what it is and where it is, is not obvious.

10 / Interview with Allen Ginsberg: "The Art of Poetry"

THOMAS CLARK

INTERVIEWER: I think Diana Trilling, speaking about your reading at Columbia, remarked that your poetry, like all poetry in English when dealing with a serious subject, naturally takes on the iambic pentameter rhythm. Do you agree?

GINSBERG: Well, it really isn't an accurate thing, I don't think. I've never actually sat down and made a technical analysis of the rhythms that I write. They're probably more near choriambic—Greek meters, dithyrambic meters—and tending toward de DA de de DA de de . . . what is that? Tending toward dactylic, probably. Williams once remarked that American speech tends toward dactylic. But it's more complicated than dactyl because dactyl is a three, three units, a foot consisting of three parts, whereas the actual rhythm is probably a rhythm which consists of five, six, or seven, like DA de de DA de de DA de de DA DA. Which is more toward the line of Greek dance rhythms—that's why they call them choriambic. So actually, probably it's not really technically correct, what she said. But— and that applies to certain poems, like certain passages of *Howl*

SOURCE: Malcolm Cowley, ed., *Writers at Work: The Paris Review Interview*, Third Series (New York: Viking Press, 1967), pp. 279–320. Copyright © 1967 by The Paris Review, Inc. All rights reserved. Reprinted by permission of The Viking Press, Inc. This selection originally appeared in *Paris Review*, No. 37 (Spring 1966), pp. 14–55.

Allen Ginsberg, a graduate of Columbia, is a poet and performer who has been involved in virtually every radical movement of the fifties and sixties; his books of poetry include *Howl and Other Poems, Kaddish and Other Poems, Empty Mirror: Early Poems*, and *Reality Sandwiches*.

and certain passages of *Kaddish*—there are definite rhythms which could be analyzed as corresponding to classical rhythms, though not necessarily *English* classical rhythms; they might correspond to Greek classical rhythms, or Sanskrit prosody. But probably most of the other poetry, like *Aether* or *Laughing Gas* or a lot of those poems, they simply don't fit into that. I think she felt very comfy, to think that that would be so. I really felt quite hurt about that, because it seemed to me that she ignored the main prosodic technical achievements that I had proffered forth to the academy, and they didn't even recognize it. I mean not that I want to stick her with being the academy.

INTERVIEWER: And in *Howl* and *Kaddish* you were working with a kind of classical unit? Is that an accurate description?

GINSBERG: Yeah, but it doesn't do very much good, because I wasn't really working with a classical unit, I was working with my own neural impulses and writing impulses. See, the difference is between someone sitting down to write a poem *in* a definite preconceived metrical pattern and filling in that pattern, and someone working with his physiological movements and *arriving* at a pattern, and perhaps even arriving at a pattern which might even have a name, or might even have a classical usage, but arriving at it organically rather than synthetically. Nobody's got any objection to even iambic pentameter if it comes from a source deeper than the mind, that is to say if it comes from the breathing and the belly and the lungs.

INTERVIEWER: American poets have been able to break away from a kind of English specified rhythm earlier than English poets have been able to do. Do you think this has anything to do with a peculiarity in English spoken tradition?

GINSBERG: No, I don't really think so, because the English don't speak in iambic pentameter either; they don't speak in the recognizable pattern that they write in. The dimness of their speech and the lack of emotional variation is parallel to the kind of dim diction and literary usage in the poetry now. But you can hear all sorts of Liverpudlian or Gordian—that's Newcastle—you can hear all sorts of variants aside from an upper-tone accent, a high-class accent, that don't fit into the tone of poetry being written right now. It's not being used like in America—I think it's just that British poets are more cowardly.

INTERVIEWER: Do you find any exception to this?

GINSBERG: It's pretty general, even the supposedly avant-garde poets. They write, you know, in a very toned-down manner.

INTERVIEWER: How about a poet like Basil Bunting?

GINSBERG: Well, he was working with a whole bunch of wild men from an earlier era, who were all breaking through, I guess. And so he had that experience—also he knew Persian, he knew Persian prosody. He was better educated than most English poets.

INTERVIEWER: The kind of organization you use in *Howl*, a recurrent kind of syntax—you don't think this is relevant any longer to what you want to do?

GINSBERG: No, but it was relevant to what I wanted to do then, it wasn't even a conscious decision.

INTERVIEWER: Was this related in any way to a kind of music or jazz that you were interested in at the time?

GINSBERG: Mmm . . . the myth of Lester Young as described by Kerouac, blowing 89 choruses of *Lady Be Good*, say, in one night, or my own hearing of Illinois Jacquet's *Jazz at the Philharmonic*, Volume 2; I think *Can't Get Started* was the title.

INTERVIEWER: And you've also mentioned poets like Christopher Smart, for instance, as providing an analogy—is this something you discovered later on?

GINSBERG: When I looked into it, yeah. Actually, I keep reading, or earlier I kept reading, that I was influenced by Kenneth Fearing and Carl Sandburg, whereas actually I was more conscious of Christopher Smart, and Blake's Prophetic Books, and

THOMAS CLARK 131

Whitman and some aspects of Biblical rhetoric. And a lot of specific prose things like Genet, Genet's *Our Lady of the Flowers* and the rhetoric in that, and Céline; Kerouac, most of all, was the biggest influence I think—Kerouac's prose.

INTERVIEWER: When did you come onto Burroughs' work?

GINSBERG: Let's see . . . Well, first thing of Burroughs I ever read was 1946 . . . which was a skit later published and integrated in some other work of his, called *So Proudly We Hail*, describing the sinking of the Titanic and an orchestra playing, a spade orchestra playing "The Star-Spangled Banner" while everybody rushed out to the lifeboats and the captain got up in woman's dress and rushed into the purser's office and shot the purser and stole all the money, and a spastic paretic jumped into a lifeboat with a machete and began chopping off people's fingers that were trying to climb into the boat, saying, "Out of the way, you foolth . . . Dirty thunthufbithes." That was a thing he had written up at Harvard with a friend named Kells Elvins. Which is really the whole key of all his work, like the sinking of America, and everybody like frightened rats trying to get out, or that was his vision of the time.

Then he and Kerouac later in 1945, '45 or '46, wrote a big detective book together, alternating chapters. I don't know where that book is now—Kerouac has his chapters and Burroughs' are somewhere in his papers. So I think in a sense it was Kerouac that encouraged Burroughs to write really, because Kerouac was so enthusiastic about prose, about writing, about lyricism, about the honor of writing . . . the Thomas Wolfe-ian delights of it. So anyway he turned Burroughs on in a *sense*, because Burroughs found a companion who could write really interestingly, and Burroughs admired Kerouac's perceptions. Kerouac could imitate Dashiell Hammett as well as Bill, which was Bill's natural style: dry, bony, factual. At that time Burroughs was reading John O'Hara, simply for facts, not for any sublime stylistic thing, just because he was a hard-nosed reporter.

Then in Mexico around 1951 he started writing *Junkie*. I've forgotten what relation I had to that—I think I wound up as the agent for it, taking it around New York trying to get it published.

I think he sent me portions of it at the time—I've forgotten how it worked out now. This was around 1949 or 1950. He was going through a personal crisis, his wife had died. It was in Mexico or South America . . . but it was a very generous thing of him to do, to start writing all of a sudden. Burroughs was always a very *tender* sort of person, but very dignified and shy and withdrawn, and for him to *commit* himself to a big autobiographical thing like that was . . . at the time, struck me as like a piece of eternity is in love with the . . . what is it, Eternity is in love with the productions of Time? So he was making a production of Time then.

Then I started taking that around. I've forgot who I took that to but I think maybe to Louis Simpson who was then working at Bobbs-Merrill. I'm not sure whether I took it to him—I remember taking it to Jason Epstein who was then working at Doubleday I think. Epstein at the time was not as experienced as he is now. And his reaction to it, I remember when I went back to his office to pick it up, was, well this is all very interesting, but it isn't really interesting, on account of if it were an autobiography of a junkie written by Winston *Churchill* then it'd be interesting, but written by somebody he'd never heard of, well then it's *not* interesting. And anyway I said what about the *prose*, the prose is interesting, and he says, oh, a difference of opinion on that. Finally I wound up taking it to Carl Solomon who was then a reader for A. A. Wynn Company, which was his uncle; and they finally got it through there. But it was finally published as a cheap paperback. With a whole bunch of frightened footnotes; like Burroughs said that marijuana was non-habit-forming which is now accepted as a fact, there'd be a footnote by the editor, "Reliable, er, responsible medical opinion does not confirm this." Then they also had a little introduction . . . literally they were afraid of the book being censored or *seized* at the time, is what they said. I've forgotten what the terms of censorship or seizure were that they were worried about. This was about 1952. They *said* that they were afraid to publish it straight for fear there would be a Congressional investigation or something, I don't know what. I think there was some noise about narcotics at the time. Newspaper noise . . . I've forgotten exactly what the arguments were. But anyway they had to write a preface which hedged on the book a lot.

INTERVIEWER: Has there been a time when fear of censorship or similar trouble has made your own expression difficult?

GINSBERG: This is so complicated a matter. The beginning of the fear with me was, you know, what would my father say to something that I would write. At the time, writing *Howl*—for instance like I assumed when writing it that it was something that *could* not be published because I wouldn't want my daddy to see what was in there. About my sex life, being fucked in the ass, imagine your father reading a thing like that, was what I thought. Though that disappeared as soon as the thing was real, or as soon as I manifested my . . . you know, it didn't make that much importance finally. That was sort of a help for writing, because I assumed that it wouldn't be published, therefore I could say anything that I wanted. So literally just for myself or anybody-that I knew personally well, writers who would be willing to appreciate it with a breadth of tolerance—in a piece of work like *Howl*. Who wouldn't be judging from a moralistic viewpoint but looking for evidences of humanity or secret thought or just actual truthfulness.

Then there's later the problem of publication—we had a lot. The English printer refused at first I think, we were afraid of customs; the first edition we had to print with asterisks on some of the dirty words, and then the *Evergreen Review* in reprinting it used asterisks, and various people reprinting it later always wanted to use the Evergreen version rather than the corrected legal City Lights version—like I think there's an anthology of Jewish writers, I forgot who edited that, but a couple of the high-class intellectuals from Columbia. I had written asking them specifically to use the later City Lights version, but they went ahead and printed an asterisked version. I forget what was the name of that—something like *New Generation of Jewish Writing*, Philip Roth, etc.

INTERVIEWER: Do you take difficulties like these as social problems, problems of communication simply, or do you feel they also block your own ability to express yourself for yourself?

GINSBERG: The problem is, where it gets to literature, is this. We all talk among ourselves and we have common understandings, and we say anything we want to say, and we talk about our assholes, and we talk about our cocks, and we talk about who we fucked last night, or who we're gonna fuck tomorrow, or what kinda love affair we have, or when we got drunk, or when we stuck a broom in our ass in the Hotel Ambassador in Prague— anybody tells one's friends about that. So then—what happens if you make a distinction between what you tell your friends and what you tell your Muse? The problem is to break down that distinction: when you approach the Muse to talk as frankly as you would talk with yourself or with your friends. So I began finding, in conversations with Burroughs and Kerouac and Gregory Corso, in conversations with people whom I knew well, whose souls I respected, that the things we were telling each other for real were totally different from what was already in literature. And that was Kerouac's great discovery in *On the Road*. The kinds of things that he and Neal Cassidy were talking about, he finally discovered were *the* subject matter for what he wanted to write down. That meant, at that minute, a complete revision of what literature was supposed to be, in *his* mind, and actually in the minds of the people that first read the book. Certainly in the minds of the critics, who had at first attacked it as not being . . . proper structure, or something. In other words, a gang of friends running around in an automobile. Which obviously is like a great picaresque literary device, and a classical one. And was *not* recognized, at the time, as suitable literary subject matter.

INTERVIEWER: So it's not just a matter of themes—sex, or any other one . . .

GINSBERG: It's the ability to commit to writing, to *write*, the same way that you . . . are! Anyway! You have many writers who have preconceived ideas about what literature is supposed to be, and their ideas seem to exclude that which makes them most charming in private conversation. Their faggishness, or their campiness, or their neurasthenia, or their solitude, or their goofiness, or their—even—masculinity, at times. Because they think that they're gonna write something that sounds like something else that they've read before, instead of sounds like them. Or comes from their own life. In other words, there's no distinction, there should be no distinction between what we write down, and what we really know, to begin with. As we know it every day, with each other. And the hypocrisy of literature has been—you know like there's supposed to be formal literature, which is supposed to be different from . . . in subject, in diction and even in organization, from our quotidian inspired lives.

It's also like in Whitman, "I find no fat sweeter than that which sticks to my own bones," that is to say the self-confidence of someone who knows that he's really alive, and that his existence is just as good as any other subject matter.

INTERVIEWER: Is physiology a part of this too—like the difference between your long breath line, and William Carlos Williams' shorter unit?

GINSBERG: Analytically, *ex post facto*, it all begins with fucking around and intuition and without any idea of *what* you're doing, I think. Later, I have a tendency to explain it, "Well, I got a longer breath than Williams, or I'm Jewish, or I study yoga, or I sing long lines . . ." But anyway, what it boils down to is this, it's my *movement*, my feeling is for a big long clanky statement—partly that's something that I share, or maybe that I even got from Kerouac's long prose line; which is really, like he once remarked, an extended poem. Like one long sentence page of his in *Doctor Sax* or *Railroad Earth* or occasionally *On the Road*—if you examine them phrase by phrase they usually have the density of poetry, and the beauty of poetry, but most of all the single elastic rhythm running from beginning to end of the line and ending "mop!"

INTERVIEWER: Have you ever wanted to extend this rhythmic feeling as far as say Artaud or now Michael McClure have taken it—to a line that is actually animal noise?

GINSBERG: The rhythm of the long line is also an animal cry.

INTERVIEWER: So you're following that feeling and not a thought or a visual image?

GINSBERG: It's simultaneous. The poetry generally is like a rhythmic articulation of feeling. The feeling is like an impulse that rises within—just like sexual impulses, say; it's almost as definite as that. It's a feeling that begins somewhere in the pit of the stomach and rises up forward in the breast and then comes out through the mouth and ears, and comes forth a croon or a groan or a sigh. Which, if you put words to it by looking around and seeing and trying to describe what's making you sigh—and sigh in words—you simply articulate what you're feeling. As simple as that. Or actually what happens is, at best what happens, is there's a definite body rhythm that has no definite words, or may have one or two words attached to it, one or two key words attached to it. And then, in writing it down, it's simply by a process of association that I find what the rest of the statement is— what can be collected around that word, what that word is connected to. Partly by simple association, the first thing that comes to my mind like "Moloch is" or "Moloch who," and then whatever comes out. But that also goes along with a definite rhythmic impulse, like DA de de DA de de DA de de DA DA. "*M*oloch whose *eyes* are a *thou*sand blind *windows*." And before I wrote "Moloch whose eyes are a thousand blind windows," I had the word, "Moloch, Moloch, Moloch," and I also had the feeling DA de de DA de de DA de de DA DA. So it was just a question of looking up and seeing a lot of windows, and saying, oh, windows, of course, but what kind of windows? But not even that—"Moloch whose eyes." "Moloch whose *eyes*"—which is beautiful in itself—but what about it, Moloch whose eyes are *what*? So Moloch whose eyes—then probably the next thing I thought was "thousands." O.K., and then thousands *what*? "Thousands blind." And I had to finish it somehow. So I hadda say "windows." It looked good *afterward*.

Usually during the composition, step by step, word by word and adjective by adjective, if it's at all spontaneous, I don't know whether it even makes sense sometimes. Sometimes I do know it makes complete sense, and I start crying. Because I realize I'm hitting some area which is absolutely true. And in that sense applicable universally, or understandable universally. In that sense able to survive through time—in that sense to be read by somebody and wept to, maybe, centuries later. In that sense prophecy, because it touches a common key . . . what prophecy actually is is not that you actually know that the bomb will fall in 1942. It's that you know and feel something which somebody knows and feels in a hundred years. And maybe articulate it in a hint—concrete way that they can pick up on in a hundred years.

INTERVIEWER: You once mentioned something you had found in Cézanne—a remark about the reconstitution of the *petites sensations* of experience, in his own painting—and you compared this with the method of your poetry.

GINSBERG: I got all hung up on Cézanne around 1949 in my last year at Columbia, studying with Meyer Schapiro. I don't know how it led into it—I think it was about the same time that I was having these Blake visions. So. The thing I understood from Blake was that it was possible to transmit a message through time which could reach the enlightened, that poetry had a definite effect, it wasn't just pretty, or just beautiful, as I had understood pretty beauty before—it was something basic to human existence, or it reached something, it reached the bottom of human existence. But anyway the impression I got was that it was like a kind of time machine through which he could transmit, Blake could transmit, his basic consciousness and communicate it to somebody else after he was dead, in other words build a time machine.

Now just about that time I was looking at Cézanne and I suddenly got a strange shuddering impression looking at his canvases, partly the effect when someone pulls a venetian blind, reverses the venetian—there's a sudden shift, a flashing that you see in Cézanne canvases. Partly it's when the canvas opens up into three dimensions and looks like wooden objects, like solid space objects, in three dimensions rather than flat. Partly it's the enormous spaces which open up in Cézanne's landscapes. And it's partly that mysterious quality around his figures, like of his wife or the card players or the postman or whoever, the local Aix characters. They look like great huge 3-D wooden dolls, sometimes. Very *uncanny* thing, like a very mysterious thing, in other words there's a strange sensation that one gets, looking at his canvases, which I began to associate with the extraordinary sensation—cosmic sensation, in fact—that I had experienced catalyzed by Blake's *Sunflower* and *Sick Rose* and a few other poems. So I began studiously investigating Cézanne's intentions and method, and looking at all the canvases of his that I could find in New York, and all the reproductions I could find, and I was writing at the time a paper on him, for Schapiro at Columbia in the Fine Arts course.

And the whole thing opened up, two ways: first, I read a book on Cézanne's composition by Earl Loran, who showed photographs, analyses and photographs of the original motifs, side by side with the actual canvases—and years later I actually went to Aix, with all the postcards, and stood in the spots, and tried to find the places where he painted Mont Ste. Victoire from, and got in his studio and saw some of the motifs he used like his big black hat and his cloak. Well, first of all I began to see that Cézanne had all sorts of literary symbolism in him, on and off. I was preoccupied with Plotinian terminology, of time and eternity, and I saw it in Cézanne paintings, an early painting of a clock on a shelf which I associated with time and eternity, and I began to think he was a big secret mystic. And I saw a photograph of his studio in Loran's book and it was like an alchemist's studio, because he had a skull, and he had a long black coat, and he had this big black hat. So I began thinking of him as you know like a magic character. Like the original version I had thought of him was like this austere dullard from Aix. So I began getting really interested in him as a hermetic type, and then I symbolically read into his canvases things that probably weren't there, like there's a painting of a winding road which turns off, and I saw that as the mystical path: it turns off into a village and the end of the path is hidden. Something he painted I guess when he went out painting with Bernard. Then there was an account of a very fantastic conversation that he had had. It's quoted in Loran's book: there's a long long long paragraph where he says, "by means of squares, cubes, triangles, I try to reconstitute the impression that I have from nature: the means that I use to reconstitute the impression of solidity that I think-feel-see when I am looking at a motif like Victoire, is to reduce it to some kind of pictorial language, so I use these squares, cubes and triangles, but I try to build them together so interknit"—*and here in the conversation he held his hands together with his fingers interknit*—"so that *no light gets through.*" And I was mystified by that, but it seemed to make sense in terms of the grid of paint strokes that he had on his canvas, so that he produced a solid two-dimensional surface which when you looked *into* it, maybe

THOMAS CLARK 139

from a slight distance with your eyes either unfocused or your eyelids lowered slightly, you could see a great three-dimensional opening, mysterious, stereoscopic, like going into a stereopticon. And I began discovering in *The Card Players* all sorts of sinister symbols, like there's one guy leaning against the wall with a stolid expression on his face, that he doesn't want to get involved; and then there's two guys who are peasants, who are looking as if they've just been dealt *Death* cards; and then the *dealer* you look at and he turns out to be a city slicker with a big blue cloak and almost rouge doll-like cheeks and a fat-faced Kafkian-agent impression about him, like he's a card sharp, he's a cosmic card sharp dealing out Fate to all these people. This looks like a great big hermetic Rembrandtian portrait in Aix! That's why it has that funny monumentality—aside from the quote plastic values unquote.

Then, I smoked a lot of marijuana and went to the basement of the Museum of Modern Art in New York and looked at his water colors and that's where I began really turning on to space in Cézanne and the way he built it up. Particularly there's one of rocks, I guess *Rocks at Garonne*, and you look at them for a while, and after a while they seem like they're rocks, just the rock parts, you don't know where they are, whether they're on the ground or in the air or on top of a cliff, but then they seem to be floating in space like clouds, and then they seem to be also a bit like they're amorphous, like kneecaps or cockheads or faces without eyes. And it has a very mysterious impression. Well, that may have been the result of the pot. But it's a definite thing that I got from that. Then he did some very odd studies after classical statues, Renaissance statues, and they're great gigantesque herculean figures with little tiny pin-heads . . . so that apparently was his comment on them!

And then . . . the things were endless to find in Cézanne. Finally I was reading his letters and I discovered this phrase again, *mes petites sensations*—"I'm an old man and my passions are not, my senses are not coarsened by passions like some *other* old men I know, and I have worked for years trying to," I guess it was the phrase, "*reconstitute* the *petites sensations* that I get from nature, and I could stand on a hill and merely by moving my head half an inch the composition of the landscape was totally changed." So apparently he'd refined his optical per-

140

ception to such a point where it's a real contemplation of optical phenomena in an almost yogic way, where he's standing there, from a specific point studying the optical field, the depth in the optical field, looking, actually looking at his own eyeballs in a sense. The attempting to reconstitute the sensation in his own eyeballs. And what does he say finally—in a very weird statement which one would not expect of the austere old workman, he said, "And this *petite sensation* is nothing other than *pater omnipotens aeterna deus.*"

So that was I felt the key to Cézanne's hermetic method . . . everybody knows his workmanlike, artisanlike, pettified-like painting method which is so great, but the really ro*man*ticistic motif behind it is absolutely marvelous, so you realize that he's really a saint! Working on his form of yoga, all that time, in obvious saintly circumstances of retirement in a small village, leading a relatively non-sociable life, going through the motions of going to church or not, but really containing in his skull these supernatural phenomena, and observations . . . you know, and it's very humble actually, because he didn't know if he was crazy or not—that is a flash of the physical, miracle dimensions of existence, trying to reduce that to canvas in two dimensions, and then trying to do it in such a way as it would look if the observer looked at it long enough it would look like as much three dimension as the actual *world* of optical phenomena when one looks through one's eyes. Actually he's *re*-constituted the whole fucking universe in his canvases—it's like a fantastic thing!—or at least the appearance of the universe.

So. I used a lot of this material in the references in the last part of the first section of *Howl*: "sensation of Pater Omnipotens Aeterna Deus." The last part of *Howl* was really an homage to art but also in specific terms an homage to Cézanne's method, in a sense I adapted what I could to writing; but that's a very complicated matter to explain. Except, putting it very simply, that just as Cézanne doesn't use perspective lines to create space, but it's a juxtaposition of one color against another color (that's one element of his space), so, I had the idea, perhaps over-refined, that by the unexplainable, unexplained non-perspective line, that is, juxtaposition of one *word* against another, a *gap* between the two words—like the space gap in the canvas— there'd be a gap between the two words which the mind would fill in with the sensation of existence. In other words when I say, oh . . . when Shakespeare says, "In the dread vast and middle of the night," something happens between "dread vast" and "middle." That creates like a whole space of, spaciness of black night. How it gets that is very odd, those words put together. Or in the haiku, you have two distinct images, set side by side without drawing a connection, without drawing a logical connection between them: the *mind* fills in this . . . this space. Like

> O ant
> crawl up Mount Fujiyama,
> but slowly, slowly.

Now you have the small ant and you have Mount Fujiyama and you have the slowly, slowly, and what happens is that you feel almost like . . . a cock in your mouth! You feel this enormous space-universe, it's almost a tactile thing. Well anyway, it's a phenomenon-sensation, phenomenon hyphen sensation, that's created by this little haiku of Issa, for instance.

So, I was trying to do similar things with juxtapositions like "hydrogen jukebox." Or . . . "winter midnight smalltown streetlight rain." Instead of cubes and squares and triangles. Cézanne is reconstituting by means of triangles, cubes and colors—I have to reconstitute by means of words, rhythms of course, and all that—but say it's words, phrasings. So. The problem is then to reach the different parts of the mind, which are existing simultaneously, the different associations which are going on simultaneously, choosing elements from both, like: jazz, jukebox and all that, and we have the jukebox from that; politics, hydrogen bomb, and we have the hydrogen of that, you see "hydrogen jukebox." And that actually compresses in one instant like a whole series of things. Or the end of *Sunflower* with "cunts of wheelbarrows," whatever that all meant, or "rubber dollar bills" —"skin of machinery"; see, and actually in the moment of composition I don't necessarily *know* what it means, but it comes to mean something later, after a year or two, I realize that it meant something clear, unconsciously. Which takes on meaning in time, like a photograph developing slowly. Because we're not really always conscious of the entire depth of our minds, in other words we just know a lot more than we're able to be aware of, normally—though at moments we're completely aware I guess.

There's some other element of Cézanne that was interesting ... oh, his patience, of course. In recording the optical phenomena. Has something to do with Blake: *with* not *through* the eye— "You're led to believe a lie when you see with not through the eye." He's seeing through his eye. One can see *through* his canvas to God, really, is the way it boils down. Or to Pater Omnipotens Aeterna Deus. I could imagine someone not prepared, in a peculiar chemical physiological state, peculiar mental state, psychic state, someone not prepared who had no experience of eternal ecstasy, passing in front of a Cézanne canvas, distracted and without noticing it his eye traveling in, to, through the canvas into the space and suddenly stopping with his hair standing on end, dead in his tracks *see*ing a whole universe. And I think that's what Cézanne really does, to a lot of people.

Where were we now. Yeah, the idea that I had was that gaps in space and time through images juxtaposed, just as in the haiku you get two images which the mind connects in a flash, and so that *flash* is the *petite sensation*; or the satori, perhaps, that the Zen haikuists would speak of—if they speak of it like that. So, the poetic experience that Housman talks about, the hair standing on end or the hackles rising whatever it is, visceral thing. The interesting thing would be to know if certain combinations of words and rhythms actually had an electro-chemical reaction on the body, which could catalyze specific states of consciousness. I think that's what probably happened to me with Blake. I'm *sure* it's what happens on a perhaps lower level with Poe's *Bells* or *Raven*, or even Vachel Lindsay's *Congo*: that there is a hypnotic rhythm there, which when you introduce it into your nervous system, causes all sorts of electronic changes—permanently alters it. There's a statement by Artaud on that subject, that certain music when introduced into the nervous system changes the molecular composition of the nerve cells or something like that, it permanently alters the being that has experience of this. Well, anyway, this is certainly true. In other words any experience we have is recorded in the brain and goes through neural patterns and whatnot: so I suppose brain recordings are done by means of shifting around of little electrons —so there is actually an electrochemical effect caused by art.

So . . . the problem is what is the maximum electrochemical effect in the desired direction. That is what I was taking Blake as having done to me. And what I take as one of the optimal possibilities of art. But this is all putting it in a kind of bullshit abstract way. But it's an interesting—toy. To play with. That idea.

INTERVIEWER: In the last five or six months you've been in Cuba, Czechoslovakia, Russia, and Poland. Has this helped to clarify your sense of the current world situation?

GINSBERG: Yeah, I no longer feel—I didn't ever feel that there was any answer in dogmatic Leninism-Marxism—but I feel very definitely now that there's no answer to my desires there. Nor do most of the people in those countries—in Russia or Poland or Cuba—really feel that either. It's sort of like a religious theory imposed from above and usually used to beat people on the head with. Nobody takes it seriously because it doesn't mean anything, it means different things in different countries anyway. The general idea of revolution against American idiocy is good, it's still sympathetic, and I guess it's a good thing like in Cuba, and obviously Vietnam. But what's gonna follow—the dogmatism that follows is a big drag. And everybody apologizes for the dogmatism by saying, well, it's an inevitable consequence of the struggle against American repression. And that may be true too.

But there's one thing I feel certain of, and that's that there's no human answer in communism or capitalism as it's practiced outside of the U.S. in any case. In other words, by hindsight the interior of America is not bad, at least for me, though it might be bad for a spade, but not too bad, creepy, but it's not impossible. But traveling in countries like Cuba and Vietnam I realize that the people that get the real evil side effects of America are there, in other words it really is like imperialism, in that sense. People in the United States all got money, they got cars, and everybody else *starves* on account of American foreign policy. Or is being bombed out, torn apart, and bleeding on the street, they get all their teeth bashed in, tear gassed, or hot pokers up their ass, things that would be, you know, considered terrible in the United States. Except for Negroes.

So I don't know. I don't see any particular answer, and *this* month it seemed to me like actually an atomic war was inevitable on account of both sides were so dogmatic, and frightened and had nowhere to go and didn't know what to do with themselves anymore except fight. Everybody too intransigent. Everybody *t*oo mean. I don't suppose it'll take place, but . . . Somebody has got to sit in the British Museum again like Marx and figure out a new system; a new blueprint. Another century has gone, technology has changed everything completely, so it's time for a new utopian system. Burroughs is almost working on it.

But one thing that's impressive is Blake's idea of Jerusalem, Jerusalemic Britain, which I think is *now* more and more valid. He, I guess, defined it. I'm still confused about Blake, I still haven't read him all through enough to understand what direction he was really pointing to. It seems to be the *naked human form divine,* seems to be Energy, it seems to be sexualization, or sexual liberation, which are the directions we all believe in. He also seems, however, to have some idea of imagination which I don't fully understand yet. That is it's something outside of the body, with a rejection of the body, and I don't quite understand that. A life after death even. Which I still haven't comprehended. There's a letter in the Fitzwilliam Museum, written several months before he died. He says, "My body is in turmoil and stress and decaying *but,* my ideas, my power of ideas and my imagination, are stronger than ever." And I find it hard to conceive of that. I think if I were lying in bed dying, with my body pained, I would just give up. I mean you know, because I don't think I could *exist* outside my body. But he apparently was able to. Williams didn't seem to be able to. In other words Williams' universe was tied up with his body. Blake's universe didn't seem to be tied up with his body. Real mysterious, like far other worlds and other seas, so to speak. Been puzzling over that today.

The Jerusalemic world of Blake seems to be Mercy-Pity-Peace. Which has human form. Mercy has a human face. So that's all clear.

INTERVIEWER: How about Blake's statement about the senses being the chief inlets of the soul in this age—I don't know what "this age" means; is there another one?

THOMAS CLARK 145

GINSBERG: What he says is interesting because there's the same thing in Hindu mythology, they speak of This Age as the Kali Yuga, the age of destruction, or an age so sunk in materialism. You'd find a similar formulation in Vico, like what is it, the Age of Gold running on to the Iron and then Stone, again. Well, the Hindus say that *this* is the Kali Age or Kali Yuga or Kali Cycle, and we are also so sunk in matter, the five senses are matter, sense, that they say there is absolutely no way out by intellect, by thought, by discipline, by practice, by sadhana, by jnana yoga, nor karma yoga, that is doing good works, no way out thru our own will or our own effort. The *only* way out that they generally now prescribe, generally in India at the moment, is through Bhakti yoga, which is Faith-Hope-Adoration-Worship, or like probably the equivalent of the Christian Sacred Heart, which I find a very lovely doctrine—that is to say, pure delight, the only way you can be saved is to sing. In other words, the only way to drag up, from the depths of this depression, to drag up your soul to its proper bliss, and understanding, is to give yourself, completely, to your heart's desire. The image will be determined by the heart's compass, by the compass of what the heart moves toward and desires. And then you get on your knees or on your lap or on your head and you sing and chant prayers and mantras, till you reach a state of ecstasy and understanding, and the bliss overflows out of your body. They say intellect, like Saint Thomas Aquinas, will never do it, because it's just like me getting all hung up on whether I could remember what happened before I was born—I mean you could get lost there very easily, and it has no relevance *anyway*, to the existent flower. Blake says something similar, like Energy, and Excess . . . leads to the palace of wisdom. The Hindu Bhakti is like excess of devotion; you just, you know, give yourself all out to devotion.

Very oddly a lady saint Shri Matakrishnaji in Brindaban, whom I consulted about my spiritual problems, told me to take Blake for my guru. There's all kinds of different gurus, there can be living and non-living gurus—apparently whoever initiates you, and I apparently was initiated by Blake in terms of at least having an ecstatic experience from him. So that when I got here to Cambridge I had to rush over to the Fitzwilliam Museum to find his misspellings in *Songs of Innocence*.

INTERVIEWER: What was the Blake experience you speak of?

GINSBERG: About 1945 I got interested in supreme reality with a capital S and R, and I wrote big long poems about a last voyage looking for Supreme Reality. Which was like a Dostoevskian or Thomas-Wolfe-ian idealization or like Rimbaud—what was Rimbaud's term, new vision, was that it? Or Kerouac was talking about a new vision, verbally, and intuitively out of longing, but also out of a funny kind of tolerance of this universe. In 1948 in East Harlem in the summer I was living—this is like the Ancient Mariner, I've said this so many times: "stoppeth one of three/ 'By thy long grey beard' . . . " Hang an albatross around your neck . . . The one thing I felt at the time was that it would be a terrible horror, that in one or two decades I would be trying to explain to people that one day something like this happened to me! I even wrote a long poem saying, "I will grow old, a grey and groaning man,/ and with each hour the same thought, and with each thought the same denial./ Will I spend my life in praise of the *idea* of God?/ Time leaves no hope. We creep and wait. We wait and go alone." Psalm II—which I never published. So anyway—there I was in my bed in Harlem . . . jacking off. With my pants open, lying around on a bed by the windowsill, looking out into the cornices of Harlem and the sky above. And I had just come. And had perhaps hardly even wiped the come off my thighs, my trousers or whatever it was. As I often do, I had been jacking off while reading—I think it's probably a common phenomenon to be noticed among adolescents. Though I was a little older than an adolescent at the time. About 22. There's a kind of interesting thing about, you know, distracting your attention while you jack off, that is, you know, reading a book or looking out of a window, or doing something else with the conscious mind which kind of makes it sexier.

So anyway, what I had been doing that week—I'd been in a very lonely solitary state, dark night of the soul sort of, reading St. John of the Cross, maybe on account of that everybody'd gone away that I knew, Burroughs was in Mexico, Jack was out in Long Island and relatively isolated, we didn't see each other, and I had been very close with them for several years. Huncke I think was in jail, or something. Anyway, there was nobody I knew. Mainly the thing was that I'd been making it with N.C., and finally I think I got a letter from him saying it was all off, no more, we shouldn't consider ourselves lovers any more on account of it just wouldn't work out. But previously we'd had an understanding that we—Neal Cassidy, I said N.C. but I suppose you can use his name—we'd had a big tender lovers' understanding. But I guess it got too much for him, partly because he was 3000 miles away and he had 6000 girl friends on the other side of the continent, who were keeping him busy, and then here was my lone cry of despair from New York. So. I got a letter from him saying, Now, Allen, we gotta move on to *new* territory. So I felt this is like a great mortal blow to all of my tenderest hopes. And I figured I'd never find any sort of psycho-spiritual sexo-cock jewel fulfillment in my existence! So, I went into . . . like I felt cut off from what I'd idealized romantically. And I was also graduating from school and had nowhere to go and the difficulty of getting a job. So finally there was nothing for me to do except to eat vegetables and live in Harlem. In an apartment I'd rented from someone. Sublet.

So, in that state therefore, of hopelessness, or dead end, change of phase you know—growing up—and in an equilibrium in any case, a psychic, a mental equilibrium of a kind, like of having no New Vision and no Supreme Reality and nothing but the world in front of me, and of not knowing what to do with *that* . . . there was a funny balance of tension, in every direction. And just after I came, on this occasion, with a Blake book on my lap—I wasn't even reading, my eye was idling over the page of *The Sunflower*, and it suddenly appeared—the poem I'd read a lot of times before, over-familiar to the point where it didn't make any particular meaning except some sweet thing about flowers—and suddenly I realized that the poem was talking about *me*. "Ah, Sunflower! weary of time, / Who countest the steps of the Sun; / Seeking that sweet golden clime, / Where the traveller's journey is done." Now, I began understanding it, the poem while looking at it, and suddenly, simultaneously with understanding it, heard a very deep earthen grave voice in the room, which I immediately assumed, I didn't think twice, was Blake's voice; it wasn't any voice that I knew, though I had previously had a conception of a voice of rock, in a poem, some image like that—or maybe that came after this experience.

And my eye on the page, simultaneously the auditory hallucination, or whatever terminology here used, the apparitional voice, in the room, woke me further deep in my understanding of the poem, because the voice was so completely tender and beautifully . . . ancient. Like the voice of the Ancient of Days. But the peculiar quality of the voice was something unforgettable because it was like God had a human voice, with all the infinite tenderness and anciency and mortal gravity of a living Creator speaking to his son. "Where the youth pined away with desire, / And the pale Virgin shrouded in snow / Arise from their graves, and aspire / Where my Sun-flower wishes to go." Meaning that there *was* a *place*, there was a sweet golden clime, and the *sweet golden*, what was that . . . and simultaneous to the voice there was also an emotion, risen in my soul in response to the voice, and a sudden *visual* realization of the same awesome phenomena. That is to say, looking out at the window, through the window at the sky, suddenly it seemed that I saw into the depths of the universe, by looking simply into the ancient sky. The sky suddenly seemed very *ancient*. And this was the very ancient place that he was talking about, the sweet golden clime, I suddenly realized that *this* existence was *it*! And, that I was born in order to experience up to this very moment that I was having this experience, to realize what this was all about—in other words that this was the moment that I was born for. This initiation. Or this vision or this consciousness, of being alive unto myself, alive myself unto the Creator. As the son of the Creator—who loved me, I realized, or who responded to my desire, say. It was the same desire both ways.

Anyway my first thought was this was what I was born for, and second thought, never forget—never forget, never renig, never deny. Never deny the voice—no, never *forget* it, don't get lost mentally wandering in other spirit worlds or American or job worlds or advertising worlds or war worlds or earth worlds. But the spirit of the universe was what I was born to realize. What I was speaking about visually was, immediately, that the cornices in the old tenement building in Harlem across the back yard court had been carved very finely in 1890 or 1910. And were like the solidification of a great deal of intelligence and care and love also. So that I began noticing in every corner where I looked evidences of a living hand, even in the bricks, in the arrangement of each brick. Some hand placed them there—that some hand had placed the whole universe in front of me. That some hand had placed the sky. No, that's exaggerating—not that some hand had placed the sky but that the sky was the living blue hand itself. Or that God was in front of my eyes—existence itself was God. Well the formulations are like that—I didn't formulate it in exactly those terms, what I was seeing was a visionary thing, it was a lightness in my body . . . my body suddenly felt *light*, and a sense of cosmic consciousness, vibrations, understanding, awe, and wonder and surprise. And it was a sudden awakening into a totally deeper real universe than I'd been existing in. So, I'm trying to avoid generalizations about that sudden deeper real universe and keep it strictly to observations of phenomenal data, or a voice with a certain sound, the appearance of cornices, the appearance of the sky say, of the great blue hand, the living hand —to keep to images.

But anyway—the same . . . *petite sensation* recurred several minutes later, with the same voice, while reading the poem *The Sick Rose*. This time it was a slightly different sense-depth-mystic impression. Because *The Sick Rose*—you know I can't interpret the poem now, but it had a meaning—I mean I can interpret it on a verbal level, the sick rose is my self, or self, or the living body, sick because the mind, which is the worm "that flies in the night, in the howling storm," or Urizen, reason; Blake's character might be the one that's entered the body and is destroying it, or let us say death, the worm as being death, the natural process of death, some kind of mystical being of its own trying to come in and devour the body, the rose. Blake's drawing for it is complicated, it's a big drooping rose, drooping because it's dying, and there's a worm in it, and the worm is wrapped around a little sprite that's trying to get out of the mouth of the rose.

But anyway, I experienced *The Sick Rose*, with the voice of Blake reading it, as something that applied to the whole universe, like hearing the doom of the whole universe, and at the same time the inevitable beauty of doom. I can't remember now, except it was very beautiful and very awesome. But a little of it slightly scary, having to do with the knowledge of death—my death and also the death of being itself, and that was the great pain. So, like a prophecy, not only in human terms but a prophecy as if Blake had penetrated the very secret core of the *entire* universe and had come forth with some little magic formula statement in rhyme and rhythm that, if properly heard in the inner inner ear, would deliver you beyond the universe.

So then, the other poem that brought this on in the same day was *The Little Girl Lost*, where there was a repeated refrain,

> Do father, mother, *weep*,
> Where can Lyca *sleep?*
>
> How can Lyca *sleep*
> If her mother *weep?*
>
> 'If her heart does *ache*
> Then let Lyca *wake;*
> If my mother *sleep,*
> Lyca shall not *weep.*'

It's that hypnotic thing—and I suddenly realized that Lyca was me, or Lyca was the self; father, mother seeking Lyca, was God seeking, Father, the Creator; and "If her heart does ache / Then let Lyca wake"—wake to what? *Wake* meaning wake to the same awakeness I was just talking about—of existence in the entire universe. The total consciousness then, of the complete universe. Which is what Blake was talking about. In other words a breakthrough from ordinary habitual quotidian consciousness into consciousness that was really seeing all of heaven in a flower. Or what was it, eternity in a flower . . . heaven in a grain of sand. As I was seeing heaven in the cornice of the building. By heaven here I mean this imprint or concretization or living form, of an intelligent hand—the work of an intelligent hand, which still had the intelligence molded into it. The gargoyles on the Harlem cornices. What was interesting about the cornice was that there's cornices like that on every building, but I never noticed them before. And I never realized that they meant spiritual labor, to anyone—that somebody had labored to make a curve in a piece of tin—to make a cornucopia out of a piece of industrial tin. Not only that man, the workman, the artisan, but the architect had thought of it, the builder had paid for it, the smelter had *smelt* it, the miner had dug it up out of the earth, the earth had gone through eons preparing it. So the little molecules had slumbered for . . . for kalpas. So out of *all* of these kalpas it all got together in a great succession of impulses, to be frozen finally in that one form of a cornucopia cornice on the building front. And God knows how many people made the moon. Or what spirits labored . . . to set fire to the sun. As Blake says, "When I look in the sun I don't see the rising sun I see a band of angels singing holy, holy, holy." Well his perception of the field of the sun is different from that of a man who just sees the sun sun, without any emotional relationship to it.

But then, there was a point later in the week when the intermittent flashes of the same . . . bliss—because the experience was quite blissful—came back. In a sense all this is described in *The Lion for Real* by anecdotes of different experiences— actually it was a very difficult time, which I won't go into here. Because suddenly I thought, also simultaneously, ooh I'm going *mad*! That's described in the line in *Howl*, "who thought they were *only* mad when Baltimore gleamed in supernatural ecstasy"—"who thought they were *only* mad . . ." If it were only that easy! In other words it'd be a lot easier if you just were crazy, instead of—then you could chalk it up, "well I'm nutty"— but on the other hand what if it's all true and you're *born* into this great cosmic universe in which you're a spirit angel— terrible fucking situation to be confronted with. It's like being woken up one morning by Joseph K's captors. Actually what I think I did was there was a couple of girls living next door and I crawled out on the fire escape and tapped on their window and said, "I've seen God!" and they *banged* the window shut. Oh, what tales I could have told them if they'd let me in! Because I was in a very exalted state of mind and the consciousness was still with me—I remember I immediately rushed to Plato and read some great image in the *Phaedrus* about horses flying through the sky, and rushed over to St. John and started reading fragments of *con un no saber sabiendo . . . que me quede balbuciendo*, and rushed to the other part of the bookshelf and picked up Plotinus about The Alone—the Plotinus I found more difficult to interpret.

But I *immediately* doubled my thinking process, quadrupled, and I was able to read almost any text and see all sorts of divine significance in it. And I think that week or that month I had to take an examination in John Stuart Mill. And instead of writing about his ideas I got completely hung up on his experience of reading—was it Wordsworth? Apparently the thing that got him back was an experience of nature that he received keyed off by reading Wordsworth, on "sense sublime" or something. That's a very good description, that sense sublime of something far more deeply interfused, whose dwelling is the light of setting suns, and the round ocean, and the . . . the *living* air, did he say? The living air—see just that hand again—*and* in the heart of man. So I think this experience is characteristic of all high poetry. I mean that's the way I began seeing poetry as the communication of the particular experience—not just any experience but *this* experience.

INTERVIEWER: Have you had anything like this experience again?

GINSBERG: Yeah . . . I'm not finished with this period. Then, in my room, I didn't know what to do. But I wanted to bring it up, so I began experimenting with it, without Blake. And I think it was one day in my kitchen, I had an old-fashioned kitchen with a sink with a tub in it with a board over the top, I started moving around and sort of shake with my body and dancing up and down on the floor and saying "Dance! dance! dance! dance! spirit! spirit! spirit! dance!" and suddenly I felt like *Faust*, calling up the devil. And then it started coming over me, this big . . . creepy feeling, cryptozoid or monozoidal, so I got all scared and quit.

Then, I was walking around Columbia and I went in the Columbia bookstore and was reading Blake again, leafing over a book of Blake, I think it was *The Human Abstract*: "Pity would be no more . . ." And suddenly it came over me in the bookstore again, and I was in the eternal place *once more*, and I looked around at everybody's faces, and I saw all these wild animals! Because there was a bookstore clerk there who I hadn't paid much attention to, he was just a familiar fixture in the bookstore scene and everybody went in the bookstore every day like me, because downstairs there was a café and upstairs there were all these clerks that we were all familiar with—this guy had a very *long* face, you know some people look like giraffes. So he looked kind of giraffish. He had a kind of a long face with a long nose. I don't know what kind of sex life he had, but he must have had something. But anyway I looked in his face and I suddenly saw like a great tormented soul—and he had just been somebody whom I'd regarded as perhaps a not particularly beautiful or sexy character, or lovely face, but you know someone familiar, and perhaps a pleading cousin in the universe. But all of a sudden I realized that *he* knew also, just like I knew. And that everybody in the bookstore knew, and that they were all hiding it! They all had the consciousness, it was like a great *un*conscious that was running between all of us that everybody *was* completely conscious, but that the fixed expressions that people have, the habitual expressions, the manners, the mode of talk, are all masks hiding this consciousness. Because almost at that moment it seemed that it would be too terrible if we communicated to each other on a level of total consciousness and awareness each of the other—like it would be too terrible, it would be the end of the bookstore, it would be the end of civ . . . not civilization, but in other words the position that everybody was in was *ridiculous*, everybody running around peddling books to each other. Here in the universe! Passing money over the counter, wrapping books in bags and guarding the door, you know, stealing books, and the people sitting up making accountings on the upper floor there, and people worrying about their exams walking through the bookstore, and all the millions of thoughts the people had you know, that I'm worrying about, whether they're going to get laid or whether anybody loves them, about their mothers dying of cancer or you know the complete death awareness that everybody has continuously with them all the time—all of a sudden revealed to me at once in the faces of the people, and they all looked like horrible grotesque masks, grotesque because *hiding* the knowledge from each other. Having a habitual conduct and forms to prescribe, forms to fulfill. Roles to play. But the main insight I had at that time was that everybody knew. Everybody knew completely everything. Knew completely everything in the terms which I was talking about.

INTERVIEWER: Do you still think they know?

GINSBERG: I'm more sure of it now. Sure. All you have to do is try and make somebody. You realize that they knew all along you were trying to make them. But until that moment you never break through to communication on the subject.

INTERVIEWER: Why not?

GINSBERG: Well, fear of rejection. The twisted faces of all those people, the faces were twisted by rejection. And hatred of self, finally. The internalization of that rejection. And finally disbelief in that shining self. Disbelief in that infinite self. Partly because the particular . . . partly because the *awareness* that we all carry is too often painful, because the experience of rejection and lacklove and cold war—I mean the whole cold war is the imposition of a vast mental barrier on everybody, a vast antinatural psyche. A hardening, a shutting off of the perception of desire and tenderness which everybody *knows* and which is the very structure of . . . the atom! Structure of the human body and organism. That desire built in. Blocked. "Where the youth pined away with desire, the Virgin shrouded in snow." Or as Blake says, "On every face I see, I meet / marks of weakness, marks of woe." So what I was thinking in the bookstore was the marks of weakness, marks of woe. Which you can just look around and look at anybody's face right next to you now always—you can see it in the way the mouth is pursed, you can see it in the way the eyes blink, you can see it in the way the gaze is fixed down at the matches. It's the self-consciousness which is a substitute for communication with the outside. This consciousness pushed back into the self and thinking of how it will hold its face and eyes and hands in order to make a mask to hide the flow that is going on. Which it's aware of, which everybody is aware of really! So let's say, shyness. Fear. Fear of like total feeling, really, total being, is what it is.

So the problem then was, having attained realization, how to safely manifest it and communicate it. Of course there was the old Zen thing, when the sixth patriarch handed down the little symbolic oddments and ornaments and books and bowls, stained bowls too . . . when the *fifth* patriarch handed them down to the sixth patriarch he told him to hide them and don't tell anybody you're patriarch because it's dangerous, they'll kill you. So there was that immediate danger. It's taken me all these years to manifest it and work it out in a way that's materially communicable to people. Without scaring them or me. Also movements of history and breaking down the civilization. To break down everybody's masks and roles sufficiently so that everybody has to face the universe *and* the possibility of the sick rose coming true and the atom bomb. So it was an immediate Messianic thing. Which seems to be becoming more and more justified. And more and more reasonable in terms of the existence that we're living.

So. Next time it happened was about a week later walking along in the evening on a circular path around what's now I guess the garden or field in the middle of Columbia University, by the library. I started invoking the spirit, consciously trying to get another depth perception of cosmos. And suddenly it began occurring again, like a sort of breakthrough again, but this time —this was the last time in that period—it was the same depth of consciousness or the same cosmical awareness but suddenly it was not blissful at all but it was *frightening*. Some like real serpent-fear entering the sky. The sky was not a blue hand anymore but like a hand of death coming down on me—some really scary presence, it was almost as if I saw God again except God was the Devil. The consciousness itself was *so* vast, much more vast than any idea of it I'd had or any experience I'd had, that it was not even human any more—and was in a sense a threat, because I was going to die into that inhuman ultimately. I don't know *what* the score was there—I was too cowardly to pursue it. To attend and experience completely the Gates of Wrath— there's a poem of Blake's that deals with that, "To find a Western Path / Right thru the Gates of Wrath." But I didn't urge my way there, I shut it all off. And got scared, and thought, I've gone too far.

INTERVIEWER: Was your use of drugs an extension of this experience?

GINSBERG: Well, since I took a vow that this was the area of, that this was my existence that I was placed into, drugs were obviously a technique for experimenting with consciousness, to get different areas and different levels and different similarities and different reverberations of the same vision. Marijuana has some of it in it, that awe, the cosmic awe that you get sometimes on pot. There are certain moments under laughing gas and aether that the consciousness does intersect with something similar—for me—to my Blake visions. The gas drugs were apparently interesting too to the Lake Poets, because there were a lot of experiments done with Sir Humphry Davy in his Pneumatic Institute. I think Coleridge and Southey and other people used to go, and De Quincey. But serious people. I think there hasn't been very much written about that period. *What went on in the Humphry Davy household on Saturday midnight when Coleridge arrived by foot, through the forest, by the lakes?* Then, there are certain states you get into with opium, and heroin, of almost disembodied awareness, looking down back at the earth from a place after you're dead. Well, it's not the same, but it's an interesting state, and a useful one. It's a normal state also, I mean it's a holy state of some sort. At times. Then, mainly, of course, with the hallucinogens, you get some states of consciousness which subjectively seem to be cosmic-ecstatic, or cosmic-demonic. Our version of expanded consciousness is as much as *un*conscious information—awareness comes up to the surface. Lysergic acid, peyote, mescaline, sylocidin, Ayahuasca. But I can't stand them anymore, because something happened to me with them very similar to the Blake visions. After about 30 times, 35 times, I began getting monster vibrations again. So I couldn't go any further. I may later on again, if I feel more reassurance.

However I did get a lot out of them, mainly like emotional understanding, understanding the female principle in a way— women, more sense of the softness and more desire for women. Desire for children also.

INTERVIEWER: Anything interesting about the actual experience, say with hallucinogens?

GINSBERG: What I do get is, say if I was in an apartment high on mescaline, I felt as if the apartment and myself were not merely on East Fifth Street but were in the middle of all space time. If I close my eyes on hallucinogens I get a vision of great scaly dragons in outer space, they're winding slowly and eating their own tails. Sometimes my skin and all the room seem sparkling with scales, and it's all made out of serpent stuff. And as if the whole illusion of life were made of reptile dream.

Mandala also. I use the mandala in an LSD poem. The associations I've had during times that I was high are usually referred to or built in some image or other to one of the other poems written on drugs. Or after drugs—like in *Magic Psalm* on lysergic acid. Or mescaline. There's a long passage about a mandala in the LSD poem. There is a good situation since I was high and I was looking at a mandala—before I got high I asked the doctor that was giving it to me at Stanford to prepare me a set of mandalas to look at, to borrow some from Professor Spiegelberg who was an expert. So we had some Sikkimese elephant mandalas there. I simply describe those in the poem— what they look like while I was high.

So—summing up then—drugs were useful for exploring perception, sense perception, and exploring different possibilities and modes of consciousness, and exploring the different versions of *petites sensations*, and useful then for composing, sometimes, while under the influence. Part II of *Howl* was written under the influence of peyote, composed during peyote vision. In San Francisco—*Moloch*. *Kaddish* was written with amphetamine injections. An injection of amphetamine plus a little bit of morphine, plus some dexedrine later on to keep me going, because it was all in one long sitting. From a Saturday morn to a Sunday night. The amphetamine gives a peculiar metaphysical tinge to things, also. Space-outs. It doesn't interfere too much there because I wasn't habituated to it, I was just taking it that one weekend. It didn't interfere too much with the emotional charge that comes through.

INTERVIEWER: Was there any relation to this in your trip to Asia?

GINSBERG: Well, the Asian experience kind of got me out of the corner I painted myself in with drugs. That corner being an inhuman corner in the sense that I figured I was expanding my consciousness and I had to go through with it but at the same time I was confronting this serpent monster, so I was getting in a real terrible situation. It finally would get so if I'd take the drugs I'd start vomiting. But I felt that I was duly bound and obliged for the sake of consciousness expansion, and this insight, and breaking down my identity, and seeking more direct contact with primate sensation, nature, to continue. So when I went to India, all the way through India, I was babbling about that to all the holy men I could find. I wanted to find out if they had any suggestions. And they all did, and they were all good ones. First one I saw was Martin Buber, who was interested. In Jerusalem, Peter and I went in to see him—we called him up and made a date and had a long conversation. He had a beautiful white beard and was friendly; his nature was slightly austere but benevolent. Peter asked him what kind of visions he'd had and he described some he'd had in bed when he was younger. But he said he was *not* any longer interested in visions like that. The kind of visions he came up with were more like spiritualistic table rappings. Ghosts coming into the room thru his window, rather than big beautiful seraphic Blake angels hitting him on the head. I was thinking like loss of identity and confrontation with non-human universe as the main problem, and in a sense whether or not man had to evolve and change, and perhaps become non-human too. Melt into the universe, let us say—to put it awkwardly and inaccurately. Buber said that he was interested in man-to-man relationships, human-to-human—that he thought it was a human universe that we were destined to inhabit. And so therefore human relationships rather than relations between the human and the non-human. Which was what I was thinking that I had to go into. And he said "Mark my word, young man, in two years you will realize that I was right." He was right—in two years I marked his words. Two years is '63—I saw him in '61. I don't know if he said two years—but he said "in years to come." This was like a real terrific classical wise man's "Mark my words young man, in several years you will realize that what I said was true!" Exclamation point.

Then there was Swami Shivananda, in Rishikish in India. He said "Your own heart is your guru." Which I thought was very sweet, and very reassuring. That is the sweetness of it I felt—in my heart. And suddenly realized it was the heart that I was seeking. In other words it wasn't consciousness, it wasn't *petites sensations*, sensation defined as expansion of mental consciousness to include more data—as I was pursuing that line of thought, pursuing Burroughs' cut-up thing—the area that I was seeking was heart rather than mind. In other words, in mind, through mind or imagination—this is where I get confused with Blake now—in mind one can construct all sorts of universes, one can construct model universes in dream and imagination, and with lysergic acid you can enter into alternative universes and with the speed of light; and with nitrous oxide you can experience several million universes in rapid succession. You can experience a whole gamut of possibilities of universes, including the final possibility that there is none. And then you go unconscious —which is exactly what happens with gas when you go unconscious. You see that the universe is going to disappear with your consciousness, that it was all dependent on your consciousness.

Anyway a whole series of India holy men pointed back to the body—getting *in* the body rather than getting out of the human form. But living in and inhabiting the human form. Which then goes back to Blake again, the human form divine. Is this clear? In other words the psychic problem that I had found myself in was that for various reasons it had seemed to me at one time or another that the best thing to do was to drop dead. Or not be afraid of death but go into death. Go into the non-human, go into the cosmic so to speak; that God was death, and if I wanted to attain God I had to die. Which *may* still be true. So I thought that what I was put up to was to therefore break out of my body, if I wanted to attain complete consciousness.

So now the next step was that the gurus one after another said live in the body: this is the form that you're born for. That's too long a narration to go into. Too many holy men and too many different conversations and they all have a little *key* thing going. But it all winds up in the train in Japan, then a year later, the poem *The Change*, where all of a sudden I renounce drugs, I don't renounce drugs but I suddenly didn't want to be *dominated* by that non-human any more, or even be dominated by the moral obligation to enlarge my consciousness any more. Or do anything any more except *be* my heart—which just desired to be and be alive now. I had a very strange ecstatic experience then and there, once I had sort of gotten that burden off my back, because I was suddenly free to love myself again, and therefore love the people around me, in the form that they already were. And love myself in my own form as I am. And look around at the other people and so it was *again* the same thing like in the bookstore. Except this time I was completely in my body and had no more mysterious obligations. And nothing more to fulfill, except to be willing to die when I am dying, whenever that be. And be willing to live as a human in this form now. So I started weeping, it was such a happy moment. Fortunately I was able to write then, too, "So that I do live I will die"—rather than be cosmic consciousness, immortality, Ancient of Days, perpetual consciousness existing forever.

Then when I got to Vancouver, Olson was saying "I am one with my skin." It *seemed* to me at the time when I got back to Vancouver that everybody had been precipitated back into their bodies at the same time. It seemed that's what Creeley had *been* talking about all along. The *place*—the terminology he used, the *place* we are. Meaning this place, here. And trying to like, be real in the real place . . . to be aware of the place where he is. Because I'd always thought that that meant that he was cutting off from divine imagination. But what that meant for him was that this place would be everything that one would refer to as divine, if one were really here. So that Vancouver seems a very odd moment, at least for me—because I came back in a sense completely bankrupt. My energies of the last . . . oh, 1948 to 1963, all completely washed up. On the train in Kyoto having renounced Blake, renounced visions—renounced *Blake!*—too. There was a cycle that began with the Blake vision which ended on the train in Kyoto when I realized that to attain the depth of consciousness that I was seeking when I was talking about the Blake vision, that in order to attain it I had to cut myself off from the Blake vision and renounce it. Otherwise I'd be hung up on a memory of an experience. Which is not the actual awareness of now, now. In order to get back to now, in order to get back to the total awareness of now and contact, sense perception contact with what was going on around me, or direct vision of the moment, now I'd have to give up this continual churning thought process of yearning back to a visionary state. It's all very complicated. And idiotic.

INTERVIEWER: I think you said earlier that *Howl* being a lyric poem, and *Kaddish* basically a narrative, that you now have a sense of wanting to do an epic . . . Do you have a plan like this?

GINSBERG: Yeah, but it's just . . . ideas, that I've been carrying around for a long time. One thing which I'd like to do sooner or later is write a long poem which is a narrative and description of all the visions I've ever had, sort of like the *Vita Nuova*. And travels, now. And another idea I had was to write a big long poem about everybody I ever fucked or slept with. Like sex . . . a love poem. A long love poem, involving all the innumerable lays of a lifetime. The epic is not that, though. The epic would be a poem including history, as it's defined. So that would be one about present-day politics, using the methods of the Blake *French Revolution*. I got a lot written. Narrative was *Kaddish*. Epic—there has to be totally different organization, it might be simple free association on political themes—in fact I think an epic poem including history, at this stage. I've got a lot of it written, but it would have to be Burroughs' sort of epic, in other words it would have to be *dis*-sociated thought stream which includes politics and history. I don't think you could do it in narrative form, I mean what would you be narrating, the history of the Korean War or something?

INTERVIEWER: Something like Pound's epic?

GINSBERG: No, because Pound seems to me to be over a course of years fabricating out of his reading and out of the museum of literature; whereas the thing would be to take all of contemporary history, newspaper headlines and all the pop art of Stalinism and Hitler and Johnson and Kennedy and Vietnam and Congo and Lumumba and the South and Sacco and Vanzetti—whatever floated into one's personal field of consciousness and contact. And then to compose like a basket—like weave a basket, basket-weaving out of those materials. Since obviously nobody has any idea where it's all going or how it's going to end unless you have some vision to deal with. It would have to be done by a process of association, I guess.

INTERVIEWER: What's happening in poetry now?

GINSBERG: I don't know yet. Despite all confusion to the contrary, now that time's passed, I think the best poet in the United States is Kerouac still. Given twenty years to settle through. The main reason is that he's the most free and the most spontaneous. Has the greatest range of association and imagery in his poetry. Also in *Mexico City Blues* the sublime as subject matter. And, in other words the greatest facility at what might be called projective verse. If you want to give it a name. I think that he's stupidly underrated by almost everybody except for a few people who are aware how beautiful his composition is—like Snyder or Creeley or people who have a taste for his tongue, for his line. But it takes one to know one.

INTERVIEWER: You don't mean Kerouac's prose?

GINSBERG: No, I'm talking about just a pure poet. The verse poetry, the *Mexico City Blues* and a lot of other manuscripts I've seen. In addition he has the one sign of being a great poet, which is he's the only one in the United States who knows how to write haikus. The only one who's written any good haikus. And everybody's been writing haikus. There are all these *dreary* haikus written by people who think for weeks trying to write a haiku, and finally come up with some dull little thing or something. Whereas Kerouac thinks in haikus, every time he writes anything—talks that way and thinks that way. So it's just natural for him. It's something Snyder noticed. Snyder has to labor for years in a Zen monastery to produce one haiku about shitting off a log! And actually does get one or two good ones. Snyder was always astounded by Kerouac's facility . . . at noticing winter flies dying of old age in his medicine chest. Medicine cabinet. "In my medicine cabinet / the winter flies / died of old age." He's never published them actually—he's published them on a record, with Zoot Sims and Al Cohn, it's a very beautiful collection of them. Those are as far as I can see the only real American haikus.

So the haiku is the most difficult test. He's the only *master* of the haiku. Aside from a longer style. Of course the distinctions between prose and poetry are broken down anyway. So much that I was saying like a long page of oceanic Kerouac is sometimes as sublime as epic line. It's there that also I think he went further into the existential thing of writing conceived of as an irreversible action or statement, that's unrevisable and unchangeable once it's made. I remember I was thinking, yesterday in fact, there was a time that I was absolutely astounded because Kerouac told me that in the future literature would consist of what people actually wrote rather than what they tried to deceive other people into thinking they wrote, when they revised it later on. And I saw opening up this whole universe where people wouldn't be able to lie any more! They wouldn't be able to *correct* themselves any longer. They wouldn't be able to hide what they said. And he was willing to go all the way into that, the first pilgrim into that new-found land.

INTERVIEWER: What about other poets?

GINSBERG: I think Corso has a great inventive genius. And also amongst the greatest *shrewdness*—like Keats or something. I like Lamantia's nervous wildness. Almost anything he writes I find interesting—for one thing he's always registering the forward march of the soul, in exploration; spiritual exploration is always there. And also chronologically following his work is always exciting. Whalen and Snyder are both very wise and very reliable. Whalen I don't *understand* so well. I did, though, earlier —but I have to sit down and study his work, again. Sometimes he seems sloppy—but then later on it always seems right.

McClure has tremendous energy, and seems like some sort of a . . . seraph is not the word . . . not herald either but a . . . not demon either. Seraph I guess it is. He's always moving—see when I came around to say getting in my skin, there I found McClure sitting around talking about being a mammal! So I suddenly realized he was way ahead of me. And Wieners . . . I always *weep* with him. Luminous, luminous. They're all old poets, everybody knows about those poets. Burroughs is a poet too, really. In the sense that a page of his prose is as *dense* with imagery as anything in St. Perse or Rimbaud, now. And it has also great repeated rhythms. Recurrent, recurrent rhythms, even rhyme occasionally! What else . . . Creeley's very stable, solid. I get more and more to like certain poems of his that I didn't understand at first. Like *The Door*, which completely baffled me because I didn't understand that he was talking about the same heterosexual problem that I was worried about. Olson, since he said "I feel one with my skin." First thing of Olson's that I liked was *The Death of Europe* and then some of his later

Maximus material is nice. And Dorn has a kind of long, *real* spare, manly, political thing—but his great quality inside also is tenderness—"Oh the graves not yet cut." I also like that whole line of what's happening with Ashbery and O'Hara and Koch, the area that they're going for, too. Ashbery—I was listening to him read *The Skaters*, and it sounded as inventive and exquisite, in all its parts, as *The Rape of the Lock*.

INTERVIEWER: Do you feel you're in command when you're writing?

GINSBERG: Sometimes I feel in command when I'm writing. When I'm in the heat of some truthful tears, yes. Then, complete command. Other times—most of the time not. Just diddling away, woodcarving, getting a pretty shape; like most of my poetry. There's only a few times when I reach a state of complete command. Probably a piece of *Howl*, a piece of *Kaddish*, and a piece of *The Change*. And one or two moments of other poems.

INTERVIEWER: By command do you mean a sense of the whole poem as it's going, rather than parts?

GINSBERG: No—a sense of being self-prophetic master of the universe.

III / Campus Agonistes:
The Students Rebel

Once looked upon as an ivory tower or medieval fortress where graying professors meditated and where their students endured a sometimes jolly period of adolescent incubation, the American university through its recent upheavals has thrust itself into the forefront of the nation's political and social life. Now the world is in the university and the university is in the world. And this curious coupling will last. This may be the main message from Columbia, Berkeley, Cornell, San Francisco State, the City College of New York, and a growing number of other colleges and universities throughout the country.

In one way or another, the writers in this section express their recognition that the central fact of contemporary American life is becoming, not business, but education—as John Dewey prophesied half a century ago. The institution that may define the style of American life in the seventies, that may shape its goals and its priorities, that certainly will provide the most informed running critique of the American experience to come is the university. And increasingly the same may be said of countries like France, Germany, and Japan, where higher education was once reserved for the elite—an education that perpetuated the values and the privileges of the upper class.

Now these institutions, especially in America, have become the proving grounds where the young define their own special qualities, measure their own development, judge the failures and successes of their elders, and prepare themselves to face a society which many of them feel, in the words of Morris Abram, the president of Brandeis University, is "now characterized by injustice, insensitivity, lack of candor and humanity." As these essays reveal, in most instances the young understand their own universities—and universe—far more profoundly than do their teachers, their administrators, and their politicians. And there is reassurance here for the older generation, for when they told their children that education was important, their children took them at their word, literally.

Anyone who reads these essays with care would be naive indeed to assume that these recent upheavals can be dismissed as temporary and unpleasant episodes inspired by communists, anarchists, madmen, spoiled brats of the affluent middle-class, father-hating sons, or criminals from the ghetto. Such accusations are a politician's cheap way of getting elected; they are the older person's apology for his own stagnation. The focus of the turmoil involves the brightest of American students, and the one necessary ingredient for trouble is a critical mass of very bright students. This generation was not sired or raised by university teachers, but by ordinary citizens, under laws and conditions we as their elders either created or permitted to stand. In brief, the unrest has been generated from within the inner core of American society, and indeed it mirrors a social, economic, moral, and even political revolution in the coming decades.

Even if the riots at the European, Japanese, and Mexican universities are far more political in complexion than those at American universities, *all* of these disruptions are truly radical in that they are recording a tremendous shift of forces—what amounts to the emergence of the university as the keystone of the modern democratic society. These upheavals have nothing in common with the old panty-raids: the student population, the largest single disenfranchised group in this nation, is finding its voice and amplifying it through its habitation, the university. We are witnessing a movement from passivity to power that mocks the sanctimoniousness of formal higher education. Despite Professor Barzun's outrage at Columbia's meddling in non-academic affairs, the university is reaching out into every aspect of American life, just as American life calls upon the university for almost everything under the sun, from the training of CIA agents to advice on international affairs. Both Columbia and Berkeley are involved in the properties adjoining the university, and, like it or not, they are landlords; Cornell and the

City College of New York may be deep into the racial crisis. The Nanterre-Sorbonne upheaval under Daniel Cohn-Bendit's leadership went furthest of all and almost toppled an authoritarian regime that was allowing higher education to stagnate while it pursued a nuclear striking force.

An informed and imaginative citizenry, aware of the conditions necessary to sustain the human spirit in a growingly one-dimensional world, can no longer exist without the university. Indeed, the thrust of the university into the realities of American life should be welcomed, not feared, encouraged, not threatened, subsidized, not undercut by state and federal investigating committees. It may not be saying too much to assert once again that the future of American civilization—and possibly the prospects of democratic, progressive regimes elsewhere—will have to be entrusted to the universities. Where else is there such a large body of people interested in justice and equity? Where else is there a massive group with sufficient time to examine itself and its environment? Where else is there a huge gathering of humanity not yet corrupted, disillusioned, and compromised?

The writers in this section sense all this, and each by implication or direction proposes new opportunities for this troubled country and its embattled campuses. Often the solution may appear to be negative, or unrealistic, but that may seem so because we are all baffled by how to translate stimulating ideas into concrete action—especially when faculties, administration, and trustees or state legislatures by nature resist change and look with suspicion at anything bearing the rubric of "radical." With press coverage inadequate or subtly muzzled by conservative owners and publishers, the facts themselves often get lost or distorted. Reading such loaded copy and rarely hearing the other side, the public is distressed by what it takes to be wanton violence and destruction, when often these are minimal or caused by overzealous forces of repression.

Kingsley Widmer, who teaches literature at San Diego State College, gives general perspective to the college situation, while Harold Taylor, formerly president of Sarah Lawrence College, counts the ways that students have been neglected by their universities until they chant, "We are students without teachers." In between, we have reports on three key schools, each representing a sizable sector of the university scene: Columbia, the City College of New York, and Berkeley. The essays are written either by students or teachers who know their own school intimately.

11 / Rebellion as Education

KINGSLEY WIDMER

We need not be at one with current campus rebels to give them sympathy and support. Granted, their rhetoric often comes out raspy, their tactics Pyrrhic and their programs simplex. All decent citizens decry the rebel's arrogant dogmatism, even when it matches official obtuseness; all deplore calling policemen "pigs," even if they do behave bestially; and all disapprove of erratic violence, even if provoked by systematic force. At worst, we may be evoking the style of revolt that we as a society deserve. History can judge the quality of a civilization by its rebels as well as by its official heroes, and that may shame us. Though good Americans all, our rebels might, and perhaps will, learn to do better if they continue their education in rebellion.

Among their present limitations one must include the current curriculum of insurrection, which is not altogether of their choosing. They seem to be as much chosen by, victimized by, as choosers of such basic issues as subordination to the military-industrial order, the structural exclusion of minorities, and the fatuous ideologies of autocratic elites. These academic side-washes of a competitively bureaucratic, militarily aggressive and smugly unjust society rarely appear evident to those who never touch them. One must, as do our militant students, wade into attempts at change, or get splashed with typical American righteousness, to realize how rough and bitter can be our social and political waters.

SOURCE: *The Nation*, April 28, 1969, pp. 537–41. Reprinted by permission of the publisher and the author.

Kingsley Widmer, professor of English at San Diego State College, is the author of *The Literary Rebel* and studies of D. H. Lawrence and Henry Miller.

But, goes the stock "liberal" retort, why should the campuses of higher education be the scenes for these rough confrontations? Why don't the deprived blacks assault the business and union leaders instead of the academic administrators; why don't the draftable young men fight the government instead of the campus police, or the leftist students attack the corporate offices instead of the university halls? Probably they would if they could. But because academic institutions half fraudulently claim to be sanctuaries from the worst aspects of this society, they become especially and justifiably vulnerable. Throughout history, revolutions have occurred more often among the half-free than among the fully oppressed. The minorities in our universities, including the few from the underclasses, the dissident middle-class students and the radical-intellectual teachers, are sufficiently well placed to revolt, though certainly not to carry out revolutionary action in the society at large. If much of this insurgency could move from the campuses and ghettos to the headquarters of power and the suburban shopping centers, this would already be a quite different society. We must understand, and critically support, dissent and protest and rebellion where we find them.

At this moment, they rightly arise in and against academic society. Ambitious efforts at higher education long ago claimed to go beyond antiquarianism and specialism to social pertinence. Now at last, in insurgency and disruption, the academies do become relevant. Student revolt as education may be epitomized in the remark of a young lady on an urban university campus: "I learned and felt more about American society in the few days of the student strike than in four years of taking courses." In our higher education it is an achievement to fuse, even briefly, social role and individual intelligence and feeling. Such responsive experience, rather than the sometimes *outré* styles and super-revolutionary mannerisms, should be the abrasive to bring out the grain of our responses. It takes rebellion, if not some official beatings, to learn many of the realities of our social order and civilization.

In and of itself, today's higher education demands its troubles and deserves its disruptions—most of which can only improve it. But even the rebellious only reluctantly learn this lesson. They, too, are compulsively entrapped in the American religiosity about education. When I taught in, and attended meetings with, the student administrators of a "free university," or listened to an SDS chapter I was advising on "university reform" (now Maoistically out of fashion), or joined debates in and on the "New Student Left," or discussed polemical targets with the editors of an "underground" newspaper, or sat through interminable quasi-therapeutic sessions of a "Student-Faculty Committee for Change," or chaired protest rallies, I often cringed at what most of the rebels thought was relevant and tough criticism of the Hired Learning. Classroom habit tempted me to rush to a blackboard and list satiric novels about academic absurdity for them to read, or to quote the lovely aphorisms, from Diogenes through Veblen to Goodman, of biting contempt for official education, or to start telling personal anecdotes of the pathology of half a dozen universities. Only as the rebels literally dramatize their yearnings for more authentic education do they discover the dishonesty and intransigence of the authorities, the selfishness and cowardice of much of the faculty, and the arbitrariness and falsity of much of academic life.

Many of the rebellious poignantly suffer shock from the lack of humane sympathy for their efforts and the righteous refusal of demands for adequate changes. Hence the increasingly disenchanted and belligerent styles of campus insurrection. Their liberal professors, the students discover, all too often provide melancholy confirmation of the usual truths about sophists, mandarins, clerics, technologues and other orthodox rationalizers. Baroque professorial ways hardly obscure the primary drive of the hirelings to self-perpetuation and self-justification. In answer to student complaints about the usual mediocre teaching and mendacious programs, my colleagues fall back on one or another appeal to "our scientific and humanistic traditions." It is disingenuous and comic, for tradition in America is like instant beverage: the bland result of a little synthetic dust and a lot of hot water. Academicians sound more sincere, I suppose, when they speak of defending from disruption universities as sanctuaries for the pursuit of truth and art and dissent in a hostile and corrupting society. Logically enough, rebellious students begin to wonder why they and their supporters can't get amnesty, much less sanctuary, when the crunch comes. Rather more than the mainline faculties, the dissidents want to create autonomous places of order and joy within America's repressive fragmentation.

The aggrandizing of institutions of higher education within the past generation obscures for the rebels what restrictive places universities have been and continue to be. The real academic tradition is that of keeping out, or only tolerating, not only the poets and saints but most of the original and critical minds. Most significant intellectual and moral work remains peripheral to formalized education or in subversion of its orderings. Though academics claim large roles for their disciplines, they tend to operate as technicians of them, and even more so these days in a society that glorifies technique. To be concerned about authentic intellectual experience still, as always, includes assaulting traditional learned disciplines, accepted and honored views and official higher education.

The odds oppose most of the academic caste doing this barnyard labor. While professors currently confuse their trade with civilization itself, most vocally in the humanities, their narrow and fearful tones belie such pretensions. There is nothing mysterious about it. Academicians are the victims of one of the most elaborate processes for inculcating subservient responses: it takes about thirty years of formalized indenture, from nursery school through assistant professorship, to become a full member. Especially these days, selection is mostly by institutional conformity rather than by any autonomous achievement.

No wonder universities suffer from ornate law-and-order arbitrariness and that so many of their members feel threatened by any criticism and disruption. Next thing you know, someone will question academic hierarchy. Are most full professors (I am one) 100 to 500 per cent more competent and harder working than assistant professors? A joke! The percentages, except for salaries and similar prerogatives, usually run the other way. However, the spread in salaries has for some years been growing even faster than the excessive general increases in academic compensation. With justice, younger faculty tend resentfully to support rebellious students. And with good reason, much of the public suspects all of us of crass self-interest. The step-by-crawling fraudulence of licking and booting one's way up the crypto-military ranks—and up the crypto-theocratic path from the provincial animal farms to the "big twenty" zoos—takes a considerable human toll. Internal exploitation creates the proper atmosphere for internal rebellion.

From their captive clientele (students) through their indentured servants (teaching assistants) into their arbitrary hierarchy (professional as well as institutional) to their dubious packaging ("sciences" and "liberal" education), the universities illustrate, as much of American advertising and foreign policy illustrate, grievous mislabeling of an ideology of competitive aggrandizement. As might therefore be expected, academic hiring exhibits all the ethical delicacy of, say, real estate brokerage. Sycophantic salesmanship controls not only the acquiring of prestigious jobs, awards and publications but reaches right down to the often miserable junior colleges and their petty prerogatives. In the current expansion of higher education, the traditional elitist and paternal (master-protégé) placement system becomes a manipulation of "connections" and "professional" images. The appropriate morals and manners for all this racketeering help determine what happens in the classrooms—and, now, on the steps of the embattled administration buildings.

Behind the rhetoric of student rebels lies the awareness that when one speaks of a "power elite" or an "authoritarian bureaucracy" or "corporate liberalism," or more generally of competitive and exploitative and unjust order, one is not referring to something "out there" but to conditions right on campus. Even when the militant focus seems mainly political, as with "student power" struggles against "militarism" and "racism," it is also a protest against faculty subservience to such order. Because of decades of institutional indoctrination and corrupt recruitment and hierarchy and production, we hardly notice the lack of an autonomous community of scholars until the students rebel in its name. They teach us what we should be teaching them.

Most of us serve large, mediocre undergraduate state institutions. (Perhaps the problems presented by the "very best" colleges and universities would require a different emphasis but, having taught in several which claim such distinction, I doubt it.) In social function, these educational bureaucracies serve to indoctrinate what used to be called the lower-middle class, now relatively affluent, in the techniques and attitudes necessary for submissive service in the middle ranges of corporate and public bureaucracies. Split between the purposes and functions of the institutions and our claims to separate moral and intellectual values, we end nastily ambivalent. Only thus can one explain some of the weird and even hysterical faculty responses to rebellious demands for clear moral choices. It is hard altogether to blame dedicated little scholars, after years of institutional processing, for themselves becoming bureaucratic devices. At our best, I suppose, many of us secretly believe that we can provide some counter-education, some involvement, for example, in literature and thought, which will work against the restricted indoctrination which the students and schools officially pursue. We fall back on such wheezing rationalizations of our roles as staying neutrally "Socratic," i.e., playing question games as a substitute for a sustained view (and as a device to avoid class preparation). But methodological excuses only midwife the rebelliousness which justly threatens to put us down and out.

For most students these days, interesting educational experience comes in inverse proportion to what passes for a "professional" or scholarly (usually meaning a technical) emphasis. But, some of my colleagues will reply, that is because the students came to college for the wrong reasons. A better case might be made that their professors, employed in one of the more lavish industries, stay in universities for the wrong reasons. Students, of course, are drawn to campuses by all sorts of motives: to remain adolescent a while longer, to look for sex, to acquire a trade the slow way, to avoid the draft, to gain social status, to play games, to join the rebellious communities, or just because they have been drilled to believe they ought to be there. Probably many students should not at their age be involved in higher education, at least in the traditional scholarly and intellectual senses. A later time of life would be much better.

The resentment of many young students, who endure years of inappropriate academicism warps the universities into doing all sorts of anti-scholarly things and the students into rebellions which reveal an unpleasant anti-intellectual element. Those colleagues who piously assume that years of submission to bureaucratic education produces socially liberal and psychologically liberating benefits reveal themselves as quacks of educationism. College may well be a net loss for many, including some who don't disgustedly drop out or arbitrarily get pushed out. Students who don't develop some resistance and some confidence in their dissatisfaction, who don't autonomously turn hip or radical, must find the processing an anxiously competitive and morally degrading effort to become less truly responsive and integral human beings. Professorial self-interest has been used to deny these students both candor and compassion.

The colleges serve partly as custodial institutions for many who lack adequate place and role in an amorphously restrictive society. Periodically, those treated as inmates do naturally rebel. Professors are well paid for their institutionalization; students are not (though they should be) and therefore feel freer to express their discontent than do the custodians. As one finds in reading most of the apologies for higher education, the basic ideology glorifies the custodial separation of knowing and doing, of culture and living. Campus rebellions, no matter what the immediate generous "cause," must be partly understood as defiance of that moral schizophrenia, which the students vehemently attempt to bridge by moral activism and lashing out against custodial treatment.

Whatever many of my colleagues might claim in scholarly allegiances, their devotion to busy work, to arbitrary requirements, to competitive procedures, to specialist propaganda, to punitive grading and to professional-class decorum reveals them as primarily keepers. The horrendous processing—requirements, courses, tests, majors, minors, patterns, units, grades, averages, honors, etc.—is even more stupid than vicious. Even at its best it rests on the fallacy that repetitive accumulation is learning. Students, unless they take to conning the mechanism as most of their professors did, can Schweikishly soldier or collectively disrupt. The white students' current enthusiastic support for the black students' autonomous control of ethnic studies programs goes beyond racist guilt and political principle to tell us something of their own longings. That rebellious students also display notable disrespect for our "scholarly" justifications means that they see them, too, as just more of the processing. Rightly enough.

In my own field of "literary scholar-criticism," in which I'm sufficiently published to confess rather than complain sourly, most of the production is hobbyism: the overelaborate doctoring of texts, the compulsive collection of historical trivia, and the willful interpretation of interpretations. I don't mean to attack this hobbyism as such, for it is a pleasant pastime which merits gracious support; but it should not be confused with the need for responsive teaching and critical intelligence. Turned into professionalist ideology and institutional aggrandizement, however, scholarship provides trivial and inhumane molds for much of teaching and thinking, and deserves to be broken. Nor am I arguing for the reduction of faculties to mere pedagogues and intellectual scoutmasters, which often seems to be the position of the "anti-publication" faction in academic departments. (In some institutions these people protectively align themselves with the milder student rebels.) Actively cultivated and contentious people—those with something to say—should be recognized as a good in themselves. Given the lack of other harboring institutions in this society, they should be a major part of higher education, rather more so than the sinecured scholar-researchers and the bureaucratic technicians. Sartre once commented that to be a teacher was to be an intellectual monk. I don't care for the desexed metaphor but the quality of intellectual commitment may be hard to describe in a post-religious way. Certainly it provides a proper contrast to our hired education, in which business and bureaucratic production, if not racketeering, replace true vocation. A seasoning of critical intellectuals among teacher-students and student-teachers suggests the best possibilities for a community of learning and change.

Otherwise we can expect rebellions to increase against faculties as well as officials. In past years, campus revolt aimed mostly at the administrators, especially when they asserted parental and police powers. The super-janitors who now administer most academic institutions often deserve and incite rebellions. On good Jeffersonian principles, one can agree that there should be student disruptions of power every generation (academically, every four or five years). However, the old rebellions simply wanted to dethrone the administrations and then carry on much as before, like the liberal theologians who admit that God is dead but want to keep the old show going. Those rebellions of the middle sixties brought some changes, which now look extreme only in their moderation. But other failures appeared. The changes didn't develop community and autonomy in education, partly because it wasn't really allowed and partly because American capacities for full participation have been deeply eroded, not least by years of phony play-yard democracy in schools and other institutions. Fighting the administration does not create sufficient conditions for change, both because the universities are subordinate to the state and because the faculties are loaded with mediocre bureaucrats. The demands then enlarge. The style of rebellion exacerbates until it fractions the faculty and incites government and public. The education in rebellion has now reached the intermediate level at which both new styles of insurgency and increased repression may be expected. An end to it would require major internal changes in universities as well as a move to other arenas for the drastic contentions all too necessary in this society.

As the student *enragés* keep trying to tell us, intellectual commitment can no longer be kept separate from moral passion. Modern academic humanism long ago settled, though not very successfully it becomes evident, for freedom from interference rather than freedom for innovation. We regular academicians may be justly accused of denaturing the professor, who no longer professes anything but a supposedly neutral methodology and submissive ideology for technicians. That may no longer get by. Students should rebel against us as well as against the administrators and the power forces in the larger society. Almost any critical éclat in the academy becomes self-justifying as a means to break the narcissistic routines and institutional denaturing. It may well be true that nothing less than disruption, however messy, will bring most of us to the perplexity and passion of a larger reality.

Can the universities bear the disruption? More grandiloquently, can our liberal humanism endure such uncouth assaults? If the institutions are so brittle, and our culture so anemic, that they can maintain themselves only by huddling in fearful unchange behind massed troopers, then there is little to be lost and, as the militants chant, "Shut it down!"

No historical evidence suggests that a culture dominated by bureaucratized intellectuals retains much vitality in the long run. We dissident professors, also quite likely warped by decades of institutionalization and excessive engagement to official culture, must make conscious efforts to support the rebellions. That does not mean forgoing criticism: black demands sometimes contain a second-rate nationalism and chauvinism; New Leftism, especially some current trends in SDS, desperately moves into a doctrinaire abstraction of reality and a destructive super-militancy; such socio-cultural rebellions as hippiedom, though delightfully realizing in a dreary academic context what Fourier called the "butterfly instinct," contains a mindless mystagogy and cultism. Discrimination is our obligation, but it should be part of a continuing radical critique to achieve the disequilibrium that allows rebellion to surface and change to come about. Academic resistance may, and must at times, take forms other than overt rebellion. However, professors cannot claim privileged sanctuary from the essential struggles of the society of which they are all too obviously an exploitative part and dishonest parcel. Only when we resist do we truly teach, turning topsy-turvy accepted values and transforming ways of life. We cannot do this by playing professional hacks and academic custodians. Nor do we really profess any humanism or science by mainly channeling students into more bureaucratic education and corporate elites and the nondimensional sensibility of the hired learning for a counterfeit society. The most distasteful deceit of professors these days comes out in those who demand intellectual and social and political change, but always somewhere else. The overwhelming majority of liberal-radical academicians, and not least the Neo-Marxists, have come out against rebellions on campus. It is sheer hypocrisy. The current rebellions should educate us, not just the students, into seeing education as rebellion.

12 / Up Against the Wall!

DOTSON RADER

"Fuck Grayson Kirk" was scrawled above the urinal in the downstairs men's room of Mathematics, a liberated building at Columbia occupied by two hundred SDS-led students, former hippies, former left-liberals, the formerly apolitical, uninvolved, apathetic, safe. I studied the graffito, trying to take my mind off the fact that I was urinating in a liberated bathroom four feet from where two Barnard freshmen were washing up. They were on the Food Committee, breakfast corps. It was six o'clock Sunday morning. We had held the building two days. This was our third morning. I needed a bath and a shave and a Bloody Mary, in that order.

I stood, it seemed for hours, cock in hand, erect, leaning tightly against the cold wall of the urinal, wishing the girls would leave. All week, and I had never learned the revolutionary art of sharing bathrooms with women. I stood planted to the tile, ignoring the girls' giggling, staring dumbly at the wall. What if they *never* leave, I thought, I'll be stuck here like the madman in *Marat/Sade*, hard cock permanently erect, while they wash and wash and wash . . .

Sunday morning. I was hung over. The night before I had attended a long meeting in the main lounge, chaired by Tom Hayden, where we had argued about negotiations with the administration and the faculty. Around midnight I had gone up to the fourth floor and found Brian and Frank and Dave—he wearing a white cardigan the police would leave stained with his young blood—sitting inside a faculty office, the lights off, drinking the Scotch and beer they had brought into the commune before it went dry. Saturday night. We climbed into the attic of

SOURCE: *Evergreen Review* 12 (August, 1968), 70–78. Copyright © 1968 by Evergreen Review, Inc. Reprinted by permission of Dotson Rader c/o IFA.
  Dotson Rader is a young graduate of Columbia University and a staff writer for *Evergreen Review*; he is also the author of *I Ain't Marchin' Any More*, an account of his experiences with the New Left, and *Government Inspected Meat*.

Math. We opened the window in the roof—you could see the stars that night, the air was cool and smelled of fish and of the sea— and Frank, his green eyes catching the light, sat under the bare bulb, with the three of us seated around him drinking, and quoted poetry by heart—his own, Ginsberg's, and Dylan Thomas'.

Six hours later, Sunday morning, the bathroom and the giggling freshmen. FUCK GRAYSON KIRK.

I went into the main floor lounge in search of coffee. My headache was growing. It would take three hours to kill it. It rumbled through the room making me literally lust after a shot of Pepto Bismol. I hurt. Most of the students were still sleeping, but a few were beginning to get up, taking their blankets off the floor, moving toward the bathrooms, waking up. I leaned against the counter, found the coffee, heated the water, looked over the room. Before we took Math the lounge had been part of the library. Now the furniture was serving as barricades before the front doors and tunnels, the library shelving was nailed against the windows, and the place—for one brief week—was being used humanly by the young.

I took the coffee and climbed two flights of stairs, maneuvering over fire hoses uncoiled down the steps, squeezing past piles of chairs waiting to be sent tumbling down when the first cop came, past little cardboard trays of vaseline and mounds of plastic bags to be used against police gas.

In the dining room lounge. In a thick, soft chair. Asleep.

"You look drunk," Roger said, shaking me awake, looking charitably at my red eyes, my shaking hands. "You shouldn't drink so much, not when you're part of a revolutionary situation." Defensively I tried out my look of startled innocence on him, eyebrows raised, mouth dropped in surprise.

"Me? Drunk? Roger, I've never been drunk in my life!" I said, sounding drunk. He mumbled something about bourgeois decadence. It was half past six. I smiled up at him, my head swimming, looking rather bleary-eyed at his homely face. Roger is not the sight one likes to see in the morning after a hard night, sleepless, for Roger has, at twenty-one, the face of a tired failure, a revolutionary who no one, not even his Detroit mother, took seriously. Until that week. That face! Hanging jowls, the muscles already weakened, the cheeks collapsing toward the nose, the entire face caving in on itself. Early. To say Roger looks like a bloodhound is to be kind. A paper bag Roger should wear over his head, especially at six thirty in the morning when you face another day inside a liberated building and your mind has to screw itself up to the task of revolutionary plotting with young yet desperate sophomores.

Roger sat down in the seat next to me and opened a paper sack, took out an orange and began peeling it. I could *smell* the paper bag, last night's peanut butter sandwiches inside, three oranges, the bottom of the bag stained wet with jelly droppings. For *this* we took five buildings and held Dean Coleman captive, for *this* we faced jail, so Roger could carry a paper sack, like a badge of martyrdom, around with him and inform anyone who asked how he *knew* from *much past experience* that jail food was uneatable? Better to be prepared at all times, he advised. Carry peanut butter sandwiches in paper bags. Be ready when the fascist bust comes.

"Want a sandwich?" Roger offered, holding a dripping, gooey glob of peanut butter and grape jelly oozing between the bread. My stomach turned. "No, Roger."

"Are you sure? I've got plenty, enough to last a couple days."

"Quite sure, Roger." Sadist.

I closed my eyes again. I woke to the sound of WKCR, the campus station, blaring out over the room. It was around ten o'clock. Roger had left, leaving only curled orange skins in the ashtray to mark his passing.

Students were relaxing in the room, some reading *The New York Times* and laughing, some playing chess, a few gathered around a card table painting posters: GYM CROW MUST GO! Over WKCR a pompous professor was bitching about the fact that the majority of the Columbia students opposed the liberation (perhaps) and that the "overwhelming number" of students in the buildings were being "duped" by SDS. So what? It mattered for nothing since this was the first event in most of our lives where we felt effective, where what we were doing belonged to us. I had been involved in the peace movement since the Student Peace Union of the early sixties, where the main concern was to oppose an SDS take-over. I had worked through countless protests, picking up friends at each: Mel and Craig at the Pentagon, Roger at Princeton, Frank and Brian at the UN, Tish at Whitehall Street—where we stood outraged, held back by the police, and watched our friends beaten up in Battery Park by ignorant, half-ass longshoremen.

I sat there and wondered where Lionel Trilling was, hoping that somehow he, who wanted to understand so badly what was happening to us, would come over to our side. I remember telling him that in relation to his generation we felt disregarded, un-consulted, powerless—powerless to affect the quality of our lives in his America. Our lives, without roots in history, seemed diminished to gesture, without power, to desperation, without probable hope, to fantasy. With that fantasy our politics and art were being created, a fantasy of revolution and ritual murder and the giving way to a clean violence and a final peace. Even sitting in Math was a bit fantastic, unreal, hopeless, for I knew that they could bust us anytime they wanted. There will be no revolution and good, rich, respected men will die, as always, in their beds. Because we knew this—the futility of our arrogance —we lost increasingly a true relationship with actuality and with history, and our responses to life became melodramatic and false and dangerous.

But it did not matter. None of it. Not the bust to come, nor the degrees and careers in jeopardy, nor the liberal faculty insulted and lost. All that counted was the two hundred of us in solidarity for the first time, together in our place in our time against the cops outside and the jocks outside and the fucking American nation hoping for our blood. HIT THOSE RED PUNK FAGGOTS AND HIT 'EM HARD! It did not matter, for if you truly believe—and we were true believers—that your hope of change is all you have, even in as narrow a situation as Columbia, and if you suspect that it is false, that you can finally do nothing effective to act on its behalf, then you have to choose between throwing it over or keeping it and acting against your suspicion. We acted against our suspicion. Our outrage grew and, in time, fermented into hatred. In five days inside the commune at Columbia I learned again to hate with a passion, to hate things I had once loved.

But I could not see any alternative to being in the building with my friends, to acting in every situation in rebellion against the System. What other choices were there? Trilling's generation had covered all the options. We were left with our resistance and, in this culture, that meant acting in danger to ourselves. It al-ways cost *us*. At the anti-Rusk demonstration I saw young men rush at mounted police in the hope of being clubbed. At the Pentagon we waited late into the night—Lowell and MacDonald had parties to attend—in the growing tension and the cold, waited around fires built on the steps before that massive, ugly building, waiting, hoping in the dark that the troopers' fingers would tighten and bullets would fly and it would be over for us. We wanted to force them to act irrevocably. We wanted a response *to us.* Any kind. And now at Columbia I waited, knowing they could not act affirmatively in regard to us, they could give nothing without endangering the whole fucking System. "We have to consider," President Kirk had said, "what effect our actions will have on other American universities." I wanted them to act as they must, to act against us, to reveal themselves for what they are—a stinking, rotten group of venal men. I and the others had reached the point where we could no longer tolerate being disregarded. I and the others had to own our lives.

Frank came into the dining lounge and asked, "When do we eat?" I told him around noon as usual. He sat down beside me, took a notebook out of his pocket, and started writing. He looked up once to ask me if I knew a word that rhymed with Trotsky. I didn't.

Frank's father is a landlord, a conservative. Frank had walked out a year ago and gone to Haight-Ashbury and become active in the Oakland anti-draft riots. When he came back he said, a bit dramatically, "I saw the face of America out there. And it is made of violence." Frank is very bright and very gifted and yet he does not want to go back to school, he does not want to go to graduate school, and he will not go into business or government. He does not want money or power. He does not want to live off someone else's labor. He does not want to sell out. He said to me that he felt like someone lying on his back in a cellar with a low ceiling. And he can hear music and laughter filter down to him. And he presses his hands against the ceiling trying to find out where it is weak, where it will break and let him into life. Yet it will not break for him.

On Friday morning when we entered the liberated building I asked him if he knew he was liable for arrest. He nodded that he knew. "It is part of the game," he said. He wants a revolution in America. He does not know how to make one. So he hangs loose. "I am looking for the inside of a jail." He thinks it is pure there

186

because he sees the outside as being corrupt and deadly. "A jail is in all our futures," he said. And he wrote, "I see my manhood in the streets." That was in Oakland in the riots.

Frank wrote. I read *The Times*. I was astonished at the inaccuracy of the reporting of the Columbia rebellion. Remembering that Sulzberger was on the Columbia Board of Trustees made it seem sinister. The radio was still blaring out reports of activities on campus; jocks had surrounded Low Library and they were mumbling about Taking The Situation Into Their Own Hands. Acting Dean Coleman, seeing a real, permanent, high-paying, high-status deanship in his future—the lure of it all shimmering just beyond those Trustee asses, bow and kiss—was going around trying to keep the boys cool, telling them that "Harlem surrounds us. They'll burn the place down if we're not careful, fellows. Let's have the police handle the situation. You can trust President Kirk, etc." The boys were getting impatient. It is no fun to be called dummy jocks by long-haired, dirty—but oh so bitterly bright—radicals and not want to beat them up. Especially when they whispered that there was something peculiar about your masculinity in your posturing love of violence.

The jocks were grouped on the lawns before the buildings. The police sat muzzled in the basement of Low and other buildings waiting to be unleashed. And outside, along the walls of Math, more cops stood in the sun, looking up now to see the students throw Sunday flowers down on them from the lounge. Faggots with their flowers. Sick!

We had tuna fish and tomatoes for lunch. After eating I went onto the ledge overlooking Broadway and sat down by Dave. He had his shirt off—well-built, handsome—and I took mine off and we sat together in the sunshine passing Coke bottles and cigarettes from mouth to mouth. Beautiful. Down below people walked by, some of them stopping to put money or food in our bucket, others calling out obscenities, most, however, simply raising their fingers in a Churchillian V, our symbol of victory. As usual there were a dozen or so cops leaning against the wall, most of them quite young, some even well disposed to us. Privately.

A contingent of Harlem demonstrators marched by with signs protesting the construction of the gym—HANDS OFF HARLEM— and shouting, "Strike! Strike!" They were the poor. In the street the middle-class, Uncle Tom niggers swept by in their shiny new cars trying to look as disdainful as possible, Thoroughly East Side Token Nigger, more white than us, giving us sliding glances of contempt as they roared by; some, playing White Tourist, slowed their cars and rolled down the windows and pointed up at us sneeringly, gracing us with queenly "we-are-amused" type smiles just like the Man does when he goes slumming in Harlem on Sunday afternoons. It was sad, their self-hatred.

A blue Ford pulled up and double-parked in front of the building. A middle-aged man, stout, gray-haired, looking like a Prussian shopkeeper or a Southern preacher, got out of the car, a Bible carried in his right hand. He strutted over and stood a few feet from the Math building, his hands on his hips, and looked up at us, trying to shrink us with his prissy contempt. He yelled up at us: "If My people which are called by My Name shall humble themselves and pray and seek My Face I will heal their land. . . ." Dave, seeing his Bible, hearing God shouted in the street, interrupted him, "Thou shalt not steal, Columbia!" The man began again, louder: "If My people which are called by My Name. . . ." "Thou shalt not kill, America!" The man stopped. He gave Dave the finger. "Fuck you commie bastards," he shouted, "God fuck you bastards!" And then seeing the girls lining the ledge with us, twenty feet above him, out of reach, casually dressed, flower children, lovely in the sun, seeing them smile down on him, he started to shout hysterically: "Bitches! Whores of Babylon! Where would you be if some big, black buck was raping you in an alley? Red sluts! Who'd you call, you commie cunts! Who'd you call for help? The *police*, that's who you'd call, you Communist. . . ." While he was spewing forth into the street a rookie cop calmly walked over to his double-parked Ford and gave him a parking ticket. We applauded. The cop grinned and bowed in reply.

Dave slapped my thigh and laughed, "Beautiful, Baby. The world's beautiful! You, the cops, life . . . life's so goddamn beautiful!" I smiled back at him. He put his hand to my head and playfully mussed my hair.

Sitting on the ledge that Sunday afternoon, caught by his friendship, I felt a great sense of oneness with the people in the commune. We were together until it was ended for us. Our building—our *home*, for Christ's sake!—where we slept and ate and talked and bathed and worked together. And our sensitivity to the goodness of the commune experience was born out of a consciousness of its contingency—that in point of fact it was bounded by time and place, fatally weak, impossible of survival. We had to make it last as long as we could. We had to make it good. Our tolerance of each other was immense. In the week, I heard not one word said in anger against anyone in the commune. And sitting with Dave on the ledge, full of love for him, I thought of Camus' celebration of human solidarity in *The Plague* and of Alyosha in *The Brothers Karamazov* with the children at the funeral, telling them to remember their sometime oneness with each other. It was a tender sentiment, new to me, and it was decidedly unusual in my America. It was, at the risk of sounding hopelessly sentimental, a precious thing.

Around five the general meeting of the commune began in the main lounge. There was one held each night. Participatory democracy. Hayden chaired them. Frank and Dave and I sat on a rug in the back of the room, not paying much attention until an announcement was made by the Steering Committee that it had broken off negotiations with the Ad Hoc Faculty Group. This frightened me since I assumed that the administration would not chance mass resignations by calling a police bust while the faculty was negotiating with the students to end the occupation of the buildings. That, of course, was precisely what happened, there being no honor among liberals or thieves. Not with so much at stake, so much *loot* to peddle one's liberal ass for— research grants, government appointments, secret funds, POWER. Not even the faculty is worth losing Percy Uris' millions. Not to mention the Rockefellers'. *Gawd!*

There was a brief debate over the accuracy of the announcement; two students disagreed about what exactly had happened at the Steering Committee meeting they had both attended. I was getting nervous so, true to left-lib form, I took the floor and made a brief and, as I remember it, magnificent speech in defense of Trilling and Westin and Anderson, the professors who had just come under attack. I remember calling them "eminent men, fair-minded," and saying that the students could act in "complete good faith" with them. The radical leaders particularly disliked the "eminent men" line, thinking, probably correctly, that it sprang from a nasty little case of intellectual elitism—most undemocratic—that I was coughing up into the room. To protect the commune from my counterrevolutionary remarks they proceeded to attack the faculty all over again, this time making it most personal. Undeterred by the evidence, I made another neat speech and offered a motion directing the Steering Committee to do what it was most unwilling to do— reopen negotiations with the faculty. I was not the only closet elitist in the room, for my motion passed overwhelmingly.

It *is* hard overnight to see your professors as enemies tainted by bloody CIA funds. It is hard but, more often than not, it is true (as I would learn as the contents of Kirk's private files began to seep out). The university was corrupt. And much of the faculty was complicit in its corruption.

Flushed with the victory of my motion I stood, not really knowing what to say, to propose other motions. *Many* of them. I did not want to let my moment of power pass. I had the Majority! I was a Leader! Not like the others who had only one gripe to bitch, I discovered as I stood to the floor, Hayden looking impatiently in my direction, that I had hundreds of silly motions whirling in my head, motions about the use of the bathrooms, the lousy food, the Defense Committee, and, *most importantly,* the ban on drinking. I could have stood the entire day offering motions to be rubber stamped by *my* majority. But Hayden interrupted me. Juan, a Puerto Rican who was an SDS marshal, came rushing in and handed the chairman a note.

"Please sit down." Is he speaking to *me*? My power went, untasted.

"This is an important announcement. We have definite word that there will be a bust before nightfall." I instinctively glanced at the window. Still light. "Anybody who has to leave may leave now. No one will think any less of you if you have to go. It's OK." No one left.

I looked at Frank and shook my head. "I guess this is it," I said. I was frightened for him and for Dave and Brian and the others, especially for the girls. I had seen the police whip into young demonstrators before, seen the delight with which they attack. The brutality of their assault almost always corresponded to the youth and weakness of the victim. And the people in the commune were young, most in their late teens and early twenties, and not strong. They would be torn apart and there was nothing I could do to help them when it came, nothing to prevent it, to make it less costly. I could do what I had to do—stand with them, share their hatred and their defeat, witness and work to make those who allowed it to happen pay. This desire for vengeance was my primary response to life in the commune. I had had enough of war and injustice. I was ashamed of my country and of its leaders. The rich had grown too rich, the poor too wretched, and it was time to demand an accounting. And if it meant destroying universities, disrupting a nation, if it meant jail and beatings, so be it. I had a deep terror of the police, but my anger was deeper and harder, and when my fear passed— and it usually passed as soon as the cops began to move—only the clean anger remained.

A member of the Legal Committee handed each of us an arraignment form which we filled out. He gave us a telephone number to call if we were isolated from the group and needed a lawyer. I wrote the number on my arm. The head of the Defense Committee stood and showed us the best position to assume if the cops attacked: fall into a fetal position on the ground, arms over your head and neck, legs drawn tightly to the stomach to protect your genitals and internal organs. Then our gas expert— an anarchist from the East Village—gave us a vivid description of the effects of tear gas and Mace, warning us that Mace only needs a small area of the skin to contact to be assimilated by the blood. Thus we were to seal our cuffs with string, put cigarette filters in our nostrils, plastic bags—air holes in the back—over our heads, and vaseline to close the pores of skin exposed to the air.

The meeting broke up. The passage window onto campus was sealed. Students started collecting bags and filters and gobs of vaseline. We were instructed to disperse ourselves throughout the building, to make it as difficult as possible for the cops to pull us out. I agreed to meet Frank, Brian and Roger—lunch bag in hand—in the attic when the cops appeared.

I went into the dining room and made a cup of coffee and sat down on the couch and waited.

About two hours later the news came that the bust was off. It was a false alarm. I was elated by the news of the reprieve. I saw Tish, blond, lovely, tough, and kissed her and said, "Isn't it great! Jesus, I'm glad!" She smiled, "So am I. It'll give us time to make more clubs." Tish, the Irish peasant wife singing her men off to war.

The whole commune was relieved that the bastards had given us more time. And, at the same moment, we were proud of ourselves because no one had walked out, no one had panicked. We had stayed solid. The barricade was taken off the passage window. The singing and dancing started. Someone got a guitar and sat down on the second floor landing and sang Bob Dylan's "It's All Right, Ma." Students sat on the steps before him like a tiered choir and sang along: *though the masters make the rules for the wisemen and the fools, I got nothing, Ma, to live up to.*

About an hour later a bagpiper came into the building and we joined hands in a long chain and danced behind him, snaking through the building, up and down the stairs, playing, shouting happily, singing about how we weren't going to study war no more. And later still I stood with Frank on the balcony beside the red flag in the coolness of that lovely night and tore sheets of paper and threw them down in lieu of rice on the couple who had been married that night in one of the liberated buildings and were walking toward us, now under the balcony, now on the lawn, lighted candles in their hands, a wedding party of tired professors, flower children, and red-banded communards dancing behind them singing. We raised our arms and shouted out into the night: "We've won! We've won!"

Sunday, feeling happy, I went to sleep upstairs on the couch listening to Frank and Brian talk about how the bust might not come at all, how they were going to hold out until the administration gave in on every demand and if they tried to bust them they would make them regret it.

Monday I left campus shortly after noon, going over to the West End Bar—deserted—for lunch and a few drinks. I tried to fortify myself to the task of meeting my parents, returning from their goy First Class Biblical Tour of the Great State of Israel, lunches included. I took a cab out to Kennedy. I felt better about the Columbia liberation, sure now the bastards would not bust us for at least a few days. I knew the tension was growing. The radicals— Roger among them—had made a pathetic charge against the hundreds of beer-happy jocks lined below Low. Fist fights had broken out. There was a chance that we would not wait until the administration acted. It is difficult to live in a tense situation, threatened, swept by rumor, the balance held by your enemies, it is tough when you are young and when you believe deeply that what you are doing is right and necessary. In spite of the growing tension and the threat of a bust—you could taste it in the air—I felt we had won.

I was mistaken.

I went back to the West End Bar, relieved my parents had left New York. It had gone easily, the past avoided, the truth skirted. Our conversation had been limited to Israel and the eighteen led through the artillery-pocked hills into Gethsemane for the service and the sunrise. My duty again would be limited to letters home. No need to justify the lust for violence to them (the politics of cultural despair, Trilling had called it, lifting Fritz Stern's term, a politics where ends had been diminished to the acts themselves), the hatred exhilarating and new, years of guilt and accumulated failure, powerlessness, the ingrown despair released daily like gism in the communes where we reassured ourselves daily of our pacific intent while we panted for the bust. Anything, however violent, to end the growing tension. I did not have to tell them that I was filled with hatred for men and institutions and, yes, for the country I had loved days before. In me and in the others I had discovered a hunger for violence, almost carnal, that admitted no reason. Put the mother-fuckers up against the goddamn wall. Them. The cops. The asshole Trustees. The bumbling, duplicitous President. The Middle Class. The Company Students. The Liberal Faculty. Up Against The Wall. Motherfuckers.

"But why?" Mother asked, Israeli-tanned and lovely, "Why get yourself hurt over a bunch of Communists?" She had not read a paper in weeks and already she saw *conspiracy* brooding over the city. She should have been an editor of *The Times*. My son the Commie dupe. "For *this* we educate and raise you, for this stealing of buildings and deans?" In her mind the St. Paul papers: LOCAL BOY ARRESTED AS RED AGENT AT COLUMBIA. Revolutions were to be read about, not made, in America. "You part of such a thing? At your age? For this we left Europe?"

I had a double Scotch at the West End. I wanted to get high before I crawled back into the liberated zone. Math was dry as an Iowa county, by democratic vote. Who needs it?

It was nearly midnight. The West End was empty of students, except for a few misplaced jocks who usually hung out at the Gold Rail or, failing that, at the Gay Way. Holding the drink in my hand I looked across the bar to the booth where four of them sat dressed like street hustlers in tight shirts and whites and sneakers. Drinking beer. They were out of place here, where Ginsberg and Kerouac drank before pot and acid and age and tiredness and fear pressed in on them, drawing them from the world (Ginsberg drunk and bugging Trilling on the phone in the back of the bar . . . *we're both Jews, man, let's admit it*). Time had taken them.

And the Liberation had taken a new generation of Columbia students, leaving in its wake their posturing indifference, their hustling, their cool, their reality, thinning in the smoke that sometimes covered an unadmitted hollowness. And the hippies inside Math, before the Liberation, had fanatically denied the actuality of the future in order to avoid judgment, had rejected political action as a sell-out. These same people, a few days inside the commune, had become obsessed by a Future and its power. Now they crouched inside Math and Avery and Fayerweather and Low waiting to meet the violence once opposed in the name of Love. Children of the Present, proud of it, hung up on it, now were captives of a Future. Buckley had said, archly, dryly, that they wanted to "imminentize the Eschaton." True. The Revolution-To-Come justified everything. All had become judgmental.

The West End was strangely quiet. Smokeless. It made me uncomfortable. The air there is usually unbreathable, but Monday night, emptied of heads and drunks spilling urine on the bathroom floors, and old lady winos, and students crowded over beers, the air was clean. I could not get high. And I wanted to in order to confront Hayden in the name of Moderation and Reason. That was my bag. But I was so politically untrained that I had to have a few drinks to convince myself I was winning him when, if ice sober, I would see I was losing miserably. All was politics. Even the West End, like the university and the community, drooped with thick rhetoric, smelled of politics. Joyless. "All within the

Revolution," Hayden had declared, half-facetiously, the age not weighing yet the resurrected terms, the retread revolutions of the East. It was still 1825 in twentieth-century America by Hayden's calendar. And he worked to press the year with decades.

The bartender asked me if I had seen Juan. I told him he was in Math. "He owes me money," he said, "the filthy spic."

Even Juan had changed. Somehow he found a grim sort of manhood, contingent though it was, situationalist, separate but equal, in darting between the communes playing Professional Puerto Rican to the whites. We listened. The blacks did not. No whites or spics welcome in Malcolm X (Hamilton) Hall.

Juan's rhetoric was limited to a hoarse but well-meant "I am for *my* America, Whitey, after we burn *your* America to the fucking ground!" Effective, especially when he delivered his speech with his greatcoat thrown over his shoulders and his red arm band glistening below his clenched fist. It was pretense, though it was delivered with such ease in telling that it made his past dissolve one week, and fiction grew inside his mind, stretching his revolutionary past back beyond last Friday to Lenin—this Puerto Rican pimp—back to Herzin and Belinsky—this pusher, pornographer, pimp—back to where his memory was lost to names and race and all violence took the name of Freedom. As I drank in the West End he was over in Math, his greatcoat discarded on the fifth floor, playing revolutionary general to the whites. Outwardly cool. His stomach tight. Feeling less white as the cops moved onto campus. "How does a black cop feel clubbing us?" Dave had asked Juan. "It makes him feel white," he had replied on Sunday.

The Liberation had taken Juan with the rest. I remembered the joints bought, the speed. I remembered the night in his pad at 124th, his old lady in the kitchen with her Gallo, a lighted candle before a saint on the wall stand, San Juan beaches nearing in the wine. Juan pinned a sheet to the wall and, at five bucks a head, I and Frank and Brian watched three blue movies, Cuban export. Dogs fucking women. Men eating each other. Old men eating little girls. During each flick his old lady wandered into the room, looked a minute and mumbled in Spanish that she had seen it, cursed, and wandered out. And now Juan was donning grease, a shield, his face too dark, and waiting for the bust. A prison record. Would the bastards give him bail?

It was twelve-thirty. I ordered another drink. When the bartender slid it across the bar to me he said, low, "They get those red punks tonight."

"Who does?"

"You haven't seen it? Christ, they're piling out of buses on Amsterdam. Looks like a goddamn army camp over there."

Tonight. Impossible. We are negotiating. They promised. Negotiate and no bust. "Are you sure?"

"Dead certain. It's for real this time. The fucking punks!"

For real. I left quickly. Outside and cool, a light breeze coming over the Hudson from the west. Fear tasted in my mouth, so soon, so soon, as I ran across Broadway toward the 116th Street gates. I had to get back inside Math. I belonged there. All I could think of as I ran was the fear that I would arrive too late, that before I could reach the entrance window into Math the blood already would have won. My friends. Frank . . . a poet's mind . . . Brian . . . who laughs at violence and believes . . . David . . . Crazy Mel . . . Tish . . . Tish who made the clubs and got the gasoline . . . they'll be cut apart, the fucking walls washed with them, bled over the floors, along the steps, broken.

At the gates. "I've got to get on to campus!" I showed my ID card.

"Campus is closed. Move or face arrest."

"This is important! I'm part of the Math commune. My friends are there. I *belong* there!" Goddamn asslicking cops.

"Move!"

I moved. Up Broadway, trying to circle the campus at 120th and over to the Amsterdam gates. The shouting of the crowds inside the campus was starting, my fear pushing like a hard knot in my chest. Running I pictured my head being clubbed by eight-foot-tall cops, swaddled in shiny leather, bulging, and my brain damaged . . . years later my limping dramatically through Leftist assemblies, people awed and drunk with sweet pity—the Martyr!—as I, a one-man Abraham Lincoln Brigade, stumbled half-wittedly through the crowd, a Crippled Veteran of the Columbia Rebellion.

Two horse vans were lined along 120th Street, across from Teachers' College and Union Theological Seminary. Horses filled the street. Twenty or so uniformed cops, smug in leather, tall, tough, strutting like leather queens on Christopher Street,

196

their hands itching to swing, to prove manhood again and again. Jogging by them, I instinctively put my hand in my pocket and covered my cock protectively. The smell of manure and piss, the smell that would cling to Broadway and the walks for days after, was there in the street. Blood has no smell.

I reached Amsterdam. There, along the walls of Columbia, hundreds of cops stood in line facing the street waiting. Five, ten city buses marked SPECIAL, filled with sadistic plainclothesmen looking like bouncers from dockside bars, or pimps ... cops in other buses ... cops inside the gates, hundreds ... cops belching and itching to kill, leaning butch under the ledges above which Trilling and Quentin and Steve Marcus wrote ... police vans, paddy wagons, two ambulances, police cars, red lights playing on the university buildings, reflecting on the windows of Philosophy Hall where the Ad Hoc faculty group had argued and lost, where the wounded would be taken that night. Crowds of whites packed across the street from the gates, along the walls under the Law Bridge, jeering the cops ... fascist motherfuckers ... and where was Harlem? Two old colored ladies—one screaming hysterically at the cops, "You's evil! You's evil!"; the other knocking over a litter basket and kicking it toward the cops. Futile anger. Harlem was asleep.

No entrance. Closed. A cop at the gates jabbed a billy club hard into my stomach. Move! Breathless. I ran to 114th and over to Broadway again, west of the fenced gym site over which the press and administration and students fought to avoid the meaning of the fight. On Broadway three ABC cameramen were laughing as they talked. The noise from the campus grew louder. The shouting would build and fade and build again. "Kill 'em!" came from the jocks gathered at Low. The bust was still to come.

Near the Broadway gates I saw a professor I knew. I went up to him and told him I had to get on campus. He understood.

Professor Dodson was an hour away, told the bust was called off, two drinks later, driving toward Sparkill ... Trilling was home exhausted ... Quentin was in front of Hamilton renewing the thirties and his credentials as a man ... Dean Platt was home ... the President and Vice President were held in the basement of Low listening to Captain Denesco reassure them of the cops' professionalism ... Coach Balquist, who had planned the attack with the cops, sat in the corridor in Low, his hands sweat-

III / CAMPUS AGONISTES

ing, waiting for the Commie bastards to get fucked but good . . . in Fayerweather the barricades were being checked once more and the commune reminded of its pledge to nonviolence . . . the cops were moving on to Low silently . . . the captain raising his bullhorn, "In the name of the Trustees of Columbia University I order. . . ." The blacks had given in in Hamilton, led like sheep by the cops through tunnels into paddy wagons, like Jews moved into the showers . . . Avery was pulling on plastic bags . . . in Mathematics the students were in the middle of their anti-gas preparations and one boy, seventeen, was sobbing out his fear in the second-floor bathroom. It was an hour to the bust.

The professor and I walked to the gates. The cop barricades were in place. A junior faculty member was in charge. He stopped us.

"No one admitted. The gates are closed." He sounded very official, smug, enjoying his power as gatekeeper.

"Do you know who I am?"

"Yes, Professor, but no one is to be admitted."

"I'm going through and he is coming with me."

The gatekeeper glanced nervously at the police a few feet away. Television lights lit the gates. "I can't, sir."

"Do you want tenure at this university?"

He let us through.

On College Walk, just before I darted up the steps toward Math, the professor grabbed my arm and stopped me. "Why, Dotson, why all this coming violence, this playing at revolution?"

I looked at him carefully. He had spoken with great sadness, almost out of defeat, and I was moved by the concern expressed in his voice. His face, the pain of it, reminded me of Lowell. "I guess because we are trying to make the world safe for our friends. At least I am. And I don't know any other way."

I ran up the steps. He called out behind me, "Protect yourself!"

The crowds of angry students were being shoved by cops away from Low Library to the steps of Earl Hall. They were militant and loud, shouting at the cops. The plainclothesmen had begun their deadly infiltration of the crowds, some of them dressed like students, carrying books. On College Walk cops were trooping onto campus, vans and paddy wagons lined from Kent to Dodge Halls. Over Alma Mater's head someone had fixed a sign that

198

read: RAPED BY THE COPS. I heard screaming in the distance and shouts that echoed through the quads across the lawns. The communes had begun to take up the defiant slogan, hurling it at the cops from the windows and roofs: UP AGAINST THE WALL MOTHERFUCKERS.

I stood on the grass in front of Math begging admission. The building was sealed. I shouted up to the windows, cupping my hands over my mouth, "I'm with you, Baby, all the way!" They shouted back encouragement.

I got in front of the Mathematics Building and leaned against the glass doors behind which tables and chairs and pathetic board barricades were built for defense. Only the barricades and the bodies of us before the door stood between the cops and the commune.

I stood before the doors, linking arms with four other young men, all of us frightened, all beginning to sweat. In front of us another line. And in front of that three professors, one with white hair, a tiny man. That was all the army of faculty—liberal, boasting that they would never allow the cops on their campus, we will stand by you, before you, behind you—that was all the army of faculty that bothered to appear before Math. We held each other's arms and waited. Hank, at the end of my line, started screaming hysterically at the cops as they came by the hundreds through the Earl Hall gates around the side of Math and another contingent came to us across from Low. As they assembled in long, tight lines before us, hundreds of them facing nine young men and three old men barring their entrance, as they grouped and waited, it seemed for hours, unmoving, the tension mounting, Hank yelled, "Motherfucking, cocksucking bastard cops! Fascists! Fascists!" over and over again. I glanced over at him and shrugged. His face was red, his hair wet with sweat. He had not shaved in five days and he looked tired and drawn. He was eighteen. And he looked utterly terrified and defiant and beautiful to me as he screamed his outrage against the fucking liberal world. The white-haired professor, after Hank had gone on for awhile, broke ranks and went up to him. "Son," he said quietly, his hand on his shoulder, "You're showing your fear. Calm yourself. We're all together. Those fascist animals will have to get through us to get to you. And I'll wear the bastards out." Hank quieted down.

I took out my contact lenses and put them in their case and shoved it in my pocket. I took off my tie to prevent strangulation. Then I waited with my friends while behind me, beguilingly, magnificently, my friends, those brave and sad young men, shouted into the night: UP AGAINST THE WALL MOTHERFUCKERS. The cry was taken up by other buildings and by the crowds and carried into the darkness.

A man in a tan trench coat stood about fifteen feet before us, and said into a bullhorn: "In the name of the Trustees of Columbia University I order you to leave. . . ."

They came at us fast and hard. The three professors were moved out quickly. Then the line of students in front of us folded quickly, some of them knocked to the ground. They were dragged away. Then the motherfuckers reached us. The boys at each end of the line braced themselves against the building. We held our arms tightly, legs spread, heads down. They kicked our legs and stomachs trying to make us break. We held for several minutes until the bastards took each of us by the hair and yanked us apart. I was thrown to the ground, kicked in the stomach, and then lifted by two plainclothesmen and thrown ten feet over the hedges onto the lawns. When I tried to get up they kicked me down. Two cops, each grabbing a leg, dragged me down the Earl Hall steps and ordered me to wait. Then Hank was dragged out. After a while we stood and ran down Broadway, the cops chasing us about a block. The motherfuckers.

While I was being pulled off campus the cops were making their way into the building, pulling the furniture out of the doorway and throwing it on the lawns. It took them fifteen minutes to clear the building; rope and hoses held the barricade in place. They were met by six boys sitting, arms locked, on the soaped stairs. They were arrested. Then Hayden and a few others were pulled out.

After the first floor was cleared, the cops went from room to room methodically axing down every door, smashing furniture and walls, beating kids, pulling them along the stone stairways face down, their heads leaving blood smeared like thin paint along the steps.

At 114th Street I climbed over the Ferris Booth gate and jumped back onto campus. Paddy wagons filled with students were being driven out College Walk, crowds of students on the lawns shouting their solidarity at the fucking cops: UP AGAINST THE WALL MOTHERFUCKERS!

The plainclothesmen started to clear South Field of thousands of students milling in rage, viciously driving them like frightened deer, trapping them between buildings and police, moving them in terror one way and then another, playing with them, dropping like animals on top of them when they fell—three, four plainclothes cops to each fallen student.

I was driven out of campus with the main contingent of students, several thousand of us running from the police to Broadway, there to be met by mounted police. The horsemen drove into us as we flooded into the street, crushing some of us against the gates and the sides of buildings.

I broke ranks and ran past a score of cops down Broadway to Furnald Hall. The French windows were open. I shouted, "I'm coming in!" and climbed the grating to the ledge and fell into the dormitory lounge, my ass being clubbed by a cop as I went inside. I saw Doug, a friend of mine, and we collected liquor from the rooms for the infirmaries in Philosophy and Ferris Booth Halls.

Then Doug and I climbed four flights and stood on the upper ledge of Furnald, the windows filled with angry students shouting at the fucking cops, and looked down Broadway, my chest constricted with anger and impotence, hating the cops and the goddamn administration and half-assed president and the cocksucking university itself, and hating—gloriously, patriotically, beautifully, cleanly—America. Hating her fucking cops and troopers and her ways and manners and indifference, her lack of human sentiment and kindness, her arrogance, her pious, *Christian* people who justified violence and spread death over the earth. Doug, his young, strong face contorted in anger, his body tense with outrage, started yelling obscenities at the cops. And I, hatred breaking me, joined his rage: UP AGAINST THE WALL MOTHERFUCKERS. ASSLICKING FASCIST FAGGOT COPS. PIMPS. GODDAMN CUNTEATING CORRUPT BASTARDS. My imagination dead, I clung to the epithet, "bastard," and hurled it monotonously, repetitively at the cops. We threw empty beer cans and lighted cigarettes down on them as they herded the terrified students up and down Broadway, allowing them no exit, whipping them with clubs, driving them into walls, making them fall again and again to be kicked and pommeled and arrested. I spit at them, shouted, hating them—and if I could I would have edged my ass over the avenue and dropped my hatred and my disgust on my America with her child-beating fascist cops and bloody, senseless wars, with her hypocritical, deadly leaders, her lack of compassion, her endless racism and inbred hatred, her balling, imperialist violence; America the violent, the disreputable, the outrageous, the incestuous land, devouring her children, feeding us bile and hunger for death; my unhappy America, my pathetic, bloody, stupid country, self-righteous and vicious, my evil land beating her sons and daughters, killing her young men in useless wars, exploiting her weak, making victims of the young and poor and powerless; my country, led by fools and ass-licking Company Men who terrorize the earth. America, how I hated you that night and how clean and good and redemptive that hatred was.

Around six thirty Tuesday morning I walked back inside of Mathematics. Empty. The floors and walls wet. I climbed the stairs. Blood smears on the walls. Broken glasses. Single shoes. Pieces of torn clothing. Bloody clumps of hair.

The place had been vandalized by the police. Ink thrown against the walls. Papers strewn everywhere. Furniture and doors and walls destroyed by axes and crowbars.

I went into the attic. "Who's there?" someone said. I stopped, standing under the light. "It's Dotson. I'm part of the Math commune."

Roger came out from behind a partition, his lunch bag in his hand. "God, you should have seen it. It was unbelievable. Oh, the fucking bastards, the bastards!"

"How did you escape?"

"I climbed out the window in the roof and hung over the side by my hands until they left. The fucking bastards. Somebody's got to pay for what they've done. Somebody's got to pay."

13 / Pride and Prejudice: The City College Crisis

LEO HAMALIAN
and JAMES V. HATCH

City College is what New York is all about.

To paraphrase Charles Dickens, these were the best of times in education, and these were the worst of times—the worst because of the many complex problems that new conditions had generated, but the best because these same new conditions offered the hope of a great future. Major modifications in social and educational institutions generally are accomplished, like childbirth, only with risk and pain.

MILTON SCHWEBEL, *Who Can Be Educated?*

Situated in the soul of Spanish Harlem, P.S. 7 was melting under 100-degree temperatures, waiting for the Memorial Day vacation to begin. The teacher looked at her fifth grade class of black and Puerto Rican children. How could she give the social studies lesson a sense of immediacy and involvement for them? She suggested "role playing" in socio-dramas.

For the first impromptu play, the kids chose to dramatize the confrontation taking place at City College between the black and Puerto Rican students (known as the "Coalition") and the "white man" who ran the college. The teacher would play "the man"

SOURCE: A shorter version of this essay appeared in *Ararat*, Summer 1969.

Leo Hamalian teaches at the City College of New York and is the author and editor of several books, including *Ten Modern Short Novels* (with E. Volpe); he is currently working on a book about D. H. Lawrence in Italy.

James V. Hatch taught film-making at UCLA and in Cairo before joining the English Department of the City College of New York. His play *Fly Blackbird!* won an Obie award in 1961, and his latest book, *The Image of the Negro in American Drama*, grew out of his course in the black theater.

and the kids would pretend to be the dissident Black and Puerto Rican Coalition.

"Why do you want to attend school here?" began the "white man."

"To git a better education," the kids parroted.

"What does that mean? Explain yourselves," responded the "white man."

"We wanna go to school. We just wanna go to school." The kids were uncertain about the benefits of advanced education.

Now the teacher reversed the roles. She took the part of the black and Puerto Rican students at City College while the kids became "the man."

"Let me in your college," demanded the teacher.

"Whut for?" asked the "white man" in unison.

"So I can train myself to be a teacher, or a social worker, or a doctor, or a lawyer, or a psychologist and earn more money and live in a nice apartment."

"No! No! No!" answered the "white man" in emphatic chorus.

"Why won't you let me in?" asked the "Coalition."

"'Cause if we do, you riot, you keep us folks out."

"I won't riot. I want to learn. I want . . ." said the "Coalition."

"Yeah, man," interrupted one of the "white men." "You riot. You lazy, you stupid. And you run 'round when you s'pose to be in class." Shouted another "white man," "Yeah, you in trouble. You got no brains. Go 'way and leave us 'lone."

This mini-drama at P.S. 7 reflected the polarities of the larger educational drama that was being enacted a few blocks away at the City College: the Black and Puerto Rican Student Coalition had locked the gates of the South Campus for almost a month while the faculty and administration of the college, the Board of Higher Education of the City University of New York, and "law-and-order" politicians improvised dialogue and melodrama in a *Lehrstücke* which an observant sociologist might have entitled "The Crisis of Rising Aspirations."

And improvisation was the key word—for the situation was unlike previous college disturbances at Berkeley, Columbia, Harvard, and Cornell. The City College was established as a free academy in 1847 to provide educational opportunity for anyone with a diploma from a city high school. But as the free tuition clause strongly implied, it would and did evolve into a college which was, by the twenties, educating city students who could not afford to attend Columbia, New York University, or schools out of town. The applicants were chiefly children of immigrant parents who for the most part had little formal education themselves. The City College degree became a prestigious passport to a middle-class career.

But there are, further, equally significant differences. The City College is a purely tax-supported institution, without endowment, located in the heart of Harlem. The rebels were not members of the SDS (although SDS took up the cause); for the most part, they were enrolled students seeking an education which would permit them to join—not to destroy—the Establishment. Indeed, the essence of their demands was simple: that more blacks and Puerto Ricans be allowed to compete for the precious degrees that have become the "open sesame" to American affluence. Finally, the "revolution" was not an impulsive act of anarchy, but the result of a long series of frustrated requests.

In November of 1968, about five months prior to the lock-out, five members of the Du Bois Club[1] appeared in Dr. Buell Gallagher's office with a petition entitled "End Racism at CCNY." Signed by 1600 students and endorsed by the Student Government and the Christian Association (among others), the petition culminated a study the group had conducted that spring, criticizing CUNY's master plan, which proposed open enrollment for all New York City high school graduates but not until 1975, seven years off. The critique charged that in setting up a three-tiered system of senior colleges, community colleges, and educational skills centers, the university would perpetuate a tracking process that discouraged non-whites from pursuing academic diplomas first in high school and then in college, the first discouragement resulting in the second. The key demands were two: "that the racial composition of all future entering classes reflect that of the high school graduating class in New York City" and "that enough new colleges be built within the next two years in New York City to accommodate all students who graduate from high school." Dr. Gallagher responded to these demands in a three-page statement disputing the accusations of

[1] The W.E.B. Du Bois Club is a Marxist, largely white organization with a nation-wide membership.

racism and arguing that the city was doing all it could to meet the most plausible of the demands. The confrontation ended at this point.

Between that November and the following January, a group calling itself The Committee of Ten prepared its own analysis of conditions at City College and a set of demands, similar to those of the Du Bois people, which were to be presented to the administration. On February 6, 1969, the first day of spring classes, members of The Committee of Ten and a group of supporters (who later became the nucleus of the Black and Puerto Rican Coalition, the name by which the occupants of the campus would be known) pushed their way into Dr. Gallagher's office with their bill of particulars. Dr. Gallagher was still on vacation and the irritated visitors presented their demands to his surprised administrative assistants, pinning extra copies to the walls of the administrative offices. These demands were as follows:

1. A separate school of black and Puerto Rican studies.

2. A separate orientation program for BPR freshmen.

3. A voice for students in SEEK (the pre-college preparatory program) in setting guidelines for the program, including a voice in the hiring and firing of the personnel.

4. Starting in September 1969 the racial composition of entering classes to reflect the black and Puerto Rican population of the city's high schools.

5. BPR history and Spanish language as a requirement for all education majors.

The Coalition circulated its demands in mimeographed form and mounted a campaign for faculty and student support. A small group of instructors, calling itself The Faculty for Action, held a series of meetings to study the grievances on which the demands were based while the English department was hiring a specialist who was to create a program of ethnic studies. But aside from these responses, few faculty members or administrators understood what the Coalition was talking about and few took the trouble to find out. The Coalition, which had given tender of its intention by briefly occupying the administration building in mid-February, continued to call for action on its demands, but Dr. Gallagher urged them to be patient. The dissidents, furious with what they termed "the old buck-passing game," issued a warning which went unnoticed: "If our demands are not met, we have no choice but to move into the next stage of the struggle."

In March, The Faculty for Action put out a position paper which concluded, after weeks of study, that the BPRC demands were based on genuine grievances. This statement from a group of very junior faculty caused a magnificent lack of stir among the more senior staff, and what desultory discussion the report managed to provoke was soon overshadowed by the momentous monetary decisions pending in Albany. Then, one rainy Tuesday morning in April, the Coalition decided to act: a group of militants seized the South Campus, barred the gates, and established "The University of Harlem" (several local cabbies still refer to the college by that name). Behind the iron gates on Convent Avenue, impassive black faces told the debarred faculty and students, "School is closed until our demands are met." When the shock wore off, the faculty did what it does best: it met. A hurried impromptu gathering of the Faculty Council of the College of Liberal Arts and Sciences yielded not only confused but angry rhetoric. What did the BPRC want? When one of the authors of this article suggested that a faculty delegate be dispatched immediately to find out, the suggestion was shouted down with irrelevant cries of "No appeasement!" All classes, except on the unaffected engineering campus, ceased for that day.

On Wednesday morning, a substantial number of faculty and students convened in the gothic Great Hall to conduct a "rational dialogue" about the demands. Invited by the self-appointed chairman of the meeting, Professor Bernie Bellush, a delegation from the BPRC marched into Great Hall and occupied the platform, the green, red, and black banner of "liberation" waving beside the Puerto Rican star and stripes. Their statements to the faculty were terse and shocking: Here are our demands! This is why they are just! They must be met before the campus can be opened again. A Che-costumed spokesman rasped into the microphone, "No more bullshit, you motherfuckers. We've had enough hypocrisy. You say one thing, you do another. That's all over." The delegation raised their fists in salute, glared defiantly at the bewildered but by now angry assembly, and marched out in crisp order, chanting "Power to the people!" A woman member of the faculty was heard to whisper indignantly, "Someone

LEO HAMALIAN and JAMES V. HATCH 207

should wash their mouths with soap." That comment caused some agitated discussion and nearly everyone deplored the tactics of disruption.

The Coalition returned behind the barricades at the South Campus, and there awaited the next move of "the man." Back at Great Hall, the faculty, by now completely demoralized by the explosion of events, jawed away indecisively. Many of the faculty wanted to follow the advice of the college ombudsman—to call the police on campus immediately—among them several professors with reputations as "liberals." One faculty member arose to tell the assembly that it was time to "call a spade a spade" and another likened the BPRC to Nazi storm-troopers. The ploy of labeling the oppressed the oppressors was cheered by a sizable faction of the faculty. The "moderates" insisted that the issues had been infected by "terrorist tactics." Other faculty used the occasion to inform their colleagues how much and for how long they had loved their black brothers. Meanwhile, one faculty member had persuaded the dean of the college and then the president himself to meet with the Coalition for talks. At first the Coalition distrusted the president, whom they felt had been very "slippery," but they agreed to meet with him and a team of three faculty-elected "observers" to "negotiate." For the next two weeks, the "opponents" met daily with the aim of hammering out an agreement. Daily the faculty and the students met to ask themselves whether police shouldn't be called to open the campus, whether the minority had the "right" to shut down the school, whether term papers could be completed by deadlines now that the library was unavailable.

Engineering students counter-demanded that classes be conducted on the North Campus, and many were held (liberal arts students met in the homes of some professors or in their own apartments). A resolution of the issues seemed near when Mario Procaccino, an alumnus running for mayor of New York City, obtained an injunction to force President Gallagher into opening the campus. Apparently Mr. Procaccino did not bother to find out that the president and his team of "negotiators" (formerly "observers") had reached accord with the BPRC on three of the demands and were making progress on the other two. It had been agreed by all negotiators, among them Joseph Copeland, that the campus would remain closed until negotiations were completed—perhaps for another day or two.

When the campus was opened by police, the negotiations ceased and the Coalition marched off the South Campus, flags flying, heads high. For the rebels, the agreement had been breached, faith had been broken. The importance of this event cannot be underestimated: it indicated to the BPRC—and a number of sympathetic but inactive students—that the president and his negotiators lacked either integrity or the power to make decisions, and at best, could no longer be taken seriously. An inspection of property revealed about $70,000 worth of damage—this is an administration estimate. Offices had been occupied, desks converted into beds, and several thousand dollars' worth of slides and films on black art taken from the art library. The campus radio station sustained about $3000 worth of damage, but it is not certain who was responsible for it.

When the Board of Higher Education (BHE) announced that negotiations would begin afresh with a different team of faculty negotiators, presumably less friendly to the black cause, the BPRC (with help from the Commune) began a series of disruptions on campus—noise in the halls during class hours, raids on the cafeteria and the bookstore. Fights broke out among students; one or two faculty-student scuffles were reported; several blacks were arrested. A strike was proclaimed by dissident students and faculty. The faculty met and debated and talked and discussed and orated and asked for "law and order," meaning by that phrase exactly what any redneck means by it.

The black and Puerto Rican faculty announced that they would "refuse to participate in the academic life of CCNY until negotiations resumed at the point from which they were broken off." Fifty white teachers sent a telegram protesting the BHE action and that week formed a picket line outside the college in support of the student demands.

More than two hundred policemen appeared Thursday morning to keep the school operating "as usual." Tension was thick and the blacks' rage could be felt and heard. The students serenaded the police: "Ol' MacDonald had a farm/Ee-ei, ee-ei, O/ And on his farm he had some pigs/Ei-ei, ee-ei, O/ A honk-honk here, a honk-honk there, here a honk, there a honk . . . ."

Eleven fires of "suspicious origin" burst out, including the costly one which destroyed Aronow Auditorium in Finley Student Center, rechristened Che Guevara Hall by the BPRC. Outside of the stone walls and iron picket fences that isolate City

College from West Harlem, hundreds of blacks moved in anger. In their eyes, the Establishment had declared war by opening the campus forcibly during negotiations despite signed agreements not to, by throwing out agreements already prepared for consideration of the faculty, and by summoning the police.

The Faculty Senate voted to hold a "convocation" that would in effect take the place of classes. The BHE voted to keep all classes in regular session. President Gallagher, who had resigned earlier in the year over another issue, resigned a second time. The associate dean of student life, James Peace, declared that he "had had it" and also resigned. Somewhat later, so did his boss, Dean of Students Nicholas Paster, who as an administrator sympathetic with the blacks and Puerto Ricans, found himself split down the middle. Riot-helmeted cops checked the ID cards of students who braved the news broadcasts to attend classes that Friday. One of the original negotiators, Joseph Copeland, a teacher of biology and the chairman of the local chapter of the Legislative Conference,[2] was appointed acting president, the police were withdrawn, a sparsely-attended "convocation" was held to air the issues, and classes were somberly or randomly resumed. (Some teachers, told that one or two of their colleagues had been threatened or roughed up, refused to come to the campus, a direct dereliction of duty.)

The semester dribbled to an end. The Faculty Senate met almost daily, often only after waiting hours for a quorum to assemble—some senators were meeting classes to make up missed work, some simply never showed up, and others boycotted the sessions.[3] At times the debate became so harrowingly intricate and involuted that even the senate parliamentarian had to improvise interpretations of Roberts' rules of order. With a number of old-line "liberals" in the van, the senate brushed one demand aside and modified three of the negotiated agreements to the point of emasculation. During one of the sessions,

---

[2] The Legislative Conference is a professors' union at the City University that has no affiliations (unlike the United Federation of College Teachers) with any organization outside of the university. It is regarded by some of its membership as well as its opponents as a conservative body.

[3] The Faculty Senate, which had been in the process of formation, was called into being during the turmoil. On a technicality, some members of the faculty, lead by the present chairman of the history department, alleged that the Faculty Senate was not a legally constituted body. Even the BPRC did not take his accusation seriously.

the acting president told the senate that he had sent the Mc-Clellan Committee the names of the students involved in the demonstrations and a list of faculty advisers of certain organizations suspected of fomenting demonstrations. The senate censured the acting president for cooperating without first consulting the senate.

To avoid the possibility of further trouble, commencement was held at Madison Square Garden. When Acting President Copeland equated black "extremists" with the Ku Klux Klan, a number of graduating black and Puerto Rican students got up and walked out of the ceremonies in protest—perhaps the first time this has happened in the history of the college. During that summer (1969), the BHE voted to set September of 1970 (instead of 1975) as the target date for open enrollment at the City University. This decision, according to Chancellor Bowker, will mean that "every June 1970 graduate of a New York City high school who wants to attend City University will be admitted and given a genuine opportunity to advance toward a degree."

Translated into statistics of enrollment, in September of 1970, this move created a freshmen class at CCNY of well over 3000 students compared to the previous year's 2200. For classroom space, the unprepared college had to rent make-shift facilities. On a city-wide level, CUNY admitted about 19,000 freshmen to its senior colleges and about 17,000 to its community colleges. Who went where was decided on the basis of class rank: half of any graduating class or anyone who earned a grade average of 80 percent was admitted to the senior colleges; the remainder are attending the two-year colleges, where, if they do well, they will become eligible for admission to the senior colleges. In effect, this plan will give seniors at heavily black and Puerto Rican high schools a chance to attend City College. Ironically, blacks and Puerto Ricans at the "integrated" high schools may find themselves shut out of the senior colleges if they happen to be in the lower 50 percent of their class.

In general, the faculty at City College has slowly swung behind the BHE's plan—according to a student newspaper poll, 54.1 percent are in favor of it, 40.5 percent against it. Students, however, are a bit more skeptical: 58.3 percent opposed the open admissions formula. The chancellor has assured those who fear that City College's high standards might be jeopardized that "we are committed to enhancing, not eroding, the academic standards."

Nevertheless, some people continue to ask, "How is it possible to have a good school if you lower standards and allow anyone to enter?" Those who have the interests of the college at heart might feel that the college is being conned into submitting to its own destruction, making itself its own executioner. A careful examination of these demands should reveal whether such fears are justified or not, whether these fears are a resistance to change rather than a resistance to chaos. Thus far, hardly anyone has troubled to correct the misimpressions that shroud the truth and which members of the faculty circulated in their effort to have Mario Procaccino elected mayor of New York in the campaign of 1969.

The fifth demand, clear and uncomplicated next to the others, was adopted by the School of Education faculty almost as soon as it was reiterated by the BPRC in April. Starting in September of 1969, black and Puerto Rican history and the Spanish language will be required of all prospective teachers. The advantages of such preparation are obvious in a city increasingly bilingual and biracial, especially as community participation in decentralized schools brings parents and teachers into closer touch.

The rationale for the other demands may be less obvious. A separate program of orientation (demand two) is needed, according to spokesmen for the Coalition, because blacks and Puerto Ricans are beginning to recognize that they know almost nothing about the "rules of academic survival"—they have been too busy learning the rules of survival that apply to the grim streets of the ghettos. When they reach college, they want to know about the tactics of survival in the new, strange environment— how to study, how to choose a career, how to drop a course without academic penalty,[4] how to get a loan that may make the difference between staying in school and dropping out, how to compete in a game in which the player sets his own pace. Last

---

[4] The part that faculty "in-breeding" plays has not been yet assessed, but it seems likely that the City College faculty, with a large percentage of its own undergraduates serving on the other side of the desk, is more prone to resist change than a college faculty developed on a less parochial principle. This is not in any way a statement about ability; it is only natural that alumni should wish to preserve a place they regard with affection.

year, one SEEK student said to one of the authors, "Man, all these cats in a room, sitting still, listening to the beard talk, writing down notes, not moving for almost an hour. Wow!" A typical white student will have been exposed to these "facts" of academic life through his parents or his guidance counselors or through his friends who have already acquired this wisdom by experience. Cut off from middle-class "informants," blacks and Puerto Ricans enter college at a subtle disadvantage, one that cannot be quantified on record cards or computer statistics. Now they want this kind of awareness offered to them in concentrated form structured with their particular problems in view. And above all, they want some sense of their own identity. If they succeed in entering the ranks of middle-class America, does it mean they must cease to be "black" in feeling? What does "black" mean anyway, aside from pigmentation? Does the prospect of integration mean the loss of whatever old identity they have brought with them from their respective "ghettos"? These are living questions that must be asked and answered before the learning process can take hold at the root of being.

Those who opposed the demand for black and Puerto Rican orientation insisted that an orientation program taught by black counselors to black students would create, so to speak, Panthers at the gates. The program would be politicized and would transform students into militants and the campus into a training ground for revolutionists. The students themselves laugh at these fears: they point out that no one will be required to take BPR orientation, nor will interested whites be debarred from the classes. Several faculty thought that acceding to this demand would mean that Sardinian, Armenian, Chinese, Greek, and Italian students would be soon asking for special orientation programs. No one from these ethnic minorities came forward to validate the faculty claim. As things stand now, freshmen who indicate that they want special sections of orientation will receive instruction from the regular staff. Presumably white instructors will be teaching black and Puerto Rican students about their own history and culture.

The original demand for a School of Black and Puerto Rican Studies, after negotiations, was modified to a plan for a School of Urban and Third World Studies. Three arguments have been advanced by the proponents of the plan:

1. "Ghetto" and urban problems have received relatively little attention at universities, and even less at a college that daily faces the downshot of such uncalculated indifference. How can better housing be planned? Financed? How can parents be stimulated to take interest in the education of their children? How can drug addiction be avoided or cured? How can the community create its own culture and encourage its own artists? If the institutions of higher learning will not devote a share of their energy and intellect to such questions, who, asks the BPRC, can be expected to do so? In effect, the BPRC is facing the City College with a crisis of conscience by asking it to recognize the community in which it exists.

2. Such a school, at City and perhaps elsewhere, would assemble under a single rubric a number of courses presently distributed throughout the curriculum. A student may now take an interdisciplinary major in Third World Studies if he wishes, but he would have to know that Swahili is offered only in the evening session, Japanese in the history department, Arabic (and soon Chinese) in the classics department, Hispanic culture of Latin America by romance languages. Black drama is given in the English department, the Middle East under Islam in history, and so on. The curriculum would gain in clarity and coordination at a point where it is sorely lacking. And like City College, probably most large universities suffering from expansion fever could benefit from the creation of a discipline that would define a new and vital program of studies pertaining to the lives of more than 30,000,000 American citizens. If we can spend hours studying a battle fought on the Dardanelles peninsula thousands of years ago simply because it was celebrated by a blind Greek bard, then we should not begrudge the time that might be given to the study of the epic of the black man in America, how he came here in bondage, how he gained his freedom, and how he survived the scars of that slavery. The history and the poetry of this epic struggle have always been slighted on the soil where it was waged and won. How do we excuse this oversight?

3. The languages, culture, and history of Latin America, Africa, and Asia (the so-called Third World) are a growingly significant part of our political and economic reality. There must be a deeper investment in such studies, instead of the tokenism we have had, before their academic value can be demonstrated.

There must be money for faculty, for facilities, for scholarships as in any other school of special purpose. And no doubt this program can serve in the area of ideas rather than action, much like the degree-granting School of International Affairs at Columbia. In turn, these ideas would have pragmatic consequences: with greater concentration in these areas at more universities, we would have trained people who could help arrest the loss of the Third World to forces which have in the past benefited from our ignorance or our implicit arrogance when confronted by Third World issues. At present, few BPR students are thinking in such ambitious terms, but it would seem axiomatic that administrators (and/or faculty) are paid to foresee and develop such possibilities.

Several misconceptions should be scotched here. First, in the plan there was no intention of restricting the enrollment to black and Puerto Rican students only—as the opponents repeatedly and erroneously charged throughout the brief discussions of the proposal. Many white students, the negotiators hoped, would soon discern the academic advantages of a good Third World program on the undergraduate level, especially in preparing them for careers in the diplomatic service or in international commerce—without the necessity of attending graduate school (the school would have been degree-granting). Second, the student planning to major in these studies would have to complete the core curriculum courses required of every student in the College of Liberal Arts and Sciences. Again, though this was reiterated, opponents of the proposal charged that the school was intended to grant cheap degrees to students who could not meet the requirements of the college. Finally, the curriculum would not have been composed of "soul courses," as Bayard Rustin and some faculty seemed to fear (Rustin's remark that such courses are "worth nothing in the real world" has been characterized by Dr. Thomas Billings, the former director of Upward Bound, as an "unfortunate, insensitive, and foolish" response to black and Puerto Rican cultural aspirations). If the City University is willing to provide funds for a School of Nursing and for a School of Police Science, then a School of Urban and Third World Studies hardly seems to its advocates to be a wild and impractical proposal. But the Faculty Senate thought that it was, and despite a severely curtailed and confused discussion of the issue (about two hours in total, during which one faculty senator asked, "What in the hell is the Third World anyway?"), it voted to send the proposal to committee—a favorite stalling tactic of faculties everywhere. Two weeks later, the Ford Foundation announced that it was giving more than a million dollars for the advancement of such studies to fifteen colleges and universities. Of course, this meant institutions that had already signified a willingness to undertake such an experiment without endless "studies" and "reports." Brooklyn College, reputedly less progressive than her older sister college with the reputation for "liberalism," received funds to start a summer program in Afro-American studies, while City College, a white enclave in the middle of Harlem, was left out in the cold. For a school beset with financial problems, City could ill afford to fumble away this chance to get foundation funds for something it must do in time anyway. As things stand, the college has a department of ethnic studies made up of two faculty members, one a former army chaplain and civil-rights advocate. More courses will be offered in the spring in addition to the two courses offered this fall. For the outside observer, there may seem to be little difference between what the BPRC asked for and what it got, but shrinking a school down to a department, in effect, emasculated the BPRC demand. A school would have its own dean, its own appointments procedure, its own faculty, its own curriculum, just as the School of Nursing or the School of Police Science has. A department at a school like the City College is subject to control in all these areas: its courses must be approved by a college committee, its promotions and policies reviewed by the administration before they can be exercised. In fact, the number of courses it can offer is subject to committee control (Curriculum and Teaching). Perhaps this is the status that Urban and Third World Studies should have—who knows for certain?—but it is a far cry from what the students of the Coalition would like. One wonders whether the BHE can disregard their wishes with impunity.

The third demand means the creation of a separate department of pre-baccalaureate studies (college preparatory courses of sufficient difficulty and sophistication that the student receives college credit for them). Such a department would be co-equal with others in the college, with its own chairman and its own tenure rules. At present, services for these students—curricular and psychological counseling, special courses in speech, writing, math, and foreign languages—are scattered over the campus. Both the students and the faculty of this program want these courses and services coordinated under coherent direction. If this were done, both the students and faculty of this new department would have something to say—at present they do not—about the selection and retention of faculty. They argue that they need teachers who understand what is going on in the head of a student scarred by years of discrimination, who know how to communicate with him. The students already in the program believe that as voting "consumers" they can help to improve the quality of what is being offered to them. The faculty recommendation that the Pre-Bac program become a department in the college, with student participation in the departmental curriculum committee, sidestepped the implications of the demand; the action by the BHE further watered down the ambiguous faculty recommendation. To the BPRC, this seemed like a blatant vitiation of student input on the most vital issue facing the program.

But the main issue was "open enrollment," promised by the CUNY master plan by 1975. The BPRC originally demanded a racial composition among the 1969 freshmen that would reflect the black and Puerto Rican population of the city high schools, a proportion they set at 60 percent BPR and 40 percent white. The negotiators worked out an arrangement whereby the entering class of 1970 would be made up of 60 percent of students chosen by normal competitive standards and 40 percent by special criteria. In supporting this dual-track proposal (which was shot down by charges of "quota system"), the BPRC asserted that guidance counselors in the high schools often steered black and Puerto Rican students toward the manual trades, toward terminal (two-year) programs at already crowded community colleges, or toward preparation for more menial employment, on the assumption that these students had been "crippled" beyond redemption by their unfortunate circumstances.

The BPRC believes that their own record of survival at City College proves the error of the last assumption (some faculty maintain that black and Puerto Rican students get preferential treatment in grades because most teachers bend over backwards to be fair). Once the doors of the college are open to them, they see new hope, new incentive, new aspirations possible for junior and senior high school students presently excluded *de facto* from the senior colleges (private colleges are too expensive for most black and Puerto Rican families unless full scholarships are granted to their children). Therefore, argues the BPRC, black and Puerto Rican students have little motivation to master such academic courses as French, geometry, or chemistry. When black and Puerto Rican students in high school have the vision of joining the mainstream of American life, a vision created by the feed-back from their older brothers in college, they will move toward it in the same manner as did the children of immigrants years ago who, knowing that the road from log cabin to presidency was open, aspired toward early academic success. Along with many respectable educational psychologists, the BPRC contends that motivation and potential, no less than the high school scholastic record, are reliable barometers of later academic success.

The last argument, radical at the core, is the crux of the contention. According to a study conducted recently in East St. Louis, a quality called "hipness" for the lack of a better term— the ability of a youngster to survive in the slums without getting "hooked"—may be an indication of educational potential. With massive supportive services, many such youngsters are performing passingly well in college. The success of Upward Bound with "hip" students is now being documented. About 80 percent of the Upward Bound students (52 percent black, 30 percent white, 18 percent Indian, Spanish-American, and other minority groups) were graduated from high school and went on to college. The number who stayed in college are near the national average—65 percent by their junior year, as against 67 percent for all American college students. A study conducted at City College in 1967 demonstrated very little correlation between composite scores used to determine admission and success during the freshman year at college.

With a horrible reflex to turn every experience into a "learning process," many professors are asking themselves what lessons can be learned from the recent events on Convent Avenue. There are several, but the following seem to us the most significant. If they seem obvious by now to those who have been tried by fire, they nevertheless need emphasis.

Traditional concepts of academia must give way to new "hard" information provided by social scientists and research psychologists, information about learning processes that must necessarily affect our pedagogical values. We may discover that the nebulous term "intelligence" may be measured in new ways and that the particular kind of intelligence and organization required to succeed in college courses may not always be reflected in high school performance, especially when grading in high school means less than it once did. The planning and strategy that went into the seizure of the campus reveals a capacity for discipline and organization that might be transferred to the way one tackles his courses. The BPRC outwitted the faculty and administration at almost every turn of the confrontation, anticipated their moves, took every precaution to avoid a bust or disorderly conduct, and maintained themselves in a state of self-imposed siege for almost two weeks. They even smelled out and expelled the informer "Broadway" from their midst. This much seems clear: if students with this kind of resourcefulness, intuition, and discipline cannot succeed in college, then perhaps we should examine the academic process and its assumptions rather than the student. Unless such information is taken into account *swiftly,* we may again in the future be treated to the spectacle of citizens fighting to be admitted to school and educators stalling to keep them out.

Higher education at the urban college can no longer ignore the community around it, any more than a neighborhood elementary or secondary school can do so (this argument does not mean that the college therefore must become a neighborhood or community college). For years the City College has pretended that the community does not exist. For instance, the students and faculty descend daily upon the neighborhood and absorb the parking space for blocks around, from 8 A.M. to 11 P.M. In this small gesture, we reveal unconsciously how we regard the community. There is no malice, no evil, no wickedness in this behavior (both authors have been guilty on occasion). It is simply a failure to be aware of others' rights; it is thoughtless insistence upon privilege based upon habit. Two swimming pools on the campus are closed to the community during the weekends, when students are not using them. Black youngsters watch white youngsters, many from Queens and Staten Island, use tennis courts forbidden to them. Most faculty drive in from Westchester, New Jersey, Long Island, and Greenwich Village. A "briefcase" faculty can hardly be expected to care very deeply about a community not its own. Students who commute to classes are similarly unconcerned with conditions beyond their academic compound. Despite this failure of imagination, we find it easy to call upon "riotous" students to show awareness of the needs and wishes of others.

It has been argued that the college cannot grapple with the overwhelming problems of the community because they are beyond the ken and competence of scholars and educators untrained in social work. But during the "occupation" some of us learned that we cannot hope to exist, *merely exist*, unless we are willing to fumble, bumble, and stumble towards some recognition that City College can no longer be a largely white enclave within a black community. The City College campus is a big piece of public real estate in the midst of Harlem. Black and Puerto Rican people pay taxes to help maintain it. We must accept these facts and must decide what they mean in determining our degree of responsibility to these citizens. Men with minds good enough to operate bubble-chambers or to criticize the Keynesian theory of money should have the ability to adapt themselves to the new realities emerging in a changing city.

Educators should make no mistake—organizations like the BPRC are not asking faculty to be "social workers" (a term of sarcasm used by faculty to describe other faculty willing to spend time teaching black and Puerto Rican classes): they want their faculty to teach at the top of its capacity, to move them, to challenge them, to enlighten them about the intellectual treasures of Western civilization, and to put these treasures under fresh scrutiny in the light of Third World cultures. They also want to know about their own past from people who are trained in the truth about that history, not in the mythology of white supremacy. They want to discover the unique character of their own cultural roots. If there is any unsoundness here, it may not be in the request, but in the response to it.

In the face of racial rage and fury born of frustration seething for years, the rhetoric of liberal and conservative alike is correct, reasonable, and *really* irrelevant unless it is coupled with activism (or whatever people who shy away from that word use for a synonym). The person who publicly praises black aspirations and then refuses to move when genuine action is required lives in a "word bag." He is isolated in ivory. He is like the image on the TV screen with the sound turned off. We must simply evolve new ways to respond to crisis or else live under the permanent condition of crisis. No longer do the answers lie in temporizing, in committee-creating, in amending amendments. In fact, Roberts' rules of order, which give extraordinary power to "parliamentarians" may be self-defeating, and the entire parliamentary approach to crisis, no matter how noble an idea, may be anachronistic. The professional ego, developed over years of expostulating before captive audiences, must seek alternatives to insisting upon points of privilege while the college is burning down. For ordinary affairs, ordinary methods may work, but for emergencies, emergency methods must be devised—the rawest intern knows this.

For instance, there should be a permanent task-force of students and faculty, operating as an ombudsman team, authorized to take immediate and direct action calculated to avoid such crises. Such a force should accept advice from the Faculty Senate and the administration, but ultimately be answerable to neither of them (red-tape and procedural matters might defeat the purpose of the idea). When its decisions prove wrong, a new team should be chosen by the faculty. If necessary, the faculty member might be compensated for his efforts and the student members given course credit for reporting the unit's activities. Such a task-force would be trained to recognize something that most students know instinctively: student complaints and grievances are an early warning system, a sort of radar that lets us know what is coming over the horizon; they should not be dismissed airily as "gripes" or symptoms of adolescent rebellion. The BPRC demonstrated once and for all the dangers of such adult smugness.

Furthermore, a governing body made up of eighty-two faculty members may be too unwieldy for dealing with crisis. And what of multiversities whose faculties number thousands! Here the example of the BPRC may be illuminating. In planning their strategy, they broke up into small groups or "cells"; each group decided upon a course of action, then the leaders of each group came together and arrived at decisions that were returned to the groups for approval. In this procedure, *everyone* gets a chance to be heard quickly and the unit becomes manageable. Any good teacher knows how difficult it is to have discussion in groups of eighty. When decisions must be made without too much delay, the numbers prove to be deadly. Four units of twenty people each (of whom fifteen would appear regularly), each with a chairman who scans for the sense of the group, might be a measure for meeting the crises which threaten to become a semipermanent part of college life unless we can neutralize the factors that cause them.

More than a year after the turmoil began, we are beginning to realize that the failure of communication and action on all levels—student, faculty, administration, BHE—has been shattering. The longer the paralysis lasted, the worse the condition became. Now we can write a formula for failure: communications gap plus crisis plus duration equals escalation (when the faculty and the administration did not respond to their demands, the BPRC broadened the terms of two of them). Escalation leads to violence and violence to bitter polarization. By now this pattern has become classic. The inability of either the faculty or the administration to act effectively, the repeated disregard of their wishes by the Board of Higher Education, and the political pressures on the BHE, suggest that the time has come to decentralize the anonymous multiversity called CUNY. The problems of the City College are different from those of a largely suburban school such as Queens College or Richmond, and it must have the maximum autonomy to resolve them as the faculty, the students, the administration, and the community see fit. The sense of impersonality can be disastrous, as educators should have learned after studying the repeated explosions on the campus of another multiversity, the University of California at Berkeley.

Even though this narrative and analysis of the City College crisis are but the bare bones of a complex situation, the full details of which will not be known until some Ph.D. student digs them out, one thing does seem clear and incontestable. When the elements of race and poverty are added to the normal student pressures for change at the university, the urban colleges are on the spot: if they hope to avoid locked gates, political exploitation, racial polarization, bloodshed, and faculty factions, they must develop methods of communication and change which do not now exist.

But like the smog, the crucial question still hovers over the campus (and perhaps others in similar settings): can the Grand Tradition of the university as a Community of Scholars dedicated to free inquiry be "sold" to the dispossessed? The dispossessed see the Grand Tradition with its emphasis on elimination through competition as an analogue of the Grand Tradition of Competitive Capitalism which has given them relatively little. The dispossessed recognize the university in one of its unconscious roles—a foremost dispenser of power and privilege. That it also encourages the Search for Truth matters little to these dispossessed when the Truth is used to further deprive them. Witness the black feeling about our landing on the moon.

Now that commercial and residential demands on the city are increasing, space grows more costly. Those who have it become even more apprehensive about the darker hordes who press upon their parks, their streets, their apartments, their children's free higher education. After every campus demonstration, these minds find more accommodation with the logic of repression, find a greater reluctance to bestow the university's mantle of power and privilege upon dark-skinned citizens—especially when some black faces question the basic internal contradictions of competitive capitalism (that some must fail so that others may succeed: the infamous bell curve for grading eliminates the "unfit" with a righteousness that would make Herbert Spencer smile).

As pressures of aspiration drive each man to a greater struggle with his neighbor for the space available at the free university of New York City, the arguments for class and racial privilege will gain in cogency. The old magic vocabulary of "equal opportunity," "free education for all," "democratic process," etc. will be preserved, but subtly the terms may be reinterpreted to mean, "Some folks gotta fall by the wayside . . . but it won't be my kids." In face of rising opposition to black ambitions,[5] the City University may be forced to defend its "standards of excellence"—a

[5] Contributions to the City College Fund from the alumni fell off to almost nothing in May, immediately after the black rebellion; after that ominous decline, they are back to normal.

term that many a cynic regards as the intellectual's synonym for the "survival of the fittest."

The BHE's decision to establish open enrollment in 1970 should mean that BPR students will have the chance to compete in the Grand Tradition at the city colleges. But the terms of the board's decision must be spelled out in dollars, facilities, and staff; until then we will not know whether the university, its faculties, and administration can be brought to tolerate a campus populated by the same kind of people who live beyond the college gates or who serve its present population. And only in time will we know whether the taxpayers will protest against the heavy taxation necessary to implement such decisions. *Real democracy, we are finding out, costs dear.*

14 / Berkeley: The Battle of People's Park

SHELDON WOLIN and JOHN SCHAAR

Shortly before 5:00 A.M., on Thursday, May 16, a motley group of about fifty hippies and "street-people" were huddled together on a lot 270 x 450 feet in Berkeley. The lot was owned by the Regents of the University of California and located a few blocks south of the Berkeley campus. Since mid-April this lot had been taken over and transformed into a "People's Park" by scores of people, most of whom had no connection with the university. Now the university was determined to reassert its legal rights of ownership. A police officer approached the group and announced

SOURCE: *The New York Review of Books*, June 19, 1969, pp. 24–31. Copyright © 1969 The New York Review. Reprinted with permission from *The New York Review of Books*.

Sheldon Wolin is a professor of political science at Berkeley and the author of *Politics and Vision*.

John Schaar teaches political science at Berkeley and is the author of *Escape from Authority*.

that it must leave or face charges of trespassing. Except for three persons, the group left and the area was immediately occupied and surrounded by about 200 police from Berkeley, Alameda county, and the campus. The police were equipped with flak jackets, tear gas launchers, shotguns, and telescopic rifles. At 6:00 A.M. a construction crew arrived and by mid-afternoon an eight-foot steel fence encircled the lot.

At noon a rally was convened on campus and about 3,000 people gathered. The president-elect of the student body spoke. He started to suggest various courses of action that might be considered. The crowd responded to the first of these by spontaneously marching toward the lot guarded by the police. (For this speech, the speaker was charged a few days later with violating numerous campus rules, and, on the initiative of university officials, indicted for incitement to riot.) The crowd was blocked by a drawn police line. Rocks and bottles were thrown at the police, and the police loosed a tear gas barrage, scattering the crowd. Elsewhere, a car belonging to the city was burned. Meanwhile, police reinforcements poured in, soon reaching around 600. A rock was thrown from a roof-top and, without warning, police fired into a group on the roof of an adjacent building. Two persons were struck in the face by the police fire, another was blinded, probably permanently, and a fourth, twenty-five-year-old James Rector, later died. Before the day was over, at least thirty others were wounded by police gunfire, and many more by clubs. One policeman received a minor stab wound and six more were reported as having been treated for minor cuts and bruises.

Meanwhile, action shifted to the campus itself, where police had herded a large crowd into Sproul Plaza by shooting tear gas along the bordering streets. The police then formed small detachments which continuously swept across the campus, breaking up groups of all sizes. Tear gas enfolded the main part of the campus and drifted into many of its buildings, as well as into the surrounding city. Nearby streets were littered with broken glass and rubble. At least six buckshot slugs entered the main library and three .38 calibre bullets lodged in the wall of a reference room in the same building. Before the day ended, more than ninety people had been injured by police guns and clubs.

Under a "State of Extreme Emergency" proclamation issued by Governor Reagan on February 5 in connection with the "Third World Strike" at Berkeley late last winter and never rescinded, a curfew was imposed on the city. Strict security measures were enforced on campus and in the nearby business districts, and all assemblies and rallies were prohibited. The proclamation also centralized control of the police under the command of Sheriff Frank Madigan of Alameda County.

Roger Heyns, the chancellor of the university, saw none of this, for he had left the previous day for a meeting in Washington. His principal vice-chancellor had gone to the Regents' meeting in Los Angeles. The Regents took notice of the events by declaring, "It is of paramount importance that law and order be upheld." The governor said that the lot had been seized by the street-people "as an excuse for a riot." A Berkeley councilman called the previous use of the lot a "Hippie Disneyland freak show."

The next day, May 17, 2,000 National Guardsmen appeared in full battle dress, armed with rifles, bayonets, and tear gas. They were called into action by the governor, but apparently the initiative came from local authorities acting in consultation with university administrators. Helicopters weaved back and forth over the campus and city. Berkeley was occupied. (The next day one helicopter landed on campus and an officer came out to ask that students stop flying their kites because the strings might foul his rotors. A collection was promptly taken and the sky was soon full of brightly colored kites.)

During the next few days a pattern emerged. Each day began quietly, almost like any other day, except that people awoke to the roar of helicopters and the rumble of transports. As university classes began (they have never been officially canceled), the Guardsmen formed a line along the south boundary of the campus. The Guard and the police would cordon off the main plaza and station smaller detachments at various points around the campus. Gradually the students crowded together, staring curiously at the Guardsmen and occasionally taunting them. The Guard stood ready with bayonets pointed directly at the crowd. This standoff would continue for an hour or two, and then the police would charge the crowd with clubs and tear gas. The

226

crowd would scatter, the police would give chase, the students and street-people would curse and sometimes hurl rocks or return the tear gas canisters, and the police would beat or arrest some of them.

On Tuesday, May 20, the pattern and tempo changed. Previously the police had sought to break up gatherings on the campus, so now the protesters left the campus and began a peaceful march through the city. This was promptly stopped by the police. The marchers then filtered back to campus and a crowd of about 3,000 assembled. The group was pressed toward the Plaza by the police and Guardsmen and, when solidly hemmed in, was attacked by tear gas. A little later a helicopter flew low over the center of the campus and spewed gas over a wide area, even though the crowd had been thoroughly scattered. Panic broke out and people fled, weeping, choking, vomiting. Gas penetrated the university hospital, imperiling patients and interrupting hospital routines. It caused another panic at the university recreation area, nearly a mile from the center of campus, where many people, including mothers and children, were swimming. The police also threw gas into a student snack bar and into an office and classroom building.

The next day, May 21, was a turning point. More than 200 faculty members announced their refusal to teach; a local labor council condemned the police action; some church groups protested; and the newspapers and television stations began to express some criticism. Controversy arose over the ammunition which the police had used the previous Thursday. Sheriff Madigan was evasive about the size of birdshot issued, but the evidence was clear that buckshot had killed James Rector. The tear gas was first identified as the normal variety (CN) for crowd disturbances, but later it was officially acknowledged that a more dangerous gas (CS) was also used. The American army uses CS gas to flush out guerrillas in Vietnam. It can cause projectile vomiting, instant diarrhea, and skin blisters, and even death, as it has to the VC, when the victim is tubercular. The Geneva Conventions outlaw the use of CS in warfare.

On the same day the chancellor issued his first statement. He deplored the death which had occurred, as well as "the senseless violence." He warned that attempts were being made "to polarize the community and prevent rational solutions," and he stated that a university has a responsibility to follow "civilized procedures." Heyns made no criticism of the police or National Guard tactics: that same day a Guardsman had thrown down his helmet, dropped his rifle, and reportedly shouted, "I can't stand this any more." He was handcuffed, taken away for a physical examination, and then rushed off to a psychiatric examination. He was diagnosed as suffering from "suppressed aggressions."

In Sacramento, where a deputation of Berkeley faculty members was meeting with the governor, aggression was more open. The governor conceded that the helicopter attack might have been a "tactical mistake," but he also insisted that "once the dogs of war are unleashed, you must expect things will happen. . . ." Meantime, the statewide commander of the Guards defended the gas attack on the grounds that his troops were threatened. He noted that the general who ordered the attack had said, "It was a Godsend that it was done at that time." The commander regretted the "discomfort and inconvenience to innocent bystanders," but added: "It is an inescapable by-product of combating terrorists, anarchists, and hard-core militants on the streets and on the campus."

The next day, May 22, a peaceful march and flower planting procession began in downtown Berkeley. With little warning, police and Guardsmen converged on the unsuspecting participants and swept them, along with a number of shoppers, newsmen, people at lunch, and a mailman, into a parking lot, where 482 were arrested, bringing the week's total near 800. As those arrested were released on bail, disturbing stories began to circulate concerning the special treatment accorded "Berkeley types" in Santa Rita prison.

These stories, supported by numerous affidavits and news accounts submitted by journalists who had been bagged in the mass arrest, told of beatings, verbal abuse, and humiliation, physical deprivations, and refusal of permission to contact counsel. Male prisoners told of being marched into the prison yard and forced to lie face down, absolutely motionless, on gravel and concrete for several hours. The slightest shift in posture, except for a head movement permitted once every half hour, was met with a blow to the kidneys or testicles. On May 24 a District

Court judge issued an order restraining Sheriff Madigan's subordinates from beating and otherwise mistreating the arrestees taken to Santa Rita prison.

Despite all the arrests, the shotguns, gas, and clubs, the protesters have thus far shown remarkable restraint. Although both police and Guards have been targets of much foul language and some hard objects, nothing remotely resembling sustained violence has been employed against the police; and the Guard has been spared from all except verbal abuse. At this writing, the only damage to campus property, other than that caused by the police, has been two broken windows and one flooded floor.

After the mass arrests, the governor lifted the curfew and the ban on assemblies, saying "a more controlled situation" existed. But he warned that no solution was likely until the trouble-making faculty and students were separated from the university. "A professional revolutionary group," he said, was behind it all. Charles Hitch, the president of the University of California, issued his first statement. (Much earlier, his own staff issued a statement protesting campus conditions of "intolerable stress" and physical danger.) The president ventured to criticize "certain tactics" of the police, but noted that these "were not the responsibility of university authorities."

In a television interview, the chancellor agreed with the president, but added that negotiations were still possible because "we haven't stopped the rational process." A published interview (May 22) with the principal vice-chancellor found him saying, "Our strategy was to act with humor and sensitivity. For instance, we offered to roll up the sod in the park and return it to the people. . . . We had no reason to believe there would be trouble." Meanwhile the governor was saying, "The police didn't kill the young man. He was killed by the first college administrator who said some time ago it was all right to break laws in the name of dissent."

The governor also accused the president of the university, a former assistant secretary of defense and RANDsman, of "trying to weasel" to the side of the street-people. Two days later the governor refused the request of the Berkeley City Council to end the state of emergency and recall the Guard—requests, it might be added, that the university itself has not yet made. At this time the mayor of Berkeley suggested that police tactics had been "clumsy and not efficient," to which Sheriff Madigan retorted: "If the mayor was capable of running the city so well without problems we wouldn't be here. I advise the mayor to take his umbrella and go to Berkeley's Munich. . . ."

On Friday, May 23, the Faculty Senate met. It listened first to a speech by the chancellor in which he defined the occupation of the lot as an act of "unjustified aggression" against the university, and declared that the "avoidance of confrontations cannot be the absolute value." He said that the fence would remain as long as the issue was one of possession and control, and, pleading for more "elbow room," he asserted that the faculty should support or at least not oppose an administrative decision once it had been made. The faculty then defeated a motion calling for the chancellor's removal (94 voted for, 737 against, and 99 abstained). It approved, by a vote of 737 to 94, a series of resolutions which condemned what was called "as irresponsible a police and military reaction to a civic disturbance as this country has seen in recent times."

The resolutions demanded withdrawal of "the massive police and military presence on campus"; the "cessation of all acts of belligerency and provocation by demonstrators"; an investigation by the attorney general of California and the Department of Justice; and the prompt implementation of a plan whereby part of the lot would become "an experimental community-generated park" and the fence would be simultaneously removed. The faculty also resolved to reconvene in a few days to reassess the situation.

There is where events now stand (May 26). But pressures from all sides are increasing. A student referendum, which saw the heaviest turnout in the history of student voting, found 85 percent of the nearly 15,000 who voted favoring the use of the lot as it had been before the occupation. The students also voted to assess themselves $1.50 each quarter to help finance an ethnic studies department previously accepted by the university but now foundering. As of this writing, college students from all over the state are planning direct protests to Governor Reagan. Leaders of the protesters are preparing for a huge march against the fence on Memorial Day. The governor remains committed to a hard line. All the issues remain unsettled.

II

What brought on this crisis? Like many of its sister institutions, the Berkeley campus has been steadily advancing its boundaries into the city. Back in 1956 it had announced its intention to purchase property in the area which includes the present disputed lot. Owing to lack of funds, very little land was actually purchased. Finally, in June, 1967, the monies were allocated and the university announced that ultimately dormitories would be built on the land, but that in the interim it would be used for recreation.

The lot itself was purchased in 1968, but no funds were then available for development. Undoubtedly the university was aware of the disastrous experience of other academic institutions which had attempted to "redevelop" surrounding areas. In fact, a short time ago the university announced, with much fanfare, its intention to mount a major attack on the problems of the cities. Despite these professions, the university's treatment of its own urban neighbors has consisted of a mixture of middle-class prejudice, aesthetic blindness, and bureaucratic callousness.

The victims in this case, however, have not been so much the blacks as another pariah group, one whose identity is profoundly influenced by the university itself. For many years, Telegraph Avenue and "the south campus area" have constituted a major irritant to the university, the city fathers, and the business interests. It is the Berkeley demi-monde, the place where students, hippies, drop-outs, radicals, and run-aways congregate. To the respectables, it is a haven for drug addicts, sex fiends, criminals, and revolutionaries. Until the university began its expansion, it was also an architectural preserve for fine old brown shingle houses and interesting shops. It is no secret that the university has long considered the acquisition of land as a means of ridding the area not of sub-standard housing, but of its human "blight." The disputed lot was the perfect symbol of the university's way of carrying out urban regeneration: first, raze the buildings; next let the land lay idle and uncared for; then permit it to be used as an unimproved parking lot, muddy and pitted; and finally, when the local people threaten to use and enjoy the land, throw a fence around it.

SHELDON WOLIN and JOHN SCHAAR   231

Around mid-April, a movement was begun by street-people, hippies, students, radicals, and a fair sprinkling of elderly free spirits to take over the parking lot and transform it. Many possibilities were discussed: a child care clinic; a crafts fair; a baseball diamond. Soon grass and shrubs were planted, playground equipment installed, benches built, and places made for eating, lounging, and occasional speechmaking. About 200 people were involved in the beginning, but soon the park was intensively and lovingly used by children, the young, students and street-people, and the elderly. A week after the park began, the university announced its intention to develop a playing field by July 1, and the park people responded by saying that the university would have to fight for it. Discussions followed, but not much else. The university said, however, that no construction would be started without proper warning and that it was willing to discuss the future design of the field.

On May 8 the chancellor agreed to form a committee representing those who were using the lot as well as the university. But he insisted as "an essential condition" of discussions about the future of the land that all work on the People's Park cease. In addition he announced certain guidelines for his committee: university control and eventual use must be assured; the field must not produce "police and other control problems"; and no political or public meetings were to be held on the land. Suddenly, on May 13, he announced his decision to fence in the area as the first step toward developing the land for intramural recreation. "That's a hard way to make a point," he said, "but that's the way it has to be. . . . The fence will also give us time to plan and consult. Regretfully, this is the only way the entire site can be surveyed, soil tested, and planned for development . . . hence the fence."

Why did it have to be this way? Because, as the chancellor explained, it was necessary to assert the university's title to ownership. Concerning the apparent lack of consultation with his own committee, he said that a plan could not be worked out because the park people had not only refused to stop cultivating and improving the land, but they had "refused to organize a responsible committee" for consultative purposes. In addition, he cited problems of health, safety, and legal liability, as well as complaints from local residents.

232

The first response came from the faculty chairman of the chancellor's committee. He declared that the chancellor had allowed only two days (the weekend) for the committee to produce a plan and that the "university didn't seem interested in negotiations." On May 14 a protest rally was held and the anarchs of the park, surprisingly, pulled themselves together and formed a negotiating committee. Although rumors of an impending fence were circulating, spokesmen for the park people insisted that they wanted discussion, not confrontation.

On May 15, the day immediately preceding the early morning police action, the chancellor placed an advertisement in the campus newspaper inviting students to draw up "ideas or designs" for the lot and to submit them by May 21. The ad was continued even after the military occupation. On May 18, three days after the occupation had begun, the chancellor announced that there would be "no negotiations in regard to the land known as People's Park," although discussions might go on "while the fence is up anyway." His principal vice-chancellor, in an interview reported on May 22, stated that the university had not turned down a negotiating committee.

He also noted—and this was after the helicopter attack—that "the fence was necessary to permit the kind of rational discussion and planning that wasn't possible before." Once more the faculty chairman had to protest that he had not been informed of meetings between the administration and representatives of the People's Park and that the chancellor had consistently ignored the committee's recommendations. However, the principal vice-chancellor had an explanation for this lack of consultation: "I guess that's because the chancellor didn't want him to get chewed up by this thing."

III

Why did the making of a park provoke such a desolating response? The bureaucratic nature of the multiversity and its disastrous consequences for education are by now familiar and beyond dispute. So, too, is the web of interdependence between it and the dominant military, industrial, and political institutions of our society. These explain much about the response of the university to the absurd, yet hopeful, experiment of People's Park.

SHELDON WOLIN and JOHN SCHAAR 233

What needs further comment is the increasingly ineffectual quality of the university's responses, particularly when its organizational apparatus attempts to cope with what is spontaneous, ambiguous, and disturbingly human. It is significant that the Berkeley administration repeatedly expressed irritation with the failure of the park people to "organize" a "responsible committee" or to select "representatives" who might "negotiate." The life-styles and values of the park people were forever escaping the categories and procedures of those who administer the academic plant.

Likewise the issue itself: the occupants of the park wanted to use the land for a variety of projects, strange but deeply natural, which defied customary forms and expectations, whereas, at worst, the university saw the land as something to be fenced, soil-tested, processed through a score of experts and a maze of committees, and finally encased in the tight and tidy form of a rational design. At best, the most imaginative use of the land which the university could contemplate was as a "field-experiment station" where faculty and graduate students could observe their fellow beings coping with their "environment." In brief, the educational bureaucracy, like bureaucracies elsewhere, is experiencing increasing difficulty, because human life is manifesting itself in forms which are unrecognizable to the mentality of the technological age.

This suggests that part of the problem lies in the very way bureaucracies perceive the world and process information from it. It was this "bureaucratic epistemology" which largely determined how the university responded to the People's Park. Bureaucracy is both an expression of the drive for rationality and predictability, and one of the chief agencies in making the world ever more rational and predictable, for the bureaucratic mode of knowing and behaving comes to constitute the things known and done themselves.

Now this rational form of organizing human efforts employs a conception of knowledge which is also rational in specific ways (cf. Kenneth Keniston's analysis in *The Uncommitted: Alienated Youth in American Society*, 1967, pp. 253–272). The only legitimate instrument of knowledge is systematic cognition, and the only acceptable mode of discourse is the cognitive mode. Other paths to knowledge are suspect. Everything tainted with the personal, the subjective, and the passionate is suppressed, or dismissed as prejudice or pathology. A bureaucrat who based his decisions upon, say, intuition, dialectical reason, empathic awareness, or even common sense, would be guilty of misconduct.

The bureaucratic search for "understanding" does not begin in wonder, but in the reduction of the world to the ordinary and the manageable. In order to deal with the world in the cognitive mode, the world must first be approached as an exercise in "problem-solving." To say there is a problem is to imply there is a solution; and finding the solution largely means devising the right technique. Since most problems are "complex," they must be broken down by bureaucrats into their component parts before the right solution can be found. Reality is parsed into an ensemble of discrete though related parts, and each part is assigned to the expert specially qualified to deal with that part. Wholes can appear as nothing more than assemblages of parts, just as a whole automobile is an assemblage of parts. But in order for wholes to be broken into parts, things that are dissimilar in appearance and quality must be made similar.

This is done by abstracting from the objects dealt with those aspects as though they were the whole. Abstraction and grouping by common attributes require measuring tools that yield comparable units for analysis: favorite ones are units of money, time, space, and power; income, occupation, and party affiliation. All such measurements and comparisons subordinate qualitative dimensions, natural context, and unique and variable properties to the common, stable, external, and reproducible. This way of thinking becomes real when campus administrators define "recreation" in fixed and restrictive terms so that it may accord with the abstract demands of "lead-time." In a way Hegel might barely recognize, the Rational becomes the Real and the Real the Rational.

When men treat themselves this way, they increasingly become this way, or they desperately try to escape the "mind-forged manacles," as Blake called them, of the bureaucratic mentality and mode of conduct. In the broadest view, these two trends increasingly dominate the advanced states of our day. On the one side, we see the march toward uniformity, predictability, and the attempt to define all variety as dissent and then to force

SHELDON WOLIN and JOHN SCHAAR 235

dissent into the "regular channels"—toward that state whose model citizen is Tocqueville's "industrious sheep," that state whose only greatness is its collective power.

On the other side we see an assertion of spontaneity, self-realization, and do-your-own-thing as the sum and substance of life and liberty. And this assertion, in its extreme form, does approach either madness or infantilism, for the only social institutions in which each member is really free to do his own thing are Bedlam and the nursery, where the condition may be tolerated because there is a keeper with ultimate control over the inmates. The opposing forces were not quite that pure in the confrontation over the People's Park, but the university and public officials nearly managed to make them so. That they could not do so is a comforting measure of the basic vitality of those who built the park and who have sacrificed to preserve it.

IV

But this still does not account for the frenzy of violence which fell on Berkeley. To understand that, we must shift focus.

Clark Kerr was perceptive when he defined the multiversity as "a mechanism held together by administrative rules and powered by money." But it is important to understand that the last few years in the university have seen more and more rules and less and less money. The money is drying up because the rules are being broken. The rules are being broken because university authorities, administrators and faculty alike, have lost the respect of very many of the students. When authority leaves, power enters—first in the form of more and tougher rules, then as sheer physical force, and finally as violence, which is force unrestrained by any thought of healing and saving, force whose aim is to cleanse by devastation.

Pressed from above by politicians and from below by students, the university administration simultaneously imposes more rules and makes continual appeals to the faculty for more support in its efforts to cope with permanent emergency. It pleads with the faculty for more "elbow room," more discretionary space in which to make the hard decisions needed when money runs short and students run amuck. That same administration is right now conducting time-and-motion studies of faculty work

236

and "productivity." Simultaneously, both faculty and administration make spasmodic efforts to give the students some voice in the governance of the institution. But those efforts are always too little, too late, too grudging.

Besides, as soon as the students get some power, unseemly things happen. Admit the blacks on campus and they demand their own autonomous departments. Give the students limited power to initiate courses and they bring in Eldridge Cleaver and Tom Hayden. The faculty sees student initiative as a revolting mixture of Agitprop and denial of professional prerogatives. The administration sees it as a deadly threat to its own precarious standing within the university and before the public. The politicians see it as concession to anarchy and revolution. The result is more rules and less trust all around—more centralization, bureaucratization, and force on one side, more despair and anger on the other.

Under these conditions, the organized system must strive to extend its control and reduce the space in which spontaneous and unpredictable actions are possible. The subjects, on the other hand, come to identify spontaneity and unpredictability with all that is human and alive, and rule and control with all that is inhuman and dead. Order and liberty stand in fatal opposition. No positive synthesis can emerge from this dialectic unless those who now feel themselves pushed out and put down are admitted as full participants. But that is not happening. More and more, we are seeing in this country a reappearance of that stage in the breakdown of political societies where one segment of the whole—in this case still the larger segment—determines to dominate by force and terror other segments which reject and challenge its legitimacy.

This dynamic largely accounts for the crushing violence and terror that hit Berkeley. When spontaneity appeared in People's Park, it was first met by a re-statement of the rules governing possession and control of land. When that re-statement did not have the desired effect, the university failed to take the next step dictated by rule-governed behavior—seeking an injunction. Nor did it take the step which would have acknowledged itself as being in a political situation—talking on a plane of equality, and acting in a spirit of generosity, with the other parties. Instead, it regressed immediately to the use of physical measures.

SHELDON WOLIN and JOHN SCHAAR   237

In the eyes of the administration, the building of People's Park was an "unjustified aggression," and the right of self-defense was promptly invoked.

Once force was called into play, it quickly intensified, and the university cannot evade its share of responsibility for what followed. He who wills the end wills the means; and no university official could have been unaware of the means necessary to keep that fence standing. But the administrators did not quite understand that their chosen agents of force, the police, would not limit their attention only to the students and street-people, who were expendable, but would turn against the university and the city as well.

Ronald Reagan reached Sacramento through Berkeley because, in the eyes of his frightened and furious supporters, Berkeley is daily the scene of events that would have shocked Sodom and revolutionary Moscow. All this came into intense focus in the behavior of the cops who were on the scene.

The police were numerous and armed with all the weapons a fertile technology can provide and an increasingly frightened citizenry will permit. Their superiority of force is overwhelming, and they are convinced they could "solve the problem" overnight if they were permitted to do it their own way: one instant crushing blow, and then license for dealing with the remaining recalcitrants. All the trouble-makers are known to the police, either by dossier and record or by appearance and attitude. But the police are kept under some restraints, and those restraints produce greater and greater rage.

The rage comes from another source as well. Demands for a different future have been welling up in this society for some years now, and while those demands have not been unheard they have gone unheeded. Vietnam, racism, poverty, the degradation of the natural and manmade environment, the bureaucratization of the academy and its active collaboration with the military and industrial state, unrepresentative and unreachable structures of domination—all these grow apace. It seems increasingly clear to those who reject this American future that the forces of "law and order" intend to defend it by any means necessary. It becomes increasingly clear to the forces of law and order that extreme means will be necessary, and that the longer they are delayed the more extreme they will have to be.

238

Those two futures met at People's Park. It should be clear that what is happening this time is qualitatively different from 1964 and the Free Speech Movement. The difference in the amount of violence is the most striking, but this is largely a symptom of underlying differences. In 1964, the issues centered around questions of civil liberties and due process within the university. The issues now are political in the largest sense.

V

The appearance of People's Park raised questions of property and the nature of meaningful work. It raised questions about how people can begin to make a livable environment for themselves; about why both the defenders and critics of established authority today agree that authority can be considered only in terms of repression, never in terms of genuine respect and affection. These questions cannot be evaded. Those who honestly and courageously ask them are not imperiling the general happiness but are working for the common redemption.

It is increasingly clear that legitimate authority is declining in the modern state. In a real sense, "law and order" *is* the basic question of our day. This crisis of legitimacy has been visible for some time in just about all of the non-political sectors of life— family, economy, religion, education—and is now spreading rapidly into the political realm. The gigantic and seemingly impregnable organizations that surround and dominate men in the modern states are seen by more and more people to have at their center not a vital principle of authority, but a hollow space, a moral vacuum. Increasingly, among the young and the rejected, obedience is mainly a matter of lingering habit, or expediency, or necessity, but not a matter of conviction and deepest sentiment.

The groups who are most persistently raising these questions are, of course, white middle-class youth and the racial and ethnic minorities. The origins of protest are different in the two cases: the former have largely seen through the American Dream of meaning in power and wealth and have found it a nightmare; the latter have been pushed aside and denied even the minimal goods of the Dream. But the ends of the protest are remarkably similar: both are fighting against distortions and denials of their humanity. Both reject the programmed future of an America whose only imperative now seems to be: more.

The people who built the park (there will be more People's Parks, more and more occasions for seemingly bizarre, perverse, and wild behavior) have pretty much seen through the collective ideals and disciplines that have bound this nation together in its conquest of nature and power. Having been victimized by the restraints and authorities of the past, these people are suspicious of all authorities and most collective ideals. Some of them seem ready to attempt a life built upon no other ideal than self-gratification. They sometimes talk as though they had found the secret which has lain hidden through all the past ages of man: that the individual can live fully and freely with no authority other than his desires, absorbed completely in the development of all his capacities except two—the capacity for memory and the capacity for faith.

No one can say where this will lead. Perhaps new prophets will appear. Perhaps the old faith will be reborn. Perhaps we really shall see the new technological Garden tended by children—kind, sincere innocents, barbarians with good hearts. The great danger at present is that the established and the respectable are more and more disposed to see all this as chaos and outrage. They seem prepared to follow the most profoundly nihilistic denial possible, which is the denial of the future through denial of their own children, the bearers of the future.

In such times as these, hope is not a luxury but a necessity. The hope which we see is in the revival of a sense of shared destiny, of some common fate which can bind us into a people we have never been. Even to sketch out that fate one must first decide that it does not lie with the power of technology or the stability of organizational society. It lies, instead, in something more elemental, in our common fears that scientific weapons may destroy all life; that technology will increasingly disfigure men who live in the city, just as it has already debased the earth and obscured the sky; that the "progress" of industry will destroy the possibility of interesting work; and that "communications" will obliterate the last traces of the varied cultures which have been the inheritance of all but the most benighted societies.

If hope is to be born of these despairs it must be given political direction, a new politics devoted to nurturing life and work.

There can be no political direction without political education, yet America from its beginnings has never confronted the question of how to care for men's souls while helping them to see the world politically. Seeing the world politically is preparatory to acting in it politically; and to act politically is not to be tempted by the puerile attraction of power or to be content with the formalism of a politics of compromise. It is, instead, a politics which seeks always to discover what men can share—and how what they share can be enlarged and yet rise beyond the banal.

People's Park is not banal. If only the same could be said of those who build and guard the fences around all of us.

15 / Students as Teachers

HAROLD TAYLOR

When a university sets out to reform its educational program in direct collaboration with students, the quality of teaching and learning is immediately affected. In the first place, the academic departments have to be much more careful in making appointments to the faculty exclusively on the basis of publication records and academic reputation. Inability to teach, or even disinterest in teaching, then becomes a potential source of embarrassment to the administration and to the departmental chairmen and their advisory committees. Too much concern with academic prestige and research ability, for even a limited period of time, means that soon there are not enough good teachers to go around, not enough scholars who enjoy working with students, or, what is worse for the departmental interest, not enough students to fill the classes and therefore not enough appointments available to sustain the size and position of the department in the university structure.

SOURCE: Harold Taylor, *Students Without Teachers* (New York: McGraw-Hill, 1969), pp. 308–21. Copyright © 1969 by McGraw-Hill, Inc. Used with permission of McGraw-Hill Book Co.

Harold Taylor, a former president of Sarah Lawrence College, has been active in writing, lecturing, research, and the development of innovative educational programs since leaving that college in 1959. His books include *On Education and Freedom, Art and the Intellect,* and *The World as Teacher.*

On the positive side, the academic faculty, when it collaborates with students in the development of courses and educational policy, has the very great advantage of working within its own disciplines with students whose talents and motivation in these fields begin to flourish at a higher level, both in teaching and in learning. Among the cooperating students, a far greater proportion than before becomes interested in working at an even higher level, with intellectual capacities of a broader range because of the experience they have had in their beginning courses and projects. The faculty thus finds itself with a breeding ground for future teaching and research talent and for the development of intellectual interests directly related to their own.

As for policy-making and government in student affairs, a great deal of this can be better arranged by students than by faculty members and administrative officers. The experimental colleges, particularly Antioch, Goddard, and Sarah Lawrence, have given students responsibilities in student affairs which in other colleges are handled entirely by college staff, and have found that not only the policy-making but the administration works in ways which call upon resources in students which would otherwise remain undeveloped. By bringing the students actively into the administration itself, the administrative problems of college life confront the students directly, and refute the idea that anyone who is an administrator belongs to the enemy camp.

The Sarah Lawrence pattern is one in which the Student Council not only has the power of deciding on the rules for the student community, from dormitory hours to chartering organizations, but the responsibility for administering their own rules through a council of vice-presidents of the student houses. In the case of student legislation which in the view of the administration or faculty is unwise or misguided, the opportunity exists for a reconsideration in a joint committee of elected faculty members, elected students, and administration. The joint committee holds the power of ultimate decision in matters of college policy in general. An appeal could of course be made beyond that body to the board of trustees, but to make such an appeal would mean to admit the failure of the very system which brings the students into a position of responsibility for their own college.

242

In view of the time and energy absorbed by the administration of student affairs by students, it is also necessary to consider that factor in planning a student schedule of education in the college, and in some cases to relieve a student of course work during a given semester or college year, and to pay a stipend for the services rendered to the community. When the educational program is arranged in such a way that the experience of organizing education on behalf of others is a genuine opportunity for the student, he may learn more from that kind of responsibility over a limited period of time than he would in the formal studies which would otherwise occupy him.

This is especially true of those who intend to become teachers or to enter one of the professions where the ability to organize oneself and to develop programs of use to others is a necessary corollary to whatever scholarship and learning one may possess in the field. The experience in personal relationships, in sustaining the delicate lines of connection which flow between persons and groups who are working in voluntary ways to achieve a common end, is a very important one for students in the entire field of the human services and the arts. The student of theater who has not learned to collaborate with others in the work of the theater, and who has not learned what is involved on the practical side in putting a production on the stage, is in the same position as a student who has not learned to do what has to be done when any useful human enterprise involving cooperative effort is set in motion.

II

This brings me to another matter basic to the reconstruction of the learning-teaching system, the matter of graduate students and their role in teaching. Their present status as teaching assistants to professors is a function of the lecture system and all its parts, not the result of an examination of how education may best be conducted through the talents which students of all kinds can bring to the teaching system. It is now a truism to say that in most cases in the big universities the graduate students provide one of the few opportunities for personal contact by the undergraduates with the teaching faculty. The rest is a matter of sitting in lectures. The graduate students know this, and are fully aware of the dependence of the present economic and cultural structure of the university on their work in teaching. At many universities they have organized Graduate Student Unions both to advance their economic interests and to influence educational policy. Their ranks contain some of the most intelligent, imaginative, and energetic educators the country has ever seen. The fact that they do not yet possess teaching credentials and higher degrees cannot disguise the fact that they are already functioning as teachers, regardless of faculty status—teachers who are working under wraps by the status they now occupy.

What is true of the graduate schools is true of the whole educational system and the society at large. Everywhere the idea of specified and certified professional and vocational skills, only available for public use after certified institutional training programs, has taken hold of the country's institutional life. It has substituted itself for the idea that anyone who can demonstrate in action the quality of what he knows and what he can do has no need of diplomas and credentials in order to do it. Except in the case of brain surgeons and a limited range of professional talents, the certification is unjustified.

A move away from the pattern of the credential society is essential as the first step toward breaking down the barriers to the full use of all human talent, certified or uncertified. Psychiatric aides, for example, who spend more time with patients than anyone in the mental hospital staff and who have a serious degree of influence on the progress of the patients' recovery, should be given the recognition and responsibility that comes with their function. So should teachers' aides, student assistants in child-care centers, community volunteers, community workers without formal education. Once the obvious fact is recognized that education is an amalgam of influences and not simply a transaction between academic professionals and pupils who appear before them, the way is open for the full use of human resources of all kinds within the schools, the colleges, and the universities.

The students who have organized store-front colleges and street academies have already recognized the ability of ordinary people, without certificates and formal training, both to teach and to learn. Among those recruited by the students as tutors for their projects are high school drop-outs, mothers of children, automobile mechanics, former convicts, college professors. Others at the University of North Carolina and elsewhere have organized "poor people's universities" and in one instance have developed a category of university professor whom they call "poor professors," which, although open to wide misinterpretation, refers to poor people in the community who come to college classes in the humanities and social sciences to talk about social issues and realities from their position in the middle of poverty.

In the case of teachers like David Riesman, in whose undergraduate courses graduate assistants are given an opportunity to collaborate directly both in the teaching and in the educational planning, there is no particular status problem, since Riesman and others like him deal with the assistants as intellectual and teaching colleagues, not as hired hands to carry out tasks for which professors have no time or inclination. But in the system as a whole the graduate assistant, whose maturity of outlook and practical teaching experience qualify him as a full-fledged teacher, finds himself in the absurd situation of acting as a handy man when he should be recognized as a major element in the conduct of university instruction.

There is no need to repeat again the account of how this situation is related to failures of graduate education in general, and the lack of connection between the requirements for the doctoral degree and the preparation of students for teaching assignments in the colleges and universities. What is needed is a conception of teaching and learning which reaches back into the undergraduate student body and considers undergraduates and graduate students as members of one community, capable of teaching each other. There are many juniors and seniors in the colleges and universities whose gifts as teachers and educational leaders are presently ignored, and, were a different attitude to the curriculum and its operation taken by the university, could become a major element in the improvement of undergraduate learning.

I have already referred to the organic unity of undergraduates and graduate students within the civil rights and activist groups, and their intellectual and practical collaboration in educational and political projects without regard to age level or academic status. There is no reason why that kind of collaboration cannot be made a regular part of the teaching system. It requires only the initiative of the faculty to set it in motion, with or without an educational plan for the whole university. A faculty member is free to call upon individual members of his undergraduate classes, both those in the present classes and those whose work in previous classes recommended itself to their teachers, to act as seminar and discussion leaders, tutors, organizers, and aides in educational planning and teaching.

A budget should be provided to allow a teacher or group of teachers to appoint undergraduates with teaching talent who had previously worked within particular courses, with the students invited to reduce their course schedule in a given semester in order to give teaching assistance as aides in a course, with a stipend to match. Freshmen entering the university could be given the advantage of choosing a student adviser from among those appointed to such a student staff; the staff could organize a seminar and tutorial plan by which the freshmen could become involved in the discussion and clarification of the problems of becoming educated at the university. This simply pushes to a larger dimension the informal advising system which already exists among students, but which at present bears the handicap of not being part of a serious effort to give the entering student a chance to find his bearings and to establish a sense of colleague-ship with students more advanced than himself in the educational system.

There are many in the ranks of the graduate students who have earned the right to teach students of their own, and who could supply the basic resources for the teaching staff of the freshman and sophomore years, as well as in the upper division. If they were invited to collaborate with the faculty in planning seminars and programs, this could replace the lecture system with one more in keeping with the needs of the undergraduates. Whenever lectures were needed, these could be supplied by calling together a number of the individual seminars into one class for a joint session to be addressed by a lecturer chosen for the particular contribution he could make to the problems under consideration in the seminars. Collaboration among the seminar teachers would be possible, not only in this way, but in many others. Individual students could combine their talents in symposia to be presented to a group of the seminars; outside visitors

246

from the community, the faculty, and the graduate-student roster could also be included.

This would entail a different kind of organization within the graduate divisions themselves. In a given semester, as part of the master of arts or doctoral degree program, a student would spend the whole of his time, with an appropriate stipend, in the work of an undergraduate seminar, with the seminar materials and supervision of undergraduate projects considered as an integral part of the work of the graduate student in developing his own body of knowledge within his chosen field. There is no more effective way of organizing such a body of knowledge of one's own than by teaching it. The rationale for the semester or year of work of a graduate student as teacher is not simply that it would give the future college professor experience in teaching as a necessary component of his preparation, but that it would deepen his scholarship and his intellectual resources by the process of discovering what it was he had learned which was useful to others in the culture.

The rationale could also be extended to the undergraduate curriculum, where, in connection with work in psychology, anthropology, literature, sociology, physics, biology, or mathematics, the students would be asked, as part of their regular work, to volunteer for tutoring assignments with children or with high school students in areas and subjects where help was needed and in which the undergraduate had competence.

When the entire educational system is seen in terms of its interconnections through teaching and learning, not as a series of interlocking social and cultural agencies separated from each other by bureaucratic rules and testing devices, the stream of consciousness which runs from the child to the adolescent to the young adult and beyond then becomes the most vital and important thing about it. Links between one consciousness and another become the crucial matter, not the discontinuities and separations which the institutions make within themselves and among each other. The continuity of experience between the internal life of the school and college and the life of the society becomes a natural educational concept, with broad implications for the union of talents found within the educational institution and the need for these talents for education in the community. The curriculum of the college is then joined to the reality of the society, and through their union the student can learn to locate himself in the wider world and to act upon it. It is this continuity in consciousness which gives the basis for planning the internal life of the university so that at every point the students are linked to others, and education for students becomes the series of influences and experiences through which they teach and are taught.

III

How then do we proceed, finally, to accomplish the reforms? Where do we take hold? Who makes the next moves?

It will be clear from what I have been saying up to now that my view is that the moves must be collaborative; they must be made by the faculty, the administration, and the students together. I would add that it does not matter who moves first, as long as the students are centrally involved in what is done. The students can become involved by invitation of the faculty or the administration, by their own initiative, by a new curriculum, by the student's natural attachment to a student organization which is itself involved in educational reform. But in the last analysis, it is the responsibility of the university of which they are a part to find ways of creating the involvement by the structure of the internal life of the college.

The movement in reform can therefore start at any point, without the necessity of another faculty report, by simply taking seriously the proposition already stated that the best place to start a reform movement to improve a student's education is directly in the area of his intellectual life as this is lived at the university—that is, in the courses, on the campus, with his teachers.

The simplest way to set in motion a reform movement which starts in the working areas of the student's intellectual life is to take the educational questions one year at a time, that is, to set a group of interested faculty members and students to work on rethinking the freshman year, with some relation between their work and that of another group considering how the freshman year develops into the sophomore year. This would be linked to plans for the junior and senior years, with students drawn into the planning from each of the years in view of the

248

recency of their experience and the degree of their talent and interest. In the case of the freshman year, many of the universities have their only connection with the high schools through the admissions office, in the review of transcripts and sometimes interviews with candidates. In some cases, the universities invite high school students to come to the campus for a day's visit, or they show films in the high schools and before community groups of football games or documentaries about the university. In other cases, in connection with some of the new programs for the relatively unprepared entrants, summer sessions are arranged to get the new students ready for entry in the fall.

An extension of the idea of linking each year of education with its preceding one, and the idea of involving students in the university curriculum, would entail the appointment of students, with an appropriate stipend, not merely to the faculty admissions committee, but to a student admissions staff drawn from a list of students recommended by the faculty. These students could visit local high schools, possibly taking a sabbatical leave during the first semester of the sophomore or junior year; they could visit high school classes, talk to the students and teachers there, and lead discussions of the courses and programs presently available to freshman students, and of other ones which the high school students would like to see organized in view of what they have already learned in high school and what they would most like to do when they first enter the university.

From the body of material collected by the student-traveller and reports made to the student-faculty committee on the freshman year, ideas for patterns of study and programs could be developed for the entering freshmen, each of whom could be asked to prepare for himself a study plan, or general outline of courses and their content, to be included among other materials presented as qualification for admission. Or the applicants could be asked to join with other students in the high school who were applying for admission, and to organize groups among themselves, on the basis of common interests, to develop ideas for projects and areas of study in which they would like to work during their freshman year at the university.

A program of this kind would have a direct effect in stimulating some new educational thinking among students and teachers in the high school about what to do with the junior and senior years aside from carrying out the obligatory academic exercises necessary to meet the present admissions requirements. There could emerge from this an internal curriculum in the high school through which the students, in order to improve their qualifications for admission to the university, could work with elementary and junior high school students as tutors and assistant teachers. Again, the rationale, as in the case of the graduate students, is that the best way to learn how to organize one's own education is to learn how to help others with theirs.

This could then serve a double purpose for the university. It would give to the faculty members who were planning the freshman year some fresh and interesting material for use in developing the freshman curriculum. It would help the admissions office to select the most promising students for admission, not exclusively in terms of their grades, rank in class, and academic credits, but by reference to the level of their intellectual interests and capacities, their talent for self-education, their potential contribution to the student community, their potential ability as teachers, community workers, artists, educational aides, and reformers once they arrived at the university.

The student appointee to the staff of the admissions office and the admissions committee, working with the committee on the freshman year, could review the study plans of high school students, along with the other admissions material from the applicants, some of which would be coming from students in the schools he had visited and whom he would know. From that material the student staff member could present ideas to the committee on the freshman year for various kinds of grouping within fields of study, distributing the freshmen throughout the university in terms of their interests, and organizing the teaching program around them.

One of the assignments for the entering freshmen could be to a seminar of the kind I have already suggested, similar to the exploratory courses taught at Sarah Lawrence by the faculty, to which freshmen are assigned on the basis of the account they have given of their past education and study plans in the admissions materials submitted to the college. The purpose of the exploratory course at Sarah Lawrence is to give a central place in the freshman year to each student, a place where, with whatever help and advice is needed from the teacher of the course, the student can explore the methods and materials for learning in an area of his interest and can raise a variety of questions on topics of concern, ranging from problems in handling the college life to issues of college policy or public affairs.

This kind of seminar provides the common intellectual experience for which the curriculum-makers have been in search, along with the sense of identification with the university, by the directly personal way in which the freshman seminar conducts its business, and the possibility of coming to know intimately and in the setting of a university class other students with similar interests and similar problems. In our experience at Sarah Lawrence, the exploratory course gave to each student a place to begin, a set of intellectual companions, and a central person in the faculty to whom one could go for advice and help on any matter connected with the experience of being in college.

When graduate students and upperclassmen are involved in advising and teaching this kind of freshman seminar, and sophomores and others are involved in the work of the admissions committee and the development of the freshman year, they create a completely new style of educational thinking. They bring to their colleagues in the faculty a wealth of empirical knowledge about students, and educational thinking can proceed on the basis of that knowledge rather than on generalizations about the student as an abstraction. They break down the barriers which separate the academic faculty from the student body, and introduce the idea of the learning-teaching community to replace the concept of the manufactured curriculum taught by hired hands.

They also produce a way of bridging the gap between the administration and the students, by carrying out some of the administrative tasks in cooperation with the administrators. In the case of the student members of the admissions staff, for example, there is no reason why such students should not correspond with high school applicants about their study plans, and prepare mimeographed material which would be useful to the high school student in understanding what would be expected of him when he comes to the university, and what he could expect to find available to him once he arrives there. Entering students can then learn to identify the university with its student body and not simply with its officials and their official pronouncements.

The same kind of approach through student-faculty planning can be taken to the sophomore year, with the returning sophomores asked to prepare preliminary study plans for themselves during the spring of the freshman year. Student members of the student-faculty committee staff could work during the summertime on the collation of the student plans into general outlines of possible courses, projects, and study groups, for use by the faculty in preparing the sophomore course offerings. In the case of the junior and senior years, when most students want to work in a major field, something approximating the student Council of Majors recommended by the Berkeley Commission on University Governance could be organized to work with the departments in making plans for courses in special fields of study.

Liberal allowances of choice could be made for students not yet ready for a full commitment to a specialized field; their programs could include a wider spread of courses, independent study under the supervision of graduate students, or work on a student research team with similar supervision. Not only would this keep the departments in touch with the changing needs of their clientele, but it would give them the benefit of many new ideas for undergraduate course offerings and different forms of organization, while linking their graduate students to the problems of the scholar-teacher.

In this way, from the freshman to the senior year and beyond, a new and sizable internal network of student teachers and policy-makers would be created on a university-wide scale. There would then be a basis for a far greater cohesion of interest in the student body as a whole and a wealth of opportunity for the undergraduates to combine forces among themselves in creating their own education and in finding close associates and colleagues who shared their interests. Out of that network can come the formal structure of student involvement in basic university policy questions, by elections from the student body, by nominations from both the students and faculty for appointments of students to the faculty bodies, administrative committees, and staff of the university. Through the existence of this internal structure, the primary elements of a true community of learning would have been assembled to carry out the tasks in which it is the business of that community to engage itself.

IV

The task of reform in education and society has no end, but only new beginnings. Reform goes on, planned or unplanned, in one way or another way, usually at a pace many years behind the need, by the efforts of those few who cannot be satisfied with what they find, and look for better ways, and by the necessities of historical change which keep pressing upon all institutions and testing their capacity for alteration and survival.

This is the first age in which so many untamed and unmanageable necessities have been pressing all at once, and the first age in which the historical circumstances have combined to produce a younger generation so fully aware of those circumstances. In other times it was possible to say that that is the way things go in the universities. The students enter and leave, the society changes and moves on, the universities stay at the quiet center, giving the mind its due, keeping the ideals of civilization alive.

It is clear that this is no longer a possible attitude, although the necessity for the quiet center continues to exist, and the protection of the ideals of civilization was never more urgent or necessary. The difference now is that the university is already engaged with the necessities and must act to engage itself with them now, on its own terms, without the time to speculate, but only time to confront. The society will not stand still, even to be studied and observed. It insists on acting.

In this situation of the university, once more the students are its greatest allies, and if some of them have declared themselves to be its enemies, let them be met by those in the universities who know and can teach that the real enemy of the university is ignorance, force, and violence, and that the way to overcome these is by knowledge, a passion for justice, and a commitment to truth.

For it is in the ideal of a community of concerned persons who share a common interest in the life of the mind and the quality of human experience that the genius of the university lies. The rest is a matter of how that community can best be constructed by the best efforts of all concerned. There is nobility and strength in the lovely old words "fraternity," "equality," "liberty and justice for all"—and the university is the place where these words can become names for the living experience of those within its environs. Unless the reality of that experience is to be found there, it is unlikely to be found in the larger world. Unless students learn through what they do there that equality is a two-edged sword, that fraternity means giving part of oneself away, that liberty is an affectionate state of mind, and that justice in a democracy is willingness to be faithful in action to agreed-upon principles, all the protest, controversy, radical action, and appeal to the big abstractions of moral enthusiasm will come to nothing but a continual attrition of the very ideals of which the young are in search.

That is why education and the university must both be redefined so that they may become instruments through which the influence of persons on each other may act to secure the elevation of spirit and quality of life which it is the purpose of all education to induce. The university should be a place where students help their teachers to teach them, where teachers help their students to learn, where administrators help both to accomplish what they have come together to do. That is why the role of the students must also be redefined, in order to make clear to them and to all others that students *are* the foundation of the university, that when everything else is taken away, as in fact it can be—the government contracts, the isolated research institutes, the alumni bodies, the services to industry, the travelling faculty, the organization men—what is left are persons working together to learn and to teach.

Learning and teaching in this sense have to do with the totality of human conduct, in which the conduct of the affairs of the mind is by turns political, social, public, private, intellectual, emotional, external, internal, and, in the last analysis, personal. Otherwise conduct has no meaning, the human act is stripped of motivation, empty of content, lacking in truth.

The education of students, therefore, means nothing less than their personal involvement in the conduct of the affairs of the mind. An equality of position in the polity of the community is a necessary condition of their involvement; otherwise they are playing a game the necessity for whose rules they never learn to understand—the commitment to play is never completely made.

What the world needs above all is a large and increasing supply of incorruptibles, men and women who have learned to act in the interest of mankind, who are capable of noble action as an outcome of unpremeditated thought, and are capable of clarity of thought as a natural and intuitive result of their experience in thinking and in acting. It is the responsibility of the university so to arrange its affairs that the experience of its students in thinking and acting can teach them what it means to serve mankind and what it means to honor the intellect.

IV / Escape from History?
The Present Imperative

IV.1 Escape from History:
The Present Imperative

While all the other sections deal directly and often concretely with the American radical experience in the sixties, this section is more abstract. It is concerned principally with what is happening to us metaphysically and historically. The writers in this section are aware that the old clichés cannot be repeated ad infinitum under the rubric of "history," that new angles of sight and new vocabularies are necessary if our visions are to catch up with our realities.

What is radical about these essays and their writers? Chiefly, it is the passionate desire to break the present off from the past, to see what is happening to us and our world, without encumbering ourselves with historical considerations. Nearly all of these writers are academics and historians, and thus they feel very heavily how many of our present perspectives are explained by means of the past. At the same time they feel, almost to a man, that such present attitudes as we hold are frequently falsified when the past is invoked. As the first essay by Frederick R. Karl makes clear, they sense that the past is often invoked—in terms of customs, traditions, patriotism, history—sometimes out of pure innocence and sometimes out of pure malice by those who want to befog the contemporary scene. Instead, the present scene must be assessed, they argue, not through the rose-colored glasses of past achievements and successes nor through the scruffy spectacles of historians who have only contempt for the contemporary scene, but by realistic analysis of history-in-the-making, of the "existential" present. Indeed, to approach the radical thought of today with nineteenth-century tools is an ex-

ercise in futility. To avoid the perpetuation of such useless calis-
thenics, we must completely remodel our educational values and
systems and incorporate into them the new styles of looking at
man.

Another insistent note in all these essays, besides the need for
reassessment, is that of self-awareness. The rejection of authority, whether of an actual person or of an abstraction like the historical past, brings with it the corollary of increased consciousness of the self in the universe. The essay by Jean-Paul Sartre,
the French novelist and philosopher, defines this quality as the
very substance of existentialism, the most influential idea of our
time. (Norman Mailer applies it to the urban crisis in the section
called "Challenge of the Environment.") Note Sartre's insistence on the responsibility of each man for his own behavior, and
his responsibility in himself for what most people assign to luck,
chance, or circumstance. Each man defines himself through his
existence itself. If there is any "essence," it is whatever vision
the individual has of himself or his nature before he acts. Thus
man in defining himself every moment lives in a kind of "perpetual crisis" which requires constant perception of the present.
If one cuts himself off from the past, then of course he cannot
escape into the past; he cannot use the past as a crutch.

So too does psychoanalyst Allen Wheelis argue that we can
change if we believe that change is possible. That is, we can release ourselves from previous postures if we really believe in
what we are at this moment and what we want to be in the future. Often a radical vision of oneself that is not unrealistic can
be the catalyst. Biological necessity or determinism is not an
argument against this conception of the individual will, except
in those instances where a person is obviously biologically dis-
advantaged.

Peter Marin's "soliloquy" touches tangentially on other themes
in this book—the values of the "Now" generation, the challenge
of the environment, and student unrest—but it belongs most
obviously in this section. Marin asserts that in educating adolescents "we make do at the moment with a set of ideas inherited
from the nineteenth century, from an industrial, relatively puritanical, repressive, and 'localized' culture; we try to gum them
like labels to new kinds of experience. But that won't do." Marin
calls for a radical reassessment of these ideas: "We must dis-

mantle them and start again from scratch." In so doing we must
discard the old vision of adolescence and education that confines us to habit and rules out perception, and preserve from the
past only that which can be internalized and harmonized with
the rhythms of the individual being. What he proposes is a combination of McLuhan, Norman O. Brown, Sartre, and his own
highly original ideas. His argument is apocalyptic in its implication that we must alter the whole social environment in which
a child grows up rather than just tinker with the schools.

An interesting gloss on these issues has been provided by
Alberto Moravia, the Italian novelist who during the forties
was debarred from both the Soviet Union and the United States
on political grounds. His introduction to *The Red Book and the
Great Wall*, an account of his second trip to China, sees that Goliath of Asia as a break with the immediate past, as the new
society of the future in which poverty, honorable poverty, will be
the standard of all—at least in the so-called Third World nations.
Along the way, Moravia pictures most of the West—with America
as leader—as obsessed with production and consumption; thus,
Western man, in this view, is caught in a cycle that "uses" him,
determines his manhood and his humanity and, if he becomes
too numerous, eliminates him through war. Although Moravia
has reservations about China's aims and progress, he perceives
the truly radical nature of its undertaking: to slice through all
past history in order to create a society without distinct variations in wealth, a life deliberately based upon equal poverty
instead of equal wealth. Moravia also senses the radical possibilities of inner cohesion that such planned poverty can create.

All of these views are suggestive of one ultimate question:
what are the possibilities of a revolution in America? That is,
have radical ideas elevated us to a point where revolution itself
can be discussed without setting off emergency alarms in educated minds? Of course, revolution now would be something
quite different from the American Revolution, which was essentially classless and which was directed against an overseas
power. Revolution at the present would spring out of class, caste,
and color, and would be fought against domestic authority if the
latter should become ruthless and repressive.

Even as the student asks himself this question, he must
grapple with several others. First, can the past and historical

reasoning itself provide guides when present situations remain fluid? Second, is discontent on a broad enough scale to warrant talk of revolution? Third, is revolution only a romantic idea in the minds of would-be revolutionaries? As Barrington Moore, Jr., in his "Revolution in America?" says: "One task of human thought is to try to perceive what the range of possibilities may be in a future that always carries on its back the burden of the present and the past."

16 / The Uselessness of the Past

FREDERICK R. KARL

One way in which a nation defines itself is by its attitudes to its own past. Most countries glorify past events and aspirations and in the process create certain inflated standards or artificial norms which they use to evaluate and revise the present. Such measures or gauges we usually call tradition, custom, convention, or myth. When these standards or attitudes are applied to contemporary events, they frequently confer a patriotic or nationalistic tone. Generally, the shakier a regime, or the more dishonest its position, the more forcefully it recalls its past, whether as glory or as shame.

At present, America seems to be glorifying its past at a time when its past never appeared more shameful. All the myths are pulled out: the myth of equality, the myth of liberty and justice for all, the myth of the melting pot, the myth of the American as Adam and the country as Paradise, the myth of America as the protector of the downtrodden and the savior of the poor, the myth of democratic political processes, and, finally, the myth that, unlike Europeans, Americans do not live by myths. Such myths are a democracy's way of rewriting history.

SOURCE: This essay was written especially for this volume.

Frederick R. Karl, who teaches at the City College of New York, has written several books on the novel, including *A Reader's Guide to Joseph Conrad, An Age of Fiction: The Nineteenth-Century British Novel*, and *The Contemporary English Novel*. He is presently editing the collected letters of Joseph Conrad.

Indeed, the past can serve many functions. In several of the new African nations, whose boundary lines are often almost the sole mark of their development, the past means colonial hypocrisy, racial indignities, humiliating and divisive tribal warfare, and economic exploitation. The present, not ripeness, is all. For the great powers who have lost their preeminent position through war, like Germany and France, the past is blocked off as either disgraceful (Germany) or unsuccessful (France) in order to prod reestablishment in a modern setting. Still another method—England's—is to fall back almost entirely on glorious rhetoric or common traditions (one's school tie, club, inheritance taxes) when the present challenge proves greater than current effort or interest. A fourth alternative—Russia's and to some extent China's—is equally desperate: the past, usually literary-cultural attainment, is rewritten to accommodate present necessity.

The American attitude toward its past is even less rooted in reality and based more on evasions and distortions in an effort to provide something—anything—as a basis for the haphazard present. The past, whether related to the Indian, the Negro, or the immigrant, is exploited almost solely for the myths of democracy and economic progress it affords rather than for the truths it might offer—as if Boosters were to accept as gospel their own lobbying. In this sense, the past has become almost totally illusory, apparently useful only for pseudo-educational purposes. Our schools nurture the young on myth, not reality. The conflict between the schools, which counsel democracy, and life outside the schools, which counsels national power, amounts to a kind of national schizophrenia, or what historian Richard Hofstadter has called "the paranoid style" in American politics. Possibly, in the light of our mythical attitudes, American historical and literary figures should be taught in the schools, not as representing ideas, philosophies, or even strivings, but as the manifestations of developing power—the way paleolithic man is presented in anthropology courses.

Perhaps, after all, it is fitting that the American view of its past should prove schizophrenic, for it is a past that has no immediate significance for half, or perhaps more, of the population. The American past, like caviar, was and is an acquired taste for 100 million people.

Such a conclusion runs counter to our romanticization of the past, especially to our sentimental gloss of American literature and institutions in the public schools. A good deal of naive scholarship has indicated that the American experience tended to draw in all people, so that the first generation of immigrants, after two or three decades, was already on the path to becoming Americans, thus creating a common past of struggle, mutual aims, and similar assumptions about freedom and individual rights. This view holds that these immigrants almost immediately accepted the American way of unlimited opportunity, leading, in one generation or another, to higher economic status and a keen sense of individual dignity. And if the first immigrants failed to come through, so the familiar reasoning runs, then certainly their children and children's children did. The conclusion was comforting, for it implied that the American way was so overwhelming that Europe's poor could hardly resist. It gave the past a gritty but palatable flavor.

The conception is, at least partially, a myth. The conformation that occurred, when it did occur, was almost solely at the economic level, which is usually the easiest place to convince people of superficial change. In those areas where real change occurs—at the cohesive level of ideas, tastes, attitudes, even philosophies—the new American accepted little, possibly nothing, except headlines. He skimmed off the top of what commonly passed as the American experience, chiefly its economic opportunities and its easy patriotism, its Protestant view of the reasonable individual, *as if* it really had meaning for him. Perhaps it did—but only as an aid to economic betterment. The cultural ideas being developed by native American poets and essayists, for example, Emerson, Thoreau, Whitman, were to remain alien until their work could be assimilated later as myth, and romanticized. Further, to the immigrant or immigrant's child, as to the Negro, what meaning do the American Revolution and Constitution have except that they give him certain legally guaranteed expectations? It is these rights he desires, leading to economic opportunity, not any understanding of the past.

In this respect, the American past is unique. The United States is the sole nation—perhaps Australia is another, but much lesser, example—in which a large part of its population has no direct or even indirect connection with the historical past it is expected

264

to honor. Surely this results from America's never having assimilated its several nationalities; they live together not because of an accepted history but by virtue of an economic truce. What is true of history is surely even more evident in literature. The American literary past provided, or provides, almost no viable meaning for the many millions who came to the United States in the last 120 years—and would have provided no meaning even if those people had been more literate than they were. It must be made perfectly clear that even if the immigrants had derived more from the middle rather than the lower and peasant classes, American literature as emanating from our nineteenth-century masters still would be without significance.

An example: One of the commonplaces of American literature and thought is that Thoreau's two years at Walden is, essentially, an archetypal experience, an instance of the triumph of human dignity over conformity and materialism. Further, Thoreau's experience is held to illustrate that even within the confines of a commercialized and industrialized society which limits individual response, there are avenues of escape to that private place where we can be ourselves, and the manipulatory bosses, those modern Fates, cannot get at us. So goes the Thoreau myth, or at least a good part of it.

Yet almost the first thing the immigrant, the Negro, and both the older and newer American wish to forsake is any sense of individual or unique self in order to cut more readily into the pie of economic goodies. The self, indeed, seems to be about the easiest thing to dispose of, particularly when it is at odds with current goals. Compromise is the keynote—of expectation, preparation, style of life—until one stands for nothing, the self annihilated by pressures one cannot begin to understand, no less control or counteract. We need look no further than recent establishment "intellectuals" to see where the sewer leaks.

Is it an exaggeration to claim that the entire educational system—from nursery school to Ph.D.—is organized to encourage collective American goals and ideals, not individual ones? In few places, to be sure, are students encouraged to go it alone, *wherever it may lead*, whatever the consequences (LSD trips, homosexuality, pacifism, antigovernment demonstrations, racial intermarriage, atheism, draft-dodging, premarital sex, religious conversion). What is true educationally is apparent in all areas. The self, we are informed, is flexible, not rigid; the individual, we are told further, can measure himself by his ability to bend with the times and with his own immediate needs. He must discipline himself, resist inner compulsions, face responsibility, go off to war or peace, as the nation needs, in any event cut his expectations. We call the process maturity. If he does not mature, we call in a psychiatrist.

For Thoreau, however, there was no equivocating. The individual of any era and any background should be undivided, inflexible in principles, unyielding in his personal vision. Thus the miniature world Thoreau embraced at Walden takes on the hues and qualities of the larger world: our wholeness, he cautions, should be intensely present in all aspects of our existence, including work and leisure. The key words are surely *wholeness* and *intensity*. Yet how unthinkable to feel intense or whole about one's activities today! There are always a happy few who feel involved and fulfilled, but for most—and often the brightest—work, leisure, even consumption are things not to throw oneself into but to escape from. Even if three-quarters of Americans say they like their jobs, their personalities are lost in the work, not refocused by it. The man is made to fit the job, not the job the man–even at the top. A kind of spoliation takes place, like the rotting of tasty fruit, with the acquiescence of the individual.

Examples abound, especially in the new world of managers and administrators, whose roles are by necessity parasitical. Professors, for instance, who become deans begin to act as they think deans should act, not as men of supposed intellectual training who must now face administrative problems. They shortly become politicians, benevolent ward bosses, gaining an "administrative personality," becoming part of the team, advocating a steady course through the rocky seas of student discontent, channeling energy into compliance, originality into acceptable modes—all out of keeping with the ideals they once had, or the assumptions of thinker and individualist.

One recalls here psychologist Erik Erikson's definition of the ambiguous but much used term "Bürger." Often translated to mean someone solid and responsible, it is applied by Erikson to a type of "adult who has betrayed youth and idealism and has sought refuge in a petty and servile kind of conservatism." From dean to Dean Rusk, the type helps define the age. Erikson also warns that when people have no human, singular basis for their lives, a nation suffers from collective anxiety and clings to absolutes. With its present a series of contradictions, its past becomes mythical, illusory, more and more a false refuge—a bomb shelter that will indefinitely prolong life amidst universal disaster.

A nation trying to lead the world while unable itself to distinguish between myth and reality is a force only for destruction. When others balk at buying our myths or beliefs about past and present, we become infuriated and even more self-righteous about our schizophrenia. In late 1969, the Vietnam War continued because of America's obsession with the myth of her invincibility, when in the last 150 years she had yet to be tested by her equals.

Even if Thoreau—that difficult, angular figure—is bypassed, then Emerson steps forth as the American Goethe. How does Emerson—that is, the man under the Boosterism—fare as a guide in contemporary America, which often regards him as its greatest natural philosopher? About as well, one might say, as did Goethe under Nazism in Germany. Emerson taught, among other things, that man is the source of all; that the individual "intellect searches out the absolute order of things as they stand in the mind of God"; that indeed "to know what God speaks, one must close himself to all else."

This advice, if pursued, should lead to spiritual awakening, to the thrust of the individual toward self-realization, to the quickening of the individual's fibers. Emerson wanted men simply to be men: solid in themselves, certain, thoughtful, meaningful. When such qualities—and such men—come to pass, then from the mind of man will flow a new world, in which the individual consciousness can successfully transform external reality. Man must become king in his own kingdom.

First things first: Emerson's abstractions about the thinking man and the spiritual life are virtually useless to our society, although we can assume that in the nineteenth century they still had the spark of working illusions. A contemporary illustration: Usually a country's leaders mirror its own inclinations or at least reflect a large segment of the population—its tastes, its attitudes, even its cultural aspirations. A president is one of us, we are told, despite his wealth and immoderate love of power. Starting with our modern era, from 1932—Franklin Roosevelt, and continuing through Truman, Eisenhower, Kennedy, and Johnson—we may ask, Which is Emersonian? Yet, with these words, we recognize the ludicrousness of the question. Emerson asked for flexibility, not rigidity; latitude, not provinciality; continual largeness of mind, not pettiness; ideas, not materiality. For many, Roosevelt was an economic god (or devil!), but spiritually and culturally he said—however truthfully—he was stirred by repeated hearings of "Home on the Range." Similarly, Johnson's ultramodern ranch features Muzak rustling through the trees, and during crises Eisenhower relaxed with cowboy stories designed for school dropouts. Only Kennedy—like Teddy Roosevelt (the historian's example)—even vaguely approaches, and yet his pragmatism, often narrow and rigid, cut off instead of opened up thought, however witty his delivery.

When Emerson's qualities have appeared for brief moments in political life, as in the earlier career of Adlai Stevenson, the word "egghead" was created to ridicule a type, to characterize a would-be bumbler, to render impotent the thoughtful man. The process is symptomatic. Eventually the "egghead" is shelled, revealed, then rerouted into powerless positions. All the time he continues to crow, even to croon, but he says nothing. Even in *his* day—before 1850—Emerson came to see that American overconfidence would lead to a restrictive pragmatism whenever problems became complicated or touchy. Under the guise of watered-down idealism (the ideological cover for pragmatism), American shortsightedness would shine forth; faced by a crisis, major or minor, only the economy, or the military, would respond.

Obviously, the Emersonian theses—despite lip service—have been stripped or ignored in order to fulfill more pressing assumptions. F. O. Matthiessen comments that Emerson's *Essays* were the favorite reading of Henry Ford! Such is the nature of the American heritage: the real Emerson may also be bunk! Yet it was Emerson's definition of the flowering self and its achievements, so alien to what could possibly appeal to the manufacturer, that gave the essayist his distinction. Quite different from Ford's economic self-righteousness, the Transcendentalist's intense awareness of inwardness created certainty, character, and uniqueness, not goon squads or anti-Semitism based on fears of a Zionist conspiracy. Emerson rerouted is apparently more comfortable.

After a rocky reception, Whitman, too, has entered the American pantheon. But which Whitman? What aspects? The Whitman who claimed that "a man only is interested in anything when he identifies with it"? The Whitman who insisted that we are redeemed by "the sexual fibre of things"? This latter is Whitman at his most Lawrentian, and his most unacceptable—hardly the man who is candidate for the most American of poets. What precisely, we may ask further, is American about him? His open-chested manliness, when his lack of manliness is precisely what bothered his contemporaries? His open-hearted acceptance of phenomena supposedly indicative of American tolerance and forebearance—this in a country that rapidly loses most of its tolerance under serious threat and remains as race-ridden a nation as any in the western world, the rather successful practitioner of 300 years of apartheid? His embracement of experience ("I was there," "America is me"), representative of the huge expanse of the American experience—when breadth of experience is precisely the commodity one must now discourage to succeed; when sharpness of focus with as little breadth as possible gains the various things of the world; when education itself discourages breadth in favor of concentration, or depth, as it is more advantageously defined?

Whitman has indeed been gutted. Even more than Wordsworth's, his poetry is agrarian, individualized, hardly suitable for a fully industrialized America. There is too little of the tragic appositeness of urban American life in Whitman, and it is just this that makes him appealing to the vast army of Americans who still wish to see America as innocent, who, in fact, hide behind innocence as others might conspire behind city walls.

The historically important part of Thoreau, Emerson, and Whitman in their day and in our own is their awareness of the dignity of man—a strangely archaic phrase called up in times of stress. Yet valuable as it is, dignity—or people's sense of mutual worthiness—is hardly the substance honored in present-day America, nor is there much chance that it will be honored in the

FREDERICK R. KARL 269

future. The tempo and tone of modern life find little need for the quality. Whose, we may ask. The Negro's? The other minority groups? The dignity of the worker? The professional's? The celebrity's? The politician's? The businessman's? Just who or what is dignified as we look over American life? To what profession can we turn to find it? How very depressing if we must restrict it to the universities! And in what capacity? Professorial? Administrative? The student himself? Even here, we may possibly find it only in a small, retiring college, where one gives up all sense of enlargement and expanse. *Restrict* the self, that is, restrict desire, and dignity is attainable.

Yet this sense of restriction or withdrawal is, of course, clearly contrary to the nineteenth-century conception of the good life— in the name of which Emerson and Thoreau inveighed so forcefully against the shivering of man into fragments. It was Emerson, after all, who said that "life was a matter of having good days." Division of labor, for them, meant division of the worker into subpieces, the sum of which were always less than the man. This was Thoreau's romantic, agrarian side, his espousal of the whole individual (at Walden or anywhere) whose labor was his culture, whose culture was his labor. Through labor, one developed mind and soul; through mind and soul, one created labor.

To recall this is to mock ourselves. As we have heard, virtually all work lacks any sense of a larger culture; virtually all work presupposes a desire to do less work, to get away from it altogether—perfectly justifiable in the light of what work normally is. To hate labor is to be cool; by that standard, one measures his temperament and status. To be interested in it for itself is a form of madness, like sea bathing in the winter ice. Only the wretched work; the rest watch. In our luxurious machinery, our abundant grants, scholarships, and bonus plans, even in the idea of our unions, we have subtly recognized that work itself must be evaded, that one measures his human condition as a working man by the amount of work he escapes. So it is that in an age of almost total work, we retain, indeed we shout schizophrenically, the aristocratic notion of free time. Our cries, needless to say, emanate from a bottomless well of confusion and self-hate.

270

Rejection of the past, unfortunately, may be irreversible. There is, possibly, no returning to the wisdom, or sins, of the fathers once the fathers have been mythified and distorted. Or else a people lives precariously and picaresquely, trading out of hand honored ideas from the past for misleading notions about the present. Seemingly, one will have it both ways, while, actually, the house may fall when the power base is challenged. Even when destruction looms, the paranoid style may prove inflexible.

One can hope, at best, for a realistic assessment of the present —founded on a tentative but conscientious rejection of the past, its myths and illusions as well as its substance. Although I do not believe that Harold Rosenberg's Tradition of the New really exists to *his* degree, we must, at some point, decide in defense that it apparently does and act accordingly.[1] Paradoxically, perhaps, we must gropingly construct myths about the present to exclude those of the past, all the time recognizing the danger of creating new illusions. Traditional philosophies—especially those offering a reasoned basis for pragmatism and naturalism —create only confusion for those who must act, so inaccurately are they understood, so completely are they fragmented and distorted. Perhaps they are no longer relevant. They may still work for those who think, but the number is too small to exert influence *when* it is needed. Even among those who think, a power base—personal or public—is necessary before the thought can begin to be translated into public relations. After all, Robert Lowell became a vocal but minor cultural force (as apart from poet) only when an intellectual journal (*New York Review of Books*) and its highly trained cadre of reviewers rallied behind him.

None of this need be quite as depressing as it first appears. We are suffering from what sociologists have traditionally called cultural lag: our power has outrun our rational means to understand and control it. The arena—political, social, intellectual—

---

[1] In *The Tradition of the New* (1959), essays on modern culture, Rosenberg writes that "In the arts an appetite for a new look is now a professional requirement. . . . The famous "modern break with tradition" has lasted long enough to have produced its own tradition. . . . Since then there have come into being an art whose history, regardless of the credos of its practitioners, has consisted of leaps from vanguard to vanguard, and political mass movements whose aim has been the total renovation not only of social institutions but of man himself."

FREDERICK R. KARL 271

takes on the hues and colors of a scene from *Alice in Wonderland,* with our hopped-up leaders, so splendidly energized, charging in from all corners, snorting, sneering, sniffing. But all is not lost, not by any means. True, the arena does appear to control *collective* destinies more tightly than ever before, but we can still gain *individual* freedom to the degree that we mock, satirize, ridicule. The wave of the future may ride on humor.

Although our present generation of fictional philosophers is not of the stature of Emerson, Thoreau, and Whitman, their sarcasm and irony indeed offer a new version of pragmatism and naturalism. They speak of course of city life, not of the "last scud of day" or of "lilac blooming perennial," but the sophisticated city now controls our imagination. We are a country of cities, not a country of country. Though rural may still suggest romantic images of nature and escape, it also entails city-prosaics like price supports, chemical feed and vegetables, low-flying planes spraying DDT, cows milked mechanically while listening to Tin Pan Alley—a heritage they share with cliff hangers.

These new comic philosophers also speak of orgasmic enrichment—resurrection of self through abundant intercourse, both normal and the far-out stuff of fantasies. They advocate fun and games. Good sex, these acute psychologists have noted, means good reason. Having rejected the old division between mind and sex (itself a myth based on guilt!), in excellent non-Freudian fashion they have plumped for the sexual man— humorous, reasonable, sensitive, decent, usually Jewish, sometimes intellectual, always humanistic. Their humor has hastily been called "black," but in America anything is called black that is not traditionally tied to the past. Anarchistic on the surface, they stand for man.

For these writers, humor is a form of cultural revisionism, a revolutionary point of view, the fictional equivalent of Norman O. Brown in history and philosophy, Marshall McLuhan in communications, Harold Rosenberg in art criticism, Jean-Luc Godard in cinema, *Ramparts* and the *New York Review of Books* in journalism. Virtually every person, idea, motive, and activity comes under the comic hammer. Only politicians, statesmen, world leaders are spared: so outrageously and evidently funny in themselves, no writer need bother. *They*—the writers—know

272

that only a clown would try to control events. What would a Barth, Friedman, Heller, Mailer, Purdy, Southern make of the marriage between Johnson and Humphrey that spawned a Ky, with Rusk as midwife and McNamara as handy supplier of deadly toys? One need only contemplate their treatment of such fellows to see that the *new* means survival through rejection of all nonsense, through concern with the individual (not the "idea" or the "cause") and support of human values *wherever* they lead.

They are not existentialists (too morbid), nor sentimentalists (too full of social illusions), nor pragmatists (too many political crimes have been committed in its name). Since they aim to get behind history, the past has little significance. The present is all; if one must connect, they would agree with Emerson's aside that life consists of having good days. In the phase is implied a new mode of life, the beginning of a contemporary myth.

Let us indeed weep over the past, we cultural diehards, as Milton wept over Lycidas, but bury it we must. We are, let us agree, so much the worse for that. But live, also, we must, and we need a present to accept and believe in. Outdated myths are dangerous when backed up by realistic military might. New myths are more accessible and, for a time, more controllable. Our nostalgia for a romantic past filled with the stalwart figures of Emerson, Thoreau, and Melville only adds to the confusion. Their values will never again prevail, and like Herodotus and Thucidydes they should be read as the historians of our buried lives. Nineteenth-century literature passes into sociology and history, even into anthropology: the delineation of the mores of a strange race of natives who, too, had their illusions. True, they produced men with vision, while we produce comics. But comedy expresses us and our aspirations, and to see ourselves still as tragic only compounds the confusion.

We are not, as Emerson thought, tragic comedians but comic tragedians, a different phrase and a different world. We have reduced tragic visions to all-purpose computers. Our man of the future wears not the garb of Emerson's scholar, but a spacesuit and lifeline to protect him against the atmosphere. Our heroes now are those who leave the earth far behind, a notable distance from the nineteenth-century creature for whom Emerson said "Life only avails." *His* man, as Hawthorne's and Thoreau's, was of the world; ours, rejecting earth as overpopulated, sealed off, somehow solved, is already stretching out toward heaven. The search for space objects, frontiers, worlds of adventure has left us caught between past myths—never rejected—and future hopes—rarely understood. Meanwhile the present presses in curious picaresque style, and we must—alas!—seek suitable structures to contain it, or else we continue to spiral, like Yeats' gyres, in painful and pitiful ambiguity.

17 / Existentialism

JEAN-PAUL SARTRE

I should like on this occasion to defend existentialism against some charges which have been brought against it.

First, it has been charged with inviting people to remain in a kind of desperate quietism because, since no solutions are possible, we should have to consider action in this world as quite impossible. We should then end up in a philosophy of contemplation; and since contemplation is a luxury, we come in the end to a bourgeois philosophy. The communists in particular have made these charges.

On the other hand, we have been charged with dwelling on human degradation, with pointing up everywhere the sordid, shady, and slimy, and neglecting the gracious and beautiful, the bright side of human nature; for example, according to Mlle. Mercier, a Catholic critic, with forgetting the smile of the child. Both sides charge us with having ignored human solidarity, with considering man as an isolated being. The communists say that the main reason for this is that we take pure subjectivity, the *Cartesian I think*, as our starting point; in other words, the moment in which man becomes fully aware of what it means to

SOURCE: Jean-Paul Sartre, *Existentialism*, trans. Bernard Frechtman (New York: Philosophical Library, 1947), pp. 275–97. Reprinted by permission of the author and publisher.

Jean-Paul Sartre is the internationally known philosopher whose chief work has been to define contemporary existentialism; he is also a novelist and short story writer of renown, and has been an influence on virtually every radical movement of the last twenty years.

him to be an isolated being; as a result, we are unable to return to a state of solidarity with the men who are not ourselves, a state which we can never reach in the *cogito*.

From the Christian standpoint, we are charged with denying the reality and seriousness of human undertakings, since, if we reject God's commandments and the eternal verities, there no longer remains anything but pure caprice, with everyone permitted to do as he pleases and incapable, from his own point of view, of condemning the points of view and acts of others.

I shall try today to answer these different charges. Many people are going to be surprised at what is said here about humanism. We shall try to see in what sense it is to be understood. In any case, what can be said from the very beginning is that by existentialism we mean a doctrine which makes human life possible and, in addition, declares that every truth and every action implies a human setting and a human subjectivity.

As is generally known, the basic charge against us is that we put the emphasis on the dark side of human life. Someone recently told me of a lady who, when she let slip a vulgar word in a moment of irritation, excused herself by saying, "I guess I'm becoming an existentialist." Consequently, existentialism is regarded as something ugly; that is why we are said to be naturalists; and if we are, it is rather surprising that in this day and age we cause so much more alarm and scandal than does naturalism, properly so called. The kind of person who can take in his stride such a novel as Zola's *The Earth* is disgusted as soon as he starts reading an existentialist novel; the kind of person who is resigned to the wisdom of the ages—which is pretty sad—finds us even sadder. Yet, what can be more disillusioning than saying "true charity begins at home" or "a scoundrel will always return evil for good?"

We know the commonplace remarks made when this subject comes up, remarks which always add up to the same thing: we shouldn't struggle against the powers-that-be; we shouldn't resist authority; we shouldn't try to rise above our station; any action which doesn't conform to authority is romantic; any effort not based on past experience is doomed to failure; experience shows that man's bent is always toward trouble, that there must be a strong hand to hold him in check, if not, there will be anarchy. There are still people who go on mumbling these melancholy old saws, the people who say, "It's only human!" whenever a more or less repugnant act is pointed out to them, the people who glut themselves on *chansons réalistes*; these are the people who accuse existentialism of being too gloomy, and to such an extent that I wonder whether they are complaining about it, not for its pessimism, but much rather its optimism. Can it be that what really scares them in the doctrine I shall try to present here is that it leaves to man a possibility of choice? To answer this question, we must re-examine it on a strictly philosophical plane. What is meant by the term *existentialism*?

Most people who use the word would be rather embarrassed if they had to explain it, since, now that the word is all the rage, even the work of a musician or painter is being called existentialist. A gossip columnist in *Clartés* signs himself *The Existentialist*, so that by this time the word has been so stretched and has taken on so broad a meaning, that it no longer means anything at all. It seems that for want of an advance-guard doctrine analogous to surrealism, the kind of people who are eager for scandal and flurry turn to this philosophy which in other respects does not at all serve their purposes in this sphere.

Actually, it is the least scandalous, the most austere of doctrines. It is intended strictly for specialists and philosophers. Yet it can be defined easily. What complicates matters is that there are two kinds of existentialist; first, those who are Christian, among whom I would include Jaspers and Gabriel Marcel, both Catholic; and on the other hand the atheistic existentialists, among whom I class Heidegger, and then the French existentialists and myself. What they have in common is that they think that existence precedes essence, or, if you prefer, that subjectivity must be the starting point.

Just what does that mean? Let us consider some object that is manufactured, for example, a book or a paper-cutter: here is an object which has been made by an artisan whose inspiration came from a concept. He referred to the concept of what a paper-cutter is and likewise to a known method of production, which is part of the concept, something which is, by and large, a routine. Thus, the paper-cutter is at once an object produced in a certain way and, on the other hand, one having a specific use; and one cannot postulate a man who produces a paper-cutter but does not know what it is used for. Therefore, let us say that, for the paper-cutter, essence—that is, the ensemble of both the production routines and the properties which enable it to be both produced and defined—precedes existence. Thus, the presence of the paper-cutter or book in front of me is determined. Therefore, we have here a technical view of the world whereby it can be said that production precedes existence.

When we conceive God as the Creator, He is generally thought of as a superior sort of artisan. Whatever doctrine we may be considering, whether one like that of Descartes or that of Leibnitz, we always grant that will more or less follows understanding or, at the very least, accompanies it, and that when God creates He knows exactly what He is creating. Thus, the concept of man in the mind of God is comparable to the concept of paper-cutter in the mind of the manufacturer, and, following certain techniques and a conception, God produces man, just as the artisan, following a definition and a technique, makes a paper-cutter. Thus, the individual man is the realisation of a certain concept in the divine intelligence.

In the eighteenth century, the atheism of the *philosophes* discarded the idea of God, but not so much for the notion that essence precedes existence. To a certain extent, this idea is found everywhere; we find it in Diderot, in Voltaire, and even in Kant. Man has a human nature; this human nature, which is the concept of the human, is found in all men, which means that each man is a particular example of a universal concept, man. In Kant, the result of this universality is that the wild-man, the natural man, as well as the bourgeois, are circumscribed by the same definition and have the same basic qualities. Thus, here too the essence of man precedes the historical existence that we find in nature.

Atheistic existentialism, which I represent, is more coherent. It states that if God does not exist, there is at least one being in whom existence precedes essence, a being who exists before he can be defined by any concept, and that this being is man, or, as Heidegger says, human reality. What is meant here by saying that existence precedes essence? It means that, first of all, man exists, turns up, appears on the scene, and, only afterwards, defines himself. If man, as the existentialist conceives him, is indefinable, it is because at first he is nothing. Only afterward will he be something, and he himself will have made what he will be. Thus, there is no human nature, since there is no God to conceive it. Not only is man what he conceives himself to be, but he is also only what he wills himself to be after this thrust toward existence.

Man is nothing else but what he makes of himself. Such is the first principle of existentialism. It is also what is called subjectivity, the name we are labeled with when charges are brought against us. But what do we mean by this, if not that man has a greater dignity than a stone or table? For we mean that man first exists, that is, that man first of all is the being who hurls himself toward a future and who is conscious of imagining himself as being in the future. Man is at the start a plan which is aware of itself, rather than a patch of moss, a piece of garbage, or a cauliflower; nothing exists prior to this plan; there is nothing in heaven; man will be what he will have planned to be. Not what he will want to be. Because by the word "will" we generally mean a conscious decision, which is subsequent to what we have already made of ourselves. I may want to belong to a political party, write a book, get married; but all that is only a manifestation of an earlier, more spontaneous choice that is called "will." But if existence really does precede essence, man is responsible for what he is. Thus, existentialism's first move is to make every man aware of what he is and to make the full responsibility of his existence rest on him. And when we say that a man is responsible for himself, we do not only mean that he is responsible for his own individuality, but that he is responsible for all men.

The word subjectivism has two meanings, and our opponents play on the two. Subjectivism means, on the one hand, that an individual chooses and makes himself; and, on the other, that it is impossible for man to transcend human subjectivity. The second of these is the essential meaning of existentialism. When we say that man chooses his own self, we mean that every one of us does likewise; but we also mean by that that in making this choice he also chooses all men. In fact, in creating the man that we want to be, there is not a single one of our acts which does not at the same time create an image of man as we think he ought to be. To choose to be this or that is to affirm at the same time the value of what we choose, because we can never choose evil. We always choose the good, and nothing can be good for us without being good for all.

If, on the other hand, existence precedes essence, and if we grant that we exist and fashion our image at one and the same time, the image is valid for everybody and for our whole age. Thus, our responsibility is much greater than we might have supposed, because it involves all mankind. If I am a working-man and choose to join a Christian trade-union rather than be a communist, and if by being a member I want to show that the best thing for man is resignation, that the kingdom of man is not of this world, I am not only involving my own case—I want to be resigned for everyone. As a result, my action has involved all humanity. To take a more individual matter, if I want to marry, to have children; even if this marriage depends solely on my own circumstances or passion or wish, I am involving all humanity in monogamy and not merely myself. Therefore, I am responsible for myself and for everyone else. I am creating a certain image of man of my own choosing. In choosing myself, I choose man.

This helps us understand what the actual content is of such rather grandiloquent words as anguish, forlornness, despair. As you will see, it's all quite simple.

First, what is meant by anguish? The existentialists say at once that man is anguish. What that means is this: the man who involves himself and who realizes that he is not only the person he chooses to be, but also a law-maker who is, at the same time, choosing all mankind as well as himself, cannot help escape the feeling of his total and deep responsibility. Of course, there are many people who are not anxious; but we claim that they are hiding their anxiety, that they are fleeing from it. Certainly, many people believe that when they do something, they themselves are the only ones involved, and when someone says to them, "What if everyone acted that way?" they shrug their shoulders and answer, "Everyone doesn't act that way." But really, one should always ask himself, "What would happen if everybody looked at things that way?" There is no escaping this disturbing thought except by a kind of double-dealing. A man who lies and makes excuses for himself by saying "not everybody does that," is someone with an uneasy conscience, because the act of lying implies that a universal value is conferred upon the lie.

Anguish is evident even when it conceals itself. This is the anguish that Kierkegaard called the anguish of Abraham. You know the story: an angel has ordered Abraham to sacrifice his son; if it really were an angel who has come and said, "You are Abraham, you shall sacrifice your son," everything would be all right. But everyone might first wonder, "Is it really an angel, and am I really Abraham? What proof do I have?"

There was a madwoman who had hallucinations; someone used to speak to her on the telephone and give her orders. Her doctor asked her, "Who is it who talks to you?" She answered, "He says it's God." What proof did she really have that it was God? If an angel comes to me, what proof is there that it's an angel? And if I hear voices, what proof is there that they come from heaven and not from hell, or from the subconscious, or a pathological condition? What proves that they are addressed to me? What proof is there that I have been appointed to impose my choice and my conception of man on humanity? I'll never find any proof or sign to convince me of that. If a voice addresses me, it is always for me to decide that this is the angel's voice; if I consider that such an act is a good one, it is I who will choose to say that it is good rather than bad.

Now, I'm not being singled out as an Abraham, and yet at every moment I'm obliged to perform exemplary acts. For every man, everything happens as if all mankind had its eyes fixed on him and were guiding itself by what he does. And every man ought to say to himself, "Am I really the kind of man who has the right to act in such a way that humanity might guide itself by my actions?" And if he does not say that to himself, he is masking his anguish.

There is no question here of the kind of anguish which would lead to quietism, to inaction. It is a matter of a simple sort of anguish that anybody who has had responsibilities is familiar with. For example, when a military officer takes the responsibility for an attack and sends a certain number of men to death, he chooses to do so, and in the main he alone makes the choice. Doubtless, orders come from above, but they are too broad; he interprets them, and on this interpretation depend the lives of ten or fourteen or twenty men. In making a decision he cannot help having a certain anguish. All leaders know this anguish. That doesn't keep them from acting; on the contrary, it is the very condition of their action. For it implies that they envisage a number of possibilities, and when they choose one they realize that it has value only because it is chosen. We shall see that this kind of anguish, which is the kind that existentialism describes, is explained, in addition, by a direct responsibility to the other men whom it involves. It is not a curtain separating us from action, but is part of action itself.

When we speak of forlornness, a term Heidegger was fond of, we mean only that God does not exist and that we have to face all the consequences of this. The existentialist is strongly opposed to a certain kind of secular ethics which would like to abolish God with the least possible expense. About 1880, some French teachers tried to set up a secular ethics which went something like this: God is a useless and costly hypothesis; we are discarding it; but, meanwhile, in order for there to be an ethics, a society, a civilization, it is essential that certain values be taken seriously and that they be considered as having an *a priori* existence. It must be obligatory, *a priori*, to be honest, not to lie, not to beat your wife, to have children, etc., etc. So we're going to try a little device which will make it possible to show that values exist all the same, inscribed in a heaven of ideas, though otherwise God does not exist. In other words—and this, I believe, is the tendency of everything called reformism in France—nothing will be changed if God does not exist. We shall find ourselves with the same norms of honesty, progress, and humanism, and we shall have made of God an outdated hypothesis which will peacefully die off by itself.

The existentialist, on the contrary, thinks it very distressing that God does not exist, because all possibility of finding values in a heaven of ideas disappears along with Him; there can no longer be an *a priori* Good, since there is no infinite and perfect consciousness to think it. Nowhere is it written that the Good exists, that we must be honest, that we must not lie; because the fact is we are on a plane where there are only men. Dostoevsky said, "If God didn't exist, everything would be possible." That is. the very starting point of existentialism. Indeed, everything is permissible if God does not exist, and as a result man is forlorn, because neither within him nor without does he find anything to cling to. He can't start making excuses for himself.

If existence really does precede essence, there is no explaining things away by reference to a fixed and given human nature. In other words, there is no determinism, man is free, man is freedom. On the other hand, if God does not exist, we find no values or commands to turn to which legitimize our conduct. So, in the bright realm of values, we have no excuse behind us, nor justification before us. We are alone, with no excuses.

That is the idea I shall try to convey when I say that man is condemned to be free. Condemned, because he did not create himself, yet, in other respects is free; because, once thrown into the world, he is responsible for everything he does. The existentialist does not believe in the power of passion. He will never agree that a sweeping passion is a ravaging torrent which fatally leads a man to certain acts and is therefore an excuse. He thinks that man is responsible for his passion.

The existentialist does not think that man is going to help himself by finding in the world some omen by which to orient himself. Because he thinks that man will interpret the omen to suit himself. Therefore, he thinks that man, with no support and no aid, is condemned every moment to invent man. Ponge, in a very fine article, has said, "Man is the future of man." That's exactly it. But if it is taken to mean that this future is recorded in heaven, that God sees it, then it is false, because it would really no longer be a future. If it is taken to mean that, whatever a man may be, there is a future to be forged, a virgin future before him, then this remark is sound. But then we are forlorn.

To give you an example which will enable you to understand forlornness better, I shall cite the case of one of my students who came to see me under the following circumstances: his father was on bad terms with his mother, and, moreover, was inclined to be a collaborationist; his older brother had been killed in the German offensive of 1940, and the young man, with somewhat immature but generous feelings, wanted to avenge him. His mother lived alone with him, very much upset by the half-treason of her husband and the death of her older son; the boy was her only consolation.

The boy was faced with the choice of leaving for England and joining the Free French Forces—that is, leaving his mother behind—or remaining with his mother and helping her to carry on.

He was fully aware that the woman lived only for him and that his going-off—and perhaps his death—would plunge her into despair. He was also aware that every act that he did for his mother's sake was a sure thing, in the sense that it was helping her to carry on, whereas every effort he made toward going off and fighting was an uncertain move which might run aground and prove completely useless; for example, on his way to England he might, while passing through Spain, be detained indefinitely in a Spanish camp; he might reach England or Algiers and be stuck in an office at a desk job. As a result, he was faced with two very different kinds of action: one, concrete, immediate, but concerning only one individual; the other concerned an incomparably vaster group, a national collectivity, but for that very reason was dubious, and might be interrupted en route. And, at the same time, he was wavering between two kinds of ethics. On the one hand, an ethics of sympathy, of personal devotion; on the other, a broader ethics, but one whose efficacy was more dubious. He had to choose between the two.

Who could help him to choose? Christian doctrine? No. Christian doctrine says, "Be charitable, love your neighbor, take the more rugged path, etc., etc." But which is the more rugged path? Whom should he love as a brother? The fighting man or his mother? Which does the greater good, the vague act of fighting in a group, or the concrete one of helping a particular human being to go on living? Who can decide *a priori*? Nobody. No book of ethics can tell him. The Kantian ethics says, "Never treat any person as a means, but as an end." Very well, if I stay with my mother, I'll treat her as an end and not as a means; but by virtue of this very fact, I'm running the risk of treating the people around me who are fighting, as means; and, conversely, if I go to join those who are fighting, I'll be treating them as an end, and, by doing that, I run the risk of treating my mother as a means.

If values are vague, and if they are always too broad for the concrete and specific case that we are considering, the only thing left for us is to trust our instincts. That's what this young man tried to do; and when I saw him, he said, "In the end, feeling is what counts. I ought to choose whichever pushes me in one direction. If I feel that I love my mother enough to sacrifice everything else for her—my desire for vengeance, for action, for adventure—then I'll stay with her. If, on the contrary, I feel that my love for my mother isn't enough, I'll leave."

But how is the value of a feeling determined? What gives his feeling for his mother value? Precisely the fact that he remained with her. I may say that I like so-and-so well enough to sacrifice a certain amount of money for him, but I may say so only if I've done it. I may say "I love my mother well enough to remain with her" if I have remained with her. The only way to determine the value of this affection is, precisely, to perform an act which confirms and defines it. But, since I require this affection to justify my act, I find myself caught in a vicious circle.

On the other hand, Gide has well said that a mock feeling and a true feeling are almost indistinguishable; to decide that I love my mother and will remain with her, or to remain with her by putting on an act, amount somewhat to the same thing. In other words, the feeling is formed by the acts one performs; so, I can not refer to it in order to act upon it. Which means that I can neither seek within myself the true condition which will impel me to act, nor apply to a system of ethics for concepts which will permit me to act. You will say, "At least, he did go to a teacher for advice." But if you seek advice from a priest, for example, you have chosen this priest; you already knew, more or less, just about what advice he was going to give you. In other words, choosing your adviser is involving yourself. The proof of this is that if you are a Christian, you will say, "Consult a priest." But some priests are collaborating, some are just marking time, some are resisting. Which to choose? If the young man chooses a priest who is resisting or collaborating, he has already decided on the kind of advice he's going to get. Therefore, in coming to see me he knew the answer I was going to give him, and I had only one answer to give: "You're free, choose, that is, invent." No general ethics can show you what is to be done; there are no omens in the world. The Catholics will reply, "But there are." Granted—but, in any case, I myself choose the meaning they have.

When I was a prisoner, I knew a rather remarkable young man who was a Jesuit. He had entered the Jesuit order in the following way: he had had a number of very bad breaks; in childhood, his father died, leaving him in poverty, and he was a scholarship student at a religious institution where he was constantly made to feel that he was being kept out of charity; then, he failed to get any of the honors and distinctions that children like; later on,

284

at about eighteen, he bungled a love affair; finally, at twenty-two, he failed in military training, a childish enough matter, but it was the last straw.

This young fellow might well have felt that he had botched everything. It was a sign of something, but of what? He might have taken refuge in bitterness or despair. But he very wisely looked upon all this as a sign that he was not made for secular triumphs, and that only the triumphs of religion, holiness, and faith were open to him. He saw the hand of God in all this, and so he entered the order. Who can help seeing that he alone decided what the sign meant?

Some other interpretation might have been drawn from this series of setbacks; for example, that he might have done better to turn carpenter or revolutionist. Therefore, he is fully responsible for the interpretation. Forlornness implies that we ourselves choose our being. Forlornness and anguish go together.

As for despair, the term has a very simple meaning. It means that we shall confine ourselves to reckoning only with what depends upon our will, or on the ensemble of probabilities which make our action possible. When we want something, we always have to reckon with probabilities. I may be counting on the arrival of a friend. The friend is coming by rail or street-car; this supposes that the train will arrive on schedule, or that the street-car will not jump the track. I am left in the realm of possibility; but possibilities are to be reckoned with only to the point where my action comports with the ensemble of these possibilities, and no further. The moment the possibilities I am considering are not rigorously involved by my action, I ought to disengage myself from them, because no God, no scheme, can adapt the world and its possibilities to my will. When Descartes said, "Conquer yourself rather than the world," he meant essentially the same thing.

The Marxists to whom I have spoken reply, "You can rely on the support of others in your action, which obviously has certain limits because you're not going to live forever. That means: rely on both what others are doing elsewhere to help you, in China, in Russia, and what they will do later on, after your death, to carry on the action and lead it to its fulfillment, which will be the revolution. You even *have* to rely upon that, otherwise you're immoral." I reply at once that I will always rely on fellow-fighters insofar as these comrades are involved with me in a common struggle, in the unity of a party or a group in which I can more or less make my weight felt; that is, one whose ranks I am in as a fighter and whose movements I am aware of at every moment. In such a situation, relying on the unity and will of the party is exactly like counting on the fact that the train will arrive on time or that the car won't jump the track. But, given that man is free and that there is no human nature for me to depend on, I cannot count on men whom I do not know by relying on human goodness or man's concern for the good of society. I don't know what will become of the Russian revolution; I may make an example of it to the extent that at the present time it is apparent that the proletariat plays a part in Russia that it plays in no other nation. But I can't swear that this will inevitably lead to a triumph of the proletariat. I've got to limit myself to what I see.

Given that men are free and that tomorrow they will freely decide what man will be, I cannot be sure that, after my death, fellow-fighters will carry on my work to bring it to its maximum perfection. Tomorrow, after my death, some men may decide to set up Fascism, and the others may be cowardly and muddled enough to let them do it. Fascism will then be the human reality, so much the worse for us.

Actually, things will be as man will have decided they are to be. Does that mean that I should abandon myself to quietism? No. First, I should involve myself; then, act on the old saw, "Nothing ventured, nothing gained." Nor does it mean that I shouldn't belong to a party, but rather that I shall have no illusions and shall do what I can. For example, suppose I ask myself, "Will socialization, as such, ever come about?" I know nothing about it. All I know is that I'm going to do everything in my power to bring it about. Beyond that, I can't count on anything. Quietism is the attitude of people who say, "Let others do what I can't do." The doctrine I am presenting is the very opposite of quietism, since it declares, "There is no reality except in action." Moreover, it goes further, since it adds, "Man is nothing else than his plan; he exists only to the extent that he fulfills himself; he is therefore nothing else than the ensemble of his acts, nothing else than his life."

According to this, we can understand why our doctrine horrifies certain people. Because often the only way they can bear their wretchedness is to think, "Circumstances have been against me. What I've been and done doesn't show my true worth. To be sure, I've had no great love, no great friendship, but that's because I haven't met a man or woman who was worthy. The books I've written haven't been very good because I haven't had the proper leisure. I haven't had children to devote myself to because I didn't find a man with whom I could have spent my life. So there remains within me, unused and quite viable, a host of propensities, inclinations, possibilities, that one wouldn't guess from the mere series of things I've done."

Now, for the existentialist there is really no love other than one which manifests itself in a person's being in love. There is no genius other than one which is expressed in works of art; the genius of Proust is the sum of Proust's works; the genius of Racine is his series of tragedies. Outside of that, there is nothing. Why say that Racine could have written another tragedy, when he didn't write it? A man is involved in life, leaves his impress on it, and outside of that there is nothing. To be sure, this may seem a harsh thought to someone whose life hasn't been a success. But, on the other hand, it prompts people to understand that reality alone is what counts, that dreams, expectations, and hopes warrant no more than to define a man as a disappointed dream, as miscarried hopes, as vain expectations. In other words, to define him negatively and not positively. However, when we say, "You are nothing else than your life," that does not imply that the artist will be judged solely on the basis of his works of art; a thousand other things will contribute toward summing him up. What we mean is that a man is nothing else than a series of undertakings, that he is the sum, the organization, the ensemble of the relationships which make up these undertakings.

When all is said and done, what we are accused of, at bottom, is not our pessimism, but an optimistic toughness. If people throw up to us our works of fiction in which we write about people who are soft, weak, cowardly, and sometimes even downright bad, it's not because these people are soft, weak, cowardly, or bad; because if we were to say, as Zola did, that they are that way because of heredity, the workings of environment, society, because of biological or psychological determinism, people would be reassured. They would say, "Well, that's what we're like, no one can do anything about it." But when the existentialist writes about a coward, he says that this coward is responsible for his cowardice. He's not like that because he has a cowardly heart or lung or brain; he's not like that on account of his physiological make-up; but he's like that because he has made himself a coward by his acts. There's no such thing as a cowardly constitution; there are nervous constitutions; there is poor blood, as the common people say, or strong constitutions. But the man whose blood is poor is not a coward on that account, for what makes cowardice is the act of renouncing or yielding. A constitution is not an act; the coward is defined on the basis of the acts he performs. People feel, in a vague sort of way, that this coward we're talking about is guilty of being a coward, and the thought frightens them. What people would like is that a coward or a hero be born that way.

One of the complaints most frequently made about *The Ways of Freedom*[1] can be summed up as follows: "After all, these people are so spineless, how are you going to make heroes out of them?" This objection almost makes me laugh, for it assumes that people are born heroes. That's what people really want to think. If you're born cowardly, you may set your mind perfectly at rest; there's nothing you can do about it; you'll be cowardly all your life, whatever you may do. If you're born a hero, you may set your mind just as much at rest; you'll be a hero all your life; you'll drink like a hero and eat like a hero. What the existentialist says is that the coward makes himself cowardly, that the hero makes himself heroic. There's always a possibility for the coward not to be cowardly any more and for the hero to stop being heroic. What counts is total involvement; some one particular action or set of circumstances is not total involvement.

Thus, I think we have answered a number of the charges concerning existentialism. You see that it cannot be taken for a philosophy of quietism, since it defines man in terms of action; nor for a pessimistic description of man—there is no doctrine more optimistic, since man's destiny is within himself; nor for an attempt to discourage man from acting, since it tells him that

---

[1] *Les Chemins de la Liberté*, M. Sartre's projected trilogy of novels, two of which, *L'Age de Raison* (*The Age of Reason*) and *Le Sursis* (*The Reprieve*), have already appeared.—Translator's note. The third, *La Mort Dans L'Ame* (*Troubled Sleep*), appeared in 1949—Editor's note.

the only hope is in his acting and that action is the only thing that enables a man to live. Consequently, we are dealing here with an ethics of action and involvement.

Nevertheless, on the basis of a few notions like these, we are still charged with immuring man in his private subjectivity. There again we're very much misunderstood. Subjectivity of the individual is indeed our point of departure, and this for strictly philosophic reasons. Not because we are bourgeois, but because we want a doctrine based on truth and not a lot of fine theories, full of hope but with no real basis. There can be no other truth to take off from than this: *I think; therefore, I exist.* There we have the absolute truth of consciousness becoming aware of itself. Every theory which takes man out of the moment in which he becomes aware of himself is, at its very beginning, a theory which confounds truth, for outside the Cartesian *cogito*, all views are only probable, and a doctrine of probability which is not bound to a truth dissolves into thin air. In order to describe the probable, you must have a firm hold on the true. Therefore, before there can be any truth whatsoever, there must be an absolute truth; and this one is simple and easily arrived at; it's on everyone's doorstep; it's a matter of grasping it directly.

Secondly, this theory is the only one which gives man dignity, the only one which does not reduce him to an object. The effect of all materialism is to treat all men, including the one philosophizing, as objects, that is, as an ensemble of determined reactions in no way distinguished from the ensemble of qualities and phenomena which constitute a table or a chair or a stone. We definitely wish to establish the human realm as an ensemble of values distinct from the material realm. But the subjectivity that we have thus arrived at, and which we have claimed to be truth, is not a strictly individual subjectivity, for we have demonstrated that one discovers in the *cogito* not only himself, but others as well.

The philosophies of Descartes and Kant to the contrary, through the *I think* we reach our own self in the presence of others, and the others are just as real to us as our own self. Thus, the man who becomes aware of himself through the *cogito* also perceives all others, and he perceives them as the condition of his own existence. He realizes that he cannot be anything (in the sense that we say that someone is witty or nasty or jealous) unless others recognize it as such. In order to get any truth about myself, I must have contact with another person. The other is indispensable to my own existence, as well as to my knowledge about myself. This being so, in discovering my inner being I discover the other person at the same time, like a freedom placed in front of me which thinks and wills only for or against me. Hence, let us at once announce the discovery of a world which we shall call inter-subjectivity; this is the world in which man decides what he is and what others are.

Besides, if it is impossible to find in every man some universal essence which would be human nature, yet there does exist a universal human condition. It's not by chance that today's thinkers speak more readily of man's condition than of his nature. By condition they mean, more or less definitely, the *a priori* limits which outline man's fundamental situation in the universe. Historical situations vary; a man may be born a slave in a pagan society or a feudal lord or a proletarian. What does not vary is the necessity for him to exist in the world, to be at work there, to be there in the midst of other people, and to be mortal there. The limits are neither subjective nor objective, or, rather, they have an objective and a subjective side. Objective because they are to be found everywhere and are recognizable everywhere; subjective because they are *lived* and are nothing if man does not live them, that is, freely determine his existence with reference to them. And though the configurations may differ, at least none of them are completely strange to me, because they all appear as attempts either to pass beyond these limits or recede from them or deny them or adapt to them. Consequently, every configuration, however individual it may be, has a universal value.

Every configuration, even the Chinese, the Indian, or the Negro, can be understood by a Westerner. "Can be understood" means that by virtue of a situation that he can imagine, a European of 1945 can, in like manner, push himself to his limits and reconstitute within himself the configuration of the Chinese, the Indian, or the African. Every configuration has universality in the sense that every configuration can be understood by every man. This does not at all mean that this configuration defines

man forever, but that it can be met with again. There is always a
way to understand the idiot, the child, the savage, the foreigner,
provided one has the necessary information.

In this sense we may say that there is a universality of man;
but it is not given, it is perpetually being made. I build the universal in choosing myself; I build it in understanding the configuration of every other man, whatever age he might have lived
in. This absoluteness of choice does not do away with the rel-
ativeness of each epoch. At heart, what existentialism shows is
the connection between the absolute character of free involvement, by virtue of which every man realizes himself in realizing
a type of mankind, an involvement always comprehensible in
any age whatsoever and by any person whosoever, and the rel-
ativeness of the cultural ensemble which may result from such
a choice; it must be stressed that the relativity of Cartesianism
and the absolute character of Cartesian involvement go together.
In this sense, you may, if you like, say that each of us performs
an absolute act in breathing, eating, sleeping, or behaving in any
way whatever. There is no difference between being free, like a
configuration, like an existence which chooses its essence, and
being absolute. There is no difference between being an absolute
temporarily localised, that is, localised in history, and being universally comprehensible.

This does not entirely settle the objection to subjectivism. In
fact, the objection still takes several forms. First, there is the
following: we are told, "So you're able to do anything, no matter
what!" This is expressed in various ways. First we are accused
of anarchy; then they say, "You're unable to pass judgment on
others, because there's no reason to prefer one configuration to
another"; finally they tell us, "Everything is arbitrary in this
choosing of yours. You take something from one pocket and pretend you're putting it into the other."

These three objections aren't very serious. Take the first objection. "You're able to do anything, no matter what" is not to the
point. In one sense choice is possible, but what is not possible is
not to choose. I can always choose, but I ought to know that if I
do not choose, I am still choosing. Though this may seem purely
formal, it is highly important for keeping fantasy and caprice
within bounds. If it is true that in facing a situation, for example,

one in which, as a person capable of having sexual relations, of having children, I am obliged to choose an attitude, and if I in any way assume responsibility for a choice which, in involving myself, also involves all mankind, this has nothing to do with caprice, even if no *a priori* value determines my choice.

If anybody thinks that he recognizes here Gide's theory of the arbitrary act, he fails to see the enormous difference between this doctrine and Gide's. Gide does not know what a situation is. He acts out of pure caprice. For us, on the contrary, man is in an organized situation in which he himself is involved. Through his choice, he involves all mankind, and he cannot avoid making a choice: either he will remain chaste, or he will marry without having children, or he will marry and have children; anyhow, whatever he may do, it is impossible for him not to take full responsibility for the way he handles this problem. Doubtless, he chooses without referring to pre-established values, but it is unfair to accuse him of caprice. Instead, let us say that moral choice is to be compared to the making of a work of art. And before going any further, let it be said at once that we are not dealing here with an aesthetic ethics, because our opponents are so dishonest that they even accuse us of that. The example I've chosen is a comparison only.

Having said that, may I ask whether anyone has ever accused an artist who has painted a picture of not having drawn his inspiration from rules set up *a priori*? Has anyone ever asked, "What painting ought he to make?" It is clearly understood that there is no definite painting to be made, that the artist is engaged in the making of his painting, and that the painting to be made is precisely the painting he will have made. It is clearly understood that there are no *a priori* aesthetic values, but that there are values which appear subsequently in the coherence of the painting, in the correspondence between what the artist intended and the result. Nobody can tell what the painting of tomorrow will be like. Painting can be judged only after it has once been made. What connection does that have with ethics? We are in the same creative situation. We never say that a work of art is arbitrary. When we speak of a canvas of Picasso, we never say that it is arbitrary; we understand quite well that he was making himself what he is at the very time he was painting, that the ensemble of his work is embodied in his life.

292

The same holds on the ethical plane. What art and ethics have in common is that we have creation and invention in both cases. We cannot decide *a priori* what there is to be done. I think that I pointed that out quite sufficiently when I mentioned the case of the student who came to see me, and who might have applied to all the ethical systems, Kantian or otherwise, without getting any sort of guidance. He was obliged to devise his law himself. Never let it be said by us that this man—who, taking affection, individual action, and kind-heartedness toward a specific person as his ethical first principle, chooses to remain with his mother, or who, preferring to make a sacrifice, chooses to go to England —has made an arbitrary choice. Man makes himself. He isn't ready made at the start. In choosing his ethics, he makes himself, and force of circumstances is such that he cannot abstain from choosing one. We define man only in relationship to involvement. It is therefore absurd to charge us with arbitrariness of choice.

In the second place, it is said that we are unable to pass judgment on others. In a way this is true, and in another way, false. It is true in this sense, that, whenever a man sanely and sincerely involves himself and chooses his configuration, it is impossible for him to prefer another configuration, regardless of what his own may be in other respects. It is true in this sense, that we do not believe in progress. Progress is betterment. Man is always the same. The situation confronting him varies. Choice always remains a choice in a situation. The problem has not changed since the time one could choose between those for and those against slavery, for example, at the time of the Civil War, and the present time, when one can side with the Maquis Resistance Party, or with the Communists.

But, nevertheless, one can still pass judgment, for, as I have said, one makes a choice in relationship to others. First, one can judge (and this is perhaps not a judgment of value, but a logical judgment) that certain choices are based on error and others on truth. If we have defined man's situation as a free choice, with no excuses and no recourse, every man who takes refuge behind the excuse of his passions, every man who sets up a determinism, is a dishonest man.

The objection may be raised, "But why mayn't he choose himself dishonestly?" I reply that I am not obliged to pass moral judgment on him, but that I do define his dishonesty as an error. One cannot help considering the truth of the matter. Dishonesty is obviously a falsehood because it belies the complete freedom of involvement. On the same grounds, I maintain that there is also dishonesty if I choose to state that certain values exist prior to me; it is self-contradictory for me to want them and at the same state that they are imposed on me. Suppose someone says to me, "What if I want to be dishonest?" I'll answer, "There's no reason for you not to be, but I'm saying that that's what you are, and that the strictly coherent attitude is that of honesty."

Besides, I can bring moral judgment to bear. When I declare that freedom in every concrete circumstance can have no other aim than to want itself, if man has once become aware that in his forlornness he imposes values, he can no longer want but one thing, and that is freedom, as the basis of all values. That doesn't mean that he wants it in the abstract. It means simply that the ultimate meaning of the acts of honest men is the quest for freedom as such. A man who belongs to a communist or revolutionary union wants concrete goals; these goals imply an abstract desire for freedom; but this freedom is wanted in something concrete. We want freedom for freedom's sake and in every particular circumstance. And in wanting freedom we discover that it depends entirely on the freedom of others, and that the freedom of others depends on ours. Of course, freedom as the definition of man does not depend on others, but as soon as there is involvement, I am obliged to want others to have freedom at the same time that I want my own freedom. I can take freedom as my goal only if I take that of others as a goal as well. Consequently, when, in all honesty, I've recognized that man is a being in whom existence precedes essence, that he is a free being who, in various circumstances, can want only his freedom, I have at the same time recognized that I can want only the freedom of others.

Therefore, in the name of this will for freedom, which freedom itself implies, I may pass judgment on those who seek to hide from themselves the complete arbitrariness and the complete freedom of their existence. Those who hide their complete freedom from themselves out of a spirit of seriousness or by means of deterministic excuses, I shall call cowards; those who try to show that their existence was necessary, when it is the very contingency of man's appearance on earth, I shall call stinkers. But cowards or stinkers can be judged only from a strictly unbiased point of view.

Therefore though the content of ethics is variable, a certain form of it is universal. Kant says that freedom desires both itself and the freedom of others. Granted. But he believes that the formal and the universal are enough to constitute an ethics. We, on the other hand, think that principles which are too abstract run aground in trying to decide action. Once again, take the case of the student. In the name of what, in the name of what great moral maxim do you think he could have decided, in perfect peace of mind, to abandon his mother or to stay with her? There is no way of judging. The content is always concrete and thereby unforeseeable; there is always the element of invention. The one thing that counts is knowing whether the inventing that has been done, has been done in the name of freedom.

For example, let us look at the following two cases. You will see to what extent they correspond, yet differ. Take *The Mill on the Floss*. We find a certain young girl, Maggie Tulliver, who is an embodiment of the value of passion and who is aware of it. She is in love with a young man, Stephen, who is engaged to an insignificant young girl. This Maggie Tulliver, instead of heedlessly preferring her own happiness, chooses, in the name of human solidarity, to sacrifice herself and give up the man she loves. On the other hand, Sanseverina, in *The Charterhouse of Parma*, believing that passion is man's true value, would say that a great love deserves sacrifices; that it is to be preferred to the banality of the conjugal love that would tie Stephen to the young ninny he had to marry. She would choose to sacrifice the girl and fulfill her happiness; and, as Stendhal shows, she is even ready to sacrifice herself for the sake of passion, if this life demands it. Here we are in the presence of two strictly opposed moralities. I claim that they are much the same thing; in both cases what has been set up as the goal is freedom.

You can imagine two highly similar attitudes: one girl prefers to renounce her love out of resignation; another prefers to disregard the prior attachment of the man she loves out of sexual desire. On the surface these two actions resemble those we've just described. However, they are completely different. Sanseverina's attitude is much nearer that of Maggie Tulliver, one of heedless rapacity.

Thus, you see that the second charge is true and, at the same time, false. One may choose anything if it is on the grounds of free involvement.

The third objection is the following: "You take something from one pocket and put it into the other. That is, fundamentally, values aren't serious, since you choose them." My answer to this is that I'm quite vexed that that's the way it is; but if I've discarded God the Father, there has to be someone to invent values. You've got to take things as they are. Moreover, to say that we invent values means nothing else but this: life has no meaning *a priori*. Before you come alive, life is nothing; it's up to you to give it a meaning, and value is nothing else but the meaning that you choose. In that way, you see, there is a possibility of creating a human community.

I've been reproached for asking whether existentialism is humanistic. It's been said, "But you said in *Nausea* that the humanists were all wrong. You made fun of a certain kind of humanist. Why come back to it now?" Actually, the word humanism has two very different meanings. By humanism one can mean a theory which takes man as an end and as a higher value. Humanism in this sense can be found in Cocteau's tale *Around the World in Eighty Hours* when a character, because he is flying over some mountains in an airplane, declares, "Man is simply amazing." That means that I, who did not build the airplanes, shall personally benefit from these particular inventions, and that I, as man, shall personally consider myself responsible for, and honored by, acts of a few particular men. This would imply that we ascribe a value to man on the basis of the highest deeds of certain men. This humanism is absurd, because only the dog or the horse would be able to make such an over-all judgment about man, which they are careful not to do, at least to my knowledge.

But it cannot be granted that a man may make a judgment about man. Existentialism spares him from any such judgment. The existentialist will never consider man as an end because he is always in the making. Nor should we believe that there is a mankind to which we might set up a cult in the manner of

Auguste Comte. The cult of mankind ends in the self-enclosed humanism of Comte, and, let it be said, of fascism. This kind of humanism we can do without.

But there is another meaning of humanism. Fundamentally it is this: man is constantly outside of himself; in projecting himself, in losing himself outside of himself, he makes for man's existing; and, on the other hand, it is by pursuing transcendent goals that he is able to exist; man, being this state of passing-beyond, and seizing upon things only as they bear upon this passing-beyond, is at the heart, at the center of this passing-beyond. There is no universe other than a human universe, the universe of human subjectivity. This connection between transcendency, as a constituent element of man—not in the sense that God is transcendent, but in the sense of passing beyond—and subjectivity, in the sense that man is not closed in on himself but is always present in a human universe, is what we call existentialist humanism. Humanism, because we remind man that there is no law-maker other than himself, and that in his forlornness he will decide by himself; because we point out that man will fulfill himself as man, not in turning toward himself, but in seeking outside of himself a goal which is just this liberation, just this particular fulfillment.

From these few reflections it is evident that nothing is more unjust than the objections that have been raised against us. Existentialism is nothing else than an attempt to draw all the consequences of a coherent atheistic position. It isn't trying to plunge man into despair at all. But if one calls every attitude of unbelief despair, like the Christians, then the word is not being used in its original sense. Existentialism isn't so atheistic that it wears itself out showing that God doesn't exist. Rather, it declares that even if God did exist, that would change nothing. There you've got our point of view. Not that we believe that God exists, but we think that the problem of His existence is not the issue. In this sense existentialism is optimistic, a doctrine of action, and it is plain dishonesty for Christians to make no distinction between their own despair and ours and then to call us despairing.

18 / How People Change

ALLEN WHEELIS

We have not far to look for suffering. It's in the streets, fills the air, lies upon our friends. Faces of pain look at us from newspaper, from TV screen. We know them: black man swinging in the warm wind, sealed cattle cars rumbling through the bitter cold, the glare of Auschwitz at midnight, the sweet smell.

And then there's always the suffering inside. But that's different. It may be very bad, this private misery, but different.

For many people pain is imposed, there's no escape. It may be impersonal, unavoidable, as by fire, flood, cancer; or man-made, as in wars, sack of cities, rape of girls. Victims still have choice; there's always a little corner of freedom. They may throw spears at the bombers or bow in prayer, may curse or plead; but they may not choose to suffer or not suffer. That choice has been foreclosed. Starving blacks of Biafra scrounge for roots, fight each other for rats; Vietnamese children with melted flesh wander homeless, orphaned, across a lunar desert.

Many of us have never known this kind of misery, have never felt a lash or club, never been shot at, persecuted, bombed, starved—yet we suffer too. Wealth and intelligence and good fortune are no protection. Having had good parents helps but guarantees nothing; misery comes equally to high-born and low, comes with the gold spoon, to prince and princess and ladies in waiting, to groom and gamekeeper, to the mighty and the humble. We feel our suffering as alien, desperately unwanted, yet nothing imposes it. We eat, often exceedingly well; the roof over our head is timber and tile; deep carpets, thin china, great music, rare wine; a woman looks at us with love; we have friends, families; our needs are met. In some way, unnoticed, unknown, we must elect our suffering, create it. It may be quite intense.

SOURCE: *Commentary* 47 (May 1969), 56–66. Copyright © 1969 by Allen Wheelis. "How People Change" is to be published in 1970 as part of a larger work, *The Desert*, by Allen Wheelis. Reprinted with permission of Basic Books, Inc., Publishers, New York.

Allen Wheelis, a San Francisco psychoanalyst, has written *The Quest for Identity*; a novel, *The Seeker*; and a book of stories, *The Illusionless Man*.

Some of it is public knowledge—madness, suicide, running amuck. Some of it is visible only to a few, to family and friends who see the withdrawal, depression, the sense of rejection, the clawing competitiveness, the bitter frustration, bafflement, and anger, year after year after year. At the concert or opera, walking about in the lobby, they bow, they smile, they glitter—show nothing of the misery inside. And some of our suffering is altogether private, known to no one but him who suffers, not even his wife, is borne with shame as some indescribable awkwardness in living, a kind of disloyalty to be in despair in the lap of plenty.

Imposed suffering has priority over elected suffering, as material needs take precedence over spiritual. "First feed the belly, then talk right and wrong," says Mac the Knife. Or Sartre: "The exploitation of men by other men, undernourishment—these make metaphysical unhappiness a luxury and relegate it to second place. Hunger—now that *is* an evil." Imposed suffering, therefore, protects from the elected kind, crowds it out. We simply cannot create despair from subjective roots if we are forced into despair by persecution. In the concentration camp, states of created despair are remembered vaguely, as if from a different life, discontinuous with the present one in which despair issues from the SS truncheons.

To those whose suffering is imposed, elected suffering seems unreal. Lacking in measurable circumstance, in objective explanation, it seems illusory, made up, "in the head." Victims of the whip feel envy of those so sheltered from pain as to be able to dream up states of misery; contempt when such fortunate ones have the arrogance to elegize their torment; a hateful mirth at existential despair hatching in a nest of IBM stock certificates.

We who compose our own misery are ambivalent toward victims of imposed suffering. We feel a subtle pride—secret, never expressed, unknown often even to ourselves—that our misery is more complicated, spiritual; as if we whispered, "The pain of being hungry, of being beaten, is very bad, we sympathize, will make a contribution to CARE; but it is, after all, a primitive suffering; anyone can feel it; just leave them alone, give them enough to eat, and they'd be happy—whereas only a poet could feel what I feel." At the same time, more openly felt, more easily expressed, we feel shame, judge our created misery to be petty in comparison.

ALLEN WHEELIS 299

In fact they are equally bad: depression or starvation is a hard choice; the terror of the ledge ten floors up matches the terror of the firing squad. In felt experience, that is: in worthiness we cannot call them equal. We who compose our own misery are ashamed at Babi Yar, at Nagasaki, on the slave ships from Africa, in the arena at Rome. They were innocent of their suffering, we are guilty of complicity with ours; they had no choice in theirs, we bear responsibility for ours.

Created suffering, except where precluded by imposed pain, affects us all. The well-adjusted lie: listen to them at your risk; listen to them long enough, declaiming the official view, being serious with their slogans, and you lose contact with your own heart. Poets tell the truth: the sadness of Greece and Gethsemane, of Sodom and Gomorrah, of the Pharaohs and their minions and their slaves, was as our own. It's part of being human, we differ from one another only in more or less. A few tranquil ones, with little conflict, suffer less; at the other extreme, stretched by despair to some dreadful cracking point, one goes berserk. In between are the rest of us, not miserable enough to go mad or jump off the bridge, yet never able if we are honest to say that we have come to terms with life, are at peace with ourselves, that we are happy.

The older I get the less I know, the darker the well of time. The enigma grows more bleak. I seek. I am concerned with suffering and with change, and I write equally for patient and therapist. What one should know will be useful, also, to the other. Here psychotherapy parts company with medicine.

The book for the surgeon is not the book for the surgical patient. One delivers one's ailing body—with its abscess or tumor or broken bone—into the hands of the surgeon, and his most elementary information and skill will transcend anything the patient need know. The patient must cooperate—one green capsule three times a day, keep the leg elevated, force fluids—but need not understand how or why. The responsibility lies with the surgeon, the problem is his, his the accountability for failure, the credit for success. Patient and surgeon do not learn from the same text.

Many patients go to psychiatrists as if to surgeons, and many psychiatrists regard themselves as psychic surgeons. When such a patient comes to such a therapist a relationship of considerable length may result, but little else. For the job can be done, if at all, only by the patient. To assign this task to anyone else, however insightful or charismatic, is to disavow the source of change. In the process of personality change the role of the psychiatrist is catalytic. As a cause he is sometimes necessary, never sufficient. The responsibility of the patient does not end with free-associating, with being on time, with keeping at it, paying his bills, or any other element of cooperation. He is accountable only to himself and this accountability extends all the way to the change which is desired, the achieving of it or the giving up on it.

So—consider one who suffers. Perhaps a woman with a warm heart but frigid. What can she do? Perhaps a mother who wants to love her children but does not. Maybe a homosexual living an endless series of hostile transient encounters. Perhaps a man in his middle fifties with a depressive character, normal to his friends, but constantly brushing away cobweb thoughts of suicide, one who is bored, finds no meaning in life, is ashamed. Consider one who suffers—anyone you know well. Consider perhaps yourself.

II

I live in a desert. Hour by hour feel myself dying. Surely I believe in something. Not much perhaps, but a little. What?

We are what we do . . . Identity is the integration of behavior. If a man claims to be honest we take him at his word. But if it should transpire that over the years he has been embezzling, we unhesitatingly discard the identity he adopts in words and ascribe to him the identity defined by his acts. "He claims to be honest," we say, "but he's really a thief."

One theft, however, does not make a thief. One act of forthrightness does not establish frankness; one tormenting of a cat does not make a sadist, nor one rescue of a fledgling a savior. Action which defines a man, describes his character, is action which has been repeated over and over, and so has come in time to be a coherent and relatively independent mode of behavior. At first it may have been fumbling and uncertain, may have required attention, effort, will—as when one first drives a car, first makes love, first robs a bank, first stands up against injustice. If one perseveres on any such course it comes in time to require less effort, less attention, begins to function smoothly; its small component behaviors become integrated within a larger pattern which has an ongoing dynamism and cohesiveness, carries its own authority. Such a mode then pervades the entire person, permeates other modes, colors other qualities, in some sense is living and operative even when the action is not being performed, or even considered. A young man who learns to drive a car thinks differently thereby, feels differently; when he meets a pretty girl who lives fifty miles away, the encounter carries implications he could not have felt as a bus rider. We may say, then, that he not only drives a car, but has *become* a driver. If the action is shoplifting, we say not only that he steals from stores but that he has *become* a shoplifter.

Such a mode of action tends to maintain itself, to resist change. A thief is one who steals; stealing extends and reinforces the identity of thief, which generates further thefts, which further strengthens and deepens the identity. So long as one lives, change is possible; but the longer such behavior is continued the more force and authority it acquires, the more it permeates other consonant modes, subordinates other conflicting modes; changing back becomes steadily more difficult; settling down to an honest job, living on one's earnings, becomes ever more unlikely. And what is said here of stealing applies equally to courage, cowardice, creativity, gambling, homosexuality, alcoholism, depression, or any other of the myriad ways of behaving, and hence of being. Identity comprises all such modes as may characterize a person, existing in varying degrees of integration and conflict. The greater the conflict the more unstable the identity; the more harmonious the various modes the more durable the identity.

The identity defined by action is present and past; it may also foretell the future, but not necessarily. Sometimes we act covertly, the eye does not notice the hand under the table, we construe the bribe to have been a gift, the running away to have been prudence, and so conceal from ourselves what we are. Then one day, perhaps, we drop the pretense, the illusion cracks. We have then the sense of an identity that has existed all along—and in some sense we knew it but would not let ourselves know that we knew it—but now we do, and in a blaze of frankness say,

"My God! I really am a crook!" or "I really am a coward!" We may then go too far and conclude that this identity is our "nature," that it was writ in the stars or in the double helix, that it transcends experience, that our actual lives have been the fulfilling of a pre-existing pattern.

In fact it was writ only in our past choices. We are wise to believe it difficult to change, to recognize that character has a forward propulsion which tends to carry it unaltered into the future, but we need not believe it impossible to change. Our present and future choices may take us upon different courses which will in time comprise a different identity. It happens, sometimes, that the crook reforms, that the coward stands to fight.

... *And may do what we choose.* The identity defined by action is not, therefore, the whole person. Within us lies the potential for change, the freedom to choose other courses. When we admit that those "gifts" were bribes and say, "Well, then, I'm a crook," we have stated a fact, not a destiny; if we then invoke the leopard that can't change his spots, saying, "That's just the way I am, might as well accept it," we abandon the freedom to change, and exploit what we have been in the past to avoid responsibility for what we shall be in the future.

Often we do not choose, but drift into those modes which eventually define us. Circumstances push and we yield. We did not choose to be what we have become, but gradually, imperceptibly became what we are by drifting into the doing of those things we now characteristically do. Freedom is not an objective attribute of life; alternatives without awareness yield no leeway. I open the door of my car, sit behind the wheel, and notice in a corner of vision an ant scurrying about on the smooth barren surface of the concrete parking lot, doomed momentarily to be crushed by one of the thousand passing wheels. There exists, however, a brilliant alternative for this gravely endangered creature: in a few minutes a woman will appear with a picnic basket and we shall drive to a sunny, hilltop meadow. This desperate ant has but to climb the wheel of my car to a safe sheltered ledge, and in a half hour will be in a paradise for ants. But this option, unknown, unknowable, yields no freedom to the ant, who is doomed; and the only irony belongs to me who observes, who reflects that options potentially as meaningful to me as this one to this ant may at this moment be eluding my awareness; so

I too may be doomed—this planet looks more like a parking lot every day.

Nothing guarantees freedom. It may never be achieved, or having been achieved may be lost. Alternatives go unnoticed; foreseeable consequences are not foreseen; we may not know what we have been, what we are, or what we are becoming. We who are the bearers of consciousness but of not very much, may proceed through a whole life without awareness of that which would have meant the most, the freedom which has to be noticed to be real. Freedom is the awareness of alternatives and of the ability to choose. It is contingent upon consciousness, and so may be gained or lost, extended or diminished.

Modern psychiatry found its image in the course of dealing with symptoms experienced as alien. A patient so afflicted seeks no alteration of character or personality, would be offended if the physician suggested such or pretended to any competence in that area. Nothing is felt to be wrong with the patient as a person, his self is not presented for examination or treatment. He is a patient only because he's sick, and his sickness consists of an ailment of which he wishes to be relieved. If the trouble is of recent onset and condenses a specific conflict of impulse and inhibition the medical model may be tenable: insight may function as medicine and dispel the symptom. On those exceedingly rare occasions when we still see such a case, we can be real doctors again and cure someone. The following is an example.

A thirty-five-year-old woman suddenly, and for the first time in her life, develops a spasm of the right foot and a left-sided migraine. Brain tumor is suspected but neurological examination is normal. On psychiatric consultation it is learned that she has been married fifteen years, no children, is devoutly religious, cannot tolerate hostile feelings, but in fact despises her alcoholic husband. At a party, on the evening before her trouble began, she went upstairs looking for a bathroom and chanced upon her husband with a woman on his lap, the two of them in deep, prolonged kissing. She watched for a few moments, then backed out without being seen. On leaving the party, as her husband was drunk, she drove the car. Reaching home he stumbled out to open the garage door and for a

moment was caught in the headlights. Just beyond him
was a concrete wall. The motor was idling fast. She felt
dizzy, passed a hand over her face. Upstairs, a few minutes later, her right foot began to twitch; during the night
she waked up with a headache.

In this case, properly prepared, the interpretation, "You wanted
to kill your husband," may effect a cure. No will is necessary,
no action, no change in being. Insight is enough.

Most psychiatrists know such cases only from reading examples like this one. The patients who actually appear in their
offices—whatever their symptoms—suffer problems of being.
When the symptom is migraine it has occurred not once but hundreds of times, over many years. It is not the somatic expression
of a specific conflict, but a response to any conflict, any tension,
a way of running from whatever seems too much; it has become
a mode of being in the world. The patient may feel it as alien,
want to be rid of it, but it has become useful in a thousand unnoticed ways; its removal would not be simple relief but would
expose the patient to conflicts which he has no other way of
handling. The symptom does not afflict the patient, it *is* the
patient.

This headache will not dissolve with insight, and here the
medical model breaks down. What is called for is not cure of illness but change in what one is. Insight is not enough. Effort and
will are crucial.

The most common illusion of patients and, strangely, even of
experienced therapists, is that insight produces change; and the
most common disappointment of therapy is that it does not. Insight is instrumental to change, often an essential component of
the process, but does not directly achieve it. The most comprehensive and penetrating interpretation—true, relevant, well expressed, perfectly timed—may lie inert in the patient's mind; for
he may always, if he be so inclined, say, "Yes, but it doesn't help."
If a therapist takes the position, as many do, that a correct interpretation is one that gets results, that the getting of results is an
essential criterion for the correctness of an interpretation, then
he will be driven to more and more remote reconstructions of
childhood events, will move further and further from present
reality, responding always to the patient's "Yes, but why?" with

further reachings for more distant antecedents. The patient will be saying, in effect, "Yes, but what are you going to do about it?" and the therapist, instead of saying, as he should, "What are *you* going to do about it?" responds according to his professional overestimate of the efficacy of insight by struggling toward some ever more basic formulation. Some patients don't want to change, and when a therapist takes up the task of changing such a one he assumes a contest which the patient always wins. The magic of insight, of unconscious psychodynamics, proves no magic at all; the most marvelous interpretation falls useless —like a gold spoon from the hand of a petulant child who doesn't want his spinach.

An anguished woman enters our office, sits down, weeps, begins to talk, and we listen. We are supposed to know what's up here, what the problem *really* is, and what to do about it. But the theories with which we have mapped the soul don't help, the life she relates is unlike any other. We may nevertheless cling to our map, telling ourselves we know where we are and all is well, but if we look up into the jungle of her misery we know we are lost. And what have we to go on? What to cling to? That people may change, that one person can help another. That's all. Maybe that's enough.

The suffering is a given, but the problem is a choice, is subjective and arbitrary, rests finally upon nothing more than the patient's will, upon his being able to say "This . . . is what I want to change."

Those psychiatrists who regard themselves in the manner of medical men would disagree, would hold that a psychic problem —homosexuality, for example, or compulsivity—is objectively verifiable, that a panel of competent therapists would concur. This view would hold that the problem "emerges" from the "material," is recognized and defined by the therapist who then presents it to the patient along with his recommendation for treatment.

But since the problem is something for which a solution is sought, only the patient can designate it. The therapist may perceive that a certain conflict leads regularly to such and such situations which cause suffering. But a cause of suffering is not a problem unless it is taken as such by the patient.

Likewise the goal of treatment must be determined by the patient. The only appropriate goal for the therapist is to assist. If the therapist cannot in good faith help to the end desired he is free to decline, but he cannot reasonably work toward goals of his own choosing. Even so benign a therapeutic aim as to "help the patient realize his potential" may be too much. It is too much if that is not what the patient wants. Sometimes, indeed, the patient may want the opposite, may feel that his trouble comes from having begun to realize incompatible potentialities, and that he must now turn away from some of them.

III

Freedom is that range of experience wherein events, courses of action, attitudes, decisions, accommodations, are seen as elective. It may be more or less, so we need to ask how much we want. In small things we always want choice. What color to paint the house? buy an Olds or a Buick? go to the Bergman film or the Ozawa concert? It would be onerous to be constrained here. In deeper matters we want to be held back. We might choose to live or die, but prefer *not* to choose, want to believe rather that we *have* to live. A kind man does not ponder becoming a sadist, an honest man does not consider whether to become a bandit; we prefer to consider such matters settled, removed from choice and hence from freedom.

In between such minor and major issues lies the middle ground of decision and action wherein some find freedom and choice while others find constraint and necessity. One man sees himself inextricably stuck in a marriage, a career, in obligations to children, relatives, colleagues, bound to his way and place of life, unable to change. Another in the same circumstances finds it possible to resign as judge of the circuit court, divorce a Philadelphia Mainline wife after twenty-four years of marriage and three children, move to Italy, live with an actress, take up painting. If we forgo the moral condemnation we generally visit upon those of greater scope and daring than ourselves, we are likely to discover great envy.

Necessity is that range of experience wherein events, courses of action, attitudes, decisions are seen as determined by forces outside ourselves which we cannot alter. A bored woman says, "I'd like to take a job, but can't leave home because of the children." With that "can't" she alleges necessity: staying home or leaving home is not open, the decision is imposed, runs counter to her wants; she designates her children's need as her necessity. Her prerogative to do this is clear, is granted, but it must be noted that nothing external to herself requires this view. Certainly her children's needs do not require it: within the same block other mothers manage somehow with babysitters and so hold jobs. The necessity that constrains her does not constrain them; it is of a different order from that which would derive from locked doors and barred windows.

The realm of necessity, therefore, must comprise two categories: the subjective or arbitrary, and the objective or mandatory. Mandatory necessity—like natural law which cannot be disobeyed—is that which cannot be suspended. It derives from forces, conditions, events which lie beyond the self, not subject to choice, unyielding to will and effort. "I wish I had blue eyes," ". . . wish I were twenty again," ". . . wish I could fly," ". . . wish I lived in the court of the Sun King." Such wishes are irrelevant, choice is inoperative; the necessity impartially constrains. And since it cannot be put aside there's not much arguing about it. "If you jump you will fall—whether or not you choose to fly." There is consensus, we don't dwell on it, we accept.

Arbitrary necessity derives from forces within the personality, but construed to be outside. The force may be either impulse or prohibition: "I didn't want to drink, but couldn't help it." That is to say, the impulse to drink does not lie within the "I." The "I," which is of course the locus of choice, does not "want" to drink, would choose otherwise, but is overwhelmed by alien force. "I want to marry you," a woman says to her lover, "want it more than anything in the world. But I can't divorce my husband. He couldn't take it . . . would break down. He depends on me. It would kill him" Here it is loyalty, caring for another's welfare, which is alleged to lie outside the deciding "I," which therefore cannot choose, cannot do what it "wants," but is held to an alien course. As though she were saying, "I do not here preside over internal conflict, do not listen to contending claims within myself to arrive finally at an anguished, fallible decision, but am coerced by mandates beyond my jurisdiction; I yield to necessity." The issue is not one of conscious versus unconscious. The contending forces are both conscious. The issue is the boundary of the self, the limits of the "I."

Arbitrary necessity, therefore—like man-made law—is that which may be suspended, disobeyed. When dealing with ourselves the constraining force seems inviolable, a solid wall before us, as though we really "can't," have no choice; and if we say so often enough, long enough, and mean it, we may make it so. But when we then look about and observe others doing what we "can't" do we must conclude that the constraining force is not an attribute of the surrounding world, not the way things are, but a mandate from within ourselves which we, strangely, exclude from the "I."

The lady who "wants" to marry her lover but "can't" divorce her husband might here object. "When I said 'can't,'" she might say, "it was just a way of speaking, a metaphor. It meant that staying with my husband represents duty, not desire, that's all. In a theoretical way I could choose . . . I know that. But it's just theoretical. Because . . . you see, the conflict is so terribly unequal, the considerations that make me stay, that absolutely demand I stay with my husband . . . they're so overwhelmingly strong, there's really no choice. That's all I mean."

We make serious record of her objection. In passing we note with surprise that the inequality of the conflict leads her to conclude there is "really no choice," whereas this same circumstance would have led us to say rather that the choice is easy, one she might arrive at promptly, with the conviction of being right.

It's only a metaphor, she says. In some theoretical way, she says, she is aware of choice. Perhaps. But we have doubt. In any event we must point out that she specifically denies this choice for which she now claims oblique awareness, that she locates the determining duty outside the "I" and its "wants." And we might add that if she continues such metaphorical speech long enough she will eventually convince even herself; her "theoretical" choice will become more and more theoretical until, with no remaining consciousness of option, it will disappear. She then will have made actual something that may once have been but a metaphor. Nothing guarantees our freedom. Deny it often enough and one day it will be gone, and we'll not know how or when.

Objective necessity is not arguable. My lover dies, I weep, beat my fists on the coffin. Everyone knows what I want; everyone knows that nothing will avail, no prayer, no curse, no desperate effort, nothing, that I shall never get her back. When there is argument about necessity, the alleged constraint is arbitrary, subjective. A house in flames, a trapped child, a restraining neighbor: "You can't go in! It's hopeless." I see it differently: I *can* go in—if I have the nerve. There may be a chance. It's not clear whether the situation permits or proscribes; the difference of opinion indicates that the necessity at issue is arbitrary. My neighbor's statement is more plea than observation; he asks me to perceive that the contemplated action is precluded, to see that there is no choice. By so deciding I can make it so. If I agree it is impossible, then—even if mistaken—my having arrived at that judgment will, in a matter of moments, make it true. Our judgments fall within the field of events being judged, so themselves become events, and so alter the field. We survey the course of history and conclude, "Wars are inevitable." The judgment seems detached, as if we observed from a distant galaxy; like all judgments, it may be mistaken. In any event it is not inert, it has consequences, shapes actions, moves interest and behavior from, for example, the politics of dissent to the connoisseurship of wine; it chips off one more fragment of the obstacle to war, and thereby makes more likely the war which, when it comes, will vindicate our original judgment and the behavior which issued from it. So we create the necessity which then constrains us, constrains ever more tightly day after day, so vindicating ever more certainly our wisdom in having perceived from the outset we were not free. Finally we are bound hand and foot and may exclaim triumphantly how right we were!

The areas of necessity and of freedom vary in proportion to each other and in absolute measure. They vary, also, from person to person, and, within the same person, from time to time. Together they comprise the total extent of available experience the range of which is a function of awareness and concern.

Adolescence, traditionally, is the time of greatest freedom, the major choices thereafter being progressively made, settled, and buried, one after another, never to be reopened. These days, however, an exhumation of such issues in later life has become quite common, with a corresponding increase in freedom which makes life again as hazardous as in youth.

Throughout our lives the proportion of necessity to freedom depends upon our tolerance for conflict: the greater our tolerance the more freedom we retain, the less our tolerance the more we jettison; for high among the uses of necessity is the pursuit of tranquility. What we can't alter we don't have to worry about; so the enlargement of necessity is a measure of economy in psychic housekeeping. The more issues we have closed the fewer we have to fret about. For many of us, for example, the issues of stealing and of homosexuality are so completely buried that we no longer have consciousness of option, and so no longer in these matters have freedom. We may then walk through Tiffany's or go to the ballet without temptation or conflict. For one to whom these are still live issues, and for whom the choice depends upon a constantly shifting balance of fallibly estimated rewards of gain or pleasure as against risks of capture or shame, such exposure may cause great tension.

Tranquility, however, has risks of its own. As we expand necessity and so relieve ourselves of conflict and responsibility, we are relieved, also, in the same measure, of authority and significance. When a crisis arises which does not fall within our limited routine we are frightened, without resources, insignificant.

For some people necessity expands cancerously, every possibility of invention and variation being transformed into inflexible routine until all freedom is eaten away. The extreme in psychic economy is an existence in which everything occurs by law. Since life means conflict, such a state is living death. When, in the other direction, the area of necessity is too much diminished we become confused, anxious, may be paralyzed by conflict, may reach eventually the extreme of panic.

The more we are threatened, fragile, vulnerable, the more we renounce freedom in favor of an expanding necessity. Observing others then who laugh at risk, who venture on paths from which we have turned back, we feel envy; they are courageous where we are timid. We come close to despising ourselves, but recover quickly, can always take refuge in a hidden determinism. "It's all an illusion," we say, "it looks like their will and daring as against my inhibition and weakness, but that *must* be illusion. Because life is lawful. Nothing happens by chance. Not a single atom veers off course at random. My inhibition is not a failure of nerve. We can't see the forces that mold us, but they are there. The genetic and experiential dice are loaded with factors unknown, unknowable, not of our intending, are thrown in circumstances over which we have no vision or control; we are stuck with the numbers that turn up. Beware the man who claims to be captain of his soul, he's first mate at the very best."

The more we are strong and daring the more we will diminish necessity in favor of an expanding freedom. "We are responsible," we say, "for what we are. We create ourselves. We have done as we have chosen to do, and by so doing have become what we are. If we don't like it, tomorrow is another day, and we may do differently."

Each speaks truly for himself, the one is just so determined, the other is just so free; but each overstates his truth in ascribing his constraint or his liberty to life at large. These truths are partial, do not contend with each other. Each expresses a quality of experience. Which view one chooses to express, to the exclusion of the other, better describes the speaker than the human condition.

In every situation, for every person, there is a realm of freedom and a realm of constraint. One may live in either realm. One must recognize the irresistible forces, the iron fist, the stone wall—must know them for what they are in order not to fall into the sea like Icarus—but, knowing them, one may turn away and live in the realm of one's freedom. A farmer must know the fence which bounds his land, but need not spend his life standing there, looking out, beating his fists on the rails; better he till his soil, think of what to grow, where to plant the fruit trees. However small the area of freedom, attention and devotion may expand it to occupy the whole of life.

Look at the wretched people huddled in line for the gas chambers at Auschwitz. If they do anything other than move on quietly, they will be clubbed down. Where is freedom? . . . But wait. Go back in time, enter the actual event, the very moment: they are thin and weak, and they smell; hear the weary shuffling steps, the anguished catch of breath, the clutch of hand. Enter now the head of one hunched and limping man. The line moves slowly; a few yards ahead begin the steps down. He sees the sign, someone whispers "showers," but he knows what happens here. He is struggling with a choice: to shout "Comrades! They will kill you! Run!"—or to say nothing. This option, in the few moments remaining, is his whole life. If he shouts he dies now, painfully; if he moves on silently he dies but minutes later. Looking back on him in time and memory, we find the moment poignant but the freedom negligible. It makes no difference in that situation, his election of daring or of inhibition. Both are futile, without consequence. History sees no freedom for him, notes only constraint, labels him victim. But in the consciousness of that one man it makes great difference whether or not he experiences the choice. For if he knows the constraint and nothing else, if he thinks "Nothing is possible," then he is living his necessity; but if, perceiving the constraint, he turns from it to a choice between two possible courses of action, then—however he chooses—he is living his freedom. This commitment to freedom may extend to the last breath.

IV

Sometimes in therapy profound change occurs spontaneously, without effort or intention. It is a rare experience—anytime, anywhere—to be known and understood without being judged, to be regarded with affection and respect, without being used. No therapist can feel this way about all his patients, though he must try. When he does genuinely so feel, he creates a nurturing context in which the patient may take in and make his own the therapist's way of thinking about problems, a certain reflectiveness about suffering, a tendency to hold conflicting motives in suspension while looking for connections, meanings, significance.

Such identification leads to slight, subtle, often unnoticed changes in action and behavior, in one's way of dealing with one's self and others; and over a period of time these changed actions may achieve a change of being. One then feels one's self to be profoundly different without knowing how or why. If one is asked, "Well, what did you learn? What was the main insight?" one may stumble about, fabricate some inadequate answer, yet may know certainly that one is a better person, more able to love.

This sort of change is rare. We can't count on it, can't make it happen; when it occurs it is great good fortune, a bonus. Usually change—when it occurs at all—follows long and arduous trying.

Neurotic suffering indicates inner conflict. Each side of the conflict is likely to be a composite of many partial forces, each one of which has been structured into behavior, attitude, perception, value. Each component asserts itself, claims priority, insists that something else yield, accommodate. The conflict therefore is fixed, stubborn, enduring. It may be impugned and dismissed without effect, imprecations and remorse are of no avail, strenuous acts of will may be futile; it causes—yet survives and continues to cause—the most intense suffering, humiliation, rending of flesh. Such a conflict is not to be uprooted or excised. It is not an ailment, it is the patient himself. The suffering will not disappear without a change in the conflict, and a change in the conflict amounts to a change in what one is and how one lives, feels, reacts.

Personality is a complex balance of many conflicting claims, forces, tensions, compunctions, distractions, which yet manages somehow to be a functioning entity. However it may have come to be what it is, it resists becoming anything else. It tends to maintain itself, to convey itself onward into the future unaltered. It may be changed only with difficulty. It may be changed from within, spontaneously and unthinkingly, by an onslaught of physiological force, as in adolescence. It may be changed from without, again spontaneously and unthinkingly, by the force of unusual circumstance, as in a Nazi concentration camp. And sometimes it may be changed from within, deliberately, consciously, and by design. Never easily, never for sure, but slowly, uncertainly, and only with effort, insight, and a kind of tenacious creative cunning.

Personality change follows change in behavior. Since we are what we do, if we want to change what we are we must begin by changing what we do, must undertake a new mode of action. Since the import of such action is change, it will run afoul of existing entrenched forces which will protest and resist. The new mode will be experienced as difficult, unpleasant, forced, unnatural, anxiety-provoking. It may be undertaken lightly but can be sustained only by a considerable effort of will. Change will occur only if such action is maintained over a long period of time.

The place of insight is to illumine: to ascertain where one is, how one got there, how now to proceed, and to what end. It is a blueprint, as in building a house, and may be essential, but no one achieves a house by blueprints alone, no matter how accurate or detailed. A time comes when one must take up hammer and nails. In building a house the making of blueprints may be delegated to an architect, the construction to a carpenter. In building the house of one's life or in its remodeling, one may delegate nothing; for the task can be done, if at all, only in the workshop of one's own mind and heart, in the most intimate rooms of thinking and feeling where none but one's self has freedom of movement or competence or authority. The responsibility lies with him who suffers, originates with him, remains with him to the end. It will be no less his if he enlists the aid of a therapist; we are no more the product of our therapists than of our genes: we create ourselves. The sequence is suffering, insight, will, action, change. The one who suffers, who wants to change, must bear responsibility all the way. "Must" because as soon as responsibility is ascribed, the forces resisting change occupy the whole of one's being, and the process of change comes to a halt. A psychiatrist may help perhaps crucially, but his best help will be of no avail if he is required to provide a kind or degree of insight which will of itself achieve change.

Should an honest man wish to become a thief the necessary action is obvious: he must steal—not just once or occasionally, but frequently, consistently, taking pains that the business of planning and executing thefts replaces other activities which in implication might oppose the predatory life. If he keeps at it long enough his being will conform to his behavior: he will have become a thief. Conversely, should a thief undertake to become an honest man, he must stop stealing and must undertake actions which replace stealing, not only in time and energy, and perhaps also excitement, but which carry implications contrary to the predatory life, that is, productive or contributive activities.

If a homosexual should set out to become heterosexual, among all that is obscure, two things are clear: he should discontinue homosexual relations, however much tempted he may be to continue on an occasional spontaneous basis, and he should undertake, continue, and maintain heterosexual relations, however little heart he may have for girls, however often he fail, and however inadequate and averse he may find himself to be. He would be well advised in reaching for such a goal to anticipate that success, if it be achieved at all, will require a long time, years not months, that the effort will be painful and humiliating, that he will discover profound currents of feeling which oppose the behavior he now requires of himself, that emerging obstacles will each one seem insuperable yet each must be thought through, that further insight will be constantly required to inform and sustain his behavior, that sometimes insight will precede and illumine action, and sometimes blind dogged action must come first, and that even so, with the best of will and good faith and determination, he still may fail. He should beware of beckoning shortcuts, such as drug therapy or hypnosis. They falsify the reality with which he must most intimately deal, that of his own thought, feeling, drive; they undermine his commitment of internal resources by encouraging him to feel that there is an easier way. There is no shortcut, no safe conduct, no easier way. He must proceed alone, on nerve. He is not entitled to much hope—just that he has a chance. He may take some bleak comfort only in knowing that no one can be sure at the outset that he will fail, and that it is his own unmeasured and unmeasurable resources of heart and mind and will which have the most bearing on the eventual outcome.

This is self-transcendence and is not to be confused with a type of coercive treatment in which the therapist acts as agent for society, and the goal is adjustment. Punishment, brainwashing, and lobotomy fall in this category. Less extreme varieties are known variously as operant conditioning, behavior therapy, or conditioned-reflex therapy. All such treatment takes the person as object and seeks to achieve the desired change by manipulation. The alcoholic may be so rigged with wires as to receive an electric shock each time he takes a drink. The homosexual man may be provided with male partners who insure that sexual experiences will be exceedingly unpleasant, while concurrently gently seductive ladies, without demands of their own, introduce him to the delights of polarized sexuality. Such things may be arranged for a fee.

We are in no position to comment on the efficacy of behavior therapy as generally practiced, but in principle we know it works. People may indeed be treated as objects and may be profoundly affected thereby. Kick a dog often enough and he will become cowardly or vicious. Men who are kicked undergo similar changes; their view of the world and of themselves is transformed. The survivors of Hitler's concentration camps testify that the treatment received did have an effect. Nor do we find any reason to doubt the alleged results of Chinese thought-control methods. People may indeed be brainwashed, for benign or exploitative reasons.

Behavior therapy is not, therefore, being contrasted to self-transcendence in terms of efficacy; the contrast is in terms of freedom. If one's destiny is shaped by manipulation one has become more of an object, less of a subject, has lost freedom. It matters little whether or not the manipulation is known to the person upon whom it acts. For even if one himself designs and provides for those experiences which are then to affect him, he is nevertheless treating himself as object—and to some extent, therefore, *becomes* an object.

If, however, one's destiny is shaped from within then one has become more of a creator, has gained freedom. This is self-transcendence, a process of change that originates in one's heart and expands outward, always within the purview and direction of a knowing consciousness, begins with a vision of freedom, with an "I want to become . . .," with a sense of the potentiality to become what one is not. One gropes toward this vision in the dark, with no guide, no map, and no guarantee. Here one acts as subject, author, creator.

Sometimes a process of character change may proceed with increasing momentum and finality to solid completion. The honest man becomes the complete thief; the thief becomes the completely honest man. When character change proceeds to such radical conclusion it is likely, not only that the old way of life has been given up, but also that a new way of life, directly opposite in implication, has been adopted. Such a change is experienced, not as a deflection of course, but as an absolute turning around, a conversion, may even call for a change of name. Saul of Tarsus had such an experience on the road to Damascus and—having been the chief persecutor of Christianity—became its greatest exponent. Malcolm X had such an experience in prison with the teachings of Elijah Muhammad, and changed not simply from thief to non-thief, but from thief to social reformer; the completeness and finality with which he transcended the old identity owed as much to his having undertaken to correct injustice with passion and commitment as it did to his giving up stealing. Had he simply "learned his lesson," decided not to steal any more, and taken an indifferently-regarded job as gas station attendant, he might never have altogether ceased being a thief. Some of the temptation, bitterness, and envy, something of the way of thought, the attitude, and outlook of a thief might have remained.

Such change as occurred in Saul or Malcolm X is rare, seems so far beyond anything we might achieve by our own efforts that, when it occurs, we usually ascribe credit—to a mystic force, to a revelation, to the hand of God. The changes we achieve with ourselves, with or without therapy, are likely to be partial and provisional. The homosexual gets married, has children, but never feels entirely safe with women; the frigid woman becomes capable of climax, but not easily and not always; the impotent man becomes able usually to make it, but can never be sure; the depressive character can work, may occasionally feel glad to be alive, but is not likely ever to be described as of sunny disposition; the phobic woman becomes less anxious, no longer has to decline invitations, but always has sweaty palms at cocktail parties. Such changes must be counted success; for more frequent in outcome, even with considerable effort, is no change at all. He who undertakes to transform himself, therefore, should think not of all or none, sick or well, miserable or happy, but of more or less, better or worse. He should undertake only to do what he can, to handle something better, to suffer less. The kingdom of heaven need not concern him.

When the thief takes a job and determines to go straight, when the homosexual gets a girl and renounces sexual relations with men, he does so with a vision of what he will become. Rarely may such direct action, in the course of time and of great effort, succeed without further insight and with no change of plan. More often the course upon which one has embarked entails so much anxiety, uncertainty, confusion, that reappraisal becomes necessary. One finds that his entire self was not known, that submerged aspects of self now rise up in terror, threat, and subversion, screaming outrage, demanding revocation. One is forced to a halt, sometimes driven back. The whole issue has to be rethought. "What I'm giving up is more important than I knew." "Maybe I don't want to change." "Am I going at it the wrong way?" Newly emerging feelings and reactions must be explored in relation to other known elements and to one's now threatened intention.

Here therapy may offer insight into bewildering experience, help with the making of new connections, give comfort and encouragement, assist in the always slippery decision of whether to hang on and try harder or to look for a different way to try. That person gains most from therapy, and gains it most quickly, who has the heart and will to go it alone in the event that therapy does not help; whereas he who clings to therapy as drowning man to ship's timber is more likely to burden therapy with a weight it can't support, and so take himself and therapy down together.

Sometimes we suffer desperately, would do anything, try anything, but are lost, find no way. We cast about, distract ourselves, search, but find no connection between the misery we feel and the way we live. The pain comes from nowhere, gives no clue. We are bored, nothing has meaning; we become depressed. What to do? How to live? Something is wrong but we cannot imagine another way of living which would free us.

Yet there must be a way, for no sustained feeling can exist as a thing in itself, independent of what we do. If the suffering is serious and intractable it must be intimately and extensively connected, in ways we do not perceive, with the way we live. We have to look for such connections. Sometimes there is nothing to be done until they are found.

Therapy may help. One may discover, for example, a simmering hatred of one's wife, not consciously felt, not expressed, but turned against one's self, experienced as depression. Such a finding may still not indicate what one should do; for that will depend on yet other feelings, connections, implications. Should one begin to express the anger? Perhaps, if the grievance is reasonable and if there is also affinity and love. Should one get a divorce? Perhaps, if there is not even that minimum affection necessary for trying to work out differences. Sometimes there is no love, and good reason for hatred, and still one does not want a divorce: then one must be struck by this curious thing, that one clings to a source of frustration and torment, must ask why, and perhaps only then may begin to uncover a profound dependence which has been both well hidden by, and fully expressed in, the hostile tie. One hates her but can't leave her because one is afraid. Afraid of what? And why? What one should do may come to be known only after this dependence is examined in its relations with various other feelings and experiences. Sometimes there is no grievance and much love, and so, gradually, one may learn that he scapegoats his wife and may realize that he must, therefore, need to feel hatred, that he is using it for ulterior purposes—perhaps to cover up feelings of inadequacy, so avoiding the awareness of what he might want to do if he weren't afraid.

Much of our suffering is just so obscure as this. Frigidity, social anxiety, isolation, boredom, disaffection with life—in all such states we may see no correlation between the inner feeling and the way we live. Yet no such feeling can be independent of behavior; and if only we find the connections we may begin to see how a change in the way we live will make for a change in the way we feel.

Since freedom depends upon awareness, psychotherapy may, by extending awareness, create freedom. When in therapy a life story of drift and constraint is reworked to expose alternatives for crucial courses of action, asking always "Why did you do that?," attaching doubt to every explanation which is cast in the form of necessary reaction to antecedent cause, always reminding the patient that "Even so . . . it was possible to have acted otherwise"—in all this one is rewriting the past, is taking the story of a life which was experienced as shaped by circumstance and which was recounted as such, and retelling it in terms of choice and responsibility. As a court may remind a defendant that ignorance of the law is no excuse, so a therapist may remind a patient that blindness to freedom does not justify constraint. And insofar as it may come to seem credible to rewrite one's life in terms of ignored choice, to assume responsibility retrospectively for what one has done and so has become, it will become possible likewise to see alternatives in the present, to become aware that one is free now in this moment to choose how to live, and that what one will become will follow upon what he now does.

When, however, in therapy a life story is reworked to expose the forces which "drove" one to do as he did, emphasizing traumas which twisted him and shaped defenses, hidden constraints, situational and libidinal, which required that he react in the way he did and in no other—in all this, too, one is rewriting the past, is taking a story which must have contained some elements of freedom and responsibility and retelling it in terms of causes lying outside one's control, so teaching the patient to see himself as the product of inner and outer forces. Where he feels himself to be the author of action, his analysis will reveal him as an object being acted upon. He then comes to regard himself as being lived by unknown and largely unknowable forces. As consolation prize he may acquire the capacity to guess at the nature of those obscure forces that move him. But only guess. He must not attempt seriously to bear witness to that which, by definition, he cannot know. He must remain forever the dilettante, making modest conjecture at the gusts which blow him this way and that. He becomes not only an object but opaque, most necessarily to himself.

A "completely analyzed" person is one who has been treated for many years by an orthodox analyst. When such a one breaks down and is hospitalized we are surprised; if he is himself a psychoanalyst we are shocked. Our reaction bespeaks the assumption that thorough analysis resolves all serious inner conflict, that thereafter—though one may expect times of sadness, uncertainty, and unrest—these will derive from reality conflicts and so will not lead to breakdown. There is little to support such a view; indeed, the most cursory glance at three generations of analysts leaves it in tatters. The surprise we feel when a "well analyzed" person breaks down derives from the wish to view man as a machine. Very delicate and complicated, to be sure, like a fine watch, and liable therefore to subtle, tricky problems of adjustment which may require the lengthy services of an expert; but when finally we get rid of all the bugs we may expect smooth and reliable function. Such an image of man is at odds with what we know life to be. If we seriously regard our private thought and feeling, our visions at night when the wind blows, when rain falls on a deserted island, then—though fine adjustments have been made by a great watchmaker—we find so much conflict, misery, confusion that we know we are never through and never safe. The suffering and the danger cannot be left behind. They are what we are.

In reconstructing a life story truth is necessary but not sufficient. Truth does not demarcate, cannot determine whether we should dwell upon cause or choice. Two histories of the same life may be radically different, yet equally true. If we have failed an examination we may say, "I would not have failed if the teacher had not asked that question on Cromwell—which, after all, had not come up in class," or "I would not have failed if I had studied harder." Both statements are addressed to the same experience, in the same effort to understand; both claim to answer the question "Why did I fail?" and both may be true. Truth does not here provide the criterion for selection; the way we understand the past is determined, rather, by the future we desire. If we want to excuse ourselves we elect the former view; if we want to avoid such failures in the future we elect the latter. (If we believe our aim to be the passing of such exams in the future, and if we nevertheless elect the former view of the present failure, then we are confused.)

Likewise in addressing ourselves to the failure of a lifetime, and asking why, we may arrive at answers significantly different but equally true. In the life most free and most aware, so much defining action still occurs without choice that it is always feasible to compose an accurate and cogent account in terms of genes, drives, and circumstance. Conversely, in the life most crushed by outside force, there nevertheless exists the potentiality for actions other than those in fact taken. With the noose around our neck there still are options—to curse God or to pray, to weep or to slap the executioner in the face.

Of two equally true accounts of the same life the one we choose will depend upon the consequences we desire, the future we intend to create. If the life is our own or one of our patients', if it involves suffering and there is desire to change, we will elect a history written in terms of choice; for this is the view that insists upon the awareness of alternatives, the freedom to make one's self into something different. If the life in question is one we observe from a distance, without contact or influence, for example a life which has ended, we may elect a history written in terms of cause. In reconstructing a life that ended at Auschwitz we usually ignore options for other courses of individual behavior, locate cause and responsibility with the Nazis; for our intent is not to appraise the extent to which one person realized existing opportunity, but to examine and condemn the social evil which encompassed and doomed him. In considering the first eighteen years in the life of Malcolm X few of us would find much point in formulating his progress from delinquency to rackets to robbery to prison in terms of choice, holding him responsible for not having transcended circumstance; most of us would find the meaning of his story to lie in the manner in which racism may be seen as the cause of his downward course.

Conflict, suffering, psychotherapy—all these lead us to look again at ourselves, to look more carefully, in greater detail, to find what we have missed, to understand a mystery; and all this extends awareness. But whether this greater awareness will increase or diminish freedom will depend upon what it is that we become aware of. If the greater awareness is of the causes, traumas, psychodynamics that "made" us what we are, then we are understanding the past in such a way as to prove that we "had" to become what we are; and, since this view applies equally to the present which is the unbroken extension of that determined past, therapy becomes a way of establishing why we must continue to be what we have been, a way of disavowing choice with the apparent blessing of science, and the net effect will be a decrease in freedom. If, however, the greater awareness is of options unnoticed, of choices denied, of other ways to live, then freedom will be increased, and with it greater responsibility for what we have been, are, and will become.

19 / The Open Truth and Fiery Vehemence of Youth: A Sort of Soliloquy

PETER MARIN

It is midnight and I am sitting here with my notes, enough of them to make two books and a half and a volume of posthumous fragments, trying to make some smaller sense of them than the grand maniacal design I have in my mind. I don't know where to begin. Once, traveling in summer across the country with a friend from Hollywood and my young son in a battered green Porsche, I stopped for lunch somewhere in Kansas on a Sunday morning. As we walked into the restaurant, bearded, wearing dark glasses and strange hats, and followed by my long-haired boy, one Kansas matron bent toward another and whispered: "I bet those two men have kidnapped that little girl." I took a deep breath and started to speak, but I did not know where to begin or how to explain just how many ways she was mistaken. Now, trying to write clearly about education and adolescence, I feel the same way.

For that reason I have chosen an eccentric method of composition, one that may seem fragmentary, jumpy, and broken. This article will be more like a letter, and the letter itself is an accumulation of impressions and ideas, a sampling of thoughts at once disconnected but related. There is a method to it that may disappear in its mild madness, but I do not know at this juncture how else to proceed. Shuffling through my notes I feel like an archeologist with a mass of uncatalogued shards. There is a pattern to all this, a coherence of thought, but all I can do here is

SOURCE: *The Center Magazine* 2 (January 1969), 61–74. *The Center Magazine* is a publication of the Center for the Study of Democratic Institutions, Santa Barbara, California.

Peter Marin was, in 1967–68, the director of Pacific High School, an experimental private day school located outside Palo Alto, California.

assemble the bits and pieces and lay them out for you and hope that you can sense how I get from one place to another.

An entire system is hiding behind this, just beginning to take form, and these notes are like a drawing, a preliminary sketch. I feel comfortable with that notion, more comfortable than with the idea of forcing them together, cutting and pasting, to make a more conventional essay. I can perceive in myself at this moment what I also see in the young: I am reluctant to deal in sequence with my ideas and experience, I am impatient with transition, the habitual ways of getting "from here to there." I think restlessly; my mind, like the minds of my students, works in flashes, in sudden perceptions and brief extended clusters of intuition and abstraction—and I have stuck stubbornly to that method of composition. There is still in me the ghost of an apocalyptic adolescent, and I am trying to move it a few steps toward the future.

One theme, as you will see, runs through what I have written or thought: we must rethink our ideas of childhood and schooling. We must dismantle them and start again from scratch. Nothing else will do. Our visions of adolescence and education confine us to habit, rule perception out. We make do at the moment with a set of ideas inherited from the nineteenth century, from an industrial, relatively puritanical, repressive, and "localized" culture; we try to gum them like labels to new kinds of experience. But that won't do. Everything has changed. The notions with which I began my job as a high-school director have been discarded one by one. They make no sense. What emerges through these children as the psyche of this culture is post-industrial, relatively unrepressed, less literate and local: a new combination of elements, almost a new strain. Adolescents are, each one of them, an arena in which the culture transforms itself or is torn between contrary impulses; they are the victims of a culture raging within itself like man and wife, a schizoid culture—and these children are the unfinished and grotesque products of that schism.

They are grotesque because we give them no help. They are forced to make among themselves adjustments to a tension that must be unbearable. They do the best they can, trying, in increasingly eccentric fashions, to make sense of things. But we adults seem to have withdrawn in defeat from that same struggle, to have given up. We are enamored, fascinated, and deluded by adolescence precisely because it is the last life left to us; only the young rebel with any real passion against media, machines, the press of circumstance itself. Their elders seem to have no options, no sense of alternative or growth. Adult existence is bled of life and we turn in that vacuum toward children with the mixed repulsion and desire of wanton puritans toward life itself.

As for me, an adult, I think of myself as I write as an observer at a tribal war—an anthropologist, a combination of Gulliver and a correspondent sending home news by mule and boat. By the time you hear of it, things will have changed. And that isn't enough, not enough at all. Somebody must step past the children, must move into his own psyche or two steps past his own limits into the absolute landscape of fear and potential these children inhabit. That is where I am headed. So these ideas, in effect, are something like a last message tacked to a tree in a thicket or tucked under a stone. I mean: we cannot *follow* the children any longer, we have to step ahead of them. Somebody has to mark a trail.

Adolescence: a few preliminary fragments . . .

(FROM MY STUDENT, V): *yr whole body moves in a trained way & you know that youve moved this way before & it contains all youve been taught its all rusty & slow something is pushing under that rusted mesh but STILL YOU CANNOT MOVE you are caught between 2 doors & the old one is much closer & you can grab it all the time but the other door it disappears that door you cant even scratch & kick (like the early settlers were stung by the new land) but this new land doesnt even touch you & you wonder if youre doing the right thing to get in*

(FROM FRANZ KAFKA): *He feels imprisoned on this earth, he feels constricted; the melancholy, the impotence, the sicknesses, the feverish fancies of the captive afflict him; no comfort can comfort him, since it is merely comfort, gentle headsplitting comfort glazing the brutal fact of imprisonment.* But if he is asked what he wants he cannot reply. . . . He has no conception of freedom.

326

(FROM TAPES RECORDED IN PACIFIC PALISADES, 1966, SEVERAL BOYS AND GIRLS AGED 12–14):—*Things are getting younger and younger. Girls twelve will do it now. One guy said I fuck a girl every Friday night. What sexual pleasure do you get out of this (he's very immature you know) and he would say, I don't know I'm just going to fuck.*

or

—How old are you? —*Twelve.* —Will you tell us your first experience with drugs, how you got into it?—*Well, the people I hung around with were big acid-heads. So one day my friend asked me if I wanted to get stoned and I said yes. That was about five months ago and I've been getting on it ever since. Started taking LSD about one month ago. Took it eleven times in one month. I consider it a good thing. For getting high, smoking grass is better, or hashish—it's about six times stronger than marijuana.*

(FROM PAUL RADIN: Primitive Man As Philosopher): *It is conceivably demanding too much of a man to whom the pleasures of life are largely bound up with the life of contemplation and to whom analysis and introspection are the self-understood prerequisites for a proper understanding of the world, that he appreciate . . . expressions which are largely non-intellectual —where life seems, predominatingly, a discharge of physical vitality, a simple and naive release of emotions or an enjoyment of sensations for their own sake. Yet . . . it is just such an absorption in a life of sensations that is the outward characteristic of primitive peoples.*

Can you see where my thought leads? It is precisely at this point, adolescence, when the rush of energies, that sea-sex, gravitation, the thrust of the ego up through layers of childhood, makes itself felt, that the person is once more like an infant, is swept once more by energies that are tidal, unfamiliar, and unyielding. He is in a sense born again, a fresh identity beset inside and out by the rush of new experience. It is at this point, too— when we seem compelled by a persistent lunacy to isolate him— that what is growing within the adolescent demands expression, requires it, and must, in addition, be received by the world and given form—or it will wither or turn to rage. Adolescence is a second infancy. It is then that a man desires solitude and at the same time contact with the vivid world; must test within social reality the new power within himself; needs above all to discover himself for the first time as a bridge between inner and outer, a maker of value, a vehicle through which culture perceives and transforms itself. It is now, ideally, that he begins to understand the complex and delicate nature of the ego itself as a thin skin between living worlds, a synaptic jump, the self-conscious point at which nature and culture combine.

In this condition, with these needs, the adolescent is like a primitive man, an apocalyptic primitive; he exists for the moment in that state of single vision in which myth is still the raw stuff of being, he knows at first hand through his own energies the possibilities of life—but he knows these in muddled, sporadic, contradictory ways. The rush of his pubescent and raw energy seems at odds with public behavior, the *order* of things, the tenor of life around him, especially in a culture just emerging—as is ours—from a tradition of evasion, repression, and fear.

The contradictions within the culture itself intensify his individual confusion. We are at the moment torn between future and past: in the midst of a process of transformation we barely understand. The development of adolescent energy and ego—difficult at any time—is complicated in our own by the increase in early sexuality, the complicated messages of the media, and the effects of strong and unfamiliar drugs. These three elements are, in themselves, the salient features of a culture that is growing more permissive, less repressive. They are profound, complex, and strong: heavy doses of experience demanding changes in attitude, changes in behavior. The direction and depth of feeling responds accordingly; the adolescent tries—even as a form of self-defense against the pressure of his own energies—to move more freely, to change his styles of life, to "grow." But it is then that he finds he is locked into culture, trapped in a web of ideas, law, and rituals that keep him a child, deprive him of a chance to test and assimilate his newer self. It is now that the culture turns suddenly repressive. His gestures are evaded or denied; at best he is "tolerated," but even then his gestures, lacking the social support of acknowledgment and reward, must seem to him lacking in authenticity—more like forms of neurosis or selfishness than the natural stages in growth.

He is thrust back upon himself. The insistent natural press within him toward becoming whole is met perpetually by unbudging resistance. Schools, rooted as they are in a Victorian century and seemingly suspicious of life itself, are his natural enemies. They don't help, as they might, to make that bridge between his private and the social worlds; they insist, instead, upon their separation. Indeed, family, community, and school all combine—especially in the suburbs—to isolate and "protect" him from the adventure, risk, and participation he needs; the same energies that relate him at this crucial point to nature result in a kind of exile from the social environment.

Thus the young, in that vivid confrontation with the thrust of nature unfolding in themselves, are denied adult assistance. I once wrote that education through its limits denied the gods, and that they would return in the young in one form or another to haunt us. That is happening now. You can sense it as the students gather, with their simplistic moral certainty, at the gates of the universities. It is almost as if the young were once more possessed by Bacchanalian gods, were once again inhabited by divinities whose honor we have neglected. Those marvelous and threatening energies! What disturbs me most about them is that we lack rituals for their use and balance, and the young—and perhaps we ourselves—now seem at their mercy. The young have moved, bag and baggage, into areas where adults cannot help them, and it is a scary landscape they face, it is crowded with strange forms and faces, and if they return from it raddled, without balance and pitched toward excess, who can pretend to be surprised—or blameless?

At times they seem almost shell-shocked, survivors of a holocaust in which the past has been destroyed and all the bridges to it bombed. I cannot describe with any certainty what occurs in their minds, but I do know that most adults must seem to the young like shrill critics speaking to them in an alien language about a Greek tragedy in which they may lose their lives. The words we use, our dress, our tones of voice, the styles of adult lives—all of these are so foreign to that dramatic crisis that as we approach them we seem to increase the distance we are trying to cross. Even our attention drives them further away, as if adolescents perceived that adults, coming closer, diminish in sense and size.

The inner events in an adolescent demand from what surrounds him life on a large scale, in a grand style. This is the impulse to apocalypse in the young, as if they were in exile from a nation that does not exist—and yet they can sense it, they know it is there—if only because their belief itself demands its presence. Their demand is absolute and unanswerable, but it exists and we seem unable at this point in time to suppress or evade it. For one reason or another, massive shifts in cultural balances, the lessening of repression for whatever reasons—economic, technological, evolutionary—those energies, like gods, have appeared among us again. But what can we make of them? The simple problem is that our institutions are geared to another century, another set of social necessities, and cannot change quickly enough to contain, receive, or direct them—and as we suppress or refuse them they turn to rage.

Primitive cultures dealt with this problem, I think, through their initiation rites, the rites of passage; they legitimized and accepted these energies and turned them toward collective aims; they were merged with the life of the tribe and in this way acknowledged, honored, and domesticated—but not destroyed. In most initiation rites the participant is led through the mythical or sacred world (or a symbolic version) and is then returned, transformed, to the secular one as a new person, with a new role. He is introduced through the rites to a dramatic reality coexistent with the visible or social one and at its root; he is put in direct touch with the sources of energy, the divinities of the tribe. In many cultures the symbolic figures in the rites are unmasked at the end, as if to reveal to the initiate the interpenetration of the secular and sacred worlds. Occasionally the initiate is asked at some point to don the ritual mask himself—joining, as he does, one world with another and assuming the responsibility for their connection. This shift in status, in *relation*, is the heart of the rite; a liturgized merging of the individual with shared sources of power.

Do you see what I am driving at? The rites are in a sense a social contract, a binding up; one occurring specifically, profoundly, on a deep psychic level. The individual is redefined in the culture by his new relation to its mysteries, its gods, to one form or another of nature. His experience of that hidden and omnipotent mythical world is the basis for his relation to the culture and his fellows, each of whom has a similar bond—deep, personal, and unique, but somehow shared, invisibly but deeply. These ritualized relationships of each man to the shared gods bind the group together; they form the substance of culture: an invisible landscape that is real and felt, commonly held, a landscape which resides in each man and in which, in turn, each man resides.

I hope that makes sense. That is the structure of the kaleidoscopic turning of culture that Blake makes in "The Crystal Cabinet," and it makes sense too, in America, in relation to adolescents. What fascinates me is that our public schools, designed for adolescents—who seem, as apocalyptic men, to demand this kind of drama, release, and support—educate and "socialize" their students by depriving them of everything the rites bestow. They manipulate them through the repression of energies; they isolate them and close off most parts of the community; they categorically refuse to make use of the individual's private experience. The direction of all these tendencies is toward a cultural schizophrenia in which the student is forced to choose between his own relation to reality or the one demanded by the institution. The schools are organized to weaken the student so that he is forced, in the absence of his own energies, to accept the values and demands of the institution. To this end we deprive the student of mobility and experience; through law and custom we make the only legal place for him the school, and then, to make sure he remains dependent, manipulable, we empty the school of all vivid life.

We appear to have forgotten in our schools what every primitive tribe with its functional psychology knows: allegiance to the tribe can be forged only at the deepest levels of the psyche and in extreme circumstance demanding endurance, daring, and awe; that the participant must be given *direct* access to the sources of cultural continuity—by and in himself; and that only a place in a coherent community can be exchanged for a man's allegiance.

I believe that it is precisely this world that drugs replace; adolescents provide for themselves what we deny them: a confrontation with some kind of power within an unfamiliar landscape involving sensation and risk. It is there, I suppose, that they hope to find, by some hurried magic, a new way of seeing, a new relation to things, to discard one identity and assume another. They mean to find through their adventures the *ground* of reality, the resonance of life we deny them, as if they might come upon their golden city and return still inside it: at home. You can see the real veterans sometimes on the street in strange costumes they have stolen from dreams: American versions of the Tupi of Brazil, who traveled thousands of miles each year in search of the land where death and evil do not exist. Theirs is a world totally alien to the one we discuss in schools; it is dramatic, it enchants them; its existence forms a strange brotherhood among them and they cling to it—as though they alone had been to a fierce land and back. It is that which draws them together and makes of them a loose tribe. It is, after all, some sort of shared experience, some kind of foray into the risky dark; it is the best that they can do.

When you begin to think about adolescence in this way, what sense can you make of our schools? None of the proposed changes makes sense to me: revision of curriculum, teaching machines, smaller classes, encounter groups, redistributions of power—all of these are stopgap measures, desperate attempts to keep the young in schools that are hopelessly outdated. The changes suggested and debated don't go deeply enough; they don't question or change enough. For what needs changing are not the methods of the school system but its aims, and what is troubling the young and forcing upon their teachers an intolerable burden is the *idea* of childhood itself; the ways we think about adolescents, their place in the culture itself. More and more one comes to see that changes in the schools won't be enough; the crisis of the young cuts across the culture in all its areas and includes the family and the community. The young are displaced; there seems no other word for it. They are trapped in a prolonged childhood almost unique.

In few other cultures have persons of fifteen or eighteen been so uselessly isolated from participation in the community, or been deemed so unnecessary (in their elders' eyes), or so limited by law. Our ideas of responsibility, our parental feelings of anxiety, blame, and guilt, all of these follow from our curious vision of the young; in turn, they concretize it, legitimize it so that we are no longer even conscious of the ways we see childhood or the strain that our vision puts upon us. That is what needs changing: the definitions we make socially and legally of the role of the young. They are trapped in the ways we see them, and the school is simply one function, one aspect, of the whole problem. What makes real change so difficult in the schools is only in part their natural unwieldiness; it is more often the difficulty we have in escaping our preconceptions about things.

In general the school system we have inherited seems to me based upon three particular things:

1. What Paul Goodman calls the idea of "natural depravity": our puritanical vision of human nature in which children are perceived as sinners or "savages" and in which human impulse or desire is not to be trusted and must therefore be constrained or "trained."

2. The necessity during the mid-nineteenth century of "Americanizing" great masses of immigrant children from diverse backgrounds and creating, through the schools, a common experience and character.

3. The need in an industrialized state for energy and labor to run the machines: the state, needing workers, educates persons to be technically capable but relatively dependent and responsive to authority so that their energies will be available when needed.

These elements combine with others—the labor laws that make childhood a "legal" state, and a population explosion that makes it necessary now to keep adolescents off both the labor market and the idle street—to "freeze" into a school system that resists change even as the culture itself and its needs shift radically. But teachers can't usually see that, for they themselves have been educated in this system and are committed to ideas that they have never clearly understood. Time and again, speaking to them, one hears the same questions and anguish:

"But what will happen to the students if they don't go to school?" "How will they learn?" "What will they do without adults?"

What never comes clear, of course, is that such questions are, at bottom, statement. Even while asking them teachers reveal their unconscious and contaminating attitudes. They can no longer imagine what children will do "outside" schools. They regard them as young monsters who will, if released from adult authority or help, disrupt the order of things. What is more, adults no longer are capable of imagining learning or child-adult relationships outside the schools. But mass schooling is a recent innovation. Most learning—especially the process of socialization or acculturation—has gone on outside schools, more naturally, in the fabric of the culture. In most cultures the passage from childhood to maturity occurs because of social necessity, the need for responsible adults, and is marked by clear changes in role. Children in the past seem to have learned the ways of the community or tribe through constant contact and interchange with adults, and it was taken for granted that the young learned continually through their place close to the heart of the community.

We seem to have lost all sense of that. The school is expected to do what the community cannot do and that is impossible. In the end, we will have to change far more than the schools if we expect to create a new coherence between the experiences of the child and the needs of the community. We will have to rethink the meaning of childhood; we will begin to grant greater freedom *and* responsibility to the young; we will drop the compulsory-schooling age to fourteen, perhaps less; we will take for granted the "independence" of adolescents and provide them with the chance to live alone, away from parents and with peers; we will discover jobs they can or want to do in the community— anything from mail delivery to the teaching of smaller children and the counseling of other adolescents. At some point, perhaps, we will even find that the community itself—in return for a minimum of work or continued schooling—will provide a minimal income to young people that will allow them to assume the responsibility for their own lives at an earlier age, and learn the ways of the community outside the school; finally, having lowered the level of compulsory schooling, we will find it necessary to provide different *kinds* of schools, a wider choice, so that students will be willing voluntarily to continue the schooling that suits their needs and aims.

All these changes, of course, are aimed at two things: the restoration of the child's "natural" place in the community and lowering the age at which a person is considered an independent member of the community. Some of them, to be sure, can be made in the schools, but my sense of things, after having talked to teachers and visited the schools, is that trying to make the changes in schools *alone* will be impossible.

One problem, put simply, is that in every school I have visited, public or private, traditional or "innovational," the students have only these two choices: to drop out (either physically or mentally) or to make themselves smaller and smaller until they can act in ways their elders expect. One of my students picked up a phrase I once used, "the larger and smaller worlds." The schools we visit together, he says, are always the smaller world: smaller at least than his imagination, smaller than the potential of the young. The students are asked to put aside the best things about themselves—their own desires, impulses, and ideas—in order to "adjust" to an environment constructed for children who existed one hundred years ago, if at all. I wonder sometimes if this condition is simply the result of poor schooling; I am more inclined to believe that it is the inevitable result of mass compulsory schooling and the fabrication of artificial environments by adults for children. Is it possible at all for adults to understand what children need and to change their institutions fast enough to keep up with changes in culture and experience? Is it possible for children to grow to their full size, to feel their full strength, if they are deprived of individual volition all along the line and forced to school? I don't know. I know only that during the Middle Ages they sometimes "created" jesters by putting young children in boxes and force-feeding them so that, as they grew, their bones would warp in unusual shapes. That is often how the schools seem to me. Students are trapped in the boxes of pedagogic ideas, and I am tempted to say to teachers again and again: more, much more, you must go further, create more space in the schools, you must go deeper in thought, create more resonance, a different feeling, a different and more human, more daring style.

Even the best teachers, with the best intentions, seem to diminish their students as they work through the public-school system. For that system is, at bottom, designed to produce what we sometimes call good citizens but what more often than not turn out to be good soldiers; it is through the schools of the state, after all, that we produce our armies. I remember how struck I was while teaching at a state college by the number of boys who wanted to oppose the draft but lacked the courage or strength to simply say no. They were trapped; they had always been taught, had always tried, to be "good." Now that they wanted to refuse to go, they could not, for they weren't sure they could bear the consequences they had been taught would follow such refusal: jail, social disgrace, loss of jobs, parental despair. They could not believe in institutions, but they could not trust themselves and their impulse and they were caught in their own impotence: depressed and resentful, filled with self-hatred and a sense of shame.

That is a condition bred in the schools. In one way or another our methods produce in the young a condition of pain that seems very close to a mass neurosis: a lack of faith in oneself, a vacuum of spirit into which authority or institutions can move, a dependency they feed on. Students are encouraged to relinquish their own wills, their freedom of volition; they are taught that value and culture reside outside oneself and must be acquired from the institution, and almost everything in their education is designed to discourage them from activity, from the wedding of idea and act. It is almost as if we hoped to discourage them from thought itself by making ideas so lifeless, so hopeless, that their despair would be enough to make them manipulable and obedient.

The system breeds obedience, frustration, dependence, and fear: a kind of gentle violence that is usually turned against oneself, one that is sorrowful and full of guilt, but a violence nonetheless, and one realizes that what is done in the schools to persons is deeply connected to what we did to the blacks or are doing now in Vietnam. That is: we don't teach hate in the schools, or murder, but we do isolate the individual; we empty him of life by ignoring or suppressing his impulse toward life; we breed in him a lack of respect for it, a loss of love—and thus we produce gently "good" but threatened men, men who will kill without passion, out of duty and obedience, men who have in themselves little sense of the vivid life being lost nor the moral strength to refuse.

From first to twelfth grade we acclimatize students to a fundamental deadness and teach them to restrain themselves for

336

the sake of "order." The net result is a kind of pervasive cultural inversion in which they are asked to separate at the most profound levels their own experience from institutional reality, self from society, objective from subjective, energy from order—though these various polarities are precisely those which must be made coherent during adolescence.

I remember a talk I had with a college student.

"You know what I love to do," he said. "I love to go into the woods and run among the trees."

"Very nice," I said.

"But it worries me. We shouldn't do it."

"Why not?" I asked.

"Because we get excited. It isn't *orderly*."

"Not orderly?"

"Not orderly."

"Do you run into the trees?" I asked.

"Of course not."

"Then it's orderly," I said.

In a small way this exchange indicates the kind of thinking we encourage in the schools: the mistaking of rigidity and stillness for order, of order as the absence of life. We try to create and preserve an order which depends upon the destruction of life both inside and out and which all life, when expressed, must necessarily threaten or weaken.

The natural process of learning seems to move naturally from experience through perception to abstraction in a fluid continuous process that cannot be clearly divided into stages. It is in that process that energy is somehow articulated in coherent and meaningful form as an act or thought or a made object. The end of learning is wisdom and wisdom to me, falling back as I do on a Jewish tradition, is, in its simplest sense, "intelligent activity" or, more completely, the suffusion of activity with knowledge, a wedding of the two. For the Hassidic Jews every gesture was potentially holy, a form of prayer, when it was made with a reverence for God. In the same way a gesture is always a form of wisdom—an act is wisdom—when it is suffused with knowledge, made with a reverence for the truth.

Does that sound rhetorical? I suppose it does. But I mean it. The end of education is intelligent activity, *wisdom*, and that demands a merging of opposites, a sense of process. Instead we produce the opposite: immobility, insecurity, an inability to act without institutional blessing or direction, or, at the opposite pole, a headlong rush toward motion without balance or thought. We cut into the natural movement of learning and try to force upon the students the end product, abstraction, while eliminating experience and ignoring their perception. The beginning of thought is in the experience through one's self of a particular environment—school, community, culture. When this is ignored, as it is in schools, the natural relation of self and knowledge is broken, the parts of the process become polar opposites, antitheses, and the young are forced to choose between them: objectivity, order, and obedience as against subjectivity, chaos, and energy. It doesn't really matter which they choose; as long as the two sets seem irreconcilable their learning remains incomplete. Caught between the two, they suffer our intellectual schizophrenia until it occupies them, too. They wait. They sit. They listen. They learn to "behave" at the expense of themselves. Or else—and you can see it happening now—they turn against it with a vengeance and may shout, as they did at Columbia, "Kill all adults," for they have allied themselves with raw energy against reason and balance—our delicate, hard-won virtues— and we should not be surprised. We set up the choices ourselves, and it is simply that they have chosen what we hold to be the Devil's side.

If this is the case, what are the alternatives? I thought at one time that changes in schooling could be made, that the school itself could become at least a microcosm of the community outside, a kind of halfway house, a preparatory arena in which students, in semi-protective surroundings, would develop not only the skill but the character that would be needed in the world. But more and more, as I have said, it seems to me impossible to do that job in a setting as isolated and restrictive as our schools. Students don't need the artificiality of schools; they respond more fully and more intelligently when they make direct contact with the community and are allowed to choose roles that have some utility for the community and themselves. What is at stake here, I suppose, is the freedom of volition, for this is the basic condition with which people must learn to deal, and the sooner they achieve within that condition wit, daring, and responsibility the stronger they will be. It seems absurd to postpone the assumption of that condition as long as we do. In most other cultures, and even in our own past, young people have taken upon themselves the responsibility of adults and have dealt with it as successfully as most adults do now. The students I have seen can do that, too, when given the chance. What a strain it must be to have that capacity, to sense in one's self a talent for adventure or growth or meaning, and have that sense continually stifled or undercut by the role one is supposed to play.

Thus, it seems inescapably clear that our first obligation to the young is to create a place in the community for them to act with volition and freedom. They are ready for it, certainly, even if we aren't. Adolescents seem to need at least some sense of risk and gain "out there" in the world: an existential sense of themselves that is vivid to the extent that the dangers faced are "real." The students I have worked with seem strongest and most alive when they are in the mountains of Mexico or the Oakland ghetto or out in the desert or simply hitchhiking or riding freights to see what's happening. They thrive on distance and motion—and the right to solitude when they want it. Many of them want jobs; they themselves arrange to be teachers in day-care centers, political canvassers, tutors, poolroom attendants, actors, governesses, gardeners. They returned from these experiences immeasurably brightened and more sure of themselves, more willing, in that new assurance, to learn many of the abstract ideas we had been straining to teach them. It was not simply the experience in itself that brought this about. It was also the feeling of freedom they had, the sense that they could come and go at will and make any choice they wanted—no matter how absurd —if they were willing to suffer what real consequences followed. Many wanted to work and travel and others did not; they wanted to sit and think or read or live alone or swim or, as one student scrawled on my office wall, "ball and goof." What they finally came to understand, of course, was that the school made no pretense at either limiting or judging their activities; we considered them free agents and limited our own activities to advice, to what "teaching" they requested, and to support when they needed it in facing community, parents, or law.

What we were after was a *feeling* to the place: a sense of intensity and space. We discarded the idea of the microcosm and

PETER MARIN 339

replaced it with an increased openness and access to the larger community. The campus itself became a place to come back to for rest or discussion or thought; but we turned things inside out to the extent that we came to accept that learning took place more naturally elsewhere, in any of the activities that our students chose, and that the school was in actuality wherever they were, whatever they did. What students learned at the school was simply the feel of things; the sense of themselves as makers of value; the realization that the environment is at best an extension of men and that it can be transformed by them into what they vitally need.

What we tried to create was a flexible environment, what a designer I know has called permissive space. It was meant to be in a sense a model for the condition in which men find themselves, in which the responsibility of a man was to make connections, value, and sense. We eliminated from the school all preconceptions about what was proper, best, or useful; we gave up rules and penalties; we refused at all levels to resort to coercive force and students were free to come and go at will, to do anything. What we were after was a "guilt-free" environment, one in which the students might become or discover what they were without having to worry about preconceived ideas of what they had to be.

What we found was that our students seemed to need, most of all, relief from their own "childhood"—what was expected of them. Some of them needed merely to rest, to withdraw from the strange grid of adult expectation and demand for lengthy periods of introspection in which they appeared to grow mysteriously, almost like plants. But an even greater number seemed to need independent commerce with the world outside the school: new sorts of social existence. Nothing could replace that. The simple fact seemed to be that our students grew when they were allowed to move freely into and around the adult community; when they were not, they languished.

We came to see that learning is natural, yes, but it results naturally from most things adolescents do. By associating learning with one particular form of intellection and insisting upon that in school we make a grave error. When students shy away from that kind of intellection it doesn't mean they are turning away forever from learning or abstractions; it means simply that

340

they are seeking another kind of learning momentarily more natural to themselves. That may be anything from physical adventure or experimental community work to withdrawn introspection and an exploration of their fantasies and dreams.

Indeed, it is hard for them to do anything without some kind of learning, but that may be what we secretly fear—that those other forms of learning will make them less manageable or less like ourselves. That, after all, may be one reason we use all those books. Levi-Strauss insists on the relation of increased literacy and the power of the state over the individual. It may well be that dependence on print and abstraction is one of the devices we use to make students manipulable, as if we meant to teach them that ideas exist in talk or on the page but rarely in activity. We tried to avoid that. When we permitted students the freedom of choice and gave them easy access to the community, we found that ideas acquired weight and value to the extent that students were allowed to try them out in action. It was in practical and social situations that their own strength increased, and the merging of the two—strengthened self and tested knowledge—moved them more quickly toward manhood than anything else I have seen.

One might make a formula of it: to the extent that students had freedom of volition and access to experience knowledge became important. But volition and access were of absolute value; they took precedence over books or parental anxiety; without them, nothing worked. So we had to trust the students to make their own choices, no matter what we thought of them. We learned to take their risks with them—and to survive. In that sense we became equals, and that equality may in the end be more educational for students than anything else. That, in fact, may be the most important thing we learned. New ways in seeing them were more effective than changes in curriculum, and without them nothing made much difference. But we must understand too that the old way of seeing things—the traditional idea of childhood—is in some way baked into the whole public-school system at almost every level and also hidden in most pedagogy.

In some ways it is compulsory schooling itself which is the problem, for without real choice students will remain locked in childhood and schools, away from whatever is vivid in life. But real choice, as we know, includes dominion over one's own time and energies, and the right to come and go on the basis of what has actual importance. And I wonder if we will ever get round, given all our fears, to granting that privilege to students.

One thing alone of all I have read has made recent sense to me concerning adolescents. That is the implicit suggestion in Erik Erikson's *Young Man Luther* that every sensitive man experiences in himself the conflicts and contradictions of his age. The great man, he suggests, is the man who articulates and resolves these conflicts in a way that has meaning for his time; that is, he is himself, as was Luther, a victim of his time and its vehicle and, finally, a kind of resolution. But all men, not only the great, have in some measure the capacity to experience in themselves what is happening in the culture around them. I am talking here about what is really shared among the members of a particular culture is a condition, a kind of internal "landscape," the psychic shape that a particular time and place assumes within a man as the extent and limit of his perceptions, dreams, and pleasure and pain.

If there is such a shared condition it seems to me a crucial point, for it means that there is never any real distance between a man and his culture, no real isolation or alienation from society. It means that adolescents are not in their untutored state cut off from culture nor outside it. It means instead that each adolescent is an arena in which the contradictions and currents sweeping through the culture must somehow be resolved, must be resolved by the person himself, and that those individual resolutions are, ideally, the means by which the culture advances itself.

Do you see where this leads? I am straining here to get past the idea of the adolescent as an isolate and deviant creature who must be joined—as if glued and clamped—to the culture. For we ordinarily think of schools, though not quite consciously, as the "culture" itself, little models of society. We try to fit the student into the model, believing that if he will adjust to it he will in some way have been "civilized." That approach is connected to the needs of the early century, when the schools were the means by which the children of immigrant parents were acculturated and moved from the European values of their parents toward more prevalent American ones. But all of that has changed now. The children in our schools, all of them, are little fragments of *this* culture; they no longer need to be "socialized" in the same ways. The specific experiences of every adolescent—his fears, his family crises, his dreams and hallucinations, his habits, his sexuality—all these are points at which the general culture reveals itself in some way. There is no longer any real question of getting the adolescent to "adjust" to things.

The problem is a different one: What kind of setting will enable him to discover and accept what is already within him; to articulate it and perceive the extent to which it is shared with others; and, finally, to learn to change it within and outside himself? For that is what I mean when I call the adolescent a "maker of value." He is a trustee, a trustee of a world that already exists in some form within himself—and we must both learn, the adolescent and his teachers, to respect it.

In a sense, then, I am calling for a reversal of most educational thought. The individual is central; the individual, in the deepest sense, *is* the culture, not the institution. His culture resides in him, in experience and memory, and what is needed is an education that has at its base the sanctity of the individual's experience and leaves it intact.

What keeps running through my mind is a line I read twelve years ago in a friend's first published story: *The Idea in that idea is: there is no one over you.* I like that line: *There is no one over you.* Perhaps that signifies the gap between these children and their parents. For the children it is true, they sense it: there is no one over them; believable authority has disappeared; it has been replaced by experience. As Thomas Altizer says, God is dead; he is experienced now not as someone above or omnipotent or omniscient or "outside," but inwardly, as conscience or vision or even the unconscious or Tillich's "ground of being." This is all too familiar to bother with here, but this particular generation is a collective dividing point. The parents of these children, the fathers, still believe in "someone" over them, insist upon it; in fact, demand it for and from their children. The children themselves cannot believe it; the idea means nothing to them. It is almost as if they are the first real Americans—suddenly free of Europe and somehow fatherless, confused, forced back on their own experience, their own sense of things, even though, at the same time, they are forced to defy their families and schools in order to keep it.

This is, then, a kind of Reformation. Arnold was wrong when he said that art would replace religion; education replaced it. Church became School, the principal vehicle for value, for "culture," and just as men once rebelled against the established Church as the mediator between God and man, students now rebel against the *public* school (and its version of things) as the intermediary between themselves and experience, between themselves and experience and the making of value. Students are expected to reach "reality" (whether of knowledge or society) through their teachers and school. No one, it is said, can participate in the culture effectively without having at one time passed through their hands, proven his allegiance to them, and been blessed. This is the authority exercised by priests or the Church. Just as men once moved to shorten the approach to God, they are moved now to do the same thing in relation to learning and to the community. For just as God was argued to appear within a man—unique, private, and yet shared—so culture is, in some way, grounded in the individual; it inhabits him. The schools, like the Church, must be the expression of that habitation, not its exclusive medium. This is the same reformative shift that occurred in religion, a shift from the institutional (the external) to the individual (the internal), and it demands, when it occurs, an agony, an apocalyptic frenzy, a destruction of the past itself. I believe it is happening now. One sees and feels it everywhere: a violent fissure, a kind of quake.

I remember one moment in the streets of Oakland during the draft demonstrations. The students had sealed off the street with overturned cars and there were no police; the gutters were empty and the students moved into them from the sidewalks, first walking, then running, and finally almost dancing in the street. You could almost see the idea coalesce on their faces: The street is ours! It was as if a weight had been lifted from them, a fog; there was not at that moment any fury in them, any vengefulness or even politics; rather, a lightness, delight, an exhilaration at the sudden inexplicable sense of being free. George Orwell describes something similar in *Homage to Catalonia*: that brief period in Barcelona when the anarchists had apparently succeeded and men shared what power there was. I don't know how to describe it, except to say that one's inexplicable sense of invisible authority had vanished: the oppressive father, who is not really there, was gone.

That sudden feeling is familiar to us all. We have all had it from time to time in our own lives, that sense of "being at home," that ease, that feeling of a Paradise which is neither behind us nor deferred but is around us, a natural household. It is the hint and beginning of Manhood: a promise, a clue. One's attention turns to the immediate landscape and to one's fellows: toward what is there, toward what can be felt as a part of oneself. I have seen the same thing as I watched Stokely Carmichael speaking to a black audience and telling them that they must stop begging the white man, like children, for their rights. They were, he said, neither children nor slaves, no, they were—and here they chanted, almost cried, in unison—a beautiful people: *yes our noses are broad and our lips are thick and our hair is kinky . . . but we are beautiful, we are beautiful, we are black and beautiful.* Watching, you could sense in that released joy an emergence, a surfacing of pride, a refusal to accept shame or the white man's dominance—and a turning to one another, to their own inherent value.

But there is a kind of pain in being white and watching that, for there is no one to say the same things to white children; no "fathers" or brothers to give them that sense of manhood or pride. The adolescents I have seen—white, middle-class—are a long way from those words *we are beautiful, we are beautiful.* I cannot imagine how they will reach them, deprived as they are of all individual strength. For the schools exist to deprive one of strength. That is why one's own worth must be proven again and again by the satisfaction of external requirements with no inherent value or importance; it is why one must satisfy a set of inexplicable demands; it is why there is a continual separation of self and worth and the intrusion of a kind of institutional guilt: failure not of God but of *the system,* the nameless "others," the authority that one can never quite see; and it explains the oppressive sense of some nameless transgression, almost a shame at Being itself.

It is this feeling that pervades both high schools and college, this Kafkaesque sense of faceless authority that drives one to rebellion or withdrawal, and we are all, for that reason, enchanted by the idea of the Trial, that ancient Socratic dream of confrontation and vindication or martyrdom. It is then, of course, that Authority shows its face. In the mid-fifties I once watched Jack Kerouac on a television show and when the interviewer asked him what he wanted he said: to see the face of God. How arrogant and childish and direct! And yet, I suppose, it is what we all want as children: to have the masks of authority, all its disguises, removed and to see it plain. That is what lies in large part behind the riots in the schools. Their specific grievances are incidental; their real purpose is to make God show his face, to have whatever pervasive and oppressive force makes us perpetual children reveal itself, declare itself, commit itself at last. It is Biblical; it is Freudian; it reminds me in some way of the initiation rites: the need to unmask the gods and assume their power, to become an equal—and to find in that the manhood one has been denied.

The schools seem to enforce the idea that there *is* someone over you; and the methods by which they do it are ritualized, pervasive. The intrusion of guilt, shame, alienation from oneself, dependence, insecurity—all these feelings are not the accidental results of schools; they are intentional, and they are used in an attempt to make children manipulable, obedient, "good citizens" we call it, and useful to the state. The schools are the means by which we deprive the young of manhood—that is what I mean to say—and we must not be surprised when they seek that manhood in ways that must of necessity be childish and violent.

But I must admit this troubles me, for there is little choice between mindless violence and mindless authority, and I am just enough of an academic, an intellectual, to want to preserve much of what will be lost in the kind of rebellion or apocalypse that is approaching. And yet, and yet . . . the rapidity of events leaves me with no clear idea, no solution, no sense of what will be an adequate change. It may be that all of this chaos is a way of breaking with the old world and that from it some kind of native American will emerge. There is no way of knowing, there no longer seems any way of estimating what is necessary or what will work. I know only that the problem now seems to be that our response to crisis is to move away or back rather than forward, and that we will surely, for the sake of some imagined order, increase in number and pressure the very approaches that have brought us to this confusion. I don't know. I believe that the young must have values, of course, be responsible, care, but I know too that most of the violence I have seen done to the young has been done in the name of value, and that the well-meaning people who have been so dead set on making things right have had a hand in bringing us to where we are now. The paradox is a deep and troubling one for me. I no longer know if change can be accomplished—for the young, for any of us, without the apocalyptic fury that seems almost upon us. The crisis of youth and education is symptomatic of some larger, deeper fault in our cities and minds, and perhaps nothing can be done consciously in those areas until the air itself is violently cleared one way or another.

So I have no easy conclusions, no startling synthesis with which to close. I have only a change in mood, a softening, a kind of sadness. It may be, given that, that the best thing is simply to close with an unfinished fragment in which I catch for myself the hint of an alternative:

...I am trying to surround you, I see that, I am trying to make with these words a kind of city so natural, so familiar, that the other world, the one that appears to be, will look by comparison absurd and flat, limited, unnecessary. What I am after is liberation, not my own, which comes often enough these days in solitude or sex, but yours, and that is arrogant, isn't it, that is presumptuous, and yet that is the function of art: to set you free. It is that too which is the end of education: a liberation from childhood and what holds us there, a kind of midwifery, as if the nation itself were in labor and one wanted to save both the future and the past—for we are both, we are, we are the thin bridge swaying between them, and to tear one from the other means a tearing of ourselves, a partial death.

And yet it may be that death is inevitable, useful. It may be. Perhaps, as in the myth, Aphrodite can rise only where Cronos' testicles have fallen into the sea. It may be that way with us. The death of the Father who is in us, the death of the old authority which is part of us, the death of the past which is also our death; it may all be necessary: a rending and purgation. And yet one still seeks another way, something less (or is it more) apocalyptic, a way in which the past becomes the future in ourselves, *in which we become the bridges between: makers of culture.*

Unless from us the future takes place, we are Death only, *said Lawrence, meaning what the Chassids do: that the world and time reside within, not outside, men; that there is no distance, no "alienation," only a perpetual wedding to the world. It is that—the presence in oneself of Time—that makes things interesting, is more gravid and interesting than guilt. I don't want to lose it, don't want to relinquish that sense in the body of another dimension, a distance, the depth of the body as it extends backward into the past and forward, as it contains and extends and transforms.*

What I am after is an alternative to separation and rage, some kind of connection to things to replace the system of dependence and submission—the loss of the self—that now holds sway, slanted toward violence. I am trying to articulate a way of seeing, of feeling, that will restore to the young a sense of manhood and potency without at the same time destroying the past. That same theme runs through whatever I write: the necessity for each man to experience himself as an extension and maker of culture, and to feel the whole force of the world within himself, not as an enemy—but as himself:

. . . An act of learning is a meeting, and every meeting is simply the discovery in the world of a part of oneself that had previously been unacknowledged by the self. It is the recovery of the extent of one's being. It is the embrace of an eternal but elusive companion, the shadowy "other" in which one truly resides and which blazes, when embraced, like the sun.

348

V / Racial Identity:
The Quest for Manhood

The very openness of American society, paradoxically, has created its severe identity crises as each minority group has struggled to achieve equity and justice for itself. For all, America has been a most difficult testing ground because its practices have never satisfactorily synchronized with its own image of itself. There has always been a conflict between the country's pride in its egalitarianism and openness—in expression, in style of living, in freedom of speech and worship—and large elements of the population which have counseled caution, conformity, and repression. Today, amid the greatest affluence ever known by a people, that cleavage looms sharper and more dangerous than at any time in our history. Thus, *any* young American growing up now must resolve this schizoid view he inherits from his society, but in addition to this burden, the young American of dark skin is deprived of any clearcut life style to which he can attach himself.

Erik Erikson, in his *Childhood and Society*, draws attention to the lack of fixed points of reference for the American:

The size and vigor of the country and the importance of the means of migration and transportation helped to create and to develop the identity of autonomy and initiative, the identity of him who is 'going places and doing things.' Historically, the over-defined past was apt to be discarded for the undefined future; geographically, migration was an ever-present fact; socially, changes and opportunities lay in daring and luck, in taking full advantage of the channels of social mobility.

In other civilizations, or among the American Indians, a youth was presented with clearly defined obstacles which he had to overcome in order to achieve his maturity. At each stage in his development, he knew where he was and what was expected of him. Until he had passed through all these expected tests, the society was closed to him; but once he had passed through, it was open to all like him equally.

In America, the tests have not been uniform. The requirements for acceptance for different groups have been very different, depending upon how the group (and hence the member) was classified. That classification has been the prerogative of the power-structure. And despite its pluralism, the society has a power-structure that is basically Anglo-Saxon in its "felt" assumptions, the WASP culture of a hundred jokes. But the WASP culture has been no joke to the diverse groups which have tried to fit themselves into an American style based on WASP assumptions. The melting pot never really melted; it simmered and, in the cities, often came to an unproductive boil. Large racial groups have not been happy with each other, although most have been able to strike a delicate balance. But each wave of immigrants had to pass through the crucible, be exploited, mocked and ridiculed before seeing their children become Americans. As long as the immigrants were white, their chances of acceptance were reasonably good. If they were Catholic, they ran into considerable persecution, and, if they were Jews, they likewise found themselves excluded and derided for several generations. But at least they were white, and white fades into the background.

For blacks, the identity problems of other minorities are meaningless. Theirs is a unique experience because black remains visible, and too much visibility provokes antagonism or, as the novelist Ralph Ellison recognized, it promotes invisibility if the individual wishes to survive. There has been no melting pot for blacks, and there is none in the foreseeable future. Federal and state governments, as well as mayors and town officials, will settle for tokenism; they will take as much action as necessary to hold off an impending riot or make enough concessions to calm stormy waters.

Young blacks know this: they say that they can expect little or nothing from the authorities; and even nonviolent blacks of every age, and in particular from the middle class, are coming to realize that they will get only what they can pre-empt for themselves. Thus, we have the proliferation of groups all concerned with Black Power, whether the black power of legalistic NAACP, of SNCC, of the Black Panthers, of CORE, of Ron Karenga's US, or Malcolm X's Muslims. In different ways, each group is trying to create a racial identity for the blacks as a means of making them aware of themselves, proud of their heritage, and strong enough to sustain themselves in an essentially hostile society. Except for the NAACP, all seem to be agreed that the black must make use of every weapon at his disposal, including disruption, blackmail, threat, and physical violence, in order to make himself felt and fit. To each group it has been driven home that white America wants the black to be invisible: that is, either exactly like the white in mind, feeling, and aspiration, or else out of sight and out of mind. Only the younger generation of Americans has stopped seeing color, and this color blindness often enrages their elders.

The reaction of black and white leaders to the moon landing was instructive. Virtually every white leader praised the effort and felt that all Americans should be proud of their astronauts' achievement; virtually every black leader said that he felt nothing or else felt shame that America could abandon its living souls in order to investigate an inert mass. The blacks have asserted repeatedly that space programs, militant foreign policies, ABM programs, economic aid to reactionary regimes throughout the world, and military commitments abroad are all subtle evasions of domestic responsibilities. On the other hand, most whites said they felt proud of the moon landing as an example of American technology, proud of the fact that this technology has also created the highest standard of living in the world. To blacks, the American achievement was that of a foreign power, for, except for a minority among them, they have enjoyed neither the freedom nor the affluence of white America.

By now, these are rather obvious statements. But they must be reiterated if the essays that follow are to have their full force.

Unless we are aware of the true situation, blacks may appear, in the eyes of whites, to be suffering from paranoia. If they are, their paranoia has solid roots in reality. Martin Duberman's essay sets forth the nature of the slogan "Black Power." The interview with Eldridge Cleaver discloses the complications that an intelligent, articulate, committed black, who has the misfortune of a criminal past, faces when he tries to pursue his vision of what blackness should mean. Cleaver and the Black Panthers are, in one strong sense, carrying on the traditions of Malcolm X. His statement, in Part II, should be read in conjunction with Cleaver's.

Although not included in this collection, Frantz Fanon, a psychiatrist born in French Martinique, was perhaps the most articulate and most intellectually radical of all black spokesmen before his death at thirty-six, in 1961. While Fanon's position is perhaps more directly applicable to Africa than to America, his subtle but tough mind attacks every aspect of racial identity, and many blacks in America have embraced him as their intellectual leader. In many ways a dangling man caught between cultures, Fanon comes close to believing that only violence, the spirit of Armageddon, will usher in the apocalyptic millennium when the unjustly crushed will rise and crush their oppressors.

All identity crises are not black. Piri Thomas, a Puerto-Rican, was born black into a light-skinned family, a kind of nether world in which he had to decide whether he was Spanish, Negro, or white American. As a ghetto-dweller, he experienced the worst aspects of the identity crisis: drugs, light crime, and, worst of all, the fear that he was wasting his life. Similarly, the interview with Julius Lester indicates what can occur when a racial group trying to find itself clashes with another group still uncertain about its assimilation. The clash here between blacks and Jews is indicative of clashes between blacks and Italians or blacks and Slavs, as each entrenched group fights to retain what it has gained. The only distinction is that many Jews have been in the forefront of the fight for Negro justice, and so the confrontation here is full of both paradox and sadness. Elements of this confrontation surfaced in the New York City school crisis of 1968–69.

The final selection, by Paul Wachtel, traces the effect that psychological discrimination and severe racial crises have on the behavior of the oppressed. Wachtel's findings indicate how complex the identity crisis is, and how futile simplistic solutions really are. If the unconscious and the consciousness of an individual are in conflict as a result of an identity crisis, we need more than social, political, and economic solutions. Radical black leaders are indeed correct: the black people need to be resurrected from within. And from within must come the radical vision that presages, with the violence of thunder and lightning, the resurrection.

20 / Black Power in America

MARTIN DUBERMAN

The slogan of "Black Power" has caused widespread confusion and alarm. This is partly due to a problem inherent in language: words necessarily reduce complex attitudes or phenomena to symbols which, in their abbreviation, allow for a variety of interpretations. Stuart Chase has reported that in the thirties, when the word "fascism" was on every tongue, he asked 100 people from various walks of life what the word meant and got 100 widely differing definitions. And in 1953 when *The Capital Times* of Madison, Wisconsin, asked 200 people "What is a Communist?" not only was there no agreement, but five out of every eight admitted they couldn't define the term at all. So it is with "Black Power." Its definition depends on whom you ask, when you ask, where you ask, and not least, who does the asking.

Yet the phrase's ambiguity derives not only from the usual confusions of language, but from a failure of clarity (or is it frankness?) on the part of its advocates, and a failure of attention (or is it generosity?) from their critics. The leaders of SNCC and CORE who invented the slogan, including Stokely Carmi-

SOURCE: *Partisan Review* 35 (Winter 1968), 34–48. Copyright © 1968 by Martin Duberman. Reprinted by permission of The Sterling Lord Agency.

Martin Duberman, a Princeton historian, is author of the documentary play *In White America* and editor of *The Antislavery Vanguard: New Essays on the Abolitionists*. His most recent play is *The Memory Bank*.

chael and Floyd McKissick, have given Black Power different definitions on different occasions, in part because their own understanding of the term continues to develop, but in part, too, because their explanations have been tailored to their audiences.[1]

The confusion has been compounded by the press, which has frequently distorted the words of SNCC and CORE representatives, harping on every connotation of violence and racism, minimizing the central call for ethnic unity.

For all these reasons, it is still not clear whether "Black Power" is to be taken as a short-term tactical device or a long-range goal —that is, a postponement or a rejection of integration; whether it has been adapted as a lever for intimidating whites or organizing blacks, for instilling race hate or race pride; whether it necessitates, permits or encourages violence; whether it is a symptom of Negro despair or of Negro determination, a reaction to the lack of improvement in the daily lives of Negro-Americans or a sign that improved conditions are creating additional expectations and demands. Whether Black Power, furthermore, becomes a constructive psychological and political tactic or a destructive summons to separatism, violence and reverse racism will depend at least as much on developments outside the control of its advocates (like the war in Vietnam) as on their conscious determination. For all these reasons, it is too early for final evaluations; only time, and perhaps not even that, will provide them. At most, certain limited, and tentative, observations are possible.

---

[1] Jeremy Larner has recently pointed out ("Initiation for Whitey: Notes on Poverty and Riot," *Dissent*, November-December, 1967) that the young Negro in the ghetto mainly seeks the kind of knowledge which can serve as a "ready-made line, a set of hard-nosed aphorisms," and that both Malcolm X and Stokely Carmichael have understood this need. In this regard Larner quotes a speech by Carmichael to the students of Morgan State College, as transcribed in *The Movement*, June, 1967:

Now then we come to the question of definitions . . . it is very, very important because I believe that people who can define are masters. I want to read a quote. It is one of my favorite quotes. It comes from *Alice in Wonderland*, Lewis Carroll. . . .
"When I use a word," Humpty Dumpty said in a rather scornful tone, "I mean just what I choose it to mean, neither more nor less." "The question is," said Alice, "whether you can make words mean so many different things." "The question is," said Humpty Dumpty, "who is to be master."
That is all. That is all. Understand that . . . the first need of a free people is to define their own terms.

As Larner comments, "Mr. Carmichael, unlike Mr. Carroll, identifies with Humpty Dumpty."

If Black Power means only that Negroes should organize politically and economically in order to develop self-regard and to exert maximum pressure, then the new philosophy would be difficult to fault, for it would be based on the truism that minorities must argue from positions of strength rather than weakness, that the majority is far more likely to make concessions to power than to justice. To insist that Negro-Americans seek their goals as individuals and solely by appeals to conscience and "love," when white Americans have always relied on group association and organized power to achieve theirs, would be yet one more form of discrimination. Moreover, when whites decry SNCC's declaration that it is tired of turning the other cheek, that henceforth it will actively resist white brutality, they might do well to remember that they have always considered self-defense acceptable behavior for themselves; our textbooks, for example, view the refusal of the revolutionaries of 1776 to "sit supinely by" as the very essence of manhood.

Although Black Power makes good sense when defined to mean further organization and cooperation within the Negro community, the results which are likely to follow in terms of political leverage can easily be exaggerated. The impact is likely to be greatest at the county unit level in the deep South and in the urban ghettos of the North. In this regard, the Black Panther party of Lowndes County, Alabama is the prototype.

There are roughly 12,000 Negroes in Lowndes County and 3,000 whites, but until 1964 there was not a single Negro registered to vote, while white registration had reached 118 percent of those eligible. Negro life in Lowndes, as Andrew Kopkind has graphically recounted[2] was—and is—wretched. The median family income for whites is $4,400, for Negroes, $935; Negro farmhands earn $3.00 to $6.00 a day; half of the Negro women who work are maids in Montgomery (which requires a 40 to 60 mile daily roundtrip) at $4.00 a day; few Negroes have farms, since 90 percent of the land is owned by about 85 white families; the one large industrial plant in the area, the new Dan River Mills textile factory, will only employ Negroes in menial capacities; most Lowndes Negroes are functional illiterates, living in squalor and hopelessness.

[2] "The Lair of the Black Panther," *The New Republic*, August 13, 1966.

The Black Panther party set out to change all this. The only path to change in Lowndes, and in much of the deep South, is to "take over the courthouse," the seat of local power. For generations the courthouse in Lowndes has been controlled by the Democratic party; indeed there is no Republican party in the county. Obviously it made little sense for SNCC organizers to hope to influence the local Democracy; no white moderates existed and no discussion of integration was tolerated. To have expected blacks to "bore from within," as Carmichael has said, would have been "like asking the Jews to reform the Nazi party."

Instead, Carmichael and his associates established the separate Black Panther party. After months of work SNCC organizers (with almost no assistance from federal agents) registered enough Negroes to hope for a numerical majority in the county. But in the election of November, 1966, the Black Panther party was defeated, for a variety of reasons which include Negro apathy or fear and white intimidation.[3] Despite this defeat, the possibility of a better life for Lowndes County Negroes does at last exist, and should the Black Panther party come into power at some future point, that possibility could become a reality.

Nonetheless, even on the local level and even in the deep South, Lowndes County is not representative. In Alabama, for example, only eleven of the state's sixty-seven counties have black majorities. Where these majorities do not exist, the only effect independent black political parties are likely to have is to consolidate the whites in opposition. Moreover, and more significantly, many of the basic ills from which Negro-Americans suffer—inadequate housing, inferior education, limited job opportunities—are national phenomena and require national resources to overcome. Whether these resources will be allocated in sufficient amounts will depend, in turn, on whether a national coalition can be formed to exert pressure on the federal govern-

---

[3] I have not seen a clear assessment of the causes for defeat. The "Newsletter" from the New York Office of SNCC of November, 1966, makes two points regarding the election: that according to a November report from the Southern Regional Council, 2,823 whites and 2,758 Negroes had registered in Lowndes County, though the white population was approximately 1900; and that "the influential Baptist Alliance told Negroes throughout Alabama to vote the straight Democratic ticket."

ment—a coalition of civil rights activists, church groups, campus radicals, New Class technocrats, unskilled, un-unionized laborers and certain elements in organized labor, such as the UAW or the United Federation of Teachers. Such a coalition, of course, would necessitate Negro-white unity, a unity Black Power at least temporarily rejects.[4]

The answer that Black Power advocates give to the "coalition argument" is of several pieces. The only kind of progressive coalition which can exist in this country, they say, is the mild, liberal variety which produced the civil rights legislation of recent years. And that kind of legislation has proven itself grossly inadequate. Its chief result has been to lull white liberals into believing that the major battles have been won, whereas in fact there has been almost no change, or change for the worse, in the daily lives of most blacks.[5]

The evidence for this last assertion is persuasive. Despite the Supreme Court decision of 1954, almost 85 percent of school-age Negroes in the South still sit in segregated classrooms. Unemployment among Negroes has actually gone up in the past ten years. Title VI of the 1964 Civil Rights Act, with its promising provision for the withdrawal of federal funds in cases of discrimination, has been used in limited fashion in regard to the schools but not at all in regard to other forms of unequal treatment, such as segregated hospital facilities. Under the 1965 Voting Rights Act, only about 40 federal registrars have been sent into the South, though many areas have less than the 50 percent registration figure which would legally warrant intervention. In short, the legislation produced by the liberal coalition of the early sixties has turned out to be little more than federally approved tokenism, a continuation of paper promises and ancient inequities.

If a *radical* coalition could be formed in this country, that is, one willing to scrutinize in depth the failings of our system, to suggest structural, not piecemeal, reforms, to see them executed with sustained rather than occasional vigor, then Black Power

[4] On this point, see what to me are the persuasive arguments made by Pat Watters, "The Negroes Enter Southern Politics," *Dissent*, July-August, 1966, and Bayard Rustin, "Black Power and Coalition Politics," *Commentary*, September, 1966.
[5] See, on this point, David Danzig, "In Defense of 'Black Power,'" *Commentary*, September, 1966.

MARTIN DUBERMAN 359

advocates might feel less need to separate themselves and to concentrate on local, marginal successes. But no responsible observer believes that in the foreseeable future a radical coalition on the Left can become the effective political majority in the United States; we will be fortunate if a radical coalition on the Right does not. And so to SNCC and CORE, talk of further cooperation with white liberals is only an invitation to further futility. It is better, they feel, to concentrate on encouraging Negroes everywhere to self-respect and self-help, and in certain local areas, where their numbers warrant it, to try to win actual political power.

As an adaptation to present realities, Black Power thus has a persuasive logic. But there is such a thing as being too present-minded; by concentrating on immediate prospects, the new doctrine may be jeopardizing larger possibilities for the future, those which could result from a national coalition with white allies. Though SNCC and CORE insist that they are not trying to cut whites out of the movement, that they merely want to redirect white energies into organizing whites so that at some future point a truly meaningful coalition of Negroes and whites can take place, there are grounds for doubting whether they really are interested in a future reconciliation, or if they are, whether some of the overtones of their present stance will allow for it. For example, SNCC's so-called position paper on Black Power attacks white radicals as well as white liberals, speaks vaguely of differing white and black "psyches," and seems to find all contact with all whites contaminating or intimidating ("whites are the ones who must try to raise themselves to our humanistic level").[6]

[6] SNCC's "position paper" was printed in *The New York Times*, August 5, 1966. It is important to point out, however, that SNCC staffers have since denied the official nature of this paper; see for example Elizabeth Sutherland's letter to the editors of *Liberation*, November, 1966, in which she insists that it was "not a S.N.C.C. position paper but a document prepared by a group of workers on one S.N.C.C. project" (she goes on to note that the *Times* refused to print a SNCC letter to this effect). For other denials of the "racist" overtones in "Black Power," see Stokely Carmichael, "What We Want," *The New York Review of Books*, September 22, 1966, and C. E. Wilson, "Black Power and the Myth of Black Racism," *Liberation*, September, 1966. But Andrew Kopkind's report on SNCC staff conferences ("The Future of Black Power," *The New Republic*, January 7, 1967) makes me believe that the dangers of black racism are real and not merely the invention of frightened white liberals (see also James Peck, "Black Racism," *Liberation*, October, 1966).

SNCC's bitterness at the hypocrisy and evasion of the white majority is understandable, yet the refusal to discriminate between degrees of inequity, the penchant instead for wholesale condemnation of all whites, is as unjust as it is self-defeating. The indictments and innuendos of SNCC's "position paper" give some credence to the view that the line between black power and black racism is a fine one easily erased, that, as always, means and ends tend to get confused, that a tactic of racial solidarity can turn into a goal of racial purity.

The philosophy of Black Power is thus a blend of varied, in part contending, elements, and it cannot be predicted with any certainty which will assume dominance. But a comparison between the Black Power movement and the personnel, programs and fates of earlier radical movements in this country can make some contribution toward understanding its dilemmas and its likely directions.

Any argument based on historical analogy can, of course, become oversimplified and irresponsible. Historical events do not repeat themselves with anything like regularity, for every event is to a large degree embedded in its own special context. An additional danger in reasoning from historical analogy is that in the process we will limit rather than expand our options; by arguing that certain consequences seem always to follow from certain actions and that therefore only a set number of alternatives ever exist, we can prevent ourselves from seeing new possibilities or from utilizing old ones in creative ways. We must be careful, when attempting to predict the future from the past, that in the process we do not straitjacket the present. Bearing these cautions and limitations in mind, some insight can still be gained from a historical perspective. For if there are large variances through time between roughly analogous events, there are also some similarities, and it is these which make comparative study possible and profitable. In regard to Black Power, I think we gain particular insight by comparing it with the two earlier radical movements of Abolition and Anarchism.

The Abolitionists represented the left wing of the antislavery movement (a position comparable to the one SNCC and CORE occupy today in the civil rights movement) because they called for an *immediate* end to slavery everywhere in the United States. Most Northerners who disapproved of slavery were not willing to go as far or as fast as the Abolitionists, preferring instead a more ameliorative approach. The tactic which increasingly won the approval of the Northern majority was the doctrine of "nonextension": no further expansion of slavery would be allowed, but the institution would be left alone where it already existed. The principle of nonextension first came into prominence in the late eighteen-forties when fear developed in the North that territory acquired from our war with Mexico would be made into new slave states. Later the doctrine formed the basis of the Republican party which in 1860 elected Lincoln to the presidency. The Abolitionists, in other words, with their demand for immediate (and uncompensated) emancipation, never became the major channel of Northern antislavery sentiment. They always remained a small sect, vilified by slavery's defenders and distrusted even by allies within the antislavery movement.

The parallels between the Abolitionists and the current defenders of Black Power seem to me numerous and striking. It is worth noting, first of all, that neither group started off with so-called "extremist" positions (the appropriateness of that word being, in any case, dubious).[7] The SNCC of 1967 is not the SNCC formed in 1960; both its personnel and its programs have shifted markedly. SNCC originally grew out of the sit-ins spontaneously begun in Greensboro, North Carolina, by four freshmen at the all-Negro North Carolina Agricultural and Technical College. The sit-in technique spread rapidly through the South, and within a few months the Student Non-Violent Coordinating Committee (SNCC) was formally inaugurated to channel and encourage further activities. At its inception SNCC's staff was interracial, religious in orientation, committed to the "American Dream," chiefly concerned with winning the right to share more equitably in that Dream and optimistic about the possibility of being allowed to do so. SNCC placed its hopes on an appeal to

---

[7] For a discussion of "extremism" and the confused uses to which the word can be and has been put, see Howard Zinn, "Abolitionists, Freedom-Riders, and the Tactics of Agitation," *The Antislavery Vanguard*, Martin Duberman, ed., (Princeton, 1965), especially pp. 421–426.

the national conscience and this it expected to arouse by the examples of nonviolence and redemptive love, and by the dramatic devices of sit-ins, freedom rides and protest marches.[8]

The Abolitionist movement, at the time of its inception, was similarly benign and sanguine. It, too, placed emphasis on "moral suasion," believing that the first order of business was to bring the iniquity of slavery to the country's attention, to arouse the average American's conscience. Once this was done, the Abolitionists felt, discussion then could, and would, begin on the particular ways and means best calculated to bring about rapid, orderly emancipation. Some of those Abolitionists who later became intransigent defenders of immediatism—including William Lloyd Garrison—were willing, early in their careers, to consider plans for preliminary apprenticeship. They were willing, in other words, to settle for gradual emancipation *immediately begun* instead of demanding that freedom itself be instantly achieved.

But this early flexibility received little encouragement. The appeal to conscience and the willingness to engage in debate over means alike brought meager results. In the North the Abolitionists encountered massive apathy, in the South massive resistance. Thus thwarted, and influenced as well by the discouraging British experiment with gradualism in the West Indies, the Abolitionists abandoned their earlier willingness to consider a variety of plans for prior education and training, and shifted to the position that emancipation had to take place at once and without compensation to the slaveholder. They also began (especially in New England) to advocate such doctrines as "Dis-Union" and "No-Government," positions which directly parallel Black Power's recent advocacy of "separation" and "decentralization," and which then as now produced discord and division within the movement, anger and denunciation without.

But the parallel of paramount importance I wish to draw between the two movements is their similar passage from "moderation" to "extremism." In both cases, there *was* a passage, a shift in attitude and program, and it is essential that this be recognized, for it demonstrates the developmental nature of these—

[8] For the shifting nature of SNCC see Howard Zinn, *SNCC: The New Abolitionists* (Boston, 1964), and Gene Roberts, "From 'Freedom High' to 'Black Power,'" *The New York Times*, September 25, 1966.

of all—movements for social change. Or, to reduce the point to individuals (and to clichés): "revolutionaries are not born but made." Garrison didn't start his career with the doctrine of "immediatism"; as a young man, he even had kind words for the American Colonization Society, a group devoted to deporting Negroes to Africa and Central America. And Stokely Carmichael did not begin his ideological voyage with the slogan of Black Power; as a teen-ager he was opposed to student sit-ins in the South. What makes a man shift from "reform" to "revolution" is, it seems to me, primarily to be explained by the intransigence or indifference of his society: either society refuses reforms or gives them in the form of tokens. Thus, *if* one views the Garrisons and Carmichaels as "extremists," one should at least place the blame for that extremism where it belongs—not on their individual temperaments, their genetic predispositions, but on a society which scorned or toyed with their initial pleas for justice.

In turning to the Anarchist movement, I think we can see between it and the new turn taken by SNCC and CORE (or, more comprehensively still, by much of the New Left) significant affinities of style and thought. These are largely unconscious and unexplored; I have seen almost no overt references to them either in the movement's official literature or in its unofficial pronouncements. Yet the affinities seem to me important.

But first I should make clear that in speaking of "Anarchism" as if it were a unified tradition, I am necessarily oversimplifying. The Anarchist movement contained a variety of contending factions, disparate personalities and differing national patterns. Some Anarchists believed in terrorism, others insisted upon nonviolence; some aimed for a communal life based on trade union "syndicates," others refused to bind the individual by organizational ties of any kind; some wished to retain private ownership of property, others demanded its collectivization.[9]

[9] In recent years several excellent histories and anthologies of Anarchism have been published: George Woodcock's brilliant *Anarchism* (New York, 1962), James Joll's *The Anarchists* (London, 1964), Irving L. Horowitz's anthology *The Anarchists* (New York, 1964) which concentrates on the "classics" of the literature, and Leonard Krimerman and Lewis Perry's collection, *Patterns of Anarchy* (New York, 1966), which presents a less familiar and more variegated selection of Anarchist writings.

Despite these differing perspectives, all Anarchists did share one major premise: a distrust of authority, the rejection of all forms of rule by man over man, especially that embodied in the State, but also that exemplified by parent, teacher, lawyer, priest. They justified their opposition in the name of the individual; the Anarchists wished each man to develop his "specialness" without the inhibiting interference imposed by authority, be it political or economic, moral or intellectual. This does not mean that the Anarchists sanctioned the idea of "each against all." On the contrary, they believed that man was a social creature—that is, that he needed the affection and assistance of his fellows—and most Anarchist versions of the good life (Max Stirner would be the major exception) involved the idea of community. The Anarchists insisted, moreover, that it was not their vision of the future, but rather society as presently constructed, which represented chaos; with privilege the lot of the few and misery the lot of the many, society was currently the essence of *dis*order. The Anarchists demanded a system which would substitute mutual aid for mutual exploitation, voluntarism for force, individual decision-making for centralized dictation.

All of these emphases find echo today in SNCC and CORE. The echoes are not perfect: "Black Power," after all, is above all a call to organization, and its acceptance of politics (and therefore of "governing") would offend a true Anarchist—as would such collectivist terms as "black psyche" or "black personality." Nonetheless, the affinities of SNCC and CORE with the Anarchist position are substantial.

There is, first of all, the same belief in the possibilities of "community" and the same insistence that community be the product of voluntary association. This in turn reflects a second and still more basic affinity: the distrust of centralized authority. SNCC and CORE's energies, and also those of other New Left groups like Students for a Democratic Society (SDS), are increasingly channeled into local, community organizing. On this level, it is felt, "participatory" democracy, as opposed to the authoritarianism of "representative" democracy, becomes possible. And in the Black Panther party, where the poor and disinherited do take a direct role in decision-making, theory has become reality (as it has, on the economic side, in the Mississippi-based "Poor

People's Corporation," which to date has formed some fifteen cooperatives).[10]

Then, too, SNCC and CORE, like the Anarchists, talk increasingly of the supreme importance of the individual. They do so, paradoxically, in a rhetoric strongly reminiscent of that long associated with the Right. It could be Herbert Hoover (or Booker T. Washington), but in fact it is Rap Brown who now reiterates the Negro's need to stand on his own two feet, to make his own decisions, to develop self-reliance and a sense of self-worth.[11] SNCC may be scornful of present-day liberals and "statism,"‐ but it seems hardly to realize that the laissez faire rhetoric it prefers, derives almost verbatim from the classic liberalism of John Stuart Mill.

A final, more intangible affinity between Anarchism and the entire New Left, including the advocates of Black Power, is in the area of personal style. Both hold up similar values for highest praise and emulation: simplicity, spontaneity, "naturalness" and "primitivism." Both reject modes of dress, music, personal relations, even intoxication, which might be associated with the dominant middle-class culture. Both, finally, tend to link the basic virtues with "the people," and especially with the poor, the downtrodden, the alienated. It is this *lumpenproletariat*—long kept outside the "system" and thus uncorrupted by its values— who are looked to as a repository of virtue, an example of a better way. The New Left, even while demanding that the lot of the underclasses be improved, implicitly venerates that lot; the desire to cure poverty cohabits with the wish to emulate it.

The Anarchist movement in the United States never made much headway. A few individuals—Benjamin Tucker, Adin Ballou, Lysander Spooner, Stephen Pearl Andrews, Emma Goldman, Josiah Warren—are still faintly remembered, but more for

---

[10] See Art Goldberg, "Negro Self-Help," *The New Republic*, June 10, 1967, and Abbie Hoffman, "Liberty House/Poor People's Corporation," *Liberation*, April, 1967.

[11] For more detailed discussions of the way in which the rhetoric of the New Left and the traditional Right have begun to merge, see Ronald Hamowy, "Left and Right Meet," *The New Republic*, March 12, 1966; Martin Duberman, "Anarchism Left and Right," *Partisan Review*, Fall, 1966; Paul Feldman, "The Pathos of 'Black Power,'" *Dissent*, Jan.-Feb., 1967; and Carl Oglesby and Richard Schaull, *Containment and Change* (Macmillan: 1967). In the latter Oglesby (p. 167) seems actually to call for a merger between the two groups, arguing that both are "in the grain of American humanist individualism and voluntaristic associational action." He confuses, it seems to me, a similarity of rhetoric and of means with a similarity of goals.

the style of their lives than for any impact on their society.[12] It is not difficult to see what prevented them from attracting a large following. Their very distaste for organization and power precluded the traditional modes for exerting influence. More important still, their philosophy ran directly counter to the national hierarchy of values, a system of beliefs, conscious and otherwise, which has always impeded the drive for rapid change in this country. And it is a system which constitutes a roadblock at least as formidable today as at any previous point in our history.

This value structure stresses, first of all, the prime virtue of "accumulation," chiefly of goods, but also of power and prestige. Any group—be it Anarchists or New Leftists—which challenges the soundness of that goal, which suggests that it interferes with the more important pursuits of self-realization and human fellowship, presents so basic a threat to our national and individual identities as to invite almost automatic rejection.

A second obstacle that our value structure places in the path of radical change is its insistence on the benevolence of history. To the average American, human history is the story of automatic progress. Every day in every way we have got better and better. *Ergo*, there is no need for a frontal assault on our ills; time alone will be sufficient to cure them. Thus it is that many whites today consider the "Negro Problem" solved by the recent passage of civil rights legislation. They choose to ignore the fact that the daily lives of most Negroes have changed but slightly— or, as in the case of unemployment, for the worse. They ignore, too, the group of hard-core problems which have only recently emerged: maldistribution of income, urban slums, disparities in education and training, the breakdown of family structure in the ghetto, technological unemployment—problems which show no signs of yielding to time, but which will require concentrated energy and resources for solution.

Without a massive assault on these basic ills, ours will continue to be a society where the gap between rich and poor widens, where the major rewards go to the few (who are not to be confused with the best). Yet it seems highly unlikely, as of 1968, that the public pressure needed for such an assault will be forth-

---

[12] The only over-all study of American Anarchism is Eunice M. Schuster, *Native American Anarchism* (Northampton: 1932). But some useful biographies exist of individual figures in the movement; see especially, Richard Drinnon, *Rebel in Paradise: A Biography of Emma Goldman* (Chicago: 1961).

coming. Most Americans still prefer to believe that ours is either already the best of all possible worlds or will shortly, and without any special effort, become such. It is this deep-seated smugness, this intractable optimism, which must be reckoned with— which indeed will almost certainly destroy any call for substantive change.

A further obstacle facing the New Left today, Black Power advocates and otherwise, is that its Anarchist style and mood run directly counter to prevailing tendencies in our national life, especially the tendencies to conformity and centralization. The conformity has been commented on too often to bear repetition, except to point out that the young radicals' unorthodox mores (sexual, social, cultural), are in themselves enough to produce uneasiness and anger in the average American. In insisting on the right of the individual to please himself and to rely on his own judgment (whether in dress, speech, music, sex or stimulants), SNCC and SDS may be solidly within the American tradition—indeed may be its main stream—but this tradition is now more central to our rhetoric than to our behavior.

The Anarchist focus in SNCC and SDS on decentralization, on participatory democracy and on community organizing, likewise runs counter to dominant national trends. Consolidation, not dispersion, is currently king. There are some signs that a counter-development has begun—such as the pending decentralization of the New York City school system—but as yet the overwhelming pattern continues to be consolidation. Both big government and big business are getting bigger and, more ominous still, are coming into ever closer partnership. As Richard J. Barber has recently documented, the federal government is not only failing to block the growth of huge "conglomerate" firms by antitrust action, but it is contributing to that growth through procurement contracts and the exchange of personnel.[13] The traditional hostility between business and government has rapidly drawn to a close. Washington is no longer interested in restraining the giant corporations, and the corporations have lost much of their fear of federal intentions. The two, in happy tandem, are moving the country still further along the road to oligopoly,

[13]Richard J. Barber, "The New Partnership: Big Government and Big Business," *The New Republic,* August 13, 1966. But see, too, Alexander Bickel's article in the same journal for May 20, 1967.

militarism, economic imperialism and greater privileges for the already privileged. The trend is so pronounced, and there is so little effective opposition to it, that it begins to take on an irrevocable, even irreversible, quality.

In the face of these monoliths of national power, Black Power in Lowndes County is pathetic by comparison. Yet while the formation of the Black Panther party in Lowndes brought out paroxysms of fear in the nation at large, the announcement that General Motors' 1965 sales totaled 21 billion dollars—exceeding the GNP of all but nine countries in the world—produced barely a tremor of apprehension. The unspoken assumption can only be something like this: It is less dangerous for a few whites to control the whole nation than for a local majority of Negroes to control their own community. The Kafkaesque dimension of life in America continues to grow.

Black Power is both a product of our society and a repudiation of it. Confronted with the continuing indifference of the majority of whites to the Negro's plight, SNCC and CORE have lost faith in conscience and time, and have shifted to a position which the white majority finds infuriating. The nation as a whole—as in the case of the Abolitionists over a hundred years ago—has created the climate in which earlier tactics no longer seem relevant, in which new directions become mandatory if frustration is to be met and hope maintained. And if the new turn proves a wrong one, if Black Power forecloses rather than animates further debate on the Negro's condition, if it destroys previous alliances without opening up promising new options, it is the nation as a whole that must bear the responsibility. There seems little likelihood that the American majority will admit to that responsibility. Let us at least hope it will not fail to recognize the rage which Black Power represents, to hear the message at the movement's core:

> *Sweethearts, the script has changed . . .*
> *And with it the stage directions which advise*
> *Lowered voices, genteel asides,*
> *And the white hand slowly turning the dark page.*[14]

[14]Kay Boyle, "On Black Power," *Liberation*, January, 1967.

MARTIN DUBERMAN 369

21 / The Minister of Information Raps: An Interview with Eldridge Cleaver[1]

CECIL M. BROWN

QUESTION: So you wanted to be a lawyer?

ANSWER: Yes, that's what I wanted to do. I was either going to be a lawyer or an economist.

Q: That's when you were in high school?

A: I went to junior college, you know, city college, and I was going there 'cause I didn't graduate from high school, but they had this thing where you could take these courses, make-up courses; you didn't even need a diploma but you'd have the credits, and you could go on and get into a college thing, you know. Transfer, that's what I wanted to do, but that didn't work out because I found that I didn't like to go to school and be up-tight with bread.

[1] Eldridge Cleaver, Minister of Information of the Black Panthers, was wounded and arrested last April 6 [1968] in a gun battle with police in Oakland, California, which left Black Panther Bobby Hutton dead and two others injured.

The author of *Soul on Ice* and the presidential candidate of the Peace and Freedom Party, Cleaver won release from jail on June 12 by order of Superior Judge Raymond Sherman who ruled he was held illegally by the police because of his political convictions.

This interview with Cleaver was taped over a period of several hours during a day early in July.–Eds.

SOURCE: *Evergreen Review* 12 (October 1968), 45–47, 75–82. Copyright © 1968 by Cecil M. Brown. Reprinted by permission of The Sterling Lord Agency.
    It was while serving a prison sentence that Eldridge Cleaver wrote his now celebrated *Soul on Ice*, a "spiritual and intellectual autobiography that stands at the exact resonant center of the new Negro writing." A former candidate for the presidency of the United States and the first Black Panther Minister of Information, Cleaver is now living abroad to avoid arrest on a parole-jumping charge. His latest book is *Black Moochie*.

Q: You mean you needed to make some money?

A: So I started cutting in marijuana, see, like my partners were into that, you know. So I started running with the bag, trying to get those coins right, and pretty soon it became clear to me that I couldn't fool around with that narcotics, as it was classified then, marijuana, and hope to be successful in school and deal with the pigs at the same time—see what I mean? Well, what I did, I said, I'll drop out of school this semester, concentrating fulltime on spreading this JOY, watching for the cops, and then next semester I'll have a bank roll and I'll go back to school and I can be cool, you know—but in the meantime I got a case; and I got shot into a nine-year forfeit.

Q: How did they catch you?

A: They caught me because I whipped some people up on their heads and shot at them and tried to ravish a woman, you know—tried to whip off some pussy, you know—and in the process of doing all that brutalizing, oh, I don't know, I thought I was on a one-man Mau Mau thing, you know. What I used to do, man, like I'd be on dope all week long, see, on weekends I'd go out and beat up somebody or something, you know, beat some Hunkies. We call it paddy-hunting, you know.

Q: Yeah, that's a weird thing. That's what we called it in the South but I didn't hear that term until I came North.

A: That didn't work out too well. And I got that case, you know, and I went to the penitentiary. First time I went to the penitentiary for pot, you know, and next time I went for assault and intent to murder.

Q: Let me ask you something about Maxwell Geismar who wrote the introduction to your book. Like that introduction is to introduce the book to white people, isn't it?

A: It seemed directed that way? I guess it might have.

Q: It reminded me of the introduction by Jean-Paul Sartre to Fanon's *The Wretched of the Earth.*

A: Yeah, I think he was into that, you know. I was embarrassed by his unrestrained praise, you know, his comparison with Fanon and everything because Fanon is out of sight.

Q: Hell, you are out of sight, too. But what I am getting at is Geismar's role, however unwitting, as the liberal introducing the Big Nigger to the white reading public, as though you were more concerned with communicating to a white audience than a black one.

A: I think there are a lot of brothers who have a grudge against white writers, you know. And rightly so, because white writers have been liars for the most part. They are falsifiers of history and justifiers of oppression. So brothers have a chance now to get back, put them down—and they should be put down, because they have to be educated, you know. At the same time, I think, you have to be careful, you know, to always kind of individualize if a given person merits that. You don't follow through with just a category of racism. You have to be careful. Like this cat Geismar, you see. I got involved with him while I was still in the penitentiary, and he helped get me out.

(Now speaking to a dog that jumped up into the window of the car as we pulled into a driveway, the dog only inches from Cleaver's face, and Cleaver speaking to the dog, jocularly: Motherfucker, I will kill you, I will kill your ass.)

I was just saying that cat Geismar has come through in some pinches: he's all right.

Q: Geismar impresses me as being that perennial white critic who always pops up when a new black writer comes on the scene and yells, with the conviction of some sociologist, this is it, this is it. We have finally "discovered" the true black writer who will give us the true Negro personality as though only one Negro personality can exist at a time. And it seems that most black writers have taken their bait and begun vying for the opportunity to present their concept of the Negro to Charlie—which explains why, at least to me, black writers are always cutting each other's throats.

A: I know what you mean. Well, what we gotta do, man, is just blow their minds from many different directions, you know.

Q: You mean what looks to them like contradictions? Confuse them?

A: Not confusion. When I say blow their minds, I mean something that's so overwhelmingly what's happening that they would have to give more than one person respect. Because, you see, respect, *unless* it's of some of these conscious conspiracies that the white people have put down on us, you know, I realize that a lot of time they recognize that a brother is saying something and they don't want it to be heard so they'll give it to somebody else that ain't saying nothing, elevate him, use him to murder the true and legitimate expression, you know. I'm not talking about that. I'm saying that people—if they're intellectually honest—will give respect where it's due, you understand? You don't have any vested interest in denying a particular person if he is saying something—I know I don't; unless it's politics, then your enemy ain't saying nothing no way, *never*. If a cat is using words to persuade people and influence people against something you are supporting, then you are not going to be persuaded by that. You are going to be trying to counter that. But if it's in this neutral realm where people discuss ideas and values and analyze experience, then if a man makes a valid analysis you welcome that, because he's enlightening you. He's adding to your tools for dealing with your environment. So you welcome that. But whites in the past have not wanted to see that happen with black people, because when black people started dealing with the evils in their environment they were dealing with the white man and his activities, so the white man was not interested in certifying an analysis that was an indictment of him and his activities. See, he would try to obscure that, or discredit it, obstruct other people from functioning on that, you know what I mean? But in this day and time we have the initiative— black people have the initiative. The Third World has the initiative. What the white man is trying to do is to stop it and defend themselves against the upthrust of oppressed people. He's got his hands full, Jack!

Q: The black writer has a moral position that the white writer does not have?

A: That's right. The black writer is in the position to essentially further the indictment, to elaborate the indictment and to keep a wary eye on the white man because he can be counted on to pretend to be changing the situation, to pretend to be doing better and to put a snow-job on us for another hundred years. See? So you gotta watch him so that every morning when we wake up we have to remind ourselves and the people that it's the same old shit warmed over.

Q: Well, then, white writers are dangerous in that respect?

A: They are by and large counter-revolutionary. They will mislead you, mistreat you; liars, propagandists for evil, everything bad that you could say about a writer who had abrogated his true function, you could say about these white writers. By and large they're criminals.

Q: What about Baldwin? He reveals himself, in this he's honest, even though what he reveals is not good, say, as an image for black men.

A: Yeah, I think the shit he be putting on paper he should be telling to a psychiatrist. Trying to get some help, trying to find his balls, you know. It's not something he should be projecting out as a model for black manhood. You see, he put that shit in his book to try to make Rufus the embodiment of black masculinity in our time. And Rufus didn't have nothing to do with the brothers that I know. Rufus was a *white* boy, a black boy with a white mind, castrated psychologically. I couldn't relate to Rufus, man. Rufus let white boys fuck him in the ass, sucking wee-wees and things, man. That ain't where this shit's at. I had a very hostile reaction to that book, you know. When I read it I just took Baldwin at face value, you know. But I don't want to say too much about Baldwin because that's been dealt with, you know. And I've met Baldwin and I consider him a friend. As long as he keeps his mouth shut.

Q: What do you see as the specific role of the black writer? Like young cats coming up, where should they look for literary models?

A: I think they need a good perspective on the history of literature, the way we got into this shit, you know, where we are now.

I think that for a black writer to *really* come to his own he needs to have as part of his working equipment some understanding of world literature, what it means, what literature means to people, and the part that it plays in helping people cope with life, in terms of explaining what some of the best minds have seen going on in the world, you know.

By and large it's to prepare oneself for battle, that's what it amounts to, because we're involved in a war. We need a fighting literature, we need to understand ways of using words to expose, to expose and to resurrect, to expose the conscious efforts the white man has made to rob us of our history, to rob us of our dignity, of understanding, of ourselves as a strong and proud people. But not just that. I'm trying to say that words, literature, is one of the categories, man, one of the essential things for survival, like music, dancing, technology. Literature is just as important as any of the other major categories of our human activity, and not just literature—literature is just a particular way of doing it, you know, putting it on paper—but the whole process of recording one's history and views of life and interpretations of human experience. There used to be a time when they had what we call the oral tradition. That is, history as the memory, the collected memory of a people, you know, and literature.

Q: So you don't have to make any distinction between history and literature because it's all . . .

A: Yes, I think it's very important to understand that even if a literary work is not designated as a piece of history, a historical work, if it's worth anything, it captures and says something about human life as someone saw it and recorded it at a given moment. And doing that is so important that writers have often been considered to be like priests or people that we can rely upon for truth.

Q: Like a poet.

A: A poet, dig?

Q: Do you write fiction?

A: Yeah, I've got some fiction. I think now I would have no trouble in putting my fiction down, see. But these motherfucking people always want to change the shit that I write, man. You know what I mean, the motherfuckers want to fuck over it, you know. I have a short story, which I know is a bad motherfucker, man. They say, "Man, there's two stories there in one—cut that up and make that two stories."

Q: Get your structure right, huh?

A: All that shit, you know. Motherfuckers. I know what I'm doing. I know I wrote this, this is one story, this ain't no two stories. This is one story, and I got it the way I want it. "No, it's too long. A short story has to be so many hundred words." It ain't no short story but I'm through with it and I want it like it is. "Well, nooo." You know what I mean? So I just kept it, man.

Q: You know that story entitled "The Allegory of the Eunuch"? It's a beautiful title, I like that. Do you consider that a short story? That's fiction, isn't it?

A: I don't know what it is, brother.

Q: It's a new form?

A: I don't know what the shit that is. I'll tell you what happened. I was at Folsom and my cell partner and a couple other cats were having dinner and we got in this argument, you know. This cat, an old motherfucker, talking that pimp talk, you know, and very disrespectful to black women, you know. He was a coward, he was everything we're trying to get out of. We're trying to explain something to him and he wouldn't understand, so I say I'm going to write this shit down, so he can read it—maybe he'll understand it. And I kind of started reconstructing the conversation, you know. Then I just went off into my thing.

Q: Did you show it to him?

A: Yeah, but a few weeks later this dude died of some liver ailment. They took him to the hospital. I believe they could have saved him, man, if they gave him attention, but they don't like to give you medicine if you talk too much, you know. They let you *die*, man. Like a lot of their medicine they have to send to Pennsylvania to get it, you know. Some of that shit's very expensive, those little pills and things. If there's something really wrong with a cat—they have to send to Canada to get a pill—"Give that nigger some aspirin. Let him sleep," you know. They ain't got no time for that. They got white folks to save, you know. That's one of the things I'd be scared of most in the penitentiary, man, is getting a bad illness going. I'd have to go to the pigs.

I gotta tell you, man, I had this skin rash, dermatitis, and I go to the pigs, and they give me some pills, you know, they got me hooked on those pills. I had to have them. I became a Muslim then, you understand; and they put me in the hole and they be bringing them pills up there and giving them to me, and it got real outta hand around there. They put me in the Jesper Center. They were coming back and forth trying to make me say that when I got out of the hole I'd be good, you know, and I wouldn't go along with that, so they stopped giving me those pills, you know. So I started breaking out. "You want your pills? Be good. I don't feel right bringing you pills, you calling me a devil and a beast and all that." So I said you take your pills, stick your pills up your motherfucking ass. Dig, I don't want your pills no more, you know. And I stopped taking those pills. I thought I wasn't going to make it, you know. I'm not taking any more of those pills; you can take those pills and stick them up your ass. I'll just lay up here and die, man, just lay up here and turn into one big sore, you know. And that shit went away, brother. It got real bad, then it went away, and I ain't been bothered with it since. I found out that my need for the pills was psychological, and the skin rash was psychological. Nervous rash, you know, there was nothing physically wrong with me.

Q: So you are going to be at the University of California at Davis. What are you going to teach?

A: As far as the name of the course, I don't know what I'm going to name it, maybe pigology. But I know what I'm gonna run down—the same shit I always be talking.

Q: What are they going to pay you?

A: Well we haven't talked about that yet. I didn't want to talk about it this morning (in the lawyer's office) because there were too many people there, and they looked uptight. Then I don't know, I got to get an understanding of the scope of this grant that they have, this money that they've got, kinda just what it's about and how it's being spread around. I'm going to get my share. It'll be enough to keep moving, you know?

Q: It'll be enough to keep the revolution on wheels?

A: Yeah.

Q: In three years, how influential will the Panther party be?

A: We'll be running the country in three years.

Q: I think in Chicago, people are very conscious of what's happening but they don't have a Panther party pulling them together. Are there any plans to move out there?

A: We plan to move into all areas where there's work to be done. We are getting a national organization that will eliminate all the splinter groups by any means necessary.

Q: So you look for specific correlation, like the Peace and Freedom party that's working here in the Bay Area?

A: That's in terms of diplomatic relations, foreign affairs, see? Relations with the mother countries. We don't merge with groups of the mother country. We form coalitions with those groups. We merge with the groups in the colleges.

Q: How much trust do you put in young white America?

A: I don't put trust in anyone in the abstract. Except when you start looking at large groupings of people and try to decide out of which group some action is more likely to come. We look upon the young white people as the likely source for reasonable men and women.

Q: Did the Berkeley students' battles with the police show any significance for the Black Panther movement?

A: You mean that uprising they had over there?

Q: Yeah, uprising . . .

A: Yes, we think that there's a heightening of consciousness going on in the Berkeley area. A process of understanding, you see, like people in the Bay Area, particularly East Bay, have tuned into what the pigs are doing; they've been sitting back watching. They've seen several outrageous incidents that has made all the rhetoric concrete reality for them, you see. After their attention was called to the activities of these pigs, they observed such things as the pigs running into Bobby Seale's house, dragging him and his wife out, charging him with conspiracy to commit murder. You know, the pigs did this at a time when community attention on them was at an all-time high. They did this nakedly and openly, and the people didn't like that; they made a public outcry against it. They came out in large numbers to show that they protested that action. Now the people in Berkeley have been listening to various analyses of how the pigs move, and then the pigs came into their own community and whipped their heads, tear-gassed them, and imposed a curfew on them, so now . . .

Q: What happened on April 6, the night of the shoot-out in which Bobby Hutton was killed?

A: We were in the process of gathering food for the picnic the next day in Sherman Park. We had a fund-raising picnic for Bobby Seale and Huey Newton and Kathleen, who was running for office. We needed funds for their campaigns and also for the Huey Newton defense fund, and a few cases in which bail money was needed. So we organized this picnic. We spent a lot of time on it and had invested $300 in meat and things like that. We were really uptight about the picnic. We wanted it to come off without any problems, you know. We put leaflets in the community, put up posters, had some spot advertising on the radio, so that it was a well-known fact that the thing was coming up. We had a little encounter with the cops over the picnic. They went to the Park Authority people and tried to get them to refuse to let us have the facility, and people didn't go along with that. The pigs did persuade the park people to impose some very stringent conditions, like no political speeches to be given in the park, no passing out of leaflets and literature during the picnic, no this, no that. Intentionally petty harassment.

We had this car that had been given to us by this white cat; he gave us two cars. A lot of people have given us things. But this particular car had a Florida license. It was a white Ford with a Florida license plate. It was quite easy to spot, you know. And none of the brothers liked to use it for that reason. I had pretty good identification. I had press cards, press passes, things of that nature, but most brothers don't have anything beyond a draft card, and possibly a driver's license. A lot of brothers have insufficient identification. Well, this car was always being stopped, you know. The pigs would spot the license plate, move in, pull the car over, stop the cat, put him through a lot of changes, ask him if he was from Florida and shit like that, just to be fucking with him. This night, about nine o'clock, the shit went down. We had been going back before, using David Henman's pad as the point where we were centralizing all the food and things so that we could take it to the park. His house was closest to the park of the pads we had available. We'd been out, dropping people off here and there, shit like that. We were on our way back to this house; I was driving this car I just described to you. There were two other cars behind me belonging to brothers, you know.

I have this thing going, you know. I have to take a leak some time. This particular night it came down on me and I had to take a piss real badly. I'm only three or four blocks away from the house, I guess, but I just about pulled down this street, you know. My reaction is I gotta take a piss, the other cats stop their cars right behind mine, and I got outta the car and started taking a piss right along the driver's side. And then this car comes around the corner down here, you know. I didn't know it was a cop car when I first saw it, so I said, Wow, there's some people coming, man, so I stopped pissing and ran around to the other side of the car—just continued—I was just trying to avoid those lights, you know, a bad scene, he might drive by.

But when the car got up there, it stopped right behind my car. I could see all these lights and shit right on top of it, then I could tell it was a cop car. Threw the spotlight on me, man; both cops jumped out, yelling, "Come out from behind there!" I zipped my pants back up; I guess I took too long to get from back there to the street, but it really wasn't that long, you dig? When I stepped out from behind my car, man, them motherfuckers start shooting, see. I don't know if they recognized me, or if they just knew I was driving, or if they had it set up and were just waiting for a chance, or what. So naturally, what I do is dive for the ground. Somebody had a gun or two (hell, I don't know), but somebody started returning that fire. By that time another cop car come from around another corner, and cops in that car start shooting, shot out all the window shields in our car. Everybody was yelling, "Let's get outta here." And so we scattered, see? We ran across the street, and they shot one brother, Warren Wells. I thought I

we were pretty fucked up, you know. Bobby was just stumbling from the shove, stumbling down this walkway, and he was scared, naturally, uptight, man, and fucked up, you know.

And they start burning him, shot him down. It sounded like fifteen, sixteen shots. He just fell, man. And then all these people who had come out from the sound of all that shooting and shit, all these people had come out and crowded around and they start yelling at the cops, you dig? "Murderers! Pigs!" All kinds of names. "Leave him alone." And they got all uptight about that, and a lieutenant came over there and then went to see the captain and told the captain, "This one here says he's wounded." The captain said to me, "Where you wounded at?" "In my foot," I said, and the motherfucker stomped me on my foot, you dig? "OK, get him outta here." And the same captain—his name is Captain McCarthy—is one of the leading troublemakers in Oakland. I had a couple of encounters with him, and he knows me, and I know him on sight.

Then they put me in a car. Then took me out of the car and into one of the big Marias, and then they began to fuck with me. One of the cops was talking on the mike. "We are bringing one in," he said, and asked what my name was. I told him and he repeated it on the microphone. Then these two cops got in the Maria and started fucking with me, hitting me, you know? They were telling the driver to drive down a dark street, you dig? And the driver turned and said, "I've already called in on that guy." Man, they cursed him, man, "Why in the fuck you do that for?" you know. The point is that they have a twenty-four-hour tape of all calls on the switchboard, so that if they had gone on and fucked with me that tape would have my name on it and they didn't dig that, see what I mean?

So they took me to the hospital. When I got there this other brother Warren Wells was laying up on the table. And a cop started fucking him up. One thing struck me as being quite significant: he (the cop) said, "You ain't goin' to no barbecue tomorrow. *You* the barbecue now!" So that indicates to me that this thing we were trying to do was very much on their minds. They took me in. There were some brothers and sisters working in this hospital, and they were trying to help us, you dig? We had so much tear gas on us, the people's eyes started burning when they brought us in. The sister did the best she could, she was washing all over my body, trying to get that gas out, which was in my hair, my beard, and my groin. All the skin was off my groin for three or four weeks. And the sister was washing me down in all these chemicals and everything. And this cop was standing there: "Say, hurry up, come on, he don't need all that." And the sister said, "Well, he goin' get all that. You don't get him until I'm through with him." So there were all kinds of conflicts like that, you know. And I'm just mentioning this to bring out the attitude of these pigs in Oakland, you see? Racist pigs, Gestapo.

Q: Let me change the discussion entirely and ask you a question about love, as you speak of it in your book. In the title essay, "Soul on Ice," you give a poetic description of the "female principle." First, is that description of women at all political? Let me explain further. In a statement before this essay, you write that: "Many whites flatter themselves that the Negro male's lust and desire for the white dream girl is purely an esthetic attraction, but nothing could be farther from the truth; his motivation is often . . . bloody." Now, *that's* a political statement—

A: Not necessarily purely political, except that everything is really political. But what I was saying there is that a lot of times when the brothers be moving to pull those white girls, you know, white people think it's just because brothers are just freaked out behind white people, you know. But really the brother is moving in terms of a triumph, that he knows the white man hates above all to see a black nigger with one of his queens, you understand. So the brother sees this as means of inflicting pain upon the white man.

Q: Does the poetic description of the "female principle," as described in "Soul on Ice," apply to white or black women, or just woman?

A: It applies to just woman, you understand. Say that there are all kinds of women on the face of the earth, you dig? You have to deal at first with nature, and then with sociology. You have to deal first with what people are in essence, and what they become after being moulded by tradition, mores, and the practices of a given civilization. So that no matter what form the moulding of this human material is, these principles, the female and male principles, will still maintain their attraction for each other, except the social structure of society tries to harness this attraction and force it to go through certain socially accepted channels—the basic human desire, the magnetism bit.

The female principle and the male principle is toward unity. The male and the female are attracted to each other, and this is what's happening. If it weren't for all these sociological considerations, then the two could move toward each other, without having to go through all these channels that are socially acceptable. So, in that essay, I was trying to uncover the basic nature. To my way of thinking, by understanding this principle, it is easier to understand and know how people are moulded by a given social structure.

Q: Then black people's attraction to whites (and vice versa) is due to social considerations?

A: Black people in mass are not attracted to white people; no, I'm not saying that. I'm saying that every man and every woman is capable of relating to each other. Now a woman has a vagina and a man a penis, you dig. And a man, everything being equal, can have a sexual relationship with any woman on the face of the earth–except, I don't know if the Watusi could have intercourse with the Pygmy. I've often thought how that would come down, you know what I mean. Given similarity of stature and so forth, I think they would make it, you know. I was just dealing there with universal masculinity and femininity without getting to all those other things that come after that—these other things are superimposed upon your true given nature.

Q: There is no contradiction between your letters to Beverly Axelrod, in *Soul on Ice,* and your letter to All Black Women, which ends the book?

A: I wouldn't go as far as to say that; I would say this: I married Kathleen. I'm not married to Beverly Axelrod, you dig it? I was in the penitentiary, and I wanted to get out. Now Beverly Axelrod was a lawyer who got me out of the penitentiary. When she came on the set, I thought that any reluctance to relate to her would be very unbecoming to me in the condition I was in. So, I just blew my soul. There are a lot of white people very uptight about that Beverly Axelrod thing. Mad with me because I didn't marry her. So, what I am going to have to do is write a little short piece, explaining just what went down.

Q: She's married, isn't she?

A: No she's been married twice, before she met me. I was to be her third husband. She married two white boys.

Q: She's angry with you too?

A: Yeah, I think so. I think she's very angry with me. If people really knew how that really went down! You see, from the moment I wrote her my first letter—you see I didn't know her, and she didn't know me; she came to see me in response to a letter I had written her. I wrote her this letter kind of based on my concept of where white women are at, and what can move them. I wanted to attract her. I didn't have any money to pay her. I only had words, and I used those words . . . and I got out of the penitentiary.

Q: At one point in a letter to her, you quite openly say that you were aware of your style, that you were jiving—

A: All her friends used to tell her that she was a fool and that I was gaming on her. And she used to come and see me and tell me that. And I would just have to leave it up to her to decide whether or not I was sincere.

Q: But you were sincere?

A: This was the way I was in prison. There are times when to take people in, to really listen to them, is to love them. And I used to love that Beverly Axelrod. Man, if somebody said something about Beverly Axelrod when I was in Folsom Prison, I'd throw his ass off the fifteenth tier. There were a lot of Muslims who didn't like it either. I'd tell them, Kiss my ass, blackass niggers!

22 / Barroom Sociology

PIRI THOMAS

That night, after a nap, we walked around the colored part of
Norfolk. The night air was cool and everything was living and
going someplace. It reminded me of Harlem. We were on our
way to the Blue Bell, a place Brew remembered from another
life. It had a dance floor, a hot combo, and some rooms nearby
for sitting out dances.

It wasn't a big place, but it swung. Inside it was dark except
for red and blue light bulbs that gave the walls the shadows of
the patrons. Brew and I got to a table and almost right away a
waiter came up to us. "May I help you, gentlemen?" he asked.

We gave him our order, and a few minutes later he returned
with our drinks. He spoke so well I asked him if he was from
New York.

"No," he said, "I'm from Pennsylvania. But I can tell you're
from New York, and," he added, looking at Brew, "you're not."

"Yuh right," Brew said, "Ah's a home boy."

"Been here long?" asked the Pennsylvanian.

"Couple of days," I lied. "We're on business. How about you?"

"Well, I've been here—excuse me, somebody's waving for service. Look," he said as he moved away, "I have my relief in a
few minutes and if you don't mind, I'll join you for a chat."

We nodded "okay," and the Pennsylvanian saluted his thanks
and drifted off through a mass of bodies. I eye-drilled a hole in
the dress of a pretty baby leaning on a jukebox across the dance
floor. "I'd like to get workin' with her like real fast," I said. "Dig,
she got my eye."

"Well, play it cool," Brew said, "'cause tha's what she's heah
fo', to ketch yo' eye an' yo' bread."

SOURCE: Piri Thomas, *Down These Mean Streets* (New York: New American Library, Signet Books, 1967), pp. 167–175. Copyright © 1967 by Piri Thomas. Reprinted by permission of Alfred A. Knopf, Inc.
Piri Thomas, a black Puerto Rican brought up in Spanish Harlem in New York
City, reached a wide audience with his first book, *Down These Mean Streets*.

As I rolled my eyes around the broad's curves, the Pennsylvanian returned with fresh drinks. He sat down and told us he had been in Norfolk about three months. He looked about twenty-five or twenty-six. "I'm writing a book on the Negro situation," he said, "and I came down for the sense of personal involvement. I wanted the feel of what it means for a Negro to live here in the South. Background and such, you know what I mean?"

"Damn, man," Brew said, "yuh sho' coulda picked a tougher place than Norfolk fo' your book. Ah means a place whar you li'ble to get a kick in yuh background."

The Pennsylvanian smiled. "Oh, I'm not looking for that kind of personal involvement," he said. "I'm not seeking violence but rather the warmth and harmony of the southern Negro, their wonderful capacity for laughter and strength, their spiritual closeness to God and their way of expressing faith through their gospel singing. I want to capture on paper the richness of their poverty and their belief in living. I want the words I write to blend with the emotions of their really fantastic ability to endure and absorb the anguish of past memories of the slavery that was the lot of their grandparents. I want to write that despite their burdens they are working with the white man toward a productive relationship."

I glanced at Brew. He was studying the shadows on the walls. I took a good look at the Pennsylvanian. He was tan-colored and not really very negroid-looking. I got a funny, almost proud feeling that I looked more negroid than he did.

The Penn State man continued, "You see, I really feel the large part of the publicity being given the southern situation is adverse and serves only to cause more misunderstanding. I realize that there have been incidents, and white men have been cruel and violent toward the Negro, but only an ignorant and small minority—"

Brew broke in quietly with a wave of his hand, "You not a southe'ner, are yuh?"

"No, I'm not."

"Evah bin down South before?"

"No, I haven't."

"Evah notice any of these problems you was talkin' 'bout up No'th?"

"Well, I suppose there is some bigotry up there, but it's not the same, or at least I find it doesn't have the same meaning as here in the South."

"Ah sees," said Brew, barely hiding a growing disgust. "You-all been any other places inna South?"

"No, but I've been making plans to go to Atlanta, and—"

"You oughta go to some of them small towns whar a rock better fuckin' well know his place."

"Well, I don't think that's totally necessary. The problem of the southern Negro is the same whether he's in the large cities or in back-wat—I mean, backwood counties. I believe that the southern Negro of today is marshaling his dignity and preparing himself for a great social revolution."

"Yuh-all gonna be a part of it?" Brew asked.

"I certainly feel that my book will contribute in some effective way to the Negro's cause."

"Ah means," said Brew, "if it comes down to fightin' an' havin' black an' white mixing their blood on big city guttahs or goddamn dirt roads?"

"If in looking for a solution to this problem," the Pennsylvanian replied, looking at me, "it comes to the point of violence, I know that many will die, especially Negroes. Those that fight, of course. And that will be their contribution to their cause. Some whites may die, and that will be their contribution to their cause. But it falls to others, black or white, to contribute in some other way. Perhaps one of these ways is by writing. By writing I will be fighting."

"About what? an' foah who?" said Brew. "Yuh gonna write 'bout Negroes' warmth an' harmony, an' their won'erful ability to laugh an' rejoice, an' that shit 'bout the richness of their poverty? Yuh gonna write 'bout their fantastick 'bility to endure fuck-up mem'ries of slavin' an' smilin'? Prissy, wha's your name? Mine's Brewster, Brewster Johnson."

"My name, Mr. Johnson, is Gerald Andrew West," the Pennsylvanian said in such a way to let Brew know that he didn't like being called "Prissy." It was like the way you let someone know your name when you think he's inferior to you.

There was a fifth of whisky on our table. It hadn't been there before, or had it? It was almost empty, and I felt high, and Brew seemed high too. "You-all don' mind if ah calls yuh by your first name, eh, Ger-rul?" he said.

"If you like—er, Mr. Johnson—I hope I haven't caused any misunderstanding between us. I didn't mean to cause any resentment. I hope . . ."

Brew didn't answer.

"Don't worry, man," I said, "say it like you feel it," and I nudged Brew to keep his cool. He smiled gently, like a hungry tiger, and I knew he'd stay cool. "*Suave, panita,*" I added to Brew.

"Oh, you speak Spanish," Gerald Andrew West said to me, "Mr.—"

"Piri—Piri Thomas. Yeah, I do."

"How wonderful! Are you of Spanish descent?"

"No, just Puerto Rican father and moms."

"I speak a little Spanish, also," said Gerald Andrew West. "*Yo estoy estudiano español.*"

"Ah di'n't order any more drinks," Brew said as another fifth of whisky found its way to the table.

"This is on me, Mr. Johnson. Uh—do you speak Spanish fluently, Mr.—Piri? May I call you by your first name?"

"You 'ready did," said Brew. "Damn p'lite prissy."

I nudged Brew again; he made pop eyes and mumbled, "'Scuse me." Gerald Andrew West looked like he hadn't heard him or like Brew wasn't there.

"Yeah, you can call me Piri—uh, Gerald," I said.

"You know, Piri, I've been taken for Spanish many times, and Indian, too. I know that many dark people say that, but it's really happened with me." Gerald smiled almost too pat and added, "So you're Puerto Rican?"

I looked at the shadows over Brew's head and then at the jukebox. Pretty baby was still leaning on it.

"A-huh," I answered, "Puerto Rican *moyeto.*"

"*Moyeto?* What does that mean?"

"Negro," I said.

"Oh—er—do Puerto Ricans—er—consider themselves—uh—Negro?"

"I can only talk 'bout me," I replied, "but *como es, es como se llama.*"

Gerald thought for a second and translated, "Like it is, is how it's called. Am I right?"

"Word for word, *amigo*," I said. "I'm a Puerto Rican Negro."

"Wha' kind is you-all, Gerald?" Brew said, smiling.

"What kind of what?" Gerald asked. "I'm afraid I don't understand you, Mr. Johnson."

"Ah means, what kinda Negro is yuh?"

"Oh! I understand now. Well, uh—according to—er—my—according to a genealogical tracer—you know, those people who trace one's family tree back as far as possible—well, according to the one my parents contracted to do the tracing, I'm really only one-eighth colored."

Brew was shaking his head slowly up and down. He made a move with his head at the bottle and Gerald said, "That's what it's there for, Mr. Johnson. By all means, please be my guest and help yourself."

"How's that work?" I asked Gerald. "I mean, tracing and all."

"Well, you see, they check back to your grandparents and get information so they can trace back to your great-grandparents and so on. For example, my great-great-grandfather was an Englishman named Robert West. He was on my father's side. His wife, my great-great-grandmother, was from Malaya. You can see my eyes have an Oriental cast about them. Well—"

"A-huh, Ah sees," Brew said absently.

"—he—my great-great-grandfather—was a ship's captain and married his wife on one of his trips to Malaya. Then his oldest son, my great-grandfather—his name was Charles Andrew West —married a woman whose father was white and mother was half Negro. They had children and their second son, my father, married my mother, who had Indian blood, from, uh, India, and uh—some Spanish blood and uh—some Negro, colored blood. I— really—I'm so blended racially that I find it hard to give myself to any, ah—well, to any one of the blends. Of course, I feel that the racial instincts that are the strongest in a person enjoying this rich mixture are the ones that—uh—should be followed."

"What is your instinks, ah, Gerald?" asked Brew, staring at our blended friend.

Gerald laughed nice-like and answered, "I—rather—feel—sort of Spanish-ish, if I may use that term. I have always had great admiration for Spanish culture and traditions. I—er—yes—feel rather impulsed toward things Spanish. I guess that's why I have this inclination to learn Castilian. Of course, I don't disregard the other blends that went into the making of me, which—"

"Yuh evah been mistook fo' a Caucasian?" Brew interrupted.

Gerald smiled politely and answered, "Well, like I said, I'm always being mistaken for one of Spanish, uh, origin, or Puerto Rican. It's the same thing, I guess, and—"

Unpolite Brew broke in again, "Ah said *Caucasian.*"

"Er, I rather think that Spaniards, even though some are swarthy like Italians from Sicily, uh—are considered Caucasians. Yes, I probably have been taken for a white."

"How 'bout gittin' mistook fo' a Negro?" Brew asked. He was tight and his voice sounded like it did that day on the stoop in Harlem when he was sounding me on the same subject.

"Well," Gerald said hesitantly, "I've seen looks of doubt, and I've had some rare unpleasant experiences. But I find that I am mostly taken for a Negro by Negroes. I guess there are many like myself who, because of their racial blends, find themselves in the same unique position."

"An' what's your answer when yuh ast?"

"By the Caucasians?"

"Naw! Ah can figger what yuh tells 'em. Ah wanna know what you says to the rock people."

"Why, I say 'yes.' I—er—couldn't possibly say anything else under the circumstances. It would at best create resentment if I attempted to explain that I don't feel one hundred per cent Negro, since I am only one-eighth Negro."

"Don' yuh-all feel a leetle bit more Negro than that?"

Gerald looked at me for assurance that this wasn't going to be one of those "under the circumstances" situations that would lead to resentment and make his "personal involvement" physically painful. I smiled at him that I'd do what I could to keep everything cool.

"Don' yuh-all feel a leetle bit more Negro than that?" Brew repeated. "Tell me, is the book you're writin' gonna be frum the Negro's point o' view? It's gonna be a great book. Yuh-all fo' sure show the true picture of the workin's toward a productive relationship 'tween the Mistuh Charlies and the rock people. Ah am sure that your book will tru'fully show who all is enjoyin' the producin' part from that there relationship."

Gerald stayed quiet for a long time, then he said, "Mr. Johnson, I'd like to tell you something." For the first time he sounded like he was going to say what he had to and fuck Brew and whatever he thought or whatever he was going to do. Brew looked at him *carapalo.* "I'm not ashamed for the so-called 'Negro' blood in me and neither am I ashamed for what I feel myself to be. Nor how I think. I believe in the right of the individual to feel and think— and choose—as he pleases. If I do not choose to be a Negro, as you have gathered, this is my right, and I don't think you can ask or fight for your rights while denying someone else's. I believe that my book will contribute. I believe that the so-called 'Negro writers' are so damned wrapped up in their skins that they can't see the white forest for the black trees. It's true I don't look like a true Caucasian, but neither do I look like a true Negro. So I ask you if a white man can be a Negro if he has some Negro blood in him, why can't a Negro be a white man if he has white blood in him?"

Gerald tenderly squeezed the flesh of his left shoulder with the fingers of his right hand. I dug the jukebox and its ornament. Brew watched Gerald.

"I believe the Negro has the burden of his black skin," Gerald continued. He was in focus now. "And I believe the white man has the burden of his white skin. But people like me have the burden of both. It's pretty funny, Mr. Johnson. The white man is perfectly willing for people like me to be Negroes. In fact, he insists upon it. Yet, the Negro won't let us be white. In fact he forbids it. Perhaps I was a bit maudlin in describing what I was looking for in the southern Negro, and this may have set you against me. But I would like you to know that if, because of genetic interbreeding, I cannot truly identify with white or black, I have the right to identify with whatever race or nationality approximates my emotional feeling and physical characteristics. If I feel comfortable being of Spanish extraction, then that's what I'll be. You might very well feel the same way, were you in my place."

People were still dancing and Gerald was still tenderly squeezing his shoulder. I was thinking that Gerald had problems something like mine. Except that he was a Negro trying to make Puerto Rican and I was a Puerto Rican trying to make Negro.

Gerald got up. "Do you know, Mr. Johnson," he said, "it's easier to pass for white down here than up North. Down here, a white man thinks twice before accusing another white openly of being a Negro for fear of getting slapped with a lawsuit or worse. And the Negro only has to think once for fear of just the 'worse.' But up North it's not an insult according to law, and I've never seen or heard of the 'worse' happening. Anyway, I've come down here to find what I couldn't find up North, and I think I've gotten what I came looking for. I've wanted to taste, feel, and identify with what was fitted for me. Even Negro. But I cannot. Not only do I not feel like a Negro, but I cannot understand his culture or feelings or his special kind of anger. Perhaps it's because I was born and raised in the North and went to white schools and white boys were my friends from childhood. I've mingled with colored boys up North, but I never felt like I was one of them, or they of me. Tonight, Mr. Johnson, I started out of place. The same feeling I've lived with a long time. And I found out tonight that I *am* out of place. Not as a human being, but as a member of your race. I will say that you hit it on the head when you insinuated that I was trying to be a Puerto Rican so I could make the next step to white. You're right! I feel white, Mr. Johnson; I look white; I think white; therefore I *am* white. And I'm going back to Pennsylvania and *be* white. I'll write the book from both points of view, white and Negro. And don't think it will be one-sided. That one eighth in me will come through; it's that potent, isn't it?"

Gerald stood there waiting for Brew or maybe me to say something. Brew was looking at a fat broad sitting at the bar. I looked at the jukebox. Gerald smiled at the shadows on the wall and said, "Good night, Mr. Johnson . . . Piri. And good-bye and good luck."

"*Adiós*, Gerald, take it smooth." I waved a hand and wasn't sure I meant it. But I found it hard to hate a guy that was hung up on the two sticks that were so much like mine. Brew just nodded his head and watched a self-chosen white man make it from a dark scene. "Ah guess he's goin' home," he said and downed his drink. "Le's go see what pussy's sellin' fo' by the pound."

I heard Lady Day singing from the jukebox. The broad was still there, still coming on. I thought, *pussy's the same in every color,* and made it over to the music.

23 / Blacks and Jews: An Interview with Julius Lester[1]

NAT HENTOFF

QUESTION: By now, that poem has become an issue not only in New York, but nationally as well. You said you expected some degree of reaction at the time, but was the extent and durability of the hostile response surprising to you?

ANSWER: Yes, very surprising, because the reaction came three weeks after the poem was read on the air. I felt, at the time, that it was simply being used as a device to get at Les Campbell, who has been under attack for some months now. And then,

[1] Leslie Campbell is a teacher in Ocean Hill-Brownsville, a focal point in the struggle for community control of schools in New York City between the black community and the predominantly white United Federation of Teachers (headed by Albert Shanker). Last December, on Julius Lester's WBAI-FM program, Campbell read a poem by a fifteen-year-old student of his. Titled "Anti-Semitism," and "dedicated to albert shanker," the poem begins: "Hey, jew boy with that yamaka on your head/ You pale faced Jew boy, I wish you were dead." The last two lines are: "I hated you jew boy cause your hang up was the Torah/ And my only hang up was my color."

The tumultuous aftermath of the reading was the filing of a complaint to the FCC by the United Federation of Teachers and demands that the station's license be revoked or suspended by the New York Board of Rabbis, the Workmen's Circle, and the Jewish Defense League, among other groups.

SOURCE: *Evergreen Review,* No. 65 (April 1969), pp. 21–25, 71–76. Copyright © 1969 by Evergreen Review, Inc. Reprinted by permission of Evergreen Review, Inc.
Julius Lester is a composer and writer, probably best known for his book, *Look Out Whitey! Black Power's Gon Get Your Mamma.* He has also written *To Be a Slave* and *Search for the New Land,* a history of America from Hiroshima to the present.
The interviewer, Nat Hentoff, is a staff writer for *Evergreen Review* who has written several novels and numerous books on contemporary issues, including a study of New York City Mayor John Lindsay, *A Political Life: The Education of John V. Lindsay.*

secondly, it was interesting that Shanker's complaint to the FCC about WBAI was made the day after the courts ruled that the principals should go back into Ocean Hill-Brownsville. I felt it was a politically inspired move. Why wait three weeks? In terms of the reaction of people who heard the program—yes, they were disturbed; they were upset. They talked about it on the air, on the show, but I didn't start receiving hate mail until after *The New York Times* came out with their story.

q: And was there much hate mail?

a: Oh, tons. Quite a bit. And, you know, threats and this type of thing.

q: Getting back to the poem itself, I'm not asking you to speak for Les Campbell, but speaking for yourself, having seen the poem, if you had been her teacher, wouldn't you then have tried to communicate with the student and explore with her the steriotypical reactions manifested in her poem? It was, after all, clearly anti-Semitic and indiscriminately made all Jews the enemy.

a: One thing people don't understand is that when you're working with blacks, there is a time when people are ready to hear certain things, and that time is not now for some things. Let's put it this way: You start where the people are and try to move from there. So, OK, you involve yourself in things which you yourself disagree with. But if there's going to be any change of attitude, then it's not going to come by preaching moralistic sermons; that's just like what white people have always done. And so, when I saw the poem—yeah, there were things wrong in terms of intellectual content. However, I'm not concerned with that. I'm concerned with the basic emotion that's there, and if all the facts are wrong, it's totally irrelevant to that basic emotional content. So it's redundant and ridiculous of me to point out that Jews have suffered for more than fifteen years; the girl who wrote the poem doesn't care. And it wouldn't change what she was feeling.

q: And that not all Jewish teachers are the kind of teachers she's talking about?

a: Right.

Q: But if this kind of feeling is allowed to grow unchallenged, won't the result be that the girl will grow up rigidly prejudiced— just as most whites, if not all, have had racism embedded in them? You say that you have to move from where the people are, but do you withhold all comment of your own?

A: I think that you have to consider the genesis of the poem. To my mind, the poem is an act of self-defense, because of the racism which was involved in the teachers' strike. The black community was attacked head-on, and specifically in Ocean Hill-Brownsville, where this girl is a student. And so, as far as I'm concerned, she is defending herself with the only weapon at her command. She is hurt, and therefore she is going to hurt back as much as she can.

I think one of the difficulties is that people are equating the poem with traditional anti-Semitism, which is rooted in God knows what—Christ-killers and what have you. That has no relationship to the black community. The black community does not fall within that. I mean, even at thirty years of age, I don't know that a person is a Jew from looking at him, or by his name, or anything like that. Now that's true of most black people, I think.

Q: Richard Wright, in *Black Boy*, said, "All of us black people who lived in the neighborhood hated Jews, not because they've exploited us, but because we have been taught at home and in Sunday School the Jews were 'Christ-killers.'" That's not analogous to your experience?

A: No. I was twenty years old before I began to have any consciousness that there was anything other than black people and white people, that there were sub-categories of white people, and that Jews were one of them. It came about through *Exodus*, and then, from that I went to a synagogue. Yes, I was aware in terms of the Bible, and in terms of spirituals—Moses, this kind of thing. It meant nothing, except later I became conscious that Einstein was a Jew, that Jews had an intellectual tradition, and being an intellectual of sorts, I could respect that. So what feelings I had were, shall we say, kindred.

Q: You came initially from the South, and I wonder whether you think that the hostility toward the Jew in some black urban communities comes from the fact that a preponderance of the merchants in these black areas are Jewish?

A: Yes, but growing up in Nashville, they were *white* people. They weren't Jews. There were crackers and there were niggers. So I came to New York in '61, and I found out—well, Jesus, there are Irish, and there are Polish, Germans, and all these other things. Each one acts differently. But I was conscious of white people, and that was all.

Q: And you don't think this identification with the Jew as merchant and then as white is as widespread as many sociologists claim?

A: Perhaps in the North it is. In terms of Harlem, yes, I would say it is.

Q: I asked because someone pointed out in an analysis that in some areas the Negro would frequently refer to his "Jew landlord," even though his name might be O'Reilly, Kowalski, or Santangelo. And, I suppose, again that comes out of the preponderance of Jewish merchants and landlords in those areas.

A: Right, yes.

Q: In another program on WBAI, and this is something you've commented on, there was a remark by a black student from N.Y.U.: "As far as I'm concerned, more power to Hitler. He didn't make enough lampshades out of them." Well, that's the kind of thing that, to a Jew listening in, even if he's totally out of the religion, out of any kind of Jewish communal feeling, immediately conjures up the very real, quite recent past. And he would ask, "How come you didn't say anything about that at the time?"

A: The reason I didn't say anything about it at the time was that I recognized he was speaking symbolically, and that he was speaking from a feeling of how can I most effectively hurt these people. It should be obvious that black people don't have the capabilities to carry out any pogrom against Jews, and then, I don't even think black people have the desire to carry out any pogrom against Jews. I took his statement totally on the symbolic level.

Q: Because he was so angry, particularly in the context of the recent teachers' strike and the various reactions after that to Les Campbell, this was the kind of thing he would say—to hurt?

A: Yes, right. And, OK, if you want to isolate it from that, yes, like it's a horrible statement; it's a horrible thing that happened. But, once again, emotionally, black people have no connection with what happened in Germany and in Eastern Europe. We were too busy fighting for our own survival.

Q: Some social scientists would say, "OK, it was symbolic. It was perhaps defensive." But it's out of symbolism, out of this use of rhetoric, that the climate in the past in places you've mentioned eventually led to political anti-Semitic movements and actual pogroms and concentration camps.

A: What really gets me angry, see, is that, for crying out loud, for six months we had a George Wallace going around the country who *created* an atmosphere that *did* provoke unwarranted attacks upon black people, that *did* create a whole climate in the country of which the UFT thing is a part. And where were these so-called friends, be they either Jews or Anglo-Saxons, when this was happening? A few of them were interested, a few of them were protesting, but they were all saying, "Oh, if Wallace ever did get elected, America would never wipe out black people"— the same thing that was said in Germany. If white people started a pogrom against Jews, then OK, Jews would be in trouble, because whites have the power to carry it out. But black people have no thought of carrying out any sort of pogrom against Jews.

Q: During the UFT strike, which closed down the schools and was, in reality, an attempt to destroy the Ocean Hill-Brownsville Experimental District and community control of the schools, there was a large amount of racist, anti-black invective on UFT picket lines, which was barely reported, and against which I don't think there was much of a record of protest by any group, certainly by none of the groups clamoring now. And after the strike, there was a teacher at Franklin K. Lane High School, who is as yet unidentified, who was quoted in the New York Post as saying, "Well, we're not going to live in fear. I think that if the black people don't get into line, then we'll have to either annihilate them or neutralize them. That's not as harsh as it sounds. It has happened in other societies. It may be the only way of dealing with this." So what I'd ask you, and I suppose it's in a sense a rhetorical question, how does one expect—let's say the girl in Les Campbell's class, the student at N.Y.U., to exist under this kind of state of siege, as they see it, and not react emotionally?

A: I react emotionally to that, you know. Because that is a reality as far as I'm concerned; the teacher at Franklin K. Lane is not joking. This country *is* capable of annihilating black people.

But how else is one to react to that? I didn't see Mayor Lindsay going around to a Baptist church, putting on the choir robes to explain to the black congregation that he wasn't going to allow that in the city. You know, like I was not even interested in Ocean Hill-Brownsville, the school fight—nothing. Until one day I was looking at TV, and all of a sudden, I hear Shanker talking about mob action and extremists.

Q: Vigilantes, Nazis.

A: Right. *That* to me means *one thing*! He's so hung up on *niggers*! They wouldn't be accusing us of anti-Semitism if we had the finesse of George Wallace and Shanker. Like, the guy who made that statement that Hitler should have made more lampshades could have got on there and said the same thing in Shanker's way. But he's the cat off the block; he said it direct from the gut. And why be dishonest about it? But you say that Shanker said he is for decentralization of the schools and all that. And so people take this and they don't hear what *I'm* hearing the man say. Hell, we were talking about decentralization and education and Shanker starts yelling anti-Semitism. Rhody McCoy was talking politics; Shanker started talking race.

Q: Then what is your explanation for so many Jews having reacted so emotionally and so vehemently to the poem and to the statement by the N.Y.U. student? In other words, why were you so surprised at this reaction?

A: Well, I guess because my knowledge of the Jewish community as such is nonexistent. I know quite a few individuals who are Jews. I expected some reaction, yes. But it was just ignorance on my part as to how deep the fear is inside the Jewish community. But that's not saying I would've done differently in this situation.

I think there's another aspect to it. For the past five or ten years in this country, Jews have sort of been "in"—the Jewish novel, *How to Be a Jewish Mother*. For the first time in world history, a country exists where Jews are "in"—*Fiddler on the Roof*, and what have you. And they were feeling good with this, and all of a sudden comes this attack from the left—or from the right, depending on where you sit—which, of course, feeds back again into what I guess is an insecurity.

Then there's the whole Israel thing. I've been thinking about the progression in terms of this whole issue of black anti-Semitism. The first column I wrote for the *Guardian*, in the fall of 1967 I think, dealt with Israel and the Mideast War and the whole thing. In that column, I said it was necessary for Jews to look upon Israel politically, at what its political role was. And, of course, the reaction I got was the same that came this time— that there's another black-Jewish division here, that naturally the Jewish attitude toward Israel was going to be very personal, very emotional, and a very moral one. And because six million Jews were killed during World War II, it sort of seems that a Jew can do no wrong, that the State of Israel can do no wrong. And I think Jews in this country have that sort of attitude. Nobody mentions the ten million who died in Stalingrad alone in World War II; there were twenty million in Russia that got wiped out, which explains a lot to me about Russia's present international position. What about these people who are just forgotten? Hell, fifteen million died in the camps. It would seem to me that Jews are falsifying history to let nine million people be forgotten.

Then the other thing is that the cat in the corner would say, "OK, six million Jews got it. *I* didn't do it. Don't tell me about it."

Q: Which, to a Jew, I think, would be the attitude of the non-Jewish population at large. I think the essential thing to keep in mind is that those Jews who still have any kind of concept of themselves as Jews are aware of the fact that it's been a long, tough pull for an awfully long time. The fact that any Jew survived is quite remarkable. Israel to them is not only the last place, but the only place, where anybody can go if he's Jewish.

NAT HENTOFF 401

It's also a radical change in Jews' attitude toward themselves. To use a term from the new movement, "It's one place where Jews don't play victims anymore."

A: Right, OK. Then why is it that they can understand Israel and can't let us have Ocean Hill-Brownsville? That's the same thing; they should understand that better than *anybody* in this country. But the reason is that they have the power now, and they don't want to relinquish their power to the black people. So therefore we fight.

Q: In an article in *Commentary*, "The Black Revolution & the Jewish Question," Earl Raab, executive director of the Jewish Community Relations Council in San Francisco, says the black movement "is developing an anti-Semitic ideology. On one coast, there's talk about how the 'Jewish establishment' is depressing the education of black students. On the other coast, a black magazine publishes a poem calling, poetically of course, for the crucifying of rabbis. 'Jew Pig' has become a common variant of the standard expressivist metaphor. On this level, there are daily signals." Do you think he is taking these "signals" out of proportion in building this case?

A: I would think so. There's a certain expression which comes from what the press would describe as militant black intellectuals. There's another expression which I think comes from black people in the community. I think he is taking it out of proportion. In a ghetto situation, the people are not adverse to the idea of sharing power. They're not at the point of, say, where Kenya is in terms of kicking out Asians. I haven't heard of any Jewish merchants being firebombed out of the ghettos since this has happened—any sort of campaign directed against them. I think the danger is that, because of the Jewish reaction to what's been going on, the blacks will move to an absolute position, which, of course, is very dangerous because then you're pitting one power against another power, and that's a war.

Q: You mean that the reaction is of such vehemence, like the demand that you be fired and WBAI be shut down, that that in itself will create anti-Semitism?

A: I don't know if you can call what blacks feel anti-Semitism. It's more of an anti-racism racism, that act of self-defense, and to call it anti-Semitism is to fail to understand it.

You see, the thing which has hurt me most in this is where has the New Left been? Where has the radical movement been? OK, you know, they say we want to be relevant in the black struggle. We want to speak to the white community. Here is opportunity busting down the door. Here it is, if you're a white who understands anything about the black framework. But what happens is that so many young kids in SDS, whose background is Jewish, hate that background so much and want to get so far away from it that they refuse to relate to where they've come from.

Q: Whereas they could have been of some help in moving around in Jewish communities, putting all this in perspective?

A: As far as black radicals go, I'm a conservative because I have a theoretical belief in coalition, and if it's possible for me to say to a cat who don't want to hear white people, "Hey man, listen, ten thousand white folks were out there on the line yesterday doing this, that, and the other," he might change his mind. But then he looks out there and sees, like *I* do, a hostile mass, and the rest silent. Hey, well, you know, fuck it!

Q: All during the teachers' strike, and all during this furor about the poem, about WBAI, I don't know of any attempt, organized, anyway, where white radicals, or people who call themselves white radicals, went into their home communities or into communities in which they can easily move, to try to explain what was going on.

A: I know of no attempt. I know of only two groups which have done anything, and that was Youth Against War and Fascism, and Coalition For An Anti-Imperialist Movement. And then it was very gratifying to me that both groups came up and counterpicketed the night others were out picketing me at the station.

I did a column on the Arab-Israeli thing and one on the school strike, both saying the same thing—that I felt the Jewish community should examine itself, and re-examine a lot of the things that it had formerly thought. One of my instincts in terms of the poem, and it was very conscious at the time—like the Zen monk who used to slap the student in the face—OK, let's try it and see what happens. But that's not my role, really. It's the responsibility of young Jews who have been in the radical movement to be the Zen monks, not me. But maybe I'm wrong.

At any rate, I think all of this has caused some self-examination inside the Jewish community and some discussions by the Jewish community, but *I* cannot really speak to the Jewish community; I don't know the Jewish community.

Q: Leonard Fein, Associate Director of the MIT-Harvard Joint Center for Urban Studies, said in *Time:* "Jews, in a perverse kind of way, need anti-Semites. Jews in this country are in fairly serious trouble spiritually and ideologically, and it is very comforting to come once again to an old and familiar problem. By confronting others, you can avoid the much more challenging confrontation with yourself." A big problem, as people always say at meetings of Jewish organizations, is that the young people are falling away from Judaism, and I would add that it is doubtful that they'll come back on a program of anti-anti-Semitism. As Rabbi Arthur Hertzberg puts it, "Negatives won't work to create a Jewish identity for our young people. The only thing that will work is a set of affirmatives that forms them as a people."

A: There seems to me to be a schizophrenia in the Jewish community. I get many letters and take many phone calls on the air and people say, "I'm white and I'm Jewish," which means that, like, when it's convenient I can be white, and then, when I'm attacked, I'm Jewish. They got to deal with that.

Q: That's a "schizophrenia" that's almost endemic to the American Jewish experience. The lower-class Jew, whose parents came from Eastern Europe, has always felt himself an outsider. I can't imagine any such Jewish kid in school pledging allegiance to the flag who really thought that it was his flag entirely. That feeling of vulnerability intensifies in time of stress.

A: I find it interesting that every other group, including blacks, will say they are Italian-American, German-American, Afro-American—except Jews. I think one of the things which is happening now, if it can be allowed to happen, is that the relationships between the Jewish community and the black community are being reordered. It's been a very patronizing relationship;

the Jews haven't realized that. OK, Shanker marches in Selma. Be serious. I mean who cares, for crying out loud! The relationship has *not* been defined by black people. And so you go around the country, and you talk and talk and talk, or you write and write and write—I just reread *The Fire Next Time*—it is fantastically contemporary, just as valid now as it was in '62. Bestseller and all that—it didn't do no good; nobody listened to it. So it takes a poem by a fifteen-year-old girl, that kick in the stomach, that Zen slap, to finally make people really take what you say seriously. Like Baldwin says in *The Fire Next Time*—is there going to be any hope, will it mean that white people, and I include Jews, are going to have to look at themselves differently, are going to have to change themselves. You know, I didn't know that Shanker was a Jew until he accused me of being an anti-Semite; I'm talking about me, as a black person. Then I figured that he was a Jew. All right, when he's going to accuse me of being something which I'm not—then my only defense is, all right, I'll go ahead and be it, goddammit!

Q: But in your own case, being an intellectual, isn't there a tension between intellect and emotion at that point?

A: Well, I think it's a question of being an intellectual who is divorced by twenty leagues from the masses of people or being divorced by five leagues. You're never going to be totally with them. And my reaction is just as a human being—I'm not much of an intellectual, you know—I had this experience: I did a TV interview in Cleveland. I *really* hated the producer and the moderator of the show. I really hated them. I hated them as people. *They* thought I hated them as *whites*. There was no way I could let them know that I hated them as *people*, because of who they were. And this is the same thing! They were the kind of liberals whose basic attitude was, "Yes, you can come here and say what you want to say, but I'm not going to listen, and it's not going to change my mind. I'm going to be nice and courteous the entire time, and you're just not going to reach me." If Shanker accuses me of being an anti-Semite, then I cannot prove that I'm not anti-Semitic. It would be futile for me to stand up and say, "Oh no, but I'm not; don't accuse me of that." Then I'm fighting the battle on his territory as he defines it, and that becomes a problem. The problem is one of the relationship of power. But Jews think it's a question of morality.

Q: But does that necessarily mean, as you said earlier, that if he's going to call you one, you're going to be one? I mean, if you're not an anti-Semite, why let him make you into one?

A: Let's put it this way: If it's very clear that he is brutalizing me for his own ends, then I'm going to retaliate, and I will retaliate in the way that will most hurt him. I don't think I have any other choice. I don't want to be called an anti-Semite for it. And that can be better understood if you understand that black people are a colonized people. You have, you know, two groups—the colonized and the colonizers. And the Jewish community is in the position of being on the side of the colonizer.

Q: This reminds me of your line on the radio the other night, which was not covered by the press, that "We are America's Jews, the Jews think we are the Germans."

A: Right. And the Jews are in the position of being Germans.

Q: Yet there is this thesis, that black people, if and when they are anti-Semitic, feel themselves, at least in that way, to be part of the majority. And there is a corollary to that, from historian Joseph Boskin, that selecting the Jew as a scapegoat fills an important psychic need for the black. To bait the Jew is to claim superiority to the Jew and to identify with the white community that still contains considerable elements of anti-Semitism.

A: You see, once again, he's hooking into traditional concepts of anti-Semitism. Jews are not being used as a scapegoat for the problems of black people. Jews happen to be in a position of power. Blacks want power, thus Jews and blacks are in conflict. There is no scapegoat involved; they are directly involved in the life and the control of the black community. We are not reaching outside. It's not that the schools are filled with Irish and we are looking over to Scarsdale or someplace, and it's the fault of the Jews. They are right there in the community. So no scapegoat; *they are the ones.* They are not the *only* ones. Every black person I've had on my show has pointed that out, and Les pointed it out, and the three guys from N.Y.U. pointed it out—they are not what's called "the enemy"; but if you are a colonized people,

then you are not going to break down the colonizer into categories of lesser or greater magnitude of enemy. The enemy is the
enemy, and you deal with him as you come to him, and right now
we are dealing with him on the level of schools, and there he is.

Q: In Ocean Hill-Brownsville, where there is at least some degree of community control, twenty-two of the Jewish teachers,
led by Chuck Isaac, said at a press conference the other day they
didn't feel any anti-Semitism there, and specifically not from Les
Campbell.

A: What really ticks me is the fact that I didn't know until I
went out to do some interviews at Ocean Hill-Brownsville that
over 50 percent of the new teachers they had hired were Jewish.
And then you find out the thing which you pointed out in your
column, about passing out a leaflet to the kids explaining what
Rosh Hashana was, and all of this. I've sat in Les' Black History
class twice. I've been amazed that Les never *once* used the word
white. He used a variety of words, slave trader, slave owner; he
never *once* used the word white. Whereas, in my class, you know,
I'm much harder than Les is in terms of talking about white
people. I spent quite a bit of time talking to the Jewish teachers
who were there, the young kids. My feeling was I wish the school
had all black teachers, but there aren't enough blacks available
who could do the job these white kids are doing. They are pulling
really fantastic poetry out of these kids, doing what seemed to
me to be good things; I had no objection to it. If the time comes
when the black community can take over the school completely
and do the same job, then I want blacks to do it, but in the meantime, I mean like, wow, these whites were really filling a role.
And these were young kids who had been politically active, politically involved, and were very aware and were working hard.
There are some beautiful kids out there.

Q: Now there comes the inevitable question. You say, if at such
time the black community can staff the schools by itself, with all
black teachers—does that mean you are opting for separatism?

A: Let me put it this way. At the present point in my own life,
and at the present point in American history, I don't see any
other alternative. We *are* separate, you know. Great Neck, L. I.,
is going to bus in some black kids to add some color. That's a

Jewish community and it's separate. It would be much better to institutionalize that as much as possible and to take care of business, rather than to keep trying to deal with a bunch of people who don't understand, who won't understand.

Q: So you would probably say that the function of the white Jewish teachers who are now in Ocean Hill-Brownsville and doing well would be to perhaps address their educational and spiritual skills to white kids if and when the time comes when black teachers will fully staff the Ocean Hill-Brownsville schools?

A: They are the only ones who can do it, and they could do a fantastic job. That's where it needs to happen. White kids need to study black history as much as black kids do. And, you know, if a white cat's running it down to white kids, white teachers who understand the black frame of reference, that black reality, that's the only way the change is going to happen. But the thing that it comes down to is that young whites don't like white people, and blacks happen to like black people, so they want to be with us. I come back to what I said before: Where has the New Left been when we needed them? Like, I'll speak to white high school students now; I will *not* speak to white college students anymore.

Q: Why?

A: Because you speak and you speak and you speak, you write books, they read books, and all that, and they understand, you know. Still, when you need them, they aren't there. There is a need which exists in the black community which I can fill. There is a need in the white community which *they* can fill. I mean, why hasn't SDS been able to run into a synagogue as quick as they ran into N.Y.U. to keep James Reston of *The Times* from speaking?

Q: You've mentioned SDS going into N.Y.U. to stop Reston from speaking; they also shouted down the South Vietnamese ambassador to the U.N. It seems to me that this, in its way, is very similar to people trying to suppress you and WBAI. So that if I am, and I am, for Les Campbell having absolute freedom to say whatever he wants to say anywhere, I have to add that apply-

408

ing "discriminative tolerance," as Herbert Marcuse would put it, anywhere, really injures anyone's right to free speech and thereby seriously limits the possibility of bringing real social and political change.

A: I've had very mixed reactions, you know, having been picketed and having that strange experience of being escorted through a police line by a cop.

Q: How did that feel?

A: It felt very normal—the people were going to kill me if they could have gotten me, but I could understand that. I felt that the cop was doing what he should be doing, helping black people. But my feeling toward the people who were picketing me was that they had a right to do that. I thought first of going to the station early, at four o'clock; they wouldn't be there until seven —and just staying inside the station. And then I said, no, they have a right. They hate me so much, they should at least have a chance to see me and really scream and yell and do whatever else. I even felt, which is my own personal whatever you want to call it, that they had a right to beat me if they could have gotten me. I wouldn't willingly have given myself to them. But I understood how they felt because if I could have gotten my hands on Dean Rusk I would have felt that I had the right to beat him. OK now, you know, there is the position that the oppressed can do no wrong. And the oppressor can do no right. On a humanistic basis, I would have to agree with you. On a revolutionary basis, I don't think that the ambassador from South Vietnam should be allowed to speak.

Q: But this is like the cliché about being slightly pregnant. Once you start limiting that right to speak—even for what you consider the best revolutionary reasons—you start precedents that other people can use against you.

A: Who am I to say who can speak and who can't speak? If I don't feel this cat has a right to say who can speak and who can't speak, then he feels that naturally I don't have the right to limit him. So to reach a compromise everybody speaks, and I support that. I have to support that, I really do, despite the fact that there are a lot of people I don't want to speak to and whom I would like to punch in the mouth once they start speaking. OK, let them talk. So that makes me an Uncle Tom revolutionary, I guess.

But there's another dimension here. One of my black listeners wrote me and said that freedom of speech is OK as long as it is white people's. I have really resented all the people who ask me, why I didn't say something to disclaim the remark the guy made —you know, about Hitler and the lampshades. There's the assumption that I was the Establishment's representative on the air. He made a flat statement. I was shocked by the statement. I would not have said it. However, knowing damn well that the black community does not have honest access to the air, I was not going to put him down. He had a perfect right to say that, you know. And that is my role in the media—to give the black community access to speak as they see fit. I'm not going to set the standards. But white folks and I guess Jews, too, expected me to be their representative, and that's what shook them up—that they had a black man at a microphone who was not going to be their representative.

Q: Probably for the first time in your life you've had this kind of instant fame, if fame is the word, in which you have become a stereotyped, faceless person to all those people who are demanding all kinds of things done to you, or because of you. How does that feel?

A: On the one hand, it makes me feel like I'm a sitting duck, because *The New York Times* can sit there and shoot at me, day after day after day, and I can't do a damn thing. I know that my listeners, however many I have, do not have the same reaction. I've been thinking a lot about Alger Hiss who is now synonymous with traitor, and will be through time immemorial—like Benedict Arnold—and Alger Hiss is probably a very beautiful cat. It doesn't matter. On the other hand, I'm glad that my listeners know me as an individual and I think they relate to me like that, not as a black individual. I'm very, very patient on the air with people. I am a person who happens to be black whom they can talk to. I won't cuss them out and all that—that's my personality, I don't cuss out people, because it takes too much energy. And also I really believe in people. I believe if you take people where they are, and don't put them down, they will move from point A to point B. It's a political decision I made a couple of years ago to

410

be that way. So to them, my listeners, I became an individual. But I'm not. For most of my life, I was a nigger. So you write a couple of books and you're on the radio and suddenly you're an individual. I was in no danger of being under any illusion about being an individual, and this only helps remind me that when I say something white folk don't like, I'm still a nigger, you know, ain't nothing changed. They will view me as they seek to view me, not as I define myself. They won't come to me and find out. I don't want my listeners or anybody to ever forget that any differences between me and the young brother on the block with a .38 in his belt are only superficial.

q: Did *The New York Times* ever contact you to find out what you thought?

a: Never, never. The story broke in the early Thursday morning edition of the *Times*. The *New York Post* called me at 3 A.M. and asked me my reaction, and they printed it. New York's Channel 2 (WCBS) has interviewed me twice, even though they only used ten or fifteen seconds once, but *The New York Times* never contacted me about any of it. They published a few sentences from the WBAI statement on it. They, more than any other news media in New York, I hold responsible for this problem, and I'm really very, very bitter about the way they have handled it. I mean, they don't realize it, not that it matters, but they have set the black community up for the most dire of consequences— given the hatred of blacks which exists and which I think Jews have been surprised to feel in themselves. What if Nixon makes any moves against the black community in toto? You see, I will never forget the *Times* editorial on the death of Malcolm X. They said he who lives by the sword shall die by the sword, and good riddance. That is exactly what they said. If anything is being created in the city, it's an anti-black hysteria which I have not even seen in the South. This is the second time it's happened since I've been here. The first time was in 1964—when the attempt was made to close the World's Fair on the first day, and was followed by the whole "Blood Brothers" myth and the Harlem Six case. I thought I was back down South. I really feel that the reaction of even sedate middle-class black people I've been in contact with has been one of "I have no choice but to go out in the streets and start shooting people." No, they don't even give us the benefit of the doubt that maybe we have a thought-out position. They hear the dog bark and so they react and they say that is what the dog is barking about.

Q: And the Jews who are now so fearful seem unable to recognize the fear that black people feel?

A: Yeah, right. I can sit down and be interviewed, talk on the radio, write and all this, but whites have to communicate with that fifteen-year-old kid on the block with the .38 in his belt; he ain't going to talk to them like I do. If he sees 100,000 white people on the street marching on City Hall, marching against *The New York Times*, that will communicate to him, but don't tell him about no good white folks or no good Jews, because he is not an individual. They are not going to ask him, did you major in English or did you shine your shoes this morning—they are going to shoot him.

Q: Do you think it is going to get worse?

A: Hey, it is election year. 1969 in New York City is going to be so bad. You know, I would not be surprised if Mayor Lindsay takes a trip to Israel before the election. And if Mayor Lindsay has totally written off the black community, he is running scared and whoever the Democrats put up—you already have hints that they are going to use the school thing, they are going to use the law and order thing, they are going to use . . .

Q: The first candidate is James Scheuer, the Congressman from the Bronx, who has a good voting record in Congress, but is so far running in part on a law and order program.

A: Right. And I think that this election is going to so further divide this city and exacerbate what now exists—and what now exists is thousands of tons of TNT—that, you know, I feel like we are sitting in this damn canoe going down the Colorado Rapids and there ain't nothin' nobody can do because they never believe what black people say anyway. We screamed racism for 400 years. It was not believed until the Kerner Commission comes out and says, hey, there's racism. Now all the white folks say, "Yeah, there's racism in America, that's right!" We've been saying it all along. So that once again, we're asking, where are those people who understand, why aren't they saying something?

24 / Change and Resistance: A Psychotherapeutic View of Race Relations

PAUL WACHTEL

The inequities in American society are so apparent and the need for broad social reform so acute that it is easy to overlook, in the plight of black Americans, what may seem like fine points in individual psychodynamics. It may seem foolish to worry about the unconscious wishes of a man who is hungry, perhaps even pernicious to suggest that Negroes in America, who have been making thunderously audible their demand for change, may actually fear and resist the very changes for which they are clamoring. Yet the experience of thousands of psychotherapists in the past half-century or so has made it clear that human beings who suffer deeply and who want change desperately do nonetheless show resistance to change and unconsciously sabotage efforts to bring change about.

It is my intention to examine below the possibility that, like psychotherapy patients, many Negroes unknowingly strive to undo the changes they seek. Such resistance is obviously not the main reason that change in American race relations has been so pitifully slow—whites have openly, or behind pious liberal words, fought to maintain their privilege at the Negro's expense. But with a problem of the complexity and magnitude of America's racial turmoil, no possible increment in understanding, no possible source of additional leverage should be overlooked.

To compare the Negro's situation to that of the psychotherapy patient is not to suggest that what most Negroes need is psychotherapy. First of all, any psychotherapy is only minimally effective when the patient continues to live in an inordinately difficult

SOURCE: *Forum* 11 (Winter 1968), 18–21. Copyright © 1968 by the Trustees of Columbia University in the City of New York.
   Paul Wachtel is on the faculty of the Psychology Department at New York University.

PAUL WACHTEL   413

environment. Effective psychotherapy requires the assistance of a milieu that encourages, or at the very least tolerates, the patient's growth. Secondly, and related, psychotherapy is a method of coping with intrapsychic difficulties, with conflicts largely internal, with neurotic distortions that force a person to work against himself. The majority of the Negro's troubles are caused and maintained by the organization of society and must be solved primarily through substantial social reform.

There are, however, some important commonalities in the life situations of Negroes and psychotherapy patients which if recognized may make such reform efforts more effective. For one, both Negroes and psychotherapy patients tend to be dissatisfied with their lot in life and wish to change the way they are living. On the surface, the nature of the change desired might appear to be radically different for patients and Negroes. Patients come to therapy to change *themselves*. Negroes want a change in an oppressive *social system*. But the complaints of many patients reveal that in many respects they feel it is not *they* who should be different, but their spouses, parents, children, bosses, etc. And with the kind of damage our society has inflicted upon the Negro psyche, many Negroes do wish that *they* could act differently, aside from how the white man behaves. The intense resentment among many Negroes of "Uncle Toms," for example, reflects how painful it is to perceive oneself as behaving in a submissive manner that aids the system one hates. The concern about and intense response to Uncle Tomism would probably be much less were there no temptations to such behavior lurking in the psyche of those who cry out against it.

Psychotherapy patients enter treatment because they are suffering. Consciously the patient wants nothing more than to change, to live differently. He is fed up with things as they are. Yet very shortly it becomes apparent that, despite his conscious wish to change and to cooperate with the therapist, he is doing a great deal to sabotage the treatment. He may miss many appointments with flimsy excuses, or be silent a good portion of the hour, or waste most of his time with frivolous gossip or gratuitous complaints and questions about the therapist. He may sense that there is something irrational and self-defeating about his behavior, and that the reasons he gives for it do not ring true. But how can it be that he is resisting getting well? This does not seem to make sense. He knows how deeply he wants to change and to cooperate with his treatment. Sometimes it becomes apparent that this kind of behavior occurs most often as progress and insight seem about to come, and the patient may begin to be aware that he is indeed fighting his own therapy.

Freud recognized the identity of those "resistances" with the forces that caused and maintained the patient's difficulty in the first place. Certain wishes, fantasies, and feelings are intolerable to the patient and would cause enormous anxiety if fully experienced in consciousness. These wishes, thoughts, and feelings are therefore repressed, kept out of awareness, and a great many other defenses are also erected in the service of keeping them from full expression. The distortion in the patient's personality resulting from his exhausting defensive efforts is the source of the patient's neurosis. The repressed impulses present far less danger to him as an adult than they did to the helpless child who could less easily control his impulses or his world. But as an adult he resists their expression as vigorously as he did as a desperate child, and he resists the efforts to release them in therapy as he does everywhere else.

One source of the patient's resistance, then, is the continuation in therapy of his constant struggle to keep offending ideas from awareness. But there is a second source of resistance, one that Freud called secondary gain. By the time a patient comes to therapy, his symptoms, or at least the personality deformations that lie behind them, have been with him for a long time. They have become a fact of life for him, a challenge to the remaining healthy trends in his personality that attempt to make the best of them. Since the healthy features of even the most troubled neurotic may still remain considerable, patients often are remarkably successful at making an asset of an unpleasant necessity. The man neurotically inhibited in expressing aggression may become extremely well liked as a "gentle" or "reasonable" man; or the woman subject to periods of anxiety and depression may manage to make her needs the concern of the entire household and elicit extraordinarily solicitous behavior from her husband and children. The price paid for these "gains" is almost always excessive, but this poor bargain may seem to the patient the best he can get. In many cases the core of his system of security and gratification is based on maintaining whatever advantages accrue from these secondary adjustments, and he is terrified of giving them up. The very limitations he comes to therapy to rid himself of are at the same time his most potent source of gratification. The more his environment rewards his symptoms and the larger the proportion of his pleasures derived in this way, the more difficult will be the task of therapy.

The readiness of troubled human beings to resist change may be further illustrated by an interesting shift in attitude toward a basic tenet of Freud's view of man: the challenge to the belief in "will power." Freud noted in 1917 that his discovery of the extreme limitation upon conscious control of behavior was a blow to man's narcissism comparable to those dealt by Copernicus and Darwin. His contemporaries were quite reluctant to view their actions as anything but freely chosen.

One must marvel at how men have come to terms with Freud's view in the ensuing half-century. Today, many people are only too willing to concede that they lack control over what they think, feel, or do; for with such an admission comes a very great reward—lack of responsibility. Many individuals seem aching to be determined, to be acted upon. Freud's great threat to man's self-esteem becomes for them a beloved security blanket to which they cling tenaciously. In therapy, efforts to talk to such individuals as fellow human beings, as subjects rather than objects, are vigorously countered, either by explicit references to Freud's views on determinism, or more subtly by focusing constantly on the events which seem to cause or influence their behavior. Psychotherapists are increasingly recognizing how tempting is the flight from responsibility, and how necessary for change is some measure of belief that a man can take charge of his own life. Many therapists are seeing their job much less as one of demonstrating to patients how they are determined and more as one of enabling them to feel free.

The Horatio Alger myth may be oppressive and intimidating as well as encouraging. One can detect wish as well as fear in the myriad complaints about how our computerized society limits human action and choice.

But there is one group in our society for which the claim that they are objects of social forces has been quite close to the whole truth: the Negroes. Until quite recently, the fact that a man's skin was black was sufficient to deny him most good jobs. Though there were some outstanding exceptions, in most cases the cards were stacked so heavily against the Negro that he had little choice but to conclude that it doesn't pay to try. Such reasoning was not rationalization; it reflected accurate perception of a social reality.

The oppressive forces to which Negroes were subjected forced them to find ways of coping with a world of restricted opportunity, and to develop some means of maintaining security within that world. These adaptive efforts, however, so vital as emergency responses to the onslaughts of ghetto life, may be a great hindrance to the acceptance and encouragement of changes that Negroes so desperately want. As Kenneth Clark has noted, "the invisible walls of a segregated society are not only damaging but protective in a debilitating way. There is considerable psychological safety in the ghetto. . . . Most Negroes take the first steps into an integrated society tentatively and torn with conflict."

Ironically, the black leaders most committed to exposing America's rapacious racism seem to be denying the most serious crime committed against American black men—the distortion of human potential. Their reaction to the Moynihan report, or to Styron's "Confessions of Nat Turner," is a reflection of this tendency. It is perhaps a valid moral diagnosis to claim that the "Negro problem" is really the white man's problem, that it is the white soul that is sick. But on a secular, practical, and psychological level it is necessary to face fully the harsh reality that many Negroes in this country have been psychologically crippled; many Negroes today, bearing the stigmata of oppression, do enter competition in many areas with limited skills and capacities that are but a tragic shadow of their natural potential.

In a seeming paradox, the opportunities now gradually opening for Negroes may be putting many ghetto dwellers into even more acute discomfort than the quiet misery to which they were accustomed. The scars of oppression remain, in the form of self-hatred and impaired capacities, but with a reduction in the visible and explicit injustices, it becomes more difficult to locate the trouble as coming totally from outside. Those Negroes who most depended for their self-esteem and identity upon their special status as victims, who managed to derive "secondary gains" from their oppressed position, must find the developing changes in society bewildering and threatening. What happens after you convince a man that he is incapable of controlling his fate, after you take away his confidence, and leave him raw except for his knowledge that you are to blame, and then you try to make it look as though you are blameless? The accomplishments of civil rights and anti-poverty legislation have clearly been pitifully small compared to the staggering need. But may not some of the intensity of the comtemptuous appraisal of such efforts by many ghetto leaders derive from the need to denigrate these efforts in order to maintain the image of a totally savage and oppressive society? It is to such an image that many ghetto dwellers are accustomed. And most men tend to feel safer with a known quantity, even if unpleasant, than with the unforeseen.

If such unconscious resistance is a part of the dynamics of our present situation, then an additional perspective is required on the riots which have become so ominous a part of American race relations. Many liberals have been discouraged that cities like Detroit and New Haven, where relatively strong efforts had been made to deal with ghetto problems, have been among the hardest hit. There is a danger that this discouragement may lessen the vigor of efforts toward enlightened social change. Certainly a major factor motivating the riots is the desire on the part of ghetto dwellers to break out of the degrading circumstances forced upon them, to call attention to their plight and express their seething rage at a social order that mocks and torments them. The above considerations suggest, however, that although much of the frenzy has derived from the feeling that change is much too slow, some of it actually may have had as its source the fear that things are changing too *fast*. Some rioters may have been acting out their terror at feeling the rug pulled out from under them, as their adaptive strategies begin to seem geared to a passing era. If this is so, then our efforts to right society's wrongs may be having more success than we realized. The turmoil in the ghettos may reflect in part the feeling (ambivalently experienced) that times *are* changing, and might well be viewed not as a discouraging sign to ditch existing efforts, but as a signal to *intensify* our efforts and take these remaining steps to the goal, finally in sight, of an equal society. Recognition of the fear and open discussion of it by blacks and whites can help promote jettisoning of outmoded adaptive patterns and building of newer

418

ones. We surely have a long way to go, but the way is made longer both when roadblocks are not recognized and when despair at the distance slows us down. The perspective on the riots offered here (and it may, within limits, be relevant to other discouraging phenomena, such as excessive school drop-out rates or unreliable job performance) may help allay some of the despair and urge us in the direction of necessary efforts.

The idea that the riots may reflect both the feeling that change is too slow and the fear that it is too fast is not as strange as it may seem at first. The cooperation of diverse and conflicting personality trends to produce a single result is quite familiar to the psychotherapist. Many symptoms and character traits are simultaneous expressions of two or more conflicting wishes. In fending off hostile feelings toward her child, a mother, for example, may become excessively solicitous, thereby fulfilling her defensive need to be a "good" mother, and at the same time expressing her hostility through a stultifying "smother love" that does not let the child grow. The riots were not only an angry warning to Whitey that he better hurry up and recognize the black man as his equal; they may also be viewed as a kind of sabotage (though no doubt mostly unconscious) of the efforts that have been made, an effective means of arousing enough fear and indignation in the white community to slow down the flow of progressive legislation and bring forth the familiar figure of a George Wallace to reinforce the stereotype of monolithic white racism. The single act of rioting could serve both wishes, the wish to speed change and the wish to slow it down.

It is the pervasive role of conflict in human behavior which is unrecognized in the simplistic thinking of racists, whose claim that "our people don't really want things to change; they like things just the way they are" may be confused with the position advanced here. Negroes in America most certainly do want things to change. They want it desperately and only a blind man could fail to perceive it. That they may also fear the change doesn't make their desire any less "real," it merely makes it human.

VI / The Challenge
of the Environment:
Control or Chaos?

"Fate is the air we breathe," writes Robert Penn Warren. Fate is environment, says the sociologist. Both may be right. Environment (or fate) is not only the air we breathe, the genes we inherit, but the food we eat, the children we propagate, the houses we live in, the politicians we elect, the weapons we design, and the schools we attend. Every change in our environment affects us, whether we live in cities or in the country, whether we marry or remain single, whether we have children or not.

When nineteenth-century England became concerned with environment, its interest was almost solely in the nature of its cities and its neighborhoods—that is, with their aesthetic value. The leading theoretician of "living amidst beauty," John Ruskin, told his audiences repeatedly that taste—how we design our buildings, streets, and cities—was "essentially a moral quality. . . . Tell me what you like and I'll tell you what you are." A nation is known, Ruskin insisted, by the structures it sanctioned; that is, by the environment it created for its citizens. A people unconcerned with the way it lives, Ruskin maintained, is a people infected by "domestic corruption."

Ruskin's views may now seem naive, but only because we so take for granted the ugliness around us. As Americans, we accept the pollution, the contamination, and desecration of water, air, and land as "natural" by-products of the technological process. And this ugliness which we accept exists in virtually every aspect of our lives. While Ruskin was concerned with aesthetics —how we live, what we build—today we find ourselves as twentieth-century creatures involved in much more complicated questions of environment than any Victorian thinker ever could have envisioned.

In many ways, beauty is not the issue, but simply survival. A growing society that does not plan for the almost infinite ramifications of its expansion is a society that hurtles out of control. When modern theoreticians like Lewis Mumford and Paul Goodman discuss our environment, they do so with the wonder of men who see chaos as being more informative than control. All of us, clearly, are implicated from the moment we are born.

Most of the time, radical ideas in science take place far from our eyes and distant from the news media; yet these revolutions, as in the current biological discoveries which Donald Fleming describes, will profoundly modify our sense of our environment. At present, a biological breakthrough is expected in the area of "genetic tailoring." Once considered inviolable, the human process of reproduction may be altered—Huxley's *Brave New World* becomes fact. The possibilities of this "tailoring" are, obviously, immense and far-reaching, and even if we are among the "untampered," we will at some stage share the world of the "new mutants."

While very divergent in their conclusions, Moshe Safdie and Norman Mailer have observed a similar phenomenon: that some pattern or plan must be imposed upon our experience to prevent deterioration of our environment. They are chiefly concerned with the cities and their development, but their ideas are widely applicable to the entire field of conservation. Deterioration in one area is symptomatic of a general deterioration. They both insist that we must care about our environment or else become its victims. Each proposes a radical surgery to check the disintegration.

As we move into the seventies, another danger is emerging with insistent clarity: not only our cities but our total environment suffers from ecological backlash. An historian of ideas, Lynn White, explores our past for the roots of this growing crisis and concludes that the attitude of "orthodox Christian arrogance" towards nature, by infiltrating science and technology, has shaped our landscapes and influenced the natural selection in human population. Unless man wants a future more disastrous than the present pollution of his environment, he must surrender the belief that he is lord and master of all he surveys and instead practice the profoundly religious doctrine of humility expressed by St. Francis, "the greatest radical in Christian history since Christ."

25 / On Living in a Biological Revolution

DONALD FLEMING

Here are a dozen things that we have discovered in the last fifteen years.

1. *We have discovered* the structure of the genetic substance DNA—the double helix of Watson and Crick—the general nature of the process by which the chromosomal strands are replicated.

2. *We have discovered* in viruses how to achieve the perfect replication of DNA molecules that are biologically effective.

3. *We have discovered* the code by which DNA specifies the insertion of amino acids in proteins.

4. *We have discovered* how to produce hybrid cells between the most diverse vertebrate species, including hybrids between man and mouse; and some of these hybrids have gone on multiplying for several (cellular) generations.

5. *We have discovered* the power of viruses to invade bacterial and other cells and to insert the genes of the virus into the genome of the host; and we have good reason to conjecture, though not yet to affirm, that this phenomenon is involved in cancer.

6. *We have discovered* hormonal contraceptives and grasped in principle the strategy for devising a contraceptive pill for *both* sexes, by knocking out certain hormones of the hypothalamus, the master sexual gland of the body.

7. *We have discovered* on a large scale in the livestock industry that deep-frozen mammalian sperm, suitably mixed with

SOURCE: *Atlantic Monthly* 223 (March 1969), 64–70. Copyright © 1969 Donald Fleming.
Donald Fleming teaches history at Harvard University.

glycerol, can be banked indefinitely and drawn upon as desired to produce viable offspring.

8. *We have discovered* in human females how to produce superovulation, the release of several eggs into the oviduct at the same time instead of the customary one, with the possibility on the horizon of withdrawing substantial numbers of human eggs for storage, culture in test tubes, or surgical manipulation, without destroying their viability.

9. *We have discovered* in rabbits how to regulate the sex of offspring by removing fertilized ova from the female before they become implanted in the wall of the uterus, "sexing" the embryos by a technique entailing the deletion of some 200 to 300 cells, flushing embryos of the "wrong" sex down the drain, and then in a substantial minority of cases, successfully reinserting in the uterus embryos of the desired sex that proceed to develop normally.

10. *We have discovered* drugs, above all the hallucinogens, that simulate psychotic states of mind; and have thereby rendered it plausible that the latter are the product of "inborn errors of metabolism" and as such remediable by the administration of drugs.

11. *We have discovered* in principle, and to a certain extent in practice, how to repress the immunological "defenses" of the body.

12. *We have discovered* a combination of immunological and surgical techniques by which the kidney, liver, or heart can be transplanted with fair prospects of the recipient's survival for months or even years—the first constructive proposal for turning our death wish on the highways to some advantage.

Each of these is a major discovery or complex of discoveries in itself, but they add up to far more than the sum of their parts. They constitute a veritable Biological Revolution likely to be as decisive for the history of the next 150 years as the Industrial Revolution has been for the period since 1750.

Definitions of what constitutes a revolution are legion. An undoctrinaire formulation would be that every full-scale revolution has three main components: a distinctive attitude toward the world; a program for utterly transforming it; and an unshakable, not to say fanatical, confidence that this program can be enacted —a world view, a program, and a faith.

In this sense, Darwinism did not usher in a full-scale biological revolution. Darwinism was a profoundly innovating world view, but one that prescribed no steps to be taken, no victories over nature to be celebrated, no program of triumphs to be successively gained. Indeed, one of the most plausible constructions to be put upon it was that nothing much *could* be done except to submit patiently to the winnowing processes of nature.

This defect was not lost upon Darwin's own cousin Sir Francis Galton, who tried to construct an applied science of eugenics for deliberately selecting out the best human stocks. But Galtonian eugenics was sadly lacking in any authentic biological foundation. Once the science of Mendelian genetics came to general notice about 1900, a more promising form of eugenics began to commend itself, the effort to induce artificial mutation of genes in desirable directions.

This was long the animating faith of one of the most extraordinary Americans of the twentieth century, the geneticist Herman J. Muller. He was the actual discoverer, in 1927, of artificial mutation through X rays. But this great achievement, for which he got the Nobel Prize, was a tremendous disappointment to Muller the revolutionary. There was no telling which genes would mutate in which direction, and he came to suspect that the vast majority of mutations were actually harmful in the present situation of the human race.

Muller at the end of his life—he died in 1967—was thrown back upon essentially Galtonian eugenics. He did bring this up to date by his proposal for sperm banks in which the sperm of exceptionally intelligent and socially useful men could be stored for decades and used for artificial insemination. He also envisioned, in the not too distant future, ova banks for storing superior human eggs. But none of these modern touches, these innovations in technique, could conceal the fact that this was still the old eugenics newly garbed, but equally subjective and imprecise.

Biological Engineering

The Biological Revolution that Muller failed to bring off was already in progress when he died, but on very different terms from his own. There is a new eugenics in prospect, not the marriage agency kind, but a form of "biological engineering." When this actually comes to pass, chromosomes, segments of chromosomes, and even individual genes will be inserted at will into the genome. Alternatively, germ cells cultured in laboratories will be enucleated and entire tailor-made DNA molecules substituted. Alternatively still, superior genes will be brought into play by hybridization of cells.

The detailed variants upon these general strategies are almost innumerable. They all have in common the fact that they cannot be accomplished at present except in viruses and bacteria or in cell cultures. But it would be a bold man who would dogmatically affirm that none of these possibilities could be brought to bear upon human genetics by the year 2000.

That is a long way off for the firebrands of the Biological Revolution. The Nobel Prize winner Joshua Lederberg in particular has been pushing the claims of a speedier remedy, christened by him "euphenics," and defined as "the engineering of human development." The part of human development that fascinates Lederberg the most is embryology, seen by him as the process of initially translating the instructions coded in the DNA into "the living, breathing organism." Embryology, he says, is "very much in the situation of atomic physics in 1900; having had an honorable and successful tradition it is about to begin!" He thinks it will not take long to mature—"from 5 to no more than 20 years." He adds that most predictions of research progress in recent times have proved to be "far too conservative."

The progress that Lederberg has in mind is the application of new embryological techniques to human affairs. He is at once maddened and obsessed by the nine-months phase in which the human organism has been exempted from experimental and therapeutic intervention—such a waste of time before the scientists can get at us. But the embryo's turn is coming. It would be incredible, he says, "if we did not soon have the basis of developmental engineering technique to regulate, for example, the size of the human brain by prenatal or early postnatal intervention."

Sex Control

Nothing as sensational as this has yet been attempted, but the new phase in embryology that Lederberg heralded is undoubtedly getting under way. The most conspicuous figure at present is

Robert Edwards of the physiology laboratory at Cambridge University. In 1966 Edwards reported the culture of immature egg cells from the human ovary up to the point of ripeness for fertilization. He made tentative claims to have actually achieved fertilization in test tubes. The incipient hullabaloo in the newspapers about the specter of "test tube babies" led Edwards to clamp a tight lid of security over his researches in progress.

In the spring of this year, however, he and Richard Gardner announced their success in "sexing" fertilized rabbit eggs before implantation in the wall of the uterus and then inducing 20 percent of the reinserted eggs to produce normal full-term infants. The aspect of these findings that attracted general attention, the prospect of regulating the sex of mammalian offspring, is not likely to be of permanent interest. For this purpose, Edwards and Gardner's technique is obviously a clumsy expedient by comparison with predetermining the "sex" of spermatozoa—presently impossible but certainly not inconceivable within the next generation.

The real importance of Edwards and Gardner's work lies elsewhere. They have opened up the possibility of subjecting the early embryo to microsurgery, with the deletion and "inoculation" of cells at the will of the investigator, *and* the production of viable offspring from the results. The manufacture of "chimeras" in the modern biological sense—that is, with genetically distinct cells in the same organism—is clearly in prospect.

Work in this vein has just begun. The only branch of euphenics that has already become something more than a promising growth stock in science is the suppression of immunological reactions against foreign tissues and the accompanying, highly limited, successes in the transplantation of organs.

Biological Revolutionaries

The technical details and immediate prospects in eugenics and euphenics, however fascinating, are less important than the underlying revolutionary temper in biology. The most conspicuous representatives of this temper are Lederberg himself, the biochemical geneticist Edward L. Tatum, and Francis Crick of the model—all of them Nobel Prize winners, with the corresponding leverage upon public opinion. Robert Edwards, though slightly singed by the blast of publicity about test tube babies, is clearly in training for the revolutionary cadre.

One of the stigmata of revolutionaries in any field is their resolute determination to break with traditional culture. For a scientist, the most relevant definition of culture is his own field of research. All of these men would angrily resent being bracketed with biologists in general. Biology has always been a rather loose confederation of naturalists and experimentalists, overlapping in both categories with medical researchers. Today even the pretense that these men somehow constitute a community has been frayed to the breaking point.

At Harvard, for example, the revolutionaries have virtually seceded from the old Biology Department and formed a new department of their own, Biochemistry and Molecular Biology. The younger molecular biologists hardly bother to conceal their contempt for the naturalists, whom they see as old fogies obsequiously attentive to the world as it is rather than bent upon turning it upside down.

In one respect, the molecular biologists do overlap with the contemporary naturalists and indeed with most creative scientists in general—in their total detachment from religion. In a way, this is a point that could have been made at any time in the last seventy-five years, but with one significant difference. Herman Muller, for example, born in 1890, had no truck with religion. But he was self-consciously antireligious.

The biological revolutionaries of today are not antireligious but simply unreligious. They give the impression not of defending themselves against religion but of subsisting in a world where that has never been a felt pressure upon them. They would agree with many devout theologians that we are living in a post-Christian world, to such an extent that some of the most doctrinaire biological revolutionaries are able to recognize without embarrassment, and even with a certain gracious condescension, that Christianity did play a useful role in defining the values of the Western world.

The operative word here is in the past tense. Francis Crick says that the facts of science are producing and must produce values that owe nothing to Christianity. "Take," he says, "the suggestion of making a child whose head is twice as big as normal. There is going to be no agreement between Christians and any humanists who lack their particular prejudice about the sanctity of the individual, and who simply want to try it scientifically."

This sense of consciously taking up where religion left off is illuminating in another sense for the revolutionary character of contemporary biology. The parallel is very marked between the original Christian Revolution against the values of the classical world and the Biological Revolution against religious values.

All the great revolutionaries, whether early Christians or molecular biologists, are men of good hope. The future may or may not belong to those who believe in it, but cannot belong to those who don't. Yet at certain points in history, most conspicuously perhaps at intervals between the close of the Thirty Years' War in 1648 and the coming of the Great Depression in 1929, the horizons seem to be wide open, and the varieties of good hope contending for allegiance are numerous. But the tidings of good hope don't become revolutionary except when the horizons begin to close in and the plausible versions of good hope have dwindled almost to the vanishing point.

For the kind of good hope that has the maximum historical impact is the one that capitalizes upon a prevalent despair at the corruption of the existing world, and then carries conviction in pointing to itself as the only possible exit from despair. Above everything else, revolutionaries are the men who keep their spirits up when everybody else's are sagging. In this sense, the greatest revolutionaries of the Western world to date have been precisely the early Christians who dared to affirm in the darkest days of the classical world that something far better was in process and could be salvaged from the ruins.

Both of these points are exemplified in the Biological Revolution that has now begun—despair at our present condition, but infinite hope for the future if the biologists' prescription is taken. Anybody looking for jeremiads on our present state could not do better than to consult the new biologists. "The facts of human reproduction," says Joshua Lederberg, "are all gloomy—the stratification of fecundity by economic status, the new environmental insults to our genes, the sheltering by humanitarian medicine of once-lethal genes."

More generally, the biologists deplore the aggressive instincts of the human animal, now armed with nuclear weapons, his lamentably low average intelligence for coping with increasingly complicated problems, and his terrible prolificity, no longer mitigated by a high enough death rate. It is precisely an aspect of the closing down of horizons and depletion of comfortable hopes in the second half of the twentieth century that conventional medicine is now seen by the biological revolutionaries as one of the greatest threats to the human race.

Yet mere prophets of gloom can never make a revolution. In fact, the new biologists are almost the only group among our contemporaries with a reasoned hopefulness about the long future—if the right path is taken. There are of course many individuals of a naturally cheerful or feckless temperament, today as always, but groups of men with an articulated hope for the future of the entire race are much rarer. The theologians no longer qualify, many Communists have lost their hold upon the future even by their own lights, and the only other serious contenders are the space scientists and astronauts. But just to get off the earth is a rather vague prescription for our ills. Few people even in the space program would make ambitious claims on this score. In a long historical retrospect, they may turn out to have been too modest.

This is not a charge that is likely ever to be leveled against the new biologists. It is well known by now that J. D. Watson begins his account of his double-helix double by saying that he had never seen Francis Crick in a modest mood. But after all, modesty is not the salient quality to be looked for in the new breed of biologists. If the world will only listen, they *know* how to put us on the high road to salvation.

Custom-Made People

What exactly does their brand of salvation entail? Perhaps the most illuminating way to put the matter is that their ideal is the manufacture of man. In a manufacturing process, the number of units to be produced is a matter of rational calculation beforehand and of tight control thereafter. Within certain tolerances, specifications are laid down for a satisfactory product. Quality-control is maintained by checking the output and replacing defective parts. After the product has been put to use, spare parts can normally be supplied to replace those that have worn out.

This is the program of the new biologists—control of numbers by foolproof contraception; gene manipulation and substitution; surgical and biochemical intervention in the embryonic and neonatal phases; organ transplants or replacements at will.

Of these, only contraception is technically feasible at present. Routine organ transplants will probably be achieved for a wide range of suitable organs in less than five years. The grafting of mechanical organs, prosthetic devices inserted in the body, will probably take longer. Joshua Lederberg thinks that embryonic and neonatal intervention may be in flood tide by, say, 1984. As for gene manipulation and substitution in human beings, that is the remotest prospect of all—maybe by the year 2000. But we must not forget Lederberg's well-founded conviction that most predictions in these matters are likely to be too conservative. We are already five to ten years ahead of what most informed people expected to be the schedule for organ transplants in human beings.

The great question becomes, what is it going to be like to be living in a world where such things are coming true? How will the Biological Revolution affect our scheme of values? Nobody could possibly take in all the implications in advance, but some reasonable conjectures are in order.

It is virtually certain that the moral sanctions of birth control are going to be transformed. Down to the present time, the battle for birth control has been fought largely in terms of the individual couple's right to have the number of babies that they want at the desired intervals. But it is built into the quantity-controls envisioned by the Biological Revolution, the control of the biological inventory, that this is or ought to be a question of social policy rather than individual indulgence.

Many factors are converging upon many people to foster this general attitude, but the issue is particularly urgent from the point of view of the biological revolutionaries. In the measure that they succeed in making the human race healthier, first by transplants and later on by genetic tailoring, they will be inexorably swamped by their own successes unless world population is promptly brought under control. The irrepressible Malthus is springing from his lightly covered grave to threaten them with catastrophic victories.

Licensed Babies

The only hope is birth control. The biologists can contribute the techniques, but the will to employ them on the requisite scale is another matter. The most startling proposal to date for actually enforcing birth control does not come from a biologist but from the Nobel-Prize-winning physicist W. B. Shockley, one of the inventors of the transistor. Shockley's plan is to render all women of childbearing age reversibly sterile by implanting a contraceptive capsule beneath the skin, to be removed by a physician only on the presentation of a government license to have a child. The mind boggles at the prospect of bootleg babies. This particular proposal is not likely to be enacted in the near future, even in India.

What we may reasonably expect is a continually rising chorus by the biologists, moralists, and social philosophers of the next generation to the effect that nobody has a right to have children, and still less the right to determine on personal grounds how many. There are many reasons why a couple may not want to be prolific anyhow, so that there might be a happy coincidence between contraception seen by them as a right and by statesmen and biologists as a duty. But the suspicion is that even when people moderate their appetite in the matter of babies, they may still want to have larger families than the earth can comfortably support. The possibility of predetermining sex would undoubtedly be helpful in this respect, but might not be enough to make people forgo a third child. That is where the conflict would arise between traditional values, however moderately indulged, and the values appropriate to the Biological Revolution.

This issue is bound to be fiercely debated. But some of the most profound implications of the Biological Revolution may never present themselves for direct ratification. In all probability, the issues will go by default as we gratefully accept specific boons from the new biology.

Take, for example, the role of the patient in medicine. One of the principal strands in Western medicine from the time of the

Greeks has been the endeavor to enlist the cooperation of the patient in his own cure. In certain respects, this venerable tradition has grown much stronger in the last century. Thus the rising incidence of degenerative diseases, like ulcers, heart trouble, and high blood pressure, has underscored the absolute necessity of inducing the patient to observe a healthful regimen, literally a way of life.

This has been the whole point of Freudian psychiatry as a mode of therapy, that cures can be wrought only by a painful exertion of the patient himself. We often forget, for good reasons, how traditional Freudianism is after the one big shock has been assimilated. In the present context, it actually epitomizes the Western tradition of bringing the patient's own personality to bear upon his medical problems.

Where do we go from here? The degenerative diseases are going to be dealt with increasingly by surgical repair of organs, by organ transplants, and later on by the installation of mechanical organs and eventually by the genetic deletion of weak organs before they occur. The incentive to curb your temper or watch your diet to keep your heart going will steadily decline.

As for mental illness, the near future almost certainly lies with psychopharmacology and the far future with genetic tailoring. Though the final pieces stubbornly decline to fall into place, the wise money is on the proposition that schizophrenia and other forms of psychosis are biochemical disorders susceptible of a pharmacological cure. If we are not presently curing any psychoses by drugs, we are tranquilizing and antidepressing many psychotics and emptying mental hospitals.

Neuroses, the theme of Freudian psychoanalysis, are another matter. It is not easy to envision a biochemical remedy for them. But even for neuroses, we already have forms of behavioral therapy that dispense with the Freudian tenet of implicating the patient in his own cure. For the *very* long future, it is certainly not inconceivable that genetic tailoring could delete neurotic propensities.

Everywhere we turn, the story is essentially the same. Cures are increasingly going to be wrought upon, done to, the patient as a passive object. The strength of his own personality, the force of his character, his capacity for reintegrating himself, are going to be increasingly irrelevant in medicine.

DONALD FLEMING   435

Genetic Tailoring, Boon or Bane?

This leads to what many people would regard as the biggest question of all. In what sense would we have a self to integrate under the new dispensation? The Princeton theologian Paul Ramsey has now been appointed professor of "genetic ethics" at the Georgetown University Medical School, presumably the first appointment of its kind. He thinks that genetic tailoring would be a "violation of man." To this it must be said that under the present scheme of things, many babies get born with catastrophic genes that are not exactly an enhancement of man. Our present genetic self is a brute datum, sometimes very brutal, and anyhow it is hard to see how we can lose our identity before we have any.

As for installing new organs in the body, there is no evident reason why the personality should be infringed upon by heart or kidney transplants per se. Brain transplants would be different, but surely they would be among the last to come. States of mind regulated by drugs we already possess, and obviously they do alter our identity in greater or lesser degree. But even here we must not forget that some identities are intolerable to their distracted possessors.

We must not conclude, however, that the importance of these developments has been exaggerated. The point is that the immediate practical consequences will probably not present themselves as threatening to the individuals involved—quite the contrary. Abstract theological speculations about genetic tailoring would be totally lost upon a woman who could be sure in advance that her baby would not be born mentally retarded or physically handicapped. The private anxieties of individuals are likely to diminish rather than increase any effective resistance to the broader consequences of the Biological Revolution.

One of these is already implicit in predicting a sense of growing passivity on the part of patients, of not participating as a subject in their own recovery. This might well be matched by a more general sense of the inevitability of letting oneself be manipulated by technicians—of becoming an article of manufacture.

The difficulty becomes to estimate what psychological difference this would make. In any Hegelian overview of history, we can only become articles of manufacture because "we" have set up as the manufacturers. But the first person plural is a slippery customer. We the manufactured would be everybody and we the manufacturers a minority of scientists and technicians. Most people's capacity to identify with the satisfactions of the creative minority is certainly no greater in science than in other fields, and may well be less.

The beneficiaries of the Biological Revolution are not likely to feel that they are in control of the historical process from which they are benefiting. But they will not be able to indulge any feelings of alienation from science without endangering the specific benefits that they are unwilling to give up.

The best forecast would be for general acquiescence, though occasionally sullen, in whatever the Biological Revolution has to offer and gradually adjusting our values to signify that we approve of what we will actually be getting. The will to cooperate in being made biologically perfect is likely to take the place in the hierarchy of values that used to be occupied by being humbly submissive to spiritual counselors chastising the sinner for his own salvation. The new form of spiritual sloth will be not to want to be bodily perfect and genetically improved. The new avarice will be to cherish our miserable hoard of genes and favor the children that resemble us.

26 / The Changing Environment —Hell or Utopia?

MOSHE SAFDIE

Speculating on the future of architecture, I dream of Utopia, of the wonderful environment we want and could have, but then I think of the fantastic, explosive problems facing us and become frightened by the implications. Actually, I couldn't care

SOURCE: *Midway* 9 (Summer 1968), 65–86. Copyright © 1969 by The University of Chicago. Reprinted by permission.

Moshe Safdie is an architect who practices in Montreal and is best known as the chief designer of Habitat at Expo '67.

less about the future of *architecture*, the word being used in its accepted meaning. I am, however, deeply concerned about the future of the *environment*, and that is what I want to consider in this article.

Utopian thinking has often been the stimulus which has given direction to our actions and aspirations. In recent years, there has been resistance to utopian thinking, resistance stemming from belief in a world that takes its own course, one which individual actions can hardly influence. This thinking has resulted in inactivity or a feeling of helplessness for many. To me, utopian thinking is still the central, unifying, motivating process, one by which we clarify to ourselves what we want, where we are going, and how we go about getting there. But this must be differentiated from prophesying. Futurism is dangerous, particularly when it becomes a substitute for present action. I never thought of Habitat as the house of tomorrow, I never thought of any of the plans or proposals which I have made as futuristic: they have always been related to available means and circumstances and existing technology, and based on an assessment of the likelihood of change in our political system.

How then is one to proceed with this task of speculating on future development without prophesying, and do so with a measure of utopianism? I think we should start with the question of change. Change rarely takes place unless some force brings it about. Let us therefore look at our environment and try to determine what forces are pressing toward change, and then let us observe what social, technical, political, or economic developments are beginning to take place in response to these forces of change, and from there let us examine the full implications of any one of these developments' being carried to its natural conclusion.

Let us first examine the question of mobility. What forces are affecting our means of movement and communication within the environment? Much is happening that would suggest change. The automobile has reached the statistical limit of efficient operation in the more concentrated areas of our urban centers. The number of people who wish to travel by car per square mile per hour is so great in these areas that no matter how many superhighways and expressways we build, they are unable to cope with the volume generated. Simultaneously, older means of mass transportation have tended to break down: our railway systems are operating on the inertia of a bygone century. Urban mass transit exists as a compromise necessity, without popular support. In the air things are just as bad. Aircraft traffic in the major metropolitan airports has reached such a state of congestion that any trip of less than five hundred miles is becoming increasingly ridiculous. Air corridors are crowded, airports are unable to handle the volume. Door-to-door travel time, including time to and from the airport, is becoming three or four hours—for a flying time of one hour for a distance of four hundred miles.

Some social symptoms affecting the need of, or wish for, mobility must be considered. The metropolitan region is thriving; notwithstanding all its problems, people continue to move into the urban centers. They do so because of the variety of social, cultural, recreational, shopping, employment, and other amenities which they desire. The great corporations are also converging on the metropolitan centers in a continued and increasing interdependency. This dependency is not so much the result of material requirements as availability of services and an employable base of professionals and technicians. The farmer as a social being, one who lives in a rural area and accepts it, is all but an image of the past. Contemporary man is reluctant to continue living in isolated rural environment. More and more farmers have moved into the metropolitan region, but agriculture as an industry must continue.

Before we look at what technical developments are taking place in the field of mobility, I think it is important to put the subject in historical perspective. One of the most constant human aspirations throughout history has been for increased mobility, the emphasis being on personal, unrestricted mobility. This force in man's history has been constant and uncompromised, has been responsible for some of the most ingenious technical evolutions, and has been directly linked to almost every major economic or technical evolution. This persistence is bound to continue. Men will never give up cars unless other means of greater mobility are substituted. By preference they will not travel by mass means that restrict personal choice.

There have been several proposals for means of transportation offering greater mobility than what we have today. Man has certainly always wanted to fly; even a car is a poor substitute for flying, where one can move in space in any direction at will. A personal flying machine has already made its appearance with James Bond and has in fact also been built and tested successfully. Such a flying machine could be attached to the individual, it would be small and light, and it would have an efficient fuel system. It would be fully maneuverable by the individual at distances up to fifty miles. It would, of course, be more difficult to employ in severe climates: rain, snow, or cold would make it hard to maneuver unless it came with an efficient, light, transparent bubble enclosing the individual in a controlled climate. It would also require efficient guiding systems and strict traffic regulations to avoid the massive collisions of thousands of individuals in midspace, the victims falling down on other individuals below. But this could be handled, and with additional electronic guiding systems any collision with another unit could be avoided. The change to our cities would be phenomenal. Great numbers of people could move about without congestion. Any point in a multistory structure would become an entrance. Any level could become accessible and equally desirable commercially. The concept of elevator buildings as we know them today would disappear. The concept of the station or stop, a place of great concentration of people and hence a focal point in city structure, would disappear. Accessibility of individuals to places of recreation, shopping, or employment would permit a degree of dispersal hitherto totally unknown. Not only would the flying man have access to any level of a multistory structure, he would be able to enter and leave group-transportation vehicles in motion for trips of greater distances. He would not be dependent on roads and hence would be able to reach secluded places—forests, hills, and lakes—and the range of such communication would make crowding unlikely.

But what about the greater distances, the three- or four- or five-hundred mile trip—Boston to Washington, Montreal to Toronto? The flying man would be too slow to travel such distances efficiently—he would have to depend on other means.

A number of prototype models of various trains have recently been designed which are capable of traveling at great speeds on ground. In fact, trains have been designed which could travel five hundred miles an hour on air-cushion types of suspension.

This would make the Boston-Washington trip take approximately one hour, and with appropriate loading and unloading systems it could make the door-to-door time not much greater than that. I think one could speculate with fair certainty that within twenty years aircraft transportation would be totally eliminated between points closer than five hundred miles and replaced by fast ground systems. These systems would introduce many unusual planning problems. It is not possible to have a train going at these high speeds stop every twenty miles to pick up passengers, and yet its influence on the planning of a regional city will not be substantial unless it has loading and unloading capability at points relatively close together. And so our ingenuity must be directed at trying to find ways in which both great speed and yet flexibility of points served can be achieved. One possible solution could be the transfer of passengers and goods in motion from one system to another. A train moving at five hundred miles an hour slows down to one hundred miles an hour, at which time a local-area train having a cruising speed of thirty miles an hour accelerates to one hundred miles an hour; both systems would then move side by side at the same speed for a time permitting passengers to get on and off. The local-area trains which have picked up passengers from the regional interurban trains would unload those to yet slower systems forming the internal mass-transportation system of the community. The effect of these speeds would be to expand the distances implied by the one-hour travel limit which has traditionally restricted the size of cities. Horse-and-buggy cities were approximately ten miles in diameter, automobile cities, thirty, and automobile with expressways, fifty. The expanded regional city would be five hundred miles across—a linear necklace of many communities, interdependent, offering amenities shared by ten, fifteen, or twenty million people and yet preserving the identity of the smaller community within the regional whole. It would also make it possible to integrate agriculture with industry. The farmer could still be in close proximity to his fields and yet be part of a regional urban community.

Other developments may even precede this. The efficiency of a particular transportation system is dependent on its relationships to others. For example, the supersonic transport aircraft may make it possible to go from Los Angeles to New York in two hours, but the overall efficiency of the trip will depend on the time taken to go to and from the airports and whether waiting time may be required by the system, which may make the total trip five hours. We may be able to reduce the travel time from Los Angeles to New York appreciably more for less expenditure by shortening the home-to-airport trip or by devising systems which would reduce the waiting time in airports. If we could eliminate all waiting time from all transfers of all systems—aircraft, trains, subways, cars, elevators—we would probably double the average speed of the individual without any change to the system itself. I believe that in the next ten to fifteen years we will go through an evolutionary process by which our entire system of transportation, personal and public, will be integrated into a single operational system totally synchronized—relating departures and arrivals and eliminating waiting time. Passengers will get out of cars onto moving walks and be picked up by trains which will transfer them to an aircraft, which will then take them a point three thousand miles away where they will be transferred to another ground system with minimum waiting at transfer points. We have a precedent for this type of planned integration: our entire telephone system is based on an integrated national network. One should expect then that the same sophisticated method will be applied to transit networks.

Practically everything we know about urban planning is based on the idea of the station—the station through which all people leave or arrive, in which there is a natural concentration of people, and around which there is a concentration of urban development. With systems such as I have described the station is eliminated—or rather changed from a point in space to a linear moving point in time—and hence the city is drastically changed.

Let us examine now the physical plan of our urban region. One observes that planning in two dimensions—the subdivision of land with streets and separate buildings—has become too restricting for a typical downtown area. In cities such as Montreal a network of underground and aboveground systems of pedestrian movement has evolved. New York is already a hidden network of three-dimensional service distribution. This pattern will continue. The flexibility and potential of three-dimensional planning is too great to ignore. It may be possible not only to plan for movement and distribution of services at any level within the multistory city, but to organize land use, housing, commercial

442

developments, and industry within a more imaginative and flex-ible three-dimensional network of subdivided space.

Technical developments in manufacturing methods are also significant. Most industries are losing the characteristics which have made them obnoxious to the community around them. Most industries today can operate (believe it or not) without emitting smoke or smell or noise. Thus they can be integrated into the community and form part of an employment base which is within closer reach than we have planned for up to now. But the movement toward the three-dimensional city would require two major developments—a basic change in our legislative struc-ture pertaining to planning and real estate, and a major tech-nical breakthrough in methods of building. On both matters, let us observe present developments in order to project what may be expected.

The builder today finds himself restricted by two main ob-stacles. First, the total lack of a suitable building material, and second, the dependency on highly primitive handcraft methods. These factors restrict building in terms of both rate of construc-tion and freedom of design, to say nothing of costs.

There has been little evolution of change in the materials available to the builder in the past fifty years. Yet it is possible to describe a material that would suit best the construction of a three-dimensional city. It ought to be a material which is ex-tremely light, possibly one-sixth or one-eighth the relative weight of concrete. At the same time it ought to have tensile strength of perhaps fifty or sixty thousand pounds per square inch—two or three times that of normal structural steel—and a compressive strength of equal measure. At the same time it ought to be a good insulator comparable with, say, the foam plas-tics in insulation value. It must have surfaces impervious to moisture on both sides so that it can form the outside and inside finish for any given space. It ought to be moldable in such a way as to lend itself to easy manufacturing of space-enclosing mod-ular cells of a variety of shapes and forms. Finally, it ought to be fireproof and it must not melt below 1,500 degrees centigrade. Such materials are available today in the laboratory. They are known to exist chemically in the intricate world of complex hy-drocarbon molecules. As other industries have organized to de-velop materials suiting their own requirements, the construction industries must work out the kind of organizational structure that will make it possible to undertake research to meet a particular material requirement. There is no doubt in my mind that such a material will be available within the next twenty years.

The three-dimensional city will not be built by handcraft methods with thousands of workers piling bricks one on top of the other, sawing millwork, and making windows on the site. It will be the product of a highly sophisticated, mechanized assembly line of centralized factories having the characteristics of other major industries, where research, planning, marketing, and design are integrated into a single process. But how is one to build the city in a factory? A city is made of thousands of components which must be brought to a particular site. The answer is the space cell—premade, manufactured, produced on an assembly line. Cells of space the size of a house, a hospital room, or a classroom, a part of an office building, a section of a bridge or street, all manufactured as complete units to be assembled with the simplest connections by specialized equipment to make up the three-dimensional city. Thus bridges, sections of roadways, harbors, and buildings would all be made up of modular components, would all resolve themselves into these subcomponents to permit the premanufacturing and assembling. The implications for the design process, which I will discuss later, are enormous.

Another restriction to the three-dimensional plan is dependence on gravity not only as it affects the loadcarrying of a building, but as it limits the services of plumbing and drainage, which are traditionally carried to the ground. This is another field where technical evolution will introduce new possibilities within the next ten years. We will undoubtedly develop pumped drainage and sewer systems which will make it possible for drainage and sewer lines to run horizontally or even vertically. This will make for much greater flexibility in planning, and designers will be free to respond to other requirements—daylight, air circulation, view, and so on. In the space industry we have already developed systems which permit all waste to be regenerated and the dwelling unit to be independent of any external connection except that for energy. This, too, will be another technical freeing device. The effect of both will not only make for more flexible design in the three-dimensional community, it will also, as Buckminster Fuller foresaw forty years ago, open up a much greater potential for a highly dispersed, open-country environment in which cheap, lightweight dwellings could be shipped to various points, probably by air. The three-dimensional city would permit a much higher concentration of people and services without the environment itself suffering. On the contrary, one could expect that in the three-dimensional city one would always be ten minutes' walking distance from an intense "meeting place"—a market place or great recreational center—and at the same time ten minutes away from a secluded, open, green park. The interwoven, interlocking network of green open parks and intense urban development would increase the choice and variety of the individual.

The three-dimensional city would require, as I mentioned earlier, legislative changes. Our entire concept of land ownership, that is, private land owned by individuals who can do with it what they want, is already disintegrating. Elaborate bylaws and building codes restrict the individual from actually doing with his land what he wants. Individual ownership of land in small parcels has made any integrated planning effort in urban centers impossible. To overcome it, the governments have had to assemble land, purchase it through expropriation at great cost, artificially reduce its cost and turn it back to private developers. I believe that within the next twenty-five years the concept of private ownership of land in the United States and Canada will be replaced by a concept of publicly owned land and space which would be leased on a ten-, fifty-, or ninety-nine-year basis to individuals or to groups for development. The length of the land lease would depend on the kind of function contemplated. Open space in the country might be leased to individuals for ten years to use for recreation. Major commercial developments might obtain land for ninety-nine years, at which time both land and improvements would return to public hands. Planning would therefore be related to the lease period. A master plan would provide for regeneration and reevaluation as leases terminated. The transition to publicly owned land would be painful. It would meet with great political resistance as one of the greatest changes of outlook in the United States and Canada in many years.

Before the full changeover took place, softer measures—which would give enough flexibility for the three-dimensional city to evolve—would be needed. I believe these would be in the form of legislation permitting governments to buy with public funds great tracts of land in both urban and nonurbanized areas and hold these for development at a later date. In such case, government would only be one of many in the land market. It would purchase land at market price, but by purchasing enormous quantities around existing centers, it could control growth, releasing land whenever it was felt that growth should take place in relation to a total plan. We could control the density of this growth, and we could avoid sprawl or the kind of growth which brings about dilapidation of existing portions of the city. This then in transition would lead to the publicly owned land resources.

It goes without saying that in our three-dimensional city everyone would be able to obtain a substantial dwelling of high standards. How is the transition to be made from the present situation, where 50 percent of the population is ill-housed and without sufficient income to purchase adequate housing? To speculate on what means would evolve within the general economy to make adequate housing available to all is beyond my ability, but there are two related developments which will probably take place simultaneously in the immediate future. One is the expenditure of a much greater proportion of our public funds on services within the city. The other is passage of a legislative program that would put adequate housing within the reach of anyone in the population. I think the new programs will replace the present subsidized rent program known as public housing. It is agreed now that ownership is the form of housing which gets the best response from the occupants. Mortgage money without down payments or interest would be made available to any family in the country to obtain a dwelling, a house within the three-dimensional city. The family would then, provided that its income is below a particular level, repay the mortgage to a maximum of 20 percent of its total income. Should the income increase they would continue to make these payments to this maximum until the mortgage was repaid. Should their income not be sufficient to cover the full mortgage, the balance would be absorbed by the public. I believe that the guaranteed environment for all will precede the guaranteed income for all.

The belief that the guaranteed environment for all will become a political and economic reality in the very near future is not based on optimistic speculation. Rather, it is the conclusion of the natural outcome of present policies which are supported by the public. The term low-cost housing has been one of the most misleading, inaccurate fabrications which has been invented to conceal or to soften for the public what in fact has been taking place for the past twenty years. Low-cost housing has never existed—there has never been such a thing. For twenty years housing for the poor has been constructed at equal and sometimes higher cost per unit than dwellings for the middle-income housing market and has been made available to low-income families at subsidized rents or by subsidized financing. To my knowledge, there has never been an actual demonstration that housing for low-income families provided on a subsidized basis costs less to build than any other form of housing. For those who are used to the terms *low-cost, middle-class*, and *luxury* housing, it is often a shock to realize how small in fact is the difference in the construction cost itself per dwelling. Land costs vary (with desirability of location), financing patterns vary, and the services provided vary, but the construction cost itself is more or less the same.

For many reasons, some of which I must leave to the economist to explain, a substantial proportion of our population is unable to obtain adequate housing within its earning power. Undoubtedly some of this relates to the inefficiency of the construction industry: while most families can afford a secondhand car or a television set, the construction industry has not been capable of producing efficiently enough to make their product available to the total population. There are also other, more complex reasons having to do with the general income distribution and the increasing cost of servicing the urban environment as against the older, lower density, or rural environment. An unappreciated fact amongst housing officials, architects, and the public is that high-density environment costs much more to build than low-density environment for the same amenities. For example, we take for granted that in the single-family house a family has a certain acoustic privacy from adjacent units. Two wood walls with an air space of six to ten feet between them

VI / THE CHALLENGE OF THE ENVIRONMENT

have produced fairly acceptable solutions. This same quality of sound insulation between two dwellings which touch each other becomes a major technical problem at considerable added cost. We take for granted that a family should have open space adjacent to its house, and when this was provided by a garden in a single-family house at land costs of, say, $1.00 a square foot, the family could have a garden of twenty by thirty feet at a cost of $600. This same open space provided in a multistory high-density environment within the structure itself may cost $7.00 a square foot, or something like $4,000 or $5,000. Most other amenities taken for granted in a single-family house double or triple their cost when provided in the denser environment, and yet there is no doubt in my own mind that the need to concentrate on higher densities is a by-product of broad economic and social forces that will not be reversed in the near future.

There is a prevailing school of thought today holding that all we need is to develop the $5,000 house and most of our problems will then be solved: this would price a dwelling within the reach of the lowest income families. This is nonsense, on two grounds. First, this point of view regards the present standards of multistory high-density housing as acceptable. By accepting them, it then suggests that with greater industrialization, and hence efficiency, one could provide a dwelling comparable to what the public-housing program has provided in, say, a thirty-story project for $5,000 per family. This I believe to be true, but the events of the past two or three summers have clearly pointed out that the denial of basic standards in housing even to the lowest income families is politically intolerable, that it is not possible to continue providing housing which is at extreme variance with the general standards of the community. Such aspects as privacy, open space, a measure of identity, and facilities close by the dwelling—a form of access compatible with raising a family —all have to be provided in the high-density environment. The problem therefore is twofold: to reduce the cost to the individual family through industrialization and mechanization (using the savings of this efficiency to increase the amenities provided) and to reduce the general cost per capita. Further, to put this minimum environment within reach of all, one of two things must take place: either the earning power of families in the lower half of the income scale in the United States and Canada must be increased substantially, or else (and certainly during the interim period, which in my opinion may be fifteen years) massive subsidies in some form or other will have to be undertaken. The fact that any environmental solution must provide for the total population as a condition to its acceptability means that economy has become a moral obligation to the designer, architect, and urbanist. We must clarify, however, what the term *economy* means. This is the ability to produce with the minimum of material and of labor an environment whose standards we consider stimulating to human development and which is within the capabilities of our economy to produce at maximum capacity. An organism in nature characteristically typifies the most economic solution possible through evolution within the confines of survival. A tree looked at out of context is an uneconomical form. It would be much more economical if the tree contained all its leaves in a small box hanging on the trunk, thereby saving several hundred feet of branches, distribution systems, and the need to resist climatic pressures. But that more economical tree would soon die, because a condition of survival is the tree's ability to expose a certain area of itself to sunlight in order to manufacture its food. It is not possible to look at the economy of the tree organism out of the context of its essential survival, and so too it is not possible to define the minimum in human environment without reaffirming what is essential to human survival.

But as physical plant changes, so does social structure. One observes today a constantly increasing mobility. The average American family, on the move with employment changes and shifting interests, spends less than four years in one dwelling. One also observes an annual migration pattern within the North American population. As the birds come from the North to the warmer South, so do thousands of individuals seeking sun and warmth. As the summer sets in, thousands migrate north or to the mountains, to cooler areas. Both this general mobility and this annual migration are constantly increasing. One ought to expect them to become significant patterns in the environment. The resort hotel will change its form and shape. It will have to preserve the qualities of resort and be capable of catering to millions. Mobility will have great effect on the house itself. More and more will basic furnishings and facilities in the house be part of a house and built into it. As it would seem too costly to move the entire house each time the family moves, the family would concentrate its belongings in objects capable of being moved easily, objects which give an environment a personal expression. But beds, cabinets, desks, chests of drawers, seating pieces, kitchen and bathroom equipment are all likely to be built in to much greater extent than before.

Within the family, there will probably be more changes than I am prepared to speculate upon. But here one can observe even today the emergence of a young, independent teenager who leaves the house at an early age producing the need of dwelling places for millions of young, independent, single people.

And there is recreation and the repeated talk of a shorter working week, of more time for pleasure. What form will it take? The day Expo 67 opened in Montreal, it was clear to everyone that so far as Montreal was concerned, this was no exhibition. It was part of environment. Expo became an extension of downtown, a place to go on a free afternoon or a free evening, to take children, to go for dinner, to go for a film, to take a class in zoology or biology, or to do any one of a hundred things. The phenomenon of Expo and Montreal is significant. It is probably the last great exhibition in the old, traditional sense; it is probably also the first environmental recreation center of urban significance and will be followed by thousands of others representing an integration of recreation, education, the arts, all grouped in an urban center, making the urban meeting place meaningful once again.

Industrialization, mass production, and public ownership of land are all means to an end. They do not guarantee a good environment. They are dependent on the design process, the decision-making complex of architect and community, out of which comes a design solution which gets built and determines our environment. Where is it going? How will this environment be determined? How will it look? In what way will it be different from what we have today?

I am totally uninterested in the single individual building, no matter how pleasant its internal environment is, if our total urban environment is not up to it. If the environment is not also inspiring and successful, then we have failed in the creation of our cities. A discipline or system which can only achieve an individual, isolated, successful building has totally failed in solving the problem of man's environment. What surrounds us today?

450

An utter mess, a disintegrating environment, one that does not work in almost any aspect we care to examine—whether it is mobility, whether it is the relationship of man to nature or of man to man, whether it is its ability to enhance social relationships or the value of the individual in his own eyes. In each aspect, one could write it off as a total failure. What is common to it all today is its total arbitrariness, its lack of any rationale, any spiritual, unifying reality for expressing the complex functions which it must serve. What characterizes it is that it could be a million things other than what it is today and be equally inadequate, dissatisfying, and destructive to human growth. The architect-planner today is often dominated by considerations of style and fashion which are totally unrelated to the morphological necessities of the environment. But even if he is not, even if he aims as best he can at the evolution of a form which satisfies the function of the organism which the building is, its relationship to the total environment—to the thousands of other buildings and roads and highways designed by other individuals—is an unintegrated hodge podge.

How then do we achieve the unarbitrary, organically whole building in the organically whole environment, the continuous building system making up the total city? This of course goes beyond the architect. It has to do with the general cultural attitudes. In a culture where women wear square-ended shoes one year and pointed shoes the next year, while the shape of the foot changes not, where men wear wool suits and ties in ninety-degree heat, get into glass boxes exposed to the sun and then employ machinery using thousands of horsepower in the attempt to keep it cool enough to survive, when a family's decision on choosing a vehicle to transport it is determined by hundreds of considerations none of which have to do with the capability or efficiency or safety of this particular machine to serve them, when man accepts spending a good part of his waking time traveling unproductively or walking between cars on the existing city streets—so long as man accepts all that, it is unlikely that his environment will improve. He is accepting the arbitrary, the unfunctional, the inorganic, that which is incompatible with survival.

Accepting such things, we could go on developing the city as it is, adopting the same arbitrary considerations and resisting any change to our political urban system. If we do, we should at least be conscious of the implications. As dispersal continues and transportation becomes forbidding, the metropolitan city would split up into a series of separate communities. These communities would be very homogeneous, grouping in them people from a single economic or ethnic background. To make up for the lack of human contact would be an elaborate network of one-way electronic communication—social tranquilizers. As these communities isolated themselves, mixing would be discouraged and conformity would become a social norm, because little tolerance for deviating from the patterns could be allowed. With all the apparent increase in mobility and in the size of the city, the amount of individual choice and therefore of freedom would continuously decrease. One would buy the goods that happened to be carried by the local chain store, send one's children to the local school regardless of quality, and continue to consume without freedom of selection the same idiotic television programs. If the same values we have expressed in our consumption of consumer goods are applied to housing, we will soon have mass-produced housing—a "Kraft cellophane jam" architecture, identically tasteless regardless of where one consumes it. Marketing, sales, and advertising people will determine what the next house will be like as they do with cars, appliances, and television programs. An advertisement of the "General Housing Corporation" in a 1982 issue of *Life* might read (I will not venture to suggest an illustration):

Introducing the improved all-new *Ranchera* for 1982, featuring:

Wristwatch house-lighting control—touch your wrist and the lights go on.

Bedrooms equipped with invisible light, requiring no natural lights or windows.

Guaranteed weather control in a hermetically sealed dwelling, filtering all smoke, odors, and poisons from your air.

Magic kitchen with infrablue cooking—including a special bonus of a one-year's supply of precooked "Worldwide" meals for the entire family—three menu series to choose from.

The new "Urite" gold finish inside and out (also copper, silver, leatherette, and six other exciting new textures).

Thus, instead of cleaning our city air, we may seal ourselves in a synthetic environment; instead of grouping dwellings with an organic relationship to the outdoors, to sunlight, to the view, to nature, we may create internal scenery and artificial lighting; instead of concentrating on a better environment, we may divert attention to hundreds of irrelevant and senseless gimmicks; and above all, we may neutralize until everything is a single common denominator and the individual is one among many statistical facts, where human alternatives do not exist.

What we need is to understand the morphology of our environment—to tackle the design of environment in an attempt to satisfy the complex program, the infinity of requirements, physical and social, thereby evolving form. The morphology of environment is the byproduct both of physical structures such as light and service distribution, aerodynamic patterns, the capability for growth, the ability to enclose space with the least material, and of psychic structures such as the need to give people a sense of location and orientation and a sense of identity. The shape of the city, its form, its structure, derives from the process of satisfying these requirements. The city is an organism, as complex as any natural organism. The leaves of the maple tree spread in spiral form to absorb the most sun, the leaves of the cactus lie parallel to the sun's rays, absorbing the least amount of light in the desert; the nautilus grows in a spiral sequence of larger and larger spaces to make it possible for the animal and its shelter to grow in the same proportions simultaneously; bees subdivide space with wax to store the maximum amount of honey with the least material; the intricate network of bones in the vulture's wing gives maximum strength with minimum weight. Each is an aspect of structure within a complex morphology. The city too is infinite structure, all of which must be considered in making an architecture of evolution where growth and progression can take place.

Building systems replacing the individual building are not only the result of the technical necessity to mass-produce; they are an essentially new way of looking at the design process of the environment. Individual buildings were finite designs, *com-*

MOSHE SAFDIE   453

positions for a limited problem at a particular given time. Building systems are an expression of the new vernacular. The Greek village on an Aegean island, the Arab hill town, the Indian pueblo were all building systems. They were not finite designs composed at one moment, they were evolutionary designs, evolved to satisfy complex climatic, physical, and social requirements, added to and changed with time, a vernacular system with great unity. Building systems can become the contemporary vernacular. Whereas the Renaissance architect tackled a building as an individual composition and had certain given, formal disciplines which were accepted in order to achieve a measure of unity within the total environment, the designer today must tackle the environment as a series of building systems, discovering the nature of the vernacular as he goes. He is trying to "break the genetic code" of that particular species of environment. When he has once discovered the genetic code, it is possible for many elements of that species to grow from it, with particular adaptations, that are themselves capable of change, capable of growth. For the new vernacular will be one that is capable of evolution. The architect will no longer regard himself as the heir of the Renaissance architect, the artist who composed a building; he will be the heir of the villagers who built their own village, a building system of repetitive components which they evolved with time.

And so will grow our city, the expanded regional city, integrating agriculture and industry, open space and urbanized space, a dispersal of concentrations, a necklace of communities. There will be great numbers for variety, small groups for identity; centralized control for planning and coordination, individual influence through the internal community; mass production and hence repetition for economy, great variety through permutations of these repetitive systems, grouped with rhythm to give a sense of location. The city organism discovered through its own morphology, with its own vernacular and hence its own unity, will become a city with its own regional characteristics, varying from the cold climate to the hot desert as the maple and pine differ from the cactus and olive tree—a three-dimensional city, an intricate assembly of modular space cells of various sizes and functions, grouped and interlocked to produce a variety of space permutation, sparkling bubbles absorbing sunlight in cold climates, cantilevering planes shading each other in hot climates—and people will be mobile, selective, with infinite choice.

27 / The Historical Roots of Our Ecologic Crisis

LYNN WHITE, JR.

A conversation with Aldous Huxley not infrequently put one at the receiving end of an unforgettable monologue. About a year before his lamented death he was discoursing on a favorite topic: Man's unnatural treatment of nature and its sad results. To illustrate his point he told how, during the previous summer, he had returned to a little valley in England where he had spent many happy months as a child. Once it had been composed of delightful grassy glades; now it was becoming overgrown with unsightly brush because the rabbits that formerly kept such growth under control had largely succumbed to a disease, myxomatosis, that was deliberately introduced by the local farmers to reduce the rabbits' destruction of crops. Being something of a Philistine, I could be silent no longer, even in the interests of great rhetoric. I interrupted to point out that the rabbit itself had been brought as a domestic animal to England in 1176, presumably to improve the protein diet of the peasantry.

All forms of life modify their contexts. The most spectacular and benign instance is doubtless the coral polyp. By serving its own ends, it has created a vast undersea world favorable to thousands of other kinds of animals and plants. Ever since man became a numerous species he has affected his environment

SOURCE: Paul Shepard and Daniel McKinley, eds., *The Subversive Science* (Boston: Houghton Mifflin, 1969), pp. 341–51. This essay originally appeared in *Science* 155 (1967), 1203–7. Copyright © 1967 by the American Association for the Advancement of Science. Reprinted by permission.

Lynn White, Jr., president of Mills College from 1943 to 1958, has taught at Princeton and Stanford and is presently at UCLA; his most recent book is *Machina ex Deo: Essays in the Dynamism of Western Culture.*

notably. The hypothesis that his fire-drive method of hunting created the world's great grasslands and helped to exterminate the monster mammals of the Pleistocene from much of the globe is plausible, if not proved. For 6 millennia at least, the banks of the lower Nile have been a human artifact rather than the swampy African jungle which nature, apart from man, would have made it. The Aswan Dam, flooding 5000 square miles, is only the latest stage in a long process. In many regions terracing or irrigation, overgrazing, the cutting of forests by Romans to build ships to fight Carthaginians or by Crusaders to solve the logistics problems of their expeditions, have profoundly changed some ecologies. Observation that the French landscape falls into two basic types, the open fields of the north and the *bocage* of the south and west, inspired Marc Bloch to undertake his classic study of medieval agricultural methods. Quite unintentionally, changes in human ways often affect nonhuman nature. It has been noted, for example, that the advent of the automobile eliminated huge flocks of sparrows that once fed on the horse· manure littering every street.

The history of ecologic change is still so rudimentary that we know little about what really happened, or what the results were. The extinction of the European aurochs as late as 1627 would seem to have been a simple case of overenthusiastic hunting. On more intricate matters it often is impossible to find solid information. For a thousand years or more the Frisians and Hollanders have been pushing back the North Sea, and the process is culminating in our own time in the reclamation of the Zuider Zee. What, if any, species of animals, birds, fish, shore life, or plants have died out in the process? In their epic combat with Neptune have the Netherlanders overlooked ecological values in such a way that the quality of human life in the Netherlands has suffered? I cannot discover that the questions have ever been asked, much less answered.

People, then, have often been a dynamic element in their own environment, but in the present state of biological scholarship we usually do not know exactly when, where, or with what effects man-induced changes came. As we enter the last third of the twentieth century, however, concern for the problem of ecologic backlash is mounting feverishly. Natural science, conceived as the effort to understand the nature of things, had flourished in several eras and among several peoples. Similarly there had been an age-old accumulation of technological skills, sometimes growing rapidly, sometimes slowly. But it was not until about four generations ago that Western Europe and North America arranged a marriage between science and technology, a union of the theoretical and the empirical approaches to our natural environment. The emergence in widespread practice of the Baconian creed that scientific knowledge means technological power over nature can scarcely be dated before about 1850, save in the chemical industries, where it is anticipated in the eighteenth century. Its acceptance as a normal pattern of action may mark the greatest event in human history since the invention of agriculture, and perhaps in nonhuman terrestrial history as well.

Almost at once the new situation forced the crystallization of the novel concept of ecology; indeed, the word *ecology* first appeared in the English language in 1873. Today, less than a century later, the impact of our race upon the environment has so increased in force that it has changed in essence. When the first cannons were fired, in the early fourteenth century, they affected ecology by sending workers scrambling to the forests and mountains for more potash, sulfur, iron ore, and charcoal, with some resulting erosion and deforestation. Hydrogen bombs are of a different order: a war fought with them might alter the genetics of all life on this planet. By 1285 London had a smog problem arising from the burning of soft coal, but our present combustion of fossil fuels threatens to change the chemistry of the globe's atmosphere as a whole, with consequences which we are only beginning to guess. With the population explosion, the carcinoma of planless urbanism, the new geological deposits of sewage and garbage, surely no creature other than man has ever managed to foul its nest in such short order.

There are many calls to action, but specific proposals, however worthy as individual items, seem too partial, palliative, negative: ban the bomb, tear down the billboards, give the Hindus contraceptives and tell them to eat their sacred cows. The simplest solution to any suspect change is, of course, to stop it, or, better yet, to revert to a romanticized past: make those ugly gasoline stations look like Anne Hathaway's cottage or (in the Far West) like ghost-town saloons. The "wilderness area" mentality invariably advocates deep-freezing an ecology, whether San Gimignano or the High Sierra, as it was before the first Kleenex was dropped. But neither atavism nor prettification will cope with the ecologic crisis of our time.

What shall we do? No one yet knows. Unless we think about fundamentals, our specific measures may produce new backlashes more serious than those they are designed to remedy.

As a beginning we should try to clarify our thinking by looking, in some historical depth, at the presuppositions that underlie modern technology and science. Science was traditionally aristocratic, speculative, intellectual in intent; technology was lower-class, empirical, action-oriented. The quite sudden fusion of these two, towards the middle of the nineteenth century, is surely related to the slightly prior and contemporary democratic revolutions which, by reducing social barriers, tended to assert a functional unity of brain and hand. Our ecologic crisis is the product of an emerging, entirely novel, democratic culture. The issue is whether a democratized world can survive its own implications. Presumably we cannot unless we rethink our axioms.

The Western Traditions of Technology and Science

One thing is so certain that it seems stupid to verbalize it: both modern technology and modern science are distinctively *Occidental*. Our technology has absorbed elements from all over the world, notably from China; yet everywhere today, whether in Japan or in Nigeria, successful technology is Western. Our science is the heir to all the sciences of the past, especially perhaps to the work of the great Islamic scientists of the Middle Ages, who so often outdid the ancient Greeks in skill and perspicacity: Al-Rāzī in medicine, for example; or ibn-al-Haytham in optics; or Omar Khāyyám in mathematics. Indeed, not a few works of such geniuses seem to have vanished in the original Arabic and to survive only in medieval Latin translations that helped to lay the foundations for later Western developments. Today, around the globe, all significant science is Western in style and method, whatever the pigmentation or language of the scientists.

458

A second pair of facts is less well recognized because they result from quite recent historical scholarship. The leadership of the West, both in technology and in science, is far older than the so-called Scientific Revolution of the seventeenth century or the so-called Industrial Revolution of the eighteenth century. These terms are in fact outmoded and obscure the true nature of what they try to describe—significant stages in two long and separate developments. By A.D. 1000 at the latest—and perhaps, feebly, as much as 200 years earlier—the West began to apply water power to industrial processes other than milling grain. This was followed in the late twelfth century by the harnessing of wind power. From simple beginnings, but with remarkable consistency of style, the West rapidly expanded its skills in the development of power machinery, labor-saving devices, and automation. Those who doubt should contemplate that most monumental achievement in the history of automation: the weight-driven mechanical clock, which appeared in two forms in the early fourteenth century. Not in craftsmanship but in basic technological capacity, the Latin West of the later Middle Ages far outstripped its elaborate, sophisticated, and esthetically magnificent sister cultures, Byzantium and Islam. In 1444 a great Greek ecclesiastic, Bessarion, who had gone to Italy, wrote a letter to a prince in Greece. He is amazed by the superiority of Western ships, arms, textiles, glass. But above all he is astonished by the spectacle of water-wheels sawing timbers and pumping the bellows of blast furnaces. Clearly, he had seen nothing of the sort in the Near East.

By the end of the fifteenth century the technological superiority of Europe was such that its small, mutually hostile nations could spill out over all the rest of the world, conquering, looting, and colonizing. The symbol of this technological superiority is the fact that Portugal, one of the weakest states of the Occident, was able to become, and to remain for a century, mistress of the East Indies. And we must remember that the technology of Vasco da Gama and Albuquerque was built by pure empiricism, drawing remarkably little support or inspiration from science.

In the present-day vernacular understanding, modern science is supposed to have begun in 1543, when both Copernicus and Vesalius published their great works. It is no derogation of their accomplishments, however, to point out that such structures as the *Fabrica* and *De revolutionibus* do not appear overnight. The distinctive Western tradition of science, in fact, began in the late eleventh century with a massive movement of translation of Arabic and Greek scientific works into Latin. A few notable books—Theophrastus, for example—escaped the West's avid new appetite for science, but within less than 200 years effectively the entire corpus of Greek and Muslim science was available in Latin, and was being eagerly read and criticized in the new European universities. Out of criticism arose new observation, speculation, and increasing distrust of ancient authorities. By the late thirteenth century Europe had seized global scientific leadership from the faltering hands of Islam. It would be as absurd to deny the profound originality of Newton, Galileo, or Copernicus as to deny that of the fourteenth century scholastic scientists like Buridan or Oresme on whose work they built. Before the eleventh century, science scarcely existed in the Latin West, even in Roman times. From the eleventh century onward, the scientific sector of Occidental culture has increased in a steady crescendo.

Since both our technological and our scientific movements got their start, acquired their character, and achieved world dominance in the Middle Ages, it would seem that we cannot understand their nature or their present impact upon ecology without examining fundamental medieval assumptions and developments.

Medieval View of Man and Nature

Until recently, agriculture has been the chief occupation even in "advanced" societies; hence, any change in methods of tillage has much importance. Early plows, drawn by two oxen, did not normally turn the sod but merely scratched it. Thus, cross-plowing was needed and fields tended to be squarish. In the fairly light soils and semiarid climates of the Near East and Mediterranean, this worked well. But such a plow was inappropriate to the wet climate and often sticky soils of northern Europe. By the latter part of the seventh century after Christ, however, following obscure beginnings, certain northern peasants were using an entirely new kind of plow, equipped with a vertical knife to cut the line of the furrow, a horizontal share to slice under the sod, and a moldboard to turn it over. The friction of this plow with the soil was so great that it normally required not two but eight oxen. It attacked the land with such violence that cross-plowing was not needed, and fields tended to be shaped in long strips.

In the days of the scratch-plow, fields were distributed generally in units capable of supporting a single family. Subsistence farming was the presupposition. But no peasant owned eight oxen: to use the new and more efficient plow, peasants pooled their oxen to form large plow-teams, originally receiving (it would appear) plowed strips in proportion to their contribution. Thus, distribution of land was based no longer on the needs of a family but, rather, on the capacity of a power machine to till the earth. Man's relation to the soil was profoundly changed. Formerly man had been part of nature; now he was the exploiter of nature. Nowhere else in the world did farmers develop any analogous agricultural implement. Is it coincidence that modern technology, with its ruthlessness toward nature, has so largely been produced by descendants of these peasants of northern Europe?

This same exploitive attitude appears slightly before A.D. 830 in Western illustrated calendars. In older calendars the months were shown as passive personifications. The new Frankish calendars, which set the style for the Middle Ages, are very different: they show men coercing the world around them—plowing, harvesting, chopping trees, butchering pigs. Man and nature are two things, and man is master.

These novelties seem to be in harmony with larger intellectual patterns. What people do about their ecology depends on what they think about themselves in relation to things around them. Human ecology is deeply conditioned by beliefs about our nature and destiny—that is, by religion. To Western eyes this is very evident in, say, India or Ceylon. It is equally true of ourselves and of our medieval ancestors.

The victory of Christianity over paganism was the greatest psychic revolution in the history of our culture. It has become fashionable today to say that, for better or worse, we live in "the post-Christian age." Certainly the forms of our thinking and language have largely ceased to be Christian, but to my eye the substance often remains amazingly akin to that of the past. Our daily habits of action, for example, are dominated by an implicit faith in perpetual progress which was unknown either to Greco-Roman antiquity or to the Orient. It is rooted in, and is indefensible apart from, Judeo-Christian teleology. The fact that Communists share it merely helps to show what can be demonstrated on many other grounds: that Marxism, like Islam, is a Judeo-Christian heresy. We continue today to live, as we have lived for about 1700 years, very largely in a context of Christian axioms.

What did Christianity tell people about their relations with the environment?

While many of the world's mythologies provide stories of creation, Greco-Roman mythology was singularly incoherent in this respect. Like Aristotle, the intellectuals of the ancient West denied that the visible world had had a beginning. Indeed, the idea of a beginning was impossible in the framework of their cyclical notion of time. In sharp contrast, Christianity inherited from Judaism not only a concept of time as nonrepetitive and linear but also a striking story of creation. By gradual stages a loving and all-powerful God had created light and darkness, the heavenly bodies, the earth and all its plants, animals, birds, and fishes. Finally, God had created Adam and, as an afterthought, Eve to keep man from being lonely. Man named all the animals, thus establishing his dominance over them. God planned all of this explicitly for man's benefit and rule: no item in the physical creation had any purpose save to serve man's purposes. And, although man's body is made of clay, he is not simply part of nature: he is made in God's image.

Especially in its Western form, Christianity is the most anthropocentric religion the world has seen. As early as the second century both Tertullian and Saint Irenaeus of Lyons were insisting that when God shaped Adam he was foreshadowing the image of the Incarnate Christ, the Second Adam. Man shares, in great measure, God's transcendence of nature. Christianity, in absolute contrast to ancient paganism and Asia's religions (except, perhaps, Zoroastrianism), not only established a dualism of man and nature but also insisted that it is God's will that man exploit nature for his proper ends.

At the level of the common people this worked out in an interesting way. In Antiquity every tree, every spring, every stream, every hill had its own *genius loci,* its guardian spirit. These spirits were accessible to men, but were very unlike men; centaurs, fauns, and mermaids show their ambivalence. Before one cut a tree, mined a mountain, or dammed a brook, it was important to placate the spirit in charge of that particular situation, and to keep it placated. By destroying pagan animism, Christianity made it possible to exploit nature in a mood of indifference to the feelings of natural objects.

It is often said that for animism the Church substituted the cult of saints. True; but the cult of saints is functionally quite different from animism. The saint is not *in* natural objects; he may have special shrines, but his citizenship is in heaven. Moreover, a saint is entirely a man; he can be approached in human terms. In addition to saints, Christianity of course also had angels and demons inherited from Judaism and perhaps, at one remove, from Zoroastrianism. But these were all as mobile as the saints themselves. The spirits *in* natural objects, which formerly had protected nature from man, evaporated. Man's effective monopoly on spirit in this world was confirmed, and the old inhibitions to the exploitation of nature crumbled.

When one speaks in such sweeping terms, a note of caution is in order. Christianity is a complex faith, and its consequences differ in differing contexts. What I have said may well apply to the medieval West, where in fact technology made spectacular advances. But the Greek East, a highly civilized realm of equal Christian devotion, seems to have produced no marked technological innovation after the late seventh century, when Greek fire was invented. The key to the contrast may perhaps be found in a difference in the tonality of piety and thought which students of comparative theology find between the Greek and the Latin Churches. The Greeks believed that sin was intellectual blindness, and that salvation was found in illumination, orthodoxy—that is, clear thinking. The Latins, on the other hand, felt that sin was moral evil, and that salvation was to be found in right conduct. Eastern theology has been intellectualist. Western theology has been voluntarist. The Greek saint contemplates; the Western saint acts. The implications of Christianity for the conquest of nature would emerge more easily in the Western atmosphere.

The Christian dogma of creation, which is found in the first clause of all the Creeds, has another meaning for our comprehension of today's ecologic crisis. By revelation, God had given man the Bible, the Book of Scripture. But since God had made nature, nature also must reveal the divine mentality. The religious study of nature for the better understanding of God was known as natural theology. In the early Church, and always in the Greek East, nature was conceived primarily as a symbolic system through which God speaks to men: the ant is a sermon to sluggards; rising flames are the symbol of the soul's aspiration. This view of nature was essentially artistic rather than scientific. While Byzantium preserved and copied great numbers of ancient Greek scientific texts, science as we conceive it could scarcely flourish in such an ambience.

However, in the Latin West by the early thirteenth century natural theology was following a very different bent. It was ceasing to be the decoding of the physical symbols of God's communication with man and was becoming the effort to understand God's mind by discovering how his creation operates. The rainbow was no longer simply a symbol of hope first sent to Noah after the Deluge: Robert Grosseteste, Friar Roger Bacon, and Theodoric of Freiberg produced startlingly sophisticated work on the optics of the rainbow, but they did it as a venture in religious understanding. From the thirteenth century onward, up to and including Leibnitz and Newton, every major scientist, in effect, explained his motivations in religious terms. Indeed, if Galileo had not been so expert an amateur theologian he would have got into far less trouble: the professionals resented his intrusion. And Newton seems to have regarded himself more as a theologian than as a scientist. It was not until the late eighteenth century that the hypothesis of God became unnecessary to many scientists.

It is often hard for the historian to judge, when men explain why they are doing what they want to do, whether they are offering real reasons or merely culturally acceptable reasons. The consistency with which scientists during the long formative centuries of Western science said that the task and the reward of the scientist was "to think God's thoughts after him" leads one to believe that this was their real motivation. If so, then modern Western science was cast in a matrix of Christian theology. The dynamism of religious devotion, shaped by the Judeo-Christian dogma of creation, gave it impetus.

An Alternative Christian View

We would seem to be headed toward conclusions unpalatable to many Christians. Since both *science* and *technology* are blessed words in our contemporary vocabulary, some may be happy at the notions, first, that, viewed historically, modern science is an extrapolation of natural theology and, second, that modern technology is at least partly to be explained as an Occidental, voluntarist realization of the Christian dogma of man's transcendence of, and rightful mastery over, nature. But, as we now recognize, somewhat over a century ago science and technology—hitherto quite separate activities—joined to give mankind powers which, to judge by many of the ecologic effects, are out of control. If so, Christianity bears a huge burden of guilt.

I personally doubt that disastrous ecologic backlash can be avoided simply by applying to our problems more science and more technology. Our science and technology have grown out of Christian attitudes toward man's relation to nature which are almost universally held not only by Christians and neo-Christians but also by those who fondly regard themselves as post-Christians. Despite Copernicus, all the cosmos rotates around our little globe. Despite Darwin, we are *not,* in our hearts, part of the natural process. We are superior to nature, contemptuous of it, willing to use it for our slightest whim. The newly elected Governor of California, like myself a churchman but less troubled than I, spoke for the Christian tradition when he said (as is alleged), "when you've seen one redwood tree, you've seen them all." To a Christian a tree can be no more than a physical fact. The whole concept of the sacred grove is alien to Christianity and to the ethos of the West. For nearly two millennia Christian missionaries have been chopping down sacred groves, which are idolatrous because they assume spirit in nature.

What we do about ecology depends on our ideas of the man-nature relationship. More science and more technology are not going to get us out of the present ecologic crisis until we find a new religion, or rethink our old one. The beatniks, who are the basic revolutionaries of our time, show a sound instinct in their affinity for Zen Buddhism, which conceives of the man–nature relationship as very nearly the mirror image of the Christian view. Zen, however, is as deeply conditioned by Asian history as Christianity is by the experience of the West, and I am dubious of its viability among us.

Possibly we should ponder the greatest radical in Christian history since Christ: Saint Francis of Assisi. The prime miracle of Saint Francis is the fact that he did not end at the stake, as many of his left-wing followers did. He was so clearly heretical that a General of the Franciscan Order, Saint Bonaventura, a great and perceptive Christian, tried to suppress the early accounts of Franciscanism. The key to an understanding of Francis is his belief in the virtue of humility—not merely for the individual but for man as a species. Francis tried to depose man from his monarchy over creation and set up a democracy of all God's creatures. With him the ant is no longer simply a homily for the lazy, flames a sign of the thrust of the soul toward union with God; now they are Brother Ant and Sister Fire, praising the Creator in their own ways as Brother Man does in his.

Later commentators have said that Francis preached to the birds as a rebuke to men who would not listen. The records do not read so: he urged the little birds to praise God, and in spiritual ecstasy they flapped their wings and chirped rejoicing. Legends of saints, especially the Irish saints, had long told of their dealings with animals but always, I believe, to show their human dominance over creatures. With Francis it is different. The land around Gubbio in the Apennines was being ravaged by a fierce wolf. Saint Francis, says the legend, talked to the wolf and persuaded him of the error of his ways. The wolf repented, died in the odor of sanctity, and was buried in consecrated ground.

What Sir Steven Ruciman calls "the Franciscan doctrine of the animal soul" was quickly stamped out. Quite possibly it was in part inspired, consciously or unconsciously, by the belief in reincarnation held by the Cathar heretics who at that time teemed in Italy and southern France, and who presumably had got it originally from India. It is significant that at just the same moment, about 1200, traces of metempsychosis are found also in western Judaism, in the Provençal *Cabbala*. But Francis held neither to transmigration of souls nor to pantheism. His view of nature and of man rested on a unique sort of pan-psychism of all things animate and inanimate designed for the glorification of their transcendent Creator, who, in the ultimate gesture of cosmic humility, assumed flesh, lay helpless in a manger, and hung dying on a scaffold.

I am not suggesting that many contemporary Americans who are concerned about our ecologic crisis will be either able or willing to counsel with wolves or exhort birds. However, the present increasing disruption of the global environment is the product of a dynamic technology and science which were originating in the Western medieval world against which Saint Francis was rebelling in so original a way. Their growth cannot be understood historically apart from distinctive attitudes toward nature which are deeply grounded in Christian dogma. The fact that most people do not think of these attitudes as Christian is irrelevant. No new set of basic values has been accepted in our society to displace those of Christianity. Hence we shall continue to have a worsening ecologic crisis until we reject the Christian axiom that nature has no reason for existence save to serve man.

The greatest spiritual revolutionary in Western history, Saint Francis, proposed what he thought was an alternative Christian view of nature and man's relation to it: he tried to substitute the idea of the equality of all creatures, including man, for the idea of man's limitless rule of creation. He failed. Both our present science and our present technology are so tinctured with orthodox Christian arrogance toward nature that no solution for our ecologic crisis can be expected from them alone. Since the roots of our trouble are so largely religious, the remedy must also be essentially religious, whether we call it that or not. We must rethink and refeel our nature and destiny. The profoundly religious, but heretical, sense of the primitive Franciscans for the spiritual autonomy of all parts of nature may point a direction. I propose Francis as a patron saint for ecologists.

28 / Architectural Excerpts
NORMAN MAILER

a) A Piece for *The New York Times*

In Lyndon Johnson's book, *My Hope for America,* the fifth chapter is titled "Toward the Great Society." It contains this paragraph:

> ... fifty years from now, ... there will be four hundred million Americans, four-fifths of them in urban areas. In the remainder of this century, ... we will have to build homes, highways, and facilities equal to all those built since this country was first settled. In the next forty years we must rebuild the entire urban United States.

It is a staggering sentence. The city we inhabit at this moment is already close to a total reconstruction of the world our parents knew in their childhood. If there is no nuclear war, if we shift from cold war to some kind of peace, and there is a worldwide rise in the standard of living, then indeed we will build a huge new country. It is possible that not one in a thousand of the buildings put up by 1899 will still be standing in the year 2000.

But what will America look like? How will its architecture appear? Will it be the architecture of a Great Society, or continue to be the architecture of an empty promiscuous panorama where no one can distinguish between hospitals and housing projects, factories and colleges, concert halls, civic centers, and airport terminals? The mind recoils from the thought of an America rebuilt completely in the shape of those blank skyscrapers forty stories high, their walls dead as an empty television screen, their

SOURCE: Norman Mailer, *Cannibals and Christians* (New York: Dial Press, 1966), pp. 233–40. Copyright © 1965, 1966 by Norman Mailer; Copyright © 1964 by Urban America, Inc. Reprinted by permission of the author and Scott Meredith Literary Agency, Inc.

Norman Mailer, a novelist (*The Naked and the Dead, An American Dream, Why Are We in Vietnam?*), has dabbled in several other careers: as city planner, as politician (running for mayor of New York City), as journalist (*The Armies of the Night*).

form as interesting as a box of cleansing tissue propped on end. They are buildings which reveal nothing so much as the deterioration in real value of the dollar bill. They are denuded of ornament (which costs money), their windows are not subtly recessed into the wall but are laid flush with the surface like a patch of collodion on the skin, there is no instance where a roof with a tower, a gable, a spire, a mansard, a ridge or even a mooring mast for a dirigible intrudes itself into the sky, reminding us that every previous culture of man attempted to engage the heavens.

No, our modern buildings go flat, flat at the top, flat as eternal monotony, flat as the last penny in a dollar. There is so much corruption in the building codes, overinflation in the value of land, featherbedding built into union rules, so much graft, so much waste, so much public relations, and so much emptiness inflated upon so much emptiness that no one tries to do more with the roof than leave it flat.

As one travels through the arbitrary new neighborhoods of the present, those high squat dormitories which imprison the rich as well as the poor, one is not surprised that the violence is greater than it used to be in the old slum, up are the statistics for juvenile delinquency and for dope addiction. To live in the old slum jungle left many half crippled, and others part savage, but it was at least an environment which asked for wit. In the prison vistas of urban renewal, the violence travels from without to within, there is no wit—one travels down a long empty corridor to reach one's door, long as the corridors in the public schools, long as the corridors in the hospitals at the end of the road; the landscape of modern man takes on a sense of endless empty communications.

Sterile as an operating table is the future vista of suburban spread, invigorating as a whiff of deodorant is the sight of new office buildings. Small elation sits upon us as we contemplate the future, for the picturesque will be uprooted with the ugly, our populations will double, and in a city like New York, the brownstone will be replaced by a cube sixteen stories high with a huge park for parking cars and a little grass. The city will go up a little and it will go out, it will spread. We will live with glass walls in a cold climate. The entire world will come to look like

Queens Boulevard. We will have been uprooted so many times that future man will come to bear the same relation to the past that a hydroponic plant bears to soil.

Yet some part of us is aware that to uproot the past too completely is a danger without measure. It must at the least produce a profound psychic discomfort. For we do not know how much our perception of the present and our estimate of the future depend upon our sense of what has gone before. To return to an old neighborhood and discover it has disappeared is a minor woe for some; it is close to a psychological catastrophe for others, an amputation where the lost nerves still feel pain. This century must appear at times like a great beast which has lost its tail, but who could argue that the amputation was not self-inflicted?

There seems at loose an impulse to uproot every vestige of the past, an urge so powerful one wonders if it is not with purpose, if it is not in the nature of twentieth-century man to uproot himself not only from his past, but from his planet. Perhaps we live on the edge of a great divide in history and so are divided ourselves between the desire for a gracious, intimate, detailed and highly particular landscape and an urge less articulate to voyage out on explorations not yet made. Perhaps the blank faceless abstract quality of our modern architecture is a reflection of the anxiety we feel before the void, a kind of visual static which emanates from the psyche of us all, as if we do not know which way to go.

If we are to spare the countryside, if we are to protect the style of the small town and of the exclusive suburb, keep the organic center of the metropolis and the old neighborhoods, maintain those few remaining streets where the tradition of the nineteenth century and the muse of the eighteenth century still linger on the mood in the summer cool of an evening, if we are to avoid a megalopolis five hundred miles long, a city without shape or exit, a nightmare of ranch houses, highways, suburbs and industrial sludge, if we are to save the dramatic edge of a city—that precise moment when we leave the outskirts and race into the country, the open country—if we are to have a keen acute sense of concentration and a breath of release, then there is only one solution: the cities must climb, they must not spread, they must build up, not by increments, but by leaps, up and up, up to the heavens.

470

We must be able to live in houses one hundred stories high, two hundred stories high, far above the height of buildings as we know them now. New cities with great towers must rise in the plain, cities higher than mountains, cities with room for 400,000,000 to live, or that part of 400,000,000 who wish to live high in a landscape of peaks and spires, cliffs and precipices. For the others, for those who wish to live on the ground and with the ground, there will then be new room to live—the traditional small town will be able to survive, as will the old neighborhoods in the cities. But first a way must be found to build upward, to triple and triple again the height of all buildings as we know them now.

Picture, if you please, an open space where twenty acrobats stand, each locking hands with two different partners. Conceive then of ten acrobats standing on the shoulders of these twenty, and five upon the ten acrobats, and three more in turn above them, then two, then one. We have a pyramid of figures: six thousand to eight thousand pounds is supported upon a base of twenty pairs of shoes.

It enables one to think of structures more complex, of pyramids of steel which rise to become towers. Imagine a tower half a mile high and stressed to bear a vast load. Think of six or eight such towers and of bridges built between them, even as huge vines tie the branches of one high tree to another; think of groups of apartments built above these bridges (like the shops on the Ponte Vecchio in Florence) and apartments suspended beneath each bridge, and smaller bridges running from one complex of apartments to another, and of apartments suspended from cables, apartments kept in harmonious stress to one another by cables between them.

One can now begin to conceive of a city, or a separate part of a city, which is as high as it is wide, a city which bends ever so subtly in a high wind with the most delicate flexing of its near-to-numberless parts even as the smallest strut in a great bridge reflects the passing of an automobile with some fine-tuned quiver. In the subtlety of its swayings the vertical city might seem to be ready to live itself. It might be agreeable to live there.

The real question, however, has not yet been posed. It is whether a large fraction of the population would find it reasonable to live one hundred or two hundred stories in the air. There is the dread of heights. Would that tiny pit of suicide, planted like the small seed of murder in civilized man, flower prematurely into breakdown, terror and dread? Would it demand too much of a tenant to stare down each morning on a flight of 2,000 feet? Or would it prove a deliverance for some? Would the juvenile delinquent festering in the violence of his monotonous corridors diminish in his desire for brutality if he lived high in the air and found the intensity of his inexpressible vision matched by the intensity of the space through a fall?

That question returns us to the perspective of twentieth-century man. Caught between our desire to cling to the earth and to explore the stars, it is not impossible that a new life lived half a mile in the air, with streets in the clouds and chasms beyond each railing could prove nonetheless more intimate and more personal to us than the present congestions of the housing-project city. For that future man would be returned some individuality from his habitation. His apartment in the sky would be not so very different in its internal details from the apartments of his neighbors, no more than one apartment is varied from another in Washington Square Village. But his situation would now be different from any other. His windows would look out on a view of massive constructions and airy bridges, of huge vaults and fine intricacies. The complexity of our culture could be captured again by the imagination of the architect: our buildings could begin to look a little less like armored tanks and more like clipper ships. Would we also then feel the dignity of sailors on a fourmaster at sea? Living so high, thrust into space, might we be returned to that mixture of awe and elation, of dignity and self-respect and a hint of dread, that sense of zest which a man must have known working his way out along a yardarm in a stiff breeze at sea? Would the fatal monotony of mass culture dissolve a hint before the quiet swaying of a great and vertical city?

b) A Statement for *Architectural Forum*

The essence of totalitarianism is that it beheads. It beheads individuality, variety, dissent, extreme possibility, romantic faith; it blinds vision, deadens instinct; it obliterates the past. It makes factories look like college campuses or mental hospitals, where once factories had the specific beauty of revealing their huge and sometimes brutal function. It makes the new buildings on college campuses look like factories. It depresses the average American with the unconscious recognition that he is installed in a gelatin of totalitarian environment which is bound to deaden his most individual efforts. This new architecture, this totalitarian architecture, destroys the past. There is no trace of the forms which lived in the centuries before us, none of their arrogance, their privilege, their aspiration, their canniness, their creations, their vulgarities. We are left with less and less sense of the lives of men and women who came before us. So we are less able to judge the psychotic values of the present: overkill, fallout shelters, and adjurations . . . to drink a glass of milk each day. . . .

People who admire the new architecture find it of value because it obliterates the past. They are sufficiently totalitarian to wish to avoid the consequences of the past. Which of course is not to say that they see themselves as totalitarian. The totalitarian passion is an unconscious one. Which liberal, fighting for bigger housing and additional cubic feet of air space in elementary schools, does not see himself as a benefactor? Can he comprehend that the somewhat clammy pleasure he obtains from looking at the completion of the new school—that architectural horror!—is a reflection of a buried and ugly pleasure, a totalitarian glee that the Gothic knots and Romanesque oppressions which entered his psyche through the schoolhouses of his youth have now been excised? But those architectural wounds, those forms from his childhood, not only shamed him and scored him, but marked upon him as well a wound from culture itself— its buried message of the cruelty and horror which were rooted in the majesties of the past. Now the flat surfaces, blank ornamentation, and pastel colors of the new schoolhouses will maroon his children in an endless hallway of the present. A school is an *arena* to a child. Let it look like what it should be, mysterious, even gladiatorial, rather than look like a reception center for war brides. The totalitarian impulse not only washes away distinctions but looks for a style in buildings, in clothing, and in the ornamentations of tools, appliances, and daily objects which will diminish one's sense of function and reduce one's sense of reality by reducing such emotions as awe, dread, beauty, pity, terror, calm, horror, and harmony. By dislocating us from the most powerful emotions of reality, totalitarianism leaves us further isolated in the empty landscapes of psychosis, precisely that inner landscape of void and dread which we flee by turning to totalitarian styles of life. The totalitarian liberal looks for new schools and more desks; the real liberal looks for more difficult books to force upon the curriculum. A good school can survive in a converted cow barn.

Yes, the people who admire the new architecture are looking to eject into their environment and landscape the same deadness and monotony life has put into them. A vast deadness and a huge monotony, a nausea without spasm, has been part of the profit of American life in the last fifteen years—we will pay in the next fifteen as this living death is disgorged into the buildings our totalitarian managers will manage to erect for us.

Our commodities are swollen in price by false, needless and useless labor. Modern architecture is the child of this fact. It works with a currency which (measured in terms of the skilled and/or useful labor going into a building) is worth half the real value of nineteenth-century money. The mechanical advances in construction hardly begin to make up for the wastes of advertising, public relations, building union covenants, city grafts, land costs, and the anemia of a dollar diminished by armaments and taxes. In this context the formulas of modern architecture have triumphed, and her bastards—those new office skyscrapers —proliferate everywhere: one suspects the best reason is that modern architecture offers a pretext to a large real-estate operator to stick up a skyscraper at a fraction of the money it should cost, so helps him to conceal the criminal fact that we are being given a stricken building, a denuded, aseptic, unfinished work, stripped of ornament, origins, prejudices, not even a peaked roof or spire to engage the heavens.

It is too cheap to separate Mafia architects with their Mussolini Modern (concrete dormitories on junior-college campuses) from serious modern architects. No, I think Le Corbusier and Wright and all the particular giants of the Bauhaus are the true villains; the Mafia architects are their proper sons; modern architecture at its best is even more anomalous than at its worst, for it tends to excite the Faustian and empty appetites of the architect's ego rather than reveal an artist's vision of our collective desire for shelter which is pleasurable, substantial, intricate, intimate, delicate, detailed, foibled, rich in gargoyle, guignol, false closet, secret stair, witch's hearth, attic, grandeur, kitsch, a world of buildings as diverse as the need within the eye. Beware: the ultimate promise of modern architecture is collective sightlessness for the species.

VII / The Arts

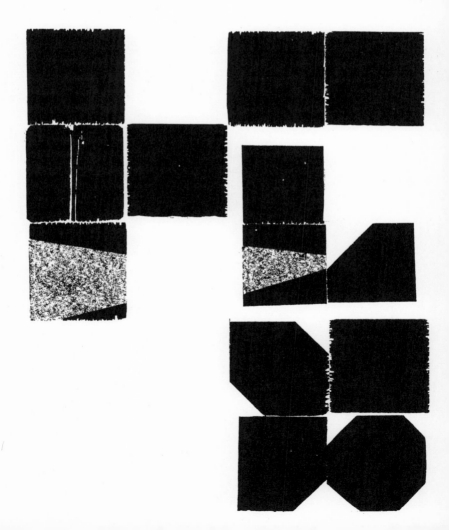

In a period of such overwhelming and rapid change, the arts have undergone radical revisions. Whether the arts have challenged the age or merely responded to it remains an issue for some future historian to settle, but the basic response of the contemporary artist (who is often an experimenter outside the system—an activist, a mystic, a dope addict, an anti-academic professor, a mutant, a madman) has been tuned to rejection of tradition and rejection of authority. So it would seem. When we speak of the arts in the late sixties and the prospects for the seventies, we are talking about a very confusing scene where the cultural experience turns over periodically like tulips or roses.

There are, nevertheless, some fundamental qualities which characterize the contemporary arts. First, there is an overriding belief in the purity of the experience which that particular art, whether plastic, literary, or aural, is conveying. This belief in purity is related to the "Now" generation's worship of self-awareness and self-consciousness. The arts today must speak to the individual, make him move to its rhythms, touch him in his soul, not his head. Second, there is a strong revulsion against the intellect or the intellectual, a persistence of an earlier trend that saw intellect as mechanical, closed, and dried out. The apostles for this view were D. H. Lawrence and Henry Miller, and their spiritual presence hangs rather heavily over the contemporary literary scene. In the plastic arts and in music, the freeing process also takes its inspiration from the first decades of this century. Third, despite the pessimism of much current art—particularly in literature—there is a belief in man's innocence, especially the conviction that man can be touched and changed by the arts. Thus, paradoxically, while the artist seems to have given up on mankind as a whole, he still believes in individual resurrection.

The next quality is often the most puzzling to the layman. Almost all of the arts are rejecting realism and everyday reality and embracing the fantastic, the apocalyptic, the fragmentary, the grotesque, elements of space-time and time-space that have little to do with the clock or the calendar. Even "pop" art, as one critic has pointed out, which deifies the ordinary, forces us to see the ordinary in a new way that questions our attitudes toward the trivial and the real. When pop art receded and "op" art replaced it, the latter carried the process even further, making obvious geometric grids into patterns of deception. Together both questioned and mocked the old definitions of art.

Fifth, all the arts seem to be working toward some statement about the space age. America has always been obsessed with space—that of seemingly endless frontiers, of the two bordering oceans, of hugeness of appetite and achievement—but the *avant garde* arts have intensified this obsession. Virtually all arts have broken with time—the drama, no less than the others, has moved towards temporal formlessness. The well-made play is now camp, no longer taken seriously. There may be a beginning, middle, and an end, but, as Godard says, they do not necessarily come in that order. The Living Theatre, as well as Godard's films, would appear to be the clearest manifestation of this development, with its free forms, its stress on individual expression, its breaking of barriers between "stage" time and "audience" time. Sixth, there appears to be a struggle in the arts to find some ground on which they can take hold when American reality is itself more fantastic than any reality art can capture. Early in the sixties, Philip Roth said that the novelist was at a terrible disadvantage, for American life made most fictional ideas pale by comparison. Thus, the writer was committed to a competition that he could never win. The artist's experiences increasingly bear out Roth's prophecy.

Finally, the arts are striving to lead a vast cultural transfiguration of the American soul, toward an untightening, opening process, away from the last vestiges of the Puritanical vision. Much of the distaste of the middle-aged generation toward the

480

new developments—see Leslie Fiedler's essay—is based on the utter disdain the new arts demonstrate toward established ideas and residual Puritanical feelings. William Burroughs has been a leading spokesman for this new vision, although his fiction has never quite aptly demonstrated his views. He is more interesting in person than in his prose. In this connection, the long interview with Allen Ginsberg in Part II is instructive: for Ginsberg both as a person and as a poet has dominated a large area of literary activity and attitude.

As a further break with tradition, the theories of Antonin Artaud, whom the French clapped into an insane asylum, have been of inestimable influence on the modern theatre, especially to dramatists and directors like Genet, Pinter, Beckett, Albee, and Peter Brook. Calling for "cruelty" as a technique of shocking his audiences, Artaud cleared the air of old texts, created a vibrant relationship between playwright and audience, and demanded that playwright, actors, and audience together seek human truth wherever it might lead. In these areas Artaud sought to establish a new theatrical process. Though Artaud remained essentially a theorist, the Living Theatre is an outgrowth of Artaud's influence as it has sifted down, and the recent *Marat-Sade* is a direct application of his conception of theater. But Artaud is far more radical than any current effort thus far would suggest.

Fiedler's essay attempts to derive some general principles from what appears to be the chaos of contemporary artistic endeavor. His position, incidentally, is influenced by several authors whose work is included in this book. Norman O. Brown, Allen Ginsberg, William Burroughs. Alan Watts, Norman Mailer, and Jerry Rubin first might clarify some of Fiedler's allusions and assumptions. The Burroughs essay exemplifies many of Fiedler's criteria for the "new mutants." There is, explicitly, the search for new forms and new ways of expression; there is, further, the willingness to forsake most models from the past, indeed a willingness to bore the reader in order to justify the search. We may be reminded of Professor Lifton's metaphor for this quasi-existential quest: "protean man."

There is little question that deliberate boredom is a factor in John Cage's music, for he weaves into his music a whole new series of sounds and pauses and even celebrates silence (see

Burroughs' statements on the "silence chambers"). Thus, if one listens to Cage hoping to hear strains of Mozart, he is bound to be disappointed and even feel "taken." What is distinctive about the "new music" is its insistence that the traditional orchestra does not limit the range of sounds; that sound may come from anywhere and anything (just as, visually, pop art does) and may be incorporated into any combination of the sounds themselves and the pauses between. The pause itself may take over: Cage has "written" a selection for the piano which requires him to sit at the piano for several minutes without touching the keys before he bows to the audience at the final "note."

While experimental music interests a relatively small though important audience, popular music, whether that of the Beatles, Bob Dylan, or The Wet Clams, has become *the* music of the "Now" generation. Only when we measure these rock groups and singers against the flat musical comedy songs or the middle-aged affection for Lawrence Welk and Liberace do they seem radical. But they do involve protest against nearly every aspect of modern society, American or otherwise. Richard Cory, E. A. Robinson's wealthy suicide, and William Butler Yeats, the occult poet, are among their heroes. Furthermore, they incorporate the anti-authoritarian styles of long hair, "acid" beat, drugs, impudence, social protest, and apocalyptic visions in their rhythms and lyrics.

Equally influential as the art form most beloved by the late sixties generation is the film. Though Fellini, Antonioni, Kubrick, Bergman, and Resnais have transformed the medium from slight entertainment into celluloid mirrors of the existential moment, Jean-Luc Godard has emerged at the end of the decade as the most influential. Of those in the vanguard, his films are not only the most individualistic and inspired, but the least predictable. Several of Godard's films made in the 1960s—*Les Carabiniers* (The Riflemen), *Band à Port* (Band of Outsiders), *Alphaville*, *Pierrot le Fou* (Pierrot the Mad), *La Chinoise*, and *Weekend*—have established this Swiss-born film maker as the most ambitious of the French "New Wave" directors. If his films are rarely satisfactory as entities, he is a genius of improvisation. In this respect, he is perhaps the most experimental within the traditional cinema forms; that is, he is not an underground film maker or a photographer. In *Weekend*, perhaps his most controversial film, he has found an apt metaphor for the mechanical, technological man of the present in the auto wrecks scattered along the French highways and in the casual way one character sets fire to another. The entire film is a critique of industrialization and the bourgeois life—through mockery, satire, and burlesque. His attacks on technology and on American militarism, his romantic defense of human values, his ironic contempt for all restrictive systems—whether totalitarian or democratic—and his flirtation with philosophical anarchy have made even his most seriously-flawed movies into cinematically exciting events, especially to the younger generation, from whose thoughts and actions his camera rarely wanders.

29 / The New Mutants

LESLIE A. FIEDLER

A realization that the legitimate functions of literature are bewilderingly, almost inexhaustibly various has always exhilarated poets and dismayed critics. And critics, therefore, have sought age after age to legislate limits to literature—legitimizing certain of its functions and disavowing others—in hope of insuring to themselves the exhilaration of which they have felt unjustly deprived, and providing for poets the dismay which the critics at least have thought good for them.

Such shifting and exclusive emphasis is not, however, purely the product of critical malice, or even of critical principle. Somehow every period is, to begin with, especially aware of certain functions of literature and especially oblivious to others: endowed with a special sensitivity and a complementary obtuseness, which, indeed, give to that period its characteristic flavor and feel. So, for instance, the Augustan Era is marked by sensi-

SOURCE: *Partisan Review* 32 (Fall 1965), 505–25. Copyright © 1965 by Partisan Review. Reprinted by permission.
Leslie A. Fiedler, the well known literary critic, teaches at the State University of New York (Buffalo) and is the author of *Love and Death in the American Novel*, *An End to Innocence*, and several other books.

tivity in regard to the uses of diction, obtuseness in regard to those of imagery.

What the peculiar obtuseness of the present age may be I find it difficult to say (being its victim as well as its recorder), perhaps toward the didactic or certain modes of the sentimental. I am reasonably sure, however, that our period is acutely aware of the sense in which literature if not invents, at least collaborates in the invention of time. The beginnings of that awareness go back certainly to the beginnings of the Renaissance, to Humanism as a self-conscious movement; though a critical development occurred toward the end of the eighteenth century with the dawning of the Age of Revolution. And we may have reached a second critical point right now.

At any rate, we have long been aware (in the last decades uncomfortably aware) that a chief function of literature is to express and in part to create not only theories of time but also attitudes toward time. Such attitudes constitute, however, a politics as well as an esthetics; or, more properly perhaps, a necessary mythological substratum of politics—as, in fact, the conventional terms reactionary, conservative, revolutionary indicate: all involving stances toward the past.

It is with the past, then, that we must start, since the invention of the past seems to have preceded that of the present and the future; and since we are gathered in a university at whose heart stands a library[1]—the latter, like the former, a visible monument to the theory that a chief responsibility of literature is to preserve and perpetuate the past. Few universities are explicitly (and none with any real degree of confidence) dedicated to this venerable goal any longer. The Great Books idea (which once transformed the University of Chicago and lives on now in provincial study groups) was perhaps its last desperate expression. Yet the shaky continuing existence of the universities and the building of new college libraries (with matching Federal funds) remind us not only of that tradition but of the literature created in its name: the neo-epic, for instance, all the way from Dante to Milton; and even the frantically nostalgic Historical Romance, out of the counting house by Sir Walter Scott.

[1] "The New Mutants" is a written version of a talk given by Mr. Fiedler at the Conference on the Idea of The Future held at Rutgers, in June, 1965. The conference was sponsored by Partisan Review and the Congress for Cultural Freedom, with the cooperation of Rutgers, The State University.

Obviously, however, literature has a contemporary as well as a traditional function. That is to say, it may be dedicated to illuminating the present and the meaning of the present, which is, after all, no more given than the past. Certainly the modern or bourgeois novel was thus contemporary in the hands of its great inventors, Richardson, Fielding, Smollett and Sterne; and it became contemporary again—with, as it were, a sigh of relief— when Flaubert, having plunged deep into the Historical Romance, emerged once more into the present of Emma Bovary. But the second function of the novel tends to transform itself into a third: a revolutionary or prophetic or futurist function; and it is with the latter that I am here concerned.

Especially important for our own time is the sense in which literature first conceived the possibility of the future (rather than an End of Time or an Eternal Return, an Apocalypse or Second Coming); and then furnished that future in joyous or terrified anticipation, thus preparing all of us to inhabit it. Men have dreamed and even written down utopias from ancient times; but such utopias were at first typically allegories rather than projections: nonexistent models against which to measure the real world, exploitations of the impossible (as the traditional name declares) rather than explorations or anticipations or programs of the possible. And, in any event, only recently have such works occupied a position anywhere near the center of literature.

Indeed, the movement of futurist literature from the periphery to the center of culture provides a clue to certain essential meanings of our times and of the art which best reflects it. If we make a brief excursion from the lofty reaches of High Art to the humbler levels of Pop Culture—where radical transformations in literature are reflected in simplified form—the extent and nature of the futurist revolution will become immediately evident. Certainly, we have seen in recent years the purveyors of Pop Culture transfer their energies from the Western and the Dracula-type thriller (last heirs of the Romantic and Gothic concern with the past) to the Detective Story especially in its hard-boiled form (final vulgarization of the realists' dedication to the present) to Science Fiction (a new genre based on hints in E. A. Poe and committed to "extrapolating" the future). This development is based in part on the tendency to rapid exhaustion inherent in popular forms; but in part reflects a growing sense of the irrelevance of the past and even of the present to 1965. Surely, there has never been a moment in which the most naïve as well as the most sophisticated have been so acutely aware of how the past threatens momentarily to disappear from the present, which itself seems on the verge of disappearing into the future.

And this awareness functions, therefore, on the level of art as well as entertainment, persuading quite serious writers to emulate the modes of Science Fiction. The novel is most amenable to this sort of adaptation, whose traces we can find in writers as various as William Golding and Anthony Burgess, William Burroughs and Kurt Vonnegut, Jr., Harry Matthews and John Barth —to all of whom young readers tend to respond with a sympathy they do not feel even toward such forerunners of the mode (still more allegorical than prophetic) as Aldous Huxley, H. G. Wells and George Orwell. But the influence of Science Fiction can be discerned in poetry as well, and even in the polemical essays of such polymath prophets as Wilhelm Reich, Buckminster Fuller, Marshall McLuhan, perhaps also Norman O. Brown. Indeed, in Fuller the prophetic–Science-Fiction view of man is always at the point of fragmenting into verse:

men are known as being six feet tall
because that is their tactile limit;
they are not known by how far we can hear them,
e.g., as a one-half mile man
and only to dogs are men known
by their gigantic olfactoral dimensions. . . .

I am not now interested in analyzing, however, the diction and imagery which have passed from Science Fiction into post-Modernist literature, but rather in coming to terms with the prophetic content common to both: with the myth rather than the modes of Science Fiction. But that myth is quite simply the myth of the end of man, of the transcendence or transformation of the human—a vision quite different from that of the extinction of our species by the Bomb, which seems stereotype rather than archetype and consequently the source of editorials rather than poems. More fruitful artistically is the prospect of the radical transformation (under the impact of advanced technology and the transfer of traditional human functions to machines) of *homo sapiens* into something else: the emergence—to use the language of Science Fiction itself—of "mutants" among us.

486

A simpleminded prevision of this event is to be found in Arthur C. Clarke's *Childhood's End*, at the conclusion of which the mutated offspring of parents much like us are about to take off under their own power into outer space. Mr. Clarke believes that he is talking about a time still to come because he takes metaphor for fact; though simply translating "outer space" into "inner space" reveals to us that what he is up to is less prediction than description; since the post-human future is now, and if not we, at least our children, are what it would be comfortable to pretend we still only foresee. But what, in fact, are they: these mutants who are likely to sit before us in class, or across from us at the dinner table, or who stare at us with hostility from street corners as we pass?

Beatniks or hipsters, layabouts and drop-outs we are likely to call them with corresponding hostility—or more elegantly, but still without sympathy, passive onlookers, abstentionists, spiritual catatonics. There resides in all of these terms an element of truth, at least about the relationship of the young to what we have defined as the tradition, the world we have made for them; and if we turn to the books in which they see their own destiny best represented (*The Clockwork Orange,* say, or *On the Road* or *Temple of Gold*), we will find nothing to contradict that truth. Nor will we find anything to expand it, since the young and their laureates avoid on principle the kind of definition (even of themselves) for which we necessarily seek.

Let us begin then with the negative definition our own hostility suggests, since this is all that is available to us, and say that the "mutants" in our midst are non-participants in the past (though our wisdom assures us this is impossible), drop-outs from history. The withdrawal from school, so typical of their generation and so inscrutable to ours, is best understood as a lived symbol of their rejection of the notion of cultural continuity and progress, which our graded educational system represents in institutional form. It is not merely a matter of their rejecting what happens to have happened just before them, as the young do, after all, in every age; but of their attempting to disavow the very idea of the past, of their seeking to avoid recapitulating it step by step—up to the point of graduation into the present.

Specifically, the tradition from which they strive to disengage is the tradition of the human, as the West (understanding the West to extend from the United States to Russia) has defined it,

Humanism itself, both in its bourgeois and Marxist forms; and more especially, the cult of reason—that dream of Socrates, re-dreamed by the Renaissance and surviving all travesties down to only yesterday. To be sure, there have long been anti-rational forces at work in the West, including primitive Christianity it-self; but the very notion of literary culture is a product of Hu-manism, as the early Christians knew (setting fire to libraries), so that the Church in order to sponsor poets had first to come to terms with reason itself by way of Aquinas and Aristotle.

Only with Dada was the notion of an anti-rational anti-liter-ature born; and Dada became Surrealism, i.e., submitted to the influence of those last neo-Humanists, those desperate Socratic Cabalists, Freud and Marx—dedicated respectively to contriving a rationale of violence and a rationale of impulse. The new ir-rationalists, however, deny all the apostles of reason, Freud as well as Socrates; and if they seem to exempt Marx, this is be-cause they know less about him, have heard him evoked less often by the teachers they are driven to deny. Not only do they reject the Socratic adage that the unexamined life is not worth living, since for them precisely the unexamined life is the only one worth enduring at all. But they also abjure the Freudian one: "Where id was, ego shall be," since for them the true rallying cry is, "Let id prevail over ego, impulse over order," or—in neg-ative terms—"Freud is a fink!"

The first time I heard this irreverent charge from the mouth of a student some five or six years ago (I who had grown up think-ing of Freud as a revolutionary, a pioneer), I knew that I was al-ready in the future; though I did not yet suspect that there would be no room in that future for the university system to which I had devoted my life. Kerouac might have told me so, or Ginsberg, or even so polite and genteel a spokesman for youth as J. D. Salinger, but I was too aware of what was wrong with such writers (their faults more readily apparent to my taste than their virtues) to be sensitive to the truths they told. It took, therefore, certain public events to illuminate (for me) the literature which might have illuminated them.

I am thinking, of course, of the recent demonstrations at Berkeley and elsewhere, whose ostensible causes were civil rights or freedom of speech or Vietnam, but whose not so secret slogan was all the time: *The Professor is a Fink!* And what an array of bad anti-academic novels, I cannot help reminding myself, written by disgruntled professors, created the mythology out of which that slogan grew. Each generation of students is invented by the generation of teachers just before them; but how different they are in dream and fact—as different as self-hatred and its reflection in another. How different the professors in Jeremy Larner's *Drive, He Said* from those even in Randall Jarrell's *Pictures from an Institution* or Mary McCarthy's *Groves of Academe.*

To be sure, many motives operated to set the students in action, some of them imagined in no book, however good or bad. Many of the thousands who resisted or shouted on campuses did so in the name of naïve or disingenuous or even nostalgic politics (be careful what you wish for in your middle age, or your children will parody it forthwith!); and sheer ennui doubtless played a role along with a justified rage against the hypocrisies of academic life. Universities have long rivaled the churches in their devotion to institutionalizing hypocrisy; and more recently they have outstripped television itself (which most professors affect to despise even more than they despise organized religion) in the institutionalization of boredom.

But what the students were protesting in large part, I have come to believe, was the very notion of man which the universities sought to impose upon them: that bourgeois-Protestant version of Humanism, with its view of man as justified by rationality, work, duty, vocation, maturity, success; and its concomitant understanding of childhood and adolescence as a temporarily privileged time of preparation for assuming those burdens. The new irrationalists, however, are prepared to advocate prolonging adolescence to the grave, and are ready to dispense with school as an outlived excuse for leisure. To them work is as obsolete as reason, a vestige (already dispensable for large numbers) of an economically marginal, pre-automated world; and the obsolescence of the two adds up to the obsolescence of everything our society understands by maturity.

Nor is it in the name of an older more valid Humanistic view of man that the new irrationalists would reject the WASP version; Rabelais is as alien to them as Benjamin Franklin. Disinterested scholarship, reflection, the life of reason, a respect for tradition stir (however dimly and confusedly) chiefly their contempt; and the Abbey of Theleme would seem as sterile to them as Robinson Crusoe's Island. To the classroom, the library, the laboratory, the office conference and the meeting of scholars, they prefer the demonstration, the sit-in, the riot: the mindless unity of an impassioned crowd (with guitars beating out the rhythm in the background), whose immediate cause is felt rather than thought out, whose ultimate cause is itself. In light of this, the Teach-in, often ill understood because of an emphasis on its declared political ends, can be seen as implicitly a parody and mockery of the real classroom: related to the actual business of the university, to real teaching only as the Demonstration Trial (of Dimitrov, of the Soviet Doctors, of Eichmann) to real justice or Demonstration Voting (for one party or a token two) to real suffrage.

At least, since Berkeley (or perhaps since Martin Luther King provided students with new paradigms for action) the choice has been extended beyond what the earlier laureates of the new youth could imagine in the novel: the nervous breakdown at home rather than the return to "sanity" and school, which was the best Salinger could invent for Franny and Holden; or Kerouac's way out for his "saintly" vagrants, that "road" from nowhere to noplace with homemade gurus at the way stations. The structure of those fictional vaudevilles between hard covers that currently please the young (*Catch 22*, *V.*, *A Mother's Kisses*), suggest in their brutality and discontinuity, their politics of mockery something of the spirit of the student demonstrations; but only Jeremy Larner, as far as I know, has dealt explicitly with the abandonment of the classroom in favor of the dionysiac pack, the turning from *polis* to *thiasos*, from forms of social organization traditionally thought of as male to the sort of passionate community attributed by the ancients to females out of control.

Conventional slogans in favor of "Good Works" (pious emendations of existing social structures, or extensions of accepted "rights" to excluded groups) though they provide the motive power of such protests are irrelevant to their form and their final significance. They become their essential selves, i.e., genuine new forms of rebellion, when the demonstrators hoist (as they did in the final stages of the Berkeley protests) the sort of slogan which embarrasses not only fellow-travelers but even the bureaucrats who direct the initial stages of the revolt: at the University of California, the single four-letter word no family newspaper would reprint, though no member of a family who could read was likely not to know it.

It is possible to argue on the basis of the political facts themselves that the word "fuck" entered the whole scene accidentally (there were only four students behind the "Dirty Speech Movement," only fifteen hundred kids could be persuaded to demonstrate for it, etc., etc.). But the prophetic literature which anticipates the movement indicates otherwise, suggesting that the logic of their illogical course eventually sets the young against language itself, against the very counters of logical discourse. They seek an anti-language of protest as inevitably as they seek anti-poems and anti-novels, end with the ultimate anti-word, which the demonstrators at Berkeley disingenuously claimed stood for FREEDOM UNDER CLARK KERR.

Esthetics, however, had already anticipated politics in this regard; porno-poetry preceding and preparing the way for what Lewis Feuer has aptly called porno-politics. Already in 1963, in an essay entitled *"Phi Upsilon Kappa,"* the young poet Michael McClure was writing: "Gregory Corso has asked me to join with him in a project to free the word FUCK from its chains and strictures. I leap to make some new freedom. . . ." And McClure's own "Fuck Ode" is a product of this collaboration, as the very name of Ed Saunders' journal, *Fuck You*, is the creation of an analogous impulse. The aging critics of the young who have dealt with the Berkeley demonstrations in such journals as *Commentary* and the *New Leader* do not, however, read either Saunders' porno-pacifist magazine or *Kulchur*, in which McClure's manifesto was first printed—the age barrier separating readership in the United States more effectively than class, political affiliation or anything else.

Their sense of porno-esthetics is likely to come from deserters from their own camp, chiefly Norman Mailer, and especially his recent *An American Dream*, which represents the entry of anti-language (extending the tentative explorations of "The Time of Her Time") into the world of the middle-aged, both on the level of mass culture and that of yesterday's ex-Marxist, post-Freudian avant-garde. Characteristically enough, Mailer's book has occasioned in the latter quarters reviews as irrelevant, incoherent, misleading and fundamentally scared as the most philistine responses to the Berkeley demonstrations, Philip Rahv and Stanley Edgar Hyman providing two egregious examples. Yet elsewhere (in sectors held by those more at ease with their own conservatism, i.e., without defunct radicalisms to uphold) the most obscene forays of the young are being met with a disheartening kind of tolerance and even an attempt to adapt them to the conditions of commodity art.

But precisely here, of course, a disconcerting irony is involved; for after a while, there will be no Rahvs and Hymans left to shock—anti-language becoming mere language with repeated use and in the face of acceptance; so that all sense of exhilaration will be lost along with the possibility of offense. What to do then except to choose silence, since raising the ante of violence is ultimately self-defeating; and the way of obscenity in any case leads as naturally to silence as to further excess? Moreover, to the talkative heirs of Socrates, silence is the one offense that never wears out, the radicalism that can never become fashionable; which is why, after the obscene slogan has been hauled down, a blank placard is raised in its place.

There are difficulties, to be sure, when one attempts to move from the politics of silence to an analogous sort of poetry. The opposite number to the silent picketer would be the silent poet, which is a contradiction in terms; yet there are these days non-singers of (perhaps) great talent who shrug off the temptation to song with the muttered comment, "Creativity is out." Some, however, make literature of a kind precisely at the point of maximum tension between the tug toward silence and the pull toward publication. Music is a better language really for saying what one would prefer not to say at all—and all the way from certain sorts of sufficiently cool jazz to Rock'n'Roll (with its minimal lyrics that defy understanding on a first hearing), music is the preferred art of the irrationalists.

But some varieties of skinny poetry seem apt, too (as practised, say, by Robert Creeley after the example of W. C. Williams), since their lines are three parts silence to one part speech:

> *My lady*
> *fair with*
> *soft*
> *arms, what*

can I say to
you— words, words . . .

And, of course, fiction aspiring to become Pop Art, say, *An American Dream* (with the experiments of Hemingway and Nathanael West behind it), works approximately as well, since clichés are almost as inaudible as silence itself. The point is not to shout, not to insist, but to hang cool, to baffle all mothers, cultural and spiritual as well as actual.

When the Town Council in Venice, California was about to close down a particularly notorious beatnik cafe, a lady asked to testify before them, presumably to clinch the case against the offenders. What she reported, however, was that each day as she walked by the cafe and looked in its windows, she saw the unsavory types who inhabited it "just standing there, looking— nonchalant." And, in a way, her improbable adjective does describe a crime against her world; for non-chaleur ("cool," the futurists themselves would prefer to call it) is the essence of their life-style as well as of the literary styles to which they respond: the offensive style of those who are not so much *for* anything in particular, as "with it" in general.

But such an attitude is as remote from traditional "alienation," with its profound longing to end disconnection, as it is from ordinary forms of allegiance, with their desperate resolve not to admit disconnection. The new young celebrate disconnection— accept it as one of the necessary consequences of the industrial system which has delivered them from work and duty, of that welfare state which makes disengagement the last possible virtue, whether it call itself Capitalist, Socialist or Communist. "Detachment" is the traditional name for the stance the futurists assume; but "detachment" carries with it irrelevant religious, even specifically Christian overtones. The post-modernists are surely in some sense "mystics," religious at least in a way they do not ordinarily know how to confess, but they are not Christians.

Indeed, they regard Christianity, quite as the Black Muslim (with whom they have certain affinities) do, as a white ideology: merely one more method—along with Humanism, technology, Marxism—of imposing "White" or Western values on the colored rest of the world. To the new barbarian, however, that would-be post-Humanist (who is in most cases the white offspring of Christian forebears) his whiteness is likely to seem if not a stigma and symbol of shame, at least the outward sign of his exclusion from all that his Christian Humanist ancestors rejected in themselves and projected mythologically upon the colored man. For such reasons, his religion, when it becomes explicit, claims to be derived from Tibet or Japan or the ceremonies of the Plains Indians, or is composed out of the non-Christian sub-mythology that has grown up among Negro jazz musicians and in the civil rights movement. When the new barbarian speaks of "soul," for instance, he means not "soul" as in Heaven, but as in "soul music" or even "soul food."

It is all part of the attempt of the generation under twenty-five, not exclusively in its most sensitive members but especially in them, to become Negro, even as they attempt to become poor or pre-rational. About this particular form of psychic assimilation I have written sufficiently in the past (summing up what I had been long saying in chapters seven and eight of *Waiting for the End*), neglecting only the sense in which what starts as a specifically American movement becomes an international one, spreading to the *yé-yé* girls of France or the working-class entertainers of Liverpool with astonishing swiftness and ease.

What interests me more particularly right now is a parallel assimilationist attempt, which may, indeed, be more parochial and is certainly most marked at the moment in the Anglo-Saxon world, i.e., in those cultural communities most totally committed to bourgeois-Protestant values and surest that they are unequivocally "white." I am thinking of the effort of young men in England and the United States to assimilate into themselves (or even to assimilate themselves into) that otherness, that sum total of rejected psychic elements which the middle-class heirs of the Renaissance have identified with "woman." To become new men, these children of the future seem to feel, they must not only become more Black than White but more female than male. And it is natural that the need to make such an adjustment be felt with especial acuteness in post-Protestant highly industrialized societies, where the functions regarded as specifically male for some three hundred years tend most rapidly to become obsolete.

494

Surely, in America, machines already perform better than humans a large number of those aggressive-productive activities which our ancestors considered man's special province, even his *raison d'être*. Not only has the male's prerogative of making things and money (which is to say, of working) been preempted, but also his time-honored privilege of dealing out death by hand, which until quite recently was regarded as a supreme mark of masculine valor. While it seems theoretically possible, even in the heart of Anglo-Saxondom, to imagine a leisurely, pacific male, in fact the losses in secondary functions sustained by men appear to have shaken their faith in their primary masculine function as well, in their ability to achieve the conquest (as the traditional metaphor has it) of women. Earlier, advances in technology had detached the wooing and winning of women from the begetting of children; and though the invention of the condom had at least left the decision to inhibit fatherhood in the power of males, its replacement by the "loop" and the "pill" has placed paternity at the mercy of the whims of women.

Writers of fiction and verse registered the technological obsolescence of masculinity long before it was felt even by the representative minority who give to the present younger generation its character and significance. And literary critics have talked a good deal during the past couple of decades about the conversion of the literary hero into the non-hero or the anti-hero; but they have in general failed to notice his simultaneous conversion into the non- or anti-male. Yet ever since Hemingway at least, certain male protagonists of American literature have not only fled rather than sought out combat but have also fled rather than sought out women. From Jake Barnes to Holden Caulfield they have continued to run from the threat of female sexuality; and, indeed, there are models for such evasion in our classic books, where heroes still eager for the fight (Natty Bumppo comes to mind) are already shy of wives and sweethearts and mothers.

It is not absolutely required that the anti-male anti-hero be impotent or homosexual or both (though this helps, as we remember remembering Walt Whitman), merely that he be more seduced than seducing, more passive than active. Consider, for instance, the oddly "womanish" Herzog of Bellow's current best seller, that Jewish Emma Bovary with a Ph.D., whose chief flaw is physical vanity and a taste for fancy clothes. Bellow, however, is more interested in summing up the past than in evoking the future; and *Herzog* therefore seems an end rather than a beginning, the product of nostalgia (remember when there were real Jews once, and the "Jewish Novel" had not yet been discovered!) rather than prophecy. No, the post-humanist, post-male, post-white, post-heroic world is a post-Jewish world by the same token, anti-Semitism as inextricably woven into it as into the movement for Negro rights; and its scriptural books are necessarily *goyish*, not least of all William Burroughs' *The Naked Lunch.*

Burroughs is the chief prophet of the post-male post-heroic world; and it is his emulators who move into the center of the relevant literary scene, for *The Naked Lunch* (the later novels are less successful, less exciting but relevant still) is more than it seems: no mere essay in heroin-hallucinated homosexual pornography—but a nightmare anticipation (in Science Fiction form) of post-Humanist sexuality. Here, as in Alexander Trocchi, John Rechy, Harry Matthews (even an occasional Jew like Allen Ginsberg, who has begun by inscribing properly anti-Jewish obscenities on the walls of the world), are clues to the new attitudes toward sex that will continue to inform our improbable novels of passion and our even more improbable love songs.

The young to whom I have been referring, the mythologically representative minority (who, by a process that infuriates the mythologically inert majority out of which they come, "stand for" their times), live in a community in which what used to be called the "Sexual Revolution," the Freudian-Laurentian revolt of their grandparents and parents, has triumphed as imperfectly and unsatisfactorily as all revolutions always triumph. They confront, therefore, the necessity of determining not only what meanings "love" can have in their new world, but—even more disturbingly—what significance, if any, "male" and "female" now possess. For a while, they (or at least their literary spokesmen recruited from the generation just before them) seemed content to celebrate a kind of *reductio* or *exaltatio ad absurdum* of their parents' once revolutionary sexual goals: The Reichian-inspired Cult of the Orgasm.

Young men and women eager to be delivered of traditional ideologies of love find especially congenial the belief that not union or relationship (much less offspring) but physical release is the end of the sexual act; and that, therefore, it is a matter of indifference with whom or by what method one pursues the therapeutic climax, so long as that climax is total and repeated frequently. And Wilhelm Reich happily detaches this belief from the vestiges of Freudian rationalism, setting it instead in a context of Science Fiction and witchcraft; but his emphasis upon "full genitality," upon growing up and away from infantile pleasures, strikes the young as a disguised plea for the "maturity" they have learned to despise. In a time when the duties associated with adulthood promise to become irrelevant, there seems little reason for denying oneself the joys of babyhood— even if these are associated with such regressive fantasies as escaping it all in the arms of little sister (in the Gospel according to J. D. Salinger) or flirting with the possibility of getting into bed with papa (in the Gospel according to Norman Mailer).

Only Norman O. Brown in *Life Against Death* has come to terms on the level of theory with the aspiration to take the final evolutionary leap and cast off adulthood completely, at least in the area of sex. His post-Freudian program for pan-sexual, non-orgasmic love rejects "full genitality" in favor of a species of indiscriminate bundling, a dream of unlimited sub-coital intimacy which Brown calls (in his vocabulary the term is an honorific) "polymorphous perverse." And here finally is an essential clue to the nature of the second sexual revolution, the post-sexual revolution, first evoked in literature by Brother Antoninus more than a decade ago, in a verse prayer addressed somewhat improbably to the Christian God:

> *Annul in me my manhood, Lord, and make*
> *Me woman sexed and weak . . .*
>   *Make me then*
> *Girl-hearted, virgin-souled, woman-docile, maiden-meek . . .*

Despite the accents of this invocation, however, what is at work is not essentially a homosexual revolt or even a rebellion against women, though its advocates seek to wrest from women their ancient privileges of receiving the Holy Ghost and pleasuring men; and though the attitudes of the movement can be adapted to the anti-female bias of, say, Edward Albee. If in

Who's Afraid of Virginia Woolf Albee can portray the relationship of two homosexuals (one in drag) as the model of contemporary marriage, this must be because contemporary marriage has in fact turned into something much like that parody. And it is true that what survives of bourgeois marriage and the bourgeois family is a target which the new barbarians join the old homosexuals in reviling, seeking to replace Mom, Pop and the kids with a neo-Whitmanian gaggle of giggling *camerados*. Such groups are, in fact, whether gathered in coffee houses, university cafeterias or around the literature tables on campuses, the peacetime equivalents, as it were, to the demonstrating crowd. But even their program of displacing Dick-Jane-Spot-Baby, etc., the WASP family of grade school primers, is not the fundamental motive of the post-sexual revolution.

What is at stake from Burroughs to Bellow, Ginsberg to Albee, Salinger to Gregory Corso is a more personal transformation: a radical metamorphosis of the Western male—utterly unforeseen in the decades before us, but visible now in every high school and college classroom, as well as on the paperback racks in airports and supermarkets. All around us, young males are beginning to retrieve for themselves the cavalier role once piously and class-consciously surrendered to women: *that of being beautiful and being loved.* Here once more the example to the Negro—the feckless and adorned Negro male with the blood of Cavaliers in his veins—has served as a model. And what else is left to young men, in any case, after the devaluation of the grim duties they had arrogated to themselves in place of the pursuit of loveliness?

All of us who are middle-aged and were Marxists, which is to say, who once numbered ourselves among the last assured Puritans, have surely noticed in ourselves a vestigial roundhead rage at the new hair styles of the advanced or—if you please—delinquent young. Watching young men titivate their locks (the comb, the pocket mirror and the bobby pin having replaced the jackknife, catcher's mitt and brass knuckles), we feel the same baffled resentment that stirs in us when we realize that they have rejected work. A job and unequivocal maleness—these are two sides of the same Calvinist coin, which in the future buys nothing.

498

Few of us, however, have really understood how the Beatle hairdo is part of a syndrome, of which high heels, jeans tight over the buttocks, etc., are other aspects, symptomatic of a larger retreat from masculine aggressiveness to female allure—in literature and the arts to the style called "camp." And fewer still have realized how that style, though the invention of homosexuals, is now the possession of basically heterosexual males as well, a strategy in their campaign to establish a new relationship not only with women but with their own masculinity. In the course of that campaign, they have embraced certain kinds of gesture and garb, certain accents and tones traditionally associated with females or female impersonators; which is why we have been observing recently (in life as well as fiction and verse) young boys, quite unequivocally male, playing all the traditional roles of women: the vamp, the coquette, the whore, the icy tease, the pure young virgin.

Not only oldsters, who had envisioned and despaired of quite another future, are bewildered by this turn of events, but young girls, too, seem scarcely to know what is happening—looking on with that new, schizoid stare which itself has become a hallmark of our times. And the crop-headed jocks, those crew-cut athletes who represent an obsolescent masculine style based on quite other values, have tended to strike back blindly; beating the hell out of some poor kid whose hair is too long or whose pants are too tight—quite as they once beat up young Communists for revealing that their politics had become obsolete. Even heterosexual writers, however, have been slow to catch up, the revolution in sensibility running ahead of that in expression; and they have perforce permitted homosexuals to speak for them (Burroughs and Genet and Baldwin and Ginsberg and Albee and a score of others), even to invent the forms in which the future will have to speak.

The revolt against masculinity is not limited, however, to simple matters of coiffure and costume, visible even to athletes; or to the adaptation of certain campy styles and modes to new uses. There is also a sense in which two large social movements that have set the young in motion and furnished images of action for their books—movements as important in their own right as porno-politics and the pursuit of the polymorphous perverse—

are connected analogically to the abdication from traditional maleness. The first of these is nonviolent or passive resistance, so oddly come back to the land of its inventor, that icy Thoreau who dreamed a love which ". . . has not much human blood in it, but consists with a certain disregard for men and their erections. . . ."

The civil rights movement, however, in which nonviolence has found a home, has been hospitable not only to the sort of post-humanist I have been describing; so that at a demonstration (Selma, Alabama will do as an example) the true hippie will be found side by side with backwoods Baptists, nuns on a spiritual spree, boy bureaucrats practicing to take power, resurrected socialists, Unitarians in search of a God, and just plain tourists, gathered, as once at the Battle of Bull Run, to see the fun. For each of these, nonviolence will have a different sort of fundamental meaning—as a tactic, a camouflage, a passing fad, a pious gesture—but for each in part, and for the post-humanist especially, it will signify the possibility of heroism without aggression, effective action without guilt.

There have always been two contradictory American ideals: to be the occasion of maximum violence, and to remain absolutely innocent. Once, however, these were thought hopelessly incompatible for males (except, perhaps, as embodied in works of art), reserved strictly for women: the spouse of the wife-beater, for instance, or the victim of rape. But males have now assumed these classic roles; and just as a particularly beleaguered wife occasionally slipped over the dividing line into violence, so do the new passive protestors—leaving us to confront (or resign to the courts) such homey female questions as: *Did Mario Savio really bite that cop in the leg as he sagged limply toward the ground?*

The second social movement is the drug cult, more widespread among youth, from its squarest limits to its most beat, than anyone seems prepared to admit in public; and at its beat limit at least inextricably involved with the civil rights movement, as the recent arrests of Peter DeLissovoy and Susan Ryerson revealed even to the ordinary newspaper reader. "Police said that most of the recipients [of marijuana] were college students," the U.P. story runs. "They quoted Miss Ryerson and DeLissovoy as saying that many of the letter packets were sent to civil rights workers." Only fiction and verse, however, has dealt with the conjunction of homosexuality, drugs and civil rights, eschewing the general piety of the press which has been unwilling to compromise "good works" on behalf of the Negro by associating it with the deep radicalism of a way of life based on the ritual consumption of "pot."

The widespread use of such hallucinogens as peyote, marijuana, the "mexican mushroom," LSD, etc., as well as pep pills, goof balls, airplane glue, certain kinds of cough syrups and even, though in many fewer cases, heroin, is not merely a matter of a changing taste in stimulants but of the programmatic espousal of an anti-puritanical mode of existence—hedonistic and detached—one more strategy in the war on time and work. But it is also (to pursue my analogy once more) an attempt to arrogate to the male certain traditional privileges of the female. What could be more womanly, as Elémire Zolla was already pointing out some years ago, than permitting the penetration of the body by a foreign object which not only stirs delight but even (possibly) creates new life?

In any case, with drugs we have come to the crux of the futurist revolt, the hinge of everything else, as the young tell us over and over in their writing. When the movement was first finding a voice, Allen Ginsberg set this aspect of it in proper context in an immensely comic, utterly serious poem called "America," in which "pot" is associated with earlier forms of rebellion, a commitment to catatonia, and a rejection of conventional male potency:

> *America I used to be a communist when I was a kid I'm not*
> *   sorry.*
> *I smoke marijuana every chance I get.*
> *I sit in my house for days on end and stare at the roses in the*
> *   closet.*
> *When I go to Chinatown I . . . never get laid . . .*

Similarly, Michael McClure reveals in his essay, "*Phi Upsilon Kappa*," that before penetrating the "cavern of Anglo-Saxon," whence he emerged with the slogan of the ultimate Berkeley demonstrators, he had been on mescaline. "I have emerged from a dark night of the soul; I entered it by Peyote." And by now, drug-taking has become as standard a feature of the literature of the young as oral-genital love-making. I flip open the first issue of yet another ephemeral San Francisco little magazine quite at random and read: "I tie up and the main pipe [the ante-cobital vein, for the clinically inclined] swells like a prideful beggar beneath the skin. Just before I get on it is always the worst." Worse than the experience, however, is its literary rendering; and the badness of such confessional fiction, flawed by the sentimentality of those who desire to live "like a cunning vegetable," is a badness we older readers find it only too easy to perceive, as our sons and daughters find it only too easy to overlook. Yet precisely here the age and the mode define themselves; for not in the master but in the hacks new forms are established, new lines drawn.

Here, at any rate, is where the young lose us in literature as well as life, since here they pass over into real revolt, i.e., what we really cannot abide, hard as we try. The mother who has sent her son to private schools and on to Harvard to keep him out of classrooms overcrowded with poor Negroes, rejoices when he sets out for Mississippi with his comrades in SNCC, but shudders when he turns on with LSD; just as the ex-Marxist father, who has earlier proved radicalism impossible, rejoices to see his son stand up, piously and pompously, for CORE or SDS, but trembles to hear him quote Alpert and Leary or praise Burroughs. Just as certainly as liberalism is the LSD of the aging, LSD is the radicalism of the young.

If whiskey long served as an appropriate symbolic excess for those who chafed against Puritan restraint without finally challenging it—temporarily releasing them to socially harmful aggression and (hopefully) sexual self-indulgence, the new popular drugs provide an excess quite as satisfactorily symbolic to the post-Puritans—releasing them from sanity to madness by destroying in them the inner restrictive order which has somehow survived the dissolution of the outer. It is finally insanity, then, that the futurists learn to admire and emulate, quite as they learn to pursue vision instead of learning, hallucination rather than logic. The schizophrenic replaces the sage as their ideal, their new culture hero, figured forth as a giant schizoid Indian (his madness modeled in part on the author's own experiences with LSD) in Ken Kesey's *One Flew Over the Cuckoo's Nest.*

The hippier young are not alone, however, in their taste for the insane; we live in a time when readers in general respond sym-

502

pathetically to madness in literature wherever it is found, in established writers as well as in those trying to establish new modes. Surely it is not the lucidity and logic of Robert Lowell or Theodore Roethke or John Berryman which we admire, but their flirtation with incoherence and disorder. And certainly it is Mailer at his most nearly psychotic, Mailer the creature rather than the master of his fantasies who moves us to admiration; while in the case of Saul Bellow, we endure the theoretical optimism and acceptance for the sake of the delightful melancholia, the fertile paranoia which he cannot disavow any more than the talent at whose root they lie. Even essayists and analysts recommend themselves to us these days by a certain redemptive nuttiness; at any rate, we do not love, say, Marshall McLuhan less because he continually risks sounding like the body-fluids man in *Dr. Strangelove*.

We have, moreover, recently been witnessing the development of a new form of social psychiatry[2] (a psychiatry of the future already anticipated by the literature of the future) which considers some varieties of "schizophrenia" not diseases to be cured but forays into an unknown psychic world: random penetrations by bewildered internal cosmonauts of a realm that it will be the task of the next generations to explore. And if the accounts which the returning schizophrenics give (the argument of the apologists runs) of the "places" they have been are fantastic and garbled, surely they are no more so than, for example, Columbus' reports of the world he had claimed for Spain, a world bounded— according to his newly drawn maps—by Cathay on the north and Paradise on the south.

In any case, poets and junkies have been suggesting to us that the new world appropriate to the new men of the latter twentieth century is to be discovered only by the conquest of inner space: by an adventure of the spirit, an extension of psychic possibility, of which the flights into outer space—moonshots and expeditions to Mars—are precisely such unwitting metaphors and analogues as the voyages of exploration were of the earlier breakthrough into the Renaissance, from whose consequences the young seek now so desperately to escape. The laureate of that new conquest is William Burroughs; and it is fitting that the final word be his:

[2] Described in an article in the *New Left Review* of November-December, 1964, by R. D. Laing who advocates "ex-patients helping future patients go mad."

"This war will be won in the air. In the Silent Air with
Image Rays. You were a pilot remember? Tracer bullets
cutting the right wing you were free in space a few sec-
onds before in blue space between eyes. Go back to
Silence. Keep Silence. Keep Silence. K.S. K.S. . . . From
Silence re-write the message that is you. You are the
message I send to The Enemy. My Silent Message."
The Naked Astronauts were free in space. . . .

30 / Journey Through Time-Space: An Interview with William S. Burroughs

DANIEL ODIER

QUESTION: Your books, since *The Ticket That Exploded* especially, are no longer "novels"; a breaking up of novelistic form is
noticeable in *Naked Lunch*. Toward what end or goal is this
breakup heading?

ANSWER: That's very difficult to say. I think the novelistic
form is probably outmoded and that we may look forward to a future in which people do not read at all or read only illustrated
books and magazines or some abbreviated form of reading matter. To compete with television and photo magazines, writers
will have to develop more precise techniques producing the
same effect on the reader as lurid action photo.

Q: What separates *Naked Lunch* from *Nova Express*? What is
the most important evolution between these two books?

A: I would say that the introduction of the cutup and foldin
method which occurred between *Naked Lunch* and *Nova Ex-*

SOURCE: *Evergreen Review* 13 (June 1969), 39–41, 78–89. Copyright © 1969 by
William Burroughs and Daniel Odier. Reprinted by permission of Harold Matson
Co., Inc.
    William S. Burroughs is the author of several "experimental" novels, including
Naked Lunch, Nova Express, and a recent collage of interviews and excerpts
called *Academy 23*.

press is undoubtedly the most important evolution between these books. In *Nova Express* I think I get further from the conventional novel form than I did in *Naked Lunch*. I don't feel that *Nova Express* was in any sense a wholly successful book.

Q: You wrote: "Writing is fifty years behind painting." How can the gap be closed?

A: I did not write that; Mr. Brion Gysin, who is both a painter and a writer, did. Why this gap? Because the painter can touch and handle his medium and the writer cannot. The writer does not yet know what words are. He deals only with abstractions from the source point of words. The painter's ability to touch and handle his medium led to montage techniques sixty years ago. It is to be hoped that the extension of cutup techniques will lead to more precise verbal experiments closing this gap and giving a whole new dimension to writing. These techniques can show the writer what words are and put him in tactile communication with his medium. This, in turn, could lead to a precise science of words and show how certain word-combinations produce certain effects on the human nervous system.

Q: Did you use the technique of foldin and cutup for a long time before moving on to the use of the tape recorder? What were your most interesting experiences with the earlier technique?

A: The first extension of the cutup method occurred through the use of tape recorders, and this extension was introduced by Mr. Brion Gysin. The simplest tape recorder cutup is made by recording some material and then cutting in passages at random —of course the words are wiped off the tape where these cutins occur—and you get very interesting juxtapositions. Some of them are very useful from a literary point of view and some are not. I would say that my most interesting experience with the earlier techniques was the realization that when you make cutups you do not get simply random juxtapositions of words, that they do mean something, and often that these meanings refer to some future event. I've made many cutups and then later recognized that the cutup referred to something I read later in a newspaper or in a book, or something that happened. To give a very simple example, I made a cutup of something Mr. Getty had written, I believe for *Time and Tide*. The following phrase emerged:

"It's a bad thing to sue your own father." About three years later his son sued him. Perhaps events are pre-written and pre-recorded, and when you cut word lines, the future leaks out. I have seen enough examples to convince me that the cutups are a

Q: For you the tape recorder is a device for breaking down the barriers which surround consciousness. How did you come to use tape recorders? What is the advantage of that technique over the foldin cutup technique?

A: I think that was largely the influence of Mr. Brion Gysin, who pointed out that the cutup method could be carried much further on tape recorders. Of course, you can do all sorts of things on tape recorders which can't be done anywhere else—effects of simultaneity, echoes, speedups, slowdowns, playing three tracks at once, and so forth. There are all sorts of things you can do on a tape recorder that cannot possibly be indicated on a printed page. The concept of simultaneity cannot be indicated on a printed page except very crudely, through the use of columns, and even so, the reader must follow one column down. We're used to reading from left to right and then back, and this conditioning is not very easy to break down.

Q: When you have arrived at a mix or montage, do you follow the channels opened by the text or do you adapt what you want to say to the mix?

A: I would say I follow the channels opened by the rearrangement of the text. This is the most important function of the cutup. I may take a page, cut it up, and get a whole new idea for straight narrative, and not use any of the cutup material at all, or I may use a sentence or two out of the actual cutup.

It's not unconscious at all; it's a very definite operation . . . the simplest way is to take a page, cut it down the middle and across the middle, and then rearrange the four sections. That's a very simple form of cutup if you just want to get some idea of one rearrangement of the words on that page. And it's quite conscious; there's nothing of automatic writing or unconscious procedure involved here.

You don't know what you're going to get, simply because of the limitations of the human mind, any more than the average person can plan five moves ahead in chess. Presumably, it would be possible for someone with a photographic memory to look at a page and cut it up in his mind, that is, put these words up here and those up there.

I've recently written a film script on the life of Dutch Schultz. Now this is perfectly straight writing. Nonetheless, I cut up every page and suddenly got a lot of new ideas that were then incorporated into the structure of the narrative. This is perfectly straight film treatment, quite intelligible to the average reader, in no sense experimental writing.

Q: Does anyone anticipate using cutup in the film?

A: Cutups have been used in films for a long time. In fact, films are assembled in the cutting room. Like the painter, film technicians can touch and handle their medium, move pieces of it around, and try out new juxtapositions. For example, in a straight narrative passage there is a delirium scene or a scene of someone in a confused state of mind, remembering past events. The writer can, of course, construct such a scene consciously and artistically. My method is to type out the material to be used and then strain it through several cutup procedures. In this way I find a more realistic picture of delirium emerges than could be achieved by artificial reconstruction. You are handling, as it were, the materials and processes of delirium. I make a number of cutups and select the ones finally that seem to me the most successful. The selection and arrangement of materials is quite conscious, but there is a random factor by which I obtain the material I use, then select and work it over into an acceptable form.

Q: To what degree do you control what you put into your montages?

A: Well, you control what you put *into* your montages; you don't fully control what comes out. That is, I select a page to cut up and I have a control over what I put in. I simply fit what comes out of the cutups back into a narrative structure.

Q: Do you work while you're traveling on trains or boats?

A: I have done this, particularly on trains, if I have a drawing room and a desk. I don't travel very often on boats . . . I attempted making montages of what I saw out the window on a train, and these attempts were described in an interview in the *Paris Review*. That is one example of a train trip in which I tried typing, incorporating what I saw in the passing stations, and also taking pictures. Merely an experiment . . .

Q: When you have taken real, raw materials from life by various means, do you always project them into another space-time?

A: Well, yes, I do in many cases. For example, you'll read something in a newspaper or see something in the street, pick up a character maybe from someone you see in the street, then you transform the character and change the setting.

Q: Do you use photographs or films along with your tape recordings? Films with a matching sound track? How does the resulting juxtaposition of different materials work out?

A: I have done quite a lot of experimentation in making tape recordings and films at the same time and have accumulated some rather odd results and experiences, all quite inconclusive, interesting, but not actually very applicable to writing. Films with matching sound tracks . . . we're talking about film actually, film with a sound track. There are many possibilities here, many suggestions and ideas I've had for new effects in film. For example, take a television set, shut off the sound, and put on any arbitrary sound track, and it will seem to fit. Show a bunch of people running for a bus in Piccadilly and put in machine-gun sound effects and it will look like Petrograd in 1917; people will assume that they are running because they're being machine-gunned. What you see is determined largely by what you hear. You can make many experiments, for example, I've taken one of these Danger . . . James Bond . . . Man from UNCLE programs and made a recording of it, then I shut off the sound track and used that sound track with another program, a similar program, and let someone watch it. They won't be able to tell the difference; you won't be able to make them believe that this is not the sound track that goes with that particular image track. Or take one politician and record his speech and substitute it for another's. Of course no one knows the difference; there isn't that much difference.

Q: In making up a text out of various materials, what is the importance of points of intersection? Starting with this material, how do the "sequences" and "rhythms" organize themselves?

A: The points of intersection are very very important certainly. In cutting up you will get a point of intersection where the new material intersects with what is there already in some very precise way, and then you start from there. As to the sequences and rhythms organizing themselves, well, they don't. The cutups will give you new materials, but they won't tell you what to do with it.

Q: Have you tried enlarging on tape-recorder techniques with, say, some kind of computer?

A: Yes. This can be done on a computer. I have a very good friend, Ian Somerville, a computer programmer, who says it is quite possible though very complicated. Certainly a computer can do any degree of cutting up or rearranging of materials that you put into it.

Q: But you haven't experimented with it?

A: To some extent, yes. Brion Gysin took some of his permutated poems and put them on a computer. Five words I think runs to about sixty-four pages. All the possible permutations of it.

Q: What do you actually record, what kind of things?

A: I haven't done much recording lately. I've been very busy with straight writing. But I have recorded all sorts of things . . . street sounds, music, parties, conversations . . .

Q: What is the important thing in music, when you use music?

A: Music is extremely important. The whole Moslem world is practically controlled by music. Certain music is played at certain times, and the association of music is one of the most powerful. John Cage and Earl Brown have carried the cutup method much further in music than I have in writing.

Q: Do you try for one kind of music rather than another?

A: I've made a lot of street recordings in Morocco that include music; I've recorded radio and television programs when I was doing a lot of work with tape recorders. In Morocco where I knew people who have quite extensive libraries of Moroccan music I have recorded that because I wanted to play it again. There's nothing special about that; it's just recording music that you want to hear.

Q: Do you think the prejudice that exists against the cutup method and its extension can be attributed to the fear of really penetrating into time and space?

A: Very definitely. The word is one of the most powerful instruments of control as exercised by the newspaper, images as well, the two together of course—there are both words and images in newspapers. . . . If you start cutting these up and rearranging them, you are breaking down the control system. Fear and prejudice are always dictated by the control system just as the church built up prejudice against heretics; it wasn't inherent in the population, it was dictated by the church which was in control at that time. If something threatens the position of the establishment, of any establishment, they will oppose it, will condition people to fear and reject or ridicule it.

Q: Is the ability "to see what is in front of us" a way of escaping from the image-prison which surrounds us?

A: Very definitely, yes. But this is an ability which very few people have, and fewer and fewer as time passes. For one thing, because of the absolute barrage of images to which we are subjected, we become blunted. Remember that a hundred years ago there were relatively few images, and people living in a more simplified environment, a farm environment, encounter very few images and those they see quite clearly. But if you're absolutely bombarded with images from passing trucks and cars and televisions and newspapers, you become blunted, and this makes a permanent haze in front of your eyes; you can't see anything.

Q: When you say that when you're in a world of simple images you see them more clearly, what do you mean by clearly?

A: There's nothing between them and the image. A farmer really sees his cows, he really sees what's in front of him quite

510

clearly. It isn't a question of familiarity, it's a question of something being between you and the image, so that you can't see it. And as I say, this continual barrage of images hazes over everything; it's like walking around in smog; we don't see anything. I don't say that the farmer has any sort of mystical identification with the cow, but he's aware whether there's anything wrong with the cow, of all sorts of things about the cow relative to how the cow is useful to him, and fits into his environment.

Q: Is the introduction of what you call "the message of resistance" the most important thing in the montage? Why?

A: I would say it's a very important factor in the montage because it does tend to break down the instruments of control, the principal instruments of control which are word and image, and, to some extent, to nullify them.

Q: Your books are rarely obscure or hard to understand, and you have mentioned to me in conversation a desire to become even more clear. Is the concern for clarity consistent with a still vaster exploration of the infinite possibilities offered by your literary methods?

A: When people speak of clarity in writing they generally mean plot, continuity, beginning, middle, and end, adherence to a "logical" sequence. But things don't happen in logical sequence and people don't think in logical sequence. Any writer who hopes to approximate what actually occurs in the mind and body of his characters cannot confine himself to such an arbitrary structure as logical sequence. Joyce was accused of being unintelligible and he was presenting only one level of cerebral events: conscious subvocal speech. I think it is possible to create multilevel events and characters that a reader could comprehend with his entire organic being.

Q: You say that tape-recorder and cinema techniques can alter or falsify reality. How is this done?

A: We think of the past as being unchangeable. Actually the past is ours to shape and change as we will. Two men talk. Two men sitting under a tree worn smooth by others who sat there before or after time switched the track through a field of little white flowers. If no recording of the conversation is made, it exists only in the memory of the two actors. Suppose I make a recording of the conversation, alter and falsify the recording, and play the altered recording back to the two actors. If my alterations have been skillfully and plausibly applied ("Yes . . . Mr. B might well have said that") the two actors will *remember* the altered recording.

Take a talking picture of you walking out in the morning to buy cigarettes and the papers. Run it back; you remember everything that happened—there it is on screen and muttering off the sound track. . . . Now, I can make you remember something that didn't happen by splicing it in. A truck passed just then: there it is on the screen, spliced in for you to remember. Always need a peg to hang it on. Well, I plant a truck passed just then and what's so strange about that? Nothing, except it didn't pass just then; it passed a year ago, and what more logical than said truck hitting a woman on a Paris corner three years later? "I wonder if the old cow died or not," he said dazedly as the medics led him away. You see what I mean? Once you have a truck on set with Larry the Lorry at the wheel, down Canal Street with no brakes, blood and tennis shoes all over the street, a limp foot dangles, or, say I splice in a little daffer asks you for the time it happens, funny I didn't remember till now. Well, once that little man who wasn't there is there on set he might well whip out a stiletto and assassinate the French Consul once the hole in reality is made and doubt consumed all the facts of history riddled with retroactive inserts all files and records of whatever nature to be immediately destroyed by order of the Emergency Sanitation Department documents are forgeries by nature before or after it is obvious.

Q: To what extent can this "new mythology," this new framework of associations and images, affect the awareness of the reader and make him move about in space and time?

A: That would depend entirely on the reader, how open he is to new experience, and how able he is to move out of his own frame of reference. Of course, most people are only able to give a very small fraction of their attention to what they read—to anything they're doing—because of their various compulsive preoccupations, and with just a tenth of their attention on something they don't move very far. Others are able to apply much more attention.

Q: Your characters are engulfed in a whirlwind of infernal happenings. They are embogged in the substance of the book. Is there a possible way to salvation for them?

A: I object to the word salvation as having a messianic Christian connotation, of final resolution . . . I don't feel that my characters, or the books in which they appear, are in any way reflecting a mood of despair. Actually, in many ways they're in the tradition of the picaresque novel. It's a question of your interpretation of "infernal happenings." Some people have much more tolerance for unusual happenings than others do. People in small towns are absolutely appalled by some very slight change, whereas people in large cities are very much less upset by change, and if riots go on and on and on, people are going to take them as a matter of course—they're already doing it.

Q: Do free men exist in your books?

A: Free men don't exist in anyone's books, because they are the author's creations. I would say that free men don't exist on this planet at this time, because they don't exist in human bodies; by the mere fact of being in a human body, you're completely controlled by all sorts of biological and environmental necessities.

Q: You often use silence as a device of terror, a "virus," as you call it, which breaks down characters into meaningless cyphers. What does this silence represent?

A: I don't think of silence as being a device of terror at all. In fact, quite the contrary. Silence is only frightening to people who are compulsively verbalizing. As you know, they have these sense withdrawal chambers and immersion chambers; there's one at the University of Oklahoma. Well, they put marines in there, and they'd be absolutely out of their minds in about ten minutes; they could not endure silence and solitude because of the inner contradictions words cover. But Gerald Heard got in there with a full dose of LSD and stayed three hours. Personally, I find nothing upsetting about silence at all. In fact it can't get too quiet for me. I would say that silence is only a device of terror for people who just can't keep their mouths shut. Because they're compulsive verbalizers and . . . they're people we can do without anyway . . .

Q: Is your interest in Mayan civilization connected with the expansion of consciousness which you try to stimulate in your reader?

A: The ancient Mayans possessed one of the most precise and hermetic control calendars ever used on this planet, a calendar that in effect controlled what the populace did, thought, and felt on any given day. A study of this model system throws light on modern methods of control. Knowledge of the calendar was the monopoly of a priestly caste who maintained their position with minimal police and military force. The priests had to start with a very accurate calendar for the tropical year, consisting of 365 days divided into 18 months of 20 days and a final period of 5 days, and these five days were considered especially unlucky and in consequence turned out to be so. An accurate calendar was essential to the foundation and maintenance of the priest's power.

The Mayans were almost entirely dependent on the maize crop, and the method of agriculture employed was slash and burn. Brush was cut down, allowed to dry, and then burned. The corn was planted with a planting stick. The Mayans had no ploughs and no domestic animals capable of pulling a plough. Since the topsoil is shallow and a stratum of limestone lies six inches under the surface, ploughs are not functional in this area and the slash and burn method is used to the present day. Slash and burn cultivation depends on exact timing. The brush must be cut and given time to dry before the rains start. Miscalculation of a few days can lose a year's crop.

In addition to the yearly calendar which regulated agricultural operations there was a sacred almanac of 260 days. This ceremonial calendar governed 13 festivals of 20 days each. The ceremonial calendar rolled through the year like a wheel, and consequently the festivals occurred at different dates each year, but always in the same sequence. The festivals consisted of religious ceremonies, music, feasts, sometimes human sacrifice. Accordingly, the priests could calculate into the future or the past exactly what the populace would be doing, hearing, seeing on a given date. This alone would have enabled them to predict

514

the future or reconstruct the past with considerable accuracy since they could determine what conditioning would be or had been applied on any given date to a population which for many years remained in hermetic seclusion, protected by impassable mountains and jungles from the waves of invaders who swept down the central plateau of Mexico.

There is every reason to infer the existence of a third, secret calendar which referred to conditioning in precise sequence applied to the populace under cover of the festivals, very much as a stage magician uses patter and spectacle to cover movements which would otherwise be apparent to the audience. There are many ways in which such conditioning can be effected, the simplest being waking suggestion, which is fully explained in a later context. Briefly, waking suggestion is a technique for implanting verbal or visual suggestions which take direct effect on the autonomic nervous system because the subject's conscious attention is directed somewhere else, in this case on the overt content of the festivals. (Waking suggestion is not to be confused with subliminal suggestion which is suggestion below the level of conscious awareness.) So the priests could calculate what the populace saw and heard on a given day and also what suggestions were secretly implanted on that day.

To obtain some idea of the secret calendar, consider the Reactive Mind (R.M.) as postulated by L. Ron Hubbard, the founder of Scientology. Mr. Hubbard described the R.M. as an ancient instrument of control designed to stultify and limit the potential for action in a constructive or destructive direction. The precise content of the R.M. as set forth in his formulation is considered confidential material since it can cause illness and upsets, so I will limit myself to general considerations without giving the exact phrases used.

The R.M. consists of consequential, sequential, and contradictory propositions that have command value at the automatic level of behavior, quite as automatic and involuntary as the metabolic commands that regulate rate of heart beats, digestion, balance of chemical constituents in the blood stream, brain waves. The regulator center of the autonomic nervous system which controls bodily processes and metabolism is the hypothalamus in the back brain. Undoubtedly the hypothalamus is the neurological intersection point where the R.M. is implanted. The

R.M. may be described as an artificially constructed and highly disadvantageous regulatory system grafted onto the natural regulatory center. The R.M., as expounded by Mr. Hubbard, is of considerable antiquity, antedating all modern languages, and yet manifesting itself through all modern languages. Consequently, it must refer to a *symbol system*. And, except for the intervention of Bishop Landa, we could infer by analogy what this symbol system consisted of since all control systems are basically similar. Bishop Landa collected all the Mayan books he could lay hands on—a stack of them six feet high—and burned the lot. To date only three authenticated Mayan codices have turned up that survived this barbarous action.

Mr. Hubbard logically postulates that the R.M. commands take effect because they relate to actual goals, needs, conditions of those affected. A consequential command is a command that one must obey in consequence of having been born: "to be here in a human body." A sequential command follows from this basic proposition: "to seek food, shelter, sexual satisfaction," "to exist in relation to other human bodies." Contradictory commands are two commands that contradict each other given at the same time. "TENSHUN!" The solider automatically stiffens to the command. "AT EASE!" The soldier automatically relaxes. Now imagine a captain who strides into the barracks snapping "TENSHUN" from one side of his face and "AT EASE" from the other (quite possible to do this with dubbing techniques). The attempt to obey two flatly contradictory commands at once, both of which have a degree of command value at the automatic level, disorients the subject. He may react with rage, apathy, anxiety, even collapse. Another example: I give the command "SIT DOWN" and when the command is obeyed promptly the subject receives a reward. If it is not obeyed promptly he receives a severe electric shock. When he has been conditioned to obey, I add the command "STAND UP" and condition him to obey this command in precisely the same way. Now I give both commands simultaneously. The results may well be complete collapse as Pavlov's dogs collapsed when given contradictory signals at such short intervals that their nervous systems could not adjust.

The aim of these commands from the viewpoint of a control system is to limit and confine. All control units employ such commands. For contradictory commands to have force, the subject must have been conditioned to obey both commands automatically, and the commands must relate to his actual goals. "TENSHUN," "AT EASE," "SIT DOWN," "STAND UP" are arbitrary commands tenuously connected to any basic goal of the subject. (Of course, "TENSHUN" relates to the goal to be a good soldier or at least to stay out of the guard house, which gives the command what strength it has.) Consider another pair of commands that contradict each other: "to make a good impression," "to make an awful impression." This relates to much more basic goals. Everyone wants to make a good impression. His self-regard, livelihood, sexual satisfaction depend on making a good impression. Why then does the subject, when he is trying most desperately to make a good impression, make the worst impression possible? Because he also has the goal to make a bad impression which operates on an involuntary automatic level. This self-destructive goal is such a threat to his being that he *reacts* against it. He may be conscious or partially conscious of the negative goal, but he cannot confront it directly. The negative goal forces him to react. The Reactive Mind consists of goals so repulsive or frightening to the subject that he compulsively reacts against them, and it is *precisely this reaction that keeps these negative goals in operation*. Negative goals are implanted by fear.

Consider a pair of contradictory commands that were undoubtedly used in some form by the Mayan priests: "to rebel stridently," "to submit meekly." Every time a worker nerved himself to rebel, the goal to submit was activated, causing him to assert rebellion more and more stridently, thus activating more and more compulsively the goal to submit. So he trembles, stammers, and collapses before an authority figure whom he consciously despises. No exercise of so-called will power affects these automatic reactions. The goal to submit was implanted by a threat so horrible that he could not confront it, and the Mayan secret books obviously consisted of such horrific pictures. The few that have survived bear witness to this. Men are depicted turning into centipedes, crabs, plants. Bishop Landa was so appalled by what he saw that his own reactive mind dictated his vandalous act. Like his modern counterparts who scream for censorship and book burning, he did not take account of the fact that any threat clearly seen and confronted loses force. The Mayan priests took care that the populace did not see the books.

Mr. Hubbard's R.M. contains about 300 items. Some are commands arranged in pairs, some are visual representations. Using the R.M. as a model—and the Mayan system must have been quite similar—postulate that during a ceremonial month of 20 days, four items were repeated or represented 20 times on the first day; 4 more items 20 times on the second day, and so on—80 items for the 20-day month. The next 20-day month of the sacred almanac, 80 more items until the items were exhausted, after which they were repeated in precisely the same sequence, thus constituting a secret calendar. The priests then could calculate precisely what reactive commands had been or would be restimulated on any date past or future, and these calculations enabled them to reconstruct the past or predict the future with considerable accuracy. They were dealing from a stacked deck. Calculations of past and future calendar juxtapositions took up a good deal of their time, and they were more concerned with the past than the future. There are calculations that go back 400,-000,000 years. These probings into the remote past may be interpreted as an assertion that the calendars always existed and always will exist. (All control systems claim to reflect the immutable laws of the universe.) These calculations must have looked like this:

year, month, day of the 365-day calendar which was calculated from 5 Ahua 8 Cumhu
a mythical date when time began
year, month, and day of the sacred almanac or ceremonial calendar
year, month, and day of the secret calendar.

Mayan students have succeeded in deciphering dates in the 365-day calendar. Lacking cross-references comparable to the Rosetta Stone, much of the writing remains unsolved. If we interpret the writing as oriented toward control, we can postulate that all the inscriptions refer to dates and the events, ceremonies, suggestions, pictures, and planetary juxtapositions correlated with dates. Any control system depends on precise timing. A picture or suggestion may be quite innocuous at one time and devastating at another. For example, "to make a splendid impression," "to make an awful impression" may have no effect on somebody when he is not in a competitive context. The same man bucking for lieutenant bars or apprentice priest can be reliably washed out by the same pair of contradictory commands brought into restimulation.

This seemingly hermetic control calendar broke down even before the Aztecs invaded Yucatan and long before the arrival of the Spaniards. All control systems work on punishment-reward. When punishment overbalances reward, when the masters have no rewards left to give, revolts occur. The continual demands for forced labor on the temples and stelae, coupled with a period of famine, may have been the precipitating factor. Or possibly some forgotten Bolivar revealed the content of the secret books. In any case, the workers rebelled, killed the priests, and defaced the stelae and temples as symbols of enslavement.

Now translate the Mayan control calendar into modern terms. The mass media of newspapers, radio, television, magazines form a ceremonial calendar to which all citizens are subjected. The "priests" wisely conceal themselves behind masses of contradictory data and vociferously deny that they exist. Like the Mayan priests, they can reconstruct the past and predict the future on a statistical basis through manipulation of media. It is the daily press preserved in newspaper morgues that makes detailed reconstruction of past dates possible. How can the modern priests predict seemingly random future events? Start with the many factors in mass media that can be controlled and predicted.

1. *Layout*: The format of newspapers and magazines can be decided in advance. The TV programs to be used in juxtaposition with news broadcasts can be decided in advance.

2. *The news to be played up and the news played down*: Ten years ago in England, drug arrests were four-line, back-page items. Today they are front-page headlines.

3. *Editorials and letters to the editors*: The letters published are of course selected in accordance with preconceived policy.

4. *Advertisements*.

So the modern ceremonial calendar is almost as predictable as the Mayan. What about the secret calendar? Any number of reactive commands can be inserted in advertisements, editorials, newspaper stories. Such commands are implicit in the layout and juxtaposition of items. Contradictory commands are an integral part of the modern industrialized environment. Stop. Go. Wait here. Go there. Come in. Stay out. Be a man. Be a woman. Be white. Be black. Live. Die. Be your real self. Be somebody else. Be a human animal. Be a superman. Yes. No. Rebel. Submit. RIGHT. WRONG. Make a splendid impression. Make an awful impression. Sit down. Stand up. Take your hat off. Put your hat on. Create. Destroy. Live now. Live in the future. Live in the past. Obey the law. Break the law. Be ambitious. Be modest. Accept. Reject. Plan ahead. Be spontaneous. Decide for yourself. Listen to others. TALK. SILENCE. Save money. Spend money. Speed up. Slow down. This way. That way. Right. Left. Present. Absent. Open. Closed. Entrance. Exit. IN. OUT. Etc., round the clock.

This creates a vast pool of statistical newsmakers. It is precisely uncontrollable, automatic reactions that make news. The controllers know what reactive commands they are going to restimulate and in consequence they know what will happen. Contradictory suggestion is the basic formula of the daily press: "Take drugs, everybody is doing it." "Drug taking is WRONG." Newspapers spread violence, sex, drugs, then come on with the old RIGHT WRONG FAMILY CHURCH AND COUNTRY sound.

It is wearing very thin. The modern control calendar is breaking down. Punishment now overbalances reward in the so-called "permissive" society, and young people no longer want the paltry rewards offered them. Rebellion is worldwide. The present controllers have an advantage which the Mayan priests did not have: an overwhelming arsenal of weapons which the rebels cannot hope to obtain or duplicate. Clubs and spears can be produced by anyone. Tanks, planes, battleships, heavy artillery, and nuclear weapons are a monopoly of those in power. As their psychological domination weakens, modern establishments are relying more and more on this advantage and now maintain their position by naked force (how permissive is the "permissive society"?). Yet the advantage of weaponry is not so overwhelming as it appears. To implement weapons the controllers need

520

soldiers and police. These guardians must be kept under reactive control. Hence the controllers must rely on people who are always stupider and more degraded by the conditioning essential to their suppressive function.

Techniques exist to erase the Reactive Mind and achieve a complete freedom from past conditioning and immunity against such conditioning in the future. Scientology processing accomplishes this. Erasure of the R.M. is carried out on the E Meter, a very sensitive reaction tester developed by Mr. Hubbard. If an R.M. item reads on the E Meter the subject is still reacting to it. When an item ceases to read he is no longer reacting to it. It may be necessary to run the entire R.M. hundreds of times to effect complete erasure. But it will erase. The method works. I can testify to that through my own experience. It takes time, at least two months of training 8 hours a day, to learn how to use the E Meter and how to run the material. It is expensive, about $3,000 for the training and processing that leads to erasure of the Reactive Mind. A reconstruction of the symbol system that must underlie the Reactive Mind would open the way for more precise and speedy erasure.

Two recent experiments indicate the possibility of mass deconditioning. In one experiment, volunteers were wired to an encephalographic unit that recorded their brain waves. When alpha brain waves, which are correlated with a relaxed state of mind and body, appeared on screen the subject was instructed to maintain this state as long as possible. After some practice alpha waves could be produced at will. The second experiment is more detailed and definitive (*Herald Tribune,* January 31, 1969): "U.S. scientist demonstrated that animals can learn to control such automatic responses as heart rate, blood pressure, glandular secretions, and brain waves in response to rewards and punishments. The psychologist is Dr. N. E. Miller. He says that his findings upset the traditional thinking that the autonomic nervous system which controls the working of the heart, digestive system, and other internal organs is completely involuntary. Dr. Miller and his coworkers were able to teach animals to increase or decrease the amount of saliva they produced, raise or lower their blood pressure, increase or decrease their intestinal contractions, stomach activity, and urinary output, and change their brain wave patterns using as a reward direct electrical stimulation of the so-called reward areas of the brain when the desired response occurred. Rats were able to learn to raise or lower their heart rates by 20 percent in 90 minutes of training. Retesting showed that they remembered their lessons well, Dr. Miller said."

In what way does this experiment differ from the experiment by which Pavlov demonstrated the conditioned reflex? I quote from *Newsweek,* February, 1969: "Until now most psychologists believed that the autonomic nervous system could be trained only by the classical conditioning techniques of Pavlov. An animal that hears a bell at the same time it is given food will eventually salivate at the sound of the bell alone. In classical conditioning, a stimulus that naturally produces a given response must always be used along with the so-called neutral stimulus (the bell). In this way a shock could be used to teach an animal to increase his heartbeat at the sound of a bell, since a shock normally causes an increase. But classical conditioning would not induce a reduced heart rate." Dr. Miller said his demonstration that the autonomic nervous system can also learn through rewards and punishments indicates that all learning is one and the same thing. He has also trained human subjects to reduce their heart rates.

Eliminate the metabolic symptoms of anxiety and you eliminate anxiety. You could not experience anxiety with a slow heartbeat, relaxed muscles, alpha brain waves, and no reaction on the E Meter. Complete control of emotional responses could be achieved by Dr. Miller's method. Anxiety reactions can be removed as they were implanted, by punishment and reward. It is now possible to decondition man from the whole punishment-reward cycle which has held him on an animal level for 500,000 years, by rewarding the manifestations of deconditioning and punishing the old automatic responses. Only those dedicated to suppressive control will oppose this deconditioning process.

Q: You mention the use of the E Meter as a deconditioning device or instrument. Could you enlarge on this point somewhat?

A: The E Meter, designed and patented by L. Ron Hubbard, the founder of Scientology, has been impounded by the Pure Food and Drug cops and ridiculed in the press as if it were a fraudulent healing device. What exactly is the E Meter and what are its uses? The E Meter is a reaction detector. It reads with a fall of the needle to the right on *resistance* to a thought. If the subject reacts to any thought presented with fear, anger, disagreement, anxiety, guilt, the Meter will read with a fall. Consequently, the E Meter, in skilled hands, is an infallible lie detector that could replace all brutal interrogation methods, and clear innocent people. If the subject tries to suppress a read, the read will be heavier.

This use of the E Meter is incidental. The essential application of this instrument is to bring conflicts and problems into precise focus, whereupon they dissolve. To show how this happens, I will define two revolutionary concepts introduced by Mr. Hubbard: to not-is and to as-is. To not-is something is to fight it, resist it, react to it, try to wipe it out by force. Not-ising always aggravates conflicts and problems. "A man who has fought evil all his life still has evil with him. A man who has fought ugliness all his life still has ugliness with him." On the other hand, to as-is something, *to see it as it is* without fear, anger, love, propitiation, or any emotional reaction will bring about the disappearance of what is as-ised in the mind of the subject and often externally, as well. This would seem to be almost impossible to achieve. You may realize that it is to your disadvantage to react with anger or anxiety to a person or a situation and yet be powerless not to react. No effort of so-called will power can prevent these involuntary emotional reactions. However, there is a means whereby any material, no matter how painful or highly charged, can be seen for what it is with no reaction. This means is the Hubbard E Meter. If you are reacting to material presented, your reaction will read by a fall to the right on the Meter. When the Meter no longer reads, you are not reacting to the material presented. The same item may read in another time and context, but for the moment it is flat. You are not reacting to it. So the seemingly impossible transformation of being able to look calmly and objectively at something that half an hour ago caused you to boil with rage, tremble with anxiety, cringe with guilt and shame can be accomplished on the E Meter.

To give an oversimplified example. Take a black militant and put him on the E Meter. Tell him to mock up a nigger-killing Southern sheriff chuckling over the notches in his gun. The needle falls off the dial. He mocks up the sheriff again. The needle falls off the dial. Again, again, again, for two hours if need be. No matter how long it takes, the time will come when he mocks up the sheriff and there is no read on the E Meter. He is looking at this creature calmly with slow heartbeat and normal blood pressure and *seeing it for what it is*. He has as-ised Big Jim Clark. As-ising *does not* mean acceptance, submission, or resignation. On the contrary, when he can look at Big Jim with no reaction, he is infinitely better equipped to deal with the external manifestation, as a calm man fights better than an angry one. If you can't bring yourself to see the target you can't hit it. When the needle reads off you are *off target*.

What causes these involuntary reactions of rage or anxiety is a hidden goal to give in and submit, which is implanted by all control systems, and all existing governments are control systems. In the face of mistreatment and injustice, the subject cannot confront this hidden goal. Once the goal to submit is as-ised it disappears. Then resistance becomes rational, controlled, and effective. As-is the goal to submit and you will overcome. As-is the goal to lose and you will win. As-is the goal to fail and you will succeed. As-is the goal to give in and you will fight very much better because you are no longer fighting on two fronts. As-ising goals to lose, give in, submit, is very painful and it may take long hours on the E Meter. But it can be done. Once you have as-ised a painful goal that resulted in humiliating defeat you will realize that all defeats can be as-ised and erased.

I have just given a simplified example of a known enemy who would be expected to read heavily on the Meter. The E Meter can also find and nullify *unknown enemies. The E Meter knows what you know and don't know that you know:* that a trusted business associate is out to cheat you, that your girlfriend is a two-timing, gold-digging bitch. If the E Meter reads with a strong fall when someone's name is called, you are in disagreement or conflict with that person whether you know it or not. In many cases the person is an active enemy. And you know who your enemies are. To find out that a close associate is actually an enemy and that you have really known this all along is, of course, a common experience. It is truly surprising to call the name of someone you have never thought of as either a friend

524

or an enemy and see the needle fall off the dial. When this happens you have found a *hidden enemy*.

When a person or situation reads strongly on the E Meter you will see that person or situation *light up* on a screen in front of you. When the item goes flat *the screen goes out and the sound track shuts off*. This suggests that persons and situations that have defeated you in the past and now keep you imprisoned in an intricate net of compulsive reactions are literally *turned on* by your resistance. As-is this resistance and the sound and image track is shut off. I have frequently found that when an item is as-ised on the E Meter the external manifestations of that item disappear as if by magic. Perhaps a battery of Negroes with E Meters could as-is Jim Clark out of existence (his photo on the dial set where the needle comes to rest) . . .

E Meters can be purchased at the New York Scientology Center, Hotel Martinique, for $150 and the instruction booklets cost about $2. However, the skill that only long practice confers is essential for successful use of this instrument. Otherwise you may bite off more than you can as-is. For one thing, you must know how to get reads. Some items are so highly charged they will not read at first. Patience and skill are needed to run an item to the flat point. And no matter how long it takes, an item that reads *must be run flat*. If you don't run the item flat you are missing your target. To run an item flat means that item no longer reads on the Meter when called aloud or brought to mind. There is no charge left on that item. A flat point may or may not result in a floating needle. A floating needle is a needle that floats from side to side over the item. A floating needle always brings a feeling of calm release, a sensation of floating. In a previous article I described how Dr. Miller taught rats (and human beings) to lower blood pressure and rate of heartbeats, to control digestion, and produce alpha brain waves by punishment and reward. The E Meter has a built-in reward, and that reward is a floating needle. It would seem probable that a floating needle is accompanied by alpha brain waves, and this supposition could easily be checked. Certainly the pulse is slow and steady, blood pressure normal, muscles and mind relaxed.

The E Meter, as a research instrument, could keep psychologists busy for many years. The Meter could of course take other forms. A dot of light on a screen could replace the needle, pictures with sound track run flat.

It is immediately apparent that all governments run on the not-is principle. Not-is the drug problem, student rebellion, obscenity, crime, communism. Pass a law. Increase penalties. Stamp it out. And the harder they stamp, the worse the situation gets. The attempt to stamp out drug addiction by police action in America has resulted in the worst addiction statistics of any Western country. And now England is following the bad example of America, like a latter-day Banana Republic. Tear gas, nightsticks, and bullets have fanned the student rebellion into an international shambles. The not-ising of communism has been equally unsuccessful. Will the politicians never learn? *All* attempts to not-is problems by force result in more problems, all insoluble because never seen for what they are. The final stage of not-ising is, of course, war. And all wars result in more wars. On the other hand, any problem seen calmly for what it is can be solved. In fact, a problem clearly seen is no problem. It will solve itself. Legislators equipped with E Meters to as-is the problems considered could change the ugly face of this planet.

Q: You write: "I am a recorder . . . I do not pretend to impose 'story,' plot, or continuity." Is it possible?

A: I can only answer that question by saying that when I said that I was perhaps going a bit far. One tries not to impose story, plot, or continuity artificially, but you do have to compose the materials; you can't just dump down a jumble of notes and thoughts and considerations and expect people to read it. So I will retract what I said then. It's simply not really true.

Q: "Words—at least as we use them—tend to hide non-physical experience from us." Once one has removed the barriers which Aristotle, Descartes and Co. put in the way, is this "non-physical experience" parallel to, i.e., interrelated with, physical experience. Is every physical experience undergone on various levels?

A: Yes, very definitely. For example, so-called psychic experiences are experienced, insofar as one experiences them at all, through the physical senses. People see or hear ghosts, feel various emanations, presences, etc.

Q: Do you think that classical philosophical thought has had a damaging effect on human life?

A: Well, it's completely outmoded. As Korzybski, the man who developed general semantics, has pointed out, the Aristotelian "either-or"—something is either this or that—is one of the great errors of Western thinking, because it's no longer true at all. That sort of thinking does not even correspond to what we now know about the physical universe.

Q: Why has it been accepted for so long?

A: There are certain formulas, word-locks, which will lock up a whole civilization for a thousand years. Another thing is Aristotle's *is* of identity: this *is* a chair. Now, whatever it may be, it's not a chair, it's not the word "chair," it's not the label "chair." The idea that the label is the thing leads to all sorts of verbal arguments; when you're just dealing with labels, you think you're dealing with objects. Yes, I would agree emphatically that Aristotle, Descartes, and all that thinking is extremely stultifying and doesn't correspond even to what we know about the physical universe, and it is particularly disastrous in that it still guides the whole academic world. They were bitterly opposed to Korzybski and his general semantics, which suggested some very obvious considerations—that labels are not the things they stand for, that when you're arguing about labels—when you're talking about things like democracy, communism, and facism that have no clear-cut references, no clear-cut thing to which they refer—you're not talking about anything.

Q: Are people, sprawled in what you call their "garbage cans of words," still capable of feeling the violence of *your* words, or is it necessary to resort to physical violence to get them out of this?

A: Generally speaking, if somebody's really tied up in words, he will not experience anything from my books at all, except automatic disapproval. It probably is necessary to resort to physical violence, which is happening everywhere. There doesn't seem to be any alternative, since the establishments just won't change their basic premises.

Q: Do you think any means, including physical violence, will actually change people who are completely tied up?

A: The point of physical violence is that it can displace them. People who are completely verbal, like lawyers and judges and politicans, just won't change their premises, and, of course, if people absolutely refuse to change their premises and the development nonetheless takes place, they're finally displaced by some violence or disaster.

Q: Where does humor fit into the scheme of your work?

A: I think of my work as being, I won't say largely humorous, but certainly as having a considerable element of humor.

Q: The hell you describe, and the accusations you make, imply their opposites and their expiations; so they might be taken as offering man a way out. It has been said that you are a great moralist. What do you think?

A: Yes, I would say perhaps too much so. There's any number of things that could be done in the present situation. The point is that they are not being done; none of them are being done. And, I don't know whether there's any possibility of their being done, given the extent of stupidity and bad intentions on the part of the people in power. You're running up against a wall even to point this out; but all sorts of things can be done that would alleviate the present situations. Perfectly simple things in terms of present techniques. What it amounts to is breaking down some basic formulas. One is the formula of a nation. You draw a line around a piece of ground and say this is a nation. Then you have to have police, customs control, armies, and eventually trouble with the people on the other side of the line. That is one formula, and any variation of that formula will come to the same thing. The U.N. is going to get nowhere. What are they doing? They're creating more of these bloody nations all the time. The next formula is, of course, the family. And nations are simply an extension of the family. And (possibly this is a matter for future techniques) the whole present method of birth and re-

An Interview with William S. Burroughs

production. Those are basic formulas that need to be broken down.

Q: You have some rather far-reaching changes in mind?

A: Yes, certainly, you have to be very far-reaching. There are ways of breaking down the family; the Chinese are on the way to it. They're the only people who've done anything about it. The Russians said they were going to and didn't, and they still guard the same old bourgeois family.

Q: What did you mean when you wrote: "A certain use of words and images can lead to silence"?

A: I think I was being over-optimistic. I doubt if the whole problem of words can ever be solved in terms of itself.

Q: Wright Morris called *Naked Lunch* a hemorrhage of the imagination. Would you take that as a complement?

A: I frankly wouldn't know how to take it.

Q: I assume he meant a fatal hemorrhage.

A: Hemorrhages do not necessarily lead to death. I wouldn't really take it as a compliment. What do you think of there? You think of a cerebral hemorrhage, of someone with fuses blowing out in his brain. No, I don't take it as a compliment at all.

Q: Who is Wright Morris?

A: I have no idea, never heard of him.

Q: You set yourself apart from the postwar American novelists who do not really know what imagination means. American writers suppose that the public is interested only in real facts, in the most material sense of the word. Your books are widely read in the United States; perhaps they describe a universe which is at the same time imaginary and real.

A: Yes, I think so. So many novels now really come under the head of journalism, that is, they try accurately to describe just what people actually do. It's more journalism and anthropology than writing. It seems to me that a novel should rework that, not just dump a lot of purely factual observations on the reader.

Q: What do you suppose accounts for the attachment of American writers to material reality?

A: Well, we had the social consciousness novels of the 1930's, and that tradition is still quite strong. The idea that a novel should deal with reality, with people, with real problems, and particularly with social problems of one sort or another, is actually not too far from the novels of Zola. It's a relatively old tradition. I don't think it's confined at all to American writers. In the case of American novelists there seems to be an idea that the more brutality, the more poverty, the more real it becomes, which I don't think is necessarily true.

Q: What is your relation to the Beat movement with which you associate yourself? What is the literary importance of this movement?

A: I don't associate myself with it at all, and never have, either with their objectives or their literary style. I have some close personal friends in the Beat movement: Jack Kerouac and Allen Ginsberg and Gregory Corso are all close personal friends of many years' standing, but we're not doing at all the same thing, either in writing or in outlook. You couldn't really find four writers more different, more distinctive. I don't associate myself with them; it's simply a matter of juxtaposition rather than any actual association of literary styles or overall objectives. The literary importance of this movement? I would say that the literary importance of the Beatnik movement is perhaps not as obvious as its sociological importance. It really has transformed the world and populated the world with these Beatniks. It has broken down all sorts of social barriers and become a worldwide phenomenon of terrific importance. The Beatniks will go to someplace like North Africa, and they contact the Arabs on a level that seems to me more fundamental than the old Arab-speaking settlers, who are still thinking in T. E. Lawrence terms. It's a terrifically important sociological phenomenon, and, as I say, worldwide.

Q: When you say they communicate on a fundamental level, do you mean that all people all over the world share certain fundamental levels?

530

A: Well, partly . . . they contact the Arabs on the subject of drugs—that is, the subject of kief—which is an important contact. How do you contact people? After all, you do contact them on certain fundamental levels, on sex, habits, etc. But more than that, you see, they're coordinated with pop music, with a way of dressing, a way of life; it is something that has influenced the youth of the world, not only in Western countries but in Eastern countries as well.

Q: Openmindedness, really, is that it? The thing that your European settler lacks?

A: Yes. The old settlers are stuck back in the nineteenth century. "Those people are quite charming really but of course we'll never understand them really." Then some anecdote to illustrate the quaintness of Arabs and how different their thinking is from ours. They see the Arabs from outside as observers with preconceptions about how Arabs think. The Beatniks do not have this folkloric viewpoint. They assume that the Arab way of thinking is not basically different from their own and make direct contact. The old settlers create a gap by assuming that it exists.

Q: What do you think of Mailer? Bellow? Capote?

A: Very difficult question . . . You have to be careful what you say about your literary colleagues. I am not too much of a reader, unfortunately, and when I read I tend to read science fiction, so I can't really speak with too much authority. I've read Mailer's early work *The Naked and the Dead,* which I thought was a very fine novel; Bellow's *Dangling Man,* which I enjoyed. I thought that Capote's earlier work showed extraordinary and very unusual talent, which I can't say for *In Cold Blood,* which seems to me could have been written by any staff editor on the *New Yorker.*

Q: American writers, like most others, seem particularly interested in judging, supporting, or condemning each other, each one having the impression of being in possession of *the truth.* How do you feel about this sort of thing?

A: Well, this has always been going on, this cliquishness of writers. I think it developed furthest in France, with the surrealists all attacking other writers. Breton spent a great deal of his time writing abusive letters to other writers. I think literary arguments are a terrific waste of time, myself. I don't care to get engaged in these sorts of polemics and manifestoes and condemnations of other writers or schools of writing.

Q: Have there been writers in the conventional, "classic" tradition who have succeeded in escaping from the imprisonment of words?

A: Escaping the imprisonment of words—that's a little bit equivocal. I think there are certain writers in the conventional classic tradition who have produced extraordinary effects with words, which sometimes went beyond words. One of my very favorite writers is Joseph Conrad, who is certainly in the classic tradition; and he's done some quite remarkable books in collaboration with Ford Madox Ford, which are very little read now. I'd mention *The Inheritors and Romance,* and there are passages there where he does seem to be escaping from words, or going beyond words, quite conventional, quite classic narrative forms.

Q: *Finnegan's Wake* is generally regarded as a magnificent literary dead end. What is your opinion?

A: I think *Finnegan's Wake* rather represents a trap into which experimental writing can fall when it becomes purely experimental. I would go so far with any given experiment and then come back; that is, I am coming back now to write purely conventional, straightforward narrative. But I am applying what I have learned from the cutup and the other techniques to the problem of conventional writing. It's simply if you go too far in one direction, you can never get back, and you're out there in complete isolation, like this anthropologist who spent the last twenty years of his life on the sweet potato controversy—whether the sweet potato was native to the New World, or whether it floated over from Indonesia, or whether it floated the other way. This went on for twenty years . . . and he would write acrimonious letters to various very specialized anthropological publications attacking the people who opposed his views on the sweet potato controversy; but I forget which way he thought the sweet potato went!

532

Q: Beckett? Genet?

A: I admire both Beckett and Genet without reservation. They're both incredible writers, I think. And, of course, Genet is not, nor does he pretend to be, a verbal innovator. He is in the classic tradition, but he is another person who, using the classic tradition, certainly seems to escape the imprisonment of words and to achieve things that you think could not be achieved in words.

Q: What is your impression of the commitments of writers who hope to achieve, by political activity, a remedy or an improvement for our civilization? Do you think that this kind of activity tends to limit one's creative capacity, or perhaps reveals its limits?

A: I think overcommitment to political objectives definitely does limit one's creative capacity; you tend to become a polemicist rather than a writer. And, of course, being very dubious of politics myself, and against the whole concept of a nation, which politics presupposes, it does seem something of a dead end, at least for me. I suppose that there are writers who really derive their inspiration from political commitments and who sometimes achieve good results: Malraux is an example. *Man's Fate*, an early work which definitely grew out of his political commitments, was a very fine novel.

Q: The literary techniques, according to Raymond Roussel, attempt to enmesh the writer in a system; yours tend on the other hand to free him. What might be the importance of a technique to a writer?

A: Well, they can be interesting experiments; some of them will work and some of them won't. About some, you can say he's done a very interesting experiment, and it's quite unreadable. I know I've done a lot of that myself. I've done writing that I thought was interesting, experimentally, but simply not readable.

Q: Do you need the reader?

A: A novelist is essentially engaged in creating character. He needs the reader in that he hopes some of his readers will turn into his characters. He needs them as vessels, on which he writes. The question frequently asked of a writer is: "Would you write if you were on a desert island and no one would ever read it?" I would say certainly, yes, I would write, in order to create characters. My characters are quite as real to me as so-called real people; which is one reason why I'm not subject to what is known as loneliness. I have plenty of company.

31 / Communication[1]

JOHN CAGE

NICHI NICHI KORE KO NICHI: EVERY DAY IS A BEAUTIFUL DAY
What if I ask thirty-two questions?
What if I stop asking now and then?
Will that make things clear?
Is communication something made clear?
What is communication?
Music, what does it communicate?
Is what's clear to me clear to you?
Is music just sounds?
Then what does it communicate?
Is a truck passing by music?
If I can see it, do I have to hear it too?

[1] The following text is made up of questions and quotations. The quotations are some from the writings of others and some from my own writings. (That from Christian Wolff is from his article "New and Electronic Music," *Audience* 5 (Summer 1958). Copyright © 1958 by Audience Press. Reprinted by permission of Wesleyan University Press.) The order and quantity of the quotations were given by chance operations. No performance timing was composed. Nevertheless, I always prescribe one before delivering this lecture, sometimes adding by chance operations indications of when, in the course of the performance, I am obliged to light a cigarette.

SOURCE: John Cage, *Silence* (Middletown, Conn.: Wesleyan University Press, 1961), pp. 41–56. Copyright © 1961 by John Cage. Reprinted by permission.
John Cage has, for several decades, experimented with chance or random musical notation; his closest collaborators have been Merce Cunningham (dance) and David Tudor (prepared piano). His second collection of lectures and writings, *A Year from Monday,* reveals the influence of Marshall McLuhan and Buckminster Fuller.

If I don't hear it, does it still communicate?

If while I see it I can't hear it, but hear something else, say an
egg-beater, because I'm inside looking out, does the truck
communicate or the egg-beater, which communicates?

Which is more musical, a truck passing by a factory or a truck
passing by a music school?

Are the people inside the school musical and the ones outside
unmusical?

What if the ones inside can't hear very well, would that change
my question?

Do you know what I mean when I say inside the school?

Are sounds just sounds or are they Beethoven?

People aren't sounds, are they?

Is there such a thing as silence?

Even if I get away from people, do I still have to listen to something?

Say I'm off in the woods, do I have to listen to a stream babbling?

Is there always something to hear, never any peace and quiet?

If my head is full of harmony, melody, and rhythm, what happens to me when the telephone rings, to my peace and quiet,
I mean?

And if it was European harmony, melody, and rhythm in my
head, what has happened to the history of, say, Javanese
music, with respect, that is to say, to my head?

Are we getting anywhere asking questions?

Where are we going?

Is this the twenty-eighth question?

Are there any important questions?

"How do you need to cautiously proceed in dualistic terms?"

Do I have two more questions?

And, now, do I have none?

Now that I've asked thirty-two questions, can I ask forty-four
more?

I can, but may I?

Why must I go on asking questions?

Is there any reason in asking why?

Would I ask why if questions were not words but were sounds?

If words are sounds, are they musical or are they just noises?

If sounds are noises but not words, are they meaningful?

Are they musical?

Say there are two sounds and two people and one of each is beautiful, is there between all four any communication?

And if there are rules, who made them, I ask you?

Does it begin somewhere, I mean, and if so, where does it stop?

What will happen to me or to you if we have to be somewhere where beauty isn't?

I ask you, sometime, too, sounds happening in time, what will happen to our experience of hearing, yours, mine, our ears, hearing, what will happen if sounds being beautiful stop sometime and the only sounds to hear are not beautiful to hear but are ugly, what will happen to us?

Would we ever be able to get so that we thought the ugly sounds were beautiful?

If we drop beauty, what have we got?

Have we got truth?

Have we got religion?

Do we have a mythology?

Would we know what to do with one if we had one?

Have we got a way to make money?

And if money is made, will it be spent on music?

If Russia spends sixty million for the Brussels Fair, lots of it for music and dance, and America spends one-tenth of that, six million about, does that mean that one out of ten Americans is as musical and kinesthetic as all the Russians put together?

If we drop money, what have we got?

Since we haven't yet dropped truth, where shall we go looking for it?

Didn't we say we weren't going, or did we just ask where we were going?

If we didn't say we weren't going, why didn't we?

If we had any sense in our heads, wouldn't we know the truth instead of going around looking for it?

How otherwise would we, as they say, be able to drink a glass of water?

We know, don't we, everybody else's religion, mythology, and philosophy and metaphysics backwards and forwards, so what need would we have for one of our own if we had one, but we don't, do we?

But music, do we have any music?

Wouldn't it be better to just drop music too?
Then what would we have?
Jazz?
What's left?
Do you mean to say it's a purposeless play?
Is that what it is when you get up and hear the first sound of each day?
Is it possible that I could go on monotonously asking questions forever?
Would I have to know how many questions I was going to ask?
Would I have to know how to count in order to ask questions?
Do I have to know when to stop?
Is this the one chance we have to be alive and ask a question?
How long will we be able to be alive?

CONTEMPORARY MUSIC   IS NOT THE MUSIC OF THE FUTURE
                      NOR THE MUSIC OF THE PAST   BUT SIMPLY
MUSIC PRESENT WITH US: THIS MOMENT,   NOW,
              THIS NOW MOMENT.

Something remarkable has happened: I was asking questions; now I'm quoting from a lecture I gave years ago. Of course I will ask some more questions later on, but not now: I have quoting to do.

THAT MOMENT IS ALWAYS CHANGING.   (I WAS SILENT: NOW
I AM SPEAKING.)   HOW CAN WE POSSIBLY TELL WHAT
CONTEMPORARY MUSIC IS, SINCE NOW WE'RE NOT LISTENING TO IT,
WE'RE LISTENING TO A LECTURE ABOUT IT. AND THAT ISN'T IT.
THIS IS "TONGUE-WAGGING." REMOVED AS WE ARE THIS MOMENT
FROM CONTEMPORARY MUSIC (WE ARE ONLY THINKING ABOUT IT)
EACH ONE OF US IS THINKING HIS OWN THOUGHTS, HIS OWN
EXPERIENCE, AND EACH EXPERIENCE IS DIFFERENT AND EACH
EXPERIENCE IS CHANGING AND WHILE WE ARE THINKING I AM
TALKING AND CONTEMPORARY MUSIC IS CHANGING.   LIKE LIFE
IT CHANGES.   IF IT WERE NOT CHANGING IT WOULD BE DEAD,
AND, OF COURSE, FOR SOME OF US,   SOMETIMES IT IS DEAD, BUT
AT ANY MOMENT IT CHANGES AND IS LIVING AGAIN.
TALKING FOR A MOMENT ABOUT CONTEMPORARY MILK: AT ROOM
TEMPERATURE IT IS CHANGING, GOES SOUR ETC., AND THEN A NEW

JOHN CAGE   537

BOTTLE ETC., UNLESS BY SEPARATING IT FROM ITS CHANGING BY POWDERING IT OR REFRIGERATION   (WHICH IS A WAY OF SLOWING DOWN ITS LIVELINESS)   (THAT IS TO SAY MUSEUMS AND ACADEMIES ARE WAYS OF PRESERVING)   WE TEMPORARILY SEPARATE THINGS FROM LIFE (FROM CHANGING) BUT AT ANY MOMENT DESTRUCTION MAY COME SUDDENLY AND THEN WHAT HAPPENS IS FRESHER

WHEN WE SEPARATE MUSIC FROM LIFE WHAT WE GET IS ART (A COMPENDIUM OF MASTERPIECES). WITH CONTEMPORARY MUSIC, WHEN IT IS ACTUALLY CONTEMPORARY, WE HAVE NO TIME TO MAKE THAT SEPARATION (WHICH PROTECTS US FROM LIVING), AND SO CONTEMPORARY MUSIC IS NOT SO MUCH ART AS IT IS LIFE AND ANY ONE MAKING IT NO SOONER FINISHES ONE OF IT THAN HE BEGINS MAKING ANOTHER JUST AS PEOPLE KEEP ON WASHING DISHES, BRUSHING THEIR TEETH, GETTING SLEEPY, AND SO ON. VERY FREQUENTLY NO ONE KNOWS THAT CONTEMPORARY MUSIC IS OR COULD BE ART.   HE SIMPLY THINKS IT IS IRRITATING. IRRITATING ONE WAY OR ANOTHER, THAT IS TO SAY KEEPING US FROM OSSIFYING.

FOR ANY ONE OF US CONTEMPORARY MUSIC IS OR COULD BE A WAY OF LIVING. SEVERAL STORIES OCCUR TO ME THAT I SHOULD LIKE TO INTERPOLATE (IN THE SAME WAY, BY THE WAY, THAT WHILE I AM WRITING THIS THAT I AM NOW TALKING, THE TELEPHONE KEEPS RINGING AND THEN CONTEMPORARY CONVERSATION TAKES PLACE INSTEAD OF THIS PARTICULAR WAY OF PREPARING A LECTURE).   THE FIRST STORY IS FROM THE *Gospel of Sri Ramakrishna.*   HIS LIVING AND TALKING HAD IMPRESSED A MUSICIAN WHO BEGAN TO THINK THAT HE SHOULD GIVE UP MUSIC AND BECOME A DISCIPLE OF RAMAKRISHNA.   BUT WHEN HE PROPOSED THIS, RAMAKRISHNA SAID, BY NO MEANS.   REMAIN A MUSICIAN: MUSIC IS A MEANS OF RAPID TRANSPORTATION. RAPID TRANSPORTATION, THAT IS, TO LIFE "EVERLASTING," THAT IS TO SAY, LIFE, PERIOD. ANOTHER STORY IS THAT WHEN I WAS FIRST AWARE THAT I WAS TO GIVE THIS TALK I CONSULTED THE *Book of Changes* AND OBTAINED BY TOSSING COINS THE HEXAGRAM TO INFLUENCE, TO STIMULATE.

SIX AT THE TOP MEANS THE INFLUENCE SHOWS ITSELF IN THE JAWS, CHEEKS, AND TONGUE AND THE COMMENTARY SAYS: THE MOST SUPERFICIAL WAY OF TRYING TO INFLUENCE OTHERS IS THROUGH TALK THAT HAS NOTHING REAL BEHIND IT. THE INFLUENCE PRODUCED BY SUCH MERE TONGUE-WAGGING MUST NECESSARILY REMAIN INSIGNIFICANT.   HOWEVER, I FIND MYSELF IN DISAGREEMENT WITH THE COMMENTARY.   I SEE NO NECESSITY TO PUT SOMETHING "REAL" BEHIND TONGUE-WAGGING.   I DO NOT SEE THAT TONGUE-WAGGING IS ANY MORE SIGNIFICANT OR INSIGNIFICANT THAN ANY THING ELSE.   IT SEEMS TO ME THAT IT IS SIMPLY A MATTER OF GOING ON TALKING, WHICH IS NEITHER SIGNIFICANT NOR INSIGNIFICANT, NOR GOOD NOR BAD, BUT SIMPLY HAPPENING TO BE THE WAY I AM RIGHT NOW LIVING WHICH IS GIVING A LECTURE IN ILLINOIS WHICH BRINGS US BACK TO CONTEMPORARY MUSIC.   BUT TAKING OFF AGAIN AND RETURNING TO THE *Book of Changes:* THE HEXAGRAM ON GRACE (WHICH IS THE HEXAGRAM ON ART)   DISCUSSES THE EFFECT OF A WORK OF ART   AS THOUGH IT WERE A LIGHT SHINING ON TOP OF A MOUNTAIN PENETRATING TO A CERTAIN EXTENT THE SURROUNDING DARKNESS.

               THAT IS TO SAY, ART IS DESCRIBED AS BEING ILLUMINATING, AND THE REST OF LIFE AS BEING DARK. NATURALLY I DISAGREE. IF THERE WERE A PART OF LIFE DARK ENOUGH TO KEEP OUT OF IT A LIGHT FROM ART, I WOULD WANT TO BE IN THAT DARKNESS, FUMBLING AROUND IF NECESSARY, BUT ALIVE   AND I RATHER THINK THAT CONTEMPORARY MUSIC WOULD BE THERE IN THE DARK TOO, BUMPING INTO THINGS, KNOCKING OTHERS OVER AND IN GENERAL ADDING TO THE DISORDER THAT CHARACTERIZES LIFE (IF IT IS OPPOSED TO ART) RATHER THAN ADDING TO THE ORDER AND STABILIZED TRUTH BEAUTY AND POWER THAT CHARACTERIZE A MASTERPIECE (IF IT IS OPPOSED TO LIFE).   AND IS IT?   YES IT IS.   MASTERPIECES AND GENIUSES GO TOGETHER AND WHEN BY RUNNING FROM ONE TO THE OTHER WE MAKE LIFE SAFER THAN IT ACTUALLY IS   WE'RE APT NEVER TO KNOW THE DANGERS OF CONTEMPORARY MUSIC   OR   EVEN TO BE ABLE TO DRINK A GLASS OF WATER.   TO HAVE SOMETHING BE A MASTERPIECE YOU HAVE TO HAVE ENOUGH TIME TO CLASSIFY IT AND MAKE IT CLASSICAL.   BUT WITH CONTEMPORARY MUSIC THERE IS NO

TIME TO DO ANYTHING LIKE CLASSIFYING.   ALL YOU CAN DO
IS SUDDENLY LISTEN   IN THE SAME WAY THAT WHEN
YOU CATCH COLD ALL YOU CAN DO IS SUDDENLY SNEEZE.
UNFORTUNATELY EUROPEAN THINKING HAS BROUGHT IT ABOUT THAT
ACTUAL THINGS THAT HAPPEN SUCH AS SUDDENLY LISTENING OR
SUDDENLY SNEEZING ARE NOT CONSIDERED PROFOUND.
IN THE COURSE OF A LECTURE LAST WINTER AT COLUMBIA, SUZUKI
SAID THAT THERE WAS A DIFFERENCE BETWEEN ORIENTAL THINKING
AND EUROPEAN THINKING, THAT IN EUROPEAN THINKING THINGS ARE
SEEN AS CAUSING ONE ANOTHER AND HAVING EFFECTS, WHEREAS IN
ORIENTAL THINKING   THIS SEEING OF CAUSE AND EFFECT
IS NOT EMPHASIZED BUT INSTEAD ONE MAKES AN IDENTIFICATION
WITH WHAT IS HERE AND NOW.   HE THEN SPOKE OF TWO
QUALITIES: UNIMPEDEDNESS   AND
INTERPENETRATION.   NOW THIS UNIMPEDEDNESS IS SEEING
THAT IN ALL OF SPACE EACH THING AND EACH HUMAN BEING IS
AT THE CENTER AND FURTHERMORE THAT EACH ONE BEING AT THE
CENTER   IS THE MOST HONORED ONE OF ALL.
INTERPENETRATION MEANS THAT EACH ONE OF THESE MOST HONORED
ONES OF ALL IS MOVING OUT IN ALL DIRECTIONS PENETRATING AND
BEING PENETRATED BY EVERY OTHER ONE NO MATTER WHAT THE
TIME OR WHAT THE SPACE.   SO THAT WHEN ONE SAYS THAT
THERE IS NO CAUSE AND EFFECT, WHAT IS MEANT IS THAT THERE
ARE AN INCALCULABLE INFINITY OF CAUSES AND EFFECTS, THAT IN
FACT EACH AND EVERY THING IN ALL OF TIME AND SPACE IS RELATED
TO EACH AND EVERY OTHER THING IN ALL OF TIME AND SPACE.
THIS BEING SO THERE IS NO NEED TO CAUTIOUSLY PROCEED IN
DUALISTIC TERMS OF SUCCESS AND FAILURE OR THE BEAUTIFUL AND
THE UGLY OR GOOD AND EVIL BUT RATHER SIMPLY TO WALK ON
"NOT WONDERING," TO QUOTE MEISTER ECKHART, "AM I RIGHT OR
DOING SOMETHING WRONG."

*This is the second Tuesday in September of 1958 and I still
have quite a lot to say: I'm nowhere near the end. I have four
questions I must ask.*

If, as we have, we have dropped music, does that mean we have
nothing to listen to?
Don't you agree with Kafka when he wrote, "Psychology—never
   again"?

540

If you had to put on ten fingers the music you would take with
you if you were going to the North Pole, what would you put?
Is it true there are no questions that are really important?

*Here's a little information you may find informative about the
information theory:*

FOURIER ANALYSIS ALLOWS A FUNCTION OF TIME (OR ANY OTHER INDE-
PENDENT VARIABLE) TO BE EXPRESSED IN TERMS OF PERIODIC (FRE-
QUENCY) COMPONENTS. THE FREQUENCY COMPONENTS ARE OVER-ALL
PROPERTIES OF THE ENTIRE SIGNAL. BY MEANS OF A FOURIER ANALYSIS
ONE CAN EXPRESS THE VALUE OF A SIGNAL AT ANY POINT IN TERMS OF THE
OVER-ALL FREQUENCY PROPERTIES OF THE SIGNAL; OR VICE VERSA, ONE
CAN OBTAIN THESE OVER-ALL PROPERTIES FROM THE VALUES OF THE
SIGNAL AT ITS VARIOUS POINTS.

What did I say?
Where is the "should" when they say you should have something to say?
Three. Actually when you drop something, it's still with you,
wouldn't you say?
Four. Where would you drop something to get it completely
away?
Five. Why do you not do as I do, letting go of each thought as
though it were void?
Six. Why do you not do as I do, letting go of each thought as
though it were rotten wood?
Why do you not do as I do, letting go of each thought as though
it were a piece of stone?
Why do you not do as I do, letting go of each thought as though
it were the cold ashes of a fire long dead, or else just making
the slight response suitable to the occasion?
Nine. Do you really think that the discovery that a measurable
entity exists, namely, the energy which can measure mechanical, electrical, thermal, or any other kind of physical activity,
and can measure potential as well as actual activity, greatly
simplifies thinking about physical phenomena?
Do you agree with Boulez when he says what he says?
Are you getting hungry?

Twelve. Why should you (you know more or less what you're going to get)?

Will Boulez be there or did he go away when I wasn't looking?

Why do you suppose the number 12 was given up but the idea of the series wasn't?

Or was it?

And if not, why not?

In the meantime, would you like to hear the very first performance of Christian Wolff's *For Piano with Preparations*?

What in heaven's name are they going to serve us for dinner, and what happens afterwards?

More music?

Living or dead, that's the big question.

When you get sleepy, do you go to sleep?

Or do you lie awake?

Why do I have to go on asking questions?

Is it the same reason I have to go on writing music?

But it's clear, isn't it, I'm not writing music right now?

Why do they call me a composer, then, if all I do is ask questions?

If one of us says that all twelve tones should be in a row and another says they shouldn't, which one of us is right?

What if a B flat, as they say, just comes to me?

How can I get it to come to me of itself, not just pop up out of my memory, taste, and psychology?

How?

Do you know how?

And if I did or somebody else did find a way to let a sound be itself, would everybody within earshot be able to listen to it?

Why is it so difficult for so many people to listen?

Why do they start talking when there is something to hear?

Do they have their ears not on the sides of their heads but situated inside their mouths so that when they hear something their first impulse is to start talking?

The situation should be made more normal, don't you think?

Why don't they keep their mouths shut and their ears open?

Are they stupid?

And, if so, why don't they try to hide their stupidity?

Were bad manners acquired when knowledge of music was acquired?

542

Does being musical make one automatically stupid and unable
   to listen?
Then don't you think one should put a stop to studying music?
Where are your thinking caps?

WE'RE PASSING THROUGH TIME AND SPACE. OUR EARS ARE IN EXCELLENT
CONDITION.

A SOUND IS HIGH OR LOW, SOFT OR LOUD, OF A CERTAIN TIMBRE, LASTS A
CERTAIN LENGTH OF TIME, AND HAS AN ENVELOPE.

Is it high?
Is it low?
Is it in the middle?
Is it soft?
Is it loud?
Are there two?
Are there more than two?
Is it a piano?
Why isn't it?
Was it an airplane?
Is it a noise?
Is it music?
Is it softer than before?
Is it supersonic?
When will it stop?
What's coming?
Is it time?
Is it very short?
Very long?
Just medium?
If I had something to see, would it be theatre?
Is sound enough?
What more do I need?
Don't I get it whether I need it or not?
Is it a sound?
Then, again, is it music?
Is music—the word, I mean—is that a sound?
If it is, is music music?
Is the word "music" music?

Does it communicate anything?
Must it?
If it's high, does it?
If it's low, does it?
If it's in the middle, does it?
If it's soft, does it?
If it's loud, does it?
If it's an interval, does it?
What is an interval?
Is an interval a chord?
Is a chord an aggregate?
Is an aggregate a constellation?
What's a constellation?
How many sounds are there altogether?
One million?
Ten thousand?
Eighty-eight?
Do I have to ask ten more?
Do I?
Why?
Why do I?
Did I decide to ask so many?
Wasn't I taking a risk?
Was I?
Why was I?
Will it never stop?
Why won't it?

THERE IS NO SUCH THING AS SILENCE. GET THEE TO AN ANECHOIC CHAMBER
AND HEAR THERE THY NERVOUS SYSTEM IN OPERATION AND HEAR THERE
THY BLOOD IN CIRCULATION.

I HAVE NOTHING TO SAY AND I AM SAYING IT.

Would it be too much to ask if I asked thirty-three more?
Who's asking?
Is it I who ask?
Don't I know my own mind?
Then why do I ask if I don't know?
Then it's not too much to ask?

544

Right?

Then, tell me, do you prefer Bach to Beethoven?

And why?

Would you like to hear *Quantitäten* by Bo Nilsson whether it's performed for the first time or not?

Has any one seen Meister Eckhart lately?

Do you think serious music is serious enough?

Is a seventh chord inappropriate in modern music?

What about fifths and octaves?

What if the seventh chord was not a seventh chord?

Doesn't it seem silly to go on asking questions when there's so much to do that's really urgent?

But we're halfway through, aren't we?

Shall we buck up?

Are we in agreement that the field of music needs to be enlivened?

Do we disagree?

On what?

Communication?

If I have two sounds, are they related?

If someone is nearer one of them than he is to the second, is he more related to the first one?

What about sounds that are too far away for us to hear them?

Sounds are just vibrations, isn't that true?

Part of a vast range of vibrations including radio waves, light, cosmic rays, isn't that true?

Why didn't I mention that before?

Doesn't that stir the imagination?

Shall we praise God from Whom all blessings flow?

Is a sound a blessing?

I repeat, is a sound a blessing?

I repeat, would you like to hear *Quantitäten* by Bo Nilsson whether it's performed for the first time or not?

The Belgians asked me about the avant-garde in America and this is what I told them:

IN THE UNITED STATES THERE ARE AS MANY WAYS OF WRITING MUSIC AS THERE ARE COMPOSERS. THERE IS ALSO NO AVAILABLE INFORMATION AS TO WHAT IS GOING ON. THERE IS NO MAGAZINE

CONCERNED WITH MODERN MUSIC. PUBLISHERS ARE NOT INQUISITIVE. THE SOCIETIES WHICH ACTIVELY EXIST (BROADCAST MUSIC INC., AMERICAN SOCIETY OF COMPOSERS, AUTHORS AND PUBLISHERS) ARE CONCERNED WITH ECONOMICS, CURRENTLY ENGAGED IN AN IMPORTANT LAWSUIT. IN NEW YORK CITY, THE LEAGUE OF COMPOSERS AND THE INTERNATIONAL SOCIETY FOR CONTEMPORARY MUSIC HAVE FUSED, THE NEW ORGANIZATION REPRESENTING THE CURRENT INTEREST IN CONSOLIDATING THE ACQUISITIONS OF SCHOENBERG AND STRAVINSKY. THIS CIRCLE HAS, NO DOUBT, AN AVANT-GARDE, BUT IT IS A CAUTIOUS ONE, REFUSING RISK. ITS MOST ACCOMPLISHED AND ADVENTUROUS REPRESENTATIVE IS PROBABLY MILTON BABBITT, WHO, IN CERTAIN WORKS, HAS APPLIED SERIAL METHOD TO THE SEVERAL ASPECTS OF SOUND. THE WORKS FOR MAGNETIC TAPE BY LUENING AND USSACHEVSKY, LOUIS AND BEBE BARRON, ARE NOT PROPERLY TERMED AVANT-GARDE, SINCE THEY MAINTAIN CONVENTIONS AND ACCEPTED VALUES. THE YOUNG STUDY WITH NEO-CLASSICISTS, SO THAT THE SPIRIT OF THE AVANT-GARDE, INFECTING THEM, INDUCES A CERTAIN DODECAPHONY. IN THIS SOCIAL DARKNESS, THEREFORE, THE WORK OF EARLE BROWN, MORTON FELDMAN, AND CHRISTIAN WOLFF CONTINUES TO PRESENT A BRILLIANT LIGHT, FOR THE REASON THAT AT THE SEVERAL POINTS OF NOTATION, PERFORMANCE, AND AUDITION, ACTION IS PROVOCATIVE. NONE OF THESE USES SERIAL METHOD. BROWN'S NOTATION IN SPACE EQUAL TO TIME TENDS CURRENTLY TO FINE PRECISION OF DIRECTIVE. WOLFF'S INTRODUCTION IN DURATIONS OF SPLIT AND PARTIAL GRUPETTOS, IN TEMPI THAT OF ZERO, TENDS OPPOSITELY. THE GRAPHS OF FELDMAN GIVE WITHIN LIMITS EXTREME FREEDOM OF ACTION TO THE PERFORMER.

They also—the Belgians, that is—asked me whether the American avant-garde follows the same direction as the European one and this is what I told them:

THE AMERICAN AVANT-GARDE, RECOGNIZING THE PROVOCATIVE CHARACTER OF CERTAIN EUROPEAN WORKS, OF PIERRE BOULEZ, KARLHEINZ STOCKHAUSEN, HENRI POUSSEUR, BO NILSSON, BENGT HAMBRAEUS, HAS IN ITS CONCERTS PRESENTED THEM IN PERFORMANCES, NOTABLY BY DAVID TUDOR, PIANIST. THAT THESE WORKS ARE SERIAL IN METHOD DIMINISHES SOMEWHAT THE INTEREST THEY ENJOIN. BUT THE THOROUGHNESS OF THE METHOD'S APPLICATION BRINGING A SITUATION REMOVED FROM CONVENTIONAL

EXPECTATION FREQUENTLY OPENS THE EAR. HOWEVER, THE EUROPEAN WORKS PRESENT A HARMONIOUSNESS, A DRAMA, OR A POETRY WHICH, REFERRING MORE TO THEIR COMPOSERS THAN TO THEIR HEARERS, MOVES IN DIRECTIONS NOT SHARED BY THE AMERICAN ONES. MANY OF THE AMERICAN WORKS ENVISAGE EACH AUDITOR AS CENTRAL, SO THAT THE PHYSICAL CIRCUMSTANCES OF A CONCERT DO NOT OPPOSE AUDIENCE TO PERFORMERS BUT DISPOSE THE LATTER AROUND-AMONG THE FORMER, BRINGING A UNIQUE ACOUSTICAL EXPERIENCE TO EACH PAIR OF EARS. ADMITTEDLY, A SITUATION OF THIS COMPLEXITY IS BEYOND CONTROL, YET IT RESEMBLES A LISTENER'S SITUATION BEFORE AND AFTER A CONCERT—DAILY EXPERIENCE, THAT IS. IT APPEARS SUCH A CONTINUUM IS NOT PART OF THE EUROPEAN OBJECTIVE, SINCE IT DISSOLVES THE DIFFERENCE BETWEEN "ART" AND "LIFE." TO THE UNEXPERIENCED, THE DIFFERENCE BETWEEN THE EUROPEANS AND THE AMERICANS LIES IN THAT THE LATTER INCLUDE MORE SILENCE IN THEIR WORKS. IN THIS VIEW THE MUSIC OF NILSSON APPEARS AS INTERMEDIATE, THAT OF BOULEZ AND OF THE AUTHOR AS IN OPPOSITION. THIS SUPERFICIAL DIFFERENCE IS ALSO PROFOUND. WHEN SILENCE, GENERALLY SPEAKING, IS NOT IN EVIDENCE, THE WILL OF THE COMPOSER IS. INHERENT SILENCE IS EQUIVALENT TO DENIAL OF THE WILL. "TAKING A NAP, I POUND THE RICE." NEVERTHELESS, CONSTANT ACTIVITY MAY OCCUR HAVING NO DOMINANCE OF WILL IN IT. NEITHER AS SYNTAX NOR STRUCTURE, BUT ANALOGOUS TO THE SUM OF NATURE, IT WILL HAVE ARISEN PURPOSELESSLY.

It's getting late, isn't it?
I still have two things to do, so what I want to know is: Would you like to hear *Quantitäten* by Bo Nilsson whether it's performed for the first time or not?

I must read a little from an article by Christian Wolff. Here's what he says:

NOTABLE QUALITIES OF THIS MUSIC, WHETHER ELECTRONIC OR NOT, ARE MONOTONY AND THE IRRITATION THAT ACCOMPANIES IT. THE MONOTONY MAY LIE IN SIMPLICITY OR DELICACY, STRENGTH OR COMPLEXITY. COMPLEXITY TENDS TO REACH A POINT OF NEUTRALIZATION: CONTINUOUS CHANGE RESULTS IN A CERTAIN SAMENESS. THE MUSIC HAS A STATIC CHARACTER. IT GOES IN NO

PARTICULAR DIRECTION. THERE IS NO NECESSARY CONCERN WITH TIME AS A MEASURE OF DISTANCE FROM A POINT IN THE PAST TO A POINT IN THE FUTURE, WITH LINEAR CONTINUITY ALONE. IT IS NOT A QUESTION OF GETTING ANYWHERE, OF MAKING PROGRESS, OR HAVING COME FROM ANYWHERE IN PARTICULAR, OF TRADITION OR FUTURISM. THERE IS NEITHER NOSTALGIA NOR ANTICIPATION. OFTEN THE STRUCTURE OF A PIECE IS CIRCULAR: THE SUCCESSION OF ITS PARTS IS VARIABLE, AS IN POUSSEUR'S *Exercises de Piano* AND STOCKHAUSEN'S *Klavierstück XI.* IN CAGE'S RECENT WORK THE NOTATION ITSELF CAN BE CIRCULAR, THE SUCCESSION OF NOTES ON A STAVE NOT NECESSARILY INDICATING THEIR SEQUENCE IN TIME, THAT IS, THE ORDER IN WHICH THEY ARE PERFORMED. ONE MAY HAVE TO READ NOTES ON A CIRCLE, IN TWO "VOICES" GOING IN OPPOSITE DIRECTIONS SIMULTANEOUSLY. AN ASPECT OF TIME DISSOLVES. AND THE EUROPEANS OFTEN VIEW ORGANIZATION AS "GLOBAL," WHEREBY BEGINNINGS AND ENDS ARE NOT POINTS ON A LINE BUT LIMITS OF A PIECE'S MATERIAL (FOR EXAMPLE, PITCH RANGES OR POSSIBLE COMBINATIONS OF TIMBRES) WHICH MAY BE TOUCHED AT ANY TIME DURING THE PIECE. THE BOUNDARIES OF THE PIECE ARE EXPRESSED, NOT AT MOMENTS OF TIME WHICH MARK A SUCCESSION, BUT AS MARGINS OF A SPATIAL PROJECTION OF THE TOTAL SOUND STRUCTURE.

AS FOR THE QUALITY OF IRRITATION, THAT IS A MORE SUBJECTIVE MATTER. ONE MIGHT SAY THAT IT IS AT LEAST PREFERABLE TO SOOTHING, EDIFYING, EXALTING, AND SIMILAR QUALITIES. ITS SOURCE IS, OF COURSE, PRECISELY IN MONOTONY, NOT IN ANY FORMS OF AGGRESSION OR EMPHASIS. IT IS THE IMMOBILITY OF MOTION. AND IT ALONE, PERHAPS, IS TRULY MOVING.

And now I have to read a story from Kwang-Tse and then I'm finished:

Yun Kiang, rambling to the East, having been borne along on a gentle breeze, suddenly encountered Hung Mung, who was rambling about, slapping his buttocks and hopping like a bird. Amazed at the sight, Yun Kiang stood reverentially and said to the other, "Venerable Sir, who are you? and why are you doing this?" Hung Mung went on slapping his buttocks and hopping like a bird, but replied, "I'm enjoying myself."

Yun Kiang said, "I wish to ask you a question." Hung
Mung lifted up his head, looked at the stranger, and
said, "Pooh!" Yun Kiang, however, continued, "The
breath of heaven is out of harmony; the breath of earth
is bound up; the six elemental influences do not act in
concord; the four seasons do not observe their proper
times. Now I wish to blend together the essential
qualities of those six influences in order to nourish all
living things. How shall I go about it?" Hung Mung
slapped his buttocks, hopped about, and shook his head,
saying, "I do not know; I do not know!"

Yun Kiang could not pursue his question; but three
years afterwards, when again rambling in the East, as
he was passing by the wild of Sung, he happened to
meet Hung Mung. Delighted with the rencontre, he
hastened to him, and said, "Have you forgotten me, O
Heaven? Have you forgotten me, O Heaven?" At the
same time, he bowed twice with his head to the ground,
wishing to receive his instructions. Hung Mung said,
"Wandering listlessly about, I know not what I seek;
carried on by a wild impulse, I know not where I am
going. I wander about in the strange manner which
you have seen, and see that nothing proceeds without
method and order—what more should I know?" Yun
Kiang replied, "I also seem carried on by an aimless
influence, and yet people follow me wherever I go. I
cannot help their doing so. But now as they thus imitate
me, I wish to hear a word from you." The other said,
"What disturbs the regular method of Heaven, comes
into collision with the nature of things, prevents the
accomplishment of the mysterious operation of Heaven,
scatters the herds of animals, makes the birds sing at
night, is calamitous to vegetation, and disastrous to all
insects; all this is owing, I conceive, to the error of
governing men." "What then," said Yun Kiang, "shall
I do?" "Ah," said the other, "you will only injure them!
I will leave you in my dancing way, and return to my
place." Yun Kiang rejoined, "It has been difficult to get
this meeting with you, O Heaven! I should like to hear
from you a word more." Hung Mung said, "Ah! your

mind needs to be nourished. Do you only take the
position of doing nothing, and things will of themselves
become transformed. Neglect your body; cast out from
you your power of hearing and sight; forget what you
have in common with things; cultivate a grand
similarity with the chaos of the plastic ether; unloose
your mind; set your spirit free; be still as if you had no
soul. Of all the multitude of things, every one returns
to its root, and does not know that it is doing so. They
all are as in the state of chaos, and during all their
existence they do not leave it. If they knew that they
were returning to their root, they would be consciously
leaving it. They do not ask its name; they do not seek
to spy out their nature; and thus it is that things come
to life of themselves."

Yun Kiang said, "Heaven, you have conferred on me the
knowledge of your operation and revealed to me the
mystery of it. All my life I have been seeking for it, and
now I have obtained it." He then bowed twice with his
head to the ground, arose, took his leave, and walked
away.

• •

One day when I was across the hall visiting Sonya
Sekula, I noticed that she was painting left-handed. I
said, "Sonya, aren't you right-handed?" She said, "Yes,
but I might lose the use of my right hand, and so I'm
practicing using my left." I laughed and said, "What if
you lose the use of both hands?" She was busy painting
and didn't bother to reply. Next day when I visited her,
she was sitting on the floor, painting with difficulty, for
she was holding the brush between two toes of her left
foot.

Morris Graves introduced Xenia and me to a miniature
island in Puget Sound at Deception Pass. To get there
we traveled from Seattle about seventy-five miles north
and west to Anacortes Island, then south to the Pass,
where we parked. We walked along a rocky beach and
then across a sandy stretch that was passable only at

low tide to another island, continuing through some luxuriant woods up a hill where now and then we had views of the surrounding waters and distant islands, until finally we came to a small foot-bridge that led to our destination—an island no larger than, say, a modest home. This island was carpeted with flowers and was so situated that all of Deception Pass was visible from it, just as though we were in the best seats of an intimate theatre. While we were lying there on that bed of flowers, some other people came across the footbridge. One of them said to another, "You come all this way and then when you get here there's nothing to see."

A composer friend of mine who spent some time in a mental rehabilitation center was encouraged to do a good deal of bridge playing. After one game, his partner was criticizing his play of an ace on a trick which had already been won. My friend stood up and said, "If you think I came to the loony bin to learn to play bridge, you're crazy."

32 / Like a Rolling Stone

RALPH J. GLEASON

Forms and rhythms in music are never changed without producing changes in the most important political forms and ways.

Plato said that.

SOURCE: Jonathan Eisen, *The Age of Rock* (New York: Random House, Vintage Books, 1969), pp. 61–76. Copyright © 1967 by Ralph J. Gleason. Reprinted by permission. This essay originally appeared in *The American Scholar* 36 (Autumn 1967).

Ralph Gleason interprets rock music for the San Francisco *Chronicle*, but he disagrees with other interpreters who see a revolutionary political message in it; in addition, he has been the producer-host of his own TV rock program, a lecturer in jazz at several schools, a contributing editor to *Ramparts*, and a consulting editor to *Rolling Stone*.

There's something happenin' here. What it is ain't exactly clear. There s a man with a gun over there tellin' me I've got to beware. I think it's time we STOP, children, what's that sound? Everybody look what's goin' down.

The Buffalo Springfield said that.

For the reality of politics, we must go to the poets, not the politicians.

Norman O. Brown said that.

For the reality of what's happening today in America, we must go to rock-'n'-roll, to popular music.

I said that.

For almost forty years in this country, which has prided itself on individualism, freedom and nonconformity, all popular songs were written alike. They had an eight-bar opening statement, an eight-bar repeat, an eight-bar middle section or bridge, and an eight-bar reprise. Anything that did not fit into that framework was, appropriately enough, called a novelty.

Clothes were basically the same whether a suit was double-breasted or single-breasted, and the only people who wore beards were absent-minded professors and Bolshevik bomb-throwers. Long hair, which was equated with lack of masculinity—in some sort of subconscious reference to Samson, I suspect—was restricted to painters and poets and classical musicians, hence the term "long-hair music" to mean classical.

Four years ago a specter was haunting Europe, one whose fundamental influence, my intuition tells me, may be just as important, if in another way, as the original of that line. The Beatles, four long-haired Liverpool teen-agers, were busy changing the image of popular music. In less than a year, they invaded the United States and almost totally wiped out the standard Broadway show/ Ed Sullivan-TV-program popular song. No more were we "flying to the moon on gossamer wings," we were now articulating such interesting and, in this mechanistic society, unusual concepts as "Money Can't Buy Me Love" and "I Want to Hold Your Hand."

"Societies, like individuals, have their moral crises and their spiritual revolutions," R. H. Tawney says in *Religion and the Rise of Capitalism*. And the Beatles appeared ("a great figure rose up from the sea and pointed at me and said 'you're a Beatle with an "a"'"—Genesis, according to John Lennon). They came at the proper moment of a spiritual cusp—as the martian in Robert Heinlein's *Stranger in a Strange Land* calls a crisis.

Instantly, on those small and sometimes doll-like figures was focused all the rebellion against hypocrisy, all the impudence and irreverence that the youth of that moment was feeling vis-à-vis his elders.

Automation, affluence, the totality of instant communication, the technology of the phonograph record, the transistor radio, had revolutionized life for youth in this society. The population age was lowering. Popular music, the jukebox and the radio were becoming the means of communication. Huntley and Brinkley were for Mom and Dad. People now sang songs they wrote themselves, not songs written *for* them by hacks in grimy Tin Pan Alley offices.

The folk-music boom paved the way. Bob Dylan's poetic polemics, "Blowin' in the Wind" and "The Times They Are A-Changin'," had helped the breakthrough. "Top-40" radio made Negro music available everywhere to a greater degree than ever before in our history.

This was, truly, a new generation—the first in America raised with music constantly in its ear, weaned on a transistor radio, involved with songs from its earliest moment of memory.

Music means more to this generation than it did even to its dancing parents in the big-band swing era of Benny Goodman. It's natural, then, that self-expression should find popular music so attractive.

The dance of the swing era, of the big bands, was the fox trot. It was really a formal dance extended in variation only by experts. The swing era's parents had danced the waltz. The fox trot was a ritual with only a little more room for self-expression. Rock-'n'-roll brought with it not only the voices of youth singing their protests, their hopes and their expectations (along with their pathos and their sentimentality and their personal affairs from drag racing to romance), it brought their dances.

"Every period which abounded in folk songs has, by the same token, been deeply stirred by Dionysiac currents," Nietzsche points out in *The Birth of Tragedy*. And Dionysiac is the word to describe the dances of the past ten years, call them by whatever name from bop to the twist to the frug, from the hully gully to the Philly dog.

In general, adult society left the youth alone, prey to the corruption the adults suspected was forthcoming from the song lyrics ("All of me, why not take all of me," from that hit of the thirties, of course, didn't mean *all* of me, it meant, well . . . er . . .) or from the payola-influenced disc jockeys. (Who ever remembers about the General Electric scandals of the fifties, in which over a dozen officials went to jail for industrial illegalities?)

The TV shows were in the afternoon anyway and nobody could stand to watch those rock-'n'-roll singers; they were worse than Elvis Presley.

But all of a sudden the *New Yorker* joke about the married couple dreamily remarking, when a disc jockey played "Hound Dog" by Elvis, "they're playing our song," wasn't a joke any longer. It was real. That generation had suddenly grown up and married and Elvis was real memories of real romance and not just kid stuff.

All of a sudden, the world of music, which is big business in a very real way, took another look at the music of the ponytail and chewing-gum set, as Mitch Miller once called the teenage market, and realized that there was one helluva lot of bread to be made there.

In a short few years, Columbia and R.C.A. Victor and the other companies that dominated the recording market, the huge publishing houses that copyrighted the music and collected the royalties, discovered that they no longer were "kings of the hill." Instead, a lot of small companies, like Atlantic and Chess and Imperial and others, had hits by people the major record companies didn't even know, singing songs written in Nashville and Detroit and Los Angeles and Chicago and sometimes, but no longer almost always, New York.

It's taken the big ones a few years to recoup from that. First they called the music trash and the lyrics dirty. When that didn't work, as the attempt more recently to inhibit songs with supposed psychedelic or marijuana references has failed, they capitulated. They joined up. R.C.A. Victor bought Elvis from the original company he recorded for—Sun Records ("Yaller Sun records from Nashville" as John Sebastian sings it in "Nashville Cats")—and then bought Sam Cooke, and A.B.C. Paramount bought Ray Charles and then Fats Domino. And Columbia, thinking it had a baby folk singer capable of some more sales of "San Francisco Bay," turned out to have a tiny demon of a poet named Bob Dylan.

So the stage was set for the Beatles to take over—"with this ring I can—dare I say it?—rule the world!"And they did take over so thoroughly that they have become the biggest success in the history of show business, the first attraction ever to have a coast-to-coast tour in this country sold out before the first show even opened.

With the Beatles and Dylan running tandem, two things seem to me to have been happening. The early Beatles were at one and the same time a declaration in favor of love and of life, an exuberant paean to the sheer joy of living, and a validation of the importance of American Negro music.

Dylan, by his political, issue-oriented broadsides first and then by his Rimbaudish nightmare visions of the real state of the nation, his bittersweet love songs and his pure imagery, did what the jazz and poetry people of the fifties had wanted to do—he took poetry out of the classroom and out of the hands of the professors and put it right out there in the streets for everyone.

I dare say that with the inspiration of the Beatles and Dylan we have more poetry being produced and more poets being made than ever before in the history of the world. Dr. Malvina Reynolds—the composer of "Little Boxes"—thinks nothing like this has happened since Elizabethan times. I suspect even that is too timid an assessment.

Let's go back to Plato again. Speaking of the importance of new styles of music, he said, "The new style quietly insinuates itself into manners and customs and from there it issues a greater force . . . goes on to attack laws and constitutions, displaying the utmost impudence, until it ends by overthrowing everything, both in public and in private."

That seems to me to be a pretty good summation of the answer to the British rock-singer Donovan's question, "What goes on? I really want to know."

The most immediate apparent change instituted by the new music is a new way of looking at things. We see it evidenced all around us. The old ways are going and a new set of assumptions is beginning to be worked out. I cannot even begin to codify them. Perhaps it's much too soon to do so. But I think there are some clues—the sacred importance of love and truth and beauty and interpersonal relationships.

When Bob Dylan sang recently at the Masonic Memorial Auditorium in San Francisco, at intermission there were a few very young people in the corridor backstage. One of them was a long-haired, poncho-wearing girl of about thirteen. Dylan's road manager, a slender, long-haired, "Bonnie Prince Charlie" youth, wearing black jeans and Beatle boots, came out of the dressing room and said, "You kids have to leave! You can't be backstage here!"

"Who are you?" the long-haired girl asked.

"I'm a cop," Dylan's road manager said aggressively.

The girl looked at him for a long moment and then drawled, "Whaaaat? With those boots?"

Clothes really do *not* make the man. But sometimes . . .

I submit that was an important incident, something that could never have happened a year before, something that implies a very great deal about the effect of the new style, which has quietly (or not so quietly, depending on your view of electric guitars) insinuated itself into manners and customs.

Among the effects of "what's goin' on" is the relinquishing of belief in the sacredness of logic. "I was a prisoner of logic and I still am," Malvina Reynolds admits, but then goes on to praise the new music. And the prisoners of logic are the ones who are really suffering most—unless they have Mrs. Reynolds' glorious gift of youthful vision.

The first manifestation of the importance of this outside music—I think—came in the works of Ken Kesey and Joseph Heller. *One Flew Over the Cuckoo's Nest*, with its delightful utilization of crackpot realism (to use C. Wright Mills's phrase) as an explanation of how things are, [was a] work of seminal importance.

No one any longer really believes that the processes of international relations and world economics are rationally explicable. Absolutely the very best and clearest discussion of the entire thing is wrapped up in Milo Minderbinder's explanation, in

Catch-22, of how you can buy eggs for seven cents apiece in Malta and sell them for five cents in Pianosa and make a profit. Youth understands the truth of this immediately, and no economics textbook is going to change it.

Just as—implying the importance of interpersonal relation and the beauty of being true to oneself—the under-thirty youth immediately understands the creed patiently explained by Yossarian in *Catch-22* that everybody's your enemy who's trying to get you killed, even if he's your own commanding officer.

This is an irrational world, despite the brilliant efforts of Walter Lippmann to make it rational, and we are living in a continuation of the formalized lunacy (Nelson Algren's phrase) of war, any war.

At this point in history, most of the organs of opinion, from the *New York Review of Books* through the *New Republic* to *Encounter* (whether or not they are subsidized by the C.I.A.), are in the control of the prisoners of logic. They take a flick like *Morgan* and grapple with it. They take *Help!* and *A Hard Day's Night* and grapple with those two beautiful creations, and they fail utterly to understand what is going on because they try to deal with them logically. They complain because art doesn't make sense! Life on this planet in this time of history doesn't make sense either—as an end result of immutable laws of economics and logic and philosophy.

Dylan sang, "You raise up your head and you ask 'is this where it is?' And somebody points to you and says 'it's his' and you say 'what's mine' and somebody else says 'well, what is' and you say 'oh my god am i here all alone?'"

Dylan wasn't the first. Orwell saw some of it, Heller saw more, and in a different way so did I. F. Stone, that remarkable journalist, who is really a poet, when he described a *Herald Tribune* reporter extracting from the Pentagon the admission that, once the first steps for the Santo Domingo episode were mounted, it was impossible to stop the machine.

Catch-22 said that in order to be sent home from flying missions you had to be crazy, and obviously anybody who wanted to be sent home was sane.

Kesey and Heller and Terry Southern, to a lesser degree in his novels but certainly in *Dr. Strangelove*, have hold of it. I suspect that they are not really a *new wave* of writers but only a *last* wave of the past, just as is Norman Mailer, who said in his Berkeley Vietnam Day speech that "rational discussion of the United States involvement in Vietnam is illogical in the way surrealism is illogical and rational political discussion of Adolf Hitler's motives was illogical and then obscene." This is the end of the formal literature we have known and the beginning, possibly, of something else.

In almost every aspect of what is happening today, this turning away from the old patterns is making itself manifest. As the formal structure of the show-business world of popular music and television has brought out into the open the Negro performer—whose incredibly beautiful folk poetry and music for decades has been the prime mover in American song—we find a curious thing happening.

The Negro performers, from James Brown to Aaron Neville to the Supremes and the Four Tops, are on an Ed Sullivan trip, striving as hard as they can to get on that stage and become part of the American success story, while the white rock performers are motivated to escape from that stereotype. Whereas in years past the Negro performer offered style in performance and content in song—the messages from Leadbelly to Percy Mayfield to Ray Charles were important messages—today he is almost totally style with very little content. And when James Brown sings, "It's a Man's World," or Aaron Neville sings, "Tell It Like It Is," he takes a phrase and only a phrase with which to work, and the Supremes and the Tops are choreographed more and more like the Four Lads and the Ames Brothers and the McGuire Sisters.

I suggest that this bears a strong relationship to the condition of the civil rights movement today in which the only truly black position is that of Stokely Carmichael, and in which the N.A.A.C.P. and most of the other formal groups are, like the Four Tops and the Supremes, on an Ed Sullivan/TV-trip to middle-class America. And the only true American Negro music is that which abandons the concepts of European musical thought, abandons the systems of scales and keys and notes, for a music whose roots are in the culture of the colored peoples of the world.

The drive behind all American popular music performers, to a greater or lesser extent, from Sophie Tucker and Al Jolson, on down through Pat Boone and as recently as Roy Head and

Charlie Rich, has been to sound like a Negro. The white jazz musician was the epitome of this.

Yet an outstanding characteristic of the new music of rock, certainly in its best artists, is something else altogether. This new generation of musicians is not interested in being Negro, since that is an absurdity.

The clarinetist Milton Mezzrow, who grew up with the Negro Chicago jazzmen in the twenties and thirties, even put "Negro" on his prison record and claimed to be more at home with his Negro friends than with his Jewish family and neighbors.

Today's new youth, beginning with the rock-band musician but spreading out into the entire movement, into the Haight-Ashbury hippies, is not ashamed of being white.

He is remarkably free from prejudice, but he is not attempting to join the Negro culture or to become part of it, like his musical predecessor, the jazzman, or like his social predecessor, the beatnik. I find this of considerable significance. For the very first time in decades, as far as I know, something important and new is happening artistically and musically in this society that is distinct from the Negro and to which the Negro will have to come, if he is interested in it at all, as in the past the white youth went uptown to Harlem or downtown or crosstown or to wherever the Negro community was centered because there was the locus of artistic creativity.

Today the new electronic music by the Beatles and others (and the Beatles' "Strawberry Fields" is, I suggest, a three-minute masterpiece, an electronic miniature symphony) exists somewhere else from and independent of the Negro. This is only one of the more easily observed manifestations of this movement.

The professional craft union, the American Federation of Musicians, is now faced with something absolutely unforeseen —the cooperative band. Briefly—in the thirties—there were co-op bands. The original Casa Loma band was one and the original Woody Herman band was another. But the whole attitude of the musicians themselves worked against the idea, and co-op bands were discouraged. They were almost unknown until recently.

Today almost all the rock groups are cooperative. Many live together, in tribal style, in houses or camps or sometimes in traveling tepees, but always, *together* as a *group;* and the young girls who follow them are called "groupies," just as the girls who in the thirties and forties followed the bands (music does more than soothe the savage breast!) were called "band chicks."

The basic creed of the American Federation of Musicians is that musicians must not play unless paid. The new generation wants money, of course, but its basic motivation is to play anytime, anywhere, anyhow. Art is first, then finance, most of the time. And at least one rock band, the Loading Zone in Berkeley, has stepped outside the American Federation of Musicians entirely and does not play for money. You may give them money, but they won't set a price or solicit it.

This seems to me to extend the attitude that gave Pete Seeger, Joan Baez and Bob Dylan such status. They are not and never have been for sale in the sense that you can hire Sammy Davis to appear, as you can hire Dean Martin to appear, any time he's free, as long as you pay his price. You have not been able to do this with Seeger, Baez and Dylan any more than Allen Ginsberg has been for sale either to *Ramparts* or the C.I.A.

Naturally, this revolt against the assumptions of the adult world runs smack dab into the sanctimonious puritan morality of America, the schizophrenia that insists that money is serious business and the acquisition of wealth is a blessing in the eyes of the Lord, that what we do in private we must preach against in public. Don't do what I do, do what I say.

Implicit in the very names of the business organizations that these youths form is an attack on the traditional, serious attitude toward money. It is not only that the groups themselves are named with beautiful imagery: the Grateful Dead, Loading Zone, Blue Cheer or the Jefferson Airplane—all dating back to the Beatles with an A—it is the names of the non-musical organizations: Frontage Road Productions (the music company of the Grateful Dead), Faithful Virtue Music (the Lovin' Spoonful's publishing company), Ashes and Sand (Bob Dylan's production firm—his music publishing company is Dwarf Music). A group who give light shows is known as the Love Conspiracy Commune, and there was a dance recently in Marin County, California, sponsored by the Northern California Psychedelic Cattlemen's Association, Ltd. And, of course, there is the Family Dog, which, despite *Ramparts*, was never a rock group, only a name under which four people who wanted to present rock 'n roll dances worked.

Attacking the conventional attitude toward money is considered immoral in the society of our fathers, because money is sacred. The reality of what Bob Dylan says—"money doesn't talk, it swears"—has yet to seep through.

A corollary of the money attack is the whole thing about long hair, bare feet and beards. "Nothing makes me sadder," a woman wrote me objecting to the Haight-Ashbury scene, "than to see beautiful young girls walking along the street in bare feet." My own daughter pointed out that your feet couldn't get any dirtier than your shoes.

Recently I spent an evening with a lawyer, a brilliant man who is engaged in a lifelong crusade to educate and reform lawyers. He is interested in the civil liberties issue of police harassment of hippies. But, he said, they wear those uniforms of buckskin and fringe and beads. Why don't they dress naturally? So I asked him if he was born in his three-button Dacron suit. It's like the newspaper descriptions of Joan Baez's "long stringy hair." It may be long, but *stringy*? Come on!

To the eyes of many of the elder generation, all visible aspects of the new generation, its music, its lights, its clothes, are immoral. The City of San Francisco Commission on Juvenile Delinquency reported adversely on the sound level and the lights at the Fillmore Auditorium, as if those things of and by themselves were threats (they may be, but not in the way the Commission saw them). A young girl might have trouble maintaining her judgment in that environment, the Commission chairman said.

Now this all implies that dancing is the road to moral ruin, that young girls on the dance floor are mesmerized by talent scouts for South American brothels and enticed away from their happy (not hippie) homes to live a life of slavery and moral degradation. It ought to be noted, parenthetically, that a British writer, discussing the Beatles, claims that "the Cycladic fertility goddess from Amorgos dates the guitar as a sex symbol to 4800 years B.C."

During the twenties and the thirties and the forties—in other words, during the prime years of the Old Ones of today—dancing, in the immortal words of Bob Scobey, the Dixieland trumpet player, "was an excuse to get next to a broad." The very least effect of the pill on American youth is that this is no longer true.

The assault on hypocrisy works on many levels. The adult society attempted to chastise Bob Dylan by economic sanction, calling the line in "Rainy Day Woman," "everybody must get stoned" (although there is a purely religious, even biblical, meaning to it, if you wish), an enticement to teen-agers to smoke marijuana. But no one has objected to Ray Charles's "Let's Go Get Stoned," which is about gin, or to any number of other songs, from the Kingston Trio's "Scotch and Soda" on through "One for My Baby and One More [ONE MORE!] for the Road." Those are about alcohol and alcohol is socially acceptable, as well as big business, even though I believe that everyone under thirty now knows that alcohol is worse for you than marijuana, that, in fact, the only thing wrong about marijuana is that it is illegal.

Cut to the California State Narcotics Bureau's chief enforcement officer, Matt O'Connor, in a TV interview recently insisting, à la Parkinson's Law, that he must have more agents to control the drug-abuse problem. He appeared with a representative of the state attorney general's office, who predicted that the problem would continue "as long as these people believe they are not doing anything wrong."

And that's exactly it. They do not think they are doing anything wrong, any more than their grandparents were when they broke the prohibition laws. They do not want to go to jail, but a jail sentence or a bust no longer carries the social stigma it once did. The civil rights movement has made a jailing a badge of honor, if you go there for principle, and to a great many people today, the right to smoke marijuana is a principle worth risking jail for.

"Make Love, Not War" is one of the most important slogans of modern times, a statement of life against death, as the Beatles have said over and over—"say the word and be like me, say the word and you'll be free."

I don't think that wearing that slogan on a bumper or on the back of a windbreaker is going to end the bombing tomorrow at noon, but it implies something. It is not conceivable that it could have existed in such proliferation thirty years ago, and in 1937 *we* were pacifists, too. It simply could not have happened.

There's another side to it, of course, or at least another aspect of it. The Rolling Stones, who came into existence really to fight jazz in the clubs of London, were against the jazz of the integrated world, the integrated world arrived at by rational processes. Their songs, from "Satisfaction" and "19th Nervous Breakdown" to "Get Off of My Cloud" and "Mother's Little Helper," were antiestablishment songs in a nonpolitical sort of way, just as Dylan's first period was antiestablishment in a political way. The Stones are now moving, with "Ruby Tuesday" and "Let's Spend the Night Together," into a social radicalism of sorts; but in the beginning, and for their basic first-thrust appeal, they hit out in rage, almost in blind anger and certainly with overtones of destructiveness, against the adult world. It's no wonder the novel they were attracted to was David Wallis' *Only Lovers Left Alive*, that Hell's Angels story of a teen-age, future jungle. And it is further interesting that their manager, Andrew Loog Oldham, writes the essays on their albums in the style of Anthony Burgess' violent *A Clockwork Orange*.

Nor is it any wonder that this attitude appealed to that section of the youth whose basic position was still in politics and economics (remember that the Rolling Stone Mick Jagger was a London School of Economics student, whereas Lennon and McCartney were artists and writers). When the Stones first came to the West Coast, a group of young radicals issued the following proclamation of welcome:

Greetings and welcome Rolling Stones, our comrades in the desperate battle against the maniacs who hold power. The revolutionary youth of the world hears your music and is inspired to even more deadly acts. We fight in guerrilla bands against the invading imperialists in Asia and South America, we riot at rock-'n'-roll concerts everywhere: We burned and pillaged in Los Angeles and the cops know our snipers will return.

They call us dropouts and delinquents and draftdodgers and punks and hopheads and heap tons of shit on our heads. In Viet Nam they drop bombs on us and in America they try to make us make war on our own comrades but the bastards hear us playing you on our little transistor radios and know that they will not escape the blood and fire of the anarchist revolution.

RALPH J. GLEASON   563

We will play your music in rock-'n'-roll marching bands as we tear down the jails and free the prisoners, as we tear down the State schools and free the students, as we tear down the military bases and arm the poor, as we tattoo BURN BABY BURN! on the bellies of the wardens and generals and create a new society from the ashes of our fires.

Comrades, you will return to this country when it is free from the tyranny of the State and you will play your splendid music in factories run by the workers, in the domes of emptied city halls, on the rubble of police stations, under the hanging corpses of priests, under a million red flags waving over a million anarchist communities. In the words of Breton, THE ROLLING STONES ARE THAT WHICH SHALL BE! LYNDON JOHNSON— THE YOUTH OF CALIFORNIA DEDICATES ITSELF TO YOUR DESTRUCTION! ROLLING STONES—THE YOUTH OF CALIFORNIA HEARS YOUR MESSAGE! LONG LIVE THE REVOLUTION!!!

But rhetoric like that did not bring out last January to a Human Be-In on the polo grounds of San Francisco's Golden Gate Park twenty thousand people who were there, fundamentally, just to see the other members of the tribe, not to hear speeches— the speeches were all a drag from Leary to Rubin to Buddah[1]— but just to *Be*.

In the Haight-Ashbury district the Love Generation organizes itself into job co-ops and committees to clean the streets, and the monks of the neighborhood, the Diggers, talk about free dances in the park to put the Avalon Ballroom and the Fillmore out of business and about communizing the incomes of Bob Dylan and the Beatles.

The Diggers trace back spiritually to those British millenarians who took over land in 1649, just before Cromwell, and after the Civil War freed it, under the assumption that the land was for the people. They tilled it and gave the food away.

---

[1] The Be-In heard speeches by Timothy Leary, the psychedelic guru, Jerry Rubin, the leader of the Berkeley Vietnam Day movement, and Buddah, a bartender and minor figure in the San Francisco hippie movement who acted as master of ceremonies.

The Diggers gave food away. Everything is Free. So is it with the Berkeley Provos and the new group in Cleveland—the Prunes—and the Provos in Los Angeles. More, if an extreme, assault against the money culture. Are they driving the money changers out of the temple? Perhaps. The Diggers say they believe it is just as futile to fight the system as to join it and they are dropping out in a way that differs from Leary's.

The Square Left wrestles with the problem. They want a Yellow Submarine community because that is where the strength so obviously is. But even *Ramparts*, which is the white hope of the Square Left, if you follow me, misunderstands. They think that the Family Dog is a rock group and that political activity is the only hope, and Bob Dylan says, "There's no left wing and no right wing, only up wing and down wing," and also, "I tell you there are no politics."

But the banding together to form job co-ops, to publish newspapers, to talk to the police (even to bring them flowers), aren't these political acts? I suppose so, but I think they are political acts of a different kind, a kind that results in the Hell's Angels being the guardians of the lost children at the Be-In and the guarantors of peace at dances.

The New Youth is finding its prophets in strange places—in dance halls and on the jukebox. It is on, perhaps, a frontier buckskin trip after a decade of Matt Dillon and *Bonanza* and the other TV folk myths, in which the values are clear (as opposed to those in the world around us) and right is right and wrong is wrong. The Negro singers have brought the style and the manner of the Negro gospel preacher to popular music, just as they brought the rhythms and the feeling of the gospel music, and now the radio is the church and Everyman carries his own walkie-talkie to God in his transistor.

Examine the outcry against the Beatles for John Lennon's remark about being more popular than Jesus. No radio station that depended on rock-'n'-roll music for its audience banned Beatles records, and in the only instance where we had a precise measuring rod for the contest—the Beatles concert in Memphis where a revival meeting ran day and date with them—the Beatles won overwhelmingly. Something like eight to five over Jesus in attendance, even though the Beatles charged a stiff price and the Gospel according to the revival preacher was free.

RALPH J. GLEASON 565

VII / THE ARTS

Was my friend so wrong who said that if Hitler were alive today, the German girls wouldn't allow him to bomb London if the Beatles were there?

"Nobody ever taught you how to live out in the street," Bob Dylan sings in "Like a Rolling Stone." You may consider that directed at a specific person, or you may, as I do, consider it poetically aimed at plastic uptight America, to use a phrase from one of the Family Dog founders.

"Nowhere to run, nowhere to hide," Martha and the Vandellas sing, and Simon and Garfunkel say, "The words of the prophets are written on the subway walls, in tenement halls." And the Byrds sing, "A time for peace, I swear it's not too late," just as the Beatles sing, "Say the word." What has formal religion done in this century to get the youth of the world so well acquainted with a verse from the Bible?

Even in those artists of the second echelon who are not, like Dylan and the Beatles and the Stones, worldwide in their influence, we find it. "Don't You Want Somebody to Love," the Jefferson Airplane sings, and Bob Lind speaks of "the bright elusive butterfly of love."

These songs speak to us in our condition, just as Dylan did with "lookout kid, it's somethin' you did, god knows what, but you're doin' it again." And Dylan sings again a concept that finds immediate response in the tolerance and the anti-judgment stance of the new generation, when he says, "There are no trials inside the Gates of Eden."

Youth is wise today. Lenny Bruce claimed that TV made even eight-year-old girls sophisticated. When Bob Dylan in "Desolation Row" sings, "At midnight all the agents and the superhuman crew come out and round up everyone that knows more than they do," he speaks true, as he did with "don't follow leaders." But sometimes it is, as John Sebastian of the Lovin' Spoonful says, "like trying to tell a stranger 'bout a rock-'n'-roll."

Let's go back again to Neitzsche.

Orgiastic movements of a society leave their traces in music [he wrote]. Dionysiac stirrings arise either through the influence of those narcotic potions of which all primitive races speak in their hymns [—dig that!—] or through the powerful approach of spring, which penetrates with joy the whole frame of nature. So stirred, the individual forgets himself completely. It is the same Dionysiac power which in medieval Germany drove ever-increasing crowds of people singing and dancing from place to place; we recognize in these St. John's and St. Vitus' dancers the bacchic choruses of the Greeks, who had their precursors in Asia Minor and as far back as Babylon and the orgiastic Sacea. There are people who, either from lack of experience or out of sheer stupidity, turn away from such phenomena, and strong, in the sense of their own sanity, label them either mockingly or pityingly "endemic diseases." These benighted souls have no idea how cadaverous and ghostly their "sanity" appears as the intense throng of Dionysiac revelers sweeps past them.

And Nietzsche never heard of the San Francisco Commission on Juvenile Delinquency or the Fillmore and the Avalon ballrooms.

"Believe in the magic, it will set you free," the Lovin' Spoonful sing. "This is an invitation across the nation," sing Martha and the Vandellas, and the Mamas and the Papas, "a chance for folks to meet, there'll be laughin', singin' and music swingin', and dancin' in the street!"

Do I project too much? Again, to Nietzsche. "Man now expresses himself through song and dance as the member of a higher community; he has forgotten how to walk, how to speak and is on the brink of taking wing as he dances . . . no longer the *artist*, he has himself become *a work of art*."

"Hail hail rock-'n'-roll," as Chuck Berry sings. "Deliver me from the days of old!"

I think he's about to be granted his wish.

33 / One or Two Things

JEAN-LUC GODARD

Yes, I'm making two films at the same time. The first is *Deux ou trois choses que je sais d'elle*, starring Marina Vlady; the other, *Made in U.S.A.*, with Anna Karina. They are completely different in style, and have nothing to do with each other, except perhaps that they let me indulge my passion for analyzing what is called modern living, for dissecting it like a biologist to see what goes on underneath. *Deux ou trois choses* was inspired by a letter in *Le Nouvel Observateur* from a woman reader replying to an inquiry into part-time prostitution in the new high-rise housing developments. *Made in U.S.A.* is the fusion in my mind of three different things: I wanted to oblige a friend, to tackle the Americanization of French life, and to do something with the Ben Barka affair.

Why did I agree to make both at the same time? Pride, I think. It's a sort of bet. A performance. As if a musician were to conduct two orchestras at once, each playing a different symphony. It is even more difficult for me than most, as I don't work from a written scenario but improvise as I go along. This sort of improvisation can only work if the ground has been thoroughly thought out in advance, and it needs absolute concentration.

I make my films not only when filming, but as I read, eat, dream, even as I talk. This is why I find making two films at once so exhausting—and so exhilarating. To tell you the truth it wasn't planned that way. I was in the middle of making *Deux ou trois choses* when Georges de Beauregard, who was in financial difficulties after the banning of *La Religieuse*,

SOURCE: Toby Mussman, ed., *Jean-Luc Godard: A Critical Anthology* (New York: E. P. Dutton, 1968), pp. 274–83. Translated by *Sight and Sound,* London, England from the French version, which appeared in *Le Nouvel Observateur,* 1966. Copyright © 1966 by Jean-Luc Godard. Reprinted by permission of *Le Nouvel Observateur.*
Swiss-born Jean-Luc Godard worked as a film critic in Paris before making films himself. The techniques he introduced into commercial cinema revolutionized the medium, and together with a few of his European contemporaries, he is the dominant force in art cinema.

asked if I couldn't run something up for him in a hurry. It was the only way to get him out of his difficulties and allow him to hang on, he said. "You're the only person who can do anything at a moment's notice." "I suppose I am," I said.

I hadn't an idea in my head when I accepted. Then I read a *Série Noire* thriller which interested me. As I had just seen *The Big Sleep* again, I thought of having the Humphrey Bogart role played by a woman—Anna Karina, as it happens. I also decided to set the action in France rather than America, and worked a marginal episode from the Ben Barka affair into the main theme. My idea was that Figon was not really dead, but had fled to the country and sent for his mistress to join him. She comes to the address given her, and finds him really dead this time. I have set the action in 1969, two years after the parliamentary elections which will be held in March this year. The character is called Politzer, not Figon. No one knows why he died, and the girl sets out to uncover his past. Among other things, she discovers that he has been the editor of an important Parisian weekly which got very worked up over the Ben Barka affair, and on which she herself was a reporter. Because of her love for him she finds herself playing detective, gets tangled in a web of crooks and cops, and in the end decides to write an article about the affair. The film closes on a discussion with a journalist—Philippe Labro—in a Europe One radio station car.

I started off intending to make a simple film; and for the first time I tried to tell a story. But it isn't my way of doing things. I don't know how to tell stories. I want to cover the whole ground, from all possible angles, saying everything at once. If I had to define myself I would say that I was a painter in letters, as one says man of letters. The result is that although I have respected story continuity for the first time in *Made in U.S.A.,* I couldn't prevent myself from filling in the sociological context. And this context is that everything now is American-influenced. Hence the title.

The other film is much more ambitious, both on the documentary level, as it is about new development schemes in the Paris region, and on the level of pure research, as it is a film in which I am constantly asking myself what I am trying to do. The pretext, of course, is the life—and sometimes the prostitution—of the new housing schemes. But my real aim is to observe the vast mutation which our civilization is undergoing at present, and to ask myself how one can best come to grips with this mutation.

I should say right away that I am particularly happy to be living in France today, in our time, because the mutations are gigantic, and for a painter in letters this is enormously exciting. In Europe today, and particularly in France, everything is stirring before our very eyes, and one must have eyes to see: the provinces, youth, urban development, industrialization. It is an extraordinary period. For me, describing modern living is not simply a matter of describing new gadgets and industrial developments as some newspapers do, but of observing these mutations. So my film opens with a commentary.

On August 17, Paul Delouvrier is appointed administrator-in-chief of the new Parisian region. As the commentary is read, we see shots of building sites, road works, housing blocks, people trying to go about the business of living. Suddenly my own voice is heard, asking myself if I have used the right words in speaking about all this. For instance, I film a house and I ask myself: "Am I right to film this house and not another, at this moment and not another?" In short, the spectator is made to share in the arbitrary nature of my particular choice, and in the quest for a general rule to justify the particular.

Why am I making this film, why am I making it this way? Is the character played by Marina Vlady representative of women on housing estates? I keep asking myself these questions. I watch myself filming, and you hear me thinking aloud. *Deux ou trois choses,* in fact, is not a film but an essay at film, presented as such and really forming part of my own personal research. A document rather than a story. Stretching a point or two, it's a film which ought to have been commissioned by M. Paul Delouvrier.

Of course, it is my secret ambition to be put in charge of French newsreels. Each of my films constitutes a report on the state of the nation: they are news reportages, treated in a quirkish way perhaps, but rooted in actuality. *Le Petit Soldat* ought to have been subsidized by the Ministry of Information, *Vivre sa Vie* by the Ministry of Health, *Pierrot le Fou* by the Minister for Culture (for the quotations), and *Masculin-Féminin* by our Minister for Youth.

570

I mention subsidy because, shocking as it may seem and taking all in all, when faced by a choice between dictatorship by money and by political censorship, I prefer the former. Advertising is another of my obsessions. In the modern world, the advertising element reigns supreme, determining everything, paralyzing everything. Advertising is allowed, or rather takes, liberties forbidden to everyone else; and in this way it is so representative of our society that it is a richer treasure trove of documentation than any archive. I buy certain papers solely to be able to read the advertisements. All of it interests me: how the slogans change, the graphics, the ways of seducing the consumer public. The importance of advertising is enormous, and so little recognized that I was attacked for being too outspoken about sex when all I did was film the posters which can be seen on any wall. I just brought them all together, and the result was thought "daring."

To return to *Deux ou trois choses que je sais d'elle*. Although it was sparked off by a newspaper anecdote, what excited me most was that this anecdote linked up with one of my pet theories, that in order to live in society in Paris today, on no matter what social level, one is forced to prostitute oneself in one way or another—or to put it another way, to live under conditions resembling those of prostitution. A worker in a factory prostitutes himself in a way three-quarters of the time, being paid for doing a job he has no desire to do. The same is true of a banker, a post office employee, a film director. In modern industrial society, prostitution is the norm: and my film endeavors to present one or two lessons on industrial society. (I quote frequently from Raymond Aron's book, *Eighteen Lessons on Industrial Society*.) No doubt you will say that I take myself very seriously. I do. I think a film director has such an enormous part to play that he can't afford not to.

When a director makes a film, he is not only the head of a great enterprise but the strategist of a great general staff, and the possibilities are fantastic. He has to deal with banks, unions, the government, he is in contact with people from all layers of society. He negotiates, controls, influences, borrows, invests. In addition his work has public repercussions, and he is not permitted to make mistakes. As far as art is concerned, he is on his own; but in its execution, he is a veritable head of state.

I am now on my thirteenth film, and yet I feel I have hardly begun really to look at the world. Curiously enough, once again I feel this because I live in France. I have traveled a good deal, and was recently planning to leave France again to make films abroad. In Cuba, for instance, about the teaching of illiterates. Or in North Vietnam, to see new ideals at war and to bear witness. Now I feel that I can do the same job by talking about Cuba and Vietnam in my films. Above all I feel that I can do the same job by talking about Cuba and Vietnam in my films. Above all I feel that a country can rarely have offered such a range of exciting subjects as France today. The choice is bewildering. I want to cover everything—sport, politics, even groceries— look at Edouard Leclerc,[1] a fantastic man whom I'd love to do a film about or with. You can put anything and everything into a film, you *must* put in everything.

When I am asked why there are references to Vietnam in my films, or to Jacques Anquetil, or to some lady who's deceiving her husband, I refer the questioner to his daily paper. It's all there. In any old order. This is why I'm so attracted by television, one of the most interesting expressions of modern living. A televised newspaper, carefully composed and documented—that would be something extraordinary. What might be even more extraordinary would be to get the various national editors to bring out their own televised newspapers. One could have a couple of hours daily of *France-Soir,* three hours of *Nouvel Observateur* every Thursday, and so on. It would be marvelous. But television in France is the voice of Power, just as it is the voice of the dollar in the United States. So, one has to make do with the cinema, attempting the impossible in order to try to do what the newsreels and programs don't.

There are other taboos in France, and one of them—no matter what they think abroad—is sex. It is extremely difficult, if not impossible, to make a frank film about sexual problems. Let's be honest: in order to make a frank film, one must oneself be affranchised, and this, I find in my own case, takes some effort. I still retain ingrained traces of my Protestant upbringing, and I have struggled to get rid of them. But each time I have tried

[1] A dynamic young revolutionary of grocery marketing—the Marx and Spencer of France.

to do something on film it shocks, and it is hard to understand why.

As a matter of fact, no one has ever made a real film about sex, except perhaps Buñuel. The difficult thing is to speak of sex as the psychologists do, coldly and clinically. In *Deux ou trois choses* (where, by the way, the "elle" is not Marina Vlady but Paris), two people who don't know each other start talking in a café. One of them says: "It's a fine day." The other replies: "We could talk about something more interesting." "But it is interesting," the first goes on. "I love fine weather and the rain, and I talk about it because it interests me."

The other then says, "It doesn't interest me. Let's talk about something else, about sex, for instance, because I think it's impossible to talk about it properly in the cinema. Actually nothing is talked about properly in the cinema. I don't know why. But sex is even less properly talked about than anything else."

—"But they're always talking about sex," the first replies.

—"Yes, but talking stupidly. Yet it's no different from the human body, legs, hair, music. So why is it considered to be so inordinately important, or conversely, not important enough? Listen, for instance, I'll ask you to repeat a sentence, and I'm sure you won't dare."

—"What sentence?"

—"First, swear to repeat it."

He refuses, then decides to swear, and the other says, "The sentence is very simple. It's: My sex is between my legs."

Then the first says, "I won't say that, I think it's stupid," etc.

Of course it's stupid, but it illustrates how sex is seen as something bizarre. Mark you, I myself will not tolerate indecency. Two people kissing, for instance. I have shown this once, with Belmondo and Seberg in *À Bout de Souffle,* but never since. The characters in my films embrace and caress each other, but never kiss. The kiss is something intimate and private, purely personal and therefore unshowable. On a huge screen it is revolting to watch. When people kiss in the street I never look at them. I respect their intimacy. But sex is a different matter. One could study it and film it, just as love is studied and filmed. Not that anyone has succeeded in discovering the mystery of love—and it is a mystery which fascinates me. How can something which is a feeling and therefore intangible, provoke such physical joy and pain? What I would like to be able to do one day is show—just show, not comment on—the moment when a feeling enters the body and becomes physiologically alive. Proust took thirty years and eight volumes on a feeling; and one still wants to know how and why it happens.

My mixed feeling of remoteness and fascination towards love also applies to actors. How can anyone be an actor? I can never understand. They are both monsters and children, and my relations with them are unhappy. I don't speak to them, and it's difficult because they are like sick children, constantly in need of reassurance. They suffer from an inability to express themselves, which is why they have become actors, of course. They are children trying to speak at birth, and because they can't, they borrow expression from others.

The plight of the actor moves me deeply because he is composed of infirmities. I don't share Camus' belief that the actor is a Don Juan, living several destinies at once. Actors have no destiny, and they know it. Far from living many roles, they are constantly made aware of their mutilation. Between the creator and the actor there is the same distance as between *is* and *has*. The actor *is* not. This said, though, I part company with Bresson when he says there can be no such thing as a good professional actor. I very much admire Bresson, who is one of our greatest directors, but I cannot help feeling that his attitude to actors smacks almost of racism. The director's ideal must certainly be to rediscover a freshness and spontaneity beyond theatricality; but that's his business.

Put another way, it seems to me that we have to rediscover everything about everything. There is only one solution, and that is to turn one's back on the American cinema. I deplore the fact that the Soviet dream now is to imitate Hollywood, just when Hollywood has nothing more to say. This, if you like, is my own personal way of deploring Soviet-American collusion. Up till now we have lived in a closed world. Cinema fed on cinema, imitating itself. I now see that in my first films I did things because I had already seen them in the cinema. If I showed a police inspector drawing a revolver from his pocket, it wasn't because the logic of the situation I wanted to describe demanded it, but because I had seen police inspectors in other films drawing revolvers at this precise moment and in this precise way. The same thing has happened in painting. There have been periods of organization and imitation, and periods of rupture. We are now in a period of rupture. We must turn to life again. We must move into modern life with a virgin eye.

VIII / Counterpoints

According to a law of physics, every action has its reaction. If the word is the deed, then the radical vision is no exception to this law; and indeed, as forcefully as it has been put forth, just as forcefully it has been opposed. By no means are all the observers of the contemporary scene aroused to approval by what meets their eyes and ears. The spectrum of disapproval is wide, and one need not be a reactionary in order to feel a reaction. For example, Theodore Roszak is politically radical even while he rejects the kind of "radical" culture that he believes to be implicit in McLuhanism. This reaction to McLuhan comes from a cultural historian, the kind of professional academic most likely to take umbrage at the freewheeling informalism of this popular professor and his followers with their blithe dismissal of history and their own emphasis on the mass media. Roszak's attack, then, is not on the radical political values of the contemporary scene, but on some of its cheap cultural side-products.

Similarly, Sir Arthur Lewis' analysis of black aspirations is not from a man uncommitted to black power. He does, however, prefer alternatives to black studies programs as the primary focus of black students in American colleges and universities. He opposes the current cultivation of these programs because he feels that they will hinder the growth of black economic power and thereby play directly into the hands of white racists who welcome any form of segregation. Once again, reaction here is not reactionaryism.

In still another "reaction," Robert Brustein's plea is for rational discourse, especially when he feels that the excesses of spontaneity may lead to chaos. Brustein implies that individual expression and honesty by themselves are not art, and that formlessness leads to superficiality. What he seeks in artistic creation is greater discipline and a more profound commitment to established forms. It may be rewarding to contrast his reactions with those of Cage, Ginsberg, and Burroughs, and to compare them with the response of Theodore Roszak as a way of differentiating between negative views.

The most thorough rejection of the current radical scene comes from a member of the older generation who has been part of the political establishment for the last two decades. George Kennan was instrumental in forging American cold-war strategy in the early 1950s, and perhaps more responsible for America's present political posture than any other theoretician. Naturally enough, his values are not only rooted in an earlier time, but rooted as well in a moralistic view of America and its role as an international leader. Kennan's attack on the political and social consequences of the radical movement, published in early 1968, remains the classic statement of the unsympathetic father ultimately rejecting even his prodigal sons.

34 / Rebels Without a Program

GEORGE F. KENNAN

There is an ideal that has long been basic to the learning process as we have known it, one that stands at the very center of our modern institutions of higher education and that had its origin, I suppose, in the clerical and monastic character of the medieval university. It is the ideal of the association of the pro-

SOURCE: George F. Kennan, *Democracy and the Student Left* (Boston: Atlantic Monthly Press, 1968), pp. 3–20. Copyright © 1968 by George F. Kennan. Reprinted by permission of Atlantic-Little, Brown and Co. This selection was originally published in the *New York Times Magazine*, January 21, 1968.

George F. Kennan is a well-known political commentator, the author of America's cold-war strategy in the 1950s, and a diplomat. His article had its origin as a speech given for the dedication of a library at Swarthmore College.

cess of learning with a certain remoteness from the contemporary scene—a certain detachment and seclusion, a certain voluntary withdrawal and renunciation of participation in contemporary life in the interests of the achievement of a better perspective on that life when the period of withdrawal is over. It is an ideal that does not predicate any total conflict between thought and action, but recognizes that there is a time for each.

No more striking, or moving, description of this ideal has ever come to my attention than that which was given by Woodrow Wilson in 1896 at the time of the Princeton Sesquicentennial.

"I have had sight," Wilson said, "of the perfect place of learning in my thought: a free place, and a various, where no man could be and not know with how great a destiny knowledge had come into the world—itself a little world; but not perplexed, living with a singleness of aim not known without; the home of sagacious men, hardheaded and with a will to know, debaters of the world's questions every day and used to the rough ways of democracy; and yet a place removed—calm Science seated there, recluse, ascetic, like a nun; not knowing that the world passes, not caring, if the truth but come in answer to her prayer. . . . A place where ideals are kept in heart in an air they can breathe; but no fool's paradise. A place where to hear the truth about the past and hold debate about the affairs of the present, with knowledge and without passion; like the world in having all men's life at heart, a place for men and all that concerns them; but unlike the world in its self-possession, its thorough way of talk, its care to know more than the moment brings to light; slow to take excitement, its air pure and wholesome with a breath of faith; every eye within it bright in the clear day and quick to look toward heaven for the confirmation of its hope. Who shall show us the way to this place?"

There is a dreadful incongruity between this vision and the state of mind—and behavior—of the radical left on the American campus today. In place of a calm science, "recluse, ascetic, like a nun," not knowing or caring that the world passes "if the truth but come in answer to her prayer," we have people utterly absorbed in the affairs of this passing world. And instead of these affairs being discussed with knowledge and without passion, we find them treated with transports of passion and with a minimum, I fear, of knowledge. In place of slowness to take excitement, we have a readiness to react emotionally, and at once, to a great variety of issues. In place of self-possession, we have screaming tantrums and brawling in the streets. In place of the "thorough way of talk" that Wilson envisaged, we have banners and epithets and obscenities and virtually meaningless slogans. And in place of bright eyes "looking to heaven for the confirmation of their hope," we have eyes glazed with anger and passion, too often dimmed as well by artificial abuse of the psychic structure that lies behind them, and looking almost everywhere else but to heaven for the satisfaction of their aspirations.

I quite understand that those who espouse this flagrant repudiation of the Wilsonian ideal constitute only a minority on any campus. But tendencies that represent the obsession of only a few may not be without partial appeal, at certain times, and within certain limits, to many others. If my own analysis is correct, there are a great many students who may resist any complete surrender to these tendencies, but who nevertheless find them intensely interesting, are to some extent attracted or morally bewildered by them, find themselves driven, in confrontation with them, either into various forms of pleasing temptation, on the one hand, or into crises of conscience, on the other.

If I see them correctly (and I have no pretensions to authority on this subject), there are two dominant tendencies among the people I have here in mind, and superficially they would seem to be in conflict one with the other. On the one side there is angry militancy, full of hatred and intolerance and often quite prepared to embrace violence as a source of change. On the other side there is gentleness, passivity, quietism—ostensibly a yearning for detachment from the affairs of the world, not the detachment Woodrow Wilson had in mind, for that was one intimately and sternly related to the real world, the objective, external world, whereas this one takes the form of an attempt to escape into a world which is altogether illusory and subjective.

What strikes one first about the angry militancy is the extraordinary degree of certainty by which it is inspired: certainty of one's own rectitude, certainty of the accuracy and profundity of one's own analysis of the problems of contemporary society, certainty as to the iniquity of those who disagree. Of course, vehemence of feeling and a conviction that right is on one's side have seldom been absent from the feelings of politically excited youth. But somehow or other they seem particularly out of place at just this time. Never has there been an era when the problems of public policy even approached in their complexity those by which our society is confronted today, in this age of technical innovation and the explosion of knowledge. The understanding of these problems is something to which one could well give years of disciplined and restrained study, years of the scholar's detachment, years of readiness to reserve judgment while evidence is being accumulated. And this being so, one is struck to see such massive certainties already present in the minds of people who not only *have not* studied very much but presumably *are not* studying a great deal, because it is hard to imagine that the activities to which this aroused portion of our student population gives itself are ones readily compatible with quiet and successful study.

The world seems to be full, today, of embattled students. The public prints are seldom devoid of the record of their activities. Photographs of them may be seen daily: screaming, throwing stones, breaking windows, overturning cars, being beaten or dragged about by police and, in the case of those on other continents, burning libraries. That these people are embattled is unquestionable. That they are really students, I must be permitted to doubt. I have heard it freely confessed by members of the revolutionary student generation of Tsarist Russia that, proud as they were of the revolutionary exploits of their youth, they never really learned anything in their university years; they were too busy with politics. The fact of the matter is that the state of being *enragé* is simply incompatible with fruitful study. It implies a degree of existing emotional and intellectual commitment which leaves little room for open-minded curiosity.

I am not saying that students should not be concerned, should not have views, should not question what goes on in the field of national policy and should not voice their questions about it. Some of us, who are older, share many of their misgivings, many of their impulses. Some of us have no less lively a sense of the dangers of the time, and are no happier than they are about a great many things that are now going on. But it lies within the power as well as the duty of all of us to recognize not only the possibility that we might be wrong but the virtual certainty that on some occasions we are bound to be. The fact that this is so does not absolve us from the duty of having views and putting them forward. But it does make it incumbent upon us to recognize the element of doubt that still surrounds the correctness of these views. And if we do that, we will not be able to lose ourselves in transports of moral indignation against those who are of opposite opinion and follow a different line; we will put our views forward only with a prayer for forgiveness for the event that we prove to be mistaken.

I am aware that inhibitions and restraints of this sort on the part of us older people would be attributed by many members of the student left to a sweeping corruption of our moral integrity. Life, they would hold, has impelled us to the making of compromises; and these compromises have destroyed the usefulness of our contribution. Crippled by our own cowardice, prisoners of the seamy adjustments we have made in order to be successfully a part of the American establishment, we are regarded-as no longer capable of looking steadily into the strong clear light of truth.

In this, as in most of the reproaches with which our children shower us, there is of course an element of justification. There is a point somewhere along the way in most of our adult lives, admittedly, when enthusiasms flag, when idealism becomes tempered, when responsibility to others, and even affection for others, compels greater attention to the mundane demands of private life. There is a point when we are even impelled to place the needs of children ahead of the dictates of a defiant idealism, and to devote ourselves, pusillanimously, if you will, to the support and rearing of these same children—precisely in order that at some future date they may have the privilege of turning upon us and despising us for the materialistic faintheartedness that made their maturity possible. This, no doubt, is the nature of the compromise that millions of us make with the imperfections of government and society in our time. Many of us could wish that it might have been otherwise—that the idealistic pursuit of public causes might have remained our exclusive dedication down into later life.

But for the fact that this is not so I cannot shower myself or others with reproaches. I have seen more harm done in this world by those who tried to storm the bastions of society in the name of utopian beliefs, who were determined to achieve the elimination of all evil and the realization of the millenium within their own time, than by all the humble efforts of those who have tried to create a little order and civility and affection within their own intimate entourage, even at the cost of tolerating a great deal of evil in the public domain. Behind this modesty, after all, there has been the recognition of a vitally important truth—a truth that the Marxists, among others, have never brought themselves to recognize—namely, that the decisive seat of evil in this world is not in social and political institutions, and not even, as a rule, in the will or iniquities of statesmen, but simply in the weakness and imperfection of the human soul itself, and by that I mean literally every soul, including my own and that of the student militant at the gates. For this reason, as Tocqueville so clearly perceived when he visited this country a hundred and thirty years ago, the success of a society may be said, like charity, to begin at home.

So much, then, for the angry ones. Now, a word about the others; the quiescent ones, the hippies and the flower people.

In one sense, my feeling for these people is one of pity, not unmixed, in some instances, with horror. I am sure that they want none of this pity. They would feel that it comes to them for the wrong reasons. If they feel sorry for themselves, it is because they see themselves as the victims of a harsh, hypocritical and unworthy adult society. If I feel sorry for them, it is because I see them as the victims of certain great and destructive philosophic errors.

One of these errors—and it is one that affects particularly those who take drugs, but not those alone—is the belief that the human being has marvelous resources within himself that can be released and made available to him merely by the passive submission to certain sorts of stimuli: by letting esthetic impressions of one sort or another roll over him or by letting his psychic equilibrium be disoriented by chemical agencies that give him the sensation of experiencing tremendous things. Well, it is true that human beings sometimes have marvelous resources within themselves. It is also true that these resources are capable, ideally, of being released and made available to the man that harbors them and through him to others, and sometimes are so released. But it is not true that they can be released by hippie means.

It is only through effort, through doing, through action—never through passive experience—that man grows creatively. It is only by volition and effort that he becomes fully aware of what he has in him of creativity and becomes capable of embodying it, of making it a part of himself, of communicating it to others. There is no pose more fraudulent—and students would do well to remember this when they look at each other—than that of the individual who pretends to have been exalted and rendered more impressive by his communion with some sort of inner voice whose revelations he is unable to describe or to enact. And particularly is this pose fraudulent when the means he has chosen to render himself susceptible to this alleged revelation is the deliberate disorientation of his own psychic system; for it may be said with surety that any artificial intervention of this sort—into the infinitely delicate balance that nature created in the form of man's psychic makeup—produces its own revenge, takes its own toll, proceeds at the cost of the true creative faculties and weakens rather than strengthens.

The second error I see in the outlook of these people is the belief in the possibility and validity of a total permissiveness. They are misjudging, here, the innermost nature of man's estate. There is not, and cannot be, such a thing as total freedom. The normal needs and frailties of the body, not to mention the elementary demands of the soul itself, would rule that out if nothing else did. But beyond that, any freedom *from* something implies a freedom to something. And because our reality is a complex one, in which conflicts of values are never absent, there can be no advance toward any particular objective, not even the pursuit of pleasure, that does not imply the sacrifice of other possible objectives. Freedom, for this reason, is definable only in terms of the obligations and restraints and sacrifices it accepts. It exists, as a concept, only in relationship to something else which is by definition its opposite; and that means commitment, duty, self-restraint.

Every great artist has known this. Every great philosopher has recognized it. It has lain at the basis of Judaic-Christian

586

teaching. Tell me what framework of discipline you are prepared to accept, and I will attempt to tell you what freedom might mean for you. But if you tell me that you are prepared to accept no framework of discipline at all, then I will tell you, as Dostoevski told his readers, that you are destined to become the most unfree of men; for freedom begins only with the humble acceptance of membership in, and subordination to, a natural order of things, and it grows only with struggle, and self-discipline, and faith.

To shun the cruelty and corruption of this world is one thing. It is not always unjustifiable. Not everyone is made to endure these things. There is something to be said for the cultivation, by the right people, and in the right way, of the virtues of detachment, of withdrawal, of unworldliness, of innocence and purity, if you will. That, as a phase of life, is just what Wilson was talking about. In an earlier age, those who are now the flower children and the hippies would perhaps have entered monastic life or scholarly life or both. But there, be it noted, they would very definitely have accepted a framework of discipline, and it would normally have been a very strict one. If it was a monastic order, their lives would have been devoted to the service of God and of other men, not of themselves and their senses. If it was the world of scholarship, their lives would have been devoted to the pursuit of truth, which never comes easily or without discipline and sacrifice. They would have accepted an obligation to cultivate order, not chaos; cleanliness, not filth; self-abnegation, not self-indulgence; health, not demoralization.

Now I have indicated that I pity these people, and in general I do. But sometimes I find it hard to pity them, because they themselves are sometimes so pitiless. There is, in this cultivation of an absolute freedom, and above all in the very self-destructiveness with which it often expresses itself, a selfishness, a hardheartedness, a callousness, an irresponsibility, an indifference to the feelings of others, that is its own condemnation. No one ever destroys just himself alone. Such is the network of intimacy in which every one of us is somehow embraced, that whoever destroys himself destroys to some extent others as well. Many of these people prattle about the principle of love; but their behavior betrays this principle in the most elementary way. Love—and by that, I mean the receiving of love as well

GEORGE F. KENNAN   587

as the bestowal of it—is itself an obligation, and as such is incompatible with the quest for a perfect freedom. Just the cruelty to parents alone, which is implicit in much of this behavior, is destructive of the purest and most creative form of love that does exist or could exist in this mortal state.

And one would like to warn these young people that in distancing themselves so recklessly not only from the wisdom but from the feelings of parents, they are hacking at their own underpinnings—and even those of people as yet unborn. There could be no greater illusion than the belief that one can treat one's parents unfeelingly and with contempt and yet expect that one's own children will some day treat one otherwise; for such people break the golden chain of affection that binds the generations and gives continuity and meaning to life.

One cannot, therefore, on looking at these young people in all the glory of their defiant rags and hairdos, always just say, with tears in one's eyes: "There goes a tragically wayward youth, striving romantically to document his rebellion against the hypocrisies of the age." One has sometimes to say, and not without indignation: "There goes a perverted and willful and stony-hearted youth by whose destructiveness we are all, in the end, to be damaged and diminished."

These people also pose a problem in the quality of their citizenship. One thing they all seem to have in common—the angry ones as well as the quiet ones—is a complete rejection of, or indifference to, the political system of this country. The quiet ones turn their backs upon it, as though it did not concern them. The angry ones reject it by implication, insofar as they refuse to recognize the validity of its workings or to respect the discipline which, as a system of authority, it unavoidably entails.

I think there is a real error or misunderstanding here. If you accept a democratic system, this means that you are prepared to put up with those of its workings, legislative or administrative, with which you do not agree as well as with those that meet with your concurrence. This willingness to accept, in principle, the workings of a system based on the will of the majority, even when you yourself are in the minority, is simply the essence of democracy. Without it there could be no system of representative self-government at all. When you attempt to alter the workings of the system by means of violence or civil disobedience, this, it seems to me, can have only one of two implications: either you do not believe in democracy at all and consider that society ought to be governed by enlightened minorities such as the one to which you, of course, belong; or you consider that the present system is so imperfect that it is not truly representative, that it no longer serves adequately as a vehicle for the will of the majority, and that this leaves to the unsatisfied no adequate means of self-expression other than the primitive one of calling attention to themselves and their emotions by mass demonstrations and mass defiance of established authority. It is surely the latter of these two implications which we must read from the overwhelming majority of the demonstrations that have recently taken place.

I would submit that if you find a system inadequate, it is not enough simply to demonstrate indignation and anger over individual workings of it, such as the persistence of the Vietnam war, or individual situations it tolerates or fails to correct, such as the condition of the Negroes in our great cities. If one finds these conditions intolerable, and if one considers that they reflect no adequate expression either of the will of the majority or of that respect for the rights of minorities which is no less essential to the success of any democratic system, then one places upon one's self, it seems to me, the obligation of saying in what way this political system should be modified, or what should be established in the place of it, to assure that its workings would bear a better relationship to people's needs and people's feelings.

If the student left had a program of constitutional amendment or political reform—if it had proposals for the constructive adaptation of this political system to the needs of our age—if it was *this* that it was agitating for, and if its agitation took the form of reasoned argument and discussion, or even peaceful demonstration accompanied by reasoned argument and discussion—then many of us, I am sure, could view its protests with respect, and we would not shirk the obligation either to speak up in defense of institutions and national practices which we have tolerated all our lives, or to join these young people in the quest for better ones.

But when we are confronted only with violence for violence's sake, and with attempts to frighten or intimidate an administra-

GEORGE F. KENNAN 589

tion into doing things for which it can itself see neither the rationale nor the electoral mandate; when we are offered, as the only argument for change, the fact that a number of people are themselves very angry and excited; and when we are presented with a violent objection to what exists, unaccompanied by any constructive concept of what, ideally, ought to exist in its place —then we of my generation can only recognize that such behavior bears a disconcerting resemblance to phenomena we have witnessed within our own time in the origins of totalitarianism in other countries, and then we have no choice but to rally to the defense of a public authority with which we may not be in agreement but which is the only one we've got and with which, in some form or another, we cannot conceivably dispense. People should bear in mind that if this—namely noise, violence and lawlessness—is the way they are going to put their case, then many of us who are no happier than they are about some of the policies that arouse their indignation will have no choice but to place ourselves on the other side of the barricades.

These observations reflect a serious doubt whether civil disobedience has any place in a democratic society. But there is one objection I know will be offered to this view. Some people, who accept our political system, believe that they have a right to disregard it and to violate the laws that have flowed from it so long as they are prepared, as a matter of conscience, to accept the penalties established for such behavior.

I am sorry; I cannot agree. The violation of law is not, in the moral and philosophic sense, a privilege that lies offered for sale with a given price tag, like an object in a supermarket, available to anyone who has the price and is willing to pay for it. It is not like the privilege of breaking crockery in a tent at the county fair for a quarter a shot. Respect for the law is not an obligation which is exhausted or obliterated by willingness to accept the penalty for breaking it.

To hold otherwise would be to place the privilege of lawbreaking preferentially in the hands of the affluent, to make respect for law a commercial proposition rather than a civic duty and to deny any authority of law independent of the sanctions established against its violation. It would then be all right for a man to create false fire alarms or frivolously to pull the emergency cord on the train, or to do any number of other things that endangered or inconvenienced other people, provided only he was prepared to accept the penalties of so doing. Surely, lawlessness and civil disobedience cannot be condoned or tolerated on this ground; and those of us who care for the good order of society have no choice but to resist attempts at its violation, when this is their only justification.

Now, being myself a father, I am only too well aware that people of my generation cannot absolve ourselves of a heavy responsibility for the state of mind in which these young people find themselves. We are obliged to recognize here, in the myopia and the crudities of *their* extremism, the reflection of our own failings: our faintheartedness and in some instances our weariness, our apathy in the face of great and obvious evils.

I am also aware that, while their methods may not be the right ones, and while their discontent may suffer in its effectiveness from the concentration on negative goals, the degree of their concern over the present state of our country and the dangers implicit in certain of its involvements is by no means exaggerated. This is a time in our national life more serious, more menacing, more crucial, than any I have ever experienced or ever hoped to experience. Not since the civil conflict of a century ago has this country, as I see it, been in such great danger; and the most excruciating aspect of this tragic state of affairs is that so much of this danger comes so largely from within, where we are giving it relatively little official attention, and so little of it comes, relatively speaking, from the swamps and jungles of Southeast Asia into which we are pouring our treasure of young blood and physical resources.

For these reasons, I do not mean to make light of the intensity of feeling by which this student left is seized. Nor do I mean to imply that people like myself can view this discontent from some sort of smug Olympian detachment, as though it were not our responsibility, as though it were not in part our own ugly and decadent face that we see in this distorted mirror. None of us could have any justification for attempting to enter into communication with these people if we did not recognize, along with the justification for their unhappiness, our own responsibility in the creation of it, and if we did not accompany our appeal to them with a profession of readiness to join them, where they want us to, in the attempt to find better answers to many of these problems.

I am well aware that in approaching them in this way and in taking issue as I have with elements of their outlook and their behavior, it is primarily myself that I have committed, not them. I know that behind all the extremisms—all the philosophical errors, all the egocentricities and all the oddities of dress and deportment—we have to do here with troubled and often pathetically appealing people, acting, however wisely or unwisely, out of sincerity and idealism, out of the unwillingness to accept a meaningless life and a purposeless society.

Well, this is not the life, and not the sort of society, that many of us would like to leave behind us in this country when our work is done. How wonderful it would be, I sometimes think to myself, if we and they—experience on the one hand, strength and enthusiasm on the other—could join forces.

35 / Monkey Business

ROBERT BRUSTEIN

As a benefit for itself, the Theatre for Ideas, a private group which arranges symposiums on a variety of subjects, organized last month a symposium called *Theatre or Therapy*. In the expectation of a large turnout, the group hired a former Friends' Meeting House near Gramercy Park, now preserved as a New York landmark. The white auditorium, in which both participants and audience were arranged in pews, provided what seemed a good atmosphere for rational discussion. The director of the Theatre for Ideas, Shirley Broughton, had invited Julian

SOURCE: *New York Review of Books*, April 24, 1969, pp. 43–46. Copyright © 1969 The New York Review. Reprinted by permission of *The New York Review of Books*.
  Robert Brustein, teacher and critic of the drama, is putting his theories into practice as dean of Yale's School of Drama. During the mid-sixties, he advocated experiment and reform in the theater in such works as *Theater of Revolt* and *Seasons of Discontent*.

Beck and Judith Malina of the Living Theatre, Paul Goodman, and myself to participate in the symposium, and I had accepted, in spite of an instinctive distaste for symposiums and a deep sense of foreboding.

I had recently published an article on the Living Theatre in these pages in which I criticized the company, along with some elements of the radical young, for mindlessness, humorlessness, and romantic revolutionary rhetoric. The meeting looked to me like a good opportunity for more extended debate on the subject, as well as for exploring the differences between those who practiced the "new theatre" and those more skeptical about its aims and aspirations. On the other hand, I had been hearing rumors that attempts would be made to disrupt this symposium. Since I don't function well under disruptive conditions, I thought it wise to make some notes, rather than run the risk of trying to extemporize during a heckling session.

Because of difficulty with the sound system—a difficulty never adequately repaired—the symposium began a half hour late. I passed the time chatting with Nat Hentoff, the moderator, Goodman, and with the Becks, whom I had not seen since their visit to Yale last fall. The Becks seemed amiable, though a little breathless, and talked about their American tour, then in its final week. Nonviolence was in trouble, they said. The "revolution" was going beyond pacifism on the assumption that only violent overthrow of the Establishment could cure its insanity and corruption. I wondered if the Becks, too, had rejected the nonviolence which they always declared to be the basis for their anarchistic program.

Hentoff worried about the proper order of speakers, Goodman about the meaning of the topic. We decided to limit our statements to ten minutes apiece, then to debate each other, and then to throw the debate open to the audience. We also decided to make some effort to interpret the vague topic title in the course of our statements. I was to speak first, Goodman second, and the Becks last.

We entered the hall past an audience that was growing restive. I caught sight of a number of friends in the house, as well as several members of The Living Theatre company stationed in the balcony and the orchestra. Hentoff started to introduce the discussion—into a dead mike; when it finally seemed in comparatively good working order, we were able to begin. Hentoff reflected on the confusing nature of the subject we were discussing, and asked me to attempt a definition. I did so, speaking from my notes, after mumbling some apology for the insecurity that had prompted them:

"*Theatre or Therapy* is a rather loaded topic title," I said, "but it does begin to indicate the kind of controversy that is occupying the theatre today where the central question seems to be: To what extent should a production be oriented toward the audience, to what extent toward the actors, and to what extent toward the playwright. One's answer to this is affected by one's attitude toward some important issues of our time: Freedom versus responsibility, activist theatre versus non-activist theatre, free improvisation versus disciplined skill, process versus presentation, and so forth."

A voice from the balcony: "What the hell is disciplined skill?"

A voice from the orchestra: "Shut up, you twerp."

From the balcony: "Fuck you, I'm asking him a question."

From the orchestra: "We'll listen to you later. He's doing the talking now."

"My own position quite simply stated is this," I continued. "I believe the theatre to be served best when it is served by supremely gifted individuals possessed of superior vision and the capacity to express this in enduring form. In short, I believe in the theatre as a place for high art."

The heckler: "We're all supremely gifted individuals."

Brustein: "I doubt that very much."

The heckler: "Up against the wall."

I decided to skip the repartee and get through the statement. "I do not believe the theatre changes anybody, politically or psychologically, and I don't believe it should try to change anybody. While necessarily concerned with social-political as well as psychological-metaphysical issues, the theatre cannot be expected to resolve these issues. . . . Chekhov, one of those supremely gifted individuals I spoke of, has said . . ."

"Fuck Chekhov!"

". . . that the correct presentation of problems, and not the solution of problems, is what is obligatory for the artist." I elaborated on this notion, describing how democratic America—and now "revolutionary" America—had always been uncomfortable

594

with the concept of high art because of its elitist and aristocratic implications. Now the practitioners of the "new theatre" have joined the old Philistines in the scandalous American contempt for art.

I concluded: "We are at the tail end of Romanticism when the spectators are on the stage, and actors are refusing to play roles that are not sufficiently close to their own personalities. The rationale behind this reluctance is a refusal of external limitations—limitations which are now called 'authoritarian.' This direction was already anticipated in the work of the Actors Studio, whose members were encouraged to examine not the lives of the characters they played but rather their own psychic eccentricities with the result that the actors invariably played themselves rather than their roles. Under such conditions, why use actors at all? This is an extension of America's love of amateurism, and looks forward to a time when there will be no more spectators, only performers—*arrogant, liberated amateurs, each tied up in his own tight bag*." I aimed these last phrases at the heckler in the balcony, though he had been relatively silent during the last part of my statement.

Paul Goodman spoke next—without notes. He reminisced affectionately about the past work of the Living Theatre company, particularly its productions of *The Connection*, of Brecht, and of his own plays. He had enjoyed my article, he said, but he couldn't understand what I was so "hot and bothered" about—he confessed that he had seen none of the work of the Living Theatre on its recent tour. Goodman then proceeded to create an analogy between contemporary unrest and the Protestant Reformation.

"Don't think you're like the Christians in the catacombs," he said. "You're not going to destroy the institutions, you're going to reform them. You talk like there's a cataclysm coming, but there isn't. . . . The institutions will survive. . . ."

"No, they won't," shouted Rufus Collins, a black member of the company who had suddenly materialized on the floor of the hall. "Because we're going to destroy them."

"You're not going to destroy them," replied Goodman, good-humoredly. "You can't destroy them. And you won't even reform them unless you can think up some ideas. I've lived through movements like this before, and I'm always struck by the poverty of ideas. In two thousand years, there hasn't been a single new revolutionary idea."

"We'll destroy them," Collins screamed. "We'll create a cataclysm."

"You're not powerful enough. You're just an idiosyncratic fringe group like the Anabaptists. You don't have the capacity even to close down the universities."

"Close them down, close them down," Collins shouted. "Fuck the universities!"

"If you start to do that," Goodman said, still maintaining his sweet reasonableness, "they'll just put you on a reservation somewhere and keep you quiet."

"They're going to put us on reservations and kill us," Collins said, his voice now cracking with fury. "They're going to exterminate us, just like the Indians—the racists, the genocides. They're going to kill all of us."

"No, they won't," Goodman answered. "They'll just feed you some LSD and keep you pacified."

Norman Mailer chose to make his entrance at this point, lumbering down the aisle to his seat just as Goodman was replying to one of Rufus Collins's assaults on America's machine culture.

"Don't blame everything on technology," Goodman said. "It's too easy. Just the other day, I listened to a young fellow sing a very passionate song about how technology is killing us and all that. . . . But before he started, he bent down and plugged his electric guitar into the wall socket."

Collins began jumping up and down in fury. "That boy has thrown away his guitar. He's taken off his clothes. He's going up to the mountains where he's using only his voice and his feet. Fuck technology!"

"Why are you wearing glasses then?" asked a man sitting nearby.

"BECAUSE I CAN'T SEE," Collins screamed. "FUCK TECHNOLOGY. FUCK TECHNOLOGY."

Mailer applauded loudly and conspicuously. Goodman shrugged and sat down on the floor in front of his seat with his back to the audience. He lit his pipe, and seemed to be listening attentively to Judith Malina, who spoke next.

But the mike went dead. "Turn her microphone on," urged Hentoff to the sound man. "Yes," said Miss Malina, "turn me on." Pleased with her witticism, she repeated it several times. "Am I turned on? Okay. . . ."

"Bob Brustein said something about freedom and responsibility, like they were different things. This is all tied up with questions I don't want to get into tonight, like are we good or bad at heart. I do want to say that when people act freely, with complete freedom, they act creatively, beautifully. Everybody has it in him to be an artist—there's no such thing as special individuals who are supremely gifted. When the audience does its thing in *Paradise Now,* it does some wild, beautiful, creative scenes. Not always, of course, but I've seen people do things as beautiful as I've ever seen in the theatre. Better than us . . . better than Shakespeare or Euripides. . . ."

"Fuck Shakespeare, fuck Euripides," yelled the balcony voice.

"I dig Shakespeare sometimes," Miss Malina replied. "But I also want to speak in my own voice, in my own person. I mean there's Hedda Gabler and there's Judith Malina, and I want to be Judith Malina."

"Let's have five minutes of Hedda Gabler," shouted one of the spectators in the orchestra pews. "We've already had five minutes of Judith Malina."

"I'll give you Hedda Gabler," yelled the heckler in the balcony, and, in a mincing voice, "'The candle is on the table.' That's Hedda Gabler. Now I'll give you me: Fuck Ibsen. Fuck all liberal intellectuals and their fucking discussions. . . ."

"Another thing," Judith Malina said. "The first night we did *Paradise Now* at Yale—the night we got busted—we all came out of the theatre on each other's shoulders and into the streets. It was a very beautiful and joyous moment, everybody was feeling like something beautiful was happening. And Bob Brustein came up to me and said: 'Judith, I hate this play. All this freedom, it could lead to fascism.' But I say, freedom is beautiful. It can never lead to fascism, it can only lead to more freedom."

This remark was the cue for pandemonium; the entire Living Theatre company proceeded to take over the Meeting House. A flamboyant actor named Olé, dressed in yards of brightly colored silk, appeared on the platform where he began doing fashion model poses while sucking on a long thin cigar. Rufus Collins was joined on the floor of the auditorium by Stephen Ben Israel (the heckler from the balcony) both shouting obscenities at the audience. The actress Jenny Hecht almost broke her neck climbing down from the balcony, her electrified hair shooting wildly in every direction. Other actors from the company began pounding on the railings and screaming at the top of their lungs. And now the audience began to scream back.

Shirley Broughton ran down the aisle in great agitation, to discuss with Hentoff the possibilities of moderating the tumult or at least returning everybody's money. Hentoff leaned back to watch the spectacle. For a few minutes Goodman attempted to discuss issues with the actors, the audience, and the Becks. Shouted down, he walked calmly off the platform and out of the hall, puffing on his pipe.

Rufus Collins was screaming: "You people all came here to have one of your discussions. Ten dollars you paid to get in here. We'll give you ten dollars worth."

"How did you get in? What about your ten dollars?"

"I got in for nothing. I don't pay for shit like this. Your money came out of my black skin and the skin of my black brothers. My own mother couldn't come here tonight. She called up and was told she couldn't attend your fucking meeting. That's when I decided to come. . . ."

After spitting into a spectator's face, Stephen Ben Israel ran to the center of the hall, holding a purse high over his head. "That lady over there hit me with her pocketbook—so I took it away from her. And this is what I am going to do with that pocketbook." He opened the purse, held it high over his head, turned it upside down, and emptied its contents on the floor.

A voice from the back, calm, sweet, and patient: "I just embraced eight members of the Living Theatre. I embraced them with love. And one of them took my wallet. You can keep the money, but would you kindly return the cards?"

"*Credit* cards? To buy things in this fucking money culture? Tear up the cards! Tear up the cards! Burn the money!"

Julian Beck's voice, above the din: "Get used to this. It's happening all over America, in every meeting house in America. Get used to this. This is what is going to happen from now on."

Ben Israel was now on the platform, chanting verses from R. D. Laing: "I'd like to turn you on, I'd like to drive you out of your wretched mind. . . ."

Collins was yelling into the microphone: "Do the Africans have theatre? When they beat their drums and do their dances?

Do the Latin Americans have theatre? Do the Cubans have theatre? Do the Vietnamese have theatre? I want Brustein to answer yes or no."

"Yes," I shouted. By this time, I was off the platform and sitting with friends.

A woman in a fur wrap pushed her way to the platform toward Rufus Collins, shouting: "You're rude, you're stupid, and you're vulgar. People paid money to come here and listen to a discussion and you. . . ." A young man came up behind her and started pinning an obscene message on the back of her wrap. A spectator came up and started pulling the message off. She continued her conversation with Julian Beck, who asked her: "Why are you wearing that loathsome fur?"

"To keep me warm."

"You musn't wear the skins of animals," Beck answered. "It's disgusting," and he tore the fur from her shoulders.

"Tell your people not to wear sheepskins then," the woman said, and picked the fur up again.

"I tell them all the time," Beck replied, taking her hat off her head and throwing it on the floor. "What are you doing about Vietnam? What are you doing for the black people?"

"Today I marched in Newark," the woman said, in a tight voice. "I am a poet, and I am as outraged as you over the treatment of the blacks in this country."

"It's not enough, it's not enough," said Beck. He was shouting now.

The woman said quietly, "Today I feel more hate than I have ever felt in my life. I'm going home now. I'm going to write a poem about the hate I feel for you."

Now Richard Schechner, former editor of *The Drama Review*, was on the platform, fondling one of the mikes. He sat cross-legged, smiling. With his moustache, long hair, and striped tee shirt, he looked like an apache dancer. "You've all got to try to understand this," he said to the angry audience. "You've got to learn to groove with it. Let's all have five minutes of meditation to think about the beautiful thing that's happening here."

By this time the noise in the Meeting House was bouncing off the walls, like a bad mix in a recording studio. Everyone was wandering around the hall or shouting. I was beginning to enjoy myself. Two private cops, both of them black, came into the room, trying to look friendly and relaxed. They were mostly concerned with preventing any smoking in the hall.

Suddenly, the wave of bodies in the aisle parted. Norman Mailer had risen, and was strutting toward the platform, pitching and rolling like a freighter in a heavy sea. He was wearing a well-made dark blue suit with a vest, and his face was flushed. He grabbed one of the mikes.

"I was one of those that applauded when Mr. Black over there said 'Fuck Technology'—so I'm not going to use this thing." He laid the mike on the pew beside him. "I'm forty-six years old. I've got a strong voice, but I don't want to waste it. So I want you all to listen, and listen hard." Some of the tumult subsided.

"This is a tough town," Mailer continued, "the toughest town in the world. Because if you think you're tough, there's always somebody who's tougher. Remember that!" The tumult was beginning again. "Now I've got a message for Mr. Black over there. You've got no surprises, and you haven't had any since the French Revolution. I've seen all this *jacquerie* before, many times before. Get it? J-a-c-q-u-e-r-i-e—it's a pun in case you don't know it." This pun was lost on most of the audience, including me.

Ben Israel grabbed a mike: "You should have sent your suit up there Mailer, and stayed home yourself." Collins started to scream at him, but Mailer remained on the platform for a short while, a faint hard smile on his face, trying to stare down his noisy antagonists. Then he said, "I guess I lost Round One," and left the platform.

About a third of the spectators had drifted out by this time. Some wandered into the back room where drinks and sandwiches were being served. Paul Goodman had returned to the hall to be told by Rufus Collins: "I don't take drugs to escape from reality. I take drugs to reach reality." Hentoff remained on the platform, a weary witness. Saul Gottlieb, the producer of the Living Theatre's American tour, was talking gently into a microphone.

"I want Bob Brustein to say why he thinks the Living Theatre is fascist."

Saul is a portly, stooped man with a fuzzy beard, a veteran of many ideological wars. I went up to the platform and gave him a kiss.

600

Judith Malina, holding a microphone, was now walking back and forth in front of her husband, like a jaguar.

"I think what happened here tonight was beautiful and good," she said. "You've had an experience—like you've never had before. This is what we should all be discussing now, how beautiful this evening was. How many people here think it was beautiful?"

"It's *boring*, IT'S BORING," came a voice from the hall. "You may think it's beautiful, but it's not what we came for. The subject was Theatre or Therapy, and all we got tonight was therapy—Living Theatre therapy. When do we get to listen to some discussion about theatre?"

"This is better than discussion, better than theatre," replied Miss Malina. "It's spontaneous, it's authentic, it's real, it's beautiful."

Stanley Kauffmann, the critic, was on his feet, and it was the only time in my life I have seen him angry. "You're lying. The whole thing was *phoney!* You staged it. You and your stooges. You brought your stooges here tonight and staged the whole dismal affair."

"No, no," Judith Malina cried. "We allow our people to do just what they want to do. Everybody should be allowed to do what he wants. That's what's so beautiful about freedom."

"You talk about *freedom!*" somebody else shouted. "What about *our* freedom? We weren't allowed to have what we paid for. Your freedom is our repression!"

Julian Beck, who all this time had been sitting silent and withdrawn, suddenly stood up. "This is the future," he said. "It's happening all over the country. And it will happen again and again whenever you try to hold a meeting. This is the future."

In one of the Marx Brothers movies, there is a scene in which Harpo picks up a book, looks it over very carefully, and then goes into a blind fury, tearing the book to bits and jumping up and down on the pages and the binding.

Groucho: "What's the matter with him?"

Chico: "He gets angry because he can't read."

36 / The Summa Popologica of Marshall McLuhan

THEODORE ROSZAK

Once when I was teaching an undergraduate survey in euro-pean history, a student came to me complaining after class that he couldn't see why I wasted his time asking him to read Cardinal Bossuet. I had to admit it was a pretty dismal assignment, wholly lacking in intellectual substance. "But," I explained, "doesn't it tell us a great deal about French society that such a mediocrity could rise to such a position of intellectual prominence? Isn't it worth knowing that the *Grand Siècle* wasn't all Molière and Pascal?"

There are people whose fate it is to be read in this spirit: not because of what they have to say, which is meager or foolish, but because of the bleaker measure they provide of their society's quality of mind and conscience. And it is in this spirit that Marshall McLuhan must be approached: as one who has little that is substantial to say, but who reveals a very great deal about the cultural permissiveness of mid-century America. For what McLuhan has discovered is the ease with which pretensious nonsense can be parleyed into a marvelously lucrative, but at the same time academically prestigious career. And, at least up to this point, he has turned the trick more neatly than anybody else on the scene.

The strategy seems to be something like this. On the one hand, one has to be just catchy and cute and simplistic enough to draw the attention and affection of the mass-cultural apparatus: *Time, Life, Fortune,* ABC, CBS, NBC. Ingratiate yourself to the publicity makers and, presto! you get publicity. But, on the other hand, if one is to avoid degenerating into another Norman Vin-

SOURCE: *New Politics* 5 (Fall 1966), 257–69. Reprinted by permission.
Theodore Roszak, author of *The Making of a Counter Culture* and editor of *The Dissenting Academy,* is chairman of the History of Western Culture program at California State College, Hayward, and at one time was editor of a British pacifist weekly.

cent Peale, one must be able to flourish some cultural savvy. Thus, McLuhan's introduction to *Understanding Media* hops, skips and jumps over Fellini, Zen, Plato, Hesiod, Burckhardt, Sartre, Beckett, Pound. . . . In this way, you keep one foot in the intellectual camp. Or more correctly, you keep your footing among the camp intellectuals. And in this respect, McLuhan's timing has been beautifully shrewd. For he has caught a fair-sized segment of the intellectual community just as it was weakening, playfully, in the direction of camp and pop. Up go posters of Batman and Bogart on living-room walls all over America, and onto the bookshelf goes McLuhan. The Campbell's soup can becomes an object of art and the Jack Paar show a subject of deep philosophical analysis. If we are to have pop art, why not pop metaphysics too?

And that is precisely what McLuhan has given us: an almost Thomistic systematization of our society's funk culture, a veritable *Weltanschauung* for the fastidious connoisseur of Smilin' Jack and Mae West. Surely the effort deserves to survive. We would want posterity to know, would we not, that America of the mid-sixties had its lighter side, that the year which produced the Johnson Administration and the Vietnam war also brought us *Understanding Media,* the *Summa Popologica.* Is it prudish to become severe about such larks? Perhaps it is. If the cultural millions American society can now afford to lay out on "exploding plastic inevitables" didn't go to the entertainments provided by the Andy Warhols and Marshall McLuhans, perhaps they would go for worse. But it *is* distressing to see so many decent minds and talents taking these oppy-poppy flirtations quite as seriously as they do. It is especially unfortunate to see so many would-be young artists—eager to gate-crash the creative life— falling for McLuhan's easy-do esthetic of media-manipulation instead of reading their Tolstoy or Shaw. And, in any case, it's always fun to pick apart pretensions, if only to see, for the record, how much in the way of intellectual murder you can get away with these days and still be treated seriously, indeed reverently, in cultural circles that should know better.

Let us, then, give a moment's attention to a few select elements in McLuhan's writing and see how they stand up to investigation. There is a very great deal more to criticize about McLuhan than what follows below. I restrict myself to only two of the many "media" McLuhan deals with. But the points I raise are central to his work and will serve our purpose here.

1. MEDIA / McLuhan's posture is that of a specialist in the field of "media." And in this respect his credentials are impressive: director of Toronto University's Centre for Culture and Technology and former chairman of the Ford Foundation Seminar on Culture and Communication. One expects the specialty to involve some order of highly technical competence, and indeed McLuhan misses no opportunity to exploit that expectation. It is as a specialist that he prefers to be approached and respected. But what are "media" as McLuhan understands them? "Media" are the "extensions of man." And as it turns out, the extensions extend a long, long way. They include all means of communication and transportation, the written and spoken word in all its forms, technology in general, fun and games, art and music, housing, fashions, weapons, social and economic systems. . . . Indeed, what do they *not* include? McLuhan's province of knowledge, quite simply, is universal. It allows him to speak, as he would have it, to everything and anything that comes his way. Last year when he was in San Francisco, the local papers carried stories of McLuhan pontificating on the subject of topless waitresses. (But perhaps this comes under the category of the extensions of women.)

Now I think it is admirable to aspire to broad-gauged intellectuality. I have no brief to make for technical specialization. But if one is a generalist, one must be prepared to say so—and to run the risks. It is really dirty pool to retire defensively, as McLuhan does under pressure, behind the barricades of a presumed specialization, when, in fact, one's "specialty" is everything under the sun. To begin with, then, one must insist that McLuhan is no sort of specialist at all. Nothing he has to say is based on esoteric knowledge or technical competence. He is best approached as a sort of social critic or perhaps a dilettante conversationalist—and his ideas stand or fall on the basis of their internal consistency or whatever evidence McLuhan can present for them. It is the plight of the generalist that he cannot expect anyone to defer to his authority on the subject at hand.

To yield to McLuhan as an "expert" on "media" is like yielding to Herman Kahn as an "expert" on "strategy." In both cases one is giving way to men whose "expertise" involves sweeping and most often profoundly ignorant opinions about the whole of human and social behavior.

2. "THE MEDIUM IS THE MESSAGE" / There is a deal of misunderstanding about this well known catchphrase. Many McLuhan devotees seem to think McLuhan, in assessing the effects of "media," is dealing with the impact technology directly has upon the social and economic environment. But if McLuhan had nothing more to tell us than that great inventions —the printing press, automobile, railroad, etc.—have vastly and unpredictably transformed society, he would be telling us nothing very new. But this isn't McLuhan's point. McLuhan's interest is in the perceptual and deep psychic impact of media. His claim is that the media "alter sense ratios or patterns of perception. . . ." And, by so doing, they radically alter the human agent. The environmental changes, then, follow from an initial transformation of the human psyche. Thus, postwar America is what it is—socially, politically, economically, culturally—because of what electronic circuitry, TV in particular, has done to the psychology of Americans. Further, these psychic transformations have *absolutely nothing* to do with the content of the media. The media have their effects because of their inherent technical characteristics, regardless of what programming they carry. For McLuhan there is no significant distinction to be made between pure static and Archibald MacLeish's *Fall of the City*— both are simply "radio"; or between Tolstoy and Mickey Spillane both are simply "typography." (One is reminded here of Jean Harlow's quip when asked what she wanted for her birthday: "Don't buy me a book; I gotta book." A perfectly sensible Mc-Luhanite response.)

If TV had never gotten beyond broadcasting test patterns, its effect upon American society would, according to McLuhan, have been precisely the same and just as total—*if* you could have gotten the whole society to watch test patterns, which you couldn't. For McLuhan "content" is "the juicy piece of meat carried by a burglar to distract the watchdog of the mind." Only that and nothing more. (One should note, however, that Mc-Luhan frequently loses his grip on this idea and—as in his treatment of photography—slides over into a discussion of content, crediting it with the significant influence. Such inconsistency at once suggests an untenable thesis.)

Now this is an extraordinary idea. And it is surely worth a few minutes' contemplation. But if we are to think any longer about it than that before rejecting it as absurd, McLuhan must offer us some evidence in support of the thesis. Alas, one searches in vain through *Understanding Media,* McLuhan's *magnum opus,* for evidence. It isn't there. McLuhan doesn't prove this thesis; he browbeats you with it. His contention is, if you don't believe me, you're hidebound, behind-the-times, bookish, square. And McLuhan delights in baiting the "conventionally literate."

It is perhaps the most remarkable aspect of McLuhan's career that so few of his critics (and of course none of his admirers) have ever asked him for proof of his central thesis. Perhaps because they are so readily intimidated? For to hear McLuhan hold forth, you would assume there is some large body of incontrovertible experimental evidence somewhere to support the assertion—and that everybody who is anybody knows all about it. *There isn't.* And yet, on the basis of this unexamined thesis, McLuhan is prepared to make extremely ambitious proposals. He tells us, for example, that the entire political character of a society can be determined by its "media mix." Thus, revolutionary discontent can be created by heavy exposure to radio and newspapers, and it can be assuaged by a hearty dosage of TV independently of anything these media say, mind!

McLuhan claims to have learned this deep truth about media from his study of post-impressionist painting. He is, of course, correct in observing that one of the directions in which Western painting has moved over the past century is toward the exploitation of paint—of its color and texture—as an autonomous medium independent of any content. The same may be said of music over a much longer period of time. Music has been, in a significant way, an autonomous sound medium, independent of any storytelling function, at least since the seventeenth century. But the fact that line, color and sound can be liberated from conceptual content does not mean that the language arts can move in a similar direction. Unlike music, which can direct itself at stimulating the auditory surface of the ear, or painting, which can direct itself at the visual surface of the eye, the written and spoken word are inseparable from what they have to say. The significant distinction to make with respect to the media is not McLuhan's distinction between "hot" and "cold"—which is largely senseless—but that between sensory media and conceptual media. A painting may only impinge on the eye, but the printed page strikes *through* the eye and into the mind. Similarly, the spoken word—whether part of a radio or television presentation—strikes *through* the ear and, again, into the mind. Such attempts as have been made to "liberate" the written or spoken word from conceptual content have always trailed off into marginal experiments that are more music or linear design than they are literature. Literature *says things*—base things or noble things, wise things or foolish things, exciting things or dull things. And in this lies its peculiar power over us, for good or ill. To the degree that any essentially literary art—poetry, the novel, the storytelling cinema, the drama—begins to manipulate itself as a "pure" medium and divests itself of having anything to say, it becomes trivial, and usually silly. The literary avant garde is littered with such misfortunate experiments, and they continue to take place. But their end is always the same: boredom and early death. In denying this fact about the nature of the word, McLuhan, himself a prodigious writer and talker, would seem to be involved in something like the paradox of Parmenides: he tells us in print that the content of print has no power over us. Thus, McLuhan's thesis and mine—which would seem to be logically contradictory—are nevertheless equivalent. For you, dear reader, are doing no more than sponging up typography, no matter which of us you read.

But in fact McLuhan's thesis is not simply unproven. It is false. There is no independent psychic effect that *any* mass medium has on an observer other than through its content. Indeed, no one witnesses a mass medium *except* for its content. In conjuring up the notion of a medium-in-itself, McLuhan is involved in a bit of metaphysics which is perhaps sensible to him as (I am given to understand) a devout Catholic, but not the least persuasive or even sensible to the skeptical mind. McLuhan's medium-in-itself is rather like the substance of the Catholic host and wine which supposedly underlies all the superficial accidents: a bladeless knife without a handle. But subtract the contents of the mass media and, like the Catholic host without its accidents, there's nothing there. Only a jabberwocky of printer's ink, static, and test patterns. To contend that these purely visual-auditory stimuli exert an independent and infinitely greater influence than any content they carry contradicts flatly the most fundamental of human experiences: that of human communication. McLuhan's thesis leads ultimately to the conclusion that human beings never communicate with one another (though I am not certain he would be willing to extend his argument to ordinary word-of-mouth communication). Mind is sealed off from mind and personality from personality. It is technology alone which intervenes between us: the printed page which conveys its own and invariable subliminal "message," the TV screen which imprints its own and always-identical psychic pattern. The reality of meaningful intercourse between people is thus abolished. Shakespeare has never spoken to us, nor Sophocles, nor Dante, but only the printing press, the radio wave, the electronic scanner.

To be sure, it *is* possible to create literature and drama and rhetoric which is empty of meaning and which does not communicate a thing: successions of words and images which baffle the understanding. Every second-rate political hack knows as much. And a great deal of contemporary theater, cinema, poetry, and prose specializes in such effects. Alas! *ad nauseam.* But not every movie is *Last Year at Marienbad.* Those of us who have been touched to the marrow by the power of an idea know better—and we ought not to let McLuhan tell us differently than our own living experience does. The thought of Socrates, of Thoreau, of Blake, of Freud has moved within our own; the trials and tragedies of Othello, of Anna Karenina, of Raskolnikov have participated significantly in our lives. (And I use the word "participate" here far more deeply than I suspect McLuhan would understand.) If McLuhan has never plumbed these depths of mind and feeling, that is indeed pathetic for one who purports to be an expert in "communication." But we *know* full well that we have been shaped by other human beings through this matrix of imagination and intellection called human culture and that in it lies all our hope of achieving wisdom. Who, then, is Marshall McLuhan that he should seek to talk us out of our richest experience with nothing more than a catchphrase? There is indeed a kind of ultimate barbarism about any conception of culture which allows itself to become obsessed with the physical

608

artifacts of communication and ignores their profoundest personal meaning.

But perhaps the best way to demonstrate the falsehood of McLuhan's thesis is to review his handling of two significant mass media and see where it leads us.

RADIO / For McLuhan, radio is "the tribal drum." The hammering of radio waves at the ears during the thirties had the effect of "retribalizing" Western society and thus producing the primitive aggressions of totalitarian mass movements. But, one observes, there were no significant totalitarian movements in Britain . . . or America . . . or, well, any number of other countries where radio was prominent in the thirties. McLuhan has an answer. The Americans and the British were further along in industrialism and literacy than the "more earthy and less visual European cultures" and so they were "immune to radio." The Germans, we are to believe, had in the thirties "only brief and superficial experience of literacy." As a matter of fact, America and Germany were at equivalent stages of industrialism and the Germans were probably far more literate—but never mind. Let's get back to those "more earthy Europeans." Unfortunately for the Germans, Hitler and the Nazis just happened to come along a generation too soon. "Had TV occurred on a larger scale during Hitler's reign, he would have vanished quickly. Had TV come first there would have been no Hitler at all."

So we are to believe that the triumph of Nazism is wholly explained by the impact of radio upon the peculiar psychology of the German people. And what was that psychology? "The tribal past," McLuhan tells us, "has never ceased to be a reality for the German psyche." Herr Goebbels, we learn, was right after all: the German people are children of the forest, possessed of a "preliterate vitality." Shall we say they "think with their blood"? Indeed, "their tribal mode gave them easy access to the new non-visual world of subatomic physics in which long-literate and long-industrialized societies are decidedly handicapped." (Apparently, the German Jews, who did so much of this work in physics, are to be assimilated to this Wagnerian *Schwärmerei*— despite their long tradition of advanced literacy.)

Thus we see where McLuhan's analysis leads us: straight back to Nazi anthropology. But how else to explain fascism in

Germany once one has discarded the historical setting of post-World War I Europe with its peculiar social and economic stresses?

For McLuhan, once you have described radio as a "hot" medium, you have said all there is to say. History and social realities are banished and the German people are left to their tragic destiny. One cannot protest that Hitler's successful use of radio had everything to do with the Nazi monopolization of the medium (indeed, the Nazis exploited *all* the media successfully by virtue of censorship) for this is to introduce the factor of content. Censorship and control of media, remarkably enough, play no part in McLuhan's system. Nor can his system account for the (apparent) fact that in England the same medium, radio, could be masterfully used by Stanley Baldwin to soothe and calm, and, with equal mastery, by Churchill to excite and arouse the identical population. (The same observation holds true in the U.S. with respect to the differing use of radio by Father Coughlin and F.D.R.) Here, again, we're introducing variables that McLuhan rejects: social setting and content.

TELEVISION / McLuhan's analysis of TV leads him to his best-known and most heroic generalizations. For McLuhan, TV is the total explanation of why America is what it is today. TV is a "cool" medium, a "mosaic mesh" of electronic dots that invites "participation in depth." It produces a "unifying synesthetic force on the sense life" and leads to a "convulsive, sensuous participation that is profoundly kinetic and tactile." From this flows everything in sight: compact cars, the Kennedy Administration, scuba diving, the twist, a "do-it-yourself pattern of living," beehive hairdos and fishnet stockings. (Incidentally, McLuhan is a great one for fashion analysis. That the fashions on which he has founded his eternal truths change by the year doesn't seem to bother him.)

Now the fact is, McLuhan's knowledge of TV is very shoddy. For the major psychic effect of TV—and it comes through the content of the medium—is a narcotic disintegration of the sensibilities. It is the standard strategy of commercial TV to frustrate continuity of thought and to screen off depth of feeling. Take the TV news, for example. What is the effect of rapid cuts from stark tragedy to trivialized "human interest," from political complexity to breezy sportscasting? Or take children's programming, where the level of artistic and linguistic imagination is kept consistently higher in the exploitative commercials (which come every three minutes) than in the so-called entertainment. These fragmenting effects show up clearly in variety programming (the Ed Sullivan show, Merv Griffin show, etc.). In the standard TV situation comedy or melodrama they take the form of canned laughter and the emotional cliché.

Now what is the result of programming techniques that chop and cut the attention span, that keep the mentality turning over at the lowest level of efficiency, that screen the emotions from all originality? The result is a mushing up of the personality, a psychic anomie that neatly lowers the resistance to merchandising—which is what TV is all about in America. What McLuhan mistakes for "participation in depth" is actually malaise: the fixed stare, the mindless drift. (One exception to this has to do with young children, for whom solitary TV viewing serves as an opportunity for masturbation. They are "participating" and "doing it themselves," but not in any way McLuhan seems to be aware of.)

Of course, what McLuhan has to tell Madison Avenue and the TV moguls about themselves is exactly what they want to hear. McLuhan gets them off the hook with respect to any kind of social or cultural responsibility. While they peddle and exploit a degraded form of sensory distraction, he tells them they are single-handedly transforming American society, and especially the kids, into vital members of a participatory cultural community. One is reminded at this point of Andrew Ure telling the world, in the dark ages of industrialization, what marvelous things the cotton mills were doing for children: improving their manual dexterity, regularizing their habits, alerting their young minds. . . . The more sophisticated the technology, the more sophisticated the apologetics. The boob tube replaces the dark satanic mill as a form of social discipline, and "participation in depth" replaces "the light play of the little elves' muscles."

But, in fact, the effect of TV has nothing to do with McLuhan's electronic dots, which at most invite a low-grade *Gestalt* response. And not very much of that, since the *Gestalts* the TV screen offers are banal and obvious. The major psychic effect of American TV has to do with the unrelenting insult it poses to human dignity by its insistent mass-marketing and its shallow, disjunctive programming.

Which is what we all knew in the first place. The country's most addicted TV viewers are not McLuhan's rebellious beat-niks, but C. Wright Mills's "cheerful robots," for whom the nar-cosis of the electric screen has become an alienation from living experience. By cheapening thought and screening off the deeps of the human condition, TV contributes to the enervating depri-vation of mind and sense which is *the* characteristic of con-temporary American life—but not only because of the existence of television in our midst.

Of all the single-factor explanations of human and social behavior I have ever come across, McLuhan's exaltation of "media" is, I fear, the most inane. But to all the objections one can make against him, McLuhan has developed a standard de-fense. McLuhan's assertions are not, he would have us believe, propositions or hypotheses. They are "probes." But what is a "probe"? It is apparently any outrageous statement for which one has no evidence at all or which, indeed, flies in the face of obvious facts. This is, no doubt, the hip version of what Wash-ington these days calls a "credibility gap" and what the squares of yesteryear used to call a falsehood.

"Probing" has served McLuhan well. It has allowed him to pose as a cultural lion while ingratiating himself with IBM and *Time* magazine. Of the latter, for example, he tells us: it is "neither narrative nor point of view nor explanation nor com-ment [surprise! surprise!]. It is a corporate image in depth of the community in action and invites maximal participation in the social process." In fact, *Time* magazine is pernicious crap. But no one who says as much winds up with his face on the million-dollar cover. "Probing" has allowed McLuhan to go barnstorm-ing the country as a Container Corporation of America lecturer and—so the London *Observer* reports—to pin down a hundred-thousand-dollar-a-year super-professorship at Fordham Uni-versity. His most recent literary effort, *The Medium Is the Mas-sage (sic.)*—a gimmicked-up non-book—is fetching $10.95 a copy in the hardbound edition. He should worry about intellec-tual respectability? About as much as Andrew Ure or Samuel Smiles, who long ago discovered the secret of becoming success-ful "fee-losophers" in an exploitative social order.

37 / The Road to the Top Is Through Higher Education —Not Black Studies

W. ARTHUR LEWIS

When a friend suggested that, since I had spent all my adult life in black-power movements and in universities, I might make some comments on the highly topical subject of black power in the American university, it did not at first seem to be a good idea. Now that I have come to grips with it I am even more conscious of my folly in tackling so difficult and controversial a subject.

I am also very conscious that my credentials are inadequate, since the black-power movements in the countries with which I am familiar differ fundamentally from black power in the United States. My stamping grounds are the West Indies, where I was born, and Africa, where I have worked, and which I shall be visiting for the fourteenth time next month. But in both those places blacks are the great majority of the people—97 percent in Jamaica, 99 percent in Nigeria. The objective of the political movements was therefore to capture the central legislature, and the executive and judicial powers. In the United States, in contrast, blacks are only 11 percent of the population, and have neither claim to nor prospect of capturing the Congress, the executive branch, or the Supreme Court for themselves alone. The objectives have to be different, and the strategy must also be different. Comparison between the colonial situation and the position of blacks in America is bound to mislead if it is suggested as a basis for deciding political strategy.

The fact of the matter is that the struggle of the blacks in America is a unique experience, with no parallel in Africa. And since it is unique, the appropriate strategies are likely to be forged only by trial and error. We are all finding the process a

SOURCE: *The New York Times Magazine*, May 11, 1969. Copyright © 1969 by The New York Times Company. Reprinted by permission.

Sir Arthur Lewis, professor of economics and international affairs at Princeton University, is the author of *Politics in West Africa*.

great trial, and since our leaders are going off in all directions at once, a great deal of error is also inevitable. I myself, in venturing onto this ground, claim the protection of the First Amendment, but do not aspire to wear the cloak of Papal infallibility.

The goals and tactics of black power in America have to be adjusted to the reality of America. Take the issue of segregation. Everywhere in the black world, except among a small minority of American blacks, the fight against segregation has been in the foreground of black-power movements. This goes without saying in countries where blacks are the great majority; yet there are situations where a minority may strengthen itself by temporary self-segregation of a limited kind.

All American minorities have passed through a stage of temporary self-segregation, not just the Afro-Americans. Foreigners speak of the United States as a "melting pot" and it may one day be that; but for the present, America is really not a melting pot but a welding shop. It is a country in which many different groups of people live and work together side by side, without coalescing. There are Poles, and Irish, and Chinese, and Jews, and Germans, and many other ethnic groups.

But their way of living together is set by the clock; there is integration between 7 o'clock in the morning and 5 o'clock at night, when all mingle and work together in the center of the city, in the banks and factories, department stores and universities. But after 5 o'clock each ethnic group returns to its own neighborhood. There it has its own separate social life. There Poles do not marry Italians, even though they are both white Catholics. The neighborhood has its own schools, its own little shops, its own doctors, and its own celebrations. Integration by day is accompanied by segregation by night.

It is important to note that this self-segregation is voluntary and not imposed by law. An Italian *can* buy a house in an Irish neighborhood if he wishes to do so, *can* marry an Irish girl, and *can* go to an Irish Catholic Church. Many people also insist that this voluntary segregation is only a temporary phase in the acculturation of ethnic groups. They live together until they have found their feet on the American way of life, after which they disperse. The immigrants from Germany and Scandinavia have for the most part already moved out of segregated neighborhoods. The Irish and the Jews are just in the process, and sooner or later the Poles, the Chinese and even the Afro-Americans may disperse. But in the meantime this voluntary self-segregation shelters those who are not yet ready to lose themselves completely in the American mainstream. Other people believe that there will always be cultural pluralism in America, and that this may even be a source of strength. Whether or not they are right about the long run, there is no disputing that voluntary social self-segregation is the current norm.

The black-power movement is therefore fully in the American tradition in recognizing that certain neighborhoods are essentially black neighborhoods, where the black politician, the black doctor, the black teacher, the black grocer and the black clergyman are going to be able to play roles which are not open to them, *de facto*, in other neighborhoods. Many southern Negroes claim vigorously that blacks are better off in the South than in the North precisely because the southern white philosophy has reserved a place for a black middle class in the black neighborhoods—for the black preacher or doctor or grocer.

Essentially, what black power is now saying in the North is that the North, too, should recognize that the middle-class occupations in the black neighborhoods belong to blacks, who are not permitted to hold such jobs in Italian, Polish, or other ethnic neighborhoods. The issue is phrased in terms of community power—that is to say, of giving to each neighborhood control over its own institutions—but this is tied inextricably to the distribution of middle-class jobs inside the neighborhood. It is unquestionably part of the American tradition that members of each ethnic group should be trained for the middle-class occupations in their neighborhoods, and that, given the training, they should have preference in employment in their own neighborhoods.

This kind of voluntary self-segregation has nothing in common with the compulsory segregation of other countries. An American neighborhood is not a ghetto. A ghetto is an area where members of an ethnic group are forced by law to live, and from which it is a criminal offense to emerge without the license of the oppressing power. This is what apartheid means in the Union of South Africa. An American neighborhood is not a place where members of an ethnic group are required by law to live; they may in the first instance have been forced to live there by circumstances, but it is soon transmuted, ideally, into a place where members of the group *choose* to live, and from which, ideally, anybody can emerge at any time that he wishes to do so. To confuse this neighborhood concept with apartheid is an egregious error.

The fundamental difference between apartheid and the American neighborhood comes out most clearly when one turns from what happens after 5 P.M. to what happens during the daytime. A neighborhood is a work place for less than half the community. The teachers, the doctors, the police, the grocers—these work where they live. But these people are supported by the labors of those who work in the factories and in other basic occupations outside the neighborhood. Some 50 to 60 percent of the labor force moves out of the neighborhood every morning to work in the country's basic industries.

So a black strategy which concentrated exclusively on building up the black neighborhoods would be dealing with less than half the black man's economic problems. The neighborhood itself will not flourish unless the man who goes out of it in the morning brings back into it from the outside world an income adequate to support its institutions.

I wrote earlier that the American pattern is segregation in *social* life after 5 P.M. but integration in the *economic* life of the country during the day. American economic life is dominated by a few large corporations which do the greater part of the country's business; indeed, in manufacturing, half the assets of the entire country are owned by just 100 corporations. The world of these big corporations is an integrated world. There will be black grocery shops in black neighborhoods, but in your lifetime and mine there isn't going to be a black General Motors, a black Union Carbide, a black Penn-Central Railroad, or a black Standard Oil Company. These great corporations serve all ethnic groups and employ all ethnic groups. American economic life is inconceivable except on an integrated basis.

The majority of Afro-Americans work not in their neighborhoods but for one of the non-neighborhood corporations or employers, and so it shall be for as far ahead as we can see. The black problem is that while we are 11 percent of the population, we have only 2 percent of the jobs at the top, 4 percent of the jobs in the middle, and are forced into 16 percent of the jobs at the bottom—indeed into as much as 40 percent of some of the jobs at the very bottom. Clearly, our minimum objective must be to capture 11 percent of the jobs in the middle, and 11 percent of the jobs at the top. Or, for those of us who have a pride in ourselves, it could even be an objective to have 15 percent of the jobs at the top and in the middle, and only 8 percent of those at the bottom, leaving the very bottom to less ambitious ethnic groups.

Not all our leaders understand that our central economic problem is not in the neighborhoods, but is in the fact that outside the neighborhoods, where most of us have to work, we are concentrated in the bottom jobs. For if they understood this they could not be as hostile as they are toward the black middle and upper classes. The measure of whether we are winning our battle is in how many of us rise to the middle and the top.

When a so-called militant abuses a successful Afro-American for having, by virtue of extreme hard work and immense self-discipline, managed to get to the top in the outside world, instead of devoting his energies to being—in the neighborhood—a social worker, or a night-school teacher, or a semi-politician, such a critic is merely being absurd. Rising from the bottom to the middle or the top, in the face of stiff white competition, prejudice and arbitrary barriers, takes everything that a man can give to it. It is our militants who should month-by-month chalk up the score of those who have broken through the barriers, should glory in their achievement, and should hold it up before our young to show them what black men can achieve.

Now, at last, I reach my central topic, which is the black man and the university. The road to the top in the great American corporations and other institutions is through higher education. Scientists, research workers, engineers, accountants, lawyers, financial administrators, presidential advisers—all these people are recruited from the university. And indeed nearly all of the top people are taken from a very small number of colleges—from not more than some 50 or 60 of the 2,000 degree-granting institutions in the United States. The Afro-American could not make it to the top so long as he was effectively excluded from this small number of select institutions. The breakthrough of the

Afro-American into these colleges is therefore absolutely fundamental to the larger economic strategy of black power.

I do not mean to suggest that the most important black strategy is to get more blacks into the best colleges. Probably the greatest contribution to black advancement would be to break the trade-union barriers which keep our people out of apprenticeships in the building and printing trades, and prevent our upgrading or promotion in other industries. The trade unions are the black man's greatest enemy in the United States.

The number of people who would be at the top, if we had our numerical share of the top, would be small. Our greatest task, in terms of numbers, is to conquer the middle—getting into skilled posts, foremen's posts, supervisory and white-collar jobs—through better use of apprenticeships, of the high schools and of technical colleges. I am going to discuss the universities not because this is numerically important, but partly because it has become so controversial, and partly because if we did conquer the top it would make much easier the conquering of the middle—both in our own minds, and in other people's minds, by altering our young people's image of themselves and of what they can achieve.

What can the good white college do for its black students that Howard or Lincoln or Fisk cannot do? It can open the road into the top jobs. It can do this only by giving our people the kinds of skills and the kind of polish which are looked for by people filling top jobs. To put it in unpopular language, it can train them to become members of the establishment.

If it is wrong for young blacks to be trained for the top jobs in the big corporations, for top jobs in the government service, for ambassadorships, for the editorial staff of *The New York Times* and so on—then there is little point in sending them to the best white colleges. On the contrary, if what one wants is people trained to live and work in black neighborhoods, they will do much better to go to the black colleges, of which there are, after all, more than one hundred, which know much better than Yale or Princeton or Dartmouth what the problems of black neighborhoods are, and how people should be trained to handle them. The point about the best white colleges is that they are a part, not of the neighborhood side of American life, but of the integrated part of American life, training people to run the economy and the administration in the integrated part of the day before 5 P.M.

But how can it be wrong for young Afro-Americans to be trained to hold superior positions in the integrated working world outside the neighborhood when in fact the neighborhood cannot provide work for even a half of its people? Whether we like it or not, most Afro-Americans *have* to work in the integrated world, and if we do not train for superior positions there, all that will happen is what happens now—that we shall be crowded into the worst-paid jobs.

If one grasps this point, that these fifty colleges are the gateway to the superior jobs, then the current attitudes of some of our black leaders to these colleges is not a little bewildering. In its most extreme form, what is asked is that the college should set aside a special part of itself which is to be the black part. There will be a separate building for black studies, and separate dormitories and living accommodations for blacks. There will be separate teachers, all black, teaching classes open only to blacks. The teachers are to be chosen by the students, and will for the most part be men whom no African or Indian or Chinese university would recognize as scholars, or be willing to hire as teachers.

Doubtless some colleges under militant pressure will give in to this, but I do not see what Afro-Americans will gain thereby. Employers will not hire the students who emerge from this process, and their usefulness even in black neighborhoods will be minimal.

I yield to none in thinking that every respectable university should give courses on African life and on Afro-American life, which are of course two entirely different subjects, and I am very anxious to see such courses developed. It is, however, my hope that they will be attended mostly by white students, and that the majority of black students will find more important uses for their time; that they may attend one or two such courses, but will reject any suggestion that black studies must be the major focus of their programs.

The principal argument for forcing black students to spend a great deal of their time in college studying African and Afro-American anthropology, history, languages and literature is that they need such studies to overcome their racial inferiority complex. I am not impressed by this argument. The youngster discovers that he is black around the age of six or seven; from then on, the whites he meets, the books he reads, and the situation of the Negro in America all combine to persuade him that he is an inferior species of Homo sapiens.

By the time he is fourteen or fifteen he has made up his mind on this one way or the other. Nothing that the college can do, after he reaches eighteen or nineteen, is going to have much effect on his basic personality. To expect the colleges to eradicate the inferiority complexes of young black adults is to ask the impossible. And to expect this to come about by segregating black students in black studies under inferior teachers suggests some deficiency of thought.

Perhaps I am wrong about this. The proposition is essentially that the young black has been brainwashed into thinking himself inferior, so now he must spend four years in some place where he will be re-brainwashed into thinking himself equal. But the prospect that the fifty best colleges in the United States can be forced to take on this re-brainwashing operation is an idle dream. Those who are now putting all their energies into working for this are doomed to disappointment.

We are knocking our heads against the wrong wall. Every black student should learn some Afro-American history, and study various aspects of his people's culture, but the place for him to do this compulsorily is in the high school, and the best age to start this seriously is even earlier, perhaps around the age of ten. By the time the student gets to a first-rate college he should be ready for business—for the business of acquiring the skills which he is going to be able to use, whether in his neighborhood, or in the integrated economy. Let the clever young black go to a university to study engineering, medicine, chemistry, economics, law, agriculture and other subjects which are going to be of value to him and his people. And let the clever white go to college to read black novels, to learn Swahili, and to record the exploits of Negro heroes of the past. They are the ones to whom this will come as an eye-opener.

This, incidentally, is very much what happens in African universities. Most of these have well-equipped departments of African studies, which are popular with visiting whites, but very few African students waste their time (as they see it) on such studies, when there is so much to be learned for the jobs they will have to do. The attitude of Africans to their past conforms to the historian's observation that only decadent peoples, on the way down, feel an urgent need to mythologize and live in their past. A vigorous people, on the way up, has visions of its future, and cares next to nothing about its past.

My attitude toward the role of black studies in the education of college blacks derives not only from an unconventional view of what is to be gained therefrom, but also from an unconventional view of the purpose of going to college. The United States is the only country in the world which thinks that the purpose of going to colleges is to be educated. Everywhere else one goes to high school to be educated, but goes to college to be trained for one's life work. In the United States serious training does not begin until one reaches graduate school at the age of twenty-two. Before that, one spends four years in college being educated—that is to say, spending twelve weeks getting some tidbits on religion, twelve weeks learning French, twelve weeks seeing whether the history professor is stimulating, twelve weeks seeking entertainment from the economics professor, twelve weeks confirming that one is not going to be able to master calculus, and so on.

If the purpose of going to college is to be educated, and serious study will not begin until one is twenty-two, one might just as well, perhaps, spend the four years reading black novels, studying black history and learning to speak Fanti. But I do not think that American blacks can afford this luxury. I think our young people ought to get down to the business of serious preparation for their life work as soon after eighteen as they can.

And I also note, incidentally, that many of the more intelligent white students are now in revolt against the way so many colleges fritter away their precious years in meaningless peregrination from subject to subject between the ages of eighteen and twenty-two.

Any Afro-American who wishes to become a specialist in black studies, or to spend some of his time on such work, should be absolutely free to do so. But I hope that, of those students who get the opportunity to attend the fifty best colleges, the proportion who want to specialize in black studies may, in their interest and that of the black community, turn out to be rather small, in comparison with our scientists, or engineers, accountants, economists or doctors.

Another attitude which puzzles me is that which requires black students in the better white colleges to mix only with each other; to have a dormitory to themselves; to eat at separate tables in the refectory, and so on. I have pointed out that these colleges are the gateway to leadership positions in the integrated part of the economy, and that what they can best do for young blacks is to prepare them to capture our 11 percent share of the best jobs at the top—one of every nine ambassadorships, one of every nine vice-presidencies of General Motors, one of every nine senior directors of engineering laboratories, and so on.

Now I am told that the reason black students stick together is that they are uncomfortable in white company. But how is one to be Ambassador to Finland or Luxembourg—jobs which American Negroes have already held with distinction—if one is uncomfortable in white company? Anybody who occupies a supervisory post, from foreman upwards, is going to have white people working under him, who will expect him to be friendly and fair. Is this going to be possible, after four years spent in boycotting white company?

Nowadays in business and in government most decisions are made in committees. Top Afro-Americans cannot hope to be more than one in nine; they will always be greatly outnumbered by white people at their level. But how can one survive as the only black vice president sitting on the executive committee of a large corporation if one is not so familiar with the ways and thoughts of other vice presidents that one can even anticipate how they are going to think?

Blacks in America are inevitably and perpetually a minority. This means that in all administrative and leadership positions we are going to be outnumbered by white folks, and will have to compete with them not on our terms but on theirs. The only way to win this game is to know them so thoroughly that we can outpace them. For us to turn our backs on this opportunity, by insisting on mingling only with other black students in college, is folly of the highest order.

This kind of social self-segregation is encouraged by two myths about the possibilities for black economic progress in the

United States which need to be nailed. One is the Nixon myth, and the other, its opposite, is the revolutionary myth.

The first postulates that the solution is black capitalism—to help as many blacks as possible to become big businessmen. To be sure, it is feasible to have more successful small businesses operating inside the protection of the neighborhood—more grocers and drug stores and lunch counters; but I have emphasized that the members of every ethnic group mostly work outside their neighborhood in the integrated economy, buying from and selling to all ethnic groups. In this part of the economy the prospects for small business are bleak.

No doubt a few Negroes, born with the special talents which success in a highly competitive business world demands, will succeed in establishing sizable and highly competitive concerns. But the great majority who start on this road, whether white or black, go bankrupt in a short time. Indeed, about half of the new white businesses go bankrupt within the first twelve months. To tell the blacks that this is the direction in which they must move is almost a form of cruelty. To pretend that black America is going to be saved by the emergence of black capitalism, competing in the integrated economy with white capitalism, is little more than a hoax.

Neither is black America going to be saved by a Marxist revolution. Revolution takes power from one set of persons and gives it to another, but it does not change the hierarchical structure of the economy. Any kind of America that you can visualize, whether capitalist, Communist, Fascist, or any other kind of ist, is going to consist of large institutions like General Motors under one name or another. It will have people at the top, people in the middle and people at the bottom. Its leading engineers, doctors, scientists and administrators—leaving out a few top professional politicians—are going to be recruited from a small number of highly select colleges.

The problem of the black will essentially be the same—that problem being whether he is going to be mostly in the bottom jobs, or whether he will also get his 11 percent share of the top and the middle. And his chance at the top is going to depend on his getting into those select schools and getting the same kind of technical training that the whites are getting—not some segregated schooling specially adapted for him, but the same kind that the whites get as their gateway to the top. Those black leaders who wish us to concentrate our efforts on working for revolution in America are living on a myth, for our problems and needed strategies are going to be exactly the same whether there is a revolution or not. In the integrated part of the American economy our essential strategy has to be to use all the normal channels of advancement—the high schools, the colleges, apprenticeships, night schools: It is only by climbing this ladder that the black man is going to escape from his concentration in the bottom jobs of the economy.

This is not, of course, simply a matter of schooling. The barriers of prejudice which keep us off the ladder still have to be broken down: the task of the civil-rights movement is still not completed, and we need all the liberal help, black and white, that we can get to help to keep the ladder clear. We need also to raise our own sights; to recognize that there are now more opportunities than there were, and to take every opportunity that offers. Here our record is good. For as the barriers came down in sports and entertainment, our young people moved swiftly to the top in baseball, football, the theater, or wherever else the road was cleared. We will do exactly the same in other spheres, given the opportunity.

The secret is to inspire our young people with confidence in their potential achievement. And psychologists tell us that the background to this is a warm and secure family life. The most successful minorities in America, the Chinese, the Japanese and the Jews, are distinguished by their close and highly disciplined family, which is the exact opposite of what has now become the stereotype of the white American family, with its undisciplined and uncontrollable children reared on what are alleged to be the principles of Dr. Spock. African families are warm, highly disciplined structures, just like Jewish or Chinese families. If black Americans are looking to Africa for aspects of culture which will distinguish them from white Americans, let them turn their backs on Spockism, and rear their children on African principles, for this is the way to the middle and the top. Given a disciplined family life and open doors to opportunity, I have no doubt that American blacks will capture one field after another, as fast as barriers come down.

624

The point which I have been trying to make is that the choice some of our leaders offer us between segregation and integration is false in the American context. America is integrated in the day and segregates itself at night. Some of our leaders who have just discovered the potential strength of neighborhood self-segregation have got drunk on it to the point of advocating segregation for all spheres of Afro-American life. But the struggle for community power in the neighborhood is not an alternative to the struggle for a better share of the integrated world outside the neighborhood, in which inevitably most of our people must earn their living. The way to a better share of this integrated economy is through the integrated colleges; but they can help us only if we take from them the same things that they give to our white competitors.

If we enter them merely to segregate ourselves in blackness, we shall lose the opportunity of our lives. Render homage unto segregated community power in the neighborhoods where it belongs, but do not let it mess up our chance of capturing our share of the economic world outside the neighborhood, where segregation weakens our power to compete.

W. ARTHUR LEWIS 625